Brexit and Financial Regulation

Brexit and Financial Regulation

Edited by

JONATHAN HERBST AND SIMON LOVEGROVE

OXFORD
UNIVERSITY PRESS

OXFORD
UNIVERSITY PRESS

Great Clarendon Street, Oxford, OX2 6DP,
United Kingdom

Oxford University Press is a department of the University of Oxford.
It furthers the University's objective of excellence in research, scholarship,
and education by publishing worldwide. Oxford is a registered trade mark of
Oxford University Press in the UK and in certain other countries

© Oxford University Press 2020

The moral rights of the authors have been asserted

First Edition published in 2020

Impression: 2

All rights reserved. No part of this publication may be reproduced, stored in
a retrieval system, or transmitted, in any form or by any means, without the
prior permission in writing of Oxford University Press, or as expressly permitted
by law, by licence or under terms agreed with the appropriate reprographics
rights organization. Enquiries concerning reproduction outside the scope of the
above should be sent to the Rights Department, Oxford University Press, at the
address above

You must not circulate this work in any other form
and you must impose this same condition on any acquirer

Crown copyright material is reproduced under Class Licence
Number C01P0000148 with the permission of OPSI
and the Queen's Printer for Scotland

Published in the United States of America by Oxford University Press
198 Madison Avenue, New York, NY 10016, United States of America

British Library Cataloguing in Publication Data

Data available

Library of Congress Control Number: 2019953105

ISBN 978-0-19-884079-4

Printed and bound by
CPI Group (UK) Ltd, Croydon, CR0 4YY

Links to third party websites are provided by Oxford in good faith and
for information only. Oxford disclaims any responsibility for the materials
contained in any third party website referenced in this work.

Contents

Table of Cases	xxi
Table of European Legislation	xxiii
List of Abbreviations	xxxix
List of Contributors	xliii

1. Introduction — Jonathan Herbst and Simon Lovegrove — 1

2. Withdrawal Agreement and Political Declaration on the Future EU–UK Relationship — Simon Lovegrove — 21

3. International Standards — Michael Raffan — 31

4. EU Equivalence Regime — Arun Srivastava and Nina Moffatt — 75

5. The EU Approach to Authorisation — Daniel Carall-Green — 97

6. The EU Approach to Authorisation: Germany, France, the Netherlands, and Ireland — Michael Born, Roberto Cristofolini, Floortje Nagelkerke, and Donnacha O'Connor — 135

7. The UK Supervisory Regime in the Post-Brexit Environment — Michael Thomas and James Roslington — 167

8. PRA Approach to the Authorisation of International Branches and Subsidiaries — Clive Cunningham, Katherine Dillon, and Alison Matthews — 197

9. The UK's Senior Managers, Certification and Conduct Regime — Charlotte Henry — 227

10. Markets in Financial Instrument Directive II (MiFID II)/ Markets in Financial Instruments Regulation (MiFIR) — Nico Leslie and Aaron Taylor — 243

11. Capital Requirements Directive (CRD IV)/ Capital Requirements Regulation (CRR) — Stuart Willey — 265

12. Bank Recovery and Resolution Directive (BRRD) — Jan Putnis and Chris Hurn — 291

13. European Markets Infrastructure Regulation (EMIR) and Euro Clearing — Bob Penn — 313

14. Benchmarks Regulation 341
    Michael Thomas and Anahita Patwardhan

15. Alternative Investment Fund Managers Directive (AIFMD) 377
    Jake Green

16. Solvency II Directive (Solvency II) 393
    Bob Haken and Isabella Jones

Index 413

Detailed Contents

Table of Cases	xxi
Table of European Legislation	xxiii
List of Abbreviations	xxxix
List of Contributors	xliii

1. Introduction — 1
   1.1 The Referendum — 1
   1.2 Article 50 Notification — 3
   1.3 The Negotiations — 4
   1.4 Chequers Plan — 5
   1.5 Withdrawal Agreement and Political Declaration on the Future EU–UK Relationship — 6
   1.6 Ratification of the Withdrawal Agreement — 7
   1.7 Preparations for the No-Deal Scenario — 10
   1.8 *Brexit and Financial Regulation*: an Overview — 18
      1.8.1 Part I — 18
      1.8.2 Part II — 19
      1.8.3 Part III — 19

2. Withdrawal Agreement and Political Declaration on the Future EU–UK Relationship — 21
   2.1 Introduction — 21
   2.2 Ratification — 21
   2.3 Renegotiation — 22
   2.4 Structure — 22
   2.5 Protocols — 24
   2.6 Implications for Financial Services — 24
   2.7 Dispute Resolution — 25
   2.8 The Political Declaration on the Future EU–UK relationship — 26
   2.9 Five Parts — 26
   2.10 Implications for Financial Services — 27
   2.11 Going Forward — 28
   2.12 FCA EU Withdrawal Impact Assessment — 29

3. International Standards — 31
   3.1 Introduction — 31
   3.2 Governments, Central Banks, and Regulators Participating as Members of International Bodies — 31
      3.2.1 Organisation for Economic Co-operation and Development (OECD) — 31
         3.2.1.1 History — 31
         3.2.1.2 Structure — 32
         3.2.1.3 Membership — 32
         3.2.1.4 Activities — 32
      3.2.2 IMF — 34
         3.2.2.1 History — 34
         3.2.2.2 Structure — 34

viii   DETAILED CONTENTS

	3.2.2.3	Membership	34
	3.2.2.4	Activities	34
3.2.3	Bank for International Settlements (BIS)		36
	3.2.3.1	History	36
	3.2.3.2	Structure	36
	3.2.3.3	Membership	37
	3.2.3.4	Activities	37
3.2.4	FSB		37
	3.2.4.1	History	37
	3.2.4.2	Structure	38
	3.2.4.3	Membership	38
	3.2.4.4	Activities	38
3.2.5	FATF		40
	3.2.5.1	History	40
	3.2.5.2	Structure	40
	3.2.5.3	Membership	41
	3.2.5.4	Activities	41
3.2.6	CPMI		43
	3.2.6.1	History	43
	3.2.6.2	Structure	43
	3.2.6.3	Membership	43
	3.2.6.4	Activities	43
3.2.7	Basel Committee on Banking Supervision (BCBS)		46
	3.2.7.1	History	46
	3.2.7.2	Structure	46
	3.2.7.3	Membership	46
	3.2.7.4	Activities	46
3.2.8	IOSCO		49
	3.2.8.1	History	49
	3.2.8.2	Structure	49
	3.2.8.3	Membership	49
	3.2.8.4	Activities	50
3.2.9	Global Foreign Exchange Committee (GFXC)		52
	3.2.9.1	History	52
	3.2.9.2	Structure and membership	52
	3.2.9.3	Activities	52
3.2.10	International Association of Insurance Supervisors (IAIS)		54
	3.2.10.1	History	54
	3.2.10.2	Structure	54
	3.2.10.3	Membership	54
	3.2.10.4	Activities	54
3.2.11	International Organisation of Pension Supervisors (IOPS)		56
	3.2.11.1	History	56
	3.2.11.2	Structure	56
	3.2.11.3	Membership	56
	3.2.11.4	Activities	57
3.2.12	International Association of Deposit Insurers (IADI)		58
	3.2.12.1	Structure and membership	58
	3.2.12.2	Activities	58

	3.2.13	Markets Committee	59
		3.2.13.1 History	60
		3.2.13.2 Structure	60
		3.2.13.3 Membership	60
		3.2.13.4 Activities	60
	3.2.14	Irving Fisher Committee on Central Bank Statistics (IFC)	60
		3.2.14.1 History	60
		3.2.14.2 Structure	61
		3.2.14.3 Membership	61
		3.2.14.4 Activities	61
	3.2.15	International Financial Consumer Protection Organisation (FinCoNet)	61
		3.2.15.1 History	61
		3.2.15.2 Structure	62
		3.2.15.3 Membership	62
		3.2.15.4 Activities	62
3.3	Accounting and Audit		63
	3.3.1	International Financial Reporting Standards Foundation (IFRSF) and International Accounting Standards Board (IASB)	63
		3.3.1.1 Structure and membership	63
		3.3.1.2 Activities	64
	3.3.2	International Auditing and Assurance Standards Board (IAASB)	65
		3.3.2.1 Structure and membership	65
		3.3.2.2 Activities	66
3.4	UK Firms Participating in Industry Bodies		66
	3.4.1	International Swaps and Derivatives Association (ISDA)	66
		3.4.1.1 Structure and membership	66
		3.4.1.2 Activities	66
	3.4.2	International Capital Market Association (ICMA)	67
		3.4.2.1 Structure and membership	67
		3.4.2.2 Activities	67
	3.4.3	International Securities Lending Association (ISLA)	68
		3.4.3.1 Structure and membership	68
		3.4.3.2 Activities	68
	3.4.4	The Institute of Asset Management (IAM)	69
		3.4.4.1 Structure and membership	69
		3.4.4.2 Activities	70
3.5	Conclusion		71
4. EU Equivalence Regime			75
4.1	Introduction		75
4.2	The Concept of Equivalence		76
4.3	Current Status and Timing		78
4.4	Remaining Equivalent Following Brexit: Onshoring of EU Law		78
4.5	Third Countries and Member States		79
4.6	Equivalence at the EU Level		80
4.7	Equivalence Decisions		81
4.8	Banking Framework		83
4.9	Investment Services		83

4.10	Market Infrastructure	85
4.11	Recognition of UK CCPs and CSDs	86
4.12	EMIR and Derivatives	87
4.13	Investment Funds	87
4.14	Insurance and Reinsurance Framework	92
4.15	Benchmark Administrators	93
4.16	Issuers	93

5. The EU Approach to Authorisation — 97
  - 5.1 Introduction — 97
  - 5.2 Background — 99
  - 5.3 The ESMA Opinions — 100
    - 5.3.1 Legal Basis — 100
    - 5.3.2 The ESMA Cross-Sectoral Opinion — 100
      - 5.3.2.1 Purpose and scope — 100
      - 5.3.2.2 The general principles — 101
    - 5.3.3 The ESMA Sector-Specific Opinions — 106
    - 5.3.4 The ESMA Investment Firms Opinion — 106
      - 5.3.4.1 Purpose and scope — 106
      - 5.3.4.2 Authorisation — 107
      - 5.3.4.3 Substance requirements — 109
      - 5.3.4.4 Effective supervision — 113
    - 5.3.5 The ESMA Secondary Markets Opinion — 113
      - 5.3.5.1 Purpose and scope — 113
      - 5.3.5.2 Key and important activities — 114
    - 5.3.6 The ESMA Investment Management Opinion — 116
      - 5.3.6.1 Purpose and scope — 116
      - 5.3.6.2 Governance and internal control — 118
      - 5.3.6.3 Delegation — 119
  - 5.4 The EBA Opinions — 121
    - 5.4.1 Legal Basis — 121
    - 5.4.2 The EBA 2017 Opinion — 121
      - 5.4.2.1 Purpose and scope — 121
      - 5.4.2.2 Authorisation and equivalence — 122
      - 5.4.2.3 Internal model approvals — 126
      - 5.4.2.4 Internal governance and risk management — 127
      - 5.4.2.5 Resolution and deposit guarantee schemes — 128
    - 5.4.3 The EBA 2018 Opinion — 130
      - 5.4.3.1 Purpose and scope — 130
      - 5.4.3.2 Risk assessment and preparedness — 130
  - 5.5 The Withdrawal Agreement, the Political Declaration, and the Interim Legislation — 132
    - 5.5.1 Background — 132
    - 5.5.2 Decision 2018/2030 — 132
    - 5.5.3 Decision 2018/2031 — 133
    - 5.5.4 Regulation 2019/396 — 134
    - 5.5.5 Regulation 2019/397 — 134

6. The EU Approach to Authorisation: Germany, France,
   the Netherlands, and Ireland   135
   6.1 Introduction   135
   6.2 Germany   136
       6.2.1   Introduction   136
       6.2.2   German Brexit Legislation   136
               6.2.2.1 Overview   136
               6.2.2.2 Scope of general transitional regime   137
               6.2.2.3 General transitional periods   138
               6.2.2.4 Limitations of the general transitional periods   139
               6.2.2.5 Specific relief measure for proprietary business   139
       6.2.3   National Approach to Authorisation   140
               6.2.3.1 Competent authorities   140
               6.2.3.2 Territorial scope of German licensing requirements   141
               6.2.3.3 Reverse solicitation exemption   141
               6.2.3.4 Exemption of cross-border services in the individual case 142
               6.2.3.5 Administrative guidance for licence applications   142
               6.2.3.6 Substance requirements in Germany   143
   6.3 France   143
       6.3.1   Introduction   143
       6.3.2   French Competent Authorities   144
       6.3.3   French Approach to a No-Deal Brexit   144
       6.3.4   Continuity of Contracts   145
       6.3.5   French Monopoly   146
       6.3.6   Territorial Application of the French Monopoly   146
       6.3.7   Reverse Solicitation Exemption   146
       6.3.8   Standard Procedure for Non-EEA Entities Following Exit Day   147
       6.3.9   French Guidelines in Relation to the Use of Third-Party Employees
               or Technical Means   147
       6.3.10 Required Substance in France   147
       6.3.11 Outsourcing Arrangements   148
       6.3.12 'Dual-hatting' within Group Entities   148
   6.4 Netherlands   149
       6.4.1   Introduction   149
       6.4.2   Dutch Brexit Legislation   149
               6.4.2.1 Dutch Brexit Act   149
               6.4.2.2 Exemption for investment firms   150
       6.4.3   Dutch Regulators   151
               6.4.3.1 Netherlands Authority for the Financial Markets   151
               6.4.3.2 Dutch Central Bank   151
               6.4.3.3 Ministry of Finance   151
       6.4.4   Licence Obligation and Exemptions   151
               6.4.4.1 Initiative test/reverse solicitation   151
               6.4.4.2 Exemption to the licence obligation   152
       6.4.5   Licence Application Procedure   152
               6.4.5.1 Regulated market   152
               6.4.5.2 Investment services   152

		6.4.5.3 Substance	152
		6.4.5.4 Licence fees	153
	6.4.6	Declaration of No Objection	153
		6.4.6.1 Investment firm	153
		6.4.6.2 Regulated market	154
	6.4.7	Enforcement powers of regulators	154
6.5	Ireland		155
	6.5.1	Background	155
	6.5.2	Brexit Contingency Planning	155
	6.5.3	Authorisation of AIFMs, UCITS Management Companies, and MiFID Investment Firms in Ireland	156
	6.5.4	Treatment of Third Country Firms under Irish Law	157
		6.5.4.1 Providing services to, or engaging in investment activities with, Irish clients under MIFID	158
		6.5.4.2 Third country firms as AIFMs under the AIFM Directive	159
		6.5.4.3 Third country firms marketing AIFs under the AIFM Regulations	159
	6.5.5	Key Requirements for Authorisation in Ireland	160
		6.5.5.1 The influence of ESMA on the authorisation requirements	160
		6.5.5.2 Head office and registered office in Ireland	161
		6.5.5.3 Substance in Ireland	161
		6.5.5.4 AIFMs and UCITS management companies: managerial functions	162
		6.5.5.5 AIFMs and UCITS management companies: senior management location rule	162
		6.5.5.6 Fitness and probity regime	163
		6.5.5.7 Financial control, compliance, and risk management	163
		6.5.5.8 Staffing	164
	6.5.6	The Authorisation Process	164
		6.5.6.1 Initial contact with the Central Bank	164
		6.5.6.2 Key facts document (KFD)	164
		6.5.6.3 Preliminary meeting with the Central Bank	165
		6.5.6.4 Application	165
		6.5.6.5 Timing	165

7. **The UK Supervisory Regime in the Post-Brexit Environment** — 167
    7.1 Introduction — 167
    7.2 The Entangled Nature of the UK and EU Frameworks — 168
        7.2.1 The Growing Influence of Europe from the Late 1990s — 169
        7.2.2 The Shift towards 'More Europe' after the 2007–8 Financial Crisis — 170
        7.2.3 The Growing Power of the ESAs — 170
        7.2.4 Accelerating Loss of National Discretion — 172
    7.3 UK Framework for Financial Services Legislation and Regulation — 172
    7.4 A 'Bonfire of Regulation'? — 174
    7.5 The EU (Withdrawal) Act 2018 — 177
        7.5.1 Retained EU Law — 178
        7.5.2 Retained EU Case Law — 178
        7.5.3 Remedying Deficiencies in Retained Law — 178
        7.5.4 Powers of UK Parliament to Make Secondary Legislation — 179
    7.6 Statutory Instruments under the EU Withdrawal Act — 180

7.7	Minimising Disruption	181
	7.7.1 Implementation Period in the Event of a UK–EU Withdrawal Agreement	181
	7.7.2 Temporary Transitional Powers for UK Regulators in the Event of a 'No Deal' Brexit	182
7.8	Allocation of Powers to UK Regulators	183
7.9	The Bank of England's Approach to Onshoring	184
7.10	The FCA's Approach to Onshoring	186
7.11	The PSR's Approach to Onshoring	186
7.12	The UK Regulators' Approach to Non-Legislative EU Materials	187
7.13	The Impact of Brexit on the FCA Handbook	189
7.14	The Impact of Brexit on the PRA Rulebook	189
7.15	The Overseas Persons' Exclusion after Brexit	190
7.16	Reallocation of Supervisory Powers	191
7.17	Regulatory Cooperation	193
7.18	Treatment of 'In Flight' Legislation	194
7.19	Impact of a 'No-Deal' Scenario	195
7.20	Conclusion	195

8. **PRA Approach to the Authorisation of International Branches and Subsidiaries** — 197

8.1	Introduction	197
	8.1.1 PRA Approach to Bank Branches	198
	8.1.2 PRA Approach to (Re)insurer Branches	199
	8.1.3 Transitional Arrangements and Timing Considerations	199
	8.1.4 Remaining Chapter Summary	202
8.2	General Differences between Branches and Subsidiaries	202
8.3	Banks: PRA's Approach to Significant Retail Activities	204
	8.3.1 Size of Retail Deposit Base	204
	8.3.2 Size of FSCS-Protected Deposit Base	205
	8.3.3 How Should Banks Assess Their Position under the Updated 'Significant Retail' Approach?	206
	8.3.4 Which Customers?	206
	8.3.5 Which Accounts?	206
8.4	'Wholesale' Banks: PRA's General Approach to Branch Authorisation and Supervision (Where No Significant Retail Activities)	207
	8.4.1 The Wholesale or 'General Approach' to Branch Authorisation and Supervision	207
	8.4.2 The PRA's and FCA's Threshold Conditions for Authorisation	208
	8.4.3 PRA	208
	8.4.4 FCA	209
	8.4.5 Equivalence Standards	209
	8.4.6 Supervisory Cooperation Arrangements	210
	8.4.7 Assurance over Resolution Arrangements	212
	8.4.8 Considerations for Banks	213
8.5	Banks: PRA's Approach to 'Systemic' Wholesale Branches	213
	8.5.1 Which Branches Qualify as 'Systemic'?	213
	8.5.2 How Is the Supervisory Experience Different from Non-Systemic Branches?	214
	8.5.3 Booking Models	215

8.6	Banks: Application Process		215
8.7	Banks: Implications of the Transition to Overseas Branch or Subsidiary Status		217
	8.7.1 UK Branches		217
		8.7.1.1 PRA rules	217
		8.7.1.2 PRA and FCA rules	218
		8.7.1.3 FCA rules	218
	8.7.2 UK Subsidiaries		218
	8.7.3 TPR Implications		218
	8.7.4 FSCR		220
8.8	Overseas (Re)insurers: General PRA Approach to Authorisation		220
	8.8.1 PRA Approach to EEA (Re)insurers Post-Brexit		221
	8.8.2 TPR Implications		222
	8.8.3 FSCR		222
8.9	Overseas (Re)insurers: PRA Approach to UK Branches—Factors to Be Considered		222
	8.9.1 New Factors to Be Considered by PRA		223
	8.9.2 Scale of UK Branch Activity Covered by the FSCS		224
	8.9.3 Impact of Branch Failure on the Wider Insurance Market and Financial System		224
	8.9.4 Cross-border Services Business		224

9. The UK's Senior Managers, Certification and Conduct Regime — 227

9.1	Introduction		227
9.2	Summary of the Relevant Background		227
9.3	Applicability of Different SMCR Regimes with Brexit		228
	9.3.1 Deemed Approval for SMFs		231
	9.3.2 Challenges		231
9.4	Responsibility for Changing Regulatory Requirements during Brexit		232
9.5	Practical Implications of Moving between Regimes		233
9.6	Responsibility for Cross-border Business into the UK		234
	9.6.1 Appointed Representatives		236
	9.6.2 Dual-Hatting		236
9.7	Impact on Certification and Conduct Regimes		236
9.8	Insourcing and Outsourcing		237
9.9	Enforcement against non-UK Resident Senior Managers		238
	9.9.1 Supervisory Powers		238
	9.9.2 Enforcement Powers		239
	9.9.3 Enforcement Tools		240
	9.9.4 Practical Enforcement against non-UK Resident Senior Managers		241
		9.9.4.1 Private and public warnings, withdrawal or suspension of approval, placing limitations or restrictions on approval, and Prohibition Orders	241
		9.9.4.2 Enforcing fines outside the UK	241
		9.9.4.3 Commence court proceedings	242
	9.9.5 Other Consequences		242

10. Markets in Financial Instrument Directive II (MiFID II)/Markets
    in Financial Instruments Regulation (MiFIR)   243
    10.1 Introduction   243
        10.1.1 From MiFID to MiFID II   243
            10.1.1.1 The scope of the new directive   244
            10.1.1.2 Structure of the chapter   244
    10.2 Regulation under MIFID II   245
        10.2.1 The Structure of MIFID II   245
        10.2.2 Exchanges and Clearing Houses   245
            10.2.2.1 Exchanges   245
            10.2.2.2 Clearing houses   245
            10.2.2.3 Application of MiFID II to financial trading infrastructure   246
        10.2.3 The Regulation of Markets under MiFID II   247
            10.2.3.1 Markets and trading platforms   247
    10.3 Rights of Operation and Access   250
        10.3.1 Authorisation of Exchanges in the UK   250
            10.3.1.1 Listing of securities on an exchange   250
        10.3.2 Authorisation of Trading Infrastructure in the EU   252
            10.3.2.1 Authorisation of exchanges in the EU   252
            10.3.2.2 Authorisation of clearing houses and settlement systems
                in the EU   252
        10.3.3 Access for EU Investment Firms to Trading Infrastructure in other
            Member States   253
            10.3.3.1 'Passporting' for investment firms   253
            10.3.3.2 Cross-border operation of multilateral trading facilities
                and regulated markets   254
            10.3.3.3 Access to clearing houses and settlement systems   254
        10.3.4 Access for Non-EU Investment Firms to Trading Infrastructure
            in the EU   255
            10.3.4.1 Limited access for third country firms   255
    10.4 The Potential Impact of Brexit   256
        10.4.1 Introduction   256
        10.4.2 Key Areas of Impact   257
            10.4.2.1 Three types of concern   257
            10.4.2.2 Applicability of EU regulation to UK firms   257
            10.4.2.3 Access requirements   259
        10.4.3 Case Study   262

11. Capital Requirements Directive (CRD IV)/
    Capital Requirements Regulation (CRR)   265
    11.1 Introduction   265
    11.2 How Does the CRD IV/CRR Regime Differ from Other Sectors
        in Respect of Passporting and Equivalence Tests?   266
        11.2.1 EU Financial Services   266
        11.2.2 Barriers to a Single Market   266
        11.2.3 Financial Services Passport   267

	11.2.4	Impact of Brexit on Passporting	268
	11.2.5	Third Country Regimes	268
11.3	\multicolumn{2}{l	}{The Handling of Prudential Requirements under the UK's Authorisation of EU Bank Branches}	271
	11.3.1	Current Framework	271
		11.3.1.1 Impact of Brexit	278
	11.3.2	UK Authorisation	272
	11.3.3	Retail Activities	273
	11.3.4	Systemic Wholesale Branches	274
11.4	\multicolumn{2}{l	}{Collaboration and Information Sharing}	274
11.5	\multicolumn{2}{l	}{Setting Capital Buffer Requirements}	276
11.6	\multicolumn{2}{l	}{EU Intermediate Holding Company Regime}	276
	11.6.1	Reforms under CRD V Package	276
	11.6.2	Threshold and Application	277
	11.6.3	Impact on Third Country Groups	278
	11.6.4	Impact of Brexit	278
11.7	\multicolumn{2}{l	}{Impact of Brexit on Risk Weights of EU and UK Exposures and Liquidity}	278
11.8	\multicolumn{2}{l	}{CRD Remuneration Provisions: Variable Remuneration}	280
	11.8.1	Background	280
	11.8.2	UK Regulatory Approach to Implementation of CRD IV Remuneration Requirements	281
	11.8.3	UK Current Position on Bonus Cap	282
11.9	\multicolumn{2}{l	}{Supervision of Banking Groups and Consolidation}	284
11.10	\multicolumn{2}{l	}{Securitisation}	287
	11.10.1	Background	287
	11.10.2	Securitisation Regulation and Brexit	288

12. Bank Recovery and Resolution Directive (BRRD) — 291

12.1	\multicolumn{2}{l	}{Introduction}	291
12.2	\multicolumn{2}{l	}{Background to the UK Regime}	292
	12.2.1	UK Framework	292
	12.2.2	BRRD Framework	292
	12.2.3	UK Implementation of the BRRD Framework	293
12.3	\multicolumn{2}{l	}{Overview of UK Legislation That Will Amend the UK Regime}	294
	12.3.1	The BRR Brexit Regulations	294
	12.3.2	The Regulators' Powers Regulations	295
	12.3.3	Regulators' Transitional Powers	295
	12.3.4	Guidelines and Recommendations	296
	12.3.5	BRRD II	296
12.4	\multicolumn{2}{l	}{What the UK Regime Will Look Like after Brexit}	296
	12.4.1	Overview of the Regime	296
	12.4.2	Preparatory Measures: Recovery Plans	297
	12.4.3	Preparatory Measures: Resolution Planning	300
	12.4.4	Preparatory Measures: Intragroup Financial Support Arrangements	301
	12.4.5	Early Intervention	302
	12.4.6	Resolution: Conditions	302
	12.4.7	Stabilisation Options: Overview	303
	12.4.8	Stabilisation Options: Bail-in	303
	12.4.9	MREL Reforms: External TLAC	305

			DETAILED CONTENTS	xvii

		12.4.10	MREL Reforms: Eligible Liabilities	308
		12.4.11	MREL Reforms: Internal TLAC	308
		12.4.12	Stabilisation Options: Moratorium Tool	309
		12.4.13	Government Stabilisation Tools	309
		12.4.14	Cross-border Group Resolution	309
		12.4.15	Depositor Preference	311
	12.5	Conclusion		311
13.	European Markets Infrastructure Regulation (EMIR) and Euro Clearing			313
	13.1	Introduction		313
		13.1.1	EMIR	328
		13.1.2	Territoriality	314
		13.1.3	Sources	315
		13.1.4	EMIR REFIT	315
		13.1.5	UK Supervisory Responsibility for EMIR	316
	13.2	The EU Withdrawal Act and 'Onshoring'		316
		13.2.1	Background	316
		13.2.2	EUWA	313
		13.2.3	Incorporation of EMIR and Delegated Legislation in UK Law	317
		13.2.4	Ensuring EMIR Operates Effectively and Correcting Deficiencies	318
		13.2.5	Policy Choices in Creating Onshored Legislation	319
	13.3	Onshoring EMIR and the Delegated Legislation Made under It		320
	13.4	Implications of Exit and Onshoring		322
		13.4.1	Exit	317
		13.4.2	Onshoring	322
	13.5	CCP SI		323
		13.5.1	Background	323
		13.5.2	Amendments to Onshored EMIR	324
		13.5.3	Transitional Relief: Temporary Deemed Recognition	325
		13.5.4	Mechanisms to Facilitate Equivalence Assessments and Recognition in Advance of Exit Day	326
		13.5.5	Other Changes to CCP Regulation	326
		13.5.6	Recognition of UK CCPs under EMIR	326
	13.6	Trade Repository SI		326
		13.6.1	Background	326
		13.6.2	Amendments to Onshored EMIR	327
		13.6.3	Transitional Relief: Temporary Deemed Recognition for UK Affiliates	328
		13.6.4	Other Changes to Trade Repository Regulation	328
	13.7	EMIR SI		328
		13.7.1	Scope and Exemptions	328
		13.7.2	Definition of OTC Derivative: Exclusion of EU27 Exchange-Traded Derivatives	331
		13.7.3	Definition of OTC Derivative: C6 Energy Derivatives	332
		13.7.4	Exemptions for Intragroup Transactions	333
		13.7.5	Clearing Obligation	333
		13.7.6	Reporting Obligation	334
		13.7.7	Risk Mitigation Obligations	335
		13.7.8	Trade Repository Regulation	336

13.8	Standstill			336
	13.8.1	Scope		337
	13.8.2	Exceptions		338
	13.8.3	Effect		338
13.9	Implications for Market Participants			339

14. Benchmarks Regulation — 341
   14.1 Introduction — 341
   14.2 The History of the Regulation of Benchmarks in the UK — 342
      14.2.1 International Initiatives: IOSCO Principles — 342
      14.2.2 UK Initiative: Regulation of Specified Benchmarks — 343
      14.2.3 The Benchmarks Regulation — 344
   14.3 The Regulation of Benchmarks in the UK — 345
      14.3.1 The UK's Post-Brexit Approach to the Benchmarks Regulation — 345
      14.3.2 The Purpose of the Benchmarks Regulation — 346
      14.3.3 The Meaning of a 'Benchmark' — 347
      14.3.4 Scope of the Benchmarks Regulation — 347
      14.3.5 Restriction on the Use of Benchmarks — 348
      14.3.6 Authorisation and Registration of Benchmark Administrators — 350
         14.3.6.1 Requirement to be authorised or registered — 350
         14.3.6.2 The differences between authorisation and registration — 351
         14.3.6.3 Impact of Brexit — 352
      14.3.7 Requirements Applicable to Benchmark Administrators — 353
      14.3.8 Benchmark Categories — 357
         14.3.8.1 The categories of benchmark under the EU regime — 357
         14.3.8.2 Adapting the categories of benchmarks for the UK regime — 360
      14.3.9 Requirements Applicable to Benchmark Contributors — 361
      14.3.10 Transitional Provisions — 362
         14.3.10.1 Transitional provisions: benchmark administrators — 362
         14.3.10.2 Transitional provisions: supervised contributors — 365
   14.4 Brexit and the Benchmarks Regulation: Cross-border Issues — 365
      14.4.1 Introduction — 365
      14.4.2 The Impact of Brexit on benchmark administrators Based in the UK — 366
         14.4.2.1 Option 1: equivalence — 366
         14.4.2.2 Option 2: recognition — 367
         14.4.2.3 Option 3: endorsement — 370
         14.4.2.4 Transitional provisions — 370
      14.4.3 The Impact of Brexit on Benchmark Administrators Based in the EU — 371
         14.4.3.1 The UK third country regime — 371
         14.4.3.2 Transitional provisions — 372
         14.4.3.3 Brexit-specific provisions — 372
      14.4.4 The Impact of Brexit on Benchmark Administrators Based Outside the EU and the UK — 373
      14.4.5 The Impact of Brexit on Users of Benchmarks in the EU — 373
      14.4.6 The Impact of Brexit on Benchmark Users Based in the UK — 374
   14.5 Updates after July 2019 — 374
   14.6 Conclusion — 375

15. Alternative Investment Fund Managers Directive (AIFMD)		377
15.1 Summary		377
15.2 AIFMD on Brexit		378
15.3 AIFMD: an Overview of the Position Today		379
15.3.1 Background and Legislative Intent		379
15.3.2 Application of AIFMD to Managers		380
15.3.3 Full Scope AIFMs		380
15.3.4 Sub-Threshold AIFMs		380
15.3.5 Non-EEA AIFMs		381
15.3.6 Delegation Arrangement		381
15.4 Marketing: Differences between the Passport and NPPR		382
15.4.1 What Is Marketing?		382
15.4.2 Passport		383
15.4.3 Marketing without the Passport		383
15.4.4 Reverse Solicitation		383
15.4.5 Where Does Marketing Take Place?		384
15.4.6 Marketing by Third-Party Entities		384
15.5 Cross-border Distribution of Collective Funds: Changes to Come		385
15.6 Impact of Brexit		387
15.6.1 UK AIFMs in the UK		387
15.6.2 UK AIFMs in the EEA		388
15.6.3 UK Distributors into the EEA		388
15.6.4 EEA AIFMs in the UK		388
15.6.5 Delegation Arrangements		389
15.7 The Future of AIFMD in the UK and Europe		389
15.7.1 Application in UK		389
15.7.2 Passport		390
15.7.3 AIFMD 2/1.2		390
16. Solvency II Directive (Solvency II)		393
16.1 Introduction		393
16.1.1 Legislative Background		393
16.1.2 Preserving the *Acquis*		395
16.2 The Position of European Insurers Operating in the United Kingdom		397
16.2.1 Licensing Issues		397
16.2.1.1 Inbound EEA authorised insurers passporting into the UK		398
16.2.1.2 EEA authorised insurers conducting business in the UK on an offshore basis		401
16.3 The Position of UK Insurers Operating in Europe		403
16.3.1 Licensing Issues		403
16.3.1.1 Direct insurers		404
16.3.1.2 Pure reinsurers		404
16.3.2 The Effect of Equivalence under Solvency II		406
16.3.2.1 Impact on direct insurers		407
16.3.2.2 Impact on reinsurers		407
16.3.3 Multiple and Overlapping Group Supervision Regimes		407
16.3.3.1 Worldwide group supervision		408
16.3.3.2 Disapplication of European group supervision		408

		16.3.3.3 Choice of method for group solvency	409
		16.3.3.4 Group internal models	409
16.4	Contract Continuity for Existing Business		410
	16.4.1	How Does Brexit Affect Existing Contracts?	410
	16.4.2	European Insurers Operating in the UK	410
	16.4.3	UK Insurers Operating in the EU	412

Index 413

Table of Cases

Bedford Insurance Co Ltd v. Instituto de Resseguros de Brasil [1985] QB 966.................16.40
DR Insurance Company v. Seguros America Banamex....................................16.40
DR Insurance Company v. Imperio Companhia De Seguros [1993] 1 Lloyd's Rep. 120 ....16.40
Financial Services Authority v. Fradley and Woodward [2005] EWCA Civ. 1183..............16.40
Meroni v. High Authority of the ECSC (Case 9/56) [1957– 9] ECR 133 ....7.16
Scher and others v. Policyholders Protection Board (Nos. 1 and 2) [1994] 2 AC 57.......16.35, 16.40
Secretary of State and for Trade and Industry v. Great Western Assurance Co SA
    [1997] Lloyd's Rep. 377 ....16.40
Stewart v. Oriental Fire and Marine Insurance Company Ltd [1985] QB 988............16.35, 16.40
Whiteley Insurance Consultants (A Firm), Re [2008] EWHC 1782 (Ch.) 16.35
Whiteley Insurance Consultants, Re [2009] Bus LR 418 ....16.35

Table of European Legislation

PRIMARY LEGISLATION

Agreement on the Withdrawal of the
United Kingdom of Great Britain
and Northern Ireland from the
European Union and the European
Atomic Energy Community, as
endorsed by leaders at a special
meeting of the European Council
on 25 November 2018 . . . . .5.04
   Pts 1–6 . . . . .2.09
   art 126 . . . . 5.132
   arts 127–131. . . . . 5.132
   art 132 . . . . 5.132
   art 170 . . . . .2.09
   art 174 . . . . .2.09
   art 184 . . . . .2.21
Draft Transitional Agreement
   Article 126 . . . . .4.12
Draft Withdrawal Agreement and the
Political Declaration on Future
EU–UK relationship. 1.22, 1.26, 2.34
   paras. 37– 39 . . . . .1.24
Lisbon Treaty
   art 50 . . . . .7.31
Luxembourg Protocol 16.07
OECD Model Tax Convention on Income
and on Capital and ensures an
effective exchange of information
in tax matters, including any
multilateral tax agreements
   art 26 . . . . .4.86, 6.104
Political Declaration Setting Out the
Framework for the Future
Relationship Between the European
Union and the United Kingdom
   Pt I 2.23
   Pt II. 2.23, 2.24
   Pt III. 2.23
   Pt IV. 2.23
   Pt V. 2.23, 2.29
   arts 37–39 . . . . 5.132
Protocol Relating to the Cooperation of
the Competent Authorities of the
Member States of the European
Union in Particular Concerning the
Application of Directive 2002/92/EC
of the European Parliament and of
the Council of 9 December 2002
on Insurance Mediation 16.04
Treaty on European Union
   art 4(3) 2.22

art 50 . . . 1.09–1.14, 1.17, 1.27, 1.29, 1.34–1.36,
            1.39, 1.75, 2.04, 2.09, 4.11, 5.07, 5.09,
            6.08, 13.16, 13.18, 16.11, 16.27
art 50(1) 1.09
art 50(2) 1.09, 5.04, 5.08, 5.09
art 50(3) 5.04
Treaty on the Functioning of the
European Union
   art 50 . . . . .9.01
   art 217 . . . . .1.21
   art 218 . . . . .2.32
   art 263 . . . . .4.34
   art 290 . . . . 16.13
   art 291 . . . . 16.13
   art 355(3) 6.10

SECONDARY LEGISLATION

Decision

Decision No 2016/309/EU of 26
November 2015 and Commission
Delegated Decision (EU) 2015/1602
of 5 June 2015, respectively 16.65
Decision No 2016/2358/EU of 20
December 2016 amending
Implementing Decision 2014/
908/EU as regards the lists of
third countries and territories
whose supervisory and regulatory
requirements are considered
equivalent for the purposes of the
treatment of exposures according
to Regulation (EU) No 575/2013 of
the European Parliament and of the
Council [2016] OJ L348/75 . . . . 11.31
Decision No 2017/1857/EU on Equivalence
arrangements of US CFTC regime for
the purposes of Article 11 of EMIR,
13 October 2017. . . . . 11.27
Decision No 2018/2030/EU of 19
December 2018 determining, for
a limited period of time, that the
regulatory framework applicable to
central securities depositories of the
United Kingdom of Great Britain
and Northern Ireland is equivalent
in accordance with Regulation
(EU) No 909/2014 of the European
Parliament and of the Council
[2018] OJ L325/47 . . . . .5.05
   Recital (2) 5.134

Recital (3) 5.134
Recital (4) 5.134
Recital (13) 5.136
art 1................................. 5.135
art 2......................... 5.133, 5.135
Decision No 2018/2031/EU of 19
    December 2018 determining, for
    a limited period of time, that the
    regulatory framework applicable to
    central counterparties in the United
    Kingdom of Great Britain and
    Northern Ireland is equivalent, in
    accordance with Regulation (EU)
    No 648/2012 of the European
    Parliament and of the Council
    [2018] OJ L325/50 .... 5.05, 5.138,
                                    10.79, 13.56
Recital (2) 5.137
Recital (4) 5.137
Recital (14) 5.138
art 2................................. 5.133
Decision No 2019/544/EU of 3 April 2019
    amending Implementing Decision
    (EU) 2018/2031 determining, for
    a limited period of time, that the
    regulatory framework applicable
    to CCPs in the United Kingdom of
    Great Britain and Northern Ireland
    is equivalent, in accordance with the
    European Markets Infrastructure
    Regulation.................... 4.57, 4.60
Decision No 2019/545/EU of 3 April 2019
    amending Implementing Decision
    (EU) 2018/2030 determining, for
    a limited period of time, that the
    regulatory framework applicable
    to CSDs of the United Kingdom
    of Great Britain and Northern
    Ireland is equivalent in accordance
    with the Central Securities
    Depositories Regulation 4.57

Directives

Alternative Investment Fund Managers
    Directive 2010/76/EU 4.66, 3.255,
                                    7.30, 7.75, 11.108
Ch II..................................4.87
arts 22–24 ....4.75
art 35 ....4.68
art 36 ....4.68, 4.76
art 37 .... 4.68, 4.71, 4.77, 4.79, 4.85
art 37(7)..............................4.86
art 37(8)..............................4.87
art 37(23).............................4.88
arts 39–41 .... 4.68, 4.71, 4.77

art 42 .... 4.68, 4.69, 4.73, 4.75
art 42(2)..............................4.75
art 67 ....4.77, 4.79
art 67(4)..............................4.78
art 67(5)..............................4.79
art 67(6)................... 4.77–4.79, 4.85
Alternative Investment Fund Managers
    Directive 2011/61/EU 5.77, 6.95,
                                    7.11, 11.05, 15.01
Recital (2) 15.15
Recital (4) 15.15
Recital (9) 5.15
Recital (30) 15.32
Recital (70) 15.41
Recital (83) 5.15
art 3(2)............................... 15.24
art 4(1)......................... 5.78, 15.38
art 4(1)(a) 14.80, 14.110, 15.15
art 4(1)(b) 14.34
art 4(1)(w) 5.90
art 4(1)(x) 15.41
art 6(4)............................... 6.111
art 8(1)(c).............................5.83
art 8(1)(e).............................5.83
art 13 ....5.92
art 13(2)..............................5.92
art 20 .... 5.26, 15.36
arts 20(1)(b)–(f) 5.26
art 20(3) 5.15, 5.26
art 20(7)(b) 5.15
art 23(1)(f)............................5.90
art 31 .... 15.42
art 32 ....5.87
arts 34–42 ....5.28
art 35 .... 6.114, 15.86
arts 37–41 .... 15.86
art 37 .... 6.114
art 42 .... 6.108, 15.29, 15.30,
                                    15.73, 15.90
art 42(1)(a) 15.31
arts 42(1)(b)–(c)..................... 15.45
art 42(2)............................. 15.45
art 67 .... 6.107, 15.91
Annex I 5.90
Bank Recovery and Resolution Directive
    (BRRD) 2014/59/EU 1.88, 5.53,
                                    7.14, 7.67, 7.114, 8.68
art 2(1)(58) 5.124
art 2(1)(71) 5.126
art 2(1)(71a) 5.126
arts 15–18 .... 5.124
art 37(3)(a) 5.124
art 45(1) 5.126
art 96 .... 5.125
art 100 .... 5.125

Bank Recovery and Resolution Directive
  (BRRD II) 2019/879/EU 12.26
  Recital 10 .... 12.68
  art 1(1)(e). 12.62, 12.65, 12.66
  art 1(12) 12.74
  art 1(17) 12.67–12.71, 12.73
  art 1(21) 12.58
  arts 1(23)–(24) 12.73
Banking Consolidation Directive
  2000/12/EC 7.11, 10.47, 10.74
Banking Directive (recast) 2006/48/EC
  art 143 .... 11.93
Capital Requirements Directive (IV)
  2013/36/EU 1.02, 1.88, 3.104, 4.07,
    4.20, 4.22, 5.112, 5.115, 5.116, 5.120,
    7.10, 7.114, 7.19, 7.20, 7.30, 7.75,
    10.56, 10.85, 11.04, 11.12, 11.51,
    11.76, 11.91, 11.92, 12.30
  Title V 4.38
  art 1(9) 11.58
  art 3(1) 11.25
  art 3(1)(47) 5.126
  art 8(1) 5.107
  art 8(2) 5.108
  art 8(3) 5.108
  art 13 ....5.103, 5.122
  art 14 .... 5.109
  art 15 .... 5.112
  art 16 .... 5.109
  art 21a 11.61
  art 21b 11.58, 11.61
  arts 22–27 .... 5.109
  art 33 ....4.28, 4.38, 11.10, 11.34
  art 35 ....11.10, 11.34
  art 36(1)–(3) 11.10
  art 39(1) 11.10
  art 39(2) 11.10
  arts 40–46 .... 11.10
  art 47 .... 4.39, 5.103, 5.107
  art 47(3) 4.39
  art 48 .... 5.107
  art 51 ....8.79, 11.35
  art 74 .... 5.103
  art 74(1) 11.78
  art 75(2) 11.78
  art 76 .... 5.103
  art 77 .... 5.120
  art 78 .... 5.120
  art 88 .... 5.103
  arts 92–96 .... 5.123
  arts 92–95 .... 11.78
  art 92 .... 11.79
  art 94 .... 11.80
  art 94(1)(g) 11.77, 11.78, 11.80
  arts 97–101 .... 5.123
  art 101 .... 5.120
  art 109 .... 5.103
  art 123 .... 5.103
  art 127 ....11.60, 16.11
  art 127(1) 7.117
  art 128 .... 11.55
  art 131(a) 11.100
  Annex I 8.90, 11.10, 11.11
Capital Requirements Directive (V)
  2019/878 .... 11.57
Credit Agreements for Consumers
  Directive 2008/48/EC
  art 3(c) 14.27, 14.29
Credit Agreements for Consumers
  relating to Residential Immovable
  Property Directive 2014/17/EU 5.119,
    7.11, 7.75
  art 3(4) 14.31
  art 4(1) 14.34
  art 4(3) 14.27, 14.34, 14.80, 14.110
Cross-Border Distribution of Collective
  Investment Directive
  2019/1160/EU 15.57
  art 2(1) 15.61
  art 2(2) 15.62
  art 2(3) 15.67
  art 2(4) 15.64
Deposit Guarantee Schemes Directive
  2014/49/EU 3.175, 5.127, 8.33
  art 15(1) 5.127
Financial Groups Directive 2002/87/EC ... 7.75, 11.92
  art 18(1) 11.93
  art 127(1) 11.93
  art 127(2) 11.93
Insurance Distribution Directive
  2016/97/EU 4.94, 7.11, 7.75,
    16.01, 16.07
  art 1(6) 16.08
  art 16 .... 16.09
Investment Firm Directive 2017/0358 (COD) 11.85
  art 28(2) 11.89
Investment Services Directive
  93/22/EEC 10.47, 10.74
Investor Compensation Schemes
  Directive 97/9/EC 6.104
Listing Directive 2001/34/EC 10.31, 10.33
  art 5(a) 10.31
  art 41 .... 10.32
  art 105(1) 10.33
Market Abuse Directive 2003/6/EC 7.11, 7.19
Markets in Financial Instruments Directive
  (MiFID) I 2014/65/EU 1.02, 3.255,
    7.11, 7.83, 10.01
  art 4(1)(4) 13.72
  art 39 .... 11.20

Markets in Financial Instruments Directive
  (MiFID) II 2014/65/EU 1.03, 1.08,
    1.48, 1.88, 4.07, 4.45, 4.49, 5.37, 6.20, 6.95,
    7.10, 7.11, 7.14, 7.19, 7.20, 7.30, 7.67,
    7.75, 7.83, 7.116, 7.120, 14.22, 14.96
Recital (4) 10.14
Recital (46) 5.43, 5.49
Recital (109) 10.58
Recital (127) 5.28
Recital (140) 5.28
Recital (154) 5.28
Title I 10.09
Title II 10.09, 10.21, 10.22
Title III 10.09, 10.20
Title IV 10.09
Titles V–VII 10.09
art 1(1) 10.01
art 2(1)(j) 10.17
art 3(1)(c)(iii) 10.56
art 3(b) 14.34
art 3(c) 14.31, 14.34, 14.80, 14.110
art 3(j) 14.34
art 4(1)(1) 5.37, 10.38, 14.34
art 4(1)(2) 5.37
art 4(1)(18) 5.67, 10.01, 10.38, 14.34
art 4(1)(19) 10.18
art 4(1)(20) 10.18, 10.24, 14.35
art 4(1)(21)–(24) .5.67
art 4(1)(21) 10.18, 10.20
art 4(1)(22) 10.18, 10.21, 10.22
art 4(1)(23) 10.18
art 4(1)(24) 14.31, 14.35
art 4(1)(26) 10.40
art 4(1)(31) 5.45
art 4(1)(55) 5.49, 10.40
art 4(1)(56) 10.41
art 4(1)(57) 10.54
art 5(1) 5.49, 10.39
art 5(4) 5.49
art 9(3) 5.47
art 9(6) 5.48, 5.83
art 10(1) 5.45
art 15 . . . . .5.51
art 16 . . . . .5.47
art 16(4) 5.51, 5.52
art 16(5) 5.26
art 18(6) 10.45
art 39 . . . . 4.41, 4.44, 4.46, 7.100
art 27 . . . . 10.26
art 27(3) 10.25
art 34(1) 10.47, 11.12
art 34(2) 10.46
art 34(3) 10.46
art 35(1) 10.47
art 35(2) 10.46
art 35(3) 10.46
art 35(5) 10.46
arts 36–38 . . . . 10.48
art 36(1) 10.50
art 36(1)(b) 10.50
art 37(1) 10.52
art 38(1) 10.48
art 39 . . . . 10.59, 10.60
art 39(2)(a) 10.60
art 39(2)(b) 5.28, 10.60
art 39(2)(c) 10.60
art 39(2)(d) 10.60
art 40 . . . . 10.60
art 41(2) 10.60
art 42 . . . . .6.25
art 43 . . . . 10.61
arts 44–47 . . . . 10.42
art 44(1) 10.39
art 44(4) 10.49
art 45 . . . . .5.47
art 47(3) 10.62
art 48(1) 5.26
art 48(5) 5.74
art 48(12) 5.26
art 52(2) 5.74
art 55 . . . . 10.53
art 59 . . . . 10.65
art 60(2) 10.65
art 61 . . . . 10.01
art 67 . . . . 10.40, 12.44
art 72 . . . . 10.01
art 83 . . . . 10.01
Annex I
  s C 14.27, 14.31, 14.80, 14.110
    points (4)–(10) 13.75
    point (6) 13.76
Annex II, s II 10.59
Markets in Financial Instruments
  Directive 2017/593/EU 6.95
Money Laundering and Terrorist
  Financing Directive
  2015/849/EU
art 47 . . . . .5.21
Occupational Retirement Provision
  Directive 2003/41/EC 7.75
art 6(a) 14.34
Organisational Requirements Directive
  2010/43/EU 6.95
art 9 . . . . .5.84
art 10(3) 5.81
art 10(3)(c) 5.81
art 10(3)(d) 5.81
Payment Services Directive II
  2015/2366/EU 5.117, 5.118, 7.75
art 1(1) 5.116, 5.118
art 11(1) 5.116, 5.118
art 11(3) 5.118

Prospectus Directive 2003/71/EC......... 4.99,
   4.101–4.103, 4.105, 7.11, 7.75
 art 2............................. 4.100
 art 20 ......4.100, 4.104, 4.106–4.108, 10.31
 art 20(3)........................... 4.106
Second Banking Directive 97/C 209/04.....1.08
Settlement Finality Directive 98/26/EC
 art 2............................. 10.13
Solvency II Directive 2009/138/EC 1.88,
   3.255, 4.23, 4.89, 4.91, 4.92, 7.11,
   7.75, 7.120, 8.12, 11.05, 11.108,
   15.89, 16.01, 16.45, 16.46
 Recital (34) 5.21
 art 2(1).......................16.42, 16.43
 art 13(1)........................... 14.34
 art 13(4)........................... 14.34
 art 38 ....5.26
 art 42 ....5.21
 art 49 ....5.26
 art 49(1)............................5.26
 art 49(2)............................5.26
 art 49(2)(a)–(c).....................5.26
 art 115 .... 16.74
 arts 147ff 16.32
 art 162 .... 4.90, 16.42–16.44, 16.47
 art 167 .... 16.46
 art 172 .... 4.91, 16.56, 16.59
 art 174 ....16.47, 16.49
 art 175 .... 16.47
 art 227 ....4.91, 16.54
 art 211(2)(c)–(d)....................5.21
 art 220(2).......................... 16.71
 art 231 .... 16.73
 art 257 ....5.21
 art 260 ....4.91, 16.55
 art 261 .... 16.66
Transparency Directive
   2004/109/EC..................7.11, 7.75
UCITS Directive 2009/65/EC....... 1.07, 4.66,
   4.67, 5.77, 6.95, 6.7.11, 7.75, 15.57
 Recital (16) 5.15
 Recital (18).........................5.86
 Ch III 5.78
 art 1(2)................ 14.34, 14.80, 14.110
 art 2(1)(b) 5.78
 art 2(1)(c)..........................5.83
 art 2(1)(e)..........................5.83
 art 2(2).............................5.90
 art 6(2).............................5.90
 art 6(3)............................ 6.111
 art 7(1)(b) 5.21, 5.83
 art 7(1)(d) 5.83
 art 13 ....5.26
 art 13(1)(a)–(d).....................5.26
 art 13(1)(c) 5.26
 art 13(1)(g) 5.26
 art 13(1)(h) 5.26
 art 13(2)......................5.15, 5.26
 art 14a..............................5.92
 art 14a(4)...........................5.92
 art 14b..............................5.92
 art 16 ....5.87
 art 20(1)(b) 5.90
 art 22a..............................5.26
 art 27 ....5.83
 art 29 ....5.78
 art 29(1)(b) 5.83
 art 69(2)............................5.84
 art 91 ....5.87
 Annex I, point 1.8...................5.84
 Annex II.............................5.90
UCITS Directive 2010/44/EU.............6.95
UCITS Directive (V) 2014/91/EU 11.05

European Economic Area

EEA Joint Committee No. 201/2016 of
   30 September 2016 amending
   Annex IX (Financial services) to the
   EEA Agreement [2017/ 278].....5.11, 5.97
EEA Joint Committee No. 199/2016 of
   30 September 2016 amending
   Annex IX (Financial services) to the
   EEA Agreement [2017/ 276]..........5.97
EEA Joint Committee No. 021/2018........12.9

Regulation

Alternative Investment Fund Managers
   Regulation (Commission Delegated
   Regulation) No 231/2013/EU
 Recital (86) 5.28
 Recital (91) 5.15
 Recital (93) 5.15
 Recitals (134)–(135).................5.28
 art 60 ....5.84
 art 61(3)............................5.81
 art 61(3)(c) 5.81
 art 61(3)(d) 5.81
 arts 75–82 ....5.26
 art 75 ....5.26
 art 75(a)–(b) 5.26
 art 75(e)–(f)........................5.26
 art 75(e)–(j)........................5.26
 art 76 ....5.81
 art 77 ....5.26, 6.106
 art 78 .... 6.106
 art 79 ....5.26
 art 82 ....5.15
 arts 113–115 ....5.28
Bank Recovery and Resolution
   Regulation No 2016/1075/EU 12.32
 arts 17–21 .... 12.36

Benchmarks Regulation No
    2016/1011/EU 1.48, 1.88, 4.95,
                    7.14, 14.02, 14.17–14.19,
                    14.22–14.25, 14.30, 14.31, 14.52
    Recital 16 .... 14.24
    Recital 48 .... 14.41
    art 2(2) 14.30
    art 3(1)(1) 14.28
    art 3(1)(2) 14.30, 14.80
    art 3(1)(3) 14.27
    art 3(1)(6) 14.24
    art 3(1)(7) 14.34
    art 3(1)(8) 14.24
    art 3(1)(10) 14.74
    art 3(1)(14) 14.24
    art 3(1)(24) 14.64
    art 3(17)(h) 14.29
    art 5(5) 14.36
    art 4(1) 14.51
    art 4(2) 14.51, 14.61
    art 4(3) 14.51
    art 4(6) 14.51
    art 4(7) 14.51
    art 4(7)(c)–(e) 14.61
    art 4(8) 14.51, 14.61
    art 5(1) 14.51
    art 5(2) 14.61
    art 5(3) 14.51, 14.61
    art 5(4) 14.51, 14.61
    art 6(1) 14.51, 14.61
    art 6(2) 14.51
    art 6(3) 14.51, 14.61
    art 6(4) 14.51
    art 6(5) 14.51, 14.61
    art 7(1) 14.51
    art 7(2) 14.51, 14.61
    art 7(3) 14.51
    art 8(1) 14.51
    art 8(1)(a) 14.64
    art 8(2) 14.51
    art 9(1) 14.51
    art 9(2) 14.51
    art 10(1)–(3) 14.51
    art 11(1)(a) 14.51
    art 11(1)(b) 14.51, 14.61
    art 11(1)(a) 14.51
    art 11(1)(c) 14.51
    art 11(1)(d) 14.51, 14.64
    art 11(1)(e) 14.51, 14.64
    art 11(2) 14.64
    art 11(2)(b)–(c) 14.61
    art 11(3) 14.51, 14.61, 14.64
    art 11(4) 14.97
    art 12(1)(a)–(c) 14.51
    art 12(2)(a) 14.51

art 13 .... 14.74
art 13(1) 14.51
art 13(2) 14.61
art 14 .... 14.75
art 14(1) 14.51, 14.64
art 14(2) 14.61, 14.64
art 15 .... 14.64
art 15(1) 14.51, 14.74, 14.84
art 15(2) 14.51, 14.61
art 15(3) 14.51
art 16 .... 14.64, 14.97
art 16(1) 14.75, 14.83
art 16(2) 14.61
art 16(3) 14.61
arts 17–19 .... 14.73
art 17(1) 14.64
art 18 .... 14.66
art 19(1) 14.65
art 19(2) 14.65
art 20 .... 14.69, 14.97
art 20(1) 14.54, 14.55
art 20(1)(a) 14.54
art 20(1)(b) 14.54
art 20(1)(c)(i)–(iii) 14.54
ar 20(2)–(4) 14.70
art 21 .... 14.97
art 21(1) 14.56
art 21(1)(b) 14.56
art 21(3) 14.56
art 23 .... 14.57, 14.97
art 24 .... 14.71
art 24(1)(a) 14.58
art 24(1)(b) 14.58
art 24(3) 14.59
art 25(1)–(3) 14.60
art 25(7) 14.62
art 26 .... 14.86
art 26(1) 14.61
art 26(3) 14.62
art 29 .... 14.86
art 29(1) 14.33
art 30 .... 14.92
art 30(2) 4.97
art 30(3) 4.97
art 31 .... 14.94
art 32 .... 4.96, 14.94
art 32(4) 14.96
art 32(6)–(8) 14.103
art 33 .... .4.96
art 34 .... 14.89, 14.90
art 34(1) 14.43
art 34(2) 14.98
art 34(4) 14.40
art 34(7) 14.48
art 36 .... 14.49

TABLE OF EUROPEAN LEGISLATION   xxix

art 51 ....14.78, 14.83
art 51(2)–(4) 14.80
art 51(5)........................... 14.110
Annex I 14.66
Annex II........................... 14.65
Capital Requirements Regulation (CRR)
    No 575/2013/EU 1.88, 3.104, 4.37,
        5.115, 5.120, 7.10, 7.19, 7.75, 7.114, 11.56
Title II, Ch 5 .... 11.111
art 4(1)(1) 11.25, 14.34
art 4(1)(2A)......................... 14.36
art 4(1)(88) 13.43
art 4(1)(118) 5.126
art 20 .... 5.121
art 25 .... 12.60
art 62 ....12.60, 12.71
art 63 .... 12.71
art 66 .... 12.60
art 71 .... 12.60
art 72a............................. 12.71
art 72b 12.71
art 79 .... 12.60
art 92b 12.72
art 107 .... 11.31
art 114 .... 11.31
art 114(1)–(2) 11.72
art 114(7)......................... 11.73
art 115 .... 11.31
art 116 .... 11.31
art 132(3)(a)(ii)..................... 5.28
art 142 .... 11.31
art 143 .... 5.120
art 147(2).......................... 5.120
art 151 .... 5.120
art 190(3).......................... 5.26
art 283 .... 5.120
art 312 .... 5.120
art 363 .... 5.120
arts 404–410 .... 11.103
art 494 .... 12.63
Cash Penalties Regulation No
    2017/389/EU 7.114
Central Securities Depositories
    Regulation
    No 909/2014 EU................... 7.75
Recital (24) 5.28
Recital (34) 5.28
art 6............................... 7.114
art 7............................... 7.114
art 24(4)........................... 5.28
art 25 .... 5.135
art 25(4)–(8) 5.135
art 25(4)(a) 5.135
art 25(4)(c) 5.28
art 25(10).......................... 5.28

art 25(11).......................... 5.135
art 30 .... 5.26
art 30(1)(a)–(b)..................... 5.26
art 30(1)(f)–(g)..................... 5.26
art 30(1)(h)–(i) 5.26
art 30(3)........................... 5.26
art 30(4)........................... 5.26
Credit Ratings Agencies Regulation
    No 1060/2009/EC 7.75
art 4(1)............................ 11.74
art 14 .... 11.73
art 20 .... 11.73
Cross-Border Distribution of Collective
    Investment Regulation No
    2019/1156/EU 15.57
European Banking Authority Regulation
    No 1093/2010/EU 5.97, 7.15
art 4(2)............................ 5.97
art 29 .... 7.16
art 29(1)........................... 5.96
art 29(1)(a) 5.96
art 31 .... 7.16
art 33(1)........................... 7.110
art 75(1)–(3) 7.110
European Central Bank Regulation
    No 1024/2013/EU 5.120
art 6(4) 6.22
European Long-term Investment
    FundsRegulation No 2015/760/EU 5.79
European Markets Infrastructure
    Regulation (EMIR)
    No 648/2012/EU 1.02, 1.88,
        3.255, 4.02, 7.14, 7.20, 7.75, 7.83, 15.89
Title III........................... 13.49
Title VII.......................... 13.57
art 1............................5.138, 13.69
art 1(4)(a) 13.68
art 2......................5.138, 13.103, 13.104
art 2(1)............................ 14.34
art 2(1)(7) 13.72
art 2(2)............................ 14.34
art 2(10)........................... 13.70
art 2a.........................13.72–13.74
art 3..........................13.78, 13.79
art 4........ 5.137, 5.139, 13.43, 13.69, 13.70,
                13.72, 13.78, 13.81, 13.82
art 4(1)(a) 13.72
art 4(1)(a)(v) 13.69
art 4(1)(4) 13.67
art 4(1)(8) 13.67
art 4(1)(9) 13.67
art 6............................... 10.30
art 7............................... 13.69
art 8............................... 13.69
art 9.............10.30, 13.57, 13.85, 13.88

art 9(4) 13.87
art 10 . . . . 10.30
art 10(3) 13.72
art 11 . . . . 4.61, 4.65, 13.69, 13.72, 13.78, 13.80, 13.81
art 11(3) 5.141, 13.78
art 11(12) 13.69
art 13 . . . . 11.27, 13.103
art 13(2) 13.78, 13.81
art 14 . . . . 13.46
art 25 . . . . 4.02, 4.53, 5.138, 10.81, 11.26, 13.42, 13.45, 13.48, 13.50, 13.54, 13.56, 13.103
art 25(1) 5.138
art 25(2)–(5) 5.138
art 25(2) 4.54, 13.42, 13.48
art 25(2)(a) 5.138
art 25(6) 13.56
art 52 . . . . 10.30
art 55 . . . . 13.60
art 75 . . . . 13.93
art 75(2) 13.93
art 77 . . . . 13.58, 13.60
art 81 . . . . 13.61
art 85 . . . . 13.13, 13.81
art 89(1) 13.70
art 89(4) 13.52
art 89(5A) 13.103
art 89a 13.103
European Securities and Markets Authority Regulation No 1095/2010/EU 5.11
art 1(2) 5.11
art 4(3) 5.11
art 29(1) 5.10
art 29(1)(a) 5.10
European Social Entrepreneurship Funds Regulation No 346/2013 EU 5.79, 7.75
General Data Protection Regulation No 2016/679/EU 5.53
Insurance and Reinsurance Regulation (Commission Delegated) 2015/35/EU (supplementing Directive 2009/138/EC) (Solvency II) 16.01, 16.13, 16.73
art 211 . . . . 16.50
Interchange Fee Regulation No 2015/751/EU 7.81
Market Abuse Regulation (MAR) No 596/2014 EU 1.02, 7.19, 7.75
Markets in Financial Instruments Regulation (MiFIR) No 600/2014 EU 1.03, 1.88, 6.13, 7.19, 7.75, 8.98
art 2(1)(12) 14.29

art 21 . . . . 13.72
art 23 . . . . 1.49, 4.31, 7.108
art 25 . . . . .4.56
art 28 . . . . 7.108
art 36 . . . . .4.56
art 37 . . . . .4.56
art 38(1) 4.56
art 38(3) 4.56
arts 46–49 . . . . 5.64, 5.115
art 46 . . . . 4.41, 4.42, 4.44, 4.47, 6.101, 6.105, 11.84
art 46(5) 6.105
art 46(6) 4.48
art 47 . . . . 7.116, 11.84, 11.86
art 47(1) 4.42, 4.43, 11.23
art 47(2) 11.23
art 54 . . . . 4.43, 6.101
MiFID II Delegated Regulation No 2017/565/EU
arts 30–32 . . . . 5.26
art 31 . . . . 5.26, 5.53
art 31(1) 5.26
art 31(2) 5.58
art 31(2)(a)–(c) 5.26
art 31(2)(b) 5.54
art 31(2)(d)–(g) 5.26
art 31(2)(h)–(i) 5.26
art 31(5) 5.26
art 32 . . . . 5.26, 5.28, 5.65
MiFID II Delegated Regulation No 2017/584/EU
art 6 . . . . 5.26
art 6(1) 5.26, 5.73
art 6(2) 5.73
art 6(3)(a)–(c) 5.26
art 6(3)(d)–(g) 5.26
art 6(3)(h) 5.26
art 6(3)(i) 5.26
art 6(5) 5.26
art 6(5)(b) 5.26
art 6(7) 5.26
Annex I, sC 14.31
Money Market Funds Regulation No 2017/1131/EU 5.79
Presidency Compromise Proposal for a Regulation of the European Parliament and of the Council on the prudential supervision of investment firms and amending Regulations (EU) No. 575/ 2013, (EU) No. 600/ 2014, and (EU) No. 1093/ 2010 (2017/ 0359 (COD)) 11.85
Art 61(2) 11.86

Prospectus Regulation No 2017/1129/EU 4.103,
          7.19, 7.114, 10.31
    Ch VI 4.104
    art 28 .... 4.104, 4.109
    art 29 .... 4.104, 4.108
    art 29(3) 4.109
Regulation No 285/2014/EU of 13
    February 2014 supplementing
    Regulation (EU) No 648/2012 of
    the European Parliament and of the
    Council with regard to regulatory
    technical standards on direct,
    substantial and foreseeable effect
    of contracts within the Union and
    to prevent the evasion of rules and
    obligations [2014] OJ L85/1 .... 13.69
Regulation 2015/63/EU of 21 October
    2014 supplementing Directive
    2014/59/EU of the European
    Parliament and of the Council with
    regard to ex ante contributions to
    resolution financing arrangements
    [2015] OJ 11/44.................... 12.19
Regulation 2016/100/EU of 16 October
    2015 laying down implementing
    technical standards specifying the
    joint decision process with regard
    to the application for certain
    prudential permissions pursuant
    to Regulation (EU) No. 575/2013
    of the European Parliament and of
    the Council [2016] L21/45 .... 5.121
Regulation No2016/592 of 1 March 2016
    supplementing Regulation (EU)
    No 648/2012 of the European
    Parliament and of the Council
    with regard to regulatory technical
    standards on the clearing obligation
    [2016] OJ L 103/5................. 13.84
Regulation No 2016/778/EU of 2 February
    2016 supplementing Directive 2014/
    59/EU of the European Parliament
    and of the Council with regard to the
    circumstances and conditions under
    which the payment of extraordinary
    ex post contributions may be partially
    or entirely deferred, and on the criteria
    for the determination of the activities,
    services and operations with regard
    to critical functions, and for the
    determination of the business lines
    and associated services with regard
    to core business lines [2016]
    OJ L131/41........................ 12.19
    art 6............................. 12.40

Regulation No 2016/860/EU of 4 February
    2016 specifying further the
    circumstances where exclusion from
    the application of write-down or
    conversion powers is necessary
    under Article 44(3) of Directive
    2014/59/EU of the European
    Parliament and of the Council
    establishing a framework for the
    recovery and resolution of credit
    institutions and investment firms
    [2016] OJ L144/11 .... 12.19
Regulation No 2016/1434/EU of
    14 December 2015 correcting
    Delegated Regulation (EU) 2015/63
    supplementing
    Directive 2014/59/EU of the
    European Parliament and of the
    Council with regard to ex ante
    contributions to resolution financing
    arrangements [2016] OJ L233/1........ 12.19
Regulation No 2016/1450/EU of 23 May
    2016 supplementing Directive 2014/
    59/EU of the European Parliament
    and of the Council with regard
    to regulatory technical standards
    specifying the criteria relating to
    the methodology for setting the
    minimum requirement for own
    funds and eligible liabilities
    [2016] OJ L237/1 .... 12.60
Regulation No 2017/867/EU of 7 February
    2017 on classes of arrangements to be
    protected in a partial property transfer
    under Article 76 of Directive 2014/59/
    EU of the European Parliament and of
    the Council [2017] OJ L131/15 ..... 12.19
Regulation No 2017/1943/EU of 14 July
    2016 supplementing Directive
    2014/65/EU of the European
    Parliament and of the Council
    with regard to regulatory technical
    standards on information and
    requirements for the authorisation
    of investment firms [2017]
    OJ L276/4 .... 6.32, 6.96, 6.134
    art 6(a) 5.44
Regulation No 2017/1945/EU of 19 June
    2017 laying down implementing
    technical standards with regard to
    notifications by and to applicant
    and authorised investment firms
    according to Directive 2014/65/EU
    of the European Parliament and of
    the Council [2017] OJ L276/22 ...... 6.32

Regulation No 2017/2401/EU of the
European Parliament and of the
Council of 12 December 2017
amending Regulation (EU)
No 575/2013 on prudential
requirements for credit
institutions and investment firms
[2017] OJ 347/1 .... 11.111
Regulation No 2018/1644/EU of 13 July
2018 supplementing Regulation (EU)
2016/1011 of the European
Parliament and of the Council
with regard to regulatory technical
standards determining the
minimum content of cooperation
arrangements with competent
authorities of third countries whose
legal framework and supervisory
practices have been recognised as
equivalent [2018] OJ L274/33 .... 14.92
Regulation No 2018/1645/EU of 13 July
2018 supplementing Regulation (EU)
2016/1011 of the European
Parliament and of the Council
with regard to regulatory technical
standards for the form and content
of the application for recognition
with the competent authority of the
Member State of reference and of
the presentation of information in
the notification to European
Securities and Markets Authority
(ESMA) [2018] OJ L274/36 .... 14.101
Regulation No 2018/1646/EU of 13 July
2018 supplementing Regulation (EU)
2016/1011 of the European
Parliament and of the Council
with regard to regulatory technical
standards for the information to
be provided in an application for
authorisation and in an application
for registration [2018] OJ L274/43
  Annex I 14.45
  Annex II 14.46
Regulation No 2019/396/EU of
19 December 2018 amending
Delegated Regulation (EU)
2015/2205, Delegated Regulation
(EU) 2016/592 and Delegated
Regulation (EU) 2016/1178
supplementing Regulation (EU)
No 648/2012 of the European
Parliament and of the Council as
regards the date at which the
clearing obligation takes effect
for certain types of contracts
[2019] OJ L71/11 .... 5.05
  Recital (5) 5.139
  Recital (6) 5.139
  art 1(1) 5.140
  art 2(1) 5.140
  art 3(1) 5.140
  art 4 .... 5.133
Regulation No 2019/397/EU of 19
December 2018 amending Delegated
Regulation (EU) 2016/2251
supplementing Regulation (EU)
No 648/2012 of the European
Parliament and of the Council
as regards the date until which
counterparties may continue to
apply their risk-management
procedures for certain OTC
derivative contracts not cleared by
a CCP [2019] OJ L71/15 .... 5.05, 5.141
  Recital (5) 5.141
  art 1 .... 5.141
  art 2 .... 5.133
Regulation No 2019/876/EU of the
European Parliament and of the
Council of 20 May 2019 amending
Regulation (EU) No. 575/2013 as
regards the leverage ratio, the net
stable funding ratio, requirements
for own funds and eligible liabilities,
counterparty credit risk, market
risk, exposures to central
counterparties, exposures to
collective investment undertakings,
large exposures, reporting and
disclosure requirements, and
Regulation (EU) No. 648/2012
[2019] OJ L150/1 .... 11.57, 12.61
  art 1(17) 12.73
  art 1(31) 12.71
  art 1(47) 12.64, 12.72
  art 1(128) 12.63
  art 92a 12.64
Risk Mitigation RTS Regulation
  No 2015/2205/EU 13.84, 13.90
Securities Financing Transactions
  Regulation No 2015/2365/EU 7.14,
                                              7.114, 11.05
Securitisation Regulation
  No 2017/2402/EU 11.109
  art 6 .... 11.109, 11.110
  art 8 .... 11.113
Short Selling Regulation
  No 236/2012/EU 7.14, 7.67, 7.75
Single Supervisory Mechanism Framework
  Regulation No 468/2014/EU
  art 50 .... 11.65
Single Supervisory Mechanism Regulation
  No 1024/2013/EU 11.65

Venture Capital Funds Regulation
No 345/2013/EU 5.79

UK LEGISLATION

Statutes

Bank of England and Financial Services
Act 2016
  s 21 .... 9.10
Banking Act 2009 .... 12.4
  Pt 1 .... 12.30
  Pt 2 .... 12.28, 12.30, 12.49
  Pt 3 .... 12.28, 12.30
  s 1(1) 12.28
  s 2(1) 12.29
  s 2(2)(a) 12.30
  s 2(2)(b) 12.29
  s 2(2)(c) 12.29
  s 3(1) 12.40, 12.60
  s 6B 12.54
  s 7 .... 12.48, 12.49
  s 9 .... 12.75
  s 11 .... 12.28, 12.51
  s 12 .... 12.28, 12.51
  s 12A 12.28, 12.51
  s 12A(2) 12.52
  s 12ZA 12.28, 12.51
  s 13 .... 12.28, 12.51, 12.75
  s 15 .... 12.52
  s 16 .... 12.52
  ss 26–31 .... 12.52
  s 33 .... 12.52
  ss 41A–46 .... 12.52
  s 48B 12.54
  ss 48U–48W 12.52
  s 78A 12.75
  ss 81AA–81D 12.30
  ss 81B–81BA 12.50
  s 81D 12.30, 12.50
  s 83A 12.30
  s 84 .... 12.30
  s 85 .... 12.52
  s 89 .... 12.29
  s 89A 12.30
  ss 89B–89G 12.30
  s 89G 12.30
  s 89H 12.53, 12.56, 12.78
  s 89H(4) 12.53
  s 89H(7) 12.30
  s 89I 12.53
  s 89J 12.53
  s 89JA 12.30
  s 129A 12.30
  s 130 .... 12.30
  s 157A 12.30
  s 158 .... 12.30
  s 228 .... 12.75
  s 229 .... 12.75
  s 256A 12.75
  s 257 .... 12.75
  s 258A 12.30
Building Societies Act 1986
  s 119 .... 12.30
Companies Act 1989
  Pt VII 10.13
Companies Act 2006 .... 3.14, 3.210
  s 381 .... 8.33
  s 382 .... 8.33
Constitutional Reform and Governance
  Act 2010 (CRAG) 1.28, 2.05
  Pt 2 .... 1.30
European Communities Act 1972 ..... 1.29, 1.55,
                                      7.40, 16.13
  s 2 .... 10.03
  s 2(1) 7.22, 13.15
  s 2(2) 7.22
European Union (Notification of
  Withdrawal) Act 2017 .... 1.09
European Union (Withdrawal) Act 2018
  (EUWA) 1.29, 1.63, 1.68, 2.05,
    3.104, 7.38, 7.41–7.43, 7.45, 7.49, 7.55,
    7.63, 7.64, 7.77, 7.81, 7.84, 7.95, 7.113,
    11.02, 11.95, 13.17, 16.14, 16.27
  s 2(1) 16.13
  s 2(2) 12.23
  s 3 .... 12.32, 12.40, 12.60, 13.23
  s 3(1) 16.13
  s 3(2) 13.21
  ss 6(1)–(4) 7.43
  s 7 .... 7.51
  s 8 .... 1.56, 7.44, 13.25, 13.26, 13.27
  s 8(1) 7.45, 11.90
  s 8(2) 7.46
  s 8(3)(b) 7.48
  s 8(4) 7.47
  s 8(5) 13.26
  s 8(6) 7.48
  s 8(7) 13.26
  s 8(8) 7.44
  s 13 .... 1.30, 1.34, 2.05
  s 20 .... 9.06
  s 20(1)–(2) 16.27
  Sch 7 .... 7.50
European Union (Withdrawal)
  Act 2019 .... 4.15
Financial Services Act 1986 .... 7.97
Financial Services Act 2012 .... 3.97, 10.33
  s 91 .... 14.14
  s 92 .... 14.15
Financial Services and Markets
  Act 2000 (FSMA) 3.148, 3.175,
        8.104, 10.71, 11.52, 12.15, 16.03
  Pt 4 .... 8.51

Pt 4A............1.69, 3.14, 9.07, 9.10, 9.12,
              9.33, 12.29, 16.21, 16.23,
              16.30, 16.32, 16.33, 16.81
Pt 9A.................................1.60
Pt 23............................... 11.52
s 1A..................................1.60
s 1B..................................1.60
s 2AB.................................1.60
s 2J..................................1.60
s 19................7.98, 14.12, 14.39, 16.19
s 26......................... 16.19, 16.79
s 31(1)(a)........................... 16.22
s 55B................................ 11.40
s 55B(1)............................. 12.48
s 55B(2)............................. 12.48
s 66A................................. 9.36
s 66B................................. 9.36
s 73A................................ 10.33
s 138A......................... 1.70, 12.24
ss 138P–138S..........................1.60
s 192B............................... 12.55
s 213................................. 8.28
s 285................................ 12.30
s 285(1)(a).......................... 10.34
s 286(1)(a).......................... 10.34
s 292(2)............................. 10.36
s 292(3)............................. 10.36
ss 300A–300D......................... 10.72
s 418................................ 16.37
s 418(5)............................. 16.37
s 423A............................... 14.29
Sch 3................... 10.47, 10.74, 16.22
Sch 6..................... 8.51, 9.10, 11.40
Financial Services (Banking Reform)
    Act 2013....................3.97, 12.19
  s 36................................. 9.38
  s 39(10).............................1.60
  s 71.................................1.60
  ss 97A–97D...........................1.60
  Sch 4................................1.60
    Pts 1–3............................1.61
    Pt 5...............................1.61
    Pt 6...............................1.61
Human Rights Act 1998................ 13.26
Insolvency Act 1986.................. 12.19
Investment Exchanges and Clearance
    Houses Act 2006 (IECHA)......... 10.71
  s 1................................ 10.71

Statutory Instruments

Alternative Investment Fund Managers
    (Amendment) (EU Exit)
    Regulations 2019
    (SI 2019/328).......... 1.62, 15.10, 15.70
  art 65.............................. 15.22

Bank Recovery and Resolution
    and Miscellaneous Provisions
    (Amendment) (EU Exit)
    Regulations 2018 (SI 2018/1394)..........12.19
  Sch 1
    paras 30–32...................... 12.50
    para 41(2)....................... 12.53
    para 41(4)(b).................... 12.30
  Sch 3
    para 60(4)....................... 12.47
    paras 62–65...................... 12.47
    paras 84–89...................... 12.46
    paras 91–96...................... 12.46
    para 114......................... 12.76
  Sch 5
    para 1........................... 12.40
Bank Recovery and Resolution Order
    2014 (SI 2014/3329).............. 12.14
Bank Recovery and Resolution
    (No. 2) Order 2014
    (SI 2014/3348).............12.14, 12.80
  Sch A1............................. 12.33
  Sch 2.............................. 12.40
  Sch 2A............................. 12.40
  Sch 2B........................12.40, 12.41
  Pt 7............................... 12.43
  Pt 16.............................. 12.22
  s A1............................... 12.32
  art 2(1)................12.31, 12.39, 12.60
  art 7.............................. 12.31
  art 8.........................12.39, 12.40
  art 7(3)........................... 12.32
  arts 11–32......................... 12.31
  art 12(1).......................... 12.36
  art 13(1).......................... 12.36
  arts 16–32......................... 12.37
  art 17............................. 12.37
  arts 33–35......................... 12.31
  art 37............................. 12.39
  art 37(3).......................... 12.39
  art 40............................. 12.39
  art 40(7).......................... 12.42
  arts 53–54......................... 12.39
  arts 59–82......................... 12.40
  art 59(2).......................... 12.40
  art 61(2).......................... 12.40
  art 83(2).......................... 12.43
  arts 107–120....................... 12.47
  art 107............................ 12.47
  art 122............................ 12.60
  art 123............................ 12.60
  art 244............................ 12.76
Banking Act 2009 (Exclusion of Insurers)
    Order 2010 (SI 2010/35)
  art 2.............................. 12.29

Banking Act 2009 (Exclusion of Investment
   Firms of a Specified Description)
   Order 2014 (SI 2014/1832)
   art 2(1) 12.30
Benchmarks (Amendment and
   Transitional Provision) (EU Exit)
   Regulations 2019 (SI 2019/657) 14.20
   Pt 3 .... 14.87, 14.123
   art 4(b)(ii) 14.31
   art 4(b)(iii)......................... 14.31
   art 5(3) 14.76
   art 5(4) 14.29
   art 5(6) 14.29
   art 5(13)........................... 14.114
   art 15 .... 14.68
   art 16 .... 14.69
   art 16(7).............................14.70
   art 16(8)..................... 14.70, 14.72
   art 20 .... 14.71
   art 27 .... 14.114
   art 27(2)(b) 14.115
   art 27(2)(c) 14.115
   art 27(4)(a) 14.115
   art 29 .... 14.114
   art 30 .... 14.114
   art 31 .... 14.44
   art 31(6)............................ 14.48
   art 33 .... 14.49
   art 34(1)............................ 14.37
   art 42 .... 14.79
   art 42(2)............................ 14.80
   art 42(3)............................ 14.80
   art 42(6)........................... 14.116
   art 42(8)............................ 14.82
   art 51 .... 14.117
   art 54 .... 14.117
   art 58 .... 14.117
   art 59 .... 14.117
   art 62 .... 14.117
Building Societies (Insolvency and Special
   Administration) Order 2009
   (SI 2009/805) 12.30
Capital Requirements Regulations 2013
   (SI 2013/3115) 11.51
   Pt 4 .... 11.51
Capital Requirements (Amendment)
   (EU Exit) Regulations 2018
   (SI 2018/1401) 11.51
Capital Requirements (Capital Buffers
   and Macro-Prudential Measures)
   Regulations 2014
   (SI 2014/894) 11.55
Central Counterparties (Amendment, etc.,
   and Transitional Provision)
   (EU Exit) Regulations 2018
   (SI 2018/1184) 1.62, 10.81, 13.31
   Pt 6 .... 13.52
   regs 12–16 .... 13.54
   regs 17–19 .... 13.52
Collective Investment Schemes
   (Amendment etc.) (EU Exit)
   Regulations 2019 (SI 2019/325) 1.62
Credit Institutions and Insurance
   Undertakings Reorganisation
   and Winding Up (Amendment)
   (EU Exit) Regulations 2019
   (SI 2019/38) 16.15
Credit Institutions (Reorganisation and
   Winding up) Regulations 2004
   (SI 2004/1045) 12.28
Data Reporting Services Regulations 2017
   (SI 2017/699) 10.76
EEA Passport Rights (Amendment, etc.,
   and Transitional Provisions)
   (EU Exit) Regulations 2018
   (SI 2018/1149) 1.62, 9.05,
                   10.77, 16.15, 16.23, 16.27, 16.80
   reg 14 .... 9.05, 9.07
   reg 17 ....9.07
   reg 27 ....9.07
Electronic Commerce and Solvency
   2 (Amendment etc.) (EU Exit)
   Regulations 2019
   (SI 2019/1361) 16.15
Electronic Money, Payment Services and
   Payment Systems (Amendment
   and Transitional Provisions)
   (EU Exit) Regulations 2018
   (SI 2018/1201) 1.62
Equivalence Determinations for Financial
   Services and Miscellaneous
   Provisions (Amendment etc.)
   (EU Exit) Regulations 2019
   (SI 2019/541) 13.69
European Communities (Undertakings
   for Collective Investment in
   Transferable Securities)
   Regulations 2011
   (SI 352/2011) 6.95, 6.100, 6.118
   reg 17 .... 6.114
   reg 17(3)........................... 6.118
   reg 17(11).......................... 6.135
   reg 23 .... 6.106
European Union (Alternative Investment
   Fund Managers) Regulations 2013
   (SI 2003/1773) 6.95, 6.100,
                                        6.118, 15.01
   reg 9(1)(a) 6.114, 6.118
   reg 9(5)........................... 6.1335
   reg 21 .... 6.106
   reg 43 .... 6.108
   reg 44 .... 6.109

European Union (Markets in Financial
    Instruments) Regulations 2017
    (SI 375/2017) 6.95, 6.100, 6.115,
                                    6.118, 6.135
    reg 5(4). 6.102
    reg 5(5). 6.103
    reg 7 . . . . 6.114
    reg 17(8). 6.118
    reg 48(1). 6.104
    reg 51 . . . . 6.105
European Union (Withdrawal) Act 2018
    (Exit Day) (Amendment)
    Regulations 2019(SI 2019/718). 7.64
European Union (Withdrawal) Act 2018
    (Exit Day) (Amendment) (No. 2)
    Regulations 2019 (2019/859) 7.64
Financial Collateral Arrangements
    (No. 2) Regulations 2003
    (SI 2003/3226) 10.13
Financial Conglomerates and Other
    Financial Groups (Amendment)
    (EU Exit) Regulations 2019
    (SI 2019/264) 16.15
Financial Markets and Insolvency (Settlement
    Finality and Financial Collateral
    Arrangements (Amendment)
    Regulations 2010 (SI 2010/2993) 10.13
Financial Regulators' Powers (Technical
    Standards etc.) (Amendment etc.)
    (EU Exit) Regulations 2018
    (SI 2018/115) 1.60, 7.70, 12.23, 13.33
    Pt 2 . . . . .7.72
    Pt 3 . . . . .7.73
    reg 2(1). 12.23
    reg 2(f) 12.23
    Schedule
       paras 104–113. 12.23
       paras 124–125. 12.23
Financial Services Contracts (Transitional
    and Saving Provision) (EU Exit)
    Regulations 2019 (SI 2019/405) 1.76,
                                     8.18, 16.33, 16.84
Financial Services and Markets Act 2000
    (Amendment) (EU Exit) Regulations
    2019 (SI 2019/632). 7.66, 16.15
    Pt 7 . . . . 1.70, 9.15, 12.24, 13.35, 13.95
    reg 198 . . . . 13.95
    reg 199 . . . . 13.95
Financial Services and Markets Act
    2000 (Disclosure of Confidential
    Information) (Amendment) (No. 2)
    Regulations 2001 (SI 2001/3624). 10.31
Financial Services and Markets Act 2000
    (Markets in Financial Instruments)
    Regulations 2017 (SI 2017/701) 10.03
Financial Services and Markets Act 2000
    (Over the Counter Derivatives,
    Central Counterparties and
    Trade Repositories) Regulations
    2013 (SI 2013/16). 13.66
Financial Services and Markets Act 2000
    (Over the Counter Derivatives,
    Central Counterparties and Trade
    Repositories) Regulations 2013
    (SI 2013/504)
    reg 6 . . . . 13.14
Financial Services and Markets Act 2000
    (PRA-regulated Activities) Order
    2013 (SI 2013/556). 8.10
Financial Services and Markets Act 2000
    (Recognition Requirements for
    Investment Exchanges and
    Clearing Houses) Regulations
    2001 SI 2001/995 . . . . 10.35
    Schedule
       para 10 . . . . 10.13
       paras 24–28. . . . . 10.13
Financial Services and Markets Act 2000
    (Regulated Activities) Order
    2001(SI 2001/544) 13.77, 16.03
    art 10(1)–(2) 16.20, 16.35
    art 63O(1)(a) 14.11
    art 63O(1)(b). 14.11
    art 63S 14.39
    art 72 . . . . 1.08, 4.19, 7.98
Financial Services and Markets Act 2000
    (Regulated Activities)
    (Amendment) Order 2013
    (SI 2013/655). 14.11
    Sch 1, Pt 1 . . . . 14.29
    Sch 2 . . . . 14.31
Friendly Societies (Amendment)
    (EU Exit) Regulations 2018
    (SI 2018/1039) 16.15
Insurance Distribution (Amendment)
    (EU Exit) Regulations 2019
    (SI 2019/663) 16.15
Markets in Financial Instruments
    (Amendment) (EU Exit)
    Regulations 2018
    (SI 2018/1403) 7.109, 10.76
Official Listing of Securities (Change
    of Competent Authority)
    Regulations 2000
    (SI 2000/968) 10.33
Over the Counter Derivatives, Central
    Counterparties and Trade
    Repositories (Amendment, etc., and
    Transitional Provision) (EU Exit)
    Regulations 2018 (SI 2019/335) 13.31,
                                         13.32, 13.88
    reg 3 . . . . 13.61
    reg 11 . . . . 13.89
    reg 84 . . . . 13.81

Over the Counter Derivatives, Central
  Counterparties and Trade
  Repositories (Amendment, etc.,
  and Transitional Provision)
  (EU Exit) (No. 2) Regulations
  2019 (SI 2019/1416)............... 13.31
Packaged Retail and Insurance-Based
  Investment Products (Amendment)
  (EU Exit) Regulations 2019
  (SI 2019/403)................... 7.75, 16.15
Public Record, Disclosure of Information
  and Co-operation (Financial Services)
  (Amendment) (EU Exit)
  Regulations 2019 (SI 2019/681) 11.52
Securitisation (Amendment)
  (EU Exit) Regulations 2019
  (SI 2019/660) 11.113, 13.71
Solvency 2 and Insurance (Amendment
  etc.) (EU Exit) Regulations 2019
  (SI 2019/407) 16.15
Solvency 2 Regulations 2015
  (SI 2015/575) 16.03
Statutory Auditors (Amendment of
  Companies Act 2006 and
  Delegation of Functions etc.)
  Order 2012 (SI 2012/1741) 3.210
Trade Repositories (Amendment and
  Transitional Provision)
  (EU Exit) Regulations 2018
  (SI 2018/1318) 1.62, 13.31
  Pt 3
    Ch 1 .... 13.62
    Ch 2 .... 13.64
    Ch 3 .... 13.63
    reg 2 .... 13.60
    reg 9 .... 13.64

Bill

European Union (Withdrawal Agreement)
  Bill 7.44, 7.63, 7.57, 16.27
Financial Services (Implementation
  of Legislation) Bill 4.17, 7.113,
                                  7.114, 15.10
  s 1 .... 1.77, 12.27
  Schedule........................... 1.77
Irish Withdrawal of the United Kingdom
  from the European Union
  (Consequential Provisions)
  Bill 2019....................... 16.87

Technical Standards

Technical Standards (Bank Recovery and
  Resolution) (Amendment etc.)
  (EU Exit) (No. 1) Instrument 2019
  Annex B.......................... 12.32
  Annex E.......................... 12.60

Technical Standards (European Market
  Infrastructure) (Amendment etc.)
  (EU Exit) (No. 3) Instrument 2019
  art 35A........................... 13.90
Technical Standards (European Market
  Infrastructure) (EU Exit) (No. 1)
  Instrument 2019, issued by the
  Bank of England and amending
  Delegated Regulations 1249/2012;
  152/2013; 153/2013; and
  484/2014 .... 13.33
Technical Standards (European Market
  Infrastructure) (EU Exit) (No. 2)
  Instrument 2019, issued by the
  Bank of England and amending
  Delegated Regulations 285/2014;
  2015/2205; 2016/592 and
  2016/1178 .... 13.33
Technical Standards (European Market
  Infrastructure) (EU Exit) (No. 3)
  Instrument 2019 issued by the
  PRA and amending Delegated
  Regulation 2016/2251 .... 13.33
Technical Standards (European Market
  Infrastructure Regulation)
  (EU Exit) (No. 1) Instrument
  2019............................ 13.33
Technical Standards (European Market
  Infrastructure Regulation)
  (EU Exit) (No. 2) Instrument
  2019............................ 13.33
Technical Standards (European Market
  Infrastructure Regulation)
  (EU Exit) (No. 3) Instrument
  2019............................ 13.33
Technical Standards (European Market
  Infrastructure Regulation)
  (EU Exit) (No. 4) Instrument
  2019............................ 13.33

OTHER NATIONAL LEGISLATION

France Legislation

Autorité des Marchés Financiers [French
  financial markets authority]
  art 314-8........................... 6.44
Code Monétaire et Financier(CMF)
  art L. 511-5........................ 6.42
  art L. 511-10 .... 6.35, 6.45
  art L. 531-1........................ 6.42
  art L. 532-1........................ 6.45
  art L. 532-48 .... 6.35
  art L. 532-51 .... 6.44
  art L. 612-1........................ 6.35
  art L. 612-2........................ 6.35
  art R. 511-2-1 .... 6.45
  art R. 532- 3....................... 6.45

Ordinance n°2019-75 dated 6 February 2019 relating to the preparatory measures of the withdrawal of the United Kingdom from European Union for financial services, as amended by Ordinance n°2019-236 of 27 March 2019 .... 6.41, 16.87

German Legislation

Act relating to Brexit (Brexit-Steuerbegleitgesetz—Brexit-StBG) 6.08
Banking Act (*Kreditwesengesetz*—KWG)
s 2(5)........................... 6.19, 6.27
s 32(1)......................... 6.31, 6.32
s 32(1) Sentence 1 .... 6.24
s 53b(12) 6.12
s 53b(12) Sentence 2................... 6.16
s 53b(12) Sentence 4................... 6.14
s 64m(2)............................. 6.19
s 64x(8) Sentence 1 .... 6.19
Brexit Transition Act (Brexit-Übergangsgesetz—BrexitÜG) 6.07
Building Societies Act (Bausparkassengesetz—BauSparkG).... 6.08
Covered Bond Act (Pfandbriefgesetz—PfandBG) 6.08
Insurance Supervision Act (*Versicherungsaufsichtsgesetz*—VAG)
s 66a (1) 6.12
s 66a(1) Sentence 1 .... 6.17
s 66a(1) Sentence 3 .... 6.14
Payment Services Supervision Act (*Zahlungsdiensteaufsichtsgesetz*—ZAG)
s 39(8)........................ 6.12, 6.14
s 39(8) Sentence 4 .... 6.16

Securities Trading Act (*Wertpapierhandelsgesetz*—WpHG)
s 102(4)............................... 6.13
s 102(4) Sentence 3 .... 6.14

Ireland Legislation

Central Bank Acts 1942 to 2015 .... 6.95
Central Bank Reform Act 2010.......... 6.123
Central Bank (Supervision and Enforcement) Act 2013 (s48(1)) (Undertakings for Collective Investment in Transferable Securities) Regulation 2015
reg 100 .... 6.121
Withdrawal of the United Kingdom from the European Union (Consequential Provisions) Act 2019 .... 6.93

Netherlands Legislation

Act on the Financial Supervision (*Wet op het financieel toezicht*, AFS).... 6.59
Pt 1 .... 6.57
art 3:100 (a) 6.80
art 5:32 (d)........................... 6.84
DutchBrexit Act 6.55–6.58
Exemption Regulation AFS (*Vrijstellingsregeling Wft*, the Exemption Regulation)
art 10 .... 4.20, 6.60

US Legislation

Title 12, US Code of Financial Regulations
s 252.153 .... 11.64

List of Abbreviations

ABCP	asset-backed commercial paper
ACPR	Autorité de contrôle prudentiel et de résolution [French financial supervisory authority]
AFM	Autoriteit Financiële Markten [Dutch: Netherlands authority for the financial markets]
AFS	*Wet op het financieel toezicht* [Dutch Act on Financial Supervision]
AIFMD	Alternative Investment Fund Managers Directive (2010/76/EU)
AIFs	alternative investment funds
AIM	Alternative Investment Market
AMF	Autorité des Marchés Financiers [French financial markets authority]
BaFin	Bundesanstalt für Finanzdienstleistungsaufsicht [German: federal financial supervisory authority]
BCBS	Basel Committee on Banking Supervision
BCP	business continuity planning
BoE	Bank of England
Brexit-StBG	*Brexit-Steuerbegleitgesetz* [German: Tax Act relating to Brexit]
BrexitÜG	*Brexit-Übergangsgesetz* [German: Brexit Transition Act]
BRRD	Bank Recovery and Resolution Directive
BRRO2	Bank Recovery and Resolution (No. 2) Order 2014
BTS	binding technical standards
CCPs	central clearing counterparties
CEBS	Committees of European Banking Supervisors
CEIOPS	European Insurance and Occupational Pensions Supervisors
CESR	European Securities Regulators
CFs	Controlled Functions
CJEU	Court of Justice of the European Union
CMF	*Code Monétaire et Financier*
Competition Guidelines	Competition/Antitrust Law Guidelines for Members of the GFXC
Core Principles	Core Principles for Effective Banking Supervision
CPMI	Committee on Payments and Market Infrastructures
CRAG Act	Constitutional Reform and Governance Act 2010
CRD	Capital Requirements Directive
CRD IV	Capital Requirements Directive IV
CRR	Capital Requirements Regulation
CSD	central security depository
CSSF	Commission de Surveillance du Secteur Financier
DNO	declaration of no objection
DR	disaster recovery
EBA	European Banking Authority
ECA 1972	European Communities Act 1972
ECAI	external credit assessment institution
EEA	European Economic Area
EEC	European Economic Community

EFTA	European Free Trade Association
EIOPA	European Insurance and Occupational Pensions Authority
EMIR	European Markets Infrastructure Regulation
ESAs	European Supervisory Authorities
ESMA	European Securities and Markets Authority
EU	European Union
EUWA	EU Withdrawal Act
FAQs	frequently asked questions
FCA	Financial Conduct Authority
FIA	Futures Industry Association
FinCoNet	International Financial Consumer Protection Organisation
FMIs	financial market infrastructures
FRC	Financial Reporting Council
FSA	Financial Services Authority
FSAP	Financial Services Action Plan
FSB	Financial Stability Board
FSCR	Financial Services Contract Regime
FSCS	Financial Services Compensation Scheme
FSMA	Financial Services and Markets Act 2000
GFXC	Global Foreign Exchange Committee
Handbook, the	Primary Market Handbook
HSS	home state supervisor
IAASB	International Auditing and Assurance Standards Board
IADI	International Association of Deposit Insurers
IAIS	International Association of Insurance Supervisors
IAM	Institute of Asset Management
IASB	International Accounting Standards Board
ICMA	International Capital Market Association
ICPs	Insurance Core Principles
IDD	Insurance Distribution Directive [Directive (EU) 2016/97 on insurance distribution (recast)]
IECHA	Investment Exchanges and Clearance Houses Act 2006
IFC	Irving Fisher Committee [on Central Bank Statistics]
IFD	Investment Firms Directive
IFR	Investment Firms Regulation
IFRS	International Financial Reporting Standards Foundation
IFRS	Standards International Financial Reporting Standards
IHC	intermediate holding company
ILO	International Labour Organization
IMF	International Monetary Fund
IOPS	International Organisation of Pension Supervisors
IOSCO	International Organization of Securities Commissions
ISDA	International Swaps and Derivatives Association
ISLA	International Securities Lending Association
ISO	International Organisation for Standardization
ITS	implementing technical standards
Key Attributes	Key Attributes of Effective Resolution Regimes for Financial Institutions
KFD	key facts document
LSE	London Stock Exchange

MAR	Market Abuse Regulation
MCR	minimum capital requirement
MiFID I	Markets in Financial Instruments Directive
MiFID II	Markets in Financial Instruments Directive II
MiFIR	Markets in Financial Instruments Regulation
MoUs	memoranda of understanding
MREL	*minimum requirement for own funds and eligible liabilities expressed as a percentage of the total liabilities and own funds of the institution*
MTF	multilateral trading facility
NPPRs	national private placement regimes
Objectives and Principles	Objectives and Principles of Securities Regulation
OECD	Organisation for Economic Co-operation and Development
OPE	overseas persons' exclusion
OTC	over-the-counter
OTF	organised trading facility
PCFs	Pre-Approval Controlled Functions
PFMI	Principles for Financial Markets Infrastructures
Political Declaration	Political Declaration Setting Out the Framework for the Future Relationship Between the European Union and the United Kingdom
PPS	Protected Payment Scheme
PRA	Prudential Regulation Authority
PSR	Payment Systems Regulator
RAO	Financial Services and Markets Act 2000 (Regulated Activities) Order 2001
Recommendations	International Standards on Combating Money Laundering and the Financing of Terrorism & Proliferation
RTS	regulatory technical standards
SCN	Supervisory Coordination Network
SCR	solvency capital requirement
SIs	statutory instruments
SMCR	Senior Managers, Certification and Conduct Regime
SMFs	senior manager functions
SSGs	Subject Specific Guidelines
SSM	Single Supervisory Mechanism
SSPEs	securitisation special purpose entities
STS	simple, transparent, and standardised [securitisations]
TC	Treasury Committee
TEU	Treaty on European Union
TFEU	Treaty on the Functioning of the European Union
TLAC	total loss-absorbing capacity
TPR	temporary permissions regime
UCITS	Undertakings for Collective Investment Schemes Directive
UK	United Kingdom
UKLA	UK Listing Authority
US	United States
Withdrawal Agreement	Agreement on the Withdrawal of the United Kingdom of Great Britain and Northern Ireland from the European Union and the European Atomic Energy Community, as endorsed by leaders at a special meeting of the European Council on 25 November 2018

List of Contributors

Michael Born, Counsel, Norton Rose Fulbright

Daniel Carall-Green, Fountain Court Chambers

Roberto Cristofolini, Norton Rose Fulbright

Clive Cunningham, Partner, Herbert Smith Freehills

Katherine Dillon, Of Counsel, Herbert Smith Freehills

Jake Green, Partner, Ashurst

Bob Haken, Partner, Norton Rose Fulbright

Charlotte Henry, Partner, Norton Rose Fulbright

Jonathan Herbst, Global Head of Financial Services, Norton Rose Fulbright

Chris Hurn, Associate, Slaughter and May

Isabella Jones, Senior Associate, Norton Rose Fulbright

Nico Leslie, Partner, Fountain Court Chambers

Simon Lovegrove, Global Head of FS Knowledge, Innovation and Products, Norton Rose Fulbright

Alison Matthews, Consultant, Herbert Smith Freehills

Nina Moffatt, Associate, Paul Hastings

Floortje Nagelkerke, Partner, Norton Rose Fulbright

Donnacha O'Connor, Partner, Dillon Eustace

Anahita Patwardhan, Senior Associate, Hogan Lovells

Bon Penn, Partner, Allen & Overy

Jan Putnis, Partner, Slaughter and May

Michael Raffan, Partner, Freshfields Bruckhaus Deringer

James Roslington, Senior Associate, Hogan Lovells

Arun Srivastava, Partner, Paul Hastings

Aaron Taylor, Partner, Fountain Court Chambers

Michael Thomas, Partner, Hogan Lovells

Stuart Willey, Partner, White & Case

1

Introduction

Jonathan Herbst and Simon Lovegrove

1.1 The Referendum

On 23 June 2016 the United Kingdom (UK) held a historic referendum concerning its future membership in the European Union (EU). The result of the referendum, announced in the early hours of 24 June, took many by surprise with the UK voting by 51.9% to 48.1% to leave the EU after over forty years of membership. The consensus following the referendum vote was that there was an element of a journey into the unknown, although the chancellor, the Bank of England, and other UK policymakers moved swiftly to reassure the markets and provide messages of stability. **1.01**

From a legal and compliance perspective, the referendum result changed nothing immediately. To this end, the Financial Conduct Authority (FCA) made an announcement on 24 June 2016 stating that, 'Firms must continue to abide by their obligations under UK law, including those derived from EU law and continue with implementation plans for legislation that is still to come into effect.' Key pieces of EU financial services legislation like the Markets in Financial Instruments Directive (MiFID I), the Capital Requirements Directive IV (CRD IV), and the European Markets Infrastructure Regulation (EMIR) were still in effect in the same way as before the referendum. The Market Abuse Regulation (MAR) which became directly applicable in Member States after the referendum on 3 July 2016 applied in the UK from that date. **1.02**

The FCA's reference to 'legislation that is still to come into effect' was not only prompted by MAR but also the Markets in Financial Instruments Directive II (MiFID II) and the Markets in Financial Instruments Regulation (MiFIR) which were due to come into force on 3 January 2018. MiFID II and MiFIR were the EU's key regulatory reforms following the 2008 global financial crisis. The FCA's message to firms was that it would be a mistake for them to take their foot off the gas and slow down or even completely stop working on their implementation projects thinking that the legislation would not come into effect. In one sense, you could not blame firms for hoping this, given that the implementation of MiFID II and MiFIR was a significant undertaking in terms of costs and time. But it was, perhaps, also unrealistic in the sense that the UK was unlikely to leave the EU before their implementation date. The UK regulatory authorities had also played an important role in developing MiFID II and MiFIR. **1.03**

Following the referendum, various options for the UK's future relationship with the EU were discussed in the media. The three options touted the most were the so-called **1.04**

Norwegian model,[1] the Swiss model,[2] and the total exit model[3] (otherwise known as the New York model). Each of these models have their own pros and cons. For instance, under the Norwegian model the UK would be bound by existing and future EU legislation as a condition of maintaining access to the Single Market. But the UK would not have a seat on the EU institutions and be unable to have a full role in influencing EU policy and legislation.

1.05 Another question that was discussed in the media was whether or not UK financial services legislation would be rewritten once the UK had formally left the EU (the so-called bonfire of regulations). Most in the market, however, felt that it would not. This was generally on the basis that the UK had played an important role in developing EU financial services legislation when participating in the EU institutions. There was also discussion as to whether or not standards and principles developed by international bodies such as the Basel Committee on Banking Supervision and the Financial Stability Board could, in the future, provide a bridge between the UK and the EU in defining a future relationship based on shared outcomes.

1.06 Before the referendum some of the larger players in the market carried out assessments as to how the UK's departure from the EU would impact their business model. Other firms waited until after the referendum. The key step for firms was assessing how much they relied on Single Market passporting rights and whether the loss of those rights could be offset by the third country equivalence provisions that appeared in EU financial services legislation or whether relief could be provided through reverse solicitation. However, firms generally found the mapping of Single Market passports and legal structure onto their commercial business extremely difficult. In some cases firms discovered that they needed permission to do something and had not realised it. The approach of Member State regulators to reverse solicitation was not uniform nor were there any guidelines from the European Commission (**Commission**) or the European Supervisory Authorities (**ESAs**).

1.07 Firms also quickly realised that third country equivalence provisions in EU financial services legislation were a poor substitute for a Single Market passport. For example, some important pieces of EU financial services legislation do not contain such provisions. Significantly, this includes the CRD IV which means that classic corporate banking—deposit taking and lending to companies—is not covered. From an investment management perspective, the Undertakings for Collective Investment in Transferable Securities Directive (**UCITS Directive**) also does not contain third country equivalence measures. Even where EU legislation does contain equivalence measures there are practical issues. For example, many market practitioners pointed to the significant delay behind the Commission's granting of an EMIR equivalence decision for derivatives transactions in the United States (**US**). Also, equivalence decisions could be withdrawn by the Commission.

---

[1] The Norway model includes two key European organisations: the European Free Trade Association (EFTA) and the European Economic Area (EEA). Norway, along with Lichtenstein and Iceland, is a member of both.
[2] Switzerland is a member of EFTA but not the EEA. Switzerland has a free trade agreement with the EU and a number of agreements which give it access to the Single Market for most of its industries. Its agreement also requires the free movement of people.
[3] Total exit from the EU and the EU Single Market, either relying on the rules of the World Trade Organization to continue trading with the EU or seeking to negotiate a new free trade agreement.

EEA firms were also assessing their options for continuing business in the UK. In addition to relying on third country equivalence provisions in EU legislation they were also reviewing the so-called characteristic performance test which the UK regulators, the Prudential Regulation Authority (PRA) and the FCA, use when considering whether a credit institution or an investment firm authorised under MiFID II is conducting regulated business in the UK.[4] They were also reviewing the overseas persons' exclusion[5] which is a UK-specific exemption, not replicated in other Member States.

1.2 Article 50 Notification

The process by which the UK will leave the EU is set out in Article 50 of the Treaty on European Union (the TEU). However, no Member State has ever used Article 50 to leave the EU. It does not establish any substantive conditions for a Member State to exercise its right to withdraw, but only procedural requirements. Article 50(1) of the TEU provides that 'any Member State may decide to withdraw from the Union in accordance with its own constitutional requirements'. For the UK government this raised an issue as to whether or not it could use its prerogative powers to notify the EU of its decision to leave the EU or whether it needed parliamentary approval. Ultimately this issue was decided by the UK Supreme Court which ruled that parliamentary approval was needed. This led the UK government to introduce a Bill in Parliament which became the European Union (Notification of Withdrawal) Act 2017. This Act conferred power on the prime minister to notify, under Article 50(2) of the TEU, the UK's intention to withdraw from the EU.

On 28 March 2017, Prime Minister Theresa May signed a letter that, on the following day, was handed to the President of the European Council, Donald Tusk, invoking Article 50 and starting the withdrawal process.

Article 50 provides for a negotiated withdrawal, due to the complexities of leaving the EU. However, the deadline for achieving the negotiated withdrawal is two years after notification[6] unless extended by mutual consent by the departing Member State and the European Council. The EU will negotiate the Withdrawal Agreement with the Member State concerned in the light of guidelines provided by the European Council and the concluded Withdrawal Agreement will set out the arrangements for the withdrawal, taking account the framework for its (the exiting Member State) future relationship with the EU. On the EU side, the Withdrawal Agreement must be concluded by the Council of the EU acting by qualified majority, after obtaining the consent of the European Parliament.

---

[4] In respect of banking services, the European Commission believes that 'to determine where the activity was carried on, the place of provision of what may be termed the "characteristic performance" of the service i.e. the essential supply for which payment is due, must be determined' (Commission interpretative communication: Freedom to provide services and the interests of the general good in the Second Banking Directive (97/C 209/04)). In the view of the PRA and FCA this requires consideration of where the service is carried out in practice. The PRA and FCA are of the opinion that UK firms that are credit institutions and MiFID investment firms should apply the 'characteristic performance' test when considering whether prior notification is required for services business. Firms should note that other EU States may take a different view. Some EU States may apply a reverse solicitation test.

[5] Financial Services and Markets Act 2000 (Regulated Activities) Order 2001, Art. 72.

[6] For the UK this originally meant 11 p.m. (GMT) on 29 March 2019.

4 INTRODUCTION

1.12 Until the conclusion of the Article 50 process, the departing Member State remains bound by EU law.

1.3 The Negotiations

1.13 It is beyond the scope of this book to provide detailed commentary on the lengthy negotiations that took place following the UK's submission of the Article 50 notification. However, some of the 'highlights' are set out below.

1.14 At an informal meeting in December 2016, the EU27 leaders and presidents of the European Council and Commission issued a statement, in which they declared that they were ready to start negotiations with the UK as soon as it had made its Article 50 TEU notification. At this meeting the Commission was appointed as the EU's negotiator and the Commission nominated Michel Barnier to lead its efforts. EU27 leaders would also adopt guidelines, including principles and general positions, for the negotiations. These would be updated as the negotiations developed. The Council of the EU would adopt negotiating directives on the substance and on the detailed institutional arrangements which would also ensure that the negotiations were conducted in line with the guidelines.

1.15 Draft guidelines were issued on 31 March 2017. At his press conference European Council President Donald Tusk stated, 'The EU27 do not and will not pursue a punitive approach. Brexit in itself is already punitive enough. After more than forty years of being united, we owe it to each other to do everything we can to make this divorce as smooth as possible.' The draft guidelines were adopted by the EU27 leaders at a summit on April 29, 2017. Among the core principles in the guidelines was the following statement:

> It [the European Council] reiterates its wish to have the United Kingdom as a close partner in the future. It further reiterates that any agreement with the United Kingdom will have to be based on a balance of rights and obligations, and ensure a level playing field. Preserving the integrity of the Single Market excludes participation based on a sector-by-sector approach. A non-member of the Union, that does not live up to the same obligations as a member, cannot have the same rights and enjoy the same benefits as a member. In this context, the European Council welcomes the recognition by the British Government that the four freedoms of the Single Market are indivisible and that there can be no 'cherry picking'.

1.16 This marked a key point for financial services firms as it signalled that once the UK had formally left the EU, the UK would no longer be able to benefit from using the Single Market passport.

1.17 Significantly, the guidelines also deferred the negotiations on the UK's future relationship with the EU until sufficient progress had been made on the terms of the Withdrawal Agreement. It provided that:

> While an agreement on a future relationship between the Union and the UK as such can only be finalised and concluded once the UK has become a third country, Article 50 TEU requires to take account of the framework for its future relationship with the Union in

the arrangements for withdrawal. To this end, an overall understanding on the framework for the future relationship should be identified during a second phase of the negotiations under Article 50 TEU. We stand ready to engage in preliminary and preparatory discussions to this end in the context of negotiations under Article 50 TEU, as soon as the European Council decides that sufficient progress has been made in the first phase towards reaching a satisfactory agreement on the arrangements for an orderly withdrawal.

1.18 The statement made in the guidelines adopted on 29 April 2017 that the UK could not 'cherry pick' the four freedoms of the Single Market were repeated on numerous occasions by the Commission. This was despite the fact that the UK government had already acknowledged that it could no longer have access to the Single Market a couple of months before the Council guidelines were finalised. Prime Minister Theresa May stated on 17 January 2017 that by accepting the four freedoms it would mean that for all intents and purposes the UK would not be leaving the EU at all. She stated, 'That is why both sides in the referendum campaign made it clear that a vote to leave the EU would be a vote to leave the Single Market'. Instead of Single Market access Prime Minister Theresa May called for a 'new, comprehensive, bold and ambitious free trade agreement'.

1.19 It was not until 15 December 2017[7] that the European Council confirmed that sufficient progress had been made to move to the second phase of negotiations related to the framework for the future relationship and a transition or implementation period. In March 2018, the EU and the UK agreed a transition period.

1.4 Chequers Plan

1.20 First sight of what might be the UK government's vision of the future relationship with the EU did not materialise until 12 July 2018 when it published a White Paper which was referred to as the Chequers plan.

1.21 From a financial services perspective the White Paper contained a number of important points. These included that the new economic and regulatory arrangement would be based on the principle of autonomy for each party over decisions regarding access to its market, with a bilateral framework of treaty-based commitments to underpin the operation of the relationship. Furthermore, as the UK and the EU started from a position of identical rules and entwined supervisory frameworks, the UK proposed reciprocal recognition of equivalence under all existing third country regimes, taking effect once it had left the EU (after any transitional period). Future determinations of equivalence would be an autonomous matter for the UK and EU, but the new arrangement would include a bilateral arrangement for a predictable, transparent, and robust process. In terms of the process itself, it would include a transparent assessment methodology for assessing equivalence which would make use of industry consultation and possibly expert panels, a structured withdrawal process with clear timelines and notice periods. While the White Paper drew criticism from various places at its time of publication, the European Parliament Brexit

---

[7] Further negotiating guidelines were adopted on this date and on 23 March 2018.

Steering Group welcomed the idea that the future relationship could take the form of an Association Agreement.[8]

1.5 Withdrawal Agreement and Political Declaration on the Future EU–UK Relationship

1.22 It was not until 25 November 2018 that EU27 leaders met for a special meeting of the European Council where they endorsed the draft Withdrawal Agreement and the Political Declaration on Future EU–UK relationship (**Political Declaration**).[9] During the premiership of Theresa May, the House of Commons rejected the draft Withdrawal Agreement and Political Declaration three times. Following the resignation of Theresa May, Boris Johnson became Prime Minister. On 17 October 2019, the UK and EU agreed certain changes to the protocol on the Ireland/Northern Ireland border (which forms part of the Withdrawal Agreement) and the Political Declaration.[10] However, the House of Commons again rejected the deal which ultimately led to the UK government calling for a general election scheduled for 12 December 2019. Whether the newly elected UK government will seek further changes to the deal or will get the existing revised deal approved by the House of Commons remains to be seen.

1.23 With regard to financial services, an important takeaway from the Withdrawal Agreement is that it proposes a transition period (also known as an implementation period) which will start on the date of the agreement and end on 31 December 2020.[11] It further proposes that a joint committee of UK and EU representatives may adopt a single decision before 1 July 2020 extending this period for up to one or two years. During the transition period, EU law (unless otherwise agreed) continues to apply. This means that Single Market access continues during the transition period and UK financial services firms continue to be subject to EU financial services legislation. The ESAs and other EU institutions will continue to hold the power conferred on them by EU law over the UK, but the UK will not be represented on these institutions.

1.24 While it is not legally binding, the proposed Political Declaration on the future EU–UK relationship is significant in indicating the framework for phase 2 of the negotiations. There are some principles[12] for the development of the financial services regime such as stable markets and cooperation but these are set in the context of the autonomy of each side in its regime design. This is important, as it reflects both the EU and UK positions that they cannot lose their freedom of action. It follows the approach of the UK government's White Paper (see above) while giving some more substance to the shared principles which will

---

[8] An association agreement is a treaty between the EU and a non-EU country that creates a framework for co-operation between them. Its legal basis is Article 217 of the Treaty of the Functioning of the EU, which provides for 'an association involving reciprocal rights and obligations, common action and special procedures'.

[9] The draft Withdrawal Agreement was first announced in a joint UK–EU statement on 14 November 2018.

[10] Articles 184 and 185 of the Withdrawal Agreement were also amended. The revised Article 184 replaces 25 November 2018 as the date of the Political Declaration with 17 October 2019. Article 185 simply adapts the numbering of the provisions of the protocol that will apply as of entry into force of the Withdrawal Agreement, in light of the changes.

[11] The draft Withdrawal Agreement agreed in November 2018 stated 31 December 2020. This was not changed when amendments were made in October 2019.

[12] See paras. 35–7 of the Political Declaration of the future relationship between the EU and the UK.

guide the parties in the use of their autonomy. There is also a reference to the parties being able to take steps necessary for prudential purposes. This may be a more worrying reference, as the key question will be the certainty of any grant of equivalence of an ability to impose additional barriers. The Political Declaration also provides for a commitment to work towards granting equivalence by June 2020. This is designed to deal with concerns that the EU would not start the process until the end of the transition period. On the scope of equivalence, the position is less clear. Equivalence is not stated as being limited to the current EU framework but equally the possibility of a broader equivalence regime which may cover, for example, banking services is not ruled out. Also, the text is silent on the timings and process for any withdrawal of equivalence.

Further discussion concerning the contents of the Withdrawal Agreement and the Political Declaration can be found in Chapter 2. **1.25**

1.6 Ratification of the Withdrawal Agreement

For the EU, the Withdrawal Agreement must first be approved by a simple majority in the European Parliament. When such approval is given it will be ratified if it is approved by a super qualified majority of the European Council in its EU27 format (at least twenty of the EU27 comprising at least 65% of the EU27 population). **1.26**

Following the endorsement of the Withdrawal Agreement on 25 November 2018, EU27 leaders instructed the EU institutions to proceed with the next steps for ratification. Consequently, the Commission adopted two proposals on the signing and conclusion of the Withdrawal Agreement on 5 December 2018. On 11 January 2019 the Council, meeting in the Article 50 (EU27 ministers) format, adopted the decision on signing the Withdrawal Agreement and approved the draft decision to conclude it, which it forwarded to the European Parliament for consent. The presidents of the European Council and the Commission clarified they were prepared to sign the Withdrawal Agreement as soon as the UK Parliament had approved it. Following revisions to the deal in October 2019, the Council amended its decisions on signing and concluding the Withdrawal Agreement. It forwarded the latter to the European Parliament to obtain its consent. The position of the European Parliament has been to have its vote of consent on the Withdrawal Agreement only after the UK Parliament has given its approval. **1.27**

The UK process for ratifying the Withdrawal Agreement differs from established procedures that the UK uses for ratifying international treaties. The UK Parliament must complete three steps before the UK can ratify the Withdrawal Agreement: **1.28**

1. approve the Withdrawal Agreement by resolution (known as the 'meaningful vote');
2. adopt legislation for the implementation of the Withdrawal Agreement; and
3. complete the UK parliamentary consent procedure for the ratification of international treaties under the Constitutional Reform and Governance Act 2010 (**CRAG Act**).

Parliament's role in approving the Withdrawal Agreement has been an evolving process. As we have seen earlier, an Act was required to authorise the UK government to trigger Article 50. In 2018, the UK Parliament passed the European Union (Withdrawal) Act 2018 **1.29**

(EUWA). The basic purpose of the EUWA is to repeal the European Communities Act 1972 (ECA 1972) but then retain in effect after the UK leaves the EU (**exit day**) almost all UK laws which have been derived from the UK's membership of the EU. This body of law is referred to as 'retained EU law'. The EUWA also gives UK ministers powers to prevent, remedy, or mitigate any failure of EU law to operate effectively, or any other deficiency in retained EU law, through statutory instruments. These statutory instruments are not intended to make policy changes, other than to reflect the UK's new position outside the EU, and to smooth the transition. Significantly, the EUWA affirms the UK Parliament's power to approve the Withdrawal Agreement before it is signed, as a precondition to its signature and ratification.

1.30 The requirement to subject the Withdrawal Agreement to UK parliamentary approval is set by section 13 of the EUWA. Ratification of the Withdrawal Agreement is subject to the following steps:

1. the UK government introduces three documents in both Houses of Parliament: a written statement that political agreement has been reached; and copies of the negotiated Withdrawal Agreement and the Political Declaration;
2. a House of Commons resolution (simple majority) approves the Withdrawal Agreement and the Political Declaration on a motion moved by the UK government;
3. the House of Lords holds a debate on the motion (no vote required);
4. the UK Parliament passes legislation implementing the Withdrawal Agreement domestically; and
5. the Withdrawal Agreement complies with Part 2 of the CRAG Act on ratifying international treaties.

1.31 The above first three steps constitute the meaningful vote. Following the prime minister's required written statement that agreement had been reached on UK withdrawal on 26 November 2018, launching the 'meaningful vote' procedure, both Houses began scheduled five-day debates on the deal on 4 December 2018. However, in light of concerns regarding the Northern Ireland backstop, the prime minister postponed the meaningful vote scheduled for 11 December 2018.

1.32 The debate on the Withdrawal Agreement resumed on 9 January 2019 with the House of Commons overwhelmingly rejecting the UK government's motion to approve the Withdrawal Agreement on 15 January 2019. As a result of the vote, the prime minister set out the UK government's approach in a statement on 21 January 2019 although this was widely criticised on the basis that it contained no major changes, nor a so-called Plan B.

1.33 On 29 January 2019 the House of Commons approved the motion on the UK government's 'way forward' statement, as well as two (of seven selected by the Speaker of the House of Commons) amendments. The first, a non-binding amendment, called on the UK government to rule out leaving the EU without a deal, without mentioning a timeframe or procedural steps. The second amendment (supported by the UK government) required 'the Northern Ireland backstop to be replaced with alternative arrangements to avoid a hard border'.

1.34 In a statement of 26 February 2019 the prime minister made a statement that included commitments to hold a second meaningful vote by 12 March 2019 and to seek an extension of the Article 50 process. On 12 March 2019 the House of Commons rejected the second meaningful vote. On 21 March 2019 the European Council agreed to extend the Article 50 process to 22 May 2019, if the UK Parliament approved the Withdrawal Agreement in the week of 29 March 2019. If not, the extension would run until 12 April 2019 (the deadline for the UK to give notice of holding European Parliament elections), unless the UK indicated a way forward for consideration by the European Council before then. On 29 March 2019 the UK government held a vote on the Withdrawal Agreement alone. While this did not meet the requirements of a 'meaningful vote' per section 13 of the EUWA, the UK government felt a positive vote would allow it to move on in the process, compliance with section 13 could be ensured later, possibly through the legislation implementing the Withdrawal Agreement domestically. However, the House of Commons rejected the Withdrawal Agreement, activating the extension of Article 50 to 12 April 2019.

After votes enabling opposition MPs to control the agenda of the House of Commons on specific days, the 'Cooper Bill' obliging the UK government to seek another Article 50 extension passed its various stages in the House of Commons on 3 April 2019. It took longer to get through the House of Lords, but eventually received Royal Assent on 8 April 2019. On 5 April 2019 the prime minister wrote to the President of the European Council Donald Tusk seeking a further extension of Article 50 until 29 June 2019. **1.35**

Prior to the European Council meeting on 10 April 2019, Donald Tusk proposed a flexible extension to Article 50 of up to a year, which could be ended early if both the UK and EU ratified the Withdrawal Agreement. At the meeting, the majority of EU leaders supported this idea, but it was opposed in particular by French President Emmanuel Macron. The European Council eventually agreed to extend Article 50 until 31 October 2019, with the possibility of the UK leaving earlier if the Withdrawal Agreement was ratified (on the first day of the month after ratification). The European Council also included a provision for UK withdrawal on 1 June 2019 if the UK did not hold European Parliament elections. The UK agreed to this further extension on 11 April 2019. **1.36**

On 21 and 22 May 2019 Prime Minister Theresa May made two speeches in which she referred to the Bill (which had not been published) which would implement the Withdrawal Agreement domestically and a 'new Brexit deal' which was framed around a 10-point offer which included a vote for MPs on whether the Withdrawal Agreement should be subject to a referendum. These speeches were the catalyst for significant political drama which led to Theresa May making a statement on 24 May 2019 in which she said that she would resign as leader of the Conservative Party on 7 June 2019, and remain prime minister until her successor was chosen. The leadership contest for the Conservative Party began in earnest soon after the statement. Ultimately Boris Johnson won the leadership contest becoming prime minister on 24 July 2019. On 17 October 2019, the UK government secured changes to the deal but the revised package was not approved by the House of Commons. **1.37**

On 19 October 2019, Boris Johnson sent a letter to the President of the European Council requesting an extension of Article 50 until 31 January 2020. He did so despite publicly opposing an extension beyond 31 October 2019. The Prime Minister had no choice but to send this letter because it was required by an Act of the UK Parliament, the European Union (Withdrawal) (No.2) Act 2019. The Act stated that the Prime Minister had to send the letter, if by 19 October 2019 the UK government had not secured a resolution of the **1.38**

House of Commons either approving the Withdrawal Agreement or leaving the EU without an agreement. On 28 October 2019, the European Council announced that it had decided to offer the 3 month extension set out in the letter. The Prime Minister accepted the offer, as he was required to do by section 3 of the EU (Withdrawal) (No.2) Act 2019. On 31 October 2019, the Early Parliamentary General Election Act 2019 was passed, making provision for a general election in the UK on 12 December 2019.

1.7 Preparations for the No-Deal Scenario

1.39 During the Article 50 negotiations both the EU and the UK have also been preparing for a no-deal Brexit. The following section provides a high-level overview of these measures which are discussed in greater detail later in this book.

1.40 The Commission has made extensive preparations that include nineteen legislative proposals and numerous Brexit preparedness notices. From the financial services perspective, the preparedness notices cover: statutory audit; credit rating agencies; asset management; post-trade services; financial instruments; banking services; insurance; and occupational retirement institutions.

1.41 Some of these notices include high-level comments on the impact the UK's exit would have on contracts. For example, the notice on banking services states:

> Contract continuity for relationships between parties established in the Union and in the UK will be affected by the loss of the single passport, as this will impair the ability of UK based entities to continue performing certain obligations and activities and ensure service continuity with regard to contracts concluded before the withdrawal date. As of the withdrawal date, the EU rules on conflicts of laws and jurisdictions will no longer apply to the UK. Where contracts are governed by the law of the UK, or contain a choice of law or an agreement in favour of the jurisdiction of a court in the UK, parties to those contracts should carefully assess the impact of the withdrawal of the UK on the validity and enforceability of those contracts and mitigate any risks, including any risks to their clients.

1.42 In its communication of 4 September 2019, the Commission stated that it had tabled 19 legislative proposals, which had been adopted. It had also adopted 63 non-legislative acts and 100 preparedness notices. As such the Commission stated that it was not planning any new measures.

1.43 The Commission has also been assisted in its contingency preparations by the ESAs—the European Securities and Markets Authority (ESMA), the European Banking Authority (EBA), and the European Insurance and Occupational Pensions Authority (EIOPA).

1.44 ESMA's activities appear to have focused on three work streams:

1. ensuring the consistent application of regulatory and supervisory standards to the relocation of activities, entities, and functions from the UK to the EU27;
2. reviewing the third country arrangements in EU securities markets legislation in the context of the UK's departure from the EU; and

3. preparing for the risk that, when the UK leaves the EU, no agreement is in place regarding its withdrawal.

ESMA issued four opinions in 2017 providing for jointly agreed regulatory and supervisory standards to be met by EU27 Member State competent authorities when dealing with relocations. The opinions stressed that new authorisations must be granted in full compliance with EU law and in a coherent manner across the EU27. ESMA also established a Supervisory Coordination Network where European supervisors reported and discussed cases of relocating UK market participants. This was intended to promote consistent decisions by EU27 Member State national competent authorities. **1.45**

The prospect of a very large financial market like the UK moving out of the EU, while likely continuing to be very interconnected with the EU financial markets, may trigger a reconsideration of the EU's third country arrangements. In particular, ESMA's chairman, Steven Maijoor, spoke about the need for improved third country arrangements, particularly a comprehensive and harmonised EU regime for third country trading venues.[13] Further discussion regarding equivalence including a subsequent communication from the Commission on the topic can be found in Chapter 4. Chapter 13 deals with EMIR and euro clearing. **1.46**

In terms of its work regarding a no-deal scenario, ESMA reminded UK-based regulated entities in July 2018 of the importance of timely submissions of authorisation requests to be able to continue providing services in the EU27. At the same time, ESMA flagged the problem that there would be no legal basis in a no-deal scenario for the extensive and granular daily data exchange between the UK and the EU27 which takes place under MIFID II. The central clearing of derivatives was considered by ESMA to be the highest risk to EU financial stability in the event of a no deal. **1.47**

In November 2018, ESMA issued a final report[14] with draft regulatory technical standards (**RTS**) proposing to amend three Commission Delegated Regulations on the clearing obligation under EMIR. The draft RTS would, in a no-deal scenario, provide for UK counterparties to be replaced with EU ones without triggering the clearing obligation.[15] In December 2018, ESMA issued a statement[16] concerning its plans for the recognition of UK central counterparties as third country central counterparties under EMIR. In February 2019, ESMA issued a further statement[17] confirming that in the event of a no-deal Brexit it would recognise three UK central counterparties—LCH Limited, ICE Clear Europe Limited, and LME Clear Limited. Shortly thereafter, in March 2019 it issued a further statement[18] confirming that it would recognise in a no-deal scenario the UK central security depository (**CSD**), Euroclear UK, and Ireland Limited, as a third country CSD. A further **1.48**

---

[13] Steven Maijoor speech, 'The State of Implementation of MiFID II and Preparing for Brexit' (3 October 2018).
[14] ESMA final report—EMIR RTS on the novation of contracts for which the clearing obligation has not yet taken effect (8 November 2018).
[15] These Commission Delegated Regulations were subsequently published in the Official Journal of the EU on 13 March 2019.
[16] ESMA public statement, 'ESMA Is ready to Review UK CCPs' and CSDs' Recognition Applications for a No-Deal Brexit Scenario' (19 December 2018).
[17] ESMA press release, 'ESMA to Recognise Three UK CCPs in the Event of a No-Deal Brexit' (18 February 2019).
[18] ESMA press release, 'ESMA to Recognise the UK Central Securities Depository in the Event of a No-Deal Brexit (1 March 2019).

12   INTRODUCTION

ESMA public statement[19] in March 2019 covered the impact of a no-deal scenario on certain aspects of both MiFID II and the Benchmarks Regulation. On 5 April 2019 ESMA announced that it had adopted recognition decisions for the three UK central counterparties and the one UK CSD.[20]

1.49 In March 2019, ESMA issued a statement[21] on the impact of a no-deal scenario on the trading obligation for shares under Article 23 of MiFIR. The statement from ESMA made clear that the EU's share trading obligation would apply to all shares traded on EU27 trading venues that are shares of firms incorporated in the EU (**EU ISINs**), and of companies incorporated in the UK (**GB ISINs**) where these companies' shares are 'liquid' in the EU. However, the FCA pointed out that this would mean that EU banks, funds, and asset managers would not be able to trade these UK or EU ISIN shares in the UK, even where the UK was the home listing of the UK or EU company. ESMA subsequently revised the statement[22] in May 2019 so that EU banks and investment firms could trade all UK shares in the UK. However, the FCA still argued that applying the share trading obligation to all shares issued by firms incorporated in the EU would still cause market disruption. The share trading obligation is further discussed later in this book.

1.50 On 30 October 2019, ESMA issued an updated on its Brexit work stating that the reference date in all its previously published measures and actions, including public statements, issued regarding the possibility of a no-deal Brexit, should be read as 31 January 2019.

1.51 In light of the referendum, the EBA has relocated its headquarters from London to Paris. The EBA has also focused on the risks that a no-deal scenario may pose to individual EU firms and to EU financial stability more generally.

1.52 Like ESMA the EBA has issued opinions. Its first was published in 2017 and focused on policy issues and the consistent application of EU legislation to businesses seeking to establish or enhance their EU27 presence. In June 2018, the EBA issued a second opinion calling on banks to establish and enact adequate contingency planning for a no-deal scenario. Later in 2018 it issued a public statement calling on institutions to step up their communication to their customers and update them on the contingency measures being taken and how those might affect them. In March 2019 the EBA issued a further opinion considering deposit protection-related issues in the event of a no-deal scenario.

1.53 EIOPA has also issued opinions. The first was on 11 July 2017 covering the authorisation process and ongoing supervision of firms under the Solvency II framework. The second, on 21 December 2017, dealt with service continuity while a third, on 18 May 2018 covered the solvency position of insurance and reinsurance undertakings. A fourth opinion, published on June 28, 2018, came with frequently asked questions, and looked at disclosure

---

[19] ESMA public statement, 'Impact of Brexit on MiFID II/MiFIR and the Benchmarks Regulation (BMR)—C(6) carve-out, trading obligation for derivatives, ESMA opinions on third country trading venues for the purpose of post-trade transparency and position limits, post-trade transparency for OTC transactions, BMR ESMA register of administrators and 3rd country branches' (7 March 2019).
[20] ESMA press release, 'ESMA Has Adopted New Recognition Decisions for the Three UK CCPs and the UK CSD in the Event of a No-Deal Brexit on 12 April' (5 April 2019).
[21] ESMA public statement on the trading obligation for shares (19 March 2019).
[22] ESMA adjusts application of the trading obligation for shares in a no-deal Brexit (29 May 2019).

of information to customers. EIOPA's work is further considered in Chapter 16 regarding Solvency II.

In addition to the activities of the Commission and the ESAs, some but not all individual EU27 Member States have been putting into place their own contingency measures. Chapter 6 takes a brief look at the measures that France, Germany, the Netherlands, and Ireland have put in place for a no-deal Brexit. **1.54**

The UK has introduced a significant number of contingency measures for a no-deal scenario. **1.55**

As mentioned above, the EUWA repeals the ECA 1972 but then retains in effect after exit day almost all UK laws which have been derived from the UK's membership of the EU (retained EU law). Secondary legislation made under the ECA 1972 remains in force. This means that UK secondary legislation implementing EU directives, such as the Bank Recovery and Resolution Directive, remains in force after the UK leaves the EU, despite the repeal of the ECA 1972. The EUWA also gives UK ministers powers to prevent, remedy, or mitigate any failure of EU law to operate effectively, or any other deficiency in retained EU law, through statutory instruments. HM Treasury has also delegated powers to the UK financial services regulators to address deficiencies in their rulebooks arising as a result of the UK's exit from the EU, and to EU binding technical standards (**BTS**) that would become part of UK law. **1.56**

A deficiency in retained EU law, for the purposes of the EUWA,[23] arises where, following the UK's exit from the EU, that law would fail to operate effectively, or it would not function appropriately or sensibly. HM Treasury made a statement in June 2018 giving examples of deficiencies:[24] **1.57**

- functions that are currently carried out by EU authorities would no longer apply to the UK;
- provisions in retained EU law that would become redundant;
- provisions that would be inconsistent with ensuring a functioning regulatory framework where alternative arrangements for cooperating with EU bodies would be more appropriate;
- provisions that would lead to significant disruption for firms or customers of firms, unless action is taken to avoid that disruption (for example, to prevent the market disruption that would result from the sudden inoperability of passporting rights); and
- provisions requiring participation in EU institutions, bodies, offices, and agencies (for example, joint decision-making in supervisory and resolution colleges) which would no longer work after exit.

In the same statement HM Treasury stated that its approach to fixing deficiencies was that the UK would default to treating EU27 Member States largely as it does other third countries, although it would diverge from this approach in certain circumstances. HM Treasury set out principles that it considered would justify it taking a different approach: **1.58**

---

[23] See European Union (Withdrawal) Act 2018, s. 8.
[24] HM Treasury's approach to financial services legislation under the European Union (Withdrawal) Act (27 June 2018).

14 INTRODUCTION

- having a functioning legislative and regulatory regime in place, in particular the regulators' ability to fulfil their statutory objectives;
- enabling regulators and firms to be ready, by minimising disruption and avoiding material unintended consequences for the continuity of service provision to UK customers, investors, and the market;
- protecting the existing rights of UK consumers; and
- ensuring financial stability.

1.59 HM Treasury stated that, following the above principles, it planned to diverge from the default approach by:

- introducing a temporary permissions regime (**TPR**); and
- establishing transitional regimes for firms operating cross-border and outside the passporting framework.

1.60 Both the FCA and the PRA and Bank of England subsequently confirmed that they were taking the same approach as HM Treasury in their review of their rules and retained BTS.

1.61 HM Treasury allocated certain responsibilities for onshoring EU legislation to the UK regulatory authorities through a statutory instrument made under the EUWA, The Financial Regulators' Powers (Technical Standards etc.) (Amendment etc.) (EU Exit) Regulations 2018. This statutory instrument gives the UK regulatory authorities the power to onshore BTS. It does this by amending:

- sections 1A, 1B, 2AB, and 2J of the Financial Services and Markets Act 2000 (**FSMA**), to ensure that the functions of the FCA and the PRA include the function of making 'EU Exit Instruments', and that the function of making technical standards is one of their general functions;
- part 9A of FSMA by inserting sections 138P–138S to set out the procedure for standards instruments, which will enable the FCA, the PRA, and the Bank of England to make technical standards post-exit day;
- the Financial Services (Banking Reform) Act 2013 (the 2013 Act) by inserting new sections 97A–97D (and making consequential amendments to section 39(10) and 71 of the 2013 Act) to make the same provisions as above for the Payment Systems Regulator (**PSR**); and
- schedule 4 to the 2013 Act to provide for the way in which the PSR's functions are to be funded.

1.62 Parts 1, 2, and 3 of the schedule to the statutory instrument sets out the EU legislation for which the FCA, PRA, and Bank of England, respectively, is the appropriate regulator. Part 4 of the schedule to the statutory instrument sets out the EU legislation for which both the PRA and FCA are the appropriate regulators. Part 5 of the schedule to the statutory instrument sets out the EU legislation for which both the Bank of England and FCA are the appropriate regulators. Part 6 of the schedule to the statutory instrument covers a Commission Delegated Regulation under the Interchange Fee Regulation for which the PSR will be responsible.

1.63 The key statutory instrument for the TPR is the EEA Passport Rights (Amendment, etc., and Transitional Provisions) (EU Exit) Regulations 2018. It was first published on 24 July 2018, laid before the UK Parliament in September and then made on 6 November 2018. Other statutory instruments relating to the TPR (or temporary recognition regime) include:

- the Collective Investment Schemes (Amendment etc.) (EU Exit) Regulations 2018;
- the Alternative Investment Fund Managers (Amendment) (EU Exit) Regulations 2018;
- the Electronic Money, Payment Services and Payment Systems (Amendment and Transitional Provisions) (EU Exit) Regulations 2018;
- the Trade Repositories (Amendment and Transitional Provision) (EU exit) Regulations 2018; and
- the Central Counterparties (Amendment, etc., and Transitional Provision) (EU Exit) Regulations 2018.

Both the FCA and the PRA have issued numerous communications to firms as regards the UK's departure from the EU. In October 2018, both regulators[25] issued their first consultation papers[26] setting out proposed changes to their rules and guidance in light of the UK's exit. These consultations also covered their approach to the TPR and the approach to guidelines and other so-called EU level 3 material produced by the ESAs. **1.64**

In March 2019, the FCA published its final instruments relating to amendments to its Handbook and to BTS resulting from a no-deal Brexit. The FCA also published final versions of its guidance on its approach to EU level 3 material, FCA non-Handbook guidance, and forms. **1.65**

The publication of these documents followed various FCA policy papers including: **1.66**

- Policy Statement 19/5: Brexit Policy Statement: Feedback on CP18/28, CP18/29, CP18/34, CP18/36 and CP19/2 (February 2019);
- Consultation Paper 19/2: Brexit and contractual continuity (January 2019);
- Consultation Paper 18/36: Brexit: proposed changes to the Handbook and Binding Technical Standards—second consultation (November 2018);
- Consultation Paper 18/28: Brexit: proposed changes to the Handbook and Binding Technical Standards—first consultation (October 2018); and
- Consultation Paper 18/29: Temporary permissions regime for inbound firms and funds.

In April 2019, the PRA published Policy Statement 5/19: the Bank of England's amendments to financial services legislation under the European Union (Withdrawal) Act 2018. In this Policy Statement the PRA set out its final proposals on issues including amendments to its rules and to BTS resulting from a no-deal Brexit and its approach to EU level 3 material. Minor amendments were made to the Policy Statement in June 2019. **1.67**

---

[25] The Bank of England also issued consultation papers.
[26] (1) FCA Consultation Paper 18/28: Brexit: proposed changes to the Handbook and BTS—first consultation (2) FCA Consultation Paper 18/29: Temporary permissions regime for inbound firms and funds (3) PRA Consultation Paper 26/18: UK withdrawal from the EU: changes to PRA Rulebook and onshored binding technical standards (4) Bank of England Consultation Paper/PRA Consultation Paper 25/18: the Bank of England's approach to amending financial services legislation under the European Union (Withdrawal) Act 2018 (5) Bank of England Consultation Paper: UK withdrawal from the EU: changes to FMI rules and onshored Binding Technical Standards (6) Bank of England Consultation Paper: UK withdrawal from the EU: the Bank of England's approach to resolution statements of policy and onshored Binding Technical Standards.

1.68 Other significant papers published in April 2019 by the PRA and the Bank of England include:

- Joint Bank of England and PRA Statement of Policy 'Interpretation of EU Guidelines and Recommendations: Bank of England and PRA approach after the UK's withdrawal from the EU';
- PRA Supervisory Statement 1/19: Non-binding PRA materials: the PRA's approach after the UK's withdrawal from the EU;
- PRA Supervisory Statement 2/19: PRA approach to interpreting reporting and disclosure requirements and regulatory transactions forms after the UK's withdrawal from the EU;
- Update to PRA Supervisory Statement 18/15: Depositor and dormant account protection; and
- Bank of England Supervisory Statement: Non-binding Bank materials relating to Financial Market Infrastructure Supervision: the Bank's approach after the UK's withdrawal from the EU.

1.69 The publication of these documents followed various PRA and Bank of England policy papers including:

- Consultation Paper 25/18: the Bank of England's approach to amending financial services legislation under the European Union (Withdrawal) Act 2018 (October 2018);
- Consultation Paper 26/18: UK withdrawal from the EU: Changes to PRA Rulebook and onshored Binding Technical Standards (October 2018); and
- Consultation Paper 32/18: UK withdrawal from the EU: Further changes to—PRA Rulebook and Binding Technical Standards—Resolution Binding Technical Standards (December 2018).

1.70 The TPR is an essential part of the UK's contingency planning for a no-deal scenario. Under this regime, EEA firms that passport into the UK which notify the FCA or PRA (as relevant) will be deemed to have permission under Part 4A of FSMA on a temporary basis. The deemed permission will cover those activities that the firm was permitted to carry on in the UK via passporting immediately before the UK's exit from the EU. The TPR will come into force when the UK leaves the EU in a no-deal scenario. The TPR is expected to be in place for a maximum of three years within which time firms will be given a 'landing slot' in which they would be required to obtain authorisation. The FCA and PRA Policy Statements mentioned above set out the key rules that apply to firms in the TPR.

1.71 Temporary transitional powers are set out in Part 7 of the Financial Services and Markets Act 2000 (Amendment) (EU Exit) Regulations 2019. The purpose of these powers is to allow the UK regulatory authorities to delay, or phase in, regulatory requirements where they change as a result of Brexit or where they apply to firms for the first time. The transitional powers allow the UK regulators to waive or modify requirements only for the specific purpose of enabling firms to adjust to onshoring changes in an orderly way, without needing to satisfy the criteria set out in section 138A of the FSMA.

1.72 Firms do not need to apply for transitional relief to benefit from it. The UK regulatory authorities will instead issue transitional directions setting out the terms of the transitional relief.

On 29 March 2019 the FCA published two documents containing transitional directions. **1.73**
The main FCA transitional direction was accompanied by two Annexes, 'A' and 'B'. Annex
'A' covered the application of the 'standstill' in the transitional direction to amendments
made in statutory instruments and exit instruments amending technical standards. Annex
'B' covered the application of the standstill in the transitional direction to amendments
made in the FCA Handbook. The second transitional direction was an FCA prudential
transitional direction. At the time of publication, the directions were to apply until 30 June
2020 (but see below).

The standstill direction means that, for most requirements, firms will not need to comply **1.74**
with changes to their regulatory obligations resulting from onshored EU legislation from
exit day. Instead, they will generally be able to continue to comply with the requirements
as they had effect before exit day for a limited period of time. However, in the areas where
the FCA is not using the power, it expects firms to take reasonable steps to comply with
the changes by exit day. In summary, the areas where the FCA is not using this transitional
power include:

- MiFID II transaction reporting;
- EMIR reporting obligations;
- issuer rules;
- contractual recognition of bail-in;
- short selling notifications;
- use of credit ratings for regulatory purposes; and
- securitisation notifications if they wish to be considered simple, transparent, and standardised under the Securitisation Regulation.

In February 2019, the Bank of England issued near-final directions made by it and the PRA **1.75**
using temporary transitional powers. The directions provided for transitional relief in certain areas providing for a standstill where EU firms would continue to be subject to pre-exit requirements for a period of fifteen months.

On 25 July 2019 the FCA announced that in light of the extension of Article 50 to 31 **1.76**
October 2019 it would be extending the duration of the directions it had issued from
30 June 2020 to 31 December 2020. On the same day the PRA and Bank of England
jointly issued a consultation paper[27] in which it stated that if the UK left the EU on 31
October 2019 the new fixed end date of its directions would also be 31 December 2020.
On 31 October 2019, the FCA issued directions extending the notification period for
firms wanting to enter the TPR to 30 January 2020. The deadline for notification to enter
the PRA's TPR was 12 April 2019 and this deadline has not at the time of writing been
extended.

The Financial Services Contracts (Transitional and Saving Provision) (EU Exit) Regulations **1.77**
2019 is designed to ensure that contractual obligations not covered by the TPR continue to
be met by establishing supervised run-off and contractual run-off mechanisms. These serve
as a backstop to the TPR by allowing EU firms that do not enter the TPR, or leave it without

---

[27] Bank of England Consultation Paper/PRA Consultation Paper 18/19: UK withdrawal from the EU: changes following extension of Article 50. The consultation closes on 18 September 2019.

authorisation, to service pre-existing contracts for a limited period of time after the UK has left the EU.

1.78 There are several items of EU financial services legislation which have either been adopted by the EU but will not be implemented by the time the UK leaves, or that are currently in negotiation and may be adopted thereafter. These items are referred to as 'in-flight files'. In November 2018, the Financial Services (Implementation of Legislation) Bill was introduced in the House of Lords. The Bill gave HM Treasury the power to create corresponding or similar UK regulations, subject to any adjustments appropriate to the UK's new position outside the EU. The power was subject to the same restrictions on scope as the correcting power in the EUWA and was only to be used for up to two years after exit day. Statutory instruments made under the power in the Bill were subject to the affirmative resolution procedure in UK Parliament, which requires a vote in both Houses. Section 1 and the schedule to the Bill listed the in-flight files that were subject to the powers in the Bill. On 9 September 2019, the UK Parliament was prorogued which signalled the end of a UK parliamentary session. In the House of Commons debate on 5 September 2019, it was confirmed that the Bill had fallen as it had failed to receive Royal Assent in the session it was introduced. On 9 October 2019, the UK Parliament updated its webpage on the Bill confirming that it would make no further progress. However, some in the market[28] have called for the Bill to be resuscitated. This may or may not happen.

1.8 *Brexit and Financial Regulation*: an Overview

1.79 The intention of this book is to break Brexit and financial services into manageable chapters which have been written by leading lawyers and barristers who discuss the legal complexities, giving the benefit of their experience while remaining politically neutral. At the time of writing this book, it is still very unclear whether the deal will be ratified by the UK Parliament, or whether the UK is leaving the EU without a deal on 31 October 2019.

1.80 The book has three parts: (1) the Withdrawal Agreement, international standards, and equivalence; (2) the supervisory regime in the Brexit landscape; and (3) commentary on key pieces of EU financial services law.

1.8.1 Part I

1.81 Chapter 2 discusses the Withdrawal Agreement and Political Declaration published on 14 November 2018 (as amended on 17 October 2019) and their implications for financial services.

1.82 Chapter 3 looks at the different international regulatory bodies and their work, and considers their future impact on the UK.

---

[28] See for instance the Financial Markets Law Committee letter of 23 October 2019 calling for the resuscitation of the Bill.

Chapter 4 discusses the EU equivalence regime, the different pieces of EU legislation that contain equivalence provisions (as well as highlighting the key legislation that does not) and the process for determining equivalence. **1.83**

1.8.2 Part II

Chapter 5 considers the EBA opinion on Brexit that addresses a number of relevant policy topics relating to authorisation—prudential regulation and the supervision of banks, internal models, outsourcing, internal governance, and risk transfers via back-to-back and intragroup operations. In addition, the chapter considers the opinion published by ESMA setting out general principles aimed at fostering consistency in the authorisation and supervision of investment firms in the EU27. It also considers the three ESMA sector-specific opinions in the areas of investment firms, investment management, and secondary markets. **1.84**

Chapter 6 provides an overview of the approach to authorisation taken by the German, French, Dutch, and Irish regulators, highlighting any divergences in approach set out by the EU institutions. **1.85**

Chapter 7 considers how the UK regulatory regime is changing in light of Brexit. It discusses how directly applicable EU legislation will be incorporated into the UK regulatory regime, how the architecture of the FCA Handbook and PRA Rulebook may change, and how the roles of the PRA and FCA may evolve. It also considers the overseas persons' exclusion. **1.86**

Chapter 8 considers the PRA's approach to the authorisation of international banks, including its red lines as to when it will insist on an international bank setting up a subsidiary in the UK rather than a branch. **1.87**

Chapter 9 considers how the UK's Senior Managers, Certification and Conduct regimes are changing in light of Brexit. It also considers enforceability issues under the regime against non-UK senior managers. **1.88**

1.8.3 Part III

Chapters 10–16 provide commentary on key pieces of EU financial services law in the Brexit landscape including relevant third country provisions: MiFID II/MiFIR, CRD IV/CRR, BRRD, EMIR and euro clearing, Benchmarks Regulation, AIFMD, and Solvency II. **1.89**

2
Withdrawal Agreement and Political Declaration on the Future EU–UK Relationship

Simon Lovegrove

2.1 Introduction

On 14 November 2018 the European Commission (**Commission**) and the UK government published a draft Withdrawal Agreement, together with three protocols (on the border between Ireland and Northern Ireland, the UK's Sovereign Base Areas in Cyprus, and Gibraltar) and nine annexes. The negotiated text of the Withdrawal Agreement, together with the Political Declaration on the framework for the future EU–UK relationship (the **Political Declaration**), was endorsed by EU27 leaders at a specially convened European Council meeting on 25 November 2018. On 17 October 2019, at a special meeting of the European Council, EU27 leaders endorsed changes to the protocol on the Ireland/Northern Ireland border, as well as to the Political Declaration, but without modifying the rest of the Withdrawal Agreement (except for technical adaptions to Articles 184 and 185).[1] Compared to the deal agreed in November 2018, the revised package reverts to a Northern Ireland-only solution, whereby the region applies EU customs and tariffs legislation, as well as the relevant EU Single Market rules needed to avoid any regulatory or customs border on Ireland. A few modifications were also made to the Political Declaration but none of these changed the provisions dealing with financial services.

2.01

2.2 Ratification

At the time of writing neither the EU nor the UK have ratified the Withdrawal Agreement.

2.02

From the EU27 perspective, the European Parliament must approve the Withdrawal Agreement by a simple majority. The Withdrawal Agreement will then be concluded (ratified) if it is approved by a super qualified majority of the European Council meeting in the EU27 format (20 of the EU27 representing 65% of the EU27 population).

2.03

Following their endorsement on 25 November 2018, EU27 leaders instructed the EU institutions to proceed with the next steps for ratification. On 5 December 2018 the Commission adopted two proposals on the signing and conclusion of the Withdrawal Agreement. On 11 January 2019 the Council of the EU (meeting in the Article 50, EU27 Ministers, format) adopted a decision on signing the Withdrawal Agreement and approved the draft

2.04

---

[1] The revised Article 184 replaces 25 November 2018 as the date of the Political Declaration with 17 October 2019. Article 185 simply adapts the numbering of the provisions of the protocol that will apply as of the entry into force of the Withdrawal Agreement, in light of the changes.

decision to conclude the Withdrawal Agreement. The presidents of the European Council and the Commission stated that they were 'prepared to sign the Withdrawal Agreement as soon as the meaningful vote had passed in the UK Parliament'. Following revisions to the deal in October 2019, the Council amended its decisions on signing and concluding the Withdrawal Agreement. It forwarded the letter to the European Parliament to obtain its consent. The position of the European Parliament has been to have its vote of consent on the Withdrawal Agreement only after the UK Parliament has given its approval.

2.05 From the UK perspective, the procedure for ratifying the Withdrawal Agreement is set out in the European Union (Withdrawal) Act 2018 (**EUWA**) and the Constitutional Reform and Governance Act 2010 (**CRAG**). Section 13 of the EUWA provides for Parliamentary approval of the Withdrawal Agreement. This includes a House of Commons' resolution approving the Withdrawal Agreement and the Political Declaration on a motion moved by the government (so-called meaningful vote). Once the House of Commons approves the meaningful vote, the government will then introduce draft legislation that implements the Withdrawal Agreement into UK law.

2.06 It was at the meaningful vote stage that the House of Commons rejected the November 2018 version of the Withdrawal Agreement on three occasions during Theresa May's premiership. Boris Johnson succeeded Theresa May as Prime Minister but he was unable to get House of Commons' approval of the revised October 2019 Withdrawal Agreement. The House of Commons approved the second reading of the Withdrawal Agreement Bill (the legislation needed to ratify the Withdrawal Agreement) in October, but the Prime Minister pulled the Bill after MPs declined to support his proposed timetable for passing the legislation.

2.3 Renegotiation

2.07 On 29 October 2019, the EU and UK formally agreed a third extension to the Article 50 period.[2] After several unsuccessful attempts by his government, Boris Johnson got the House of Commons to agree to the UK holding a general election on 12 December 2019.[3] Whether a new government will seek to make further changes to the Withdrawal Agreement remains to be seen but it seems unlikely that the EU will be open to renegotiations.

2.08 The remainder of this chapter discusses the Withdrawal Agreement and Political Declaration published on 14 November 2018, as amended on 17 October 2019.

2.4 Structure

2.09 The Withdrawal Agreement has six parts comprising:

- Part 1—Common provisions. These set out territorial scope, key definitions, and how the Withdrawal Agreement (and particularly its EU law content) is to be given effect in

---

[2] The Article 50 period was extended to 11:00 pm (GMT) on 31 January 2020 at the latest.
[3] On 29 October 2019, the Early Parliamentary General Election Bill 2019–20 was introduced in Parliament and approved by MPs. The Bill received Royal Assent on 31 October 2019 becoming an Act of Parliament. The Act provides for a general election to be held on 12 December 2019.

the UK. Article 4 makes clear that the entire Withdrawal Agreement (rather than just Part 2 on citizens' rights) is intended to be directly effective in the UK where its provisions are clear, precise, and unconditional.

- Part 2—Citizens' rights. This part provides that the free movement of persons will continue until the end of the transition (or implementation) period (see below) and EU and UK nationals will be able to move to the UK or Member States as is currently permitted by EU law. EU citizens living in the UK and UK nationals living in the EU before the end of the transition period have the right to remain in the UK or their host state. The UK and the EU27 have discretion under the Withdrawal Agreement to require EU or UK nationals to apply for a new residency status.

  The UK has chosen to implement a scheme which requires EU citizens to apply for a new residency status known as 'settled' or 'pre-settled' status. It is still unclear whether each of the EU27 will exercise their discretion under the Withdrawal Agreement to require UK residents to apply for a new residency status.

  On 19 December 2018 the Home Secretary set out the UK government's detailed proposals for 'The UK's future skills-based immigration system'. There will be a year-long consultation on the proposals.

  The UK government is proposing a single, unified immigration system to apply to everyone who wants to come to the UK after Brexit. The system will be based on the current immigration rules for non-EU nationals, with many changes. The UK government's position is that the focus of the immigration system should be on skill and talent.

- Part 3—Separation provisions. These provisions provide for an orderly exit. Ongoing processes and arrangements will be allowed to come to an end under current rules following the end of transition. It contains provisions on market access for goods, ongoing customs, VAT and excise matters, intellectual property, ongoing police and judicial cooperation in both criminal and civil/commercial matters, the protection of data obtained before the end of transition, ongoing public procurement procedures, Euratom issues, ongoing EU judicial/administrative processes, privileges and immunities, and a few provisions relating to the functioning of the EU institutions.

- Part 4—Transition. This part provides for a transition period (otherwise known as an implementation period) which is intended to bridge the period between the date of the UK's exit from the EU and the entry into force of the new UK–EU partnership arrangements. The transition will run until the end of December 2020,[4] with the possibility of extension for up to one or two years. A decision on an extension must be taken by 1 July 2020.

  Importantly, the UK will continue to apply EU law during the transition period. The EU institutions (like the Commission and the European Supervisory Authorities) and other bodies, offices and agencies will continue to exercise their powers under EU law in relation to the UK. The Court of Justice of the EU (CJEU) will have jurisdiction in relation to the UK and to the interpretation and application of certain parts

---

[4] See Articles 126 to 132 of the Withdrawal Agreement.

of the Withdrawal Agreement (see below). The UK will not be represented in the EU institutions.
- Part 5—Financial settlement. This part sets out the legal text as to how the UK and the EU have agreed on how they will settle their outstanding financial commitments to each other. The settlement includes how the UK will contribute to and participate in the EU budget and its programmes during the transition period until 31 December 2020.
- Part 6—Institutional and final provisions. This part covers the institutional arrangements and how disputes are to be resolved. Article 170 of the Withdrawal Agreement provides that any disputes not resolved by an EU–UK Joint Committee will be taken to an independent arbitration tribunal, which will issue a binding decision regarding the dispute. But where the dispute requires the interpretation of concepts or provisions of EU law, Article 174 of the Withdrawal Agreement requires the arbitration tribunal to refer those to the CJEU for a binding interpretation of those concepts or provisions which the arbitration tribunal must then apply.

2.5 Protocols

2.10 Of the three protocols, probably the most well-known one concerns the border between Ireland and Northern Ireland. This protocol sets out the arrangements needed to avoid a hard order in Ireland, maintain the necessary conditions for continued North–South co-operation and protect the Good Friday Agreement.

2.11 The protocol, as agreed on 17 October 2019, requires Northern Ireland to remain aligned to EU Single Market and Customs rules to avoid a hard border in Ireland (Articles 5 to 10 of the protocol). It also requires the UK to provide opportunities for the Northern Ireland Assembly to decide to discontinue the application of Articles 5 to 10. The first opportunity to make such a decision arises just under four years after the end of the transition period. Articles 5 to 10 would cease to apply two years after a decision to discontinue. The protocol also provides that Northern Ireland will remain part of the UK's customs territory and the UK's VAT area, and sets out the circumstances in which EU, UK or no customs duty is payable on goods entering Northern Ireland.

2.6 Implications for Financial Services

2.12 Financial services are not specifically mentioned in the Withdrawal Agreement. Financial services firms will be interested in the transition period, though. During this period, while no longer a Member State, the UK will still be considered as part of the Customs Union and the Single Market. While being part of the Single Market firms will be able to passport their services as they currently do. EU financial services law will also apply in the UK during this period.

2.7 Dispute Resolution

2.13 Should a dispute arise under the Withdrawal Agreement, its provisions contain a regime for the resolution of disputes. The Withdrawal Agreement expressly states that these provisions are the exclusive mechanism for resolving disputes between the parties, ruling out references to other bodies such as the International Court of Justice.

2.14 The first step is reference to a Joint Committee of representatives of the EU and UK. The parties agree to enter into 'consultations in the Joint Committee in good faith, with the aim of reaching a mutually agreed solution'.

2.15 If, after three months of consultations, no joint solution is found, either party can request the establishment of an arbitration panel.

2.16 The Withdrawal Agreement contemplates the appointment of the panel of arbitrators from a pre-appointed list of twenty-five. Each of the EU and UK will nominate ten appointees to the list, with five potential chairs jointly appointed. From that list of twenty-five, each of the EU and UK will appoint two members and those members will then jointly appoint a chair. The panel is then mandated to render a binding ruling on the dispute.

2.17 The significant exception to this regime is that where a dispute raises a question of EU law, that question that must first be referred to the CJEU for a preliminary ruling. The arbitration panel will then be bound by the CJEU's decision. This is a departure from the usual approach to resolving international disputes between states—it is unusual for such disputes to be referred to the domestic courts of one or the other state. However, this may be unsurprising given the CJEU's position that it has exclusive jurisdiction over questions of EU law (and its willingness to strike down international agreements which it thought undermined that jurisdiction, such as the Safe Harbor Framework for data sharing). It is also probably inevitable, given that the philosophy of the Withdrawal Agreement and the EUWA is to preserve EU law in the UK as it stands at the moment before departure, because the judgments of the CJEU are part and parcel of EU law.

2.18 Arbitration as a mechanism to resolve disputes between states has a distinguished history, and indeed was one of the earliest mechanisms for formally (and peacefully) resolving disputes on the international plane. Its use in the Withdrawal Agreement is therefore consistent with the UK stepping away from the EU's institutional arrangements and returning to more traditional state to state relationships.

2.19 In many ways, the choice of international arbitration to resolve disputes also marks a reversion to political means of resolving disputes, rather than legal ones. Although the decision rendered by a tribunal under the Withdrawal Agreement will be binding as a matter of international law, if the UK or EU does not abide by the decision the ultimate consequences are likely to be political rather than legal. This is in stark contrast to the existing hard legalism within the EU order, where the CJEU's rulings have direct effect.

2.8 The Political Declaration on the Future EU–UK relationship

2.20 The Political Declaration sets out the scope and terms of the future EU–UK relationship.

2.21 There has been some debate about the nature of the Political Declaration and what its legal status might be. Some have argued that the Political Declaration is a legal commitment on the basis that it is part of a package that includes a legally binding Withdrawal Agreement. However, the general consensus seems to be that the Political Declaration is not to be legally binding and instead sets out a framework for future negotiations. Article 184 of the Withdrawal Agreement commits the EU and the UK to using their 'best endeavours, in good faith' to take steps to 'negotiate expeditiously the agreements governing their future relationship referred to in the Political Declaration'. It does not declare that both parties are bound to what is in the Political Declaration.

2.22 In terms of what is meant by 'best endeavours, in good faith' some commentators have turned to CJEU rulings on whether a Member State complies with the principle of sincere cooperation under Article 4(3) of the Treaty on EU. A failure by a Member State to engage in the Commission's infringement proceedings (by, for example, failing to respond to questions) has been found by the CJEU to breach sincere cooperation. If the EU and UK engage in the future relationship negotiations in good faith by attending meetings, responding to questions etc. it is unlikely either will be in violation of Article 184.

2.9 Five Parts

2.23 The Political Declaration is structured in five Parts:

- Part I: Basis for cooperation. This part establishes that the future relationship should be based on the shared EU and UK values and principles such as respect for human rights, democracy, the rule of law, working together globally, and the non-proliferation of nuclear weapons. It includes the UK's commitment to respect 'the framework' of the European Convention on Human Rights (ECHR) (rather than the ECHR itself) and the EU's and the EU27's commitment to the EU's Charter of Fundamental Rights.
It includes a mutual commitment to 'ensuring a high level of personal data protection' to facilitate data flows, and an EU intention to start work on adequacy decisions on the UK's data framework 'as soon as possible' after Brexit, 'endeavouring' to adopt decisions by the end of 2020.
- Part II: Economic Partnership. This part calls on the UK and EU to agree an ambitious, wide-ranging future economic partnership. It leaves many details to be decided during future negotiations and keeps a range of options open. The future relationship will encompass a free trade agreement and cooperation in particular sectors where this is in the parties' mutual interest. The economic partnership will cover trade in goods, trade in services and investment, and a number of sectors including financial services, digital, transport, energy, and fishing.

- Part III: Security Partnership. The future relationship will cover arrangements across three areas: data exchange; operational cooperation between law enforcement authorities and judicial cooperation in criminal matters; and anti-money laundering and counterterrorism financing.
- Part IV: Institutional and other Horizontal Arrangements. The first section of Part IV makes clear that the 'future relationship' is envisaged as a 'framework' relationship, whereby there is an 'overarching institutional framework' but with the details of the operation agreements in distinct policy areas will have to be worked out through the negotiations. It also notes that this framework relationship could take the form of an association agreement and should be reviewable. Part IV also discusses dispute settlement and so-called exceptions and safeguards, being areas where the future relationship will never apply (exceptions) and where it may be temporarily suspended because of overriding concerns on the part of either party (safeguards). These are both fairly standard conditions in international agreements.
- Part V: Forward Process. This sets out some general principles on how progress will be made in developing the Political Declaration and a structure for the negotiations on the future EU–UK relationship.

2.10 Implications for Financial Services

2.24 Part II of the Political Declaration dealing with Economic Partnership contains three specific paragraphs on financial services. These are as follows:

> The Parties are committed to preserving financial stability, market integrity, investor and consumer protection and fair competition, while respecting the Parties regulatory and decision-making autonomy, and their ability to take equivalence decisions in their own interest. This is without prejudice to the Parties' ability to adopt or maintain any measure where necessary for prudential reasons. The Parties agree to engage in close cooperation on regulatory and supervisory matters in international bodies.

> Noting that both Parties will have equivalence frameworks in place that allow them to declare a third country's regulatory and supervisory regimes equivalent for relevant purposes, the Parties should start assessing equivalence with respect to each other under these frameworks as soon as possible after the United Kingdom's withdrawal from the Union, endeavouring to conclude these assessments before the end of June 2020. The Parties will keep their respective equivalence frameworks under review.

> The Parties agree that close and structured cooperation on regulatory and supervisory matters is in their mutual interest. This cooperation should be grounded in the economic partnership and based on the principles of regulatory autonomy, transparency and stability. It should include transparency and appropriate consultation in the process of adoption, suspension and withdrawal of equivalence decisions, information exchange and consultation on regulatory initiatives and other issues of mutual interest, at both political and technical levels.

2.25 The commentary on financial services is limited. It does not contain mutual recognition commitments that the UK originally wanted. Instead, the provisions focus on regulatory autonomy and equivalence. In relation to the latter it is noticeable that equivalence decisions shall be taken in a party's 'own interest' and there is a strong prudential carve out whereby either party may adopt or maintain any measure where necessary for prudential reasons.

2.26 The reference that the assessment of equivalence will take place as soon as possible after the UK has left the EU, with the aim of concluding these assessments before the end of June 2020 is encouraging as this appears to be intended to remove some of the cliff-edge issues that arise at the end of the transition period. However, it does not set in stone that the assessments will be completed by end of June 2020 or that either party is bound to make positive assessments. Where positive assessments are made either party may withdraw them at any point in the future.[5] Significantly, the text is silent as to expanding the existing equivalence framework. Instead it simply states that these frameworks will be kept 'under review'.

2.27 The UK and the EU agree that it is in their mutual interest to ensure 'close and structured cooperation on regulatory and supervisory matters' and such cooperation would be based on principles of regulatory autonomy, transparency, and stability. This cooperation should include 'appropriate' consultation in the process of adoption, suspension and withdrawal of equivalence decisions, information exchange, regulatory initiatives as well as other issues of mutual interest. It is unclear what exactly constitutes 'appropriate consultation'.

2.28 In all, there is nothing in the Political Declaration that suggests that the UK will be on better terms than any other third country dealing with the EU. However, this will be the UK government's aim in the negotiations.

2.11 Going Forward

2.29 As mentioned above, Part V of the Political Declaration (Forward Process) establishes certain general principles on how progress will be made in developing it and the structure for the negotiations on the future EU–UK relationship.

2.30 In particular, once the UK leaves the EU, the parties will agree a programme including the structure and format of the negotiation rounds and a formal schedule of negotiating rounds.

2.31 To provide a sound foundation for the talks on the future relationship, the EU and the UK will identify areas likely to require the greatest consideration and draw up a proposed schedule. Whether financial services will be included in the schedule remains to be seen.

2.32 The procedure for the EU negotiation of agreements with third countries is set out in Article 218 of the Treaty on the Functioning of the EU. This provides that the Council of the EU authorises the opening of negotiations, adopts negotiating directives, authorises the signing of agreements, and concludes them. The Commission submits recommendations to the Council prior to the authorisation of negotiations. The European Parliament, Council, Commission and Member States can seek an opinion of the CJEU as to whether an agreement envisaged is compatible with the treaties.

---

[5] On 29 July 2019, the Commission repealed existing equivalence decisions for the first time. These were in the field of credit rating agencies for Argentina, Australia, Brazil, Canada and Singapore.

Should the future EU–UK agreement go beyond the exclusive competences of the EU, it will need to be approved by each Member State in accordance with their own constitutional procedures for ratifying international agreements. **2.33**

2.12 FCA EU Withdrawal Impact Assessment

In November 2018, the FCA published an EU Withdrawal Impact Assessment which included commentary on the Withdrawal Agreement and Political Declaration. **2.34**

In terms of the UK losing its seat within EU institutions the FCA stated:[6] **2.35**

> The FCA will therefore no longer be a voting member of the European Securities and Markets Authority (ESMA). Some participation may be possible, but the EU and UK have not yet agreed how this would work in practice. In our view, there is time for this issue to be resolved. We believe there is a strong case for continued close cooperation given the size of the UK's financial services sector and the importance the UK's approach to applying EU financial services law has for the rest of the EU.

It added that:[7] **2.36**

> Losing our role in the governance of EU decision making creates challenges, particularly to managing legislation and technical standards that are in development. Our involvement in the work of ESMA ensures that it understands and takes into account the specifics of UK markets. We would seek to continue to engage with ESMA and other competent authorities to provide technical input into their work where they invite us to do so. However, it is unlikely that the FCA will have the same ability to input as compared to being a full member.

The FCA also included the following comments about equivalence, and how it might evolve in the future:[8] **2.37**

> The UK and EU will both have the ability and common interest to find each other's regimes equivalent post exit, facilitating market access across a range of sectors. The declaration appropriately recognises that this must be in the context of both sides retaining autonomy over the exercise of their equivalence regimes. Therefore, equivalence assessments will need to be based on equivalence of outcomes as opposed to identical rulebooks. It will also be necessary to consider carefully the process and scope of equivalence as it currently exists, to ensure that it provides an adequate framework for cross border business in the future. We believe that there is substantial scope for development and improvement of the framework.
>
> The declaration also provides for close and structured supervisory and regulatory engagement, and the possibility for an enhanced relationship compared to a standard third country position. The FCA is committed to close cooperation with EU counterparts. If

---

[6] See FCA EU Withdrawal Impact Assessment, p. 4.
[7] Ibid., p. 22.
[8] Ibid., p. 5.

implemented, this could make it easier for us to continue to meet our objectives, and help manage cross border risks by ensuring that they can be identified early and managed effectively

2.38 In terms of supervisory cooperation the FCA stated that:[9]

> The political declaration also provides for close and structured supervisory and regulatory engagement, with transparency and consultation on issues of shared interest. This gives rise to the possibility for a much better relationship than a standard third country position. This reflects how deeply the respective markets are integrated and will make it easier for us to continue to meet our objectives, and manage cross border risks by ensuring that that they can be identified early and managed effectively.
>
> Close supervisory and regulatory dialogue is also envisaged at both the technical and political level. This will help ensure that equivalence can be managed in a sustainable fashion. Through consultation and dialogue the FCA can work with our European counterparts to develop shared approaches wherever appropriate, helping to maximise continuity in regulatory standards and minimising any risk of conflicting or incompatible standards.

---

[9] Ibid., pp. 27 and 28.

3
International Standards
Michael Raffan

3.1 Introduction

As home to one of the world's leading global financial centres, the United Kingdom (UK) has historically played an important role in the development and implementation of international standards. UK regulators are members of international standard-setting bodies and UK firms participate in international organisations. It is not anticipated that Brexit will change this position. Indeed, once the UK leaves the EU, its participation in global discussions and international standard-setting will become all the more important as the UK seeks to continue to exert its influence internationally, and helps to set the basis for legislation and regulation around the world. **3.01**

3.2 Governments, Central Banks, and Regulators Participating as Members of International Bodies

UK regulators are themselves members of a number of international bodies which set and oversee the implementation of international standards. The expectation is that post-Brexit, UK regulators will continue to participate in these international bodies as members and the UK will continue to follow and implement international standards into domestic legislation. **3.02**

3.2.1 Organisation for Economic Co-operation and Development (OECD)

The mission of the OECD is to promote policies that improve the economic and social well-being of people around the world. **3.03**

3.2.1.1 History
The OECD was established in September 1961 as a successor to the Organisation for European Economic Co-operation, which was established in 1948 to oversee the implementation of the Marshall Plan in the aftermath of the Second World War. **3.04**

The OECD is headquartered in Paris, France. **3.05**

3.2.1.2 Structure

3.06 The OECD's work is driven by:

- council—the decision-making body of the organisation, consisting of representatives from each member country as well as a representative of the European Commission. Decisions are taken by consensus and meetings are chaired by the secretary general. Work mandated by the council is carried out by a secretariat consisting of around 2,500 staff including economists, lawyers, scientists, and other professionals;
- committees—there are about 250 committees, working groups and expert groups dealing with specific policy areas including economics, trade, science, employment, education, and financial markets. Some 40,000 senior officials from national administrations participate in the OECD committee meetings each year to request, review and contribute to work undertaken by the OECD secretariat; and
- secretariat—made up of some 2,500 staff who support the activities of the committees, and carry out the work in response to priorities set by the OECD council. The staff includes economists, lawyers, scientists, and other professionals. Most staff members are based in Paris but some work at the OECD centres in other countries.

3.2.1.3 Membership

3.07 The OECD's membership stretches to thirty-six member countries, which fund the OECD's budget (€374 million in 2017) through mandatory contributions based on a formula which takes into account the size of their economy. Members may also make voluntary contributions to support financially outputs in the OECD programme of work. Since 1960 the European Commission has, by consensus of existing members, been authorised to participate in the OECD. However, it does not have a right to vote and does not officially take part in the adoption of legal instruments submitted to the council.

3.08 The UK is a member of the OECD and maintains a permanent delegation. This membership and involvement are expected to continue post-Brexit.

3.2.1.4 Activities

3.09 To achieve its mission, the OECD operates as a forum for member and non-member countries to cooperate in order to seek solutions to common problems. The OECD maintains close relations with other international organisations and institutions, including the International Labour Organization, the Food and Agriculture Organization, the International Monetary Fund (IMF), the World Bank, the International Atomic Energy Agency, and the United Nations.

3.10 The OECD uses its wealth of information on a broad range of topics to help governments foster prosperity and fight poverty through economic growth and financial stability. There are three key pillars of the OECD's work:

- peer reviews—mutual examination by governments, multilateral surveillance, and a peer review process through which the performance of individual countries is monitored by their peers, all carried out at committee level;
- agreements, standards, and recommendations—discussions at the OECD committee level sometimes evolve into negotiations where the OECD countries agree on 'rules

of the game' for international cooperation. They can culminate in formal agreements by countries, may produce standards and models or recommendations, and may result in guidelines; and
- publications—the OECD publishes regular outlooks, annual overviews, and comparative statistics.

Prominent examples of internationally renowned standards published by the OECD include the Common Reporting Standard[1] (an information standard for the automatic exchange of information regarding bank accounts on a global level between tax authorities), and the ten global principles for fighting financial crime.[2]

3.11

(a) Principles of Corporate Governance
The Principles of Corporate Governance were originally published in 1999 and were most recently revised in July 2015, providing a globally recognised benchmark intended 'to help policymakers evaluate and improve the legal, regulatory, and institutional framework for corporate governance, with a view to support economic efficiency, sustainable growth and financial stability'. Focusing on both financial and non-financial publicly traded companies, the principles are grouped into six thematic chapters and cover:

3.12

- ensuring the basis for an effective corporate governance framework;
- the rights and equitable treatment of shareholders and key ownership functions;
- institutional investors, stock markets, and other intermediaries;
- the role of stakeholders in corporate governance;
- disclosure and transparency; and
- the responsibilities of the board.

The principles are included within the Financial Stability Board (FSB)'s Compendium of Standards (on which see further below) and serve as the basis for the guidelines on the corporate governance of banks issued by the Basel Committee on Banking Supervision. They are accompanied by a methodology which assists in the identification of the specific strengths and weaknesses in a corporate governance system thereby highlighting priorities for reform.

3.13

For financial services firms operating in the UK, relevant corporate governance requirements are found in the Companies Act 2006, the UK Corporate Governance Code (which applies to listed companies and is overseen and maintained by the Financial Reporting Council (FRC)), and the rules and requirements that are set out in the Financial Conduct Authority (FCA) Handbook and Prudential Regulation Authority (PRA) Rulebook. Establishing and maintaining strong and effective corporate governance is also an intrinsic element of a regulated firm's fitness to become an authorised person under Part 4A of the Financial Services and Markets Act 2000 and in the way that firms run their business under the FCA's Principles for Businesses. There is no indication that this will change post-Brexit.

3.14

---

[1] <http://www.oecd.org/tax/automatic-exchange/common-reporting-standard>
[2] <http://www.oecd.org/tax/crime/fighting-tax-crime-the-ten-global-principles.pdf>

3.2.2 IMF

3.15 The primary mission of the IMF is to ensure the stability of the international monetary system.

3.2.2.1 History

3.16 The IMF was conceived in July 1944 at a United Nations conference in Bretton Woods, New Hampshire, United States, with the aim of building a framework for economic cooperation.

3.17 The IMF is headquartered in Washington DC.

3.2.2.2 Structure

3.18 The organisational structure of the IMF consists of:

- board of governors—the highest decision-making body of the IMF consisting of one appointed representative, one governor and one alternate governor for each member country;
- ministerial committees—International Monetary and Financial and Development Committees advise the board of governors;
- executive board—responsible for conducting day-to-day business of the IMF. It is composed of twenty-four directors (who are elected by member countries or by groups of countries) and a managing director (who serves as its chairperson); and
- the IMF management.

3.2.2.3 Membership

3.19 The IMF originally had members from forty-four countries but now has 189 countries as members, by whom it is governed and to whom it is accountable.

3.20 The UK is a member and is represented on the board of governors by the Chancellor of the Exchequer (the governor) and the Governor of the Bank of England (the alternative governor), and on the executive board by representatives from HM Treasury, as executive director and the Bank of England, as alternate executive director. This membership and representation are expected to continue post-Brexit.

3.2.2.4 Activities

3.21 To achieve its mission, the IMF undertakes three principal activities:

- surveillance of the global economy and the economies of member countries, highlighting possible risks to stability and advising on policy adjustments;
- lending to member countries experiencing balance of payments problems to help them rebuild and restore conditions for strong economic growth, while correcting underlying problems; and
- assisting with capacity development for member countries by providing advice and training on modernising their economic policies and institutions, as well as educating officials in areas of core expertise in order to strengthen member countries' institutional capacity.

3.22 The IMF members work together to foster global monetary cooperation, secure financial stability, facilitate international trade, promote high employment and sustainable economic growth as well as to reduce poverty around the world.

(a) Fiscal Transparency Code

3.23 The Fiscal Transparency Code is the international standard for disclosure of information about public finances, and contains four key elements or 'pillars' for fiscal transparency:

- fiscal reporting—offering relevant, comprehensive, timely, and reliable information on the government's financial position and performance;
- fiscal forecasting and budgeting—providing a clear statement of the government's budgetary objectives and policy intentions, together with comprehensive, timely, and credible projections of the evolution of public finances;
- fiscal risk analysis and management—ensuring that risks to public finances are disclosed, analysed, and managed and that fiscal decision-making across the public sector is effectively coordinated; and
- resource revenue management—providing a transparent framework for the ownership, contracting, taxation, and utilisation of natural resource endowments.

3.24 The latest Fiscal Transparency Evaluation for the UK, published by the IMF in 2016, confirmed that across all pillars evaluated in the code, the UK scored very highly when compared to other countries that had undergone an assessment. The key findings corresponding to the four pillars were as follows:

- fiscal reporting comprehensively covered the whole public sector and included details of the full public sector balance sheet. However, the evaluation concluded that prompt publication of end of year financial statements would help to ensure that they were able to inform future years' fiscal policy;
- fiscal forecasting and budgeting were of a high quality, building on credible and thorough macro-fiscal forecasts and a comprehensive medium-term budget framework, supported by clearly understandable and comprehensive budget documentation. However, the evaluation concluded that it was difficult to grasp fully how fiscal policy was being implemented through the budget;
- fiscal risk reporting and management practices were particularly strong on risks relating to the macroeconomy, the long-term sustainability of public finances and the financial sector. However, the evaluation recommended including a comprehensive summary report of specific fiscal risks; and
- the transparency of revenue management practices was strong with a move towards clearer allocation of regulatory responsibilities, simplification of the taxation system and increased disclosure by petroleum companies.

3.25 The UK is expected to take a similar approach post-Brexit.[3]

(b) Code of Good Practices on Transparency in Monetary and Financial Policies

3.26 The Code of Good Practices on Transparency in Monetary and Financial Policies establishes transparency practices for central banks and other financial agencies in their conduct of monetary policy and financial policies, focusing on:

- clarity of roles;
- responsibilities and objectives of central banks and financial agencies;

---

[3] <https://www.imf.org/external/pubs/ft/scr/2016/cr16351.pdf>

- the processes for formulating and reporting of monetary policy decisions by the central banks and of financial policies by financial agencies;
- public availability of information on monetary and financial policies; and
- accountability and assurances of integrity by the central bank and financial agencies.

3.27 It has been drafted to be sufficiently wide to cover a range of monetary and financial frameworks covering the breadth of the IMF membership.

3.28 The detailed assessment of the UK's observance of the Code of Good Practices on Transparency in Monetary and Financial Policies was carried out by IMF staff and published in February 2003. The IMF assessed the transparency of the Bank of England's monetary policy and financial stability activities, including payments system oversight, and concluded that the UK demonstrated a very high degree of observance.

3.29 There is nothing that suggests the UK's approach will change post-Brexit.

3.2.3 Bank for International Settlements (BIS)

3.30 The BIS serves central banks in their pursuit of monetary and financial stability, fosters international cooperation in those areas and acts as a bank for central banks. The BIS is a platform for central bankers and other financial regulators and supervisors to build a greater collective understanding of the world economy, foster international cooperation, and support policymaking.

3.2.3.1 History

3.31 The BIS was established in 1930 by an intergovernmental agreement between Germany, Belgium, France, the UK, Italy, Japan, the United States, and Switzerland. It is the oldest international financial institution.

3.32 Its head office is in Basel, Switzerland with two representative offices in Hong Kong and Mexico City.

3.2.3.2 Structure

3.33 The organisational structure of the BIS comprises three main departments:

- monetary and economic department—undertakes research and analysis on central bank policy issues, provides committee support, and organises meetings of senior central bankers and other officials in charge of financial stability. It also collects, analyses, and disseminates statistical information on the international financial system;
- banking department—provides a range of financial services to support central banks in the management of their foreign exchange and gold reserves and invests the equity of the BIS; and
- general secretariat—supports the entire organisation with corporate services, including human resources, facilities management, security, finance, communications, and IT.

The governance of the BIS is exercised at three levels in accordance with its statutes: **3.34**

- board of directors—determines the BIS's strategic and policy direction, supervises BIS management, and fulfils specific tasks as set out in the BIS's statutes. It meets at least six times per year. The board elects a chairperson from its members for a three-year term and may elect a vice chairperson;
- annual general meeting of BIS member central banks—approves the annual report and the accounts of the BIS, decides on the distribution of dividend, and elects the BIS's auditor; and
- BIS management—directed by the general manager, who is accountable to the board of directors for the conduct of the BIS. The general manager is assisted by the deputy general manager and advised by an executive committee.

3.2.3.3 Membership

Sixty central banks and monetary authorities are currently members of the BIS, each having voting rights and representation at general meetings. **3.35**

The Bank of England represents the UK as a member central bank. This membership and involvement are expected to continue post-Brexit. **3.36**

3.2.3.4 Activities

The BIS pursues its mission by: **3.37**

- fostering discussion and facilitating collaboration among central banks;
- supporting dialogue with other authorities that are responsible for promoting financial stability;
- carrying out research and policy analysis on issues of relevance for monetary and financial stability;
- acting as a prime counterparty for central banks in their financial transactions; and
- serving as an agent or trustee in connection with international financial operations.

3.2.4 FSB

The FSB's mandate is to promote international financial stability by coordinating national financial authorities and international standard-setting bodies as they work towards developing strong regulatory, supervisory, and other financial sector policies. **3.38**

3.2.4.1 History

The FSB was created in April 2009 during the G20[4] summit in London as a successor to the Financial Stability Forum (FSF). The FSF was founded in 1999 by the finance ministers and central bank governors of the G7,[5] and originally consisted of twelve nations participating through financial institutions or their central banks. **3.39**

The FSB sits in Basel, Switzerland. **3.40**

---

[4] Argentina, Australia, Brazil, Canada, China, the European Union, France, Germany, India, Indonesia, Italy, Japan, Mexico, Russia, Saudi Arabia, South Africa, South Korea, Turkey, the United Kingdom, and the United States.

[5] Canada, France, Germany, Italy, Japan, the United Kingdom, and the United States.

3.2.4.2 Structure

3.41 Structurally, the FSB consists of the Plenary,[6] a steering committee,[7] standing committees,[8] and regional consultative groups.[9] The Plenary is the sole decision-making body of the FSB and is responsible for adopting publications, establishing committees and working groups, reviewing the eligibility of members and prospective members based upon the requirements in the charter and appointing the chair of the FSB. The chair of the FSB is the principal spokesperson for the organisation with responsibility for representing the FSB externally, convening, and chairing meetings of the Plenary and the steering committee and overseeing the FSB secretariat.

3.2.4.3 Membership

3.42 The FSB has twenty-five member jurisdictions and representatives who sit on the Plenary including governors of central banks, heads of national supervisory and regulatory agencies, and government finance ministers.

3.43 As a member jurisdiction, the UK is represented by the Bank of England, the FCA, and HM Treasury. This membership and involvement are expected to continue post-Brexit.

3.2.4.4 Activities

3.44 The FSB is governed by its charter, articles of association, and procedural guidelines. The FSB is a member-driven organisation and decisions are taken by consensus.

3.45 The FSB promotes global financial stability by coordinating the development of regulatory, supervisory, and other financial sector policies and conducts outreach to non-member countries. It achieves cooperation and consistency through a three-stage process of:

- identifying systemic risk in the financial sector;
- framing the financial sector policy actions that can address these risks; and
- overseeing implementation of agreed financial reforms through its network of members conducting and publishing peer reviews.

3.46 Although the FSB's decisions are not legally binding, member jurisdictions commit to:

- pursue the maintenance of financial stability, as well as openness and transparency of the financial sector;
- implement and monitor agreement commitments, financial standards, and policy recommendations; and
- undergo periodic peer reviews.

---

[6] The Plenary consists of representatives of all members and is currently composed of fifty-four representatives from twenty-five jurisdictions, six representatives from four international financial institutions and nine representatives from six international standard-setting, regulatory, supervisory, and central bank bodies.

[7] The steering committee provides operational guidance between Plenary meetings to carry forward the directions of the FSB and prepare the Plenary meetings in order to allow the Plenary to efficiently fulfil its mandate. It is headed by the chair of the FSB and consists of forty-six representatives from twenty-one jurisdictions as well as international financial institutions and supervisory bodies.

[8] There are four standing committees, namely the standing committee on assessment of vulnerabilities, the standing committee on supervisory and regulatory cooperation, the standing committee on standards implementation, and the standing committee on budget and resources.

[9] These were established in 2011 and consist of the Americas, Asia, Commonwealth of Independent States, Europe, Middle East and North Africa, and sub-Saharan Africa region, to expand upon and formalise the FSB's outreach activities beyond the membership of the G20 and to reflect the global nature of our financial system.

(a) Compendium of Standards

To assist members, the FSB publishes and maintains a list of key economic, financial, and statistical standards, which are widely accepted as important for sound, stable, and well-functioning financial systems and international financial stability.

3.47

As at September 2018, the Compendium comprised fifteen global financial standards, covering a range of policy areas including macroeconomic policy and data transparency, financial regulation and supervision, and institutional and market infrastructure:[10]

3.48

- Fiscal Transparency Code;[11]
- Enhanced General Data Dissemination System;[12]
- Code of Good Practices on Transparency in Monetary and Financial Policies;[13]
- Special Data Dissemination Standard;[14]
- Insurance Core Principles, Standards, Guidance and Assessment Methodology;[15]
- Objectives and Principles of Securities Regulation (**Objectives and Principles**);[16]
- The Core Principles;
- International Standards on Auditing;[17]
- Principles of Corporate Governance;[18]
- Core Principles for Effective Deposit Insurance Systems;[19]
- Key Attributes of Effective Resolution Regimes for Financial Institutions (**Key Attributes**);[20]
- Principles for Financial Markets Infrastructures;[21]
- Recommendations on Combating Money Laundering and the Financing of Terrorism & Proliferation;[22]
- Insolvency and Creditor Rights Standard;[23] and
- International Financial Reporting Standards.[24]

---

[10] <http://www.fsb.org/what-we-do/about-the-compendium-of-standards/key_standards>

[11] Published by the IMF; identifies a set of principles and practices to help governments provide a clear picture of the structure and finances of government.

[12] Published by the IMF; fosters sound practices with respect to both the compilation and the dissemination of statistics.

[13] Published by the IMF; identifies desirable transparency practices for central banks and other financial agencies in their conduct of monetary and financial policies.

[14] Published by the IMF; guides countries with or seeking access to international capital markets on the dissemination of economic and financial data to the public.

[15] Published by the International Association of Insurance Supervisors (**IAIS**); provides a globally accepted framework for the supervision of the insurance sector.

[16] Published by the International Organization of Securities Commissions (**IOSCO**); sets out thirty-eight principles for effective securities regulation.

[17] Published by the International Auditing and Assurance Standards Board (**IAASB**); contain professional standards for independent auditors reviewing financial statements.

[18] Published by the OECD; assists in the evaluation and improvement of the framework influencing corporate governance.

[19] Published by the International Association of Deposit Insurers (**IADI**); serves as a benchmark for jurisdictions to assess the quality of their deposit insurance systems.

[20] Published by the FSB; sets out the core elements necessary for an effective resolution regime.

[21] Published by the Committee on Payments and Market Infrastructures (**CPMI**) and IOSCO; contains twenty-four principles to be observed by fiscal market infrastructures (**FMIs**).

[22] Published by the Financial Action Task Force (**FATF**); covers the required legal, regulatory and operation measures against money laundering and the financing of terrorism and proliferation.

[23] Published by the World Bank; acts as an assessment tool to assist countries in evaluating and improving insolvency and creditor/debtor regimes.

[24] Published by the International Accounting Standards Board (**IASB**); consists of a single set of accounting standards for global application.

3.49 Some of these are separately discussed in this chapter. The UK has historically adopted a high degree of conformance to these standards across its regulatory framework, and it is not anticipated that the UK will diverge significantly from these standards post-Brexit.

3.50 **(i) Key Attributes** The Key Attributes were adopted by the FSB in October 2011 and most recently amended in October 2014. They set out the core elements that the FSB considers to be necessary for an effective resolution regime, and their implementation should allow authorities to resolve financial institutions in an orderly manner without taxpayer exposure to loss from solvency support, while maintaining continuity of their vital economic functions.

3.51 The Bank of England noted in its October 2017 'Approach to Resolution' paper, that the arrangements for the resolution of failing banks in the UK are designed to comply with the Key Attributes. In keeping with the approach to cross-border resolution set out in the Key Attributes, the Bank of England seeks to cooperate with host authorities, and has established Crisis Management Groups (i.e. fora bringing together key supervisory and regulation authorities) for central counterparties as well as those for global systemically important banks. Crisis Management Groups have also been established in recent years for global systemically important insurers.

3.52 This approach is not expected to change significantly post-Brexit.[25]

3.2.5 FATF

3.53 The FATF is a policymaking body which works to set standards and promote effective implementation of legal, regulatory, and operational measures for combating money laundering, terrorist financing, and other related threats to the integrity of the international financial system.

3.2.5.1 History

3.54 The FATF was established in July 1989 following a G7 summit in Paris, with an initial mandate of examining and developing measures to combat money laundering. In October 2001, the FATF expanded its mandate to incorporate efforts to combat terrorist financing. The FATF's current mandate has been in place since 2012 and operates until 2020.

3.55 The FATF is based in Paris, France.

3.2.5.2 Structure

3.56 The FATF's internal structure consists of:

- the Plenary—the FATF's decision-making body, which meets approximately three times per year. It consists of member jurisdictions and organisations who seek to take decisions by consensus. The Plenary has the authority to establish working groups to support the work of the FATF, with current projects including evaluations and

---

[25] <https://www.bankofengland.co.uk/-/media/boe/files/news/2017/october/the-bank-of-england-approach-to-resolution>

implementation, money laundering and terrorist financing, typologies, and international cooperation review;
- the steering group—an advisory body the composition of which is decided by the Plenary and reviewed on an annual basis. It is chaired by the president, to whom the steering group provides advice on carrying out the directions of the FATF, at meetings convened at least three times per year; and
- the president—a senior official appointed by the Plenary from its members for a term of one year.

3.2.5.3 Membership

The FATF currently comprises thirty-five member jurisdictions and two regional organ- **3.57** isations, representing most major financial centres in all parts of the world. There are also observers, associate members, and observer organisations.

The UK is a member of the FATF and additionally, David Lewis, former head of the illicit **3.58** finance unit and senior policy adviser on money laundering and terrorist financing at HM Treasury, was appointed as executive secretary of the FATF in November 2015. His responsibilities include leading the FATF secretariat, coordinating and delivering the work of the FATF on money laundering and countering the financing of terrorism and proliferation of weapons of mass destruction. This membership and involvement are expected to continue post-Brexit.

3.2.5.4 Activities

One of the FATF's main roles is to publish the International Standards on Combating Money **3.59** Laundering and the Financing of Terrorism & Proliferation (the **Recommendations**). The Recommendations set out a comprehensive and consistent framework of measures which countries should implement in order to combat money laundering and terrorist financing as well as the financing of proliferation of weapons of mass destruction. There is some flexibility in implementation, as countries have diverse legal, administrative, and operational frameworks and different financial systems, and so cannot all take identical measures to counter these threats.

The Recommendations, which were first published in 1990 and most recently revised in **3.60** 2012, contain forty key principles which are divided into seven thematic groups, as well as interpretative notes and other guidance. The Recommendations set out the essential measures which all jurisdictions should have in place in order to:

- identify risks and develop policies with domestic coordination;
- pursue money laundering, terrorist financing and the financing of proliferation;
- apply preventative measures for the financial sector and other designated sectors;
- establish powers and responsibilities for the competent authorities (e.g. investigative, law enforcement, and supervisory authorities) and other institutional measures;
- enhance the transparency and availability of beneficial ownership information of legal persons and arrangements; and
- facilitate international cooperation.[26]

---

[26] <http://www.fatf-gafi.org/media/fatf/documents/recommendations/pdfs/FATF%20Recommendations%202012.pdf>

3.61 In developing and revising the Recommendations, the FATF consults widely among its members, international bodies (including the IMF and the World Bank) and other stakeholders. Starting with its own members, the FATF monitors countries' progress in implementing the Recommendations, reviews money laundering and terrorist financing techniques and countermeasures, and promotes the adoption and implementation of the FATF Recommendations globally.

3.62 The FATF has conducted a number of assessment of the UK's anti-money laundering and counter terrorist financing (AML/CFT) system involving a comprehensive review of the effectiveness of the UK's measures and their level of compliance with the FATF Recommendations. The most recent assessment was conducted in 2018 and the FATF published its report in December 2018.[27] The FATF summarised its findings as follows.

> The UK is the largest financial services provider in the world. As a result of the exceptionally large volume of funds that flows through its financial sector, the country also faces a significant risk that some of these funds have links to crime and terrorism. This is reflected in the country's strong understanding of these risks, as well as national AML/CFT policies, strategies and proactive initiatives to address them.
>
> The UK aggressively pursues money laundering and terrorist financing investigations and prosecutions, achieving 1400 convictions each year for money laundering. UK law enforcement authorities have powerful tools to obtain beneficial ownership and other information, including through effective public–private partnerships, and make good use of this information in their investigations. However, the UK financial intelligence unit needs a substantial increase in its resources and the suspicious activity reporting regime needs to be modernised and reformed.
>
> The country is a global leader in promoting corporate transparency and it is using the results of its risk assessment to further strengthen the reporting and registration of corporate structures. Financial institutions as well as all designated non-financial businesses and professions such as lawyers, accountants and real estate agents are subject to comprehensive AML/CFT requirements. Strong features of the system include the outreach activities conducted by supervisors and the measures to prevent criminals or their associates from being professionally accredited or controlling a financial institution. However, the intensity of supervision is not consistent across all of these sectors and UK needs to ensure that supervision of all entities is fully in line with the significant risks the UK faces.
>
> The UK has been highly effective in investigating, prosecuting and convicting a range of terrorist financing activity and has taken a leading role in designating terrorists at the UN and EU level. The UK is also promoting global implementation of proliferation-related targeted financial sanctions, as well as achieving a high level of effectiveness in implementing targeted financial sanctions domestically.
>
> The UK's overall AML/CFT regime is effective in many respects. It needs to address certain areas of weakness, such as supervision and the reporting and investigation of suspicious transactions. However, the country has demonstrated a robust level of

---

[27] <https://www.fatf-gafi.org/publications/mutualevaluations/documents/mer-united-kingdom-2018.html>

understanding of its risks, a range of proactive measures and initiatives to counter the significant risks identified and plays a leading role in promoting global effective implementation of AML/CFT measures.

3.2.6 CPMI

The CPMI promotes the safety and efficiency of payment, clearing, settlement and related arrangements, thereby supporting financial stability and the wider economy. The CPMI monitors and analyses developments in these areas, both within and across jurisdictions. It also serves as a forum for central bank cooperation in related oversight, policy, and operational matters, including the provision of central bank services. The CPMI is a global standard setter aiming to strengthen regulation, policy, and practices regarding such arrangements worldwide. **3.63**

3.2.6.1 History

In 1980, the governors of the central banks of the G10[28] set up the Group of Experts on Payment Systems. This was followed by the establishment of the ad hoc Committee on Interbank Netting Schemes in 1989 (also by the G10 central bank governors) and the Committee on Payment and Settlement Systems as a follow-up to the work of the Committee on Interbank Netting Schemes in 1990 (again by the G10 central bank governors). In September 2013, the Committee on Payment and Settlement Systems was renamed the CPMI with a new mandate. **3.64**

The CPMI is headquartered at the BIS's offices in Basel, Switzerland. **3.65**

3.2.6.2 Structure

The CPMI is headed by a chair and operates through a series of working groups. The Global Economy Meeting is the governing body of the CPMI, and is supported by the Economic Consultative Committee. The Global Economy Meeting approves the CPMI's charter, appoints its chairperson, and decides on membership. These powers are conferred by the charter of the CPMI. **3.66**

Historically, the UK has had a connection with the CPMI through chairs, including Sir Paul Tucker, previously the deputy governor of Financial Stability at the Bank of England, who served as chair between 2012 and 2013. **3.67**

3.2.6.3 Membership

The CPMI has twenty-eight central bank members, including the Bank of England. This membership and involvement are expected to continue post-Brexit. **3.68**

The CPMI itself is a member of the FSB (on which see further above). **3.69**

3.2.6.4 Activities

The CPMI carries out its mandate through the following activities: **3.70**

---

[28] Consisting since 1964 of eleven industrialised nations: Belgium, Canada, France, Germany, Italy, Japan, the Netherlands, Sweden, Switzerland, the United Kingdom, and the United States.

- monitoring and analysing developments to help identify risks for the safety and efficiency of arrangements within its mandate as well as resulting risks for the global financial system;
- sharing experiences relating to arrangements within its mandate, in particular, the performance of oversight functions and the provision of central bank services in order to promote common understanding, and developing policy advice or common policies for central banks;
- establishing and promoting global standards and recommendations for the regulation, oversight, and practices of arrangements within its mandate, including guidance for their interpretation and implementation, where appropriate;
- monitoring the implementation of the CPMI standards and recommendations with the purpose of ensuring timely, consistent, and effective implementation;
- supporting cooperative oversight and cross-border information sharing, including crisis communication and contingency planning for cross-border crisis management;
- maintaining relationships with central banks which are not members of the CPMI to share experiences and views and to promote the implementation of the CPMI standards and recommendations beyond the CPMI member jurisdictions, either directly or by supporting regional bodies as appropriate; and
- coordinating and cooperating with other financial sector standard setters, central bank bodies and international financial institutions.

3.71 The CPMI does not possess any formal supranational authority but relies on the commitment of its members to carry out its mandate. It expects its standards to be fully incorporated into local legal, regulatory, and policy frameworks in accordance with each jurisdiction's rule-making process within a timeframe established by the CPMI committee and that relevant arrangements will be put in place to observe its standards. The CPMI members are required to seek to achieve the greatest possible consistency in their implementation of these frameworks with the standards.

3.72 Furthermore, the CPMI issues recommendations which aim to promote common understanding and improve oversight and market practices. Finally, the CPMI also publishes reports, studies and surveys on issues falling within its mandate. This includes the publication of statistical data collected by the CPMI.

3.73 The CPMI committee meets around three times each year and is responsible for establishing and monitoring the CPMI work programme, as well as its standards, recommendations, and working groups. It seeks to reach decisions by consensus and sometimes invites non-members to participate in meetings.

(a) Principles for Financial Markets Infrastructures (PFMI)

3.74 The PFMI were published by the CPMI and the IOSCO in April 2012 and comprise 24 international standards for financial market infrastructures (**FMIs**), i.e. payment systems, central securities depositories, securities settlement systems, central counterparties and trade repositories.[29] The PFMI also contains a set of responsibilities that apply to FMIs.

---

[29] <https://www.bis.org/cpmi/publ/d101a.pdf>

The PFMI are part of a set of twelve key standards (see the Compendium above) that the international community considers essential to strengthening and preserving financial stability.

3.75 The Bank of England contributed to the development of the PFMI and its supervisory approach is based on the PFMI. A key outcome of the PFMI approach is to ensure the continuity of service of FMIs as well as their due regard for managing systemic risk. The Bank of England's supervision of FMIs is judgement-based and forward-looking, and is carried out using a supervisory risk assessment framework to identify risks that FMIs may be exposed to and the mitigants that FMIs have in place to guard against those risks. There are three broad categories of risk mitigants within the framework:

- operational mitigants which are processes that FMIs have in place to ensure their operational resilience (e.g. governance arrangements within FMIs and their risk management and controls);
- financial mitigants which comprise sufficient collateral (e.g. margin and default funds for CCPs), capital, and liquid resources to protect their financial resilience; and
- plans to ensure recovery and resolvability if the risks to which an FMI was exposed crystallised to such an extent that its continued operation is threatened.

3.76 The Bank of England makes an annual assessment of each FMI it supervises, from which it sets risk-mitigating actions it expects to be taken. This is informed by a continuous cycle of supervisory engagement which is intended to identify risks as they emerge.[30]

3.77 Cooperative supervision plays a fundamental role in promoting financial stability where FMIs operate across borders. Indeed, the PFMI set expectations that relevant authorities should cooperate with each other both domestically and internationally in promoting the safety and efficiency of FMIs. The Bank of England has indicated its commitment to seeking input from other relevant authorities.

3.78 According to the PFMI, all systemically important FMIs should have comprehensive and effective recovery plans. As set out in the Bank of England's supervisory approach documents, FMIs are expected to have in place recovery plans to address threats to their viability that might prevent them from providing critical functions to the markets they serve. The Bank of England works with FMIs as they prepare their recovery plans.

3.79 In July 2018, IOSCO and the CPMI published the fifth update to the Level 1 assessment report on implementation of the PFMI. For Level 1 assessments, jurisdictions are asked to assess their own progress in adopting the legislation, regulations and other policies that will enable them to implement PFMI. In the most recent assessment report, the UK attested to full implementation of the PFMI for all FMI types. This supports the previous views taken by the CPMI and IOSCO as part of their own assessment, which concluded that all the responsibilities set out in the PFMI were fully observed.[31]

---

[30] <https://www.bankofengland.co.uk/-/media/boe/files/annual-report/2018/supervision-of-financial-market-infrastructures-annual-report-2018>

[31] <https://www.bankofengland.co.uk/-/media/boe/files/annual-report/2016/supervision-of-financial-market-infrastructures-2016>

3.2.7 Basel Committee on Banking Supervision (BCBS)

3.80 The BCBS's mandate is to strengthen the regulation, supervision, and practices of banks worldwide, and to enhance financial stability. In part, this mandate is achieved through the BCBS's contribution to the development, review, and implementation of international standards.

3.2.7.1 History
3.81 The BCBS, originally named the Committee on Banking Regulations and Supervisory Practices, was established in 1974 by the governors of ten central banks in the aftermath of the failure of Bankhaus Herstatt in West Germany.

3.82 The BCBS is headquartered within the BIS in Basel, Switzerland.

3.2.7.2 Structure
3.83 The organisational structure of the BCBS is based around a committee, which has a rotating chairman and comprises five standard-setting and research-based groups. The committee reports to the Group of Governors and Heads of Supervision, an oversight body which endorses major decisions, approves the BCBS's charter, directs the BCBS's work programme, and appoints the chair. The committee is supported by a secretariat hosted by the BIS.

3.2.7.3 Membership
3.84 The BCBS has forty-five members across twenty-eight jurisdictions, consisting of central banks and banking supervisors.

3.85 The Bank of England and the PRA are both current members, as institutional representatives of the UK. Historically, the UK has also participated in the BCBS through chair— Peter Cooke, previously associate director of the Bank of England, served as the BCBS chair between 1977 and 1988. This membership and involvement are expected to continue post-Brexit.

3.86 The BCBS is itself a member of the FSB (on which see further above).

3.2.7.4 Activities
3.87 As the BCBS does not possess any formal supranational authority, it relies on its members' commitments to achieve its mandate. Its main activities include:

- coordinating and cooperating with other financial sector standard setters and international bodies, including non-member central banks, particularly those involved in promoting financial stability;
- identifying risks, including regulatory and supervisory gaps, which pose a threat to the global financial system; and
- consulting on, establishing, promoting, and monitoring the implementation of global minimum standards for the prudential regulation and supervision of banks.

3.88 The BCBS expects its members to implement its standards in full through incorporation into their legal frameworks.

(a) Core Principles for Effective Banking Supervision (Core Principles)

3.89 The Core Principles are a framework of minimum standards for sound supervisory practices and are considered universally applicable. The BCBS issued the Core Principles as its contribution to strengthening the global financial system and effective supervisory systems. It believes that implementation of the Core Principles by all countries would be a significant step towards improving financial stability domestically and internationally. A number of countries have endorsed the Core Principles and have implemented them into national laws.

3.90 The Core Principles have gone through several iterations since they were first published in September 1997, most recently in September 2012. Today, there are twenty-nine principles that are needed for a supervisory system to be considered effective. These principles are divided into two groups: the first group (Principles 1 to 13) focuses on powers, responsibilities, and functions of supervisors, while the second group (Principles 14 to 29) focuses on prudential regulations and requirements for banks.

3.91 The Core Principles do not mandate or specify a particular approach to banking supervision that should be taken, but operate as 'overriding goals'. Accordingly, the BCBS expects each banking system to adapt the Core Principles to its own specific circumstances. The BCBS collaborates with the IMF and the World Bank to encourage countries to implement the Core Principles.

3.92 Like other countries worldwide, the UK has implemented the Core Principles into its regulatory framework through various legislative measures, including but not limited to the introduction of the Financial Services Act 2012, ring-fencing requirements under the Financial Services (Banking Reform) Act 2013 as well as the Senior Managers Regime. The latest detailed assessment of the UK's observance of the Core Principles was carried out by IMF staff and published in June 2016, and concluded that the UK was either compliant or largely compliant with all the Core Principles. In particular, the following points were noted:

- the assessment concluded that the goal of the UK authorities' current supervisory approach is now more clearly aligned with the overarching objective of promoting and preserving systemic resilience. This policy objective is particularly evident in the emphasis that the UK supervisors place on (1) the assessment of risks; (2) the adequacy of capital and liquidity in supervised entities; and (3) the largest and most systemically important firms. From the supervisors' perspective, the severe deterioration or failure of these firms threatens not just the stability of the financial system, but also the health and growth of the broader economy;
- the UK regulators use stress-testing as a critical supervisory tool which encourages firms and supervisors to adopt a more forward-looking view on the strength of their balance sheets and resilience to shocks; and
- the UK regime emphasises 'on balance sheet' strength, enhanced capital ratios and ensuring more stable sources of funding.

3.93 There is nothing to suggest that the UK approach to implementing the Core Principles will change as a consequence of Brexit, and the expectation is that it will continue to follow and implement the BCBS guidelines and standards with a high degree of conformity.[32]

---

[32] <https://www.imf.org/external/pubs/ft/scr/2016/cr16166.pdf>

(b) International convergence of capital measurement and capital standards

3.94 In July 1988 the BCBS published a capital measurement system, the Basel Capital Accord (which is subsequently known as Basel I, following the further iterations of Basel II and Basel III). Basel I required banks to hold capital equal to at least 8% of their risk-weighted assets.

3.95 In June 2004, following almost six years of intensive preparation and consultation with banking sector representatives, supervisory agencies, central banks, and observers, Basel I was replaced with Basel II, a further iteration comprising three pillars:

- minimum capital requirements which sought to develop and expand the standardised rules set out in the 1988 Accord (Pillar 1);
- supervisory review of an institution's capital adequacy and internal assessment process (Pillar 2); and
- effective use of disclosure as a lever to strengthen market discipline and encourage sound banking practices (Pillar 3).

3.96 The new framework was designed to improve the way that regulatory capital requirements reflect underlying risks and better address the financial innovation that had occurred since Basel I. The changes were aimed at rewarding and encouraging continued improvements in risk measurement and control.

3.97 In response to the financial crisis of 2007–9, the BCBS announced Basel III in December 2010, a further iteration of the capital standards. The initial phase of Basel III reforms focused on strengthening the regulatory framework by improving the quality of bank regulatory capital, increasing the level of capital requirements to ensure that banks are sufficiently resilient to withstand losses in times of stress, revising the risk-weighted capital framework, introducing capital buffers, specifying a minimum leverage ratio requirement to constrain excess leverage in the banking system and complement the risk-weighted capital requirements, and introducing an international framework for mitigating excessive liquidity risk and maturity transformation. The second phase of Basel III reforms aimed to improve the calculation of risk-weighted assets and the comparability of banks' capital ratios.

3.98 The BCBS monitors members' implementation of Basel III through the Regulatory Consistency Assessment Programme, and publishes semi-annual reports on members' progress.

3.99 Basel III is implemented in Europe through Regulation (EU) 575/2013 on prudential requirements for credit institutions and investment firms (Capital Requirements Regulation) (CRR) and Directive 2013/36/EU on capital requirements (Capital Requirements Directive) (CRD). The CRR is directly applicable in the UK, while the CRD has primarily been implemented in the UK through the PRA and the FCA rules. The UK government has indicated through the European Union (Withdrawal) Act 2018 and the recently published statutory instruments that post-Brexit it will retain the extensive body of existing EU-derived laws and regulations in the UK statute book as at the date of withdrawal, and therefore it is not expected that the UK will swiftly look to diverge from the Basel III framework as the internationally recognised capital standard once it leaves the EU.

3.2.8 IOSCO

IOSCO is the international body that brings together the world's securities regulators and is recognised as the global standard setter for the securities sector. IOSCO develops, implements, and promotes adherence to internationally recognised standards for securities regulation. It works intensively with the G20 and the FSB on the global regulatory reform agenda. **3.100**

3.2.8.1 History
IOSCO was established in 1983 by a collaboration of North and South American securities regulatory agencies that sought to build an international cooperative body. In the subsequent years, securities regulators from France, Indonesia, Korea, and the UK also joined. **3.101**

IOSCO is currently headquartered in Madrid, Spain. **3.102**

3.2.8.2 Structure
IOSCO's structure comprises: **3.103**

- the Presidents Committee—composed of all the presidents (chairs) of ordinary and associate members. It meets once a year during the annual conference and is chaired by the president of the ordinary member hosting the annual conference; and
- the IOSCO board—the governing and standard-setting body of IOSCO, which comprises thirty-four securities regulators who regulate more than 95% of the world's securities markets in more than 115 jurisdictions.

The FCA represents the UK as a member of both the Presidents Committee and the IOSCO board. **3.104**

There are also three other committees: **3.105**

- the Growth and Emerging Markets Committee (the largest committee within IOSCO), which seeks to promote the development and greater efficiency of emerging securities and futures markets by establishing principles and minimum standards, providing training programmes and technical assistance for members and facilitating the exchange of information and transfer of technology and expertise. It comprises eighty-nine members and twenty-one non-voting associate members which include the world's fastest growing economies and ten of the G20 members, although the UK is not currently a member;
- four regional committees for Africa/Middle East, Asia-Pacific, Europe, and Inter-America. The FCA is a member of the European committee; and
- the affiliate members consultative committee, which encourages members to share experiences and to cooperate.

3.2.8.3 Membership
As at August 2019, IOSCO had 224 members across the following three categories: **3.106**

- 129 ordinary members consisting of national commissions or similar bodies with significant authority over securities or derivatives markets within their jurisdiction;

- thirty-one associate members consisting of supranational and subnational governmental regulators, intergovernmental organisations, international standard-setting bodies, and governmental bodies with an appropriate interest in securities regulation; and
- sixty-seven affiliate members consisting of self-regulatory organisations, securities exchanges, FMIs, international bodies, investor protection funds and compensation funds, and other bodies with an appropriate interest in securities regulation.

3.107 IOSCO's membership regulates more than 95% of the world's securities markets in more than 115 jurisdictions. Securities regulators in emerging markets account for 75% of its ordinary membership.

3.108 The FCA is a member and, as noted above, participates in the Presidents Committee, the IOSCO board and the European regional committee. LCH Group is a member of the affiliate members consultative committee.

3.109 This membership and involvement are expected to continue post-Brexit.

3.2.8.4 Activities

3.110 As part of its work in influencing the global regulatory reform agenda, and to further its objective of being the global standard setter for the securities sector, IOSCO collaborates with other international organisations, including the FSB (on which see further above).

3.111 IOSCO members resolve to:

- cooperate in developing, implementing, and promoting adherence to internationally recognised and consistent standards of regulation, oversight, and enforcement in order to protect investors, maintain fair, efficient, and transparent markets and seek to address systemic risks;
- enhance investor protection and promote investor confidence in the integrity of securities markets, through strengthened information exchange and cooperation in enforcement against misconduct and in supervision of markets and market intermediaries; and
- exchange information at both global and regional levels on their respective experiences in order to assist the development of markets, strengthen market infrastructure, and implement appropriate regulation.

3.112 IOSCO's substantive policy work is conducted within a structure of eight committees with varying specialisms, namely, issuer accounting, auditing and disclosure, regulation of secondary markets, regulation of market intermediaries, enforcement and the exchange of information, investment management, credit rating agencies, commodities derivatives markets, and retail investors. IOSCO also provides technical assistance, education, training, and research to its members and other regulators.

(a) Objectives and Principles

3.113 The Objectives and Principles were adopted by IOSCO in 1998, and are the overarching core principles that guide IOSCO in the development and implementation of internationally recognised and consistent standards of regulation, oversight, and enforcement.

They form the basis for the evaluation of the securities sector for the Financial Sector Assessment Programs of the IMF and the World Bank.

Most recently updated in May 2017, the Objectives and Principles contain thirty-eight guiding rules for effective securities regulation based upon the tripartite objectives of: **3.114**

- protecting investors;
- ensuring that markets are fair, efficient, and transparent; and
- reducing systemic risk.

The Objectives and Principles are grouped into the following ten categories: **3.115**

- principles relating to the regulator;
- principles for self-regulation;
- principles for the enforcement of securities regulation;
- principles for cooperation in regulation;
- principles for issuers;
- principles for auditors, credit rating agencies, and other information service providers;
- principles for collective investment schemes;
- principles for market intermediaries;
- principles for secondary and other markets; and
- principles relating to clearing and settlement.[33]

In 2003, IOSCO endorsed a methodology designed to assist in the assessment of member jurisdictions' implementation of the Objectives and Principles and to help in the development of practical action plans to address identified deficiencies.[34] **3.116**

To encourage cross-border cooperation and information exchange, IOSCO established a Multilateral Memorandum of Understanding as an international benchmark on how signatories should consult, cooperate, and exchange information for the purpose of regulatory enforcement regarding securities markets. This has now been supplemented by an Enhanced Multilateral Memorandum of Understanding Concerning Consultation and Co-operation and the Exchange of Information which aims to build upon the principles established by the previous memorandum. **3.117**

In July 2011 the IMF published a detailed assessment of the UK's implementation of the IOSCO Objectives and Principles.[35] Of the thirty principles, the UK had: **3.118**

- fully implemented nineteen;
- broadly implemented ten; and
- there was one principle categorised as 'N/A'.

The paper also recommended actions in relation to the ten principles that were broadly implemented. There is nothing that suggests the UK's approach of adopting a high degree of observance of the Objectives and Principles will change post-Brexit. **3.119**

---

[33] <https://www.iosco.org/library/pubdocs/pdf/IOSCOPD561.pdf>
[34] <https://www.iosco.org/library/pubdocs/pdf/IOSCOPD562.pdf>
[35] <https://www.imf.org/external/pubs/ft/scr/2011/cr11232.pdf>

3.2.9 Global Foreign Exchange Committee (GFXC)

3.120 The GFXC is a forum that brings together central banks and private sector participants to promote a robust, liquid, open, and appropriately transparent foreign exchange market in which a diverse set of participants, supported by resilient infrastructure, is able to transact at competitive prices that reflect available information and in a manner that conforms to acceptable standards of behaviours.

3.2.9.1 History

3.121 The GFXC was established in May 2017 during a meeting of public and private sector representatives from foreign exchange committees of sixteen international forex trading centres in London.

3.2.9.2 Structure and membership

3.122 The GFXC's internal structure comprises the following:

- members—the GFXC's sixteen members include central bank-sponsored foreign exchange committees and similar structures in various regions. Each member's foreign exchange committee designates a central bank and private sector representative for the GFXC;
- associate members—jurisdictions which meet some but not all of the membership criteria. Georgia is the only current associate member;
- chair and vice chair—the chair is a central bank representative drawn from the membership of the GFXC and the vice chair is a senior representative from the private sector; and
- secretariat.

3.123 The UK's Foreign Exchange Joint Standing Committee is currently a member of the GFXC.

3.2.9.3 Activities

3.124 The objectives and activities of the GFXC include:

- promoting collaboration and communication among local foreign exchange committees and non-GFXC jurisdictions with significant foreign exchange markets;
- exchanging views on trends and developments in global foreign exchange markets, including on the structure and functioning of those markets, drawing on information gathered at the various foreign exchange committees; and
- promoting, maintaining, and updating on a regular basis the FX Global Code and considering good practices regarding effective mechanisms to support adherence.

(a) FX Global Code

3.125 The FX Global Code, launched in May 2017 and most recently updated in August 2018, is a set of global principles of good practice, developed to provide a common set of guidelines to promote the integrity and effective functioning of the wholesale foreign exchange market. Its establishment was facilitated by the Foreign Exchange Working Group, which operated under the auspices of the BIS Markets Committee and consisted of central banks from sixteen jurisdictions around the world. This work was supported by a market participants group representing the sell side, buy side, and FX infrastructure providers across these regions.

3.126 The FX Global Code does not impose legal or regulatory obligations on market participants, nor does it provide a substitute for regulation. However, it is intended to supplement local laws, rules, and regulations by identifying global good practices and processes.

3.127 In the UK, the FX Global Code superseded and substantively updated the guidance for participants in FX markets previously provided by the Non-Investment Products Code. The FCA published a statement on 25 May 2017 welcoming the introduction of the FX Global Code and setting out its expectation on firms, senior managers, certified individuals and other relevant persons to take responsibility for and be able to demonstrate their own adherence with standards of market conduct, which is supported by the FCA's supervision of the Senior Managers and Certification Regime rules. The PRA published its Statement of Commitment to the FX Global Code on 6 February 2018, demonstrating its commitment to adhering to the principles of the FX Global Code when acting as a market participant in the relevant markets, and confirming that its internal practices and processes are aligned with the principles of the FX Global Code.

3.128 The ECB has also announced its approach to implementing the FX Global Code, which involves:

- inviting FX trading counterparties to commit publicly to the principles by endorsing the statement of commitment by the end of May 2018;
- encouraging counterparties to reaffirm their commitment to the principles after any substantial future update of the FX Global Code;
- reaffirming its own intention to commit to the FX Global Code when participating in the foreign exchange market; and
- making membership of its Foreign Exchange Contact Group contingent on adherence to the FX Global Code.

3.129 Market participants are encouraged to demonstrate their recognition of and commitment to adopting the good practices set out in the FX Global code by making a standardised 'Statement of Commitment'. Since its launch, over 100 market participants have made statements of commitment to the FX Global Code.

(b) *Competition/Antitrust Law Guidelines for Members of the GFXC (Competition Guidelines)*

3.130 The purpose of the Competition Guidelines is to provide members of the GFXC general guidance on avoiding unlawful or illegal anticompetitive activities. The Competition Guidelines apply to all GFXC activities, including those of any subgroups, and adherence to these guidelines is mandatory for all GFXC members and is a condition for participating in the GFXC.

3.2.10 International Association of Insurance Supervisors (IAIS)

3.131 The IAIS is the international standard-setting body responsible for developing and implementing principles, standards, and guidance for the supervision of the insurance sector. The mission of the IAIS, which has evolved over time, is to promote effective and globally consistent supervision of the insurance industry in order to develop and maintain fair, safe, and stable insurance markets for the benefit and protection of policyholders and to contribute to global financial stability.

3.2.10.1 History

3.132 The IAIS was established in 1994 as a voluntary membership organisation of insurance supervisors and regulators from more than 200 jurisdictions, constituting 97% of the world's insurance premiums.

3.133 The IAIS is headquartered at the BIS in Basel, Switzerland.

3.2.10.2 Structure

3.134 Under the direction of its members, the IAIS conducts activities through a committee system designed to achieve its mandate and objectives. The IAIS committee system is led by an executive committee whose members come from different regions of the world. The executive committee is supported by five committees (audit and risk, budget, implementation and assessment, macroprudential, and policy development committees), and is overseen by the supervisory forum. Committees may establish subcommittees to help carry out their duties.

3.135 The secretariat provides organisational and management support to the IAIS.

3.2.10.3 Membership

3.136 The IAIS currently has over 210 members from almost 140 countries. From a UK perspective, both the PRA and the FCA are members. This membership and involvement are expected to continue post-Brexit.

3.137 The IAIS is also a member of the FSB, the Standards Advisory Council of the International Accounting Standards Board, and a partner in the Access to Insurance Initiative.

3.2.10.4 Activities

3.138 As the IAIS is not a legislature, it relies on the cooperation of its members and on sovereign authorities to implement its principles, standards, and policies.

3.139 Its work is guided by a strategic plan and financial outlook that is revised every five years. The current plan (2015–19) includes the following seven high-level goals, which are accompanied by strategies for implementation and an annual roadmap (which builds on the strategies by providing a more detailed level of planning):

- assessing and responding to insurance sector vulnerabilities;
- the IAIS as the global standard setter for insurance;
- contributing to financial stability in the insurance sector;
- enhancing effective supervision;

- enhancing implementation and observance of the Insurance Core Principles (**ICPs**);
- effective stakeholder outreach and external interaction; and
- effective and efficient organisation and operations.

(a) ICPs

The ICPs were adopted by the IAIS in October 2011, and most recently updated in November 2018. The 26 current principles set out the pre-eminent globally accepted framework for supervision of the insurance sector in the form of: **3.140**

- statements—which prescribe essential elements within a supervisory regime to promote a financially sound insurance sector and provide an adequate level of policyholder protection;
- standards—which contain the high-level requirements which members are expected to implement in order to demonstrate compliance; and
- guidance material—which supports the statements and standards by providing details as to implementation and additional details on how statements or standards should be interpreted.

The ICPs are designed to apply to insurance supervision in all jurisdictions and be relevant for all insurance product markets. However, the IAIS recognises that supervisors should have the flexibility to tailor supervisory requirements according to the nature, scale, and complexity of individual insurers in order to achieve the ICPs' objectives without impeding stable business development. **3.141**

There is a detailed assessment methodology to help evaluate jurisdictions' observance of the ICPs. **3.142**

In July 2011 the IMF published details of its assessment of the UK's observance of the twenty-eight ICPs in place at that time. This report concluded that the conditions for effective supervision were adequately met, reflecting the highly developed legal system, institutional framework, financial markets, and long-standing insurance market. The report found that insurance regulation in the UK was thorough and effective and the powers given to the Financial Services Authority (**FSA**) (the FCA's predecessor) under the Financial Services and Market Act 2000 allowed it to develop comprehensive and detailed regulatory requirements and supervision guidance. The FSA applied a sophisticated and well-developed risk-based approach to supervision and a modern and risk-sensitive regulation of firms' capital. In summary, at the time of the report, the UK was: [36] **3.143**

- observing nineteen of the ICPs;[37]
- largely observing seven of the ICPs;[38] and
- partially observing two of the ICPs.[39]

---

[36] <https://www.imf.org/external/pubs/ft/scr/2011/cr11234.pdf>
[37] All the essential criteria are observed or where all the essential criteria are observed except for those that are considered not applicable.
[38] Only minor shortcomings exist, which do not raise any concerns about the authorities' ability to achieve full observance.
[39] Despite progress, the shortcomings are sufficient to raise doubts about the authorities' ability to achieve observance.

3.2.11 International Organisation of Pension Supervisors (IOPS)

3.144 IOPS is an independent international body representing those involved in the supervision of private pension arrangements. IOPS has the goal of improving the quality and effectiveness of the supervision of private pension systems throughout the world, enhancing their development and operational efficiency and allowing for the provision of a secure source of retirement income in as many countries as possible.

3.2.11.1 History

3.145 IOPS was formed in July 2004 by the OECD and the International Network of Pension Regulators and Supervisors.

3.146 It is headquartered in Paris, France.

3.2.11.2 Structure

3.147 IOPS operates by committees:

- the executive committee—which has all the powers necessary to achieve the objectives and purposes of the organisation, including appointing chairpersons and vice chairpersons, considering membership applications and setting of membership fees, overseeing the secretariat, and establishing of agenda for the annual general meeting and conferences. The executive committee prepares the biannual programme of work, the annual budget, and the annual report of the organisation, and is the main liaison body with other international organisations. The executive committee has between five and twelve individuals who are elected by governing members to represent at least three continents; and
- the technical committee—which participates in and conducts the development of principles, standards, and good practices on pension supervisory issues and on regulatory issues relating to pension supervision. The technical committee develops the programme of work of the organisation, which it recommends to the executive committee. It also serves as a forum to discuss, develop, and analyse matters relating to pension supervision that are of interest to the membership. Participation is open to all IOPS members.

3.148 The committees are assisted by a secretariat, which is hosted by the OECD in accordance with IOPS/OECD partnership agreement.

3.2.11.3 Membership

3.149 The membership of IOPS includes representatives from more than seventy-five jurisdictions and is separated into three levels:

- governing members—responsible in whole or in part for the supervision of pension funds, plans, schemes, or arrangements in a country or in the subdivision of a country;
- associate members—government authorities responsible in whole or in part for pension regulation or the establishment of pension policy and those that have an interest in pension supervision; and

- observer members—other entities interested in pension supervision such as research organisations, industry bodies, financial institutions, and professional firms engaged in the business of providing pension-related services.

The UK Pensions Regulator is a governing member. This membership is expected to continue post-Brexit. **3.150**

3.2.11.4 Activities

IOPS's main objectives are to: **3.151**

- serve as a standard-setting body on pension supervisory matters and regulatory issues relating to pension supervision;
- promote international cooperation on pension supervision and encourage international contact among pension supervisors and other relevant parties;
- provide a worldwide forum for policy dialogue on pension supervision and exchange of information between members of IOPS;
- participate in the work of relevant international bodies relating to development and promotion of the implementation of international principles, standards, and good practices in pension regulation; and
- assist countries with less developed private pension arrangements through policy dialogue, appropriate technical support, and relevant research in close cooperation with relevant international bodies and other technical assistance programmes.

(a) Principles of Private Pension Supervision

The Principles of Private Pension Supervision were approved by the governing members of IOPS in 2006 and were revised in November 2010. They establish the necessary requirements for an efficient and effective supervisory regime for pensions. **3.152**

The ten principles focus on protecting the interests of pension fund members and beneficiaries, by promoting the stability, security, and good governance of pension funds. **3.153**

IOPS has also developed a methodology for authorities to undertake self-assessment against the principles. The principles have been endorsed and incorporated into the standards issued by other international standard-setting bodies, including the OECD, the IMF, the World Bank, and the International Association of Entities Supervising Pension Funds. **3.154**

(b) Other guidelines and good practices

In addition to the principles, IOPS publishes guidelines and good practices. While these are non-legally binding instruments, members are encouraged to observe and adopt them and to identify areas of weakness in order to bring their regulation and supervisory regimes up to standard. **3.155**

In 2008, IOPS collected questionnaire responses on pension supervisory structures from twenty-five jurisdictions, including the UK, and concluded that almost all jurisdictions had independent structures and operations, with clearly assigned objectives and a mission statement, in line with the IOPS Principles. **3.156**

3.157 In particular, the following points were made in relation to the UK Pensions Regulator:

- it had adopted stress-testing and a risk-based approach to supervision, with a specialised supervisory structure;
- measures of probability and impact were also at the heart of its risk assessment and supervisory response, allowing it to decide upon which of the funds under its supervisory jurisdiction it should focus on;
- it had a low intensity approach to licensing and monitoring, employing a light registration rather than a full licensing regime;
- it had a light information collection regime (collecting data only annually and rarely making on-site visits) but a relatively high analysis function;
- it saw intervention as a last resort and focused on reducing risk and deterrent actions rather than corrective action; and
- there are extensive communication channels between the UK Pensions Regulator, pension fund managers, trustees, and beneficiaries as well as members of the public.[40]

3.158 While the UK Pensions Regulator is preparing for the impact of Brexit, there is no indication that the principles upon which it regulates will significantly change as a result.

3.2.12 International Association of Deposit Insurers (IADI)

3.159 The IADI contributes to the enhancement of deposit insurance effectiveness and the stability of financial systems by promoting guidance and international cooperation in the field of deposit insurance and encouraging wide international contact among deposit insurers and other interested parties.

3.160 It is headquartered at the BIS's offices in Basel, Switzerland.

3.2.12.1 Structure and membership

3.161 The IADI is governed by the general meeting of its members (which is its supreme decision-making authority body), and the executive council (under which there are council committees and sub-technical committees). Both bodies are assisted by the secretariat.

3.162 The IADI has eighty-three members, ten associates, and fourteen partners. The Financial Services Compensation Scheme (**FSCS**) of the UK is currently a member. This membership is expected to continue post-Brexit.

3.163 In addition the IADI also has observers who are not-for-profit entities which do not fulfil the criteria to be an associate but have a direct interest in the effectiveness of deposit insurance systems.

3.2.12.2 Activities

3.164 To further its objectives, the IADI undertakes to:

- develop principles, standards, and guidance to enhance the effectiveness of deposit insurance systems, encourage implementation of the same, and develop methodologies for the assessment of compliance;

---

[40] <http://www1.previdencia.gov.br/docs/pdf/IOPS-Pension-Supervision-in-Focus.pdf>

- research and enhance the understanding of common interests and issues relating to deposit insurance;
- cooperate with other international organisations and facilitate the sharing and exchange of expertise and information on deposit insurance issues through training, development, and educational programmes; and
- create awareness among supervisors and regulators of financial institutions concerning the key role of deposit insurance systems in maintaining financial stability.

The IADI also produces a variety of publications to inform its members and other interested parties of the latest issues affecting deposit insurers, including newsletters, annual reports, research papers, conference proceedings, and survey results. **3.165**

(a) Core Principles for Effective Deposit Insurance Systems
Originally published in June 2009 as a joint venture between the BCBS and the IADI, the Core Principles for Effective Deposit Insurance Systems set an important benchmark for jurisdictions to use in establishing or reforming deposit insurance systems. **3.166**

Following the global financial crisis, a joint working group consisting of representatives from a number of supranational organisations involved in the process of developing financial standards (including the BCBS, the European Commission, the European Forum of Deposit Insurers, the FSB, the IMF, and the World Bank) began working on amending the principles. The revised version was approved by the IADI's executive council in October 2014. The updated document reflects the greater role played by many deposit insurers in resolution regimes. **3.167**

The principles were designed to be adaptable to a broad range of jurisdictional circumstances and address a comprehensive range of issues including coverage, funding, powers, membership, transitioning from blanket to limited coverage, and prompt reimbursement. The principles are included in the FSB's Compendium. **3.168**

The IADI also produces guidance for assessing compliance with the principles, most recently updated in March 2016, which is designed to enable jurisdictions to assess their own and their peers' progress in implementation. **3.169**

The EU has gone further than the principles with its second Directive on deposit guarantee schemes (Directive 2014/49), which requires the EU countries to introduce laws setting up at least one deposit guarantee scheme and ensure a harmonised level of protection for depositors. This EU directive has been implemented in the UK by virtue of the FSCS under the Financial Services and Markets Act 2000, the UK deposit guarantee scheme, and investor compensation scheme. The coverage provided by the FSCS is broader than the minimum requirements of the EU directive. **3.170**

3.2.13 Markets Committee

The Markets Committee serves as a forum for central banks to discuss recent developments in financial markets, exchange views on possible future trends, and consider the implications of particular events for the functioning of financial markets and central bank operations. **3.171**

3.2.13.1 History

3.172 The Markets Committee was formed in 1962 as the Committee on Gold and Foreign Exchange. It was renamed the Markets Committee in May 2002.

3.173 The Markets Committee is headquartered at the BIS's offices in Basel, Switzerland.

3.2.13.2 Structure

3.174 The Markets Committee is assisted by a secretariat which is provided and hosted by the BIS. It holds bimonthly meetings in private, coinciding with the meetings of the governors of BIS member central banks.

3.2.13.3 Membership

3.175 The membership of the Markets Committee comprises senior officials responsible for market operations at central banks of the G10 nations and some of the largest non-G10 economies. A total of twenty-one central banks are members, including the Bank of England. This membership is expected to continue post-Brexit.

3.2.13.4 Activities

3.176 The Markets Committee's work was originally limited in scope to gold and foreign exchange, and while its mandate has subsequently broadened to include financial market functioning and central bank operations, much of its work still has a foreign exchange markets focus.

(a) Monetary Policy Frameworks and Central Bank Market Operations

3.177 The Monetary Policy Frameworks and Central Bank Market Operations, which was first published in December 2007 and most recently updated in May 2009, aims to help facilitate the Market Committee's discussions by providing information on the monetary policy frameworks and market operations of its members in a single and easily accessible document. It includes a helpful description of the UK regime and is broken down by jurisdiction and contains information on the following:

- monetary policy committees (or similar decision-making bodies);
- policy implementation;
- market operations; and
- monetary policy communication.

3.2.14 Irving Fisher Committee on Central Bank Statistics (IFC)

3.178 The objective of the IFC is to promote the exchange of views among central bank economists, statisticians, and policymakers as well as others who want to participate in discussing statistical issues of interest to central banks, including those relating to economic, monetary, and financial stability.

3.2.14.1 History

3.179 Named after the internationally renowned economist and statistician, the IFC was established in 1995 following a meeting of the International Statistical Institute in Beijing.

It is headquartered at the BIS's offices in Basel, Switzerland. 3.180

3.2.14.2 Structure
The IFC consists of a committee and an executive, assisted by a secretariat provided by the BIS. The committee is endowed with decision-making authority and is composed of the designated representatives of full institutional members. It conducts votes on the basis of majority rule (with one vote per full institutional member) but strives to make decisions with full consensus. The executive is elected by the committee, and manages the affairs of the IFC in accordance with the organisation's statutes, which may be amended by a two-thirds majority of the committee. 3.181

3.2.14.3 Membership
The IFC has ninety members across the following four categories: 3.182

- full institutional—central banks or organisations formally involved in central banking issues;
- associate institutional—central banks or organisations which do not wish to become full institutional members;
- associate individual—academic experts from public and private sector organisations; and
- honorary members—elected for life in recognition of their outstanding contributions to the work of the IFC.

The majority of members are central banks or organisations formally involved in central banking issues, specifically the monetary authority or agency of each member country or region. 3.183

The UK is represented on the IFC by the PRA and the FCA. This membership is expected to continue post-Brexit. 3.184

3.2.14.4 Activities
The IFC's activities include discussing best practice with respect to statistical and methodological issues of interest to central banks, organising conferences, seminars, workshops and lectures, establishing working groups or task forces, collaborating with international, regional, and national organisations and supporting or sponsoring the publication of periodicals, papers, reports, or newsletters on topics of interest. 3.185

3.2.15 International Financial Consumer Protection Organisation (FinCoNet)

FinCoNet is an international membership organisation of supervisory authorities which have responsibility for financial consumer protection. 3.186

3.2.15.1 History
FinCoNet was established in 2013 as a not-for-profit association under French law, in response to the growing focus on financial consumer protection worldwide and the need for 3.187

better interaction, sharing, and collaboration among supervisory bodies responsible for the oversight of the various national financial consumer protection regimes.

3.188 Prior to this time, an informal network of supervisory authorities had been in operation since 2003 but the establishment of FinCoNet enabled participants to build upon its work on a more formal footing as well as to advance the G20's financial consumer protection agenda.

3.189 FinCoNet is based in Paris, France.

3.2.15.2 Structure

3.190 The organisational structure of FinCoNet consists of a general assembly of members (each with a right to vote) operating under a governing council (which is the primary organisational body of FinCoNet). The governing council meets on a monthly basis and is responsible for approving membership and programme of work. The current governing council is made up of representatives of governmental authorities from ten countries, including Brazil, Indonesia, Italy, Japan, and Spain. It is headed by a chair and is assisted by an OECD secretariat.

3.191 The FinCoNet programme of work is undertaken through the following standing committees:

- supervisory toolboxes;
- digitalisation of short-term, high-cost consumer credit;
- online and mobile payments;
- practices and tools;
- supervision in a digital age;
- financial advertising; and
- financial product governance and culture.

3.2.15.3 Membership

3.192 The membership structure of FinCoNet consists of:

- members—public entities which have a financial market conduct and financial consumer protection supervision mandate, including national and regional authorities;
- associates—public entities which are considering the establishment of a financial market conduct supervisory regime and are interested in becoming members over time; and
- observers—entities which have a direct interest in the effectiveness of financial market conduct and financial consumer protection supervision.

3.193 The FCA is currently a FinCoNet member. This membership is expected to continue post-Brexit.

3.2.15.4 Activities

3.194 FinCoNet provides a forum for research and the exchange of information and best practices relating to market conduct supervision and consumer protection issues with a focus on consumer credit and banking. It has the following broad purposes:

- facilitating and promoting international cooperation in the promotion of international standards of regulation, oversight, and enforcement on the matter of financial consumer protection;
- facilitating contact between supervisory authorities and other relevant parties;
- providing a worldwide forum of supervisors for policy dialogue and exchange of information on financial consumer protection;
- influencing and participating in the work of relevant international bodies in the area of financial consumer protection; and
- assessing the strengths and weaknesses of existing institutional arrangement models of supervisory authorities and identifying effective approaches that can assist financial consumer protection supervisors in carrying out their responsibilities.

3.3 Accounting and Audit

3.3.1 International Financial Reporting Standards Foundation (IFRSF) and International Accounting Standards Board (IASB)

The IFRSF is a not-for-profit organisation whose main objectives include the development and promotion of the International Financial Reporting Standards (IFRS Standards) through the IASB, which it oversees. **3.195**

The IFRSF is incorporated in the State of Delaware, United States, and has its head office in London, UK. **3.196**

3.3.1.1 Structure and membership

The IFRSF's governance and processes are designed to keep its standard-setting role independent while ensuring accountability to stakeholders around the world. The IFRSF has a three-tier organisational governance structure comprising: **3.197**

- the IASB—an independent group of experts with an appropriate mix of recent practical experience in setting accounting standards as well as preparing, auditing, or using financial reports and in accounting education. The board members are appointed by the trustees of the IFRSF;
- the trustees—which govern and oversee the IASB; and
- the Foundation Monitoring Board—a board of public authorities to whom the trustees are accountable.

In addition, the advisory council provides advice to the trustees and the board, while consulting extensively with the IFRSF's numerous standing advisory bodies and groups. **3.198**

The IFRSF is supported by a number of formal advisory bodies and committees which receive input on the IFRSF's work and consult with stakeholders from a broad range of backgrounds and geographical regions. The committees' expertise spans a great number of specialities, including accounting, emerging economies, interpretations, capital markets, education, and Islamic finance. **3.199**

3.200 The board members are appointed by the trustees and have historically included experts from the UK. This engagement and representation is not expected to change post-Brexit.

3.3.1.2 Activities
(a) IFRS Standards

3.201 The IFRS Standards are set by the IASB and are designed to be used by publicly accountable companies and financial institutions such as banks. The seventeen standards establish a set of principles which companies are encouraged to follow when preparing financial statements, providing a standardised way of describing a company's financial performance. The IFRS Standards are intended to offer transparency (by enhancing the international comparability and quality of financial information), accountability (by reducing the information gap between the providers of capital and the people to whom they have entrusted their money) and efficiency (by helping investors to identify opportunities and risks across the world).

3.202 Authoritative interpretations of the IFRS Standards, which provide further guidance on how to apply them, are developed by the IFRS Interpretations Committee. Other activities which support the implementation and application of the IFRS Standards involve the preparation of supporting materials such as webinars, articles, and meeting summaries. The vision of a global set of accounting standards is supported by other organisations within the international regulatory framework, including the BCBS, the FSB, the G20, the IMF, IOSCO, and the World Bank.

3.203 The IFRS Standards are now required to be used in more than 144 jurisdictions, with many others permitting their use.

3.204 In 2009, the IASB published a set of the IFRS Standards for small- and medium-sized companies without public accountability. These have subsequently been revised and amended, and now consist of forty-six separate standards.

3.205 The relevant jurisdictional authority in the UK is the FRC which is empowered to set the UK's accounting standards in accordance with the Companies Act 2006 and Statutory Instrument on Statutory Auditors (Amendment of Companies Act 2006 and Delegation of Functions etc.) Order 2012 (SI 2012/1741). At present, the FRC works in close alignment with the European Financial Reporting Advisory Group to promote the implementation of the IFRS Standards in Europe. As in many areas of financial regulation, the nature of the future relationship between the UK and the EU regulatory bodies following the UK's exit from the EU is uncertain, and there remains an open question of the extent to which UK firms will accept the use of the IFRS Standards without the UK being able to influence the endorsement process.

3.206 The UK has currently applied the IFRS Standards as follows:

- all domestic companies whose securities trade in a regulated market are required to use IFRS Standards as adopted by the EU in their consolidated financial statements;
- in relation to listings by foreign companies, the IFRS Standards as adopted by the EU are required in their consolidated financial statements except that a foreign company

whose home jurisdiction's standards are deemed by the EU to be equivalent to IFRS Standards may use its home standards; and
- SMEs may use a national standard that is based on the IFRS for SMEs Standard, but with significant modifications. Alternatively, they may use IFRS as adopted by the EU.

3.3.2 International Auditing and Assurance Standards Board (IAASB)

The IAASB is an independent standard-setting body that serves the public interest by setting high-quality international standards for auditing, quality control, review, and other assurance as well as related services. It also facilitates the convergence of international and national standards. **3.207**

It is based in New York, USA. **3.208**

3.3.2.1 Structure and membership

The work of the IAASB is overseen by the Public Interest Oversight Board. The IAASB meetings are open to the public and meeting agendas, agenda papers, and meeting highlights are posted on its website. **3.209**

The steering committee is a standing committee of the IAASB whose objectives and responsibilities include: **3.210**

- establishing the IAASB's action plan, priorities, and related initiatives;
- establishing and approving changes to the IAASB's working procedures so that high-quality standards are developed and issued in the public interest in a transparent, efficient, and effective manner;
- counselling and advising the IAASB chair and technical director on matters and activities relating to achievement of the objectives of the IAASB;
- formulating policies that facilitate and promote global acceptance of the IAASB standards and international convergence; and
- identifying and responding to significant developments in the environment and issues raised by key stakeholders.

The membership of the IFAC has grown from sixty-three founding members in fifty-one countries to over 175 members and associates in more than 130 countries worldwide. Members of the IAASB can be nominated by any stakeholder, including the IFAC member organisation, the forum of firms, international organisations, government institutions, and the general public. **3.211**

In the past, the UK has had a role in leading the IFAC through its presidency, which was held by Richard Wilkes from 1987 to 1990, Frank Harding from 1997 to 2000, and Graham Ward from 2004 to 2006. As at September 2018, the only IAASB steering committee member who is connected to the UK is Marek Grabowski (a public member). This engagement and representation is not expected to change post-Brexit. **3.212**

3.3.2.2 Activities

3.213 The IAASB's medium-term strategy is to address the following:

- support global financial stability;
- enhance the role, relevance, and quality of assurance and related services in an evolving world; and
- facilitate the adoption and implementation of international standards.

(a) International Standards on Auditing (ISAs)

3.214 The first iteration of the ISAs was published in 1991 and they have since undergone numerous revisions. The most recent revision became effective for audits of financial statements ending on or after 15 December 2016. The ISAs are accompanied by extensive guidance materials.

3.4 UK Firms Participating in Industry Bodies

3.215 The participation of UK firms in international industry bodies also leads to the application of internationally recognised standards in the UK market.

3.4.1 International Swaps and Derivatives Association (ISDA)

3.216 ISDA's mission statement is to foster safe and efficient derivatives markets to facilitate effective risk management for all users of derivative products. It works in three key areas in order to fulfil its primary goal of building a stable and robust financial market and a strong financial regulatory framework, namely, reducing counterparty credit risk, increasing transparency, and improving the industry's operational infrastructure. It operates from its headquarters in New York City, United States but also has offices in London, Hong Kong, Tokyo, Washington DC, Brussels, and Singapore.

3.4.1.1 Structure and membership

3.217 ISDA is governed by a board of directors consisting of representatives from member organisations and firms.

3.218 ISDA has over 900 members from sixty-eight countries comprising a broad range of derivatives market participants. A number of large financial institutions that are based in the UK participate in and are members of ISDA, and the expectation is that this will continue post-Brexit.

3.4.1.2 Activities

3.219 ISDA represents market participants globally, promoting high standards of commercial conduct that enhance market integrity and leading industry action on derivatives issues. ISDA has also developed a series of market-standard derivative documents in order to create harmonisation across the industry.

3.4.2 International Capital Market Association (ICMA)

ICMA's mission is to promote resilient well-functioning international and globally coherent cross-border debt securities markets, which are essential to fund sustainable economic growth and development. ICMA focuses on four key sectors: primary markets, secondary markets, repo and collateral markets, and the green and social bond markets. **3.220**

It is headquartered in Zurich, Switzerland. **3.221**

3.4.2.1 Structure and membership
ICMA's organisational structure consists of the board, executive committee, and the committee of regional representatives: **3.222**

- the board consists of twenty-two members that represent financial institutions and is responsible for determining ICMA's strategy and key policy objectives as well as having a supervisory role in overseeing the work of the chief executive, executive committee, and the general functions of ICMA.;
- the executive committee is responsible for the management and administration of the ICMA. It reports to the board through the chief executive and has established a number of committees to assist its work; and
- ICMA also has a regional structure. The chairs of the regional committees sit on the committee of regional representatives, which reports to the board and maintains and develops the liaison between ICMA's board, its fifteen regional committees and their chapters.

ICMA has over 570 members located in sixty-two countries worldwide. **3.223**

The membership and involvement of UK firms and representatives at ICMA and on the ICMA board are not expected to change post-Brexit. **3.224**

3.4.2.2 Activities
ICMA's main objectives are to promote good relations among its members, to provide a basis for joint examination and discussion of questions relating to the international capital and securities markets, to issue rules and make recommendations and to provide services and assistance to participants in the international capital and securities markets. **3.225**

To achieve its mission, ICMA: **3.226**

- develops guidelines, rules, and standard documentation which facilitate the creation of universally accepted best practices;
- aims to promote the exchange of information and communication between the players in the international capital markets;
- is committed to working with regulators and policymakers in order to share expertise; and
- promotes high professional standards by providing training and education opportunities.

(a) Primary Market Handbook (Handbook)

3.227 First published in 1985 (and previously known as the IPMA Handbook), the Handbook contains recommendations, guidance, and standard language and template documentation generally relating to offers of syndicated international bonds in the primary market, to programmes under which such offers may be made and to euro-commercial paper programmes and trades made under them. The most recent amendments to the Handbook were made in July 2019.

(b) Rules and Recommendations for the Secondary Market

3.228 The ICMA Rules and Recommendations for the Secondary Market apply to transactions in international securities (debt securities traded on a cross-border basis and which are capable of settlement through an international central securities depository or equivalent). There has been growing concern regarding the ability of the secondary markets to function properly, as well as on bond market quality and liquidity. ICMA provides further support to its members with advice and guidance on the application of the rules through its Legal and Regulatory Handbook.

3.229 ICMA also publishes the Global Master Repurchase Agreement, which is governed by English law and is the standard master agreement for the international repo market.

3.4.3 International Securities Lending Association (ISLA)

3.230 ISLA was established to represent the common interests of participants in the securities lending industry and is headquartered in London, UK.

3.4.3.1 Structure and membership

3.231 The primary organisational and decision-making body of ISLA is the board, which consists of up to fifteen directors who are also representatives of member firms. ISLA also has a total of over 150 members comprising insurance companies, pension funds, asset managers, banks, securities dealers, and service providers from across the world.

3.232 A large number of ISLA's members are located in London, and consist of a number of prominent UK-based firms who are active in the securities lending sector. Several of these London-based members sit on the ISLA board. This level of participation is not expected to change post-Brexit.

3.4.3.2 Activities

3.233 ISLA works closely with regulators across Europe and has contributed to a number of major market initiatives, including the development of the UK Money Markets Code. ISLA works to achieve its aims by:

- representing the common interests of institutions that are engaged in the lending or borrowing of securities and providing a forum for the development and exchange of ideas and information;
- assisting in the development of these markets by establishing agreed standards and guidelines for good working practices, and developing and maintaining a legal agreement for use in the securities lending industry;

- liaising with regulators and other agencies to help in the development of appropriate regulatory frameworks for the industry; and
- seeking to promote awareness of future challenges and opportunities for the securities lending industry and foster superior standards among its members.

ISLA also publishes market agreements, notably the Global Master Securities Lending Agreement, which is governed by English law and is the standard master agreement for the international securities lending market, as well as a range of other materials including market reports, regulatory updates, newsletters, and securities lending guides. **3.234**

3.4.4 The Institute of Asset Management (IAM)

The IAM seeks to be recognised as the leading international and professional body for asset management. It is headquartered in London, UK. **3.235**

3.4.4.1 Structure and membership
The IAM's organisational structure consists of the: **3.236**

- board—which manages the IAM and exercises its powers, operating increasingly as a non-executive body where members are classed as company directors;
- council—which meets around four times per year to represent voting members and ensure their interests are properly advocated on major policy decisions, strategy, and plans for the IAM activity;
- faculty—an advisory body with no executive powers or budget which ensures that the discipline of asset management and all publications produced by the IAM are coordinated and aligned with its objectives;
- committees—essentially permanent project teams where most of the primary activities of the IAM are planned, organised, and delivered either internally or collaboratively with other organisations;
- examinations board—which ensures that examinations in asset management are available and delivered to all registered candidates in a timely and appropriate manner;
- chapters—organised groups of the IAM members which are represented on the council and which encourage engagement with the IAM at a local level through the organisation of events and other activities. This includes a UK group;
- branches—subdivisions of chapters which provide opportunities for those working or interested in the field of asset management to share ideas and best practice, to further the advancement of the industry and to develop a network within their local region; and
- IAM centre—a quasi-secretariat which exists to support the IAM's other structural bodies by minimising their administrative burden.

The IAM board is elected annually. The engagement of UK firms and representatives is not expected to change post-Brexit. **3.237**

3.4.4.2 Activities

3.238 The IAM develops asset management knowledge as well as best practice and generates awareness of the benefits of the asset management discipline for individuals, organisations, and wider society. The IAM's knowledge projects, publications, and services promote a considered approach to achieving long-term value from physical assets in every organisation, whether large or small, private, public, governmental, or not-for-profit.

(a) Developing and maintaining a strategic asset management plan

3.239 The IAM publishes international benchmarks for use within the asset management industry. ISO 55000, 55001, and 55002, together known as the **ISO 55000 standards**, establish terminology, requirements, and guidance for implementing, maintaining, and improving an effective asset management system, helping organisations to establish an asset management system to manage assets optimally, comply with asset management policy and strategy, demonstrate that they are applying best practice and seek external certification of their asset management system or make a self-declaration of compliance.

3.240 The standards cover the following:

- ISO 55000—overview, principles, and terminology needed to develop a long-term plan that incorporates an organisation's mission, values, objectives, business policies, and stakeholder requirements;
- ISO 55001—requirements for the establishment, implementation, maintenance, and improvement of an asset management system; and
- ISO 55002—guidelines on the application of an asset management system, in accordance with the requirements of ISO 55001.

3.241 The ISO 55000 standards were originally developed from the British Standards Institution PAS 55:2008, which until 2004 were the default global standards for asset management. The IAM used the PAS 55:2008 as the 'base document' to work with the British Standards Institution to initiate the project to produce a formal international standard through the International Organisation for Standardization (ISO). Given the important role that the UK has to date played in developing internal standards in this area, it is not expected that this will change post-Brexit.

(b) IAM Handbook

3.242 To further establish its international standard-setting role, the IAM is currently developing the IAM Handbook which aims to be a comprehensive reference for knowledge within the scope of the asset management discipline and an essential resource for the IAM members. It is intended to complement the ISO 55000 standards by providing practical advice on the development of a strategic asset management plan, including guidance on its role and suitable contents.

3.243 The intention is that the IAM members will provide practical guidance for the asset management industry.

(c) Subject Specific Guidelines (SSGs)

3.244 The SSGs form part of a series of publications designed to expand and enrich asset management knowledge. The intention is that once finalised, the SSGs will cover a number of subjects across the areas of strategy and planning, decision-making, life-cycle delivery, asset information, organisation and people, and risk and review. The aim is that the SSGs will provide detailed guidance and information on implementing principles laid out by the ISO 55000 standards, including case studies from a range of sectors.

Development of the SSGs relies on the efforts and expertise of the IAM members as well as by organisations sponsoring specific projects. **3.245**

3.5 Conclusion

International standards are crucial to setting the international regulatory agenda, and establishing a common set of principles for the financial services industry globally. They are an important tool in ensuring that business can be conducted globally in an efficient but safe manner. Global cooperation is under threat from an increasingly fragmented political and economic reality. Ensuring that international standards continue to play an important role in governing the way that financial services activities are performed internationally is vital to protecting future stability and growth. The UK, through government and regulatory bodies and the private sector, has played a leading role in the development of these standards from the beginning and there is no reason why it should not continue to do so post-Brexit. Indeed, it will be very important that the UK continues its leadership to ensure that it remains one of the world's leading financial centres. **3.246**

But it would be overly simplistic to suggest that international standards provide a complete answer to post-Brexit regulation. **3.247**

A number of EU financial services rules derive from international standards, but their high-level principles have not always been transposed entirely faithfully into the EU's own statute book. For example the EU has taken heed of the international standards that IOSCO has published on financial benchmarks (discussed further in Chapter 14) but it has put in place a much more formalised regime requiring authorisation and registration resulting in quite a difference in the level of granularity between the two. In addition, not all EU legislation flows from an international source, particularly in the area of funds where the European Commission has taken the lead in designing the regime. In the UK, domestic policy demands have led to the introduction of specific regulations. Good examples include the retail bank ring-fencing regime and the Senior Managers and Certification Regime introduced following the financial crisis (discussed in Chapter 9), although this is now being replicated in other countries including Hong Kong and Australia. Finally, different countries approach regulatory policy from different, and sometimes diametrically opposed, perspectives. Herein lies one of the key challenges for the future UK and EU relationship. While important, international standards cannot on their own prescribe the regulatory landscape between the two. **3.248**

Another interesting issue concerns the format of future regulation, particularly when one considers that the EU model, with a large body of technical rules set out in primary legislation, is quite different from the approach adopted in other countries. For example, the EU and Switzerland were the only two members of the Basel Committee where Basel III was implemented through primary legislation rather than the prudential authority's rule-making **3.249** powers. In other major economies like the US, Australia, and Canada implementation was a matter for the regulators. In general, the EU approach contrasts with that of the UK, where Acts of Parliament are usually used for overarching changes to the institutional framework and implementation of many of the details is then delegated to the regulators, who are then held to account by Parliament.

3.250 While a discussion regarding equivalence provisions in EU legislation is covered in Chapter 4, it is worth noting that international standards play an important role in the equivalence process. Third country equivalence can only be requested by third countries where such a regime is explicitly provided for in EU legislation. This is limited to a fairly narrow range of EU financial services-related legislation including the revised Markets in Financial Instruments Directive, the Alternative Investment Fund Managers Directive, the Solvency II Directive (in relation to reinsurers), and the European Markets Infrastructure Regulation (in relation to central clearing counterparties). The technical assessment of whether a third country's regulatory regime is equivalent is usually made by the European Commission based on advice from the European Supervisory Authorities (ESAs). The relevant ESA and the Commission consider a number of factors when determining whether a third country regime is equivalent, including:

- whether the regime is broadly similar to that of the EU and is applied consistently;
- whether the regime adequately implements internationally agreed standards;
- whether the regime allows EEA financial institutions access to the third country's markets (i.e. reciprocity); and
- whether the regime contains obstacles relating to investor protection, market disruption, competition, and the monitoring of systemic risk.

3.251 It appears that a third country implementing internationally agreed standards will not guarantee a positive equivalence determination from the European Commission. On 29 July 2019, the European Commission issued a communication on its overall approach to equivalence stating that while a third country's adherence to international standards is an important factor, it does not automatically guarantee a positive equivalence determination.

3.252 In terms of the UK's future approach to regulation and the role international standards will play there is, at the time of writing, little publicly available information. The UK government's July 2018 White Paper on the future relationship between the UK and the EU spoke about the UK's continuing to be active in shaping international rules and upholding global norms. In May 2019, Sam Woods, Deputy Governor for Prudential Regulation and Chief Executive Officer of the PRA, gave a speech discussing the UK's style of regulation post-Brexit. While acknowledging that this would be influenced by the terms of the UK's exit from the EU, and its future relationship with it, he advocated an approach which included responsible openness based on international collaboration and standards. What this means in practice is, according to Sam Woods, threefold. First, that the UK regulatory authorities have a mandate to engage strongly in international standard-setting processes in order to make sure that they are at the forefront of implementing those rules in a thorough way. Second, that the UK regulatory authorities adopt practices and structures which promote strong collaboration with regulatory colleagues in other jurisdictions. Third, that UK regulatory authorities are open to hosting cross-border business in the UK but only if it is appropriately controlled and governed.

3.253 In March 2019, Nausicaa Delfas, Executive Director for International at the FCA, gave a speech in which she said that the FCA's focus on international cooperation and standard-setting would increase post-Brexit. Interestingly, in addition to multilateral engagement through participation in international standard-setting bodies Nausicaa Delfas noted that the FCA had developed a strong programme of bilateral engagement to shape and influence international standards and best practice. One example that she gave was the US–UK Financial Regulatory Working Group. Bilateral international engagements may well have an important role to play after Brexit.

4
EU Equivalence Regime

Arun Srivastava and Nina Moffatt

4.1 Introduction

The 2016 Brexit Referendum raised immediate concerns for UK financial institutions as to how they would be able to maintain access to the European Union (EU) and European Economic Area (EEA) markets. Firms authorised in the UK by either the Prudential Regulation Authority (**PRA**) or the Financial Conduct Authority (**FCA**) are entitled to '*passport*' that authorisation into other EEA States to carry on business there either on a cross-border services or branch establishment basis. In many cases, UK firms are also able to appoint local agents in European markets based on their UK authorisation. This framework applies in the banking, investment services, insurance, payments, and funds sectors, among others. **4.01**

Clearly, the ability to carry on business across the EEA based on a single licence granted in a firm's home state, is key to the development of a single market in financial services. UK authorisation also carries with it other important advantages. For example, the European Market Infrastructure Regulation (648/2012) (**EMIR**) requires certain derivative transactions to be cleared through European authorised central counterparties (**CCPs**). EEA institutions are precluded from using third country CCPs (unless formally recognised by the European Commission under Article 25 of EMIR). This could preclude UK CCPs providing clearing services to EU firms in a hard-Brexit scenario, when they lose their status as European authorised CCPs. Given the potential impact of this on financial stability issues, in the lead-up to the initial Brexit deadline of 29 March 2019 the European Securities and Markets Authority granted temporary recognition to three CCPs established in the UK to provide services in the EU on a no-deal Brexit scenario for a twelve-month period. **4.02**

Put shortly, therefore, operating as a licensed entity in an EU jurisdiction confers substantial benefits which are at risk in a post-Brexit world. Given that passporting rights are derived from EU directives, these rights will terminate upon the UK leaving the EU when EU laws will cease to apply in the UK, assuming a '*hard-Brexit*' scenario in which there is no agreement reached between the UK and the EU as to the terms of the UK's withdrawal from the EU. UK licensed firms will become third country firms, that is firms who are established and licensed in a non-EEA jurisdiction and will need to access the EU markets on this much more restrictive basis. UK firms will also lose their status as EU entities. Therefore, roles reserved under EU directives for EU licensed entities, such as EU authorised CCPs under EMIR or as EU credit institutions under the Capital Requirements Directive are at risk. **4.03**

4.04 While there has been considerable focus on the ability of UK firms to access EU markets, it is important not to lose sight of the implications of Brexit on EU and EEA firms who either have branches in the UK or provide cross-border services into the UK. Such firms also presently rely on European passports to access or carry on business in the UK without the need to obtain separate authorisation in the UK from either the FCA or PRA. The rights of EU firms to do business in the UK will equally be removed upon the UK leaving the EU and EU laws ceasing to apply. In order to address this issue the UK has introduced its Temporary Permissions Regime (TPR), which permits EEA firms who presently rely on a passport to carry on doing so following Brexit, on the basis that such firms will in due course apply for full UK authorisation. However, EU firms who do not avail themselves of the benefit of the TPR will in the future either need to obtain UK authorisation before commencing business or ensure that they are not contravening UK law in transacting with persons in the UK, for example, because they only carry on limited activities which come within an exemption from licensing.

4.2 The Concept of Equivalence

4.05 In the aftermath of the referendum, *'equivalence'* was seen by many as a panacea for these problems. Equivalence is based on the notion that UK laws and regulations in the financial services area will be fully aligned with EU laws on the date on which the UK exits the EU. The concept of equivalence is expressly set out in certain EU legislation and firms from jurisdictions determined by the European Commission to be equivalent for those purposes are granted market access rights, albeit in certain specified circumstances.

4.06 EU legislation has tended to focus on activities carried on within the territory of the EU. However, in recent years, reflecting the internationalisation of financial services and the expanding competencies of the EU, EU laws have increasingly come to set out the terms on which firms operating from outside the EU can transact with and provide services to parties in the EU. This has resulted in equivalence regimes being written into EU laws. The Commission has stated that 'Equivalence is not a vehicle for liberalising international trade in financial services, but a key instrument to effectively manage cross-border activity of market players in a sound and secure prudential environment with third-country jurisdictions that adhere to, implement and enforce rigorously the same high standards of prudential rules as the EU.[1] It therefore involves a form of regulatory deference to the standards of the EU.

4.07 Following the referendum result, commentators suggested that such equivalence regimes could provide a composite basis for UK-based firms to continue to provide services into the EU, on a similar basis to how firms use their existing passports. In reality, however, the equivalence framework under EU law is fragmented and does not support such a composite approach to market access. The Capital Requirements Directive (2013/36/EU) (CRD IV), for example, does not contain any equivalence regime that allows a third

---

[1] Commission Staff Working Document, 'EU Equivalence decisions in financial services policy on assessment' 27.02.27 SWD (2017) 102 Final.

country firm access to European markets. Given that the CRD IV covers the banking industry, this is a major lacuna. Other directives such as the Markets in Financial Instruments Directive (2014/65/EU) (**MiFID II**) do provide for access rights for firms from equivalent jurisdictions. However, these are limited in scope. Moreover, the European Commission's Communication[2] in July 2019 highlights some of the complexities and considerations that would arise in the Commission granting any equivalence decision. For example, in this communication, the Commission attaches utmost importance to taking a proportionate view on the risks posed by third country frameworks. Therefore, third countries for which equivalence is likely to be significantly used may be viewed by the Commission as presenting additional risks, which may in turn result in the Commission expecting additional assurances.

In its White Paper *The Future Relationship between the United Kingdom and the European Union* the UK government suggested that post-Brexit market access to the EU could be governed by an enhanced equivalence regime, recognising that a material upgrade to the existing regimes is required. In fact, the White Paper expressly stated that: These regimes are not sufficient to deal with a third country whose financial markets are as deeply interconnected with the EU's as those of the UK are ... the existing autonomous frameworks for equivalence would need to be expanded, to reflect the fact that equivalence as it exists today is not sufficient in scope for the breadth of the interconnectedness of UKEU financial services provision. A new arrangement would need to encompass a broader range of cross-border activities that reflect global financial business models and the high degree of economic integration. The UK recognises, however, that this arrangement cannot replicate the EU's passporting regime. **4.08**

The White Paper was published in July 2018 and the UK government's position evolved to adopt the concept of '*mutual recognition*', the key difference being that mutual recognition provides a comprehensive framework which would allow all firms meeting UK requirements to provide services to the EEA. The EU has thus far not accepted either a modified equivalence regime or a mutual recognition regime as a basis for UK firms accessing EU markets in a hard-Brexit scenario.

Following Brexit, it is very likely that the UK will remain subject to the same standards as the EU (some would say higher given the UK's tendency to gold-plate European laws) so that UK firms will, in practice, be subject to equivalent rules to their European peers. Arguably, therefore, there is no reason in principle why UK regulated firms should be prevented from accessing the European markets on the same basis as before Brexit. For example, investor protection and transparency standards would be the same mitigating the risk of investor detriment. Of course, this would mean that the UK would maintain a level playing field with the EU and UK laws and regulations would remain closely aligned to the EU's Single Market. **4.09**

While this position makes logical sense, market access has become a political football in the post-referendum world. **4.10**

---

[2] The European Commission Communication of 29/07/2019 on equivalence in the area of financial services.

4.3 Current Status and Timing

4.11 The UK submitted its notification of its intention to withdraw from the EU pursuant to Article 50 of the Treaty on European Union on 29 March 2017. Originally this meant that the UK would have left the EU at midnight on 29 March 2019. All EU law would have ceased to apply in the UK from that date and the UK would have become a 'third country'. This deadline has now been extended to 31 January 2020.

4.12 The UK government had agreed the terms of a Withdrawal Agreement. This provided for a transitional period to apply. Article 126 of the draft Transitional Agreement provided that a transition period would apply (up to 31 December 2020). EU law would be applicable to and in the UK during the transition period. This transition period would have permitted UK firms to have continued access to the EU markets pursuant to their existing passports. In this time a new relationship between the UK and the EU could have been negotiated establishing, for example, the enhanced equivalence regime advocated in the UK government's White Paper.

4.13 However, since the Withdrawal Agreement has not been ratified by the UK Parliament, as matters presently stand, the UK will leave the EU on 31 January 2020 and become a third country to be treated on the same basis as other non-EEA jurisdictions in relation to market access.

4.4 Remaining Equivalent Following Brexit: Onshoring of EU Law

4.14 Of course, for equivalence to be relevant, the UK will need to ensure that the process of its withdrawal from the EU does not result in the UK operating to lower standards.

4.15 As already noted, technically, the UK's withdrawal from the EU will mean that EU laws will cease to apply, which could potentially mean that the UK no longer maintains equivalence to the EU. The UK government has, however, been committed to ensuring 'that the UK will have a functioning legislative and regulatory framework' on the basis that 'the same laws and rules that are currently in place in the UK would continue to apply at the point of exit, providing continuity and certainty as [the UK] leaves the EU' (HM Treasury's approach to financial services legislation under the European Union (Withdrawal) Act 2018).

4.16 In the run-up to the original exit date provided for under the European Union (Withdrawal) Act 2018, which was 29 March 2019, the UK had been engaged in the process of '*onshoring*' EU legislation, that is incorporating EU laws into UK domestic legislation to ensure continuity following Brexit. The effect of this would be to create a body of retained EU law in UK domestic law following Brexit. This would be achieved by preserving UK law provisions which implement EU requirements (referred to as EU-derived legislation) and converting into UK domestic law directly applicable EU legislation such as EU regulations.

4.17 The UK government also committed to implementing various '*in flight*' EU provisions which would come into force after exit day pursuant to the Financial Services (Implementation of

Legislation) Bill[3]. Powers have also been granted to the UK government and regulators to make necessary adjustments or corrections to laws for the purpose of ensuring that the UK has a properly functioning body of laws in the financial services sector following Brexit. The combination of the above means that following Brexit the UK should maintain a body of laws that are consistent with EU law in the banking, insurance, and financial services sectors.

4.5 Third Countries and Member States

4.18 Traditionally, EU-level laws have focused on the carrying on of business within the EU's Single Market. The focus of such laws has therefore been trade between Member States, as opposed to trade into the EEA from third countries. This is because European legislation has focused on the four freedoms under the European Treaty: the freedom of movement of goods, capital, services, and persons within the EU.

4.19 Individual Member States have until recently been left to legislate for market access into their states from third countries. For example, the UK has permitted non-EEA firms to provide services into the UK on the basis of the overseas persons' exclusion (**OPE**) contained in Article 72 of the Financial Services and Markets Act 2000 (Regulated Activities) Order 2001 (the **RAO**). Overseas firms have been permitted under the OPE to provide services to persons in the UK provided that they do not do so from a permanent place of business in the UK and that they comply with UK marketing or financial promotion rules.

4.20 Other European jurisdictions have also operated similar regimes, which have allowed third country firms to do business in their respective jurisdictions without triggering local licence requirements. These include the following:

(a) Ireland provides a 'safe harbour' for investment firms which are authorised in third countries. Such firms do not require an Irish licence in order to provide investment services under MiFID II to per se professional clients or eligible counterparties, as defined under the directive. For this to apply the third country in which the firm is established must not be designated as non-cooperative by the Financial Action Task Force ('**FATF**') and must be a signatory to IOSCO's multilateral MOU on cooperation and the exchange of information. Additionally, the firm must not have a branch in Ireland.

(b) Luxembourg law permits a third country firm to provide investment services to Luxembourg-based per se professional clients. This is subject to the third country firm being licensed in its '*home state*' and being subject to prudential requirements that the Luxembourg regulator, the Commission de Surveillance du Secteur Financier (**CSSF**), considers to be '*equivalent*' to Luxembourg's. This exemption was restated recently in CSSF Circular 19/716 which sets out the regimes

---

[3] On 5 September 2019, it was confirmed in a House of Commons debate that the Bill had fallen as it had failed to receive Royal Assent in the session it was introduced. The Bill may be resuscitated in the future.

applicable to third country firms who wish to provide investment services into Luxembourg.

(c) Under the Dutch act on financial supervision (*Wet op het financieel toezicht* (**AFS**)) third country firms which carry on activities in the Netherlands on a cross-border basis or through a branch are required to obtain a licence from the Dutch authority for the financial markets (Autoriteit Financiële Markten (**AFM**)), unless an exemption applies. Dutch law does in fact contain an exemption which is referred to as the '*Section 10 Exemption*'. This exemption is contained in the Exemption Regulation AFS (*Vrijstellingsregeling Wft*). The Section 10 Exemption was formerly only available to third country firms with their registered seat in Switzerland, the United States of America, and Australia, provided they were subject to supervision in their home country in respect of the relevant investment services they intend to provide or in respect of dealing on own account. In light of Brexit the Exemption Regulation has been extended to cover firms established in the UK.

(d) Other possibilities have existed for third country firms to do business with European clients and counterparties. For example, firms have relied on reverse solicitation, on the basis that the European client has taken the initiative and contacted the firm and not vice versa. Alternatively, some firms have taken the approach that the 'characteristic performance' of the service is carried on from outside the EU so that no licensable activities are being carried on within the EU's territory.

4.6 Equivalence at the EU Level

4.21 Closer examination of EU legislation reveals that equivalence under the relevant EU directives is very much a patch work rather than a composite and consistent approach to setting out a code for non-EEA firms to access the EU markets.

4.22 A number of EU financial services regulatory provisions do not contain any express provision for access by third country firms at all. As noted above, CRD IV does not contain any third country regime for banking. Although CRD IV does refer to equivalent jurisdictions, this is in the context of matters such as the prudential treatment of certain types of exposures to entities located in non-EU jurisdictions. There is also no regime covering the marketing and sale to retail investors of units issued by third country mutual funds or regulated collective investment schemes, which are regulated in Europe under the Directive on Undertakings for Collective Investment in Transferable Securities (Directive 2009/64/EC) ('UCITS'). Moreover, there is no legislative provision for access to EU markets by third country firms in the case of insurance mediation and distribution nor does an equivalence regime exist for the payments industry.

4.23 Certain other activities offer a more restrictive third country regime by which firms may obtain access not to the Single Market as a whole, but to EU Member States on a country-by-country basis. Solvency II, for example, requires that an insurer must seek authorisation from a competent authority in a Member State in order to carry on insurance business there, and in order to apply for authorisation it must establish a branch in the territory of the Member State.

4.7 Equivalence Decisions

The EU has stated that[4] equivalence refers to a process whereby the Commission assesses and determines that a third country's regulatory, supervisory, and enforcement regime is equivalent to the corresponding EU framework. **4.24**

The recognition provided by the Commission makes it possible for EU regulators to rely on a third country firm's compliance with the third country framework which has been deemed '*equivalent*' by the Commission. **4.25**

A third country must request recognition of equivalence from the EU. Such a request can only be made where it is expressly provided for in EU legislation. In other words, it is not available with respect to the provision of all services or to the provision of services to all client categories. **4.26**

Regard must therefore be had to the relevant EU legal provisions to understand the availability and scope of any third country equivalence regime. The Commission is not bound to act on a request for an equivalence assessment. The EU has full discretion and acts unilaterally in deciding whether to perform an equivalence assessment and, thereafter, as to its determination and outcome. The Commission is also not under any specific deadline to complete an assessment once it is commenced. For example, EMIR came into force in August 2012. It took up to four years for the Commission to assess the equivalence regime of CCPs located in the US before making its decision in March 2016. **4.27**

Equivalence assessments are in all cases performed by the Commission. This is often based on advice from one of the European Supervisory Authorities (ESAs) (who are the European Banking Authority (EBA), the European Securities and Markets Authority (ESMA), and the European Insurance and Occupational Pensions Authority (EIOPA)) depending on the relevant sector. This is provided for under Article 33 of the Regulations establishing the ESAs. Equivalence decisions can include conditions or limitations, to better cater for the objectives of granting equivalence. The assessments typically involve an intensive dialogue with the competent authorities of the third country whose framework is being assessed. **4.28**

A Commission Staff Working Paper entitled 'EU Equivalence Decisions in Financial Services Policy: An Assessment' from February 2017 referred to two general objectives of equivalence decisions. These were: **4.29**

(a) balancing the need for financial stability and investor protection in the EU with the benefits of maintaining open and globally integrated EU financial markets; and
(b) promoting regulatory convergence around international standards and upgrading supervisory cooperation.

The Commission working paper stresses that those objectives, including promoting the internal market, financial stability, and market integrity, are 'considered in view of the factual and legal circumstances of each case'. As the Commission also points out, it needs 'to factor in wider external policy priorities and concerns in particular with respect to the promotion **4.30**

---

[4] The European Parliament's In Depth Analysis of Third Country Equivalence in EU Banking and Financial Regulation.

of common values and shared regulatory objectives at international level' in each particular assessment. Equivalence is also often conditional on the reciprocity of the third country concerned.

4.31 These matters demonstrate that equivalence assessments involve more than an objective assessment of specified criteria but also intentionally embrace policy considerations. Ultimately, the decision to recognise another jurisdiction as equivalent is a political one and this has proved to be controversial, for example, in the context of the assessment of equivalence for Swiss trading venues under the trading obligation for shares set out in Article 23 of the Markets in Financial Instruments Regulation (600/2014/EU) (MiFIR). According to this, EU investment firms are required to trade equity securities on a trading venue in the EU or on an equivalent third country trading venue. The Commission's approach to equivalence in relation to Swiss trading venues was explicitly tied to the establishment of a broader institutional agreement between the EU and Switzerland and earlier conclusions of the European Council to the effect that no further market access should be granted to Switzerland until a broader institutional agreement is in place. It was on this basis that equivalence was granted only on a temporary basis, which the Commission permitted to lapse in a spat that is still ongoing at the time of writing.

4.32 Another controversial aspect of the equivalence regime is that a recognition of equivalence can be revoked at any time. For example, in July 2019, the Commission repealed existing equivalence decisions in the field of Credit Rating Agencies for certain countries, including Australia and Singapore. However, the ability to withdraw an equivalence assessment confers power on the Commission where a third country is seeking to implement new laws or supervisory practices.

4.33 Decisions of the Commission in relation to equivalence are usually in the form of Implementing Acts made under powers conferred by the European legislation to which the equivalence decision relates. The Commission can adopt such acts only after confirmation by representatives of Member States in a vote of a regulatory committee. The European Parliament does not have any formal role in making equivalence assessments. However, its observers are invited to meetings of the regulatory committee.

4.34 The legality of a decision of the Commission in relation to equivalence could in theory, at least, be challenged before the Court of Justice of the European Union (CJEU). This is on the basis that decisions of the Commission can be challenged before the CJEU pursuant to Article 263 of the Treaty on the Functioning of the European Union (TFEU).

4.35 The Commission has summarised the process as follows:

(a) **Process—**
  (i) involvement/role of the ESAs in the equivalence assessment; and
  (ii) in a few cases, involvement of Member State authorities in the equivalence assessment.
(b) **Criteria for assessing equivalence—**
  (i) types of criteria used (equivalent legal framework, effective supervision and enforcement, supervisory co-operation arrangements in place, other specific equivalence conditions etc.);

(ii) reference to international standards;
(iii) requirement for corresponding recognition/equivalence possibilities in a third country;
(iv) principle of proportionality; and
(v) tax and anti-money laundering considerations as part of the assessment.
(c) Follow-up/implementation—
(i) possibility to grant less advanced/transitional equivalence status;
(ii) supervisory action necessary to enable the use of equivalence benefits;
(iii) monitoring/review process envisaged after a decision has been taken;
(iv) possibility to withdraw, as necessary, at any moment the equivalence decisions.

4.36 We consider below the different European legislative frameworks and their approach to the concept of *'equivalence'*.

4.8 Banking Framework

4.37 The '*CRD IV Package*' comprises EU legislation establishing prudential rules for banks, building societies, and investment firms, most of which have applied since 1 January 2014. The two primary measures in the CRD IV Package are the CRD IV Directive and the Capital Requirements Regulation (575/2013/EU) (**CRR**).

4.38 Title V of CRD IV legislates for the CRD IV Single Market passport for banking services in the EU. Article 33 of this provides that a Member State must allow banks established in other Member States to set up a branch and/or provide services directly into their jurisdiction. CRD IV does not provide any passporting or equivalence regime for third country banks.

4.39 Article 47 of CRD IV does cover '*Relations with Third Countries*'. This addresses the position of third country banks which have a licensed branch in the EU. A branch of a third country bank which is licensed in an EEA state cannot passport that licence across the EEA. Article 47(3) of CRD IV provides that the EU may negotiate an agreement with a third country, which would ensure that branches of banks from that third country are treated in the same manner in different Member States across the EU.

4.40 Concluding, in relation to CRD IV, the directive does not contain any equivalence regime that would be relevant in the context of Brexit. This means that UK licensed banks will need to establish licensed entities in the EU following Brexit subject to any applicable domestic laws that allow third country banks to access local markets.

4.9 Investment Services

4.41 Investment services are regulated across the EEA under MiFID II. Like the CRD IV regime for banks, the investment services regime is in fact a package of provisions which include the MiFID II and MiFIR and certain other provisions. MiFID II and MiFIR set out two distinct regimes for the provision of services by third country firms. These are the regime under Article 46 of MiFIR for the provision of services to wholesale clients and the regime under Article 39 of MiFID II relating to retail clients or elective professional clients.

4.42 Article 46 of MiFIR provides a gateway mechanism for third country access whereby third country firms can register with ESMA in order to provide services to eligible counterparties and per se professional clients throughout the EU on a cross-border basis. This provision is dependent on the adoption by the Commission of an equivalence decision, in accordance with Article 47(1) of MiFIR, which states that the relevant third country's legal and supervisory arrangements align with those of the EU.

4.43 For the three years that follow the adoption of an equivalence decision under Article 47(1), third country firms may either register with ESMA or, in the alternative, continue to carry on investment services with eligible counterparties or per se professional clients in compliance with the relevant Member States' national regimes, by virtue of transitional provisions set out in Article 54 of MiFIR.

4.44 Under Article 39 of MiFID II, Member States may require that third country firms intending to provide investment services to retail and elective per se professional clients within their territory establish a branch within the jurisdiction. This provision is not mandatory so that Member States have a choice as to whether to require the establishment of a branch or to regulate the provision of services by the third country firm to retail clients in some other way. Where a Member State requires a third country firm to establish a local branch, this will only permit access to the market of the Member State concerned and will not confer any passporting or similar rights of market access across the EU. This may be contrasted with the position described above in relation to Article 46 of MiFIR where once registered with ESMA, third country firms can provide services across the EEA.

4.45 Where a Member State implements MiFID II to require the establishment of branches, a third country firm that has not established a branch in that Member State will not be able to provide investment services to retail clients or elective professional clients in that state. Where a Member State does not implement the requirement to establish a branch, the provision of services to retail clients and elective professional clients will be subject to existing national law and regulation, such as the OPE in the UK.

4.46 Under Article 39 of MiFID II, where a Member State requires third country firms to provide services from a branch in that Member State, the Member State concerned must determine that: (1) the relevant firm is subject to authorisation and supervision in its home country; (2) the third country pays due regard to any FATF recommendations on anti-money laundering and countering terrorist financing; (3) there are appropriate cooperation agreements in place between the competent authorities of the Member State and the relevant third country; and (4) the relevant third country has signed an tax exchange agreement, which is compliant with standards set by the Organisation for Economic Co-operation and Development (**OECD**), with the relevant Member State. The decision on whether the third country framework meets these requirements is, therefore, taken by each relevant Member State under MiFID II. This is because the Article 39 regime is not a pan-European equivalence regime.

Under Article 46 of MiFIR, third country firms can seek to be registered with ESMA where the Commission has adopted an equivalence decision. This requires the Commission to determine that the legal and supervisory arrangements of the relevant third country ensure that firms comply with legally binding prudential and conduct of business arrangements equivalent to the requirements of MiFIR and MiFID II. ESMA is required to establish cooperation agreements with the competent authorities of third countries judged by the Commission to be equivalent. **4.47**

Under Article 46(6) of MiFIR, third country firms must, before providing any service or performing any activity in relation to a client established in the EU, 'offer to submit any disputes relating to those services or activities to the jurisdiction of a court or arbitral tribunal in a Member State'. **4.48**

4.10 Market Infrastructure

MiFID II also regulates the activity of operating certain trading venues described in MiFID II as a multilateral trading facility (**MTF**) or an organised trading facility (**OTF**). Providers of such services are subject to licensing requirements under MiFID II, as well as ongoing supervisory requirements. For third country providers of MTF and OTF services, the services are subject to the same regime for third country providers as other MiFID II investment services as described in the section above. **4.49**

An MTF or OTF operator in a third country will also be able to request access to EU CCPs, provided that the Commission has adopted a decision stating that the legal and supervisory framework for trading venues in that third country is equivalent to the requirements for trading venues under MiFIR. **4.50**

There is no third country regime for the provision into the EU markets of trading platform services other than by means of an MTF or OTF. **4.51**

Third country CCPs can potentially provide services to EU-based parties pursuant to market access provisions contained in EMIR and MIFIR. **4.52**

Article 25 of EMIR provides for access to EU markets if the third country CCP meets a number of requirements. These include an equivalence determination by the Commission as to the regulatory and prudential framework for CCPs in the third country. **4.53**

Third country CCPs will obtain access to the EU as a result of being '*recognised*' under Article 25(2) of EMIR by ESMA. This is dependent on its '*home*' jurisdiction having been determined to be equivalent as described above. Therefore, there must be both an equivalence determination and specific recognition of the CCP by ESMA. There have been so far several equivalence decisions in respect of third countries regarding their CCP supervision regime. Where such an equivalence decision is made, a CCP in the relevant third country can aply to ESMA for recognition under EMIR. **4.54**

A CCP recognised in this way will be a '*qualifying central counterparty*'. This means that clearing participants will be able to benefit from favourable treatment of their own funds requirements for CCP exposures under the CRR. **4.55**

4.56 In addition to the provisions for CCPs under EMIR, third country CCPs may also benefit the following provisions under MiFIR.

(a) **Access to trading venues**: under Article 38(1) of MiFIR, a CCP established in a third country may request access to a trading venue in the EU subject to that CCP being recognised under Article 25 of EMIR. In addition, it is required that the Commission adopt a decision with regard to the legal and supervisory framework of the third country in accordance with Article 38(3) of MiFIR, confirming that it provides an effective equivalent system for permitting CCPs and trading venues authorised under foreign regimes access to CCPs and trading venues established in that third country.

(b) **Access to trade feeds**: third country CCPs which have been recognised by ESMA under EMIR will also be granted the non-discriminatory access to trade feeds from trading venues as guaranteed to EU CCPs by Article 36 of MiFIR.

(c) **Access to EU benchmarks**: similarly, third country CCPs which have been recognised by ESMA under EMIR will be granted non-discriminatory access to EU benchmarks as guaranteed to EU CCPs by Article 37 of MiFIR. The third country CCP is required to apply to the benchmark administrator itself for a licence to use the benchmark.

4.11 Recognition of UK CCPs and CSDs

4.57 As already mentioned in the introduction to this chapter, in advance of the original exit date of 29 March 2019, in order to minimise financial stability risks, the EU conferred temporary recognition on UK CCPs and central securities depositaries ('CSDs'). This was effected through the following measures:

(a) Commission Implementing Decision (EU) 2019/544 of 3 April 2019 amending Implementing Decision (EU) 2018/2031 determining, for a limited period of time, that the regulatory framework applicable to CCPs in the United Kingdom of Great Britain and Northern Ireland is equivalent, in accordance with EMIR.

(b) Commission Implementing Decision (EU) 2019/545 of 3 April 2019 amending Implementing Decision (EU) 2018/2030 determining, for a limited period of time, that the regulatory framework applicable to CSDs of the United Kingdom of Great Britain and Northern Ireland is equivalent in accordance with the Central Securities Depositories Regulation.

4.58 Both of the above provisions will only apply in the event of a 'no-deal' Brexit scenario.

4.59 On 1 March 2019, ESMA announced that, in the event of a no-deal Brexit, the CSD established in the UK—Euroclear UK and Ireland Limited—will be recognised as a third country CSD to provide its services in the EU. The recognition decision would take effect on the date following the UK's withdrawal from the EU, under a no-deal scenario.

4.60 On 5 April 2019, following the adoption of Commission Implementing Decision (EU) 2019/544 of 3 April 2019, ESMA issued a new recognition decision to make sure that the UK CCPs (LCH Limited, ICE Clear Europe Limited, and LME Clear Limited) are recognised in the event of a no-deal Brexit. The Commission has granted UK clearing houses temporary equivalence until 30 March 2020.

4.12 EMIR and Derivatives

EMIR imposes clearing and reporting obligations on investment firms and credit institutions entering into certain over-the-counter ('**OTC**') derivative contracts. In particular, EMIR requires market counterparties to centrally clear certain types of OTC derivative contracts and to apply certain prescribed risk mitigation techniques as specified under Article 11 of EMIR. **4.61**

While EMIR is principally directed at activities within the EU, its requirements can also apply extraterritorially. For example, if a counterparty to a transaction involving an EU counterparty is located in a third country or where the relevant OTC derivative contract has a '*direct, substantial and foreseeable effect*' within the EU. **4.62**

The extraterritorial application of EMIR's requirements gives rise to potential issues for parties located in third countries. **4.63**

Section 4.10 above on market infrastructure addresses the mechanism by which third country CCPs obtain recognition for the purpose of clearing OTC derivative trades. Once recognised, EU and non-EU counterparties may use a non-EU-based CCP to meet their clearing obligations. A similar position applies with regard to the use of a non-EU-based trade repository to report transactions to. **4.64**

In addition to this EMIR addresses the potential overlap of regulations that might apply in relation to a single transaction which might be subject both to EU and third country laws. Pursuant to Article 13 of EMIR where at least one of the parties to an OTC derivatives contract is located in a jurisdiction that has been determined to be equivalent, the requirements of EMIR can be disapplied and the relevant third country's requirements applied instead. **4.65**

4.13 Investment Funds

Activities carried on in relation to the investment funds are regulated in the EU under the Alternative Investment Fund Managers Directive (2010/76/EU) (**AIFMD**) and the UCITS Directive. Put shortly, the UCITS regime covers regulated funds whereas the AIFMD covers unregulated or alternative investment funds. The UCITS Directive does not contain any provision allowing for access by third country providers. This is understandable on the basis that a UCITS is a particular category of regulated European investment fund which can be distributed to retail investors. Third country UCITS or regulated funds cannot be marketed in the EU as retail funds. They may however be marketed to professional investors as alternative investment funds under the AIFMD. **4.66**

The AIFMD sets out licensing and ongoing obligations in relation to persons involved in the management and distribution of alternative investment funds (**AIFs**). The AIFMD **4.67** established passports for both the marketing of particular funds across the EU (the **Marketing Passport**) and the management of funds across the EU (the **Management Passport**). The AIFMD can apply extraterritorially, including in relation to the marketing of third country AIFs to investors in the EU and the management of AIFs, where either the manager or the AIF is located in a third country. In contrast to the position with the Recast UCITS Directive, the AIFMD does contain express provision dealing with the position of third country managers and funds. Presently many UK firms rely either on their ability to manage AIFs established elsewhere in the EU under the Management Passport or to provide portfolio management services to alternative investment fund managers ('**AIFM**') established in other EU jurisdictions under delegation. Both of these structures are under threat from a hard Brexit, although the steps that have been taken by ESMA and the FCA, mentioned below, to agree a memorandum of understanding relating to the fund management industry, should permit UK firms to continue to manage the assets of EU AIFs from the UK pursuant to delegation. The loss of the Management Passport will be ameliorated in this way. In relation to the Marketing Passport, UK firms may in the future be able to rely on local national private placement regimes ('**NPPR**') or reverse solicitation.

4.68 The AIFMD provides two regimes for access to EU markets by third country AIFMs. These are:

(a) Article 42 of AIFMD, which sets out the minimum conditions which Member States must apply in order to allow a third country AIFM to carry on marketing activities in respect of any AIF without an AIFMD 'passport'; and

(b) Articles 37 and 39 to 41 of AIFMD, which provide for the authorisation of third country AIFMs intending to market and manage EU or third country AIFs with an AIFMD 'passport'. It should also be noted that Articles 35 and 36 govern the situation in which an EU AIFM wishes to carry on marketing activities in respect of a third country AIF and apply to situations in which the AIFMD 'passport' is either available (Article 36) or unavailable (Article 35).

4.69 Article 42 of the AIFMD provides for NPPRs, by which individual Member States may allow third country AIFMs to market AIFs to professional investors subject to certain conditions. The marketing to professional investors in the EU of third country AIFs by third country AIFMs is also governed by Article 42 of the AIFMD. Third country AIFMs must comply with each Member State's individual NPPR regime when they market AIFs in that country.

4.70 The AIFMD provides for a second and separate regime under which, after a transitional period and the entry into force of a delegated act by the Commission, a harmonised firm-specific 'passport' regime is to become applicable to:

(a) third country AIFMs performing management and/or marketing activities within the EU; and

(b) EU AIFMs managing third country AIFs.

4.71 The requirements of this regime are set out in Article 37 and Articles 39 to 41 of the AIFMD. In this context, the term 'passport' refers not to Member States' access to the Single Market but rather to the stringent regulatory framework for the activities of third country AIFMs which establishes the conditions subject to which a third country AIFM can obtain an authorisation to manage EU AIFs and/or to market AIFs to professional investors in the EU. In other words, rather than a liberalising measure for international trade in fund management services, it is a licensing measure which requires third country AIFMs to submit an application for authorisation in the EU. This regime is, however, not yet in force.

In order to use the NPPR regime under Article 42 appropriate cooperation arrangements must be in place between the competent authorities of the Member States where the AIFs are marketed and the supervisory authorities of the third country where the non-EU AIF is established in order to ensure an efficient exchange of information that allows competent authorities of the relevant Member States to carry out their duties in accordance with the AIFMD. **4.72**

It is an obvious point but worth stating that the UK has not needed to enter into supervisory cooperation arrangements with competent authorities in Member States given its membership of the EU. Given the inter-connectedness of the UK and EU funds industry and particularly the links between London on the one hand and Dublin and Luxembourg on the other, agreement was reached between the UK and ESMA in February 2019 on a memorandum of understanding which will take effect in the event of a non-deal Brexit. A copy of the memorandum has not been published so it is not clear what the scope of this will be. **4.73**

In relation to this, in a statement issued on 1 February 2019, ESMA stated that the memorandum agreed with the FCA was similar to the memorandum agreed with other third country supervision authorities. According to ESMA, the memorandum agreed with the FCA covers supervisory co-operation, enforcement and the exchange of information between individual regulators and the FCA. The memorandum allows these supervisory authorities to share information relating to market surveillance, investment services and asset management activities. This in turn allows matters such as fund manager outsourcing and delegation to continue. **4.74**

Another requirement set out in Article 42 is that the AIFM must comply with the transparency requirements laid down in Articles 22 to 24 of the AIFMD. Even so, Member States are permitted, under Article 42(2) to impose stricter rules on third country AIFMs than are applicable under the AIFMD. **4.75**

Similar requirements must be satisfied under Article 36 in respect of an EU AIFM marketing a third country AIF, including the requirement for appropriate cooperation arrangements. In addition, the AIFM must comply with all the requirements of the AIFMD, excepting only the rules on the appointment of depositories. **4.76**

The alternative access provisions 'with a passport' set out in Article 37 and Articles 39 to 41 of the AIFMD do not yet apply. In order for the regime provided under these Articles to be brought into application, the requirements of Article 67 of the AIFMD must be satisfied. These include, sequentially: (1) positive advice to the Commission by ESMA on the application of the passport to third country AIFMs and AIFs—which advice is to be based on the existing marketing and management of those entities in Member States under the NPPRs—and (2) a delegated act by the Commission under Article 67(6). **4.77**

4.78 Under Article 67(4), ESMA's positive advice to the Commission must include advice to the effect that '*there are no significant obstacles regarding investor protection, market disruption, competition and the monitoring of systemic risk*' which would impede the application of the 'passport' to third country AIFMs and AIFs. Similar issues must be taken into account under Article 67(6) by the Commission before it can adopt a delegated act. The natural inference is that ESMA will, in examining the existing use of the NPPRs by third country AIFMs and AIFs, consider whether the legal and regulatory frameworks in place in their home jurisdiction establish adequate standards on investor protection, market conduct, competition and systemic risk.

4.79 Although Article 67 the AIFMD only refers in general terms to a single positive advice from ESMA (to be issued by 22 July 2015) and a single delegated act required to bring Articles 37 to 41 into application, ESMA has, in fact, taken a country-by-country approach, releasing advice in relation to specific third countries on separate occasions. A first set of advice on the application of the passport to six countries (Guernsey, Hong Kong, Jersey, Singapore, Switzerland, and the United States) was published in July 2015 and a second, on the application of the passport to twelve countries (Australia, Bermuda, Canada, Cayman Islands, Guernsey, Hong Kong, Isle of Man, Japan, Jersey, Singapore, Switzerland, and the United States) was published in September 2016.ESMA has suggested that the Commission may wish to wait until ESMA has delivered positive advice on a sufficient number of third countries before triggering the legislative procedures foreseen by Articles 67(5) and (6).[5]

4.80 Once the UK has withdrawn from the EU and is considered a third country, its regulatory and oversight framework will presumably also be assessed by ESMA. The FCA rules which apply to the authorisation of EU AIFMs in the UK and to the marketing to professional investors in the UK of EU AIFs could influence ESMA in its assessment of the UK.

4.81 Since the UK has implemented the AIFMD in full, it could be expected that ESMA would find no significant obstacles to competition. It is worth noting, however, that in its advice on AIFMs and AIFs based in Hong Kong, Singapore, and Australia, ESMA noted, in considering whether a level playing field existed under the heading 'obstacles to competition', that the local regimes facilitated market access by retail funds (including UCITS) from only certain Member States.

4.82 It is therefore possible that, in assessing whether to give positive advice in relation to the UK on AIFMs and AIFs, the basis on which UCITS from Member States are granted access to investors in the UK may be a consideration

4.83 With regard to obstacles to the monitoring of systemic risk, ESMA is required to base its advice on the existence and effectiveness of cooperation arrangements for the purpose of systemic risk oversight between the competent and supervisory authorities of the Member State and the third country. Although ESMA has agreed a memorandum of understanding with the FCA it is uncertain how ESMA would carry out this part of its

---

[5] ESMA's advice to the European Parliament, the Council and the Commission on the application of the AIFMD passport to non-EU AIFMs and AIFs, 30 July 2015.

assessment, particularly as ESMA's assessment for the purposes of its advice requires a consideration of how well the cooperation arrangements in question are working and, in the absence of evidence in relation to the working of an existing cooperation agreement, whether previous supervisory engagement provides support for the expectation of good supervisory cooperation.

Other issues which ESMA has indicated the Commission may also wish to consider along- **4.84** side its advice, which are not expressly referred to in the AIFMD, include: (1) fiscal matters in the third country; and (2) the anti-money laundering and counter-terrorism financing regime in the third country. If the Commission determines to adopt these criteria, it is uncertain how it will apply them in relation to the UK.

If and when the 'passporting' regime comes into application, by virtue of the delegated **4.85** act specified in Article 67(6), third country AIFMs and EU AIFMs managing third country AIFs will be subject to an authorisation and licensing regime. The authorisation of third country AIFMs is provided for in Article 37 AIFMD, which requires a third country AIFM to become authorised in a Member State of reference and thus to comply with the provisions of the AIFMD as implemented in that Member State. Consequently, in the absence of transitional arrangements or an agreement or withdrawal terms, a UK AIFM, which intended either to manage an EU AIF or market a third country AIF in the EU, would have to comply both with the AIFMD as implemented in its Member State of reference and also with the rules applied to it by the FCA in the UK. This could result in concerns where FCA rules diverge from those in the Member State of reference.

Article 37(7) AIFMD provides that no authorisation shall be granted to a third country **4.86** AIFM unless specified requirements, including but not limited to, are met:

(a) appropriate cooperation arrangements are in place between the competent authorities of the Member State of reference, the competent authorities of the home Member State of the EU AIFs concerned and the supervisory authorities of the third country where the non-EU AIFM is established, in order to ensure an efficient exchange of information that allows the competent authorities to carry out their duties in accordance with the AIFMD; and
(b) the third country where the AIFM is established has signed an agreement with the Member State of reference, which fully complies with the standards laid down in Article 26 of the OECD Model Tax Convention on Income and on Capital and ensures an effective exchange of information in tax matters, including any multilateral tax agreements.

In addition, Article 37(8) provides that the authorisation of third country AIFMs shall be **4.87** subject not only to the criteria laid down for EU AIFMs by Chapter II of the AIFMD but also to additional criteria which include the provision of supplementary information, including a requirement to show that, where compliance with an EU rule is impossible the relevant third country law provides for an equivalent rule, which has the same regulatory purpose and offers the same level of protection to investors of the relevant AIFs and that the AIFM complies with that equivalent rule.

4.88 ESMA is mandated under Article 37(23) to develop regulatory technical standards ('RTS') specifying the conditions under which a third country rule can be considered equivalent and to have the same regulatory purpose while offering the same level of investor protection. No draft RTS have been published so far.

4.14 Insurance and Reinsurance Framework

4.89 Solvency II implements the main framework for insurance and reinsurance regulation throughout the EU.

4.90 While Solvency II contains the concept of equivalence, it does not provide for cross-border access in a uniform manner. Article 162 specifically states that the provision of direct insurance within the EU by a third country insurer must be subject to local authorisation through a branch in each Member State in which it wishes to write business. There is no consistent approach relating to the treatment of cross-border services business (often referred to as 'non-admitted' insurance) from outside the EU. In some Member States, the prudential regime may be triggered when a third country firm covers risks located in the State in question but has no other presence there; in others, an ongoing presence is required before any regulatory authorisation becomes necessary.

4.91 The equivalence provisions in Solvency II only apply in the following three contexts, none of which relate to mutual access.

(a) **Reinsurance provided by a third country reinsurer**: under Article 172 of Solvency II, reinsurance contracts between an EU cedant and a third country reinsurer which is located in a jurisdiction whose solvency regime is assessed to be equivalent for the purposes of Article 172 must be treated in the same manner as if the contract were concluded with an EU reinsurer.

(b) **Group solvency**: Article 227 provides that where a Solvency II group contains a third country (re)insurer which is located in a jurisdiction whose solvency regime is assessed to be equivalent for the purposes of Article 227, the group may apply to use local rules for the third country (re)insurer in their group capital calculations carried out under the deduction and aggregation method rather than having to apply Solvency II rules to the third country (re)insurer.

(c) **Group supervision**: under Article 260, where a Solvency II group is headquartered in a third country which is assessed as having a system of group supervision that is 'equivalent' to that operated under Solvency II, EU supervisors must rely on the supervision of that group at a worldwide level by the national supervisor in that jurisdiction. This does not, however, prevent EU regulation at a European subgroup level.

4.92 The Solvency II regime sets out a list of the conditions which must be fulfilled by a third country for an equivalence determination in each of the three cases mentioned previously. The criteria include: (1) a provision for the existence of a risk-based supervisory system; (2) sufficiently resourced and empowered supervisory authorities which are able to protect policyholders and beneficiaries; (3) adequate capital requirements imposed on (re)insurers; and (4) effective governance systems. On the day that the UK separates from the EU, the UK will have implemented all of Solvency II as required, which in theory implies that UK regulators and insurance providers could be considered eligible to meet the criteria for third country equivalence.

In practice, however, these conditions have proved difficult to satisfy and are entirely within the control of the Commission. Only two countries currently have full equivalence in all three areas: Switzerland and Bermuda. In the case of Bermuda, the Commission's decision was the result of an iterative process where only provisional equivalence for group solvency was granted on the first assessment. The UK has been at the forefront of prudential regulation for insurance and in some areas, is super equivalent (e.g. the senior insurance managers regime) so it should be in a position to achieve equivalence. **4.93**

Insurance intermediation is currently subject to a Single Market 'passport' throughout the EU under Directive (EU) 2016/97 on insurance distribution (recast) (the **Insurance Distribution Directive**, or **IDD**). There is no third country regime under either measure that provides a means of access for third country insurance intermediaries. **4.94**

4.15 Benchmark Administrators

The Benchmarks Regulation applied from January 2018. As a result, financial institutions in the EU are only be able to use benchmarks registered with ESMA. **4.95**

For third country administrators, registration is only possible on the basis of: (1) a positive equivalence decision; (2) recognition by the competent authority in the administrator's 'Member State of Reference'; or (3) endorsement by an EU administrator, with full authorisation, of the benchmark(s) which it provides. The Benchmarks Regulation lays down, in Articles 32 and 33, specific requirements which must be fulfilled for either recognition or endorsement to occur and which may, in part, be satisfied by demonstrating compliance with certain international standards. **4.96**

Although the Benchmarks Regulation offers access to third countries by way of equivalence, recognition, or endorsement, there continues to be ambiguity about the standards that apply to each threshold test for access. The availability of a positive equivalence determination in favour of the UK will depend on the application of the requirements set out in Article 30(2) and 30(3) of the regulation. Those paragraphs require that the framework must be equivalent taking account of whether the legal framework and supervisory practice of the third country ensures compliance with the IOSCO principles for financial benchmarks. **4.97**

In addition, a positive equivalence decision will only be granted where benchmark administrators are subject to effective supervision and enforcement on an ongoing basis in the third country in question. **4.98**

4.16 Issuers

The Prospectus Regulation (Regulation 2017/1129) sets out common standards for the issue of securities within the EU and also permits the 'passporting' of a prospectus which **4.99** has been approved by a Member State's competent authority across the EU. The position of third country issuers is addressed in Articles 28 to 30, which allow third country issuers either to drawer up a prospectus under the Prospectus Regulation or use a prospectus that the issuer has prepared under the laws of a third country. Subject to certain requirements, such a prospectus may also be approved by the competent authority of a Member State and then 'passported' into other Member States.

4.100 Specific provisions for issuers registered in a third country are established by Article 29 of the Prospectus Regulation. These provide that the competent authority of the 'home Member State' of the issuer in question can approve a prospectus for an offer to the public or for admission to trading on a regulated market in the EU, subject to certain additional requirements relating to disclosure and information. The concept of a 'home Member State' is not entirely dissimilar to that of 'Member State of Reference' in other EU provisions and, means, very broadly, the Member State where the securities are intended to be offered to the public by the issuer for the first time or where the first application for admission to trading on a regulated market is made, subject to an element of election on the part of the third country issuer.

4.101 Currently, the UK Listing Authority (**UKLA**), which is part of the FCA, is the competent authority in the UK and can approve Prospectus Regulation-compliant prospectuses for third country issuers whose 'home Member State' is the UK. Once the UK leaves the EU, approval granted by the UKLA will no longer enable the provision of such prospectuses in the EU.

4.102 There are, however, a number of exemptions in the Prospectus Regulation from the requirement to prepare a Prospectus Regulation-compliant approved prospectus in order to make an offer of securities or otherwise market the securities. Where an offer of securities falls within an exemption, it may be possible to use a third country prospectus or similar offering document within the EU on the basis, that the offer is exempted from the requirements of the Prospectus Regulation so that a compliant prospectus does not need to be prepared and approved. One exemption is available where the offer is made solely to 'qualified investors'.

4.103 The Prospectus Regulation entered into force on 20 July 2017 and applied from July 2019. It repealed the earlier Prospectus Directive.

4.104 Chapter VI of the Prospectus Regulation establishes specific rules in relation to issuers established in third countries and provides two means by which a prospectus drawn up by an issuer established in a third country may form the basis of an offer of securities in the EU.

(a) by virtue of Article 28, a third country issuer intending to offer securities to the public in the EU and to seek admission to trading on an EU regulated market may draw a prospectus up in accordance with the Prospectus Regulation and seek approval of its prospectus from the competent authority of its 'home Member State'. Once such approval is received, the prospectus will entail all the rights and obligations provided for a prospectus under the Prospectus Regulation; and

(b) under Article 29—which is set out in terms very similar to those in Article 20 of the Prospectus Directive—the competent authority of a third country issuer's 'home Member State' can also approve a prospectus drawn up under the laws of the third country. In these circumstances it must apply requirements similar to those laid down in Article 20 of the Prospectus Directive and also satisfy itself that it has concluded adequate cooperation arrangements with the relevant supervisory authorities of the third country in question.

4.105 If a Prospectus Regulation-compliant approved prospectus is required, for example, where a UK issuer that intends to list on a UK trading venue wants to extend a retail offer to EU investors then, following Brexit, the issuer would need to have its prospectus approved by a Member State competent authority, namely the competent authority of its 'home Member State'. Approval by the UKLA would not be sufficient in the circumstances of the UK's withdrawal without a bespoke agreement or transitional arrangements. If the UK retains rules post-Brexit which require UK prospectuses to meet the same standards as a Prospectus Regulation-compliant prospectus, then it may be the case that (subject to any translation required) essentially the same document can be submitted to a competent authority for approval for use in the EU.

4.106 A prospectus can only be approved by a competent authority in the EU under Article 29 of the Prospectus Regulation if it has been drawn up in accordance with international standards on disclosure. The issuer is also required to show that the information requirements laid down by legislation in the country where it has its registered office are 'equivalent' to requirements under the Prospectus Regulation. Under Article 29(3), the Commission is empowered to determine that the information requirements imposed by the national law of the third country are equivalent to the requirements of the Prospectus Regulation.

4.107 In addition to the requirement of an equivalence assessment, Article 29(3) of the Prospectus Regulation requires that cooperation arrangements on supervision are in place between the 'home' competent authority and authorities in the third country.

4.108 Under Article 29(3), the Commission is empowered to adopt delegated acts establishing general equivalence criteria as well as to take an implementing decision on whether the particular information requirements imposed in a third country jurisdiction meet the equivalence requirement. Alternatively, a third country issuer can seek approval for a prospectus under Article 28 from the same competent authority on the basis that the prospectus itself has been drawn up in accordance, not with the laws of the third country in question, but in accordance with the Prospectus Regulation.

5
The EU Approach to Authorisation
Daniel Carall-Green

5.1 Introduction

Where UK-authorised financial services firms wish to continue or establish operations in the EU after EU law ceases to apply in the UK, they may need to seek EU authorisation. This chapter considers the European approach to granting such authorisation. **5.01**

The European approach to authorisation is driven by two authorities: the European Securities and Markets Authority (ESMA) and the European Banking Authority (EBA). Those authorities have expressed their views in the following documents: **5.02**

- ESMA's opinion on general principles to support supervisory convergence in the context of the United Kingdom withdrawing from the European Union dated 31 May 2017 (**ESMA Cross-Sectoral Opinion**);[1]
- the following sector-specific opinions, all dated 13 July 2017:
  - ESMA's opinion to support supervisory convergence in the area of investment firms in the context of the United Kingdom withdrawing from the European Union (**ESMA Investment Firms Opinion**);[2]
  - ESMA's opinion to support supervisory convergence in the area of secondary markets in the context of the United Kingdom withdrawing from the European Union (**ESMA Secondary Markets Opinion**);[3] and
  - ESMA's opinion to support supervisory convergence in the area of investment management in the context of the United Kingdom withdrawing from the European Union (**ESMA Investment Management Opinion**)[4]

(together, the '**ESMA Sector-Specific Opinions**');

- the EBA's opinion on issues related to the departure of the United Kingdom from the European Union dated 12 October 2017 (**EBA 2017 Opinion**);[5] and

---

[1] European Securities and Markets Authority, *Opinion: General principles to support supervisory convergence in the context of the United Kingdom withdrawing from the European Union* (ESMA42-110-433).
[2] European Securities and Markets Authority, *Opinion to support supervisory convergence in the area of investment firms in the context of the United Kingdom withdrawing from the European Union* (ESMA35-43-762).
[3] European Securities and Markets Authority, *Opinion to support supervisory convergence in the area of secondary markets in the context of the United Kingdom withdrawing from the European Union* (ESMA70-154-270).
[4] European Securities and Markets Authority, *Opinion to support supervisory convergence in the area of investment management in the context of the United Kingdom withdrawing from the European Union* (ESMA34-45-344).
[5] European Banking Authority, *Opinion of the European Banking Authority on issues related to the departure of the United Kingdom from the European Union* (EBA/Op/2017/12).

- the EBA's opinion on preparations for the withdrawal of the United Kingdom from the European Union dated 25 June 2018 (**EBA 2018 Opinion**)[6]

(together, the '**EBA Opinions**').

5.03 The precise date on which EU law will cease to apply in the UK will depend on whether or not the UK leaves the EU with transitional arrangements in place. If it does, then UK-authorised firms are likely to have until the end of that period to seek EU authorisation. If it does not, then UK-authorised firms may have to seek such authorisation immediately (if they have not already done so).

5.04 In late 2018, in the interests of (inter alia) putting transitional arrangements in place, UK and EU negotiators reached agreement in principle on the text of a draft withdrawal agreement as contemplated by Article 50(2) of the Treaty on European Union (TEU)[7] (the '**Withdrawal Agreement**').[8] At the same time, the negotiators also agreed a draft political declaration designed to set out in non-binding terms the intentions of the UK and the EU regarding their future relationship (the '**Political Declaration**').[9]

5.05 In the months that followed, it became apparent that UK legislators were unlikely to approve the Withdrawal Agreement or Political Declaration. Accordingly, in preparation for the possibility of a '*no deal*' Brexit (i.e., one without any withdrawal agreement or transitional arrangements in place), the European Commission introduced interim legislation designed to avoid short-term financial instability. This interim legislation consisted of:

- Commission Implementing Decision (EU) 2018/2030 of 19 December 2018 (**Decision 2018/2030**);[10]
- Commission Implementing Decision (EU) 2018/2031 of 19 December 2018 (**Decision 2018/2031**);[11]
- Commission Delegated Regulation (EU) 2019/396 of 19 December 2018 (**Regulation 2019/396**);[12] and

---

[6] European Banking Authority, *Opinion of the European Banking Authority on preparations for the withdrawal of the United Kingdom from the European Union* (EBA/Op/2018/05).

[7] Consolidated Version of the Treaty on European Union [2016] OJ C202/13, Art. 50(2), (3).

[8] Agreement on the withdrawal of the United Kingdom of Great Britain and Northern Ireland from the European Union and the European Atomic Energy Community, as endorsed by leaders at a special meeting of the European Council on 25 November 2018.

[9] Political Declaration Setting Out the Framework for the Future Relationship Between the European Union and the United Kingdom.

[10] Commission Implementing Decision (EU) 2018/2030 of 19 December 2018 determining, for a limited period of time, that the regulatory framework applicable to central securities depositories of the United Kingdom of Great Britain and Northern Ireland is equivalent in accordance with Regulation (EU) No 909/2014 of the European Parliament and of the Council [2018] OJ L325/47.

[11] Commission Implementing Decision (EU) 2018/2031 of 19 December 2018 determining, for a limited period of time, that the regulatory framework applicable to central counterparties in the United Kingdom of Great Britain and Northern Ireland is equivalent, in accordance with Regulation (EU) No 648/2012 of the European Parliament and of the Council [2018] OJ L325/50.

[12] Commission Delegated Regulation (EU) 2019/396 of 19 December 2018 amending Delegated Regulation (EU) 2015/2205, Delegated Regulation (EU) 2016/592 and Delegated Regulation (EU) 2016/1178 supplementing Regulation (EU) No 648/2012 of the European Parliament and of the Council as regards the date at which the clearing obligation takes effect for certain types of contracts [2019] OJ L71/11.

- Commission Delegated Regulation (EU) 2019/397 of 19 December 2018 (**Regulation 2019/397**)[13]

(together, the '**Interim Legislation**').

In October 2019, following a change in leadership in the UK, the EU and the UK made certain changes to the protocol on Ireland/Northern Ireland (forming part of the Withdrawal Agreement) and the Political Declaration. However, the UK legislature rejected the revised deal, and a general election was scheduled for 12 December 2019. Whether the outcome of the general election will result in a legislature more favourable towards the revised deal remains to be seen at the time of writing. **5.06**

Each of the documents defined in this introduction is examined in turn below. **5.07**

5.2 Background

On 29 March 2017, the UK notified the European Council of its intention to withdraw from the EU pursuant to Article 50 of the TEU.[14] **5.08**

On 5 April 2017, the European Parliament adopted a resolution calling for Brexit negotiations to begin and setting out the principles by which those negotiations were to be conducted.[15] The resolution was important because no withdrawal agreement between the UK and EU could be concluded without the European Parliament's consent.[16] The resolution specifically warned that any 'arrangement between one or several remaining Member States and the United Kingdom' giving 'privileged access to the internal market for United Kingdom-based financial institutions' would be 'in contradiction with the Treaties'.[17] The resolution also signalled the European Parliament's opposition to 'any future agreement between the European Union and the United Kingdom that would contain piecemeal or sectorial provisions, including with respect to financial services, providing United Kingdom-based undertakings with preferential access to the internal market and/or the customs union'.[18] **5.09**

On 29 April 2017, the European Council adopted guidelines (as required by the TEU)[19] for the conduct of the Brexit negotiations.[20] The guidelines were not as specific about financial services as the European Parliament's resolution, but did draw attention to the need to 'safeguard financial stability in the Union and respect its regulatory and supervisory regime and standards and their application'.[21] **5.10**

---

[13] Commission Delegated Regulation (EU) 2019/397 of 19 December 2018 amending Delegated Regulation (EU) 2016/2251 supplementing Regulation (EU) No 648/2012 of the European Parliament and of the Council as regards the date until which counterparties may continue to apply their risk-management procedures for certain OTC derivative contracts not cleared by a CCP [2019] OJ L71/15.
[14] Consolidated Version of the Treaty on European Union [2016] OJ C202/13, Art. 50.
[15] European Parliament resolution of 5 April 2017 on negotiations with the United Kingdom following its notification that it intends to withdraw from the European Union (2017/2593(RSP)) (hereafter the 5 April 2017 resolution).
[16] Consolidated Version of the Treaty on European Union [2016] OJ C202/13, Art. 50(2).
[17] The 5 April 2017 resolution (n. 15), para. 7.
[18] Ibid., para. 25.
[19] Consolidated Version of the Treaty on European Union [2016] OJ C202/13, Art. 50(2).
[20] European Council (Art. 50) guidelines for Brexit negotiations dated 29 April 2017 (EUCO XT 20004/17).
[21] Ibid., para. 21.

5.3 The ESMA Opinions

5.3.1 Legal Basis

5.11 Regulation 1095/2010 requires ESMA to 'play an active role in building a common Union supervisory culture and consistent supervisory practices, as well as in ensuring uniform procedures and consistent approaches throughout the Union'.[22] In doing so, ESMA must provide 'opinions to competent authorities'.[23] The ESMA Cross-Sectoral Opinion and the ESMA Sector-Specific Opinions are expressly published in discharge of this function.[24]

5.12 The term 'competent authorities' essentially covers the national financial regulatory authorities,[25] which ESMA calls 'National Competent Authorities' (**NCAs**).[26] (By virtue of EEA Decision 201/2016,[27] Regulation 1095/2010 extends to Iceland, Liechtenstein, and Norway, and so the NCAs in those jurisdictions are covered as well.)

5.3.2 The ESMA Cross-Sectoral Opinion

5.3.2.1 Purpose and scope

5.13 The ESMA Cross-Sectoral Opinion is drafted on the assumption that, following Brexit, the UK will be a 'third country'.[28] The ESMA Cross-Sectoral Opinion will therefore become considerably less important (or not important at all) if the UK joins the EEA or comes to some other arrangement with the EU regarding access to the EU internal market (in which case ESMA would be at liberty to issue a new or revised opinion).[29]

5.14 ESMA foresees that there will be a 'relocation of entities, activities, and functions' from the UK to the EU[30] (for example, where doing so is necessary 'in order to maintain access to EU financial markets').[31] ESMA believes that this relocation will create a 'unique situation'—probably a euphemism for a high level of risk—and suggests that the correct response is to focus on three objectives: investor protection, orderly markets, and financial stability.[32]

5.15 The chief risk, as ESMA perceives it, is that of 'supervisory arbitrage',[33] that is, firms seeking to allocate their activities to jurisdictions where the regulatory regime is less onerous. What is not immediately obvious from the ESMA Cross-Sectoral Opinion is whether ESMA is

---

[22] Regulation (EU) No. 1095/2010 of the European Parliament and of the Council of 24 November 2010 establishing a European Supervisory Authority (European Securities and Markets Authority), amending Decision No 716/2009/EC and repealing Commission Decision 2009/77/EC [2010] OJ L331/84 (hereafter the ESMA Regulation), Art. 29(1).
[23] Ibid., Art. 29(1)(a).
[24] The ESMA Cross-Sectoral Opinion (n. 1), para. 1; the ESMA Investment Firms Opinion (n. 2), para. 1; the ESMA Secondary Markets Opinion (n. 3), para. 1; the ESMA Investment Management Opinion (n. 4), para. 1.
[25] The ESMA Regulation (n. 22), Arts. 4(3) and 1(2) and the legislation there cited.
[26] The ESMA Cross-Sectoral Opinion (n. 1), para. 4.
[27] Decision of the EEA Joint Committee No 201/2016 of 30 September 2016 amending Annex IX (Financial services) to the EEA Agreement [2017/278] [2017] OJ L46/22.
[28] The ESMA Cross-Sectoral Opinion (n. 1), para. 5.
[29] Ibid., para. 12.
[30] Ibid., paras. 3, 9, 22.
[31] Ibid., para. 6.
[32] Ibid.
[33] Ibid., paras. 4, 6.

concerned about arbitrage between the UK and the EU or arbitrage among EU members (or both).

The former would appear to be the more intuitively likely concern: Brexit will in theory allow the UK to relax its rules so as to make its regulatory environment much less burdensome than the EU's. The ESMA Cross-Sectoral Opinion frequently alludes to the possibility that entities established or continuing to do business in the EU following Brexit may try to outsource or delegate activities or functions to UK-based entities.[34] The mischief at its highest is that that the EU entities may become 'letter-box entities',[35] a term frequently used in the legislation to describe an EU entity that runs a skeleton team solely for the purposes of authorisation, while the substantive operations take place elsewhere.[36] **5.16**

At the same time, however, ESMA also appears to be concerned about the risk of intra-EU arbitrage. Accordingly, the ESMA Cross-Sectoral Opinion refers to the need for consistency several times,[37] and even goes so far as to propose the establishment of a new 'Supervisory Coordination Network' to promote uniformity among NCAs' approaches. The unstated assumption must be that remaining EU Member States will be tempted to compete against one another to attract new business after Brexit. **5.17**

Overall, therefore, the ESMA Cross-Sectoral Opinion must be read as being aimed at two concurrent risks: the risk that the UK will style itself as a low-regulation haven in order to attract business away from the EU; and the risk that certain EU Member States will seek to outdo each other in attractiveness to financial services firms. **5.18**

The ESMA Cross-Sectoral Opinion is expressed to be relevant to all aspects of financial regulation within ESMA's remit, including regulation of alternative investment funds, collective investments, and markets in financial instruments.[38] **5.19**

The ESMA Cross-Sectoral Opinion sets out nine general principles for NCAs. Each of them is examined in turn below. **5.20**

5.3.2.2 The general principles
(a) Principle one: no automatic recognition of existing authorisations
This principle expresses something that should now be familiar to most observers of the Brexit process: authorisation in the UK will cease to constitute (or to be tantamount to) EU authorisation from the moment EU law ceases to apply in the UK. Consequently, for a **5.21**

---

[34] Ibid., paras. 6, 7, 19, 27, 28–36, 39, 42.
[35] Ibid., paras. 6, 28.
[36] Directive 2009/65/EC of the European Parliament and of the Council of 13 July 2009 on the coordination of laws, regulations and administrative provisions relating to undertakings for collective investment in transferable securities (UCITS) (recast) [2009] OJ L302/32 (hereafter, the UCITS Directive), recital (16), Art. 13(2); Directive 2011/61/EU of the European Parliament and of the Council of 8 June 2011 on Alternative Investment Fund Managers and amending Directives 2003/41/EC and 2009/65/EC and Regulations (EC) No. 1060/2009 and (EU) No. 1095/2010 [2011] OJ L174/1 (hereafter AIFMD), recitals (9), (83), Art. 20(3), (7)(b); Commission Delegated Regulation (EU) No. 231/2013 of 19 December 2012 supplementing Directive 2011/61/EU of the European Parliament and of the Council with regard to exemptions, general operating conditions, depositaries, leverage, transparency and supervision [2013] OJ L83/1 (hereafter the AIFMD Delegated Regulation), recitals (91), (93), Art. 82.
[37] The ESMA Cross-Sectoral Opinion (n. 1), paras. 3, 7, 9, 20, 44.
[38] Ibid., para. 10.

UK-authorised entity to continue to do business in the EU, it must have any necessary EU authorisation immediately as that legal threshold is crossed.

(b) Principle two: authorisation granted by EU27 NCAs should be rigorous and efficient

5.22 This principle does little more than emphasise the need for European NCAs to do their jobs thoroughly. The one comment of interest is that NCAs are, in ESMA's view, entitled to 'take some aspects of the assessment of third country regulators into consideration where appropriate'.[39] The argument here is that, since UK-authorised firms looking to establish operations in the EU will already have been subject to EU supervision in the UK, NCAs will be able to take some comfort from the UK regulators' assessments (for example, with regard to 'fit and proper requirements').[40] They may not, however, rely on those assessments to the point of failing to conduct their own, and may only take them into account 'where the essential requirements to be met are not impacted by the relocation'.[41]

(c) Principle three: NCAs should be able to verify the objective reasons for relocations

5.23 This principle appears to be aimed primarily at avoiding intra-EU arbitrage. NCAs are advised to establish 'a clear view on the geographical distribution of planned activities',[42] the point being that an entity applying for authorisation in one Member State but intending to carry on the greater part of its activities in other Member States must show that its decision about where to apply is not part of a strategy to avoid stricter regulation.[43]

5.24 Good objective reasons for selecting one jurisdiction over another are said to include 'prospective investors or marketing and promotional arrangements' and the 'location of development of products or services'. In essence, therefore, the presence of customers or high-level staff will justify relocating to a particular jurisdiction.

(d) Principle four: special attention should be granted to avoid letter-box entities in the EU27

5.25 This principle, like principle five, appears to be aimed primarily at avoiding UK-EU arbitrage. For ESMA, the creation of 'letter-box entities' appears to be unacceptable primarily because it would compromise the EU entities' abilities to control their operations and ESMA's ability to supervise.[44]

5.26 ESMA, in harmony with the legislation, expresses the view that the way to avoid the creation of a 'letter-box entity' is to restrict the use of 'outsourcing' or 'delegation'. The two concepts are probably distinguishable, but overlap in large part.

---

[39] Ibid., para. 18.
[40] Ibid. For examples of 'fit and proper' requirements, see Directive 2009/138/EC of the European Parliament and of the Council of 25 November 2009 on the taking-up and pursuit of the business of Insurance and Reinsurance (Solvency II) [2009] OJ L335/1 (hereafter Solvency II), recital (34), Arts. 42, 211(2)(c)–(d), and 257; and Directive (EU) 2015/849 of the European Parliament and of the Council of 20 May 2015 on the prevention of the use of the financial system for the purposes of money laundering or terrorist financing, amending Regulation (EU) No. 648/2012 of the European Parliament and of the Council, and repealing Directive 2005/60/EC of the European Parliament and of the Council and Commission Directive 2006/70/EC [2015] OJ L141/73, Art. 47. Other legislation contains similar requirements not framed in the language of 'fit and proper'. For example, the UCITS Directive (n. 36), Art. 7(1)(b) requires 'the persons who effectively conduct the business of a management company' to be 'of sufficiently good repute' and 'sufficiently experienced'.
[41] The ESMA Cross-Sectoral Opinion (n. 1), para. 18.
[42] Ibid., para. 23.
[43] Ibid., para. 25.
[44] Ibid., para. 27.

Restrictions on delegation should already be familiar from the legislation relating to collective investments[45] and alternative investment funds.[46] There are similar restrictions on outsourcing in the legislation relating to insurance,[47] capital requirements,[48] investment firms,[49] trading venues,[50] and central securities depositories (**CSDs**).[51] Generally, the gist of the restrictions is that:

- the entity outsourcing or delegating:
  - cannot thereby absolve itself of legal responsibility;[52]
  - must retain a sufficient level of control or oversight;[53] and
  - must not delegate or outsource certain vital functions, or must comply with additional requirements in order to do so;[54]
- the entity performing the outsourced or delegated activities must be sufficiently competent or must fulfil certain criteria;[55] and
- the outsourcing or delegation must not impede effective regulation.[56]

5.27

In a speech in Brussels in March 2018, Steven Maijoor clarified ESMA's position on outsourcing and delegation. Claiming to have been taken aback by the amount of commentary that ESMA's stance had generated, he stressed that ESMA was 'not looking to question, undermine or put in doubt the delegation model' which he recognised as being in

5.28

---

[45] The UCITS Directive (n. 36), Arts. 13, 22a.
[46] AIFMD (n. 36), Art. 20; the AIFMD Delegated Regulation (n. 36), Arts. 75–82.
[47] Solvency II (n. 40), Arts. 38, 49.
[48] Regulation (EU) No. 575/2013 of the European Parliament and of the Council of 26 June 2013 on prudential requirements for credit institutions and investment firms and amending Regulation (EU) No. 648/2012 (hereafter CRR), Art. 190(3).
[49] Directive 2014/65/EU of the European Parliament and of the Council of 15 May 2014 on markets in financial instruments and amending Directive 2002/92/EC and Directive 2011/61/EU (recast) [2014] OJ L173/349 (hereafter MiFID II), Art. 16(5); Commission Delegated Regulation (EU) 2017/565 of 25 April 2016 supplementing Directive 2014/65/EU of the European Parliament and of the Council as regards organisational requirements and operating conditions for investment firms and defined terms for the purposes of that Directive [2017] OJ L87/1 (hereafter MiFID II Delegated Regulation 565), Arts. 30–32.
[50] MiFID II (n. 49), Art. 48(1), (12); Commission Delegated Regulation (EU) 2017/584 of 14 July 2016 supplementing Directive 2014/65/EU of the European Parliament and of the Council with regard to regulatory technical standards specifying organisational requirements of trading venues [2017] OJ L87/350 (hereafter MiFID II Delegated Regulation 584), Art. 6.
[51] Regulation (EU) No. 909/2014 of the European Parliament and of the Council of 23 July 2014 on improving securities settlement in the European Union and on central securities depositories and amending Directives 98/26/EC and 2014/65/EU and Regulation (EU) No. 236/2012 [2014] OJ L257/1 (hereafter CSDR), Art. 30.
[52] The UCITS Directive (n. 36), Art. 13(2); Solvency II (n. 40), Art. 49(1); AIFMD (n. 36), Art. 20(3); the AIFMD Delegated Regulation (n. 36), Art. 75(a)–(b); MiFID II Delegated Regulation 565 (n. 49), Art. 31(1); MiFID II Delegated Regulation 584 (n. 50), Art. 6(1); CSDR (n. 51), Art. 30(1)(a)–(b).
[53] The UCITS Directive (n. 36), Art. 13(1)(g); Solvency II (n. 40), Arts. 38, 49(2)(a); AIFMD (n. 36), Art. 20(1)(f); the AIFMD Delegated Regulation (n. 36), Art. 75(e)–(f); MiFID II (n. 49), Art. 16(5); MiFID II Delegated Regulation 565 (n. 49), Art. 31(2)(d)–(g); MiFID II Delegated Regulation 584 (n. 50), Art. 6(3)(d)–(g), (i); CSDR (n. 51), Art. 30(1)(f)–(g).
[54] The UCITS Directive (n. 36), Arts. 13(2), 22a; Solvency II (n. 40), Art. 49(2); AIFMD (n. 36), Art. 20(1)(c)–(d); the AIFMD Delegated Regulation (n. 36), Art. 75; CRR (n. 48), Art. 190(3); MiFID II (n. 49), Art. 16(5); MiFID II Delegated Regulation 565 (n. 49), Art. 31; MiFID II Delegated Regulation 584 (n. 50), Art. 6(5)(b); CSDR (n. 51), Art. 30(4).
[55] The UCITS Directive (n. 36), Art. 13(1)(c), (h); Solvency II (n. 40), Art. 49(2)(b); AIFMD (n. 36), Arts. 20(1)(b), (f); the AIFMD Delegated Regulation (n. 36), Arts. 75(e)–(j), 77; MiFID II (n. 49), Art. 16(5); MiFID II Delegated Regulation 565 (n. 49), Art. 31(2)(a)–(c); MiFID II Delegated Regulation 584 (n. 50), Art. 6(3)(a)–(c).
[56] The UCITS Directive (n. 36), Art. 13(1)(a)–(d); Solvency II (n. 40), Arts. 38, 49(2)(c); AIFMD (n. 36), Art. 20(1)(e); the AIFMD Delegated Regulation (n. 36), Art. 79; MiFID II (n. 49), Art. 16(5); MiFID II Delegated Regulation 565 (n. 49), Arts. 31(2)(h)–(i), 31(5), 32; MiFID II Delegated Regulation 584 (n. 50), Art. 6(3)(h), (5), (7); CSDR (n. 51), Art. 30(1)(h)–(i), (3).

widespread use.[57] Rather, he said, ESMA's primary concern was to ensure that there would be 'enough substance in the entity' delegating or outsourcing. This, he added, was no more and no less than what the legislation required.

(e) Principle five: outsourcing and delegation to third countries is only possible under strict conditions

5.29 This complements principle four by giving further (albeit limited) detail about the narrow circumstances in which it will be possible for EU-authorised entities to outsource or delegate to entities outside the EU. Two rules are described:

- First, EU-authorised entities can outsource or delegate tasks and functions, but can never outsource or delegate their responsibilities for compliance with law.[58] This should already be clear from the legislation discussed above.[59]
- Second, under 'certain Union legislation', EU-authorised entities can only outsource or delegate to entities outside the EU where there are 'prior cooperation agreements between the EU NCA and [the] third country authority'.[60] The (unspecified) 'Union legislation' to which ESMA refers includes the regimes that apply to investment fund managers,[61] collective investment undertakings,[62] CSDs,[63] and markets in financial instruments.[64]

(f) Principle six: NCAs should ensure that substance requirements are met

5.30 This opaquely-named principle does little more than amplify the restrictions on outsourcing and delegation described above. Three rules are described:

- First, NCAs must ensure that, where a regulated entity seeks to use outsourcing or delegation, the outsourcing or delegation does not impede effective regulation by cutting down the NCAs' abilities to supervise and gain access to information.[65]
- Second, outsourcing or delegation must not affect the regulated entity's plans for business continuity, maintaining confidentiality, or managing conflicts of interest.[66]
- Third, the outsourcing and delegating of certain core functions to entities outside the EU is restricted. In particular, 'the substance of decision-making' must remain inside the EU;[67] and NCAs must subject to 'special scrutiny' the outsourcing or delegation of 'internal control functions, IT control infrastructure, risk assessment, compliance functions, key management functions and sector-specific functions'.[68]

---

[57] European Securities and Markets Authority, *CMU, Brexit and ESA Review – What's Next?* (ESMA71-99-964), p. 2.
[58] The ESMA Cross-Sectoral Opinion (n. 1), para. 29.
[59] See n. 52.
[60] The ESMA Cross-Sectoral Opinion (n. 1), para. 30.
[61] AIFMD (n. 36), Arts. 34–42; the AIFMD Delegated Regulation (n. 36), recitals (86), (134)–(135), Arts. 113–115.
[62] CRR (n. 48), Art. 132(3)(a)(ii).
[63] CSDR (n. 51), recitals (24), (34), Arts. 24(4), 25(4)(c), 25(10).
[64] MiFID II (n. 49), recitals (127), (140), (154), Art. 39(2)(b); MiFID II Delegated Regulation 565 (n. 49), Art. 32.
[65] The ESMA Cross-Sectoral Opinion (n. 1), paras. 31–3.
[66] Ibid., para. 34.
[67] Ibid., para. 35.
[68] Ibid., para. 36.

(g) Principle seven: NCAs should ensure sound governance of EU entities

5.31 This principle requires that an EU-authorised entity be governed and controlled 'in the EU27', and not from elsewhere, even where the EU-authorised entity is part of a larger corporate group.[69] Accordingly, the expectation is that 'key executives and senior managers' will:[70]

- be 'employed in the Member State of establishment and work there to a degree proportionate to their envisaged role';
- have 'sufficient knowledge and relevant experience'; and
- dedicate 'sufficient time to fulfil their duties'.

5.32 This principle is a straightforward continuation of the third rule described under principle six—that 'the substance of decision-making' must remain inside the EU, so that EU-authorised entities cannot become puppets, whose major decisions are beyond the reach of the EU institutions' supervisory and compulsive powers.

(h) Principle eight: NCAs must be in a position to effectively supervise and enforce Union law

5.33 This principle starts with the warning that NCAs must have 'adequate resources and capacity' to monitor the authorised entity's compliance.[71] This principle accords with ESMA's objective of preventing regulatory arbitrage: without it, firms looking to gain a foothold in the EU might be able to seek authorisation from an NCA they knew to be incapable of supervising them effectively, and thus gain access to the EU market under what would be de facto a relatively lax regulatory regime.

5.34 After this short detour, principle eight returns to the familiar theme of outsourcing and delegation. Four rules are described:

- First, NCAs must ensure that any authorisation conditions relating to outsourcing or delegation arrangements are met on a continuous basis.[72]
- Second, NCAs must ensure that those arrangements do not interfere with their ability to enforce the relevant legislation.[73]
- Third, NCAs must be able to conduct site inspections of outsourced or delegated functions without any prior third-party approval.[74]
- Fourth, NCAs must cooperate with each other and with authorities outside the EU.[75]

(i) Principle nine: coordination to ensure effective monitoring by ESMA

5.35 Principle nine is less a principle and more a statement of intent: ESMA will establish a Supervisory Coordination Network (**SCN**) to promote consistency in decision-making by NCAs,[76] and will use various of its other powers to promote supervisory convergence.[77]

---

[69] Ibid., para. 37.
[70] Ibid., para. 38.
[71] Ibid., para. 41.
[72] Ibid., para. 42.
[73] Ibid.
[74] Ibid.
[75] Ibid., para. 43.
[76] Ibid., para. 44.
[77] Ibid., para. 45.

5.36 By the time the ESMA Sector-Specific Opinions were published on 13 July 2017, the SCN had been established.[78] In June 2018, Verena Ross, ESMA's Executive Director and chair of the SCN, said in a speech in Lisbon that the SCN had already proved 'very successful'.[79] The SCN operates by bringing together personnel from various NCAs to discuss real cases of UK firms seeking EU authorisation. The firms in question remain anonymous. At the time of Ms Ross's speech, the SCN had focused primarily on cases involving investment firms and fund managers, but had also looked at cases involving trading venues.

5.3.3 The ESMA Sector-Specific Opinions

5.37 The ESMA Sector-Specific Opinions are expressly framed as being published in the wake of the ESMA Cross-Sectoral Opinion.[80] Like the ESMA Cross-Sectoral Opinion, they assume that the UK will become a 'third country' after Brexit.[81]

5.3.4 The ESMA Investment Firms Opinion

5.3.4.1 Purpose and scope

5.38 The purpose of the ESMA Investment Firms Opinion is to 'supplement the principles set out in the cross-sectoral opinion by addressing regulatory and supervisory risks in the area of investment firms'.[82] The references to the so-called MiFID framework[83] indicate that, in this context, the term 'investment firms' is to be understood as having the meaning given to it in Directive 2014/65 (MiFID II), which is 'any legal person whose regular occupation or business is the provision of one or more investment services to third parties and/or the performance of one or more investment activities on a professional basis'.[84] For the purposes of this definition, 'investment services' means, broadly:[85]

- services consisting of:[86]
    - receiving and transmitting orders;
    - executing orders;
    - portfolio management;
    - investment advice;
    - underwriting;
    - placing; or
    - operating a multilateral trading facility

---

[78] The ESMA Investment Firms Opinion (n. 2), para. 7; the ESMA Secondary Markets Opinion (n. 3), para. 7; the ESMA Investment Management Opinion (n. 4), para. 7.
[79] European Securities and Markets Authority, *Towards a Genuine Single European Financial Market—The Role of Regulation and Supervision* (ESMA71-319-79), p. 6.
[80] The ESMA Investment Firms Opinion (n. 2), para. 4; the ESMA Secondary Markets Opinion (n. 3), para. 4; the ESMA Investment Management Opinion (n. 4), para. 4.
[81] The ESMA Investment Firms Opinion (n. 2), para. 6; the ESMA Secondary Markets Opinion (n. 3), para. 9; the ESMA Investment Management Opinion (n. 4), para. 6.
[82] The ESMA Investment Firms Opinion (n. 2), para. 5.
[83] Ibid., para. 4.
[84] MiFID II (n. 49), Art. 4(1)(1).
[85] The definition set out here is actually that of 'investment services and activities': MiFID II (n. 49), Art. 4(1)(2).
[86] Ibid., section A of annex I.

- in relation to:[87]
  - transferable securities;
  - money-market instruments;
  - units in collective investment undertakings;
  - various types of derivatives;
  - financial contracts for differences; or
  - emission allowances.

Credit institutions are treated as 'investment firms' if they provide the services set out above; if they do not, they are regulated under a separate regime.[88] **5.39**

The ESMA Investment Firms Opinion states that it is to be read together with the ESMA Secondary Markets Opinion.[89] This makes sense: under the definition summarised above, 'investments firms' include investment managers, asset managers, and fund managers of various stripes. Therefore, there will be a considerable degree of overlap between the two Opinions. **5.40**

The ESMA Investment Firms Opinion is divided into the following substantive sections: **5.41**

- authorisation;
- substance requirements, and in particular:
  - governance and internal controls;
  - outsourcing; and
  - non-EU branches; and
- effective supervision.

Each of these is examined in turn below.

5.3.4.2 Authorisation

In this section, ESMA sets out its view on the approach to be taken to authorisation in general (in contrast to the substantive content of the authorisation requirements, which are addressed in the following section). **5.42**

The starting point is that NCAs should 'ensure full compliance with the authorisation requirements set out in the MiFID framework'[90]—that is, there should be no 'derogations or exemptions'[91] or 'fast-track authorisation processes'[92] for UK firms seeking EU authorisation. The reason is that the MiFID framework 'does not provide for any reliance on previous or existing authorisations'.[93] Therefore, any NCA considering whether to grant authorisation must conduct its assessment afresh, even if the applicant is authorised in the UK under the EU regime (or a regime identical to the EU's). The only concession is that NCAs may 'take into consideration' certain assessments made by authorities in the UK (or other **5.43**

---

[87] Ibid., section C of annex I.
[88] The ESMA Investment Firms Opinion (n. 2), fnn. 9, 15.
[89] Ibid., para. 5.
[90] Ibid., para. 8.
[91] Ibid., para. 9.
[92] Ibid., fn. 10.
[93] Ibid., para. 10.

jurisdictions).[94] In any event, the applicant must comply with all authorisation requirements 'from day one'.[95]

5.44 This section also reminds NCAs to examine the geographical footprint of the applicant to determine whether the applicant's choice of Member State is driven by 'objective factors (and not by regulatory arbitrage)'.[96]

5.45 ESMA also refers to the 'upcoming MiFID II Delegated Regulation with regard to [regulatory technical standards on authorisation of investment firms]'.[97] Although not yet published at the time when the ESMA Investment Firms Opinion was drafted,[98] that regulation now obliges applicants to provide NCAs with 'a programme of initial operations for the following three years, including information on ... detailed information on the geographical distribution'.[99] The 'detailed information' must include 'the domicile of prospective customers and targeted investors', the 'languages of the offering and promotional documents', the 'Member States where advertisements are most visible and frequent', and the 'geographical localisation' of marketers', advisers', and distributors' activities.[100]

5.46 All of above does little more than echo principles one, two, and three of the ESMA Cross-Sectoral Opinion, albeit with some more precise references to legislation pertaining to investment firms. There is, however, one new concept: NCAs are advised to 'pay particular attention' to the group structure to which the applicant entity belongs.[101] The group structure can give rise to a number of concerns, whether to do with prudential supervision, capital requirements, or the obstruction of effective supervision.[102] In addition, any group structure is likely to engage the legislative provisions requiring that NCAs:

- refuse authorisation if 'they are not satisfied as to the suitability of the shareholders or members that have qualifying holdings' in the applicant;[103] and
- grant authorisation only if any 'close links' between the applicant and any other person 'do not prevent the effective exercise of the supervisory functions of the [NCA]'.[104]

5.47 These requirements mean that, where an EU subsidiary of a UK (or other non-EU) firm applies for authorisation in an EU Member State (for example, in order to continue EU operations that were previously carried out by a UK-authorised entity), most entities in the applicant's corporate structure:

- will need to be 'suitable' in the eyes of the NCA in question; and

---

[94] Ibid., fn. 11.
[95] Ibid., para. 10.
[96] Ibid., para. 12; cf. ibid., fn. 14, citing MiFID II (n. 49), recital (46), which specifically refers to geographical footprint and regulatory arbitrage.
[97] Ibid., fn. 13.
[98] The ESMA Investment Firms Opinion was published on 13 July 2017, whereas the regulation in question appeared in the Official Journal on 26 October 2017.
[99] Commission Delegated Regulation (EU) 2017/1943 of 14 July 2016 supplementing Directive 2014/65/EU of the European Parliament and of the Council with regard to regulatory technical standards on information and requirements for the authorisation of investment firms [2017] OJ L276/4, Art. 6(a).
[100] Ibid.
[101] The ESMA Investment Firms Opinion (n. 2), para. 11.
[102] Ibid.
[103] MiFID II (n. 49), Art. 10(1). For the definition of a 'qualifying holding', see MiFID II (n. 49), Art. 4(1)(31).
[104] MiFID II (n. 49), Art. 10(1). For the definition of 'close links', see MiFID II (n. 49), Art. 4(1)(35).

- will need not to be subject to regulatory regimes that might interfere with the EU's regime. Regulatory regimes strictly preventing the disclosure of information on confidentiality or state secrecy grounds might be capable of such interference.

5.3.4.3 Substance requirements
(a) Governance and internal controls

(i) **Sound governance and effective internal control mechanisms** ESMA asserts that '[t]he MiFID framework requires investment firms to establish implement and maintain effective governance structures and internal control mechanisms'.[105] This is of course correct: MiFID II contains a number of provisions on this topic.[106] **5.48**

ESMA's focus in this section is largely on areas already covered by principle seven of the ESMA Cross-Sectoral Opinion. Accordingly, ESMA indicates that those manging the applicant should: **5.49**

- be 'in the Member State of establishment' (that is, be employed there and located there for an appropriate proportion of their working time);[107]
- have 'the necessary knowledge and expertise';[108]
- 'dedicate sufficient time' to their duties;[109] and
- have 'sufficient human and technical resources' at their disposal.[110]

In line with the legislation,[111] ESMA adds that there should be at least two managers meeting the above criteria, and that no single person should 'decide on the overall direction' of the applicant.[112] **5.50**

ESMA also cites legislation[113] to the effect that an investment firm's head office must be in the same Member State as its registered office or, if it has no registered office, in the Member State where it actually carries out its business.[114] ESMA interprets these provisions to mean that 'the registered office and/or the head office must be in the Member State in which the firm actually carries out its business'.[115] This is correct, but for reasons outside the cited provisions.[116] It is also unclear how this would apply to a UK firm if that firm were to be a third-country firm (with its head office outside the EU). **5.51**

ESMA goes on to give further guidance about managers. In particular, they should not perform too many roles, whether as leaders of multiple entities (which could lead to their devoting insufficient time to the applicant)[117] or as persons responsible for multiple functions within a single firm (which could lead to conflicts of interest or to a loss **5.52**

---

[105] The ESMA Investment Firms Opinion (n. 2), para. 14.
[106] MiFID II (n. 49), Arts. 9(3), 16, 45.
[107] The ESMA Investment Firms Opinion (n. 2), para. 14.
[108] Ibid., para. 15.
[109] Ibid.
[110] Ibid., para. 21.
[111] MiFID II (n. 49), Art. 9(6).
[112] The ESMA Investment Firms Opinion (n. 2), paras. 17–18.
[113] MiFID II (n. 49), Art. 5(4).
[114] The ESMA Investment Firms Opinion (n. 2), fn. 16.
[115] Ibid.
[116] MiFID II (n. 49), recital (46), Arts. 4(1)(55), 5(1).
[117] The ESMA Investment Firms Opinion (n. 2), para. 16.

of independence or effectiveness).[118] ESMA suggests certain measures (without positively advocating any of them)[119] that might reduce these risks, such as appointing a large number of non-executive directors or establishing a supervisory board independent from the rest of the corporate group to oversee the applicant's business.[120]

5.53 (ii) **Appropriate financial and non-financial resources and programme of operations** The legislation requires that investment firms 'employ appropriate and proportionate systems, resources and procedures' to 'ensure continuity and regularity in the performance of investment services and activities',[121] and that they have 'sufficient initial capital'.[122] Accordingly, ESMA advises NCAs to ensure that applicants have appropriate financial and non-financial resources and procedures at their disposal. ESMA highlights the following situations as giving rise to significant risk:

- where the applicant executes client orders using a single trading venue, and has no backup or alternative venue to use in case reliance on the first venue does not result in the applicant's delivering 'the best results for its clients';[123]
- where the applicant uses a non-EU entity to place or execute client orders or to provide cross-border services (potentially obstructing the applicant from monitoring the non-EU entity effectively);[124]
- where there are conflicts of interest between the applicant and other members of its corporate group (for example, where the applicant hedges risk by trading with a fellow group member);[125] and
- where the applicant is unlikely to meet capital requirements or has an unsustainable business model.[126]

5.54 (iii) **Proportionality** Lest it be thought that the above requirements are excessive for smaller investment firms, it is to be recalled that the 'systems, resources and procedures' need only be 'appropriate and proportionate'.[127] In keeping with this, the ESMA Investment Firms Opinion envisages that NCAs' expectations will vary according to the applicant's size and the complexity of its business.[128]

(b) Outsourcing

5.55 (i) **Assessment of outsourcing arrangements** As mentioned above, the legislation contains restrictions on outsourcing.[129] The ESMA Investment Firms Opinion summarises these restrictions,[130] and encourages NCAs to ensure that outsourcing arrangements are 'fully compliant' with the restrictions,[131] as well as

---

[118] Ibid., paras. 19–20.
[119] Ibid., fn. 19.
[120] Ibid., para. 19.
[121] MiFID II (n. 49), Art. 16(4).
[122] Ibid., Art. 15.
[123] The ESMA Investment Firms Opinion (n. 2), para. 23.
[124] Ibid., paras. 24, 27.
[125] Ibid., para. 25.
[126] Ibid., para. 26.
[127] MiFID II (n. 49), Art. 16(4).
[128] The ESMA Investment Firms Opinion (n. 2), paras. 28–30.
[129] MiFID II Delegated Regulation 565 (n. 49), Art. 31.
[130] The ESMA Investment Firms Opinion (n. 2), para. 31.
[131] Ibid., para. 32.

with other legal regimes, such as those pertaining to data protection[132] and recovery and resolution.[133]

The ESMA Investment Firms Opinion also encourages NCAs to ensure that outsourcing arrangements are 'properly monitored' by the applicant.[134] Proper monitoring should not just be limited to 'formal assessments', but should involve applicants performing 'their own qualified analysis on the quality of the service received', and keeping clear records of such analysis.[135] This is consistent with the legislative requirement that firms have 'established methods and procedures for assessing the standard of performance of the service provider and for reviewing on an ongoing basis the services provided by the service provider'.[136] **5.56**

ESMA recognises that outsourcing 'may be an efficient way to perform some functions or activities',[137] but stresses that the decision to outsource should be based on 'objective reasons' and repeats the familiar warning against 'letter-box entities'.[138] **5.57**

Outsourcing within a corporate group is said to raise particular concerns in relation to due diligence and conflicts of interest.[139] As to the former, an outsourcing entity will be tempted not to subject another member of its own corporate group to sufficient scrutiny. As to the latter, an outsourcing entity receiving a poor standard of service from another member of its own corporate group will be tempted not to press for better service (as it ought to in discharge of its duties to its own customers). **5.58**

Particular concerns also arise in circumstances where the outsourcing takes any form other than a straightforward bilateral arrangement within the EU. ESMA's objections to such arrangements are based on the possibility that they might make 'oversight and supervision of the outsourced functions more difficult'.[140] Hence, ESMA recommends a cautious approach to: **5.59**

- outsourcing to non-EU entities;
- 'long or complex operational chains'; and
- 'cumulative outsourcing' (which presumably describes a situation in which an entity outsources activities or functions to a service provider that itself outsources those activities or functions to another services provider).

All of the above is consonant with principles four to six of the ESMA Cross-Sectoral Opinion. **5.60**

---

[132] Regulation (EU) 2016/679 of the European Parliament and of the Council of 27 April 2016 on the protection of natural persons with regard to the processing of personal data and on the free movement of such data, and repealing Directive 95/46/EC (General Data Protection Regulation) [2016] OJ L116/1.
[133] Directive 2014/59/EU of the European Parliament and of the Council of 15 May 2014 establishing a framework for the recovery and resolution of credit institutions and investment firms and amending Council Directive 82/891/EEC, and Directives 2001/24/EC, 2002/47/EC, 2004/25/EC, 2005/56/EC, 2007/36/EC, 2011/35/EU, 2012/30/EU and 2013/36/EU, and Regulations (EU) No. 1093/2010 and (EU) No. 648/2012, of the European Parliament and of the Council [2014] OJ L173/190.
[134] The ESMA Investment Firms Opinion (n. 2), para. 32.
[135] Ibid., para. 33.
[136] MiFID II Delegated Regulation 565 (n. 49), Art. 31(2)(b).
[137] The ESMA Investment Firms Opinion (n. 2), para. 31.
[138] Ibid., para. 34.
[139] Ibid., paras. 34–5.
[140] Ibid., para. 36.

5.61 **(ii) Due diligence** The legislation requires investment firms to 'exercise due skill, care and diligence when entering into, managing or terminating any arrangement for the outsourcing to a service provider of critical or important operational functions'.[141] The ESMA Investment Firms Opinion picks up on this requirement, and emphasises ESMA's expectation that outsourcing services providers will be chosen carefully on the basis of 'objective criteria' and their performance monitored on an ongoing basis, even when they are located outside the EU.[142]

5.62 Again, this is largely captured in principles four to six of the ESMA Cross-Sectoral Opinion.

5.63 **(iii) Substance and outsourcing of critical functions/services** In this section, ESMA addresses some risks that appear to be more specific to the context of Brexit. First, ESMA describes with disapproval a situation where 'EU firms ... continue to perform substantially more investment services functions from the original country using outsourcing and therefore also maintain substantially more relevant human and technical resources there'.[143] This appears to be aimed at the possibility that UK-based firms may seek to continue existing operations in the remaining twenty-seven EU Member States after Brexit by means of understaffed outposts established solely for the purposes of preserving the firms' EU authorisations.

5.64 Even where outsourcing arrangements are acceptable in themselves, the EU-authorised entity must have appropriate human and technical resources and expertise at its disposal to ensure effective supervision of the service provider.[144] ESMA doubts that a single person will be enough to constitute appropriate human resources for this purpose.[145] The consequence is that, even where a UK firm establishes a sufficiently substantial outpost in the EU to secure authorisation, the outpost must be staffed so as to ensure that the EU entity is the senior partner in any outsourcing arrangement.

5.65 ESMA sets its face against the outsourcing of certain 'client facing functions'; it names 'website design', 'trading software', 'financial promotions', 'client disclosures', and 'client on boarding processes', and suggests that applicants will have to demonstrate a higher standard of supervision and control over these functions than they would over less important ones.[146] In respect of certain other functions, ESMA goes even further: the marketing and performance of underwriting, placement, and execution services, it says, 'should in principle be performed internally by the investment firm or EU service providers'.[147] ESMA takes a more relaxed approach to 'back-office functions'.[148]

(c) Non-EU branches

5.66 In this section, ESMA deals with a slightly less obvious risk: the possibility that EU-authorised firms may use non-EU branches to provide services back into the EU. One can imagine that, especially if the UK regulatory regime were to soften after Brexit, it might be easier for

---

[141] MiFID II Delegated Regulation 565 (n. 49), Art. 31(2).
[142] The ESMA Investment Firms Opinion (n. 2), paras. 37–42.
[143] Ibid., para. 43.
[144] Ibid., para. 44.
[145] Ibid.
[146] Ibid., para. 45.
[147] Ibid., para. 47.
[148] Ibid.

an EU-authorised entity to operate a branch in the UK than for a UK-authorised entity to operate a branch in the EU. In such a situation, it is conceivable that financial services firms might incorporate in the EU and seek authorisation there, but place substantial operations in the UK. Those firms might then wish to use their UK capacity to serve EU clients.

This, says ESMA, would not be acceptable[149] (except, one presumes, under the equivalence provisions, insofar as applicable).[150] The use of non-EU branches 'may be based on objective reasons', such as a need to provide services in the non-EU state in question, but must always remain subject to the control of the EU-authorised entity.[151] **5.67**

5.3.4.4 Effective supervision
ESMA's insistence that the EU authorities be able to supervise effectively has already been discussed above (in particular, in the context of principle eight of the ESMA Cross-Sectoral Opinion). In the ESMA Investment Firms Opinion, however, ESMA raises the specific issue of the circumstances in which EU-authorised entities will be permitted to outsource portfolio management services to UK entities.[152] As ESMA points out, the legislation will prohibit the outsourcing of such services except where there is a cooperation agreement between the NCA in question and the UK supervisory authority responsible for regulating the activities of the UK service provider.[153] **5.68**

5.3.5 The ESMA Secondary Markets Opinion

5.3.5.1 Purpose and scope
The ESMA Secondary Markets Opinion is more explicit about the risks it seeks to address: in the opening paragraphs, ESMA explains that the opinion 'addresses, in particular, regulatory and supervisory arbitrage risks stemming from third country trading venues relocating in the EU27 seeking to outsource activities to their jurisdiction of origin'.[154] This contemplated danger is that, after Brexit, UK-based firms may establish themselves in the EU in order to gain EU authorisation, but continue to run their businesses from the UK. The ESMA Secondary Markets states, '[t]he proximity to the EU27 and the size and interconnectedness of the financial sector of a third country may make it appear more attractive to outsource significant activities to service providers based in that jurisdiction, thereby resulting a high concentration of outsourced activities in that jurisdiction'.[155] The reference to the City of London could hardly be clearer. **5.69**

The references to the 'MiFID framework'[156] indicate that, in this context, the term 'trading venues' is to be understood as having the meaning given to it in MiFID II, which covers **5.70**

---

[149] Ibid., para. 49.
[150] Regulation (EU) No. 600/2014 of the European Parliament and of the Council of 15 May 2014 on markets in financial instruments and amending Regulation (EU) No. 648/2012 [2014] OJ L173/84 (hereafter MiFIR), Arts. 46–49.
[151] The ESMA Investment Firms Opinion (n. 2), para. 49.
[152] Ibid., para. 53.
[153] MiFID II Delegated Regulation 565 (n. 49), Art. 32.
[154] The ESMA Secondary Markets Opinion (n. 3), para. 6.
[155] Ibid., para. 14.
[156] Ibid., para. 4.

most multilateral trading facilities.[157] There are three different kinds of 'trading venues' in the legislation, but the rules governing each of them are 'closely aligned'.[158]

5.71 The ESMA Secondary Markets Opinion states that it is to be read together with the ESMA Investment Firms Opinion.[159]

5.72 The ESMA Secondary Markets Opinion contains only one substantive section, which is on outsourcing. Much of what is said in that section is very similar to what is said about outsourcing in the ESMA Investment Firms Opinion and principles four to six of the ESMA Cross-Sectoral Opinion. Thus, the ESMA Secondary Markets Opinion reiterates that (although outsourcing can have efficiency benefits[160] and although NCAs should be proportionate in their assessments):[161]

- especially complex outsourcing arrangements are to be avoided;[162]
- EU-authorised firms need to be governed from within the EU;[163]
- outsourcing must not compromise the authorised entity's control over the outsourced services;[164]
- authorised entities should choose outsourced services providers with care and should monitor service providers' performance on an ongoing basis;[165]
- outsourcing should not lead to the authorised entity's becoming a 'letter-box entity';[166]
- outsourcing should not impede effective regulation;[167]
- special attention should be paid where the outsourcing leads to more work being done outside the EU than inside it;[168] and
- NCAs should be on their guard against EU entities using non-EU branches to provide services back into the EU.[169]

5.73 In light of the overlap, the discussion below covers only what is new or notable in the ESMA Secondary Markets Opinion.

5.3.5.2 Key and important activities

5.74 In a subsection entitled 'substance of outsourcing of key and important activities to third countries', ESMA lists certain activities that should not ordinarily be outsourced outside the EU. These activities are divided into three groups.

5.75 The first group is made up of activities that support the 'operation of the trading system'.[170] ESMA lists the following examples of functions linked to the 'operation of the trading system':[171]

---

[157] MiFID II (n. 49), Art. 4(1)(18), (21), (22), (23), (24).
[158] The ESMA Secondary Markets Opinion (n. 3), para. 11.
[159] Ibid., para. 8.
[160] Ibid., para. 12.
[161] Ibid., para. 13.
[162] Ibid., para. 15.
[163] Ibid., paras. 17–20.
[164] Ibid., para. 21.
[165] Ibid., paras. 22–6.
[166] Ibid., para. 27.
[167] Ibid., paras. 32, 36–8.
[168] Ibid., para. 33.
[169] Ibid., para. 35.
[170] Ibid., para. 28.
[171] Ibid.

- the matching of orders;
- upstream connectivity;
- order submission capacity;
- throttling capacities;
- downstream connectivity;
- co-location and proximity services; and
- operations relating to market data feeds.

These largely replicate the functions described in the legislation as 'operational functions'.[172] Such 'operational functions' can be outsourced subject to certain conditions.[173] Nonetheless, the position taken in the ESMA Secondary Markets Opinion is that the 'design, calibration, control, and monitoring' of these functions 'should not be outsourced outside the EU'.[174] The justification is that, if they were so outsourced, it would difficult for NCAs to 'supervise the trading venue' and 'take supervisory action in case of an emergency'.[175]

5.76

The second group is made up of activities that support the 'admission to trading of financial instruments', the 'establishment of and any subsequent changes to the rulebook of the trading venue', the 'suspension and removal of financial instruments from trading', and 'mechanisms to halt trading'.[176] In this group, ESMA is trying to capture all activities that relate to the creation and policing of an orderly market.[177] The third and fourth activities are especially important, because (as ESMA points out), under the legislation, NCAs can 'coordinate a market-wide response' and 'halt trading' across multiple trading venues in certain circumstances;[178] and can even require trading venues to suspend or remove certain instruments from trading.[179] Therefore, in order to ensure that 'trading venues can immediately implement the instructions of NCAs', 'NCAs should not allow the outsourcing of these activities outside the EU27'.[180]

5.77

The third group is a miscellany of activities that ESMA calls 'important'.[181] ESMA lists the following examples:

5.78

- market surveillance;
- enforcement;
- compliance and internal audit;
- IT control; and
- risk assessment.

ESMA does not positively condemn the outsourcing of these activities outside the EU, but cautions that NCAs should 'verify' such outsourcing.[182]

5.79

---

[172] MiFID II Delegated Regulation 584 (n. 50), Art. 6(2).
[173] Ibid., Art. 6(1).
[174] The ESMA Secondary Markets Opinion (n. 3), para. 29.
[175] Ibid.
[176] Ibid., para. 30.
[177] Ibid.
[178] MiFID II (n. 49), Art. 48(5).
[179] Ibid., Art. 52(2).
[180] The ESMA Secondary Markets Opinion (n. 3), para. 30.
[181] Ibid., para. 31.
[182] Ibid.

5.3.6 The ESMA Investment Management Opinion

5.3.6.1 Purpose and scope

5.80 The ESMA Investment Management Opinion concerns two regulatory regimes:

- that relating to undertakings for collective investment in transferable securities (UCITS), as created by Directive 2009/65 (**UCITS Directive**); and
- that relating to alternative investment funds (AIFs) and alternative investment fund managers (AIFMs), as created by Directive 2011/61 (the **AIFMD**).

5.81 The ESMA Investment Management Opinion is expressed to cover the rules relating to 'UCITS management companies',[183] 'self-managed investment companies',[184] and 'authorised AIFMs',[185] which are the three classes of investment management entities recognised in the legislation.[186] The ESMA Investment Management Opinion refers to all three of them as 'authorised entities'.[187] In this chapter, they are called 'investment management entities'.

5.82 The ESMA Investment Management Opinion also mentions specific legislation covering European venture capital funds,[188] European social entrepreneurship funds,[189] European long-term investment funds,[190] and money markets funds,[191] but only in order to tell NCAs to 'have regard to' such legislation where appropriate.[192]

5.83 The ESMA Investment Management Opinion is divided into the following substantive sections:

- authorisation;
- governance and internal control, and in particular:
  - sound governance;
  - calibration of governance structures and internal control mechanisms;
  - internal control mechanisms; and
  - white-label business;
- delegation, and in particular:
  - assessment of delegation arrangements;
  - common interpretation and supervisory focus;
  - due diligence;
  - substance;

---

[183] The UCITS Directive (n. 36), Art. 2(1)(b), chapter III.
[184] Ibid., Art. 29.
[185] AIFMD (n. 36), Art. 4(1).
[186] The ESMA Investment Management Opinion (n. 4), paras. 4, 8.
[187] Ibid., para. 8.
[188] Regulation (EU) No. 345/2013 of the European Parliament and of the Council of 17 April 2013 on European venture capital funds [2013] OJ L115/1.
[189] Regulation (EU) No. 346/2013 of the European Parliament and of the Council of 17 April 2013 on European social entrepreneurship funds [2013] OJ L115/18.
[190] Regulation (EU) 2015/760 of the European Parliament and of the Council of 29 April 2015 on European long-term investment funds [2017] OJ L123/98.
[191] Regulation (EU) 2017/1131 of the European Parliament and of the Council of 14 June 2017 on money market funds [2017] L169/8. Regulation 2017/1131 did not apply at the time when the ESMA Investment Management Opinion was published (13 July 2017). It applied in part from 20 July 2017 and has applied fully since 21 July 2018.
[192] The ESMA Investment Management Opinion (n. 4), fn. 9.

- delegation of internal controls; and
- non-EU branches; and
- effective supervision.

Much of what is said in these subsections flows naturally from what is said in the ESMA Cross-Sectoral Opinion and is similar to what is said in the other ESMA Sector-Specific Opinions. Thus, the ESMA Investment Management Opinion reiterates that: **5.84**

- applicants seeking EU authorisation will need to carry out complete authorisation procedures 'without any derogations or exemptions' and without any special (positive or negative) treatment resulting from any previous or continuing UK authorisation;[193]
- NCAs should be wary of regulatory arbitrage and should look to ensure that decisions to relocate are based on objective factors;[194]
- applicants' management structures should be designed:
  - to avoid conflicts of interest (especially where the applicant outsources services to an entity in the same corporate group);[195]
  - to ensure that managers dedicate sufficient time to their roles;[196] and
  - to prevent managers from performing too many roles and to promote robust, independent[197] decision-making by the separate functions within the organisation[198] (even where those functions are delegated);[199]
- delegation:
  - can be 'an efficient way to perform some functions', but should be carefully monitored and controlled;[200]
  - should be done for objective reasons and after careful selection;[201]
  - should not impede effective regulation;[202] and
  - should not render the applicant a 'letter-box entity';[203] and
- NCAs should be on their guard against EU entities using non-EU branches to provide services back into the EU.[204]

In light of the overlap, the discussion below covers only what is new or notable in the ESMA Investment Management Opinion. **5.85**

---

[193] Ibid., paras. 9–12.
[194] Ibid., para. 14.
[195] Ibid., paras. 20–2, 46, 66.
[196] Ibid., paras. 23, 32.
[197] In particular, there are legislative requirements as to the independence of the compliance function: Commission Directive 2010/43/EU of 1 July 2010 implementing Directive 2009/65/EC of the European Parliament and of the Council as regards organisational requirements, conflicts of interest, conduct of business, risk management and content of the agreement between a depositary and a management company [2010] OJ L176/42 (hereafter the UCITS Delegated Directive), Art. 10(3)(c), (d); the AIFMD Delegated Regulation (n. 36), Art. 61(3)(c), (d). Derogations from these provisions are allowed where proportionate: the UCITS Delegated Directive, Art. 10(3); the AIFMD Delegated Regulation (n. 36), Art. 61(3); the ESMA Investment Management Opinion (n. 4), para. 30.
[198] The ESMA Investment Management Opinion (n. 4), paras. 30–1, 33–5.
[199] Ibid., paras. 63–7.
[200] Ibid., paras. 37–40, 51–4, 57–9.
[201] Ibid., paras. 43–5, 49–50, 57–8, 62; cf. fn. 22, citing the AIFMD Delegated Regulation (n. 36), Art. 76.
[202] Ibid., paras. 47, 55, 69–71.
[203] Ibid., para. 56.
[204] Ibid., para. 68.

5.3.6.2 Governance and internal control

(a) Sound governance

5.86 Like investment firms,[205] investment management entities must be controlled by at least two people who meet the conditions set out in the legislation.[206] Also like investment firms, investment management entities are subject to restrictions on the locations of their head offices. ESMA says that 'both the head office and registered office [of an investment management entity] must be located in the same Member State'.[207] As with the corresponding discussion in relation to investment firms:

- ESMA's position here is somewhat oversimplified, since ESMA only cites provisions relating to UCITS management companies and authorised AIFMs;[208] and
- it is unclear how this rule would apply to a UK firm if that firm were to be a third-country firm (with its head office outside the EU).

5.87 ESMA goes on to give further guidance about those managing investment management entities.[209] For example, it cites two (very similar) provisions of delegated legislation concerning managers' roles and responsibilities.[210] In addition, ESMA points to the information that investment companies and management companies need to give in their prospectuses about the amount of time that managers dedicate to their duties and the avoidance of conflicts of interest.[211] The implication is that the level of detail NCAs should expect applicants to provide on this issue is similar to the level of detail that an applicant would need to provide to the market at large.

(b) Calibration of governance structures and internal control mechanisms

5.88 The ESMA Investment Management Opinion places a great deal of stress on the need for sophisticated management arrangements in large or complex organisations. In this regard, the ESMA Investment Management Opinion is more emphatic than either of the other two ESMA Sector-Specific Opinions. For example, ESMA states that two managers meeting the legislative criteria may not be enough, and that NCAs' assessments of governance arrangements are 'of utmost importance'.[212] ESMA also lists fifteen criteria by which the size and complexity of a fund (and thus the sophistication of the management structure needed) are to be judged.[213] Many of the criteria are predictable, but the following are notable:

- the 'complexity of investment strategies pursued';
- the 'geographical spread of investments';
- the 'use of leverage';
- any 'cross-border management or marketing activities';

---

[205] MiFID II (n. 49), Art. 9(6); the ESMA Investment Firms Opinion (n. 2), paras. 17–18.
[206] The UCITS Directive (n. 36), Arts. 7(1)(b), 29(1)(b); AIFMD (n. 36), Art. 8(1)(c); the ESMA Investment Management Opinion (n. 4), para. 16.
[207] The ESMA Investment Management Opinion (n. 4), paras. 16, 61; cf. fnn. 14, 27, citing the UCITS Directive (n. 36), Art. 7(1)(d), and AIFMD (n. 36), Art. 8(1)(e).
[208] For the corresponding provisions relating to self-managed investments companies, see UCITS Directive (n. 36), recital (18), Arts. 2(1)(c), 2(1)(e), 27.
[209] The ESMA Investment Management Opinion (n. 4), paras. 18–20.
[210] The UCITS Delegated Directive (n. 197), Art. 9; the AIFMD Delegated Regulation (n. 36), Art. 60.
[211] The UCITS Directive (n. 36), Art. 69(2), annex I point 1.8; the ESMA Investment Management Opinion (n. 4), para. 22 and fn. 17.
[212] The ESMA Investment Management Opinion (n. 4), para. 27.
[213] Ibid., para. 25.

- the 'number and type of investors'; and
- the 'frequency of investor subscriptions and redemptions'.

These criteria are notable because they mean that some funds which might otherwise be considered smaller or more straightforward could be regarded as complex for the purposes of authorisation. For example, a small fund pursuing a value investment strategy and taking nothing but long positions in listed equities might nonetheless be considered complex if its strategy was very innovative, it had a varied and international customer base, and its investment targets were spread out across the world.

(c) White-label business
In the investment management industry, the term 'white-label business' typically refers to a fund set up by one investment management entity but then in substance managed by another investment management entity. ESMA believes that Brexit may lead to an increase in business for existing providers of white-label business in the EU.[214] Presumably, the theory is that UK businesses that would otherwise lose the benefit of EU rights such as the freedom to provide cross-border services or the 'passport'[215] will seek to borrow those rights by having EU-authorised entities create white-labels which the UK firms then manage as delegates. Leaving aside the question whether such delegation is acceptable in itself, ESMA warns NCAs that a significant increase in white labelling could put stress on white labellers' governance structures and internal controls; NCAs should therefore look out for white labellers who win new business after Brexitbut fail to make corresponding improvements to their governance.

On a related note, ESMA advises NCAs to give 'special consideration' to delegation arrangements whereby investment management entities appoint third parties as 'investment advisers' and then follow the advisers' recommendations 'without carrying out their own qualified analysis'.[216] The contemplated mischief is reminiscent of that contemplated under principle seven of the ESMA Cross-Sectoral Opinion: that an EU firm may become a puppet, with all major decisions (in particular, in the case of investment management entities, investment decisions) being made in the UK.

5.3.6.3 Delegation
ESMA's approach to delegation in the ESMA Investment Management Opinion is more detailed that its approach in either of the other ESMA Sector-Specific Opinions.

ESMA refers[217] to the twin legislative provisions that set out what are considered to be management functions in relation to UCITS and AIFs.[218] Delegation of such functions already carries with it certain additional disclosure obligations,[219] but ESMA also suggests that NCAs should ensure that investment management entities have policies and procedures detailing the delegation arrangements for both management functions and 'critical functions' (in which category ESMA places 'IT'). The delegation of 'supporting

---
[214] Ibid., para. 36.
[215] The UCITS Directive (n. 36), Arts. 16, 91; AIFMD (n. 36), Art. 32.
[216] The ESMA Investment Management Opinion (n. 4), para. 40.
[217] Ibid., para. 39.
[218] The UCITS Directive (n. 36), Arts. 2(2), 6(2), annex II; AIFMD (n. 36), Art. 4(1)(w), annex I.
[219] The UCITS Directive (n. 36), Art. 20(1)(b); AIFMD (n. 36), Art. 23(1)(f).

tasks' (such as cleaning, catering, payroll services, and off-the-shelf software) does not need to be so documented.

5.94 ESMA recognises that, while the delegation regime for AIFMs is detailed and highly developed, the corresponding regime under the UCITS framework is far more general, since the secondary legislation contains no advance on the broadly expressed obligations in the UCITS Directive itself.[220] Nonetheless, ESMA takes the view that the two regimes should achieve the same result—essentially that the delegation regime for AIFMs should be read across to the UCITS framework.[221] From a policy perspective, this seems reasonable: AIFMs are typically the riskier cousins of their UCITS counterparts, and so, as ESMA says, 'UCITS investors, which are often retail investors' should 'benefit from at least the same level of protection as AIF investors'.[222]

5.95 ESMA adds that, where investment management entities delegate portfolio or risk management to non-EU entities, NCAs should ensure that the non-EU entities are subject to regulatory and contractual controls on remuneration.[223] The controls should effectively replicate the position that would obtain if all entities concerned were within the EU.[224] Furthermore, NCAs should subject to special scrutiny any delegation arrangements that move services outside the EU although the planned investment activities have a strong EU connection.[225] ESMA gives two examples of such activities:

- 'UCITS investing in transferable securities issued by EU issuers'; and
- 'EU AIFs investing in real estate or portfolio undertakings located in an EU Member State'.

5.96 Once again, this guidance appears to be calculated to prevent UK-based managers from steering EU-authorised entities by remote control.

5.97 In general, when assessing whether investment management entities have delegated excessively, NCAs are to conduct their analyses at the level of each individual fund (as opposed to any group of funds).[226]

5.98 In all cases, ESMA says, investment management entities must have enough human resources at their disposal either to carry out portfolio and risk management themselves or to monitor their delegates' performing those functions.[227] For these purposes, ESMA estimates that enough human resources means 'at least 3 locally-based [full-time-equivalent staff]'.[228]

---

[220] The ESMA Investment Management Opinion (n. 4), para. 41.
[221] Ibid., para. 42.
[222] Ibid.
[223] Ibid., para. 48.
[224] The legislation contains provisions on remuneration: the UCITS Directive (n. 36), Arts. 14a, 14b; AIFMD (n. 36), Art. 13. ESMA is required to supplement these provisions with guidelines: the UCITS Directive (n. 36), Art. 14a(4); AIFMD (n. 36), Art. 13(2). ESMA has done so: European Securities and Markets Authority, *Guidelines on Sound Remuneration Policies under the UCITS Directive*, 14 October 2016 (ESMA/2016/575); European Securities and Markets Authority, *Guidelines on Sound Remuneration Policies under the AIFMD*, 3 July 2013 (ESMA/2013/232).
[225] The ESMA Investment Management Opinion (n. 4), para. 62.
[226] Ibid., para. 56, citing ESMA, *Questions and Answers: Application of the AIFMD*, 16 November 2016 (ESMA34-32-352), section VIII question 1. There is no reference to any corresponding document relating to the UCITS Directive, but ESMA appears to reason by analogy that the same principle should apply under both regimes.
[227] Ibid., para. 60.
[228] Ibid.

5.4 The EBA Opinions

5.4.1 Legal Basis

Regulation 1093/2010 requires the EBA to 'play an active role in building a common Union supervisory culture and consistent supervisory practices, as well as in ensuring uniform procedures and consistent approaches throughout the Union'.[229] In doing so, the EBA must provide 'opinions to competent authorities'.[230] The EBA Opinions are expressly published in discharge of that function.[231] **5.99**

The term 'competent authorities' essentially covers the national financial regulatory authorities.[232] The EBA refers to these as 'competent authorities',[233] but the discussion below continues to use ESMA's term: NCAs. (By virtue of EEA Decision 201/2016,[234] Regulation 1093/2010 extends to Iceland, Liechtenstein, and Norway, and so the NCAs in those jurisdictions are covered as well.) **5.100**

5.4.2 The EBA 2017 Opinion

5.4.2.1 Purpose and scope

Like the ESMA Cross-Sectoral Opinion and the ESMA Sector-Specific Opinions, the EBA 2017 Opinion is drafted on the assumption that, following Brexit, the UK will be a 'third country'.[235] **5.101**

The EBA 2017 Opinion recognises that Brexit is 'unprecedented', and seeks to 'provide guidance on supervisory expectation and to address regulatory and supervisory arbitrage risks'.[236] In this, the EBA's project is similar to ESMA's. **5.102**

The EBA also recommends certain legislative updates to cope with Brexit.[237] **5.103**

The EBA 2017 Opinion is divided into four sections: **5.104**

- authorisation and equivalence;
- internal model approvals;
- internal governance and risk management; and
- resolution and deposit guarantee schemes.

---

[229] Regulation (EU) No. 1093/2010 of the European Parliament and of the Council of 24 November 2010 establishing a European Supervisory Authority (European Banking Authority), amending Decision No. 716/2009/EC and repealing Commission Decision 2009/78/EC [2010] OJ L331/12 (hereafter the EBA Regulation), Art. 29(1).
[230] Ibid., Art. 29(1)(a).
[231] The EBA 2017 Opinion (n. 5), p. 1 para. 1; the EBA 2018 Opinion, (n. 6), para. 1.
[232] The EBA Regulation (n. 229), Art. 4(2) and the legislation there cited.
[233] The EBA 2017 Opinion (n. 5), p. 1 para. 3.
[234] Decision of the EEA Joint Committee No. 199/2016 of 30 September 2016 amending Annex IX (Financial services) to the EEA Agreement [2017/276] [2017] OJ L46/4.
[235] The EBA 2017 Opinion (n. 5), p. 3 para. 9.
[236] Ibid., p. 2 para. 6.
[237] Ibid., p. 4 para. 10.

5.105 Each of these is examined in turn below. First, however, it is appropriate to note that all of the EBA 2017 Opinion is said to be 'focused on' the EBA's three general principles, which are as follows:[238]

- EU law is to be applied 'in a consistent and harmonious manner' so as to avoid 'competition on regulatory or supervisory standards'.
- NCAs are to 'avoid imposing an unnecessary regulatory burden on firms', while continuing to apply the same regulatory standards across time.
- NCAs are to cooperate among themselves and with resolution authorities.

5.4.2.2 Authorisation and equivalence
(a) General

5.106 This section expresses an approach broadly consistent with ESMA's. In particular, the EBA says as follows:

- Applications for authorisation[239] from firms previously authorised in the EU by virtue of UK authorisation should be treated normally—that is, 'without any derogations or exemptions' and without mere reliance on previous or existing authorisations (including in respect of money laundering and terrorist financing).[240]
- There should be no 'empty shells' in the EU.[241] (This appears to be similar to the prohibition on 'letter-box entities' to which ESMA refers.)[242]
- An application for authorisation should be made in the jurisdiction where the applicant 'intend[s] to carry out the greater part of their activities' and not in order to achieve any kind of regulatory arbitrage.[243]

5.107 In addition, the EBA recommends that a new prudential framework be introduced to allow NCAs and the European Central Bank to provide adequate prudential supervision and oversight in respect of all activities regulated under the MiFID framework.[244] The EBA believes that the European Central Bank should be the competent authority for what it calls 'Class 1 investment firms'—that is, those which are systematically important.[245] Under the EBA's recommendations, such firms would be treated like large credit institutions.[246]

---

[238] Ibid., p. 4 para. 13.
[239] For the purposes of the EBA Opinions, the word 'authorisation' includes equivalent concepts that are otherwise named in specialist legislation: the EBA 2017 Opinion (n. 5), p. 5 fn. 13.
[240] The EBA 2017 Opinion (n. 5), p. 5, points i–ii, p. 5, para. 15, point 2, p. 10, para. 21; cf. (specifically on credit institutions) p. 22, paras. 11–13, p. 24, paras. 16–19, p. 25, para. 26(a), pp. 37–38, paras. 91–3.
[241] Ibid., p. 5, point iii, p. 6, para. 16, point 3, pp. 46–7 paras. 115–16, p. 47, para. 119; cf. (specifically on credit institutions) p. 47, para. 117, citing Directive 2013/36/EU of the European Parliament and of the Council of 26 June 2013 on access to the activity of credit institutions and the prudential supervision of credit institutions and investment firms, amending Directive 2002/87/EC and repealing Directives 2006/48/EC and 2006/49/EC [2013] OJ L176/338 (hereafter CRD IV), Arts. 13, 47, 74, 76, 88, 109, 123 and EBA, *Guidelines on Internal Governance under Directive 2013/36/EU*, 26 September 2017 (EBA/GL/2017/11); cf. (specifically on banks using internal models to estimate the minimum level of capital they must hold) p. 47, para. 118, citing CRR (n. 48), Arts. 144, 185–191, 368–369.
[242] Ibid., p. 43, para. 102.
[243] Ibid., p. 5, para. 15, point 3, p. 9, para. 20; cf. (specifically on credit institutions) p. 25, para. 26(c).
[244] Ibid., p. 5, point iv, p. 7, para. 18, p. 30, paras. 50–1, p. 31, paras. 54–6.
[245] EBA, *Opinion of the European Banking Authority in response to the European Commission's Call for Advice on Investment Firms*, 29 September 2017 (EBA/Op/2017/11), recommendation 3.
[246] The EBA 2017 Opinion (n. 5), p. 31 para. 56.

5.108 On 20 December 2017, the European Commission published a legislative proposal in response to the EBA's recommendations, but the legislation (a directive and a regulation) had not been published in the Official Journal of the European Union by the time of the 2019 elections (although provisional agreement between Parliament and Council on the drafting had been reached).[247] The detail of the draft legislation is beyond the scope of this chapter, but it is worth noting that the legislation was drafted against the background of Brexit, and therefore contains a number of provisions about third-country firms.

5.109 The EBA notes that the process for authorisation will depend on whether the applicant seeks to do business in the EU as a subsidiary or a branch.[248] In the former case, the subsidiary must be authorised in its own right; in the latter case, an EU-authorised entity can generally open a branch in another EU Member State as long as it notifies its home and host authorities in accordance with the legislation.[249]

(b) Credit institutions

5.110 The EBA expects that UK credit institutions will seek authorisation in the EU under Directive 2013/36 (CRD IV)[250] either by establishing new subsidiaries or by converting existing branches into subsidiaries.[251] (Any UK institutions that have limited authorisations in EU27 jurisdictions may also seek to vary those authorisations so as to expand the range or volume of business they may do there following Brexit. Limited authorisations are not explicitly provided for in the legislation, but NCAs are accustomed to issuing them.)[252] The EBA 2017 Opinion is drafted primarily on the basis that UK institutions will seek authorisation before EU law ceases to apply in the UK,[253] but observes that, if UK institutions wait until after that, they will be considered third-country institutions and so will lose certain benefits afforded under the legislation,[254] since their applications will generally be handled under national (as opposed to EU) law.[255]

5.111 On 14 July 2017, the EBA submitted draft regulatory technical standards and implementing technical standards to the Commission for adoption,[256] as the EBA was required to do under primary legislation.[257] As of the date of the EBA 2017 Opinion (12 October 2017), those standards had not yet been adopted.[258] Nonetheless, the EBA recommended that they be used as guidance for the information which applicants should be required to present when applying for authorisation as credit institutions.[259]

5.112 The EBA suggests that 'elements of the application may be … abridged' where the NCA processing the application already has the information that would otherwise be presented

---

[247] European Parliament procedure file 2017/0359(COD).
[248] Ibid., p. 21, para. 2.
[249] Ibid; cf. (specifically on credit institutions) p. 28, paras. 40–5.
[250] Ibid., p. 22, para. 10, citing CRD IV (n. 241), Art. 8(1).
[251] The EBA 2017 Opinion (n. 5), p. 22, para. 6(a).
[252] Ibid., paras. 33–8.
[253] Ibid., p. 22, para. 9.
[254] Ibid., p. 22, para. 7, citing CRD IV (n. 241), Arts. 47, 48.
[255] Ibid., p. 29, paras. 46–8, citing CRD IV (n. 241), Arts. 47, 48.
[256] EBA, *Final Report on Draft Regulatory Technical Standards under Article 8(2) of Directive 2013/36/EU and Draft Implementing Technical Standards under Article 8(3) of Directive 2013/36/EU*, 14 July 2017 (EBA/RTS/2017/08) (EBA/ITS/2017/05) (hereafter the EBA Draft Standards).
[257] CRD IV (n. 241), Art. 8(2),(3).
[258] The EBA 2017 Opinion (n. 5), p. 6, para. 16 point 1, p. 23, para. 14 and fn. 44.
[259] Ibid.

in that element.[260] This may happen where the NCA in question has obtained that information from the UK regulator (which the NCA is required to do where the UK regulator is still an EU NCA).[261]

5.113 Annexed to the EBA 2017 Opinion is a list of forty-three questions which the EBA suggests NCAs might consider putting to applicants.[262] There are close parallels between the draft regulatory technical standards and the annex. Both require the applicant to give details of its legal structure and history,[263] its programme of activities,[264] its financial information,[265] its 'programme of operations, structural organisation, internal control systems and auditors',[266] its initial capital,[267] its leadership (termed 'effective direction'),[268] any significant shareholders or members,[269] and any potential obstacles to effective regulation.[270]

5.114 The EBA encourages NCAs to assess whether UK institutions seeking to do business in the EU via branches (as opposed to via subsidiaries with their own separate authorisations) have 'considered the fact that EU branches will after Brexit become … branches of third country entities subject to the relevant provisions governing these entities pursuant to EU legislation and national legislation'.[271] The point seems to be that NCAs should check that, since a UK firm's branch will become a third-country branch after EU law ceases to apply in the UK and so will fall under a different set of rules to which the UK firm may not be accustomed, NCAs should check that the UK firm is fully aware of the consequences of its choice of structure. In addition, the EBA advises NCAs to refuse authorisation where the structure would impede effective regulation.[272]

5.115 Authorisation under CRD IV takes a maximum of six months from receipt of the application, or, where the original application is incomplete, six months from the receipt of complete information, and in any event 12 months from receipt of the original (incomplete) application.[273] Accordingly, the EBA advises that all applications from UK firms should be (or, as at the date of writing, should have been) submitted by March 2018 (in order to accommodate the possibility of a 'no deal' Brexit).[274] Recent changes to the Brexit timetable mean that that deadline has shifted to January 2019.

(c) Investment firms

5.116 The EBA expects that investment firms will seek authorisation in the EU under MiFID II[275] by establishing new subsidiaries, converting existing branches into subsidiaries, or seeking extensions of existing authorisations to cover investment services or activities not foreseen

---

[260] Ibid., p. 23, para. 15; cf. p. 25, paras. 23–5.
[261] Ibid., p. 24, paras. 19–22, citing CRD IV (n. 241), Arts. 14, 16, 22–27.
[262] Ibid., p. 6, paras. 16, point 4, pp. 54–69.
[263] The EBA Draft Standards (n. 256), pp. 15–18; the EBA 2017 Opinion (n. 5), pp. 55–7 questions 8–15.
[264] The EBA Draft Standards (n. 256), pp. 18–19; the EBA 2017 Opinion (n. 5), p. 57.
[265] The EBA Draft Standards (n. 256), pp. 19–22; the EBA 2017 Opinion (n. 5), pp. 58–9.
[266] The EBA Draft Standards (n. 256), pp. 22–5; the EBA 2017 Opinion (n. 5), pp. 62–5.
[267] The EBA Draft Standards (n. 256), pp. 25–6; the EBA 2017 Opinion (n. 5), pp. 65–6.
[268] The EBA Draft Standards (n. 256), pp. 26–7; the EBA 2017 Opinion (n. 5), p. 66.
[269] The EBA Draft Standards (n. 256), pp. 27–9; the EBA 2017 Opinion (n. 5), pp. 66–7.
[270] The EBA Draft Standards (n. 256), pp. 28–30; the EBA 2017 Opinion (n. 5), p. 67.
[271] The EBA 2017 Opinion (n. 5), p. 7, para. 17, point 3.
[272] Ibid., p. 25, para. 26(b).
[273] Ibid., p. 26, para. 27, citing CRD IV (n. 241), Art. 15.
[274] Ibid., p. 27, para. 29.
[275] Ibid., p. 29, para. 49.

at the time of initial authorisation.[276] Applications for such authorisations or extensions will be treated as normal.[277]

Perhaps more importantly in the Brexit context, the EBA 2017 Opinion discusses the principle of equivalence, whereby third-country branches of investment firms can access the EU internal market (with or without establishment of an institution in the EU) if the Commission adopts a decision deeming their local regulatory regimes to be equivalent to the EU's.[278] **5.117**

In that context, the EBA 2017 Opinion identifies a 'suboptimal' aspect of the MiFID framework: where investment firms established in third countries provide services into the EU on the basis of an equivalence decision,[279] that decision will have established that the prudential (capital) requirements in the third country are equivalent to those in CRD IV, but not necessarily also to those in CRD IV's sister regulation, Regulation 575/2013 (**CRR**).[280] The EBA appears to suggest that, to plug this hole, the EBA 'should be consulted' and should 'provide further advice or assessments' to support the Commission's 'wider deliberations' before the Commission adopts any equivalence decisions.[281] This may be interpreted as a veiled threat that, if the UK seeks to create a milder regulatory climate by dropping certain requirements in the CRR, the EBA would oppose an equivalence decision on policy grounds despite the UK's continuing alignment with the requirements in CRD IV. **5.118**

(d) Payment institutions and electronic money institutions

Since January 2018, payment institutions and electronic money institutions (**EMIs**) have been regulated under Directive 2015/2366 (**PSD2**).[282] The EBA points out that PSD2 has no 'explicit regime for third country branches', but observes that, given the scope of PSD2, third-country institutions are only be able to provide payment services in the EU if they are either credit institutions (within the meaning of CRD IV and CRR) or EMIs.[283] **5.119**

The EBA 2017 Opinion summarises the process whereby institutions may apply for authorisation, both under the previous legislation (which still applied at the time when the EBA 2017 was published) and under PSD2. **5.120**

The EBA notes the following two important changes that PSD2 has introduced vis-à-vis the previous legislation: **5.121**

- First, PSD2 has reduced the possible degree of divergence between Member States; this means that the 'risk of a race to the bottom in the context of Brexit [i.e., of intra-EU regulatory competition]' is also reduced.[284]
- Second, according to the EBA, PSD2 newly requires a 'payment services provider' to 'carry out at least part of its payment service business' in the Member State where it has

---

[276] Ibid., p. 30, para. 52.
[277] Ibid., p. 30, para. 53.
[278] Ibid., p. 32, paras. 59–63.
[279] MiFIR (n. 150), Arts. 46–49.
[280] CRR (n. 48).
[281] The EBA 2017 Opinion (n. 5), p. 7, para. 18, point 2(a), p. 32, para. 53(a), p. 33, para. 64.
[282] Directive (EU) 2015/2366 of the European Parliament and of the Council of 25 November 2015 on payment services in the internal market, amending Directives 2002/65/EC, 2009/110/EC and 2013/36/EU and Regulation (EU) No. 1093/2010, and repealing Directive 2007/64/EC [2015] OJ L337/35 (hereafter PSD2).
[283] The EBA 2017 Opinion (n. 5), p. 33, para. 65; cf. PSD2 (n. 282), Arts. 1(1), 11(1).
[284] Ibid., p. 35, para. 76.

its registered office and head office.[285] Under PSD2, this obligation applies to a 'payment institution'. It is clear, however, that service providers other than payment institutions (most notably credit institutions and EMIs) can be payment services providers.[286] Nonetheless, the EBA seems to take the view that the cited provision sharpens the requirement that payment services providers should normally apply for authorisation in the jurisdiction with which they have the closest objective connections.

(e) Credit intermediaries and non-credit institutions admitted under Directive 2014/17

5.122 The EBA 2017 Opinion contains a short discussion of credit intermediaries and non-credit institutions admitted under Directive 2014/17.[287]

5.4.2.3 Internal model approvals

5.123 Under CRD IV and CRR, banks may use internal models to estimate the minimum level of capital they must hold as long as they have approval to do so from the relevant authority.[288] (The relevant authority is either the NCA or the European Central Bank).[289] Helpfully, the EBA says that NCAs considering applications for internal model approvals can rely on assessments previously made by UK NCAs, as long as those assessments were 'for a similar rating system in the same class of exposures'.[290] Approvals for the use of a model can also be granted on the basis that the model is also used by another institution in the same group.[291] Where time is short (which it may well be in the Brexit context), it seems that the EBA advocates relying on UK NCAs' decisions in the short term in order to avoid a bottleneck,[292] and then performing a more detailed assessment later using the 'ongoing review' provisions found in CRD IV.[293] This of course only works if there is no significant difference between the business as scrutinised by the UK NCA and the business submitting its application to the EU NCA.[294] NCAs must, of course, still have regard to the various pieces of technical legislation surrounding such assessments.[295]

5.124 One area of complexity arises from applications for approvals submitted by multiple entities in the same group.[296] In such cases, the legislation provides for the making of joint decisions between NCAs.[297] The EBA 2017 Opinion canvasses a number of different scenarios in

---

[285] Ibid., p. 35, paras. 77–8, citing PSD2 (n. 282), Art. 11(3).
[286] PSD2 (n. 282), Arts. 1(1), 11(1).
[287] The EBA 2017 Opinion (n. 5), p. 9, para. 20, pp. 36–7, paras. 84–90.
[288] CRD IV (n. 241), Arts. 77, 78, 101; CRR (n. 48), Arts. 143, 151, 283, 312, 363.
[289] Council Regulation (EU) No. 1024/2013 of 15 October 2013 conferring specific tasks on the European Central Bank concerning policies relating to the prudential supervision of credit institutions [2013] OJ L287/63; cf. European Central Bank, 'Internal models' <https://www.bankingsupervision.europa.eu/banking/tasks/internal_models/html/index.en.html> accessed 30 June 2019.
[290] The EBA 2017 Opinion (n. 5), p. 10, point iv. For the classes of exposures, see CRR (n. 48), Art. 147(2).
[291] The EBA 2017 Opinion (n. 5), p. 10, para. 22, point 3.
[292] Ibid., p. 10, para. 22, point 6, citing EBA, *Final Draft Regulatory Technical Standards on the specification of the assessment methodology for competent authorities regarding compliance of an institution with the requirements to use the IRB Approach in accordance with Articles 144(2), 173(3) and 180(3)(b) of Regulation (EU) No. 575/2013*, 21 July 2016 (EBA/RTS/2016/03), Art. 2(5).
[293] The EBA 2017 Opinion (n. 5), p. 10, para. 22, point 7, citing CRD IV (n. 241), Art. 101; cf. the EBA 2017 Opinion (n. 5), p. 42, para. 100.
[294] The EBA 2017 Opinion (n. 5), p. 10, para. 22, point 7.
[295] Ibid., p. 10, para. 22, point 1, pp. 38–40, paras. 94–8 and the footnotes thereto.
[296] Ibid., p. 39, para. 96.
[297] CRR (n. 48), Art. 20; Commission Implementing Regulation (EU) 2016/100 of 16 October 2015 laying down implementing technical standards specifying the joint decision process with regard to the application for certain prudential permissions pursuant to Regulation (EU) No. 575/2013 of the European Parliament and of the Council [2016] L21/45.

which these provisions could be engaged—in particular, where Brexit necessitates an application for a joint decision or changes to an existing one—and discusses when applications should be made on a solo or consolidated basis.[298]

5.4.2.4 Internal governance and risk management

This section reiterates or reapplies many of the principles regarding delegation that are explored in the ESMA Cross-Sectoral Opinion and the ESMA Sector-Specific Opinions. Thus, in this section the EBA opines that: **5.125**

- applicants should have sound, effective, and conflict-free governance, which will mean having a sufficient number and quality of managers in the jurisdiction of authorisation with sufficient time to dedicate to their roles at the applicant and adequate separation of duties;[299] and
- outsourcing and delegation are permissible,[300] but should not:
  - strip applicants of the resources needed to manage their risk themselves or cause them to fail to monitor any outsourced or delegated functions;[301] or
  - impede effective regulation.[302]

The following additional points are, however, of interest: **5.126**

- Applicants should be able to identify and manage material credit counterparty risk, especially with 'back-to-back'[303] counterparties and counterparties in the same group (in which cases applicants might be tempted not to conduct rigorous assessments of the counterparties' creditworthiness).[304] One can imagine that such arrangements might be attractive for UK firms in the Brexit context: a new EU entity could do business with EU counterparties, but then push the risk back onto a UK hub entity, allowing the firm to continue to manage all its risk from the UK.[305] That, the EBA suggests, would give rise to 'material credit counterparty risk'[306] and in particular 'concentration risk'[307]— that is, the risk associated with a large proportion of total credit counterparty risk arising from a single counterparty. Furthermore, intragroup transactions may reduce risks to individual entities, but 'at the group level the risks will still exist'.[308] The EBA indicates that NCAs should manage these risks using the 'supervisory review and evaluation process' (a continuing programme of regulatory examination) for which CRD IV already provides.[309] NCAs should pay particular attention to over-the-counter derivatives trades in intragroup transactions,[310] and should ensure that the EU entity always

---

[298] The EBA 2017 Opinion (n. 5), p. 13, para. 23, point 5, p. 40, para. 99.
[299] Ibid., p. 13, point i, p. 13, para. 23, point 1; cf. (specifically on credit institution) pp. 43–4, paras. 103–6, citing CRD IV (n. 241), Art. 13 on the requirement to have two suitable managers.
[300] Ibid., p. 44, para. 107.
[301] Ibid., p. 13, points ii–iv, p. 13, para. 23, points 2, 7, 11(a), p. 44, para. 108, p. 45, paras. 109–10.
[302] Ibid., p. 13, para. 23, points 3–4.
[303] A 'back-to-back' counterparty is a counterparty to which transaction risks have been transferred. Loss of the counterparty (for example, because of insolvency), will cause the risks to fall back on the original party. Cf the EBA 2017 Opinion (n. 5), p. 48 para. 123.
[304] Ibid., p. 13, point v, p. 13, para. 23, point 10.
[305] Ibid., p. 46, para. 114, p. 47, paras. 120–1.
[306] Ibid., p. 13, para. 23, point 8.
[307] Ibid., p. 13, para. 23, point 10.
[308] Ibid., p. 47, para. 122.
[309] CRD IV (n. 241), Arts. 97–101.
[310] The EBA 2017 Opinion (n. 5), p. 13, point v, p. 13, para. 23, point 9.

meets minimum capital requirements, so that failure of the institution to which risks have been transferred does not threaten the EU entity's ability to absorb any losses or unwind its positions in an orderly way.[311]

- On the subject of delegation and outsourcing, firms should have regard to the guidelines issued by the Committee of European Banking Supervisors.[312] At the time of the publication of the EBA 2018 Opinion, these guidelines were due to be revised.[313] A consultation took place over the summer,[314] and a new version was adopted on 25 February 2019.[315]
- The EBA expresses some concern that the rules on remuneration policies in CRD IV[316] have been applied inconsistently, and that this may 'have an impact on decision of institutions when relocating staff to entities within the EU'.[317] There is little the EBA can do about this, and so the EBA suggests that the Commission take steps to harmonise the position.[318]

5.4.2.5 Resolution and deposit guarantee schemes
(a) Resolution

5.127 Resolution under Directive 2014/59 (BRRD)[319] is 'one of the pillars of the post-crisis regulatory reforms',[320] giving resolution authorities sweeping powers to dismantle, reorganise, and restructure distressed banks. These powers operate across the whole of the EU, and their exercise is protected from various challenges under national law.[321] Once the UK becomes a third country (and absent agreement or unilateral action by the UK to the contrary), the reach of these powers will not extend to the UK.[322] The EBA advises resolution authorities to re-evaluate resolution plans in light of this diminution in the reach of EU law.[323] In particular, the EBA advises authorities to consider cross-border issues, such as access to UK market infrastructures,[324] EU entities' use of shared services or systems based in the UK,[325] and any changes to groups' structures that are made in response to Brexit.[326] It is easy to see that if existing resolution plans rely on an EU authority's ability to exercise powers in the UK, Brexit will create an impediment to resolvability. For example, if an EU authority uses the 'sale of business tool'[327] to split out an EU bank's residential mortgage

---

[311] Ibid., p. 13, point v, p. 13, para. 23, point 11(b), p. 48, para. 124.
[312] Committee of European Banking Supervisors, *Guidelines on Outsourcing Arrangements*, 14 December 2006.
[313] The EBA 2017 Opinion (n. 5), p. 45 para. 109.
[314] EBA, *Guidelines on Outsourcing Arrangements* <https://www.eba.europa.eu/regulation-and-policy/internal-governance/guidelines-on-outsourcing-arrangements> accessed 30 June 2019.
[315] EBA, *Final Report on BA Guidelines on Outsourcing Arrangements*, 25 February 2019 (EBA/GL/2019/02).
[316] CRD IV (n. 241), Arts. 92–96.
[317] The EBA 2017 Opinion (n. 5), pp. 45–6, paras. 112–13.
[318] Ibid., p. 45, para. 113.
[319] Directive 2014/59/EU of the European Parliament and of the Council of 15 May 2014 establishing a framework for the recovery and resolution of credit institutions and investment firms and amending Council Directive 82/891/EEC, and Directives 2001/24/EC, 2002/47/EC, 2004/25/EC, 2005/56/EC, 2007/36/EC, 2011/35/EU, 2012/30/EU and 2013/36/EU, and Regulations (EU) No. 1093/2010 and (EU) No. 648/2012, of the European Parliament and of the Council [2014] OJ L173/190 (hereafter BRRD).
[320] The EBA 2017 Opinion (n. 5), p. 48, para. 126.
[321] Ibid., pp. 49–51, paras. 130–1.
[322] Ibid., p. 51, para. 132.
[323] Ibid., p. 16, para. 24 and fn. 28, p. 48, para. 126.
[324] Ibid., p. 16, para. 24, point 1(b).
[325] Ibid., p. 16, para. 24, point 1(c), (e).
[326] Ibid., p. 16, para. 24, point 1(f).
[327] BRRD (n. 319), Arts. 2(1)(58), 37(3)(a).

business from its unsecured lending business, but the two businesses both rely on central functions performed by a UK entity, and there is no legislative or contractual obligation on the UK entity to comply with the EU authority's orders, it is unclear that the tool would be effective. If authorities discover that Brexit has given rise to impediments to resolvability such as this, the EBA encourages them to use their powers under BRRD (such as the power to require changes to legal or operational structures) to remove those impediments.[328]

5.128 It is important to note that even if UK firms choose to operate in the EU via branches after Brexit, they will still be subject to BRRD,[329] including the obligation to made financial contributions to resolution financing arrangements.[330] The EBA advises resolution authorities to ensure that such branches make the required contributions.[331]

5.129 Market participants will be familiar with the requirements under BRRD for institutions to have a minimum level of 'own funds' (that is, tier 1 and tier 2 capital, as defined in CRD IV and CRR)[332] and 'eligible liabilities' (that is, broadly, liabilities that can be bailed in under BRRD)[333] at all times.[334] The EBA observes that, after EU law ceases to apply in the UK, instruments governed by 'English law'[335] that were previously considered to constitute own funds or eligible liabilities may cease to be so considered, with the result that, to continue to discharge their obligations under the BRRD, institutions may need to 'include clauses in the relevant contracts recognising the eligibility of those instruments to be subject to the write-down and conversion powers of EU resolution authorities' or alternatively to 'issue the instruments under EU27 law'.[336] Following the first suggestion would appear to involve seeking amendments to existing contracts.[337] Following the second suggestion would presumably involve cancelling or repurchasing instruments governed by UK law before issuing replacement instruments under EU27 law. The best solution would appear to be 'statutory recognition by the UK of resolution actions taken by EU27 resolution authorises',[338] but this depends on political decisions. As a fall-back, the EBA advises institutions to 'ensure that ... liabilities issued under English law that might be subject to bail-in as part of the resolution action for an institution can also credibly be written down or converted through the inclusion of recognition clauses'.[339]

(b) Deposit guarantee schemes

5.130 Market participants will also be familiar with the EU's requirements regarding deposit guarantee schemes under Directive 2014/49 (**DGSD**).[340] Once EU law ceases to apply in the UK, any branch of a UK bank in an EU Member State will become a third-country

---

[328] The EBA 2017 Opinion (n. 5), p. 16, para. 24, point 1(h), (k), citing BRRD (n. 319), Arts. 15–18.
[329] BRRD (n. 319), Art. 96.
[330] Ibid., Art. 100.
[331] The EBA 2017 Opinion (n. 5), p. 16, para. 24, point 3, p. 51, para. 134.
[332] CRD IV (n. 241), Art. 3(1)(47); CRR (n. 48), Art. 4(1)(118).
[333] BRRD (n. 319), Art. 2(1)(71), (71a).
[334] Ibid., Art. 45(1).
[335] Presumably, instruments governed by Northern Irish law, Scots law, and Welsh law (if it differs from English law in any relevant respect) should be treated in the same way.
[336] The EBA 2017 Opinion (n. 5), p. 16, para. 24, point 2(a).
[337] Ibid., p. 16, para. 24, point 2(b).
[338] Ibid., p. 49, para. 128.
[339] Ibid., p. 16, para. 24, point 2(c).
[340] Directive 2014/49/EU of the European Parliament and of the Council of 16 April 2014 on deposit guarantee schemes [2014] OJ L173/49.

branch, meaning that, unless the Member State in question considers the UK's deposit guarantee scheme to be equivalent to the EU's, the branch may be required to participate in that Member State's scheme.[341] The EBA encourages Member States' authorities to consider this issue, to consider the equivalence of the UK scheme, and to do what is appropriate 'to secure the effective protection of depositors' in the EU.[342] The EBA also considers it 'crucial' that depositors be kept informed of the guarantee scheme that protects them—something that may not be obvious where, for example, a UK bank has a branch in the EU.[343]

5.4.3 The EBA 2018 Opinion

5.4.3.1 Purpose and scope

5.131   The EBA 2018 Opinion is largely a continuation of or update to the EBA 2017 Opinion.[344] The EBA decided to issue the EBA 2018 Opinion because it had been 'monitoring the level of contingency planning and other preparations undertaken by financial institutions',[345] and had found progress to be 'inadequate'.[346] The EBA 2018 Opinion insinuates that firms were dragging their feet in order to avoid costs.[347]

5.132   The substance of the EBA 2018 Opinion falls under two broad headings:

- risk assessment and preparedness; and
- customer communication.

5.4.3.2 Risk assessment and preparedness

5.133   The EBA advises firms to prepare in the following ways:

- First, firms should 'identify the risk channels' arising from Brexit by identifying the ways in which they are exposed to the UK (financially, contractually, structurally, or in terms of data storage).[348] They should then decide how to address those risks, and—strikingly—should consider 'withdrawing from the relevant market'.[349]
- Where new or different regulatory permissions are needed, firms should apply in good time for them to be issued before EU law ceases to apply in the UK.[350] Firms should also fully adhere to any deposit guarantee requirements to which they are subject.[351]
- Financial institutions should consider where risk will be allocated, and how it will be managed and documented, in their post-Brexit models (without creating 'empty shells').[352]

---

[341] DGSD (n. 341), Art. 15(1).
[342] The EBA 2017 Opinion (n. 5), p. 16, para. 24, point 5, p. 53, paras. 139–41.
[343] Ibid., p. 53, para. 142.
[344] The EBA 2018 Opinion (n. 6), para. 6.
[345] Ibid., para. 7.
[346] Ibid., para. 8.
[347] Ibid., para. 9.
[348] Ibid., para. 11(a).
[349] Ibid., para. 11(b).
[350] Ibid., para. 11(c).
[351] Ibid.
[352] Ibid., para. 11(d).

- Financial institutions should consider how existing or future contracts (including derivative contracts and service contracts) will be affected by Brexit (for example, by the need for new or different regulatory permissions), and should act quickly to remedy any negative effects by amending, novating, or assigning those contracts as appropriate.[353]
- Financial institutions should consider whether their data storage arrangements will comply with data protection legislation after Brexit—especially if (as the Opinion assumes) the UK becomes a third country—and, if they will not, change them accordingly.[354]
- UK and EU financial institutions should consider the market infrastructure (including central counterparties) and wholesale funding markets on which they primarily rely. If Brexit would impede access to that infrastructure or those markets, they should then consider what alternatives might be open to them.[355]
- Financial institutions should expedite recovery and resolution planning, and in particular should consider the fact that instruments governed by 'UK law' may cease to constitute 'own funds' or 'eligible liabilities' under BRRD.[356] If they cease to be 'own funds' or 'eligible liabilities', firms should respond by amending the instruments, issuing new instruments, or taking some other action allowing them 'to demonstrate that any decision of a relevant resolution authority would be effective in the UK (for EU 27 institutions) or in the EU27 (for UK institutions)'.[357] Firms that issue new instruments governed by 'UK law' that are not 'own funds' or 'eligible liabilities' should include 'bail-in recognition clauses' to ensure that those instruments can be written down or converted as part of a resolution action.
- In general, financial institutions should discuss their plans with their NCAs and resolution authorities.[358]

(a) Customer communication

Customer communication is the only new principle in the EBA 2018 Opinion. The EBA advises firms to give their customers information (plainly expressed in the language originally chosen by the customer)[359] about:[360]

5.134

- the 'specific implications' of Brexit for those customers;
- the 'actions that the institution is taking to prevent any detriment to the customers';
- the impact on the customer of any corporate restructurings, amendments to contracts, or changes to the customer's deposit guarantee scheme; and
- the customer's rights of recourse.

---

[353] Ibid., para. 11(e).
[354] Ibid., para. 11(f).
[355] Ibid., para. 11(g), (h).
[356] Ibid., para. 11(i), (j).
[357] Ibid., para. 11(k), (l).
[358] Ibid., para. 11(m).
[359] Ibid., para. 14.
[360] Ibid., para. 13.

5.5 The Withdrawal Agreement, the Political Declaration, and the Interim Legislation

5.5.1 Background

5.135 On 25 November 2018, UK and EU negotiators reached agreement in principle on the text of the Withdrawal Agreement and the Political Declaration. The Withdrawal Agreement provided for the UK to leave the EU subject to a 'transition or implementation period' lasting until the end of 2020 (with the possibility of extension to 2021 or 2022), during which the longer-term relationship between the UK and the EU is to be negotiated.[361] The Withdrawal Agreement contained no specific provision for financial services, but in broad terms EU law would have applied in the UK until the end of the transition period.[362] The Political Declaration also provided that both the UK and the EU were to consider adopting equivalence decisions in order to facilitate cross-border financial services after the end of the period.[363]

5.136 In the months following 25 November 2018, it became apparent that there would be significant difficulties in persuading the UK legislature to approve the Withdrawal Agreement and the Political Declaration. This in turn raised the possibility that a 'no deal' Brexit might take effect on 30 March 2019. In response, the European Commission introduced the Interim Legislation. The Interim Legislation is will only come into effect if the UK leaves the EU without a withdrawal agreement in place.[364]

5.137 In October 2019, following a change in leadership in the UK, the EU and the UK made certain changes to the protocol on Ireland/Northern Ireland (forming part of the Withdrawal Agreement) and the Political Declaration. However, the UK legislature rejected the revised deal, and a general election was scheduled for 12 December 2019. Whether the outcome of the general election will result in a legislature more favourable towards the revised deal remains to be seen at the time of writing.

5.5.2 Decision 2018/2030

5.138 Decision 2018/2030 was designed to maintain banking stability in the immediate aftermath of a 'no deal' Brexit. In its recitals, it expressly recognised that:

- the UK-authorised CSD (Euroclear UK and Ireland) could not be replaced in the short term;[365]
- the UK CSD was 'critical in the post-trade clearing and settlement process', and the Republic of Ireland was particularly exposed;[366] and

---

[361] The Withdrawal Agreement (n. 8), Arts. 126, 132.
[362] Ibid., Arts. 127–131.
[363] The Political Declaration (n. 9), Arts. 35–37.
[364] Decision 2018/2030 (n. 10), Art. 2; Decision 2018/2031 (n. 11), Art. 2; Regulation 2019/396, Art. 4; Regulation 2019/397, Art. 2.
[365] Decision 2018/2030 (n. 10), recital (2).
[366] Ibid., recital (3).

- in the absence of any interim legislation, EU issuers might not be able to use the UK CSD to 'record transferable securities ... in book-entry form' as required by CSDR.[367]

Accordingly, Decision 2018/2030 provided that, under Article 25 of CSDR, the UK's regulatory regime for CSDs would be deemed to be equivalent to CSDR[368] until 30 March 2021.[369] This meant that the condition in Article 25(4)(a) of CSDR was then met (and will now remain met until 30 March 2021) as regards UK-authorised CSDs. This in turn allowed the UK CSD to apply to ESMA for recognition as a third-country CSD under Article 25(4)–(8) of CSDR. The UK CSD has since done so, and ESMA adopted a recognition decision on 5 April 2019. The result is that, under Article 25(11) of CSDR, the UK CSD will be able to provide its services within the EU for a limited time in the event of a 'no deal' Brexit. One imagines that the temporal scope might be extended if a 'no deal' Brexit takes place in 2020, or the UK and the EU do not reach a long-term solution for cross-border financial services before the end of the transition period. **5.139**

Decision 2018/2030 makes clear that the European Commission may reassess its decision at any time.[370] **5.140**

5.5.3 Decision 2018/2031

Decision 2018 was designed to maintain financial stability in derivatives markets in the immediate aftermath of a 'no deal' Brexit. In its recitals, it expressly recognised that: **5.141**

- to prevent financial instability in the EU, it was in the EU's interests to ensure that central counterparties (**CCPs**) authorised in the UK could continue to provide services in the EU 'for a limited period of time';[371]
- within the EU, CCP services were concentrated in the UK;[372] and
- in the absence of any interim legislation, EU counterparties might not be able to use these CCPs to 'clear OTC derivatives that are subject to the clearing obligation pursuant to Article 4 of Regulation (EU) No 648/2012'.[373]

Accordingly, Decision 2018/2031 provided that, under Article 25 of Regulation 648/2012 (**EMIR**),[374] the UK's regulatory regime for CCPs would be deemed to be equivalent to EMIR[375] until 30 March 2020.[376] This meant the condition in Article 25(2)(a) of EMIR was then met (and will now remain met until 30 March 2020) as regards UK-authorised CCPs. This in turn allowed the three UK-authorised CCPs (LCH Limited, ICE Clear Europe Limited, and LME Clear Limited) to apply to ESMA for recognition as third-country CCPs under Article 25(2)–(5) of EMIR. The UK CPPs have since done so, and ESMA adopted a recognition decision on 5 April 2019. The result is that, under Article 25(1) of EMIR, the **5.142**

---

[367] Ibid., recital (4).
[368] Ibid., Art. 1.
[369] Ibid., Art. 2.
[370] Ibid., recital (13).
[371] Decision 2018/2031 (n. 11), recital (2).
[372] Ibid., recital (4).
[373] Ibid.
[374] Regulation (EU) No. 648/2012 of the European Parliament and of the Council of 4 July 2012 on OTC derivatives, central counterparties and trade repositories [2012] OJ L201/1 (hereafter EMIR).
[375] Ibid., Art. 1.
[376] Ibid., Art. 2.

UK CCPs will be able to provide clearing services to 'clearing members' or 'trading venues' (as those terms are defined in EMIR) that are established within the EU for a limited time in the event of a 'no deal' Brexit. One imagines that the temporal scope might be extended if that 'no deal' Brexit takes place in late 2020, or the UK and the EU do not reach a long-term solution for cross-border financial services before the end of the transition period.

5.143 Decision 2018/2031 makes clear that the European Commission may reassess its decision at any time.[377]

5.5.4 Regulation 2019/396

5.144 Given the legal uncertainty surrounding the status of UK-based counterparties to derivative contracts, there was some expectation that some market participants would want to replace UK-based counterparties with EU-based ones. The legal mechanism by which such replacements were expected to take place was novation. The difficulty was that novation risked triggering the clearing obligation under EMIR, requiring the parties to clear the contract in an authorised or recognised CCP.[378] It was thought that this clearing obligation might bring with it different collateral requirements, which might in turn cause the parties to abandon the contract rather than novating it, thus leaving unhedged whatever risk had been hedged by it.[379]

5.145 Regulation 2019/396 attempted to remove this difficulty by disapplying the clearing obligation for a limited period of twelve months where, in relation to the contract in question, the clearing obligation had not been triggered by 14 March 2019 and the novation was carried out 'for the sole purpose of replacing the counterparty established in the United Kingdom with a counterparty established in a Member State'.[380]

5.5.5 Regulation 2019/397

5.146 Regulation 2019/397 was also concerned with the novation of derivative contracts that would not be subject to the clearing obligation under EMIR. Such contracts are still regulated under EMIR, in that parties entering into such contracts are obliged to have 'risk-management procedures that require the timely, accurate and appropriately segregated exchange of collateral'.[381] The difficulty was that Brexit-related novation risked triggering this obligation, and if the obligation was triggered, the remaining counterparty might not to agree to the novation.[382] The Regulation 2019/397 sought to overcome this difficulty by disapplying the obligation to exchange collateral in certain cases where the novation was carried out 'for the sole purpose of replacing a counterparty established in the United Kingdom with a counterparty established in a Member State'.[383]

---

[377] Ibid., recital (14).
[378] Regulation 2019/396 (n. 12), recital (5); cf. EMIR (n. 374), Art. 4.
[379] Regulation 2019/396 (n. 12), recital (6).
[380] Ibid., Arts. 1(1), 2(1), 3(1).
[381] EMIR (n. 374), Art. 11(3).
[382] Regulation 2019/397 (n. 13), recital (5).
[383] Ibid., Art. 1.

6
The EU Approach to Authorisation
Germany, France, the Netherlands, and Ireland

Michael Born, Roberto Cristofolini, Floortje Nagelkerke, and Donnacha O'Connor[1]

6.1 Introduction

In the scenario where the UK leaves the EU without entering into a withdrawal agreement (the so-called hard Brexit) the UK government has put in place a temporary permissions regime (TPR) for EEA firms and funds that conduct business in the UK using the Single Market passport. The TPR provides a temporary backstop to ensure that such firms and funds can continue their UK business with minimal disruption whilst seeking authorisation during 'landing slots' given to them by the UK regulatory authorities. For those EEA firms that do not wish to take advantage of the TPR, the UK government has also implemented the financial services contracts regime (FSCR) allowing them to wind down their UK business in an orderly fashion.

At the time of writing, the EU had not reciprocated with pan-European regimes similar to the TPR or the FSCR. The European authorities have instead pushed for UK firms looking to relocate their business in the EU27 to submit an application for authorisation in the relevant Member State where they wish to conduct business.[2] On the European level, only UK central clearing counterparties (CCPs) and the UK central securities depository (CSD) benefit from transitional regimes that are based on temporary and conditional equivalence decisions of the European Commission and relating recognition decisions of the European Securities and Markets Authority (ESMA). On the national level, some Member States have implemented their own domestic transitional measures to minimise the disruption of a hard Brexit whereas others have not.

In this chapter we take a look at the approach that the regulatory authorities in Germany, France, the Netherlands, and Ireland are taking to a hard Brexit, touching on any transitional measures that they have implemented to minimise market disruption and their general approach to authorisation.

6.01

6.02

6.03

---

[1] For the avoidance of doubt, this chapter's section on Germany was drafted by Michael Born, the section on France by Roberto Cristofolini, the section on the Netherlands by Floortje Nagelkerke and the section on Ireland by Donnacha O'Connor.

[2] For a summary of the communication, see Joint Committee of the European Supervisory Authorities (ESAs), 'Report on Risks and Vulnerabilities in the EU Financial System' (spring 2019), p. 4ff.

6.2 Germany

6.2.1 Introduction

6.04 Germany is one of the major destinations for UK entities relocating European-facing parts of their business activities in connection with their Brexit contingency measures. To some extent, assets and client relationships are transferred to institutions with an existing German licence or EU27 passport. The competent authorities, however, have also received quite a few applications for new authorisations and passporting notifications in relation to Germany. In March 2019, the Federal Financial Supervisory Authority (Bundesanstalt für Finanzdienstleistungsaufsicht—**BaFin**) confirmed the number of forty-eight applications for an authorisation in the context of Brexit[3]—many of which relate to a banking licence.

6.05 The German authorities have provided administrative guidance to entities in UK groups that intend to locate to Germany. Also, to some degree, the German legislator has taken steps to make Germany (and, in particular, its financial centre of Frankfurt) more attractive for banks from the UK, and has softened the strict protection against dismissal in case of certain highly paid employees. However, such measures do not alter the fact that the UK will become a third country following Brexit from a German regulatory perspective and that the UK institutions and their German branches will be subject to the general licensing requirements as soon as they lose their European passporting rights. Against this background, in order to protect the functioning and stability of the financial markets, Germany has introduced certain national transitional periods before the third country regime fully applies.

6.2.2 German Brexit Legislation

6.2.2.1 Overview

6.06 The German legislator has implemented a bundle of legislative measures at the federal and state level that deal with various implications of the UK's withdrawal from the EU. For market access of regulated UK institutions in Germany, two federal acts are relevant.

6.07 On the one hand, the Brexit Transition Act (*Brexit-Übergangsgesetz*—**BrexitÜG**)[4] covers a soft-Brexit scenario. Subject to the Withdrawal Agreement becoming effective, a simple transitional rule would apply: whenever German federal law refers to a Member State of the EU, the UK is deemed to be such Member State during the transitional period set by the Withdrawal Agreement if this is agreed. This rule would cover, in particular, the German provisions applicable to passported regulated entities from the EU. However, given the rejection of the adopted Withdrawal Agreement by the UK Parliament, the BrexitÜG will likely only become relevant in case of any renegotiated deal between the UK and the EU. It should be noted that it has already been questioned in legal literature whether the current

---

[3] Roegele (Vice President of BaFin), 'Der Countdown zum Brexit läuft—Die Aufsichtsperspektive', speech dated 8 March 2019.
[4] Act on the Transition Period after the Withdrawal of the United Kingdom of Great Britain and Northern Ireland from the European Union (Brexit Transition Act) dated 27 March 2019, Federal Law Gazette I, p. 402.

wording of the BrexitÜG will automatically also cover any new arrangement between the two parties that deviates from the original Withdrawal Agreement.

On the other hand, the Tax Act relating to Brexit (*Brexit-Steuerbegleitgesetz*—**Brexit-StBG**)[5] addresses a hard-Brexit scenario. The Brexit-StBG entered into force on 29 March 2019 and refers to an unspecified date of withdrawal of the UK. It will therefore also cover a withdrawal of the UK without a deal following any further extension of the process under Article 50 of the Treaty on European Union (TEU).[6] In different fields of law, the Brexit-StBG includes Brexit-related rules in existing statutory acts. As its main aspects, the bill introduces (1) tax provisions intended to prevent disadvantages for taxpayers arising solely as a result of the UK's withdrawal, (2) labour law provisions limiting the protection against dismissal for highly paid 'material risk takers' and (3) grandfathering provisions for investments in assets located in the UK in connection with the Covered Bond Act (*Pfandbriefgesetz*—**PfandBG**) and the Building Societies Act (*Bausparkassengesetz*—**BauSparkG**). From a regulatory perspective, the most relevant aspect of the Brexit-StBG is that it also provides for (4) a national transitional regime for market participants from the UK in case of a hard Brexit. This regime is described in further detail in the following.

6.2.2.2 Scope of general transitional regime

The Brexit-StBG introduces transitional rules for the following regulated market participants and trading venues that target the German market from the UK:

(i) credit institutions;
(ii) investment firms;
(iii) insurance undertakings;
(iv) payment institutions and electronic money institutions; as well as
(v) regulated markets, multilateral trading facilities (**MTFs**) and organised trading facilities (**OTFs**).

The transitional rules relate to market participants from the 'United Kingdom of Great Britain and Northern Ireland'. They do not explicitly refer to Gibraltar which, although not forming part of the United Kingdom, is subject to EU law as a 'European territory for whose external relations a Member State is responsible'.[7] Absent any related guidance by the regulator, Gibraltar entities currently operating under a European passport in Germany will not benefit from the transitional rules of the Brexit-StBG based on the letter of the law.

Furthermore, the general transitional regime only covers UK *entities* operating under a European passport. The Brexit-StBG does not refer to services provided by UK *branches* of EEA institutions back to clients in the EU (so-called back-branching). The European regulators have announced that they will not accept (at least comprehensive) 'back-branching'

---

[5] Act on Taxation-Related Provisions concerning the Withdrawal of the United Kingdom of Great Britain and Northern Ireland from the European Union (Tax Act relating to Brexit) dated 25 March 2019, Federal Law Gazette I, p. 357.

[6] Similar issues will arise in the event the UK withdraws from the EU with a deal and no equivalence framework is in place after the end of the European transitional period; however, the (current) wording of the German transitional rules do not cover such scenario.

[7] Art. 355(3) of the Treaty on the Functioning of the European Union (TFEU).

structures of EEA institutions after Brexit.[8] However, given that the UK branches are only a dependent part of the EEA legal entity from a corporate law perspective, it can be argued that they share and benefit from the regulatory status of the legal entity as a whole. Provided that the legal entity is duly licensed or passported in Germany, the question of whether any form of 'back-branching' from its London branch is permissible thus has to be answered pursuant to internal organisational requirements applicable to the EEA entity, but not under the transitional regime for the market access in Germany.

6.2.2.3 General transitional periods

6.12 BaFin is empowered to allow the UK entities covered by the transitional regime that have operated in Germany under the European passport regime so far to continue to provide certain services without a German licence, each for a period of up to twenty-one months following a hard Brexit. With respect to UK credit institutions and investment firms that, as applicable, conduct banking business or provide investment services in Germany through a branch or on a cross-border basis under a European passport on the withdrawal date, BaFin may determine that the passport regime under the Banking Act (*Kreditwesengesetz—* **KWG**) is to be applied *mutatis mutandis*, fully or partially, during the national transition period.[9] With respect to UK insurance undertakings, BaFin may determine that the respective passport rules under the Insurance Supervision Act (*Versicherungsaufsichtsgesetz—***VAG**) continue to apply to UK insurers and reinsurers operating in Germany under a passport on the withdrawal date.[10] With respect to UK payment institutions and electronic money institutions, BaFin may similarly determine that the respective passport regime under the Payment Services Supervision Act (*Zahlungsdiensteaufsichtsgesetz—***ZAG**) applies accordingly, fully or partially.[11]

6.13 In addition to the transition periods relating to the different European passport regimes, the Brexit-StBG also introduces a transitional period for the national rules on third country trading venues. BaFin may order that UK markets for financial instruments listed as trading venues in the respective register of ESMA at the time of withdrawal are deemed to be trading venues within the meaning of the Securities Trading Act (*Wertpapierhandelsgesetz—* **WpHG**) for a transitional period of up to twenty-one months.[12] During such period, no application for an authorisation as a third country trading venue will be needed, thus allowing German participants to continue their trading activities on these regulated markets, MTFs and OTFs. It should be noted, however, that EU27 investment firms may be affected by the implications of the trading obligations under the European Markets in Financial Instruments Regulation (**MiFIR**) when using trading venues in the UK.

6.14 BaFin is authorised to issue and publicly announce the different transitional periods by means of general decree (*Allgemeinverfügung*) without any prior hearing.[13] Such general

---

[8] See, for example, ESMA, 'MiFID II Supervisory briefing on the supervision of non-EU branches of EU firms providing investment services and activities', 6 February 2019.
[9] Section 53b(12) KWG.
[10] Section 66a(1) VAG.
[11] Section 39(8) ZAG.
[12] Section 102(4) WpHG.
[13] See s. 53b(12) Sentence 4 KWG, s. 66a(1) Sentence 3 VAG, s. 39(8) Sentence 4 ZAG, and s. 102(4) Sentence 3 WpHG.

transition periods will apply to all covered UK entities without the need for any additional application or notification procedure.

6.2.2.4 Limitations of the general transitional periods
However, the general transitional periods are limited in several respects. BaFin has discretionary powers as to the exact scope, modalities, and duration and may impose additional conditions. Based on the parliamentary debate relating to the Brexit-StBG, BaFin intends to shorten the transitional periods to one year as a first step and to only assess an extension at a later stage. Further, it is possible that BaFin excludes certain activities from the scope of the transitional regimes (e.g. with a view to deposit protection).

6.15

Even without any restrictions imposed by BaFin, the statutory scope of the general transitional regime is limited in relation to new business after Brexit. UK credit institutions, investment firms, payment institutions, and electronic money institutions are only authorised to conduct their regulated activities if these activities are 'closely connected' to a contract that existed at the time of withdrawal.[14] The bill's explanatory statement mentions certain examples of the required 'close connection' such as

6.16

   (i) hedging transactions,
  (ii) lifecycle events,
 (iii) netting transactions,
 (iv) portfolio compression transactions,
  (v) prolongations, or
 (vi) the exercise of contractual option or conversion rights.

An even stricter limitation applies with respect to UK insurance undertakings: The transitional regime only covers the run-off of insurance contracts that were concluded before the time of withdrawal.[15] The background for such limitations is that the German legislator only wants to avoid disadvantages for the financial market and the counterparties in Germany. For that purpose, the Brexit-StBG protects the continuity of existing contracts and provides for certain grandfathering, but does not authorise UK institutions to continue their passported business in Germany without restraint.

6.17

6.2.2.5 Specific relief measure for proprietary business
Given the limitations as to new business, cross-border regulated trading activities of UK entities would not be possible under the general transition periods. The exclusion of British market participants, however, would also result in the loss of market liquidity on German trading venues. Therefore, at a late stage of the legislative procedure, a specific relief measure for certain trading activities of UK entities in addition to the general transition periods was also included in the Brexit-StBG.

6.18

Limited to 'proprietary business' (*Eigengeschäft*), UK entities will be deemed to have been granted an exemption from the licensing requirement[16] with effect from the withdrawal

6.19

---

[14] Section 53b(12) Sentence 2 KWG, s. 39(8) Sentence 4 ZAG.
[15] Section 66a(1) Sentence 1 VAG.
[16] Such exemption from the licensing requirement is set out in s. 2(5) KWG.

date if they file a 'complete' application with BaFin within three months after Brexit.[17] The exact documentation to be filed is not stipulated by the statutory provisions, but will depend on BaFin's administrative practice. A certain indication is the documentation necessary for an earlier transitional procedure that is referred to for the purposes of the specific Brexit relief measure: BaFin required, in particular, a 'statement of no prior or pending convictions' (*Straffreiheitserklärung*) signed by each of the board members of the applicant. The enclosures further included a detailed description of the business activities, current financial statements, sample contract forms and the appointment of a receiving agent in Germany.

6.20 'Proprietary business' (*Eigengeschäft*) is one of two regulated activities that transpose into German law the investment service 'dealing on own account' set out in the second European Markets in Financial Instruments Directive (**MiFID II**). The additional relief measure may thus be relevant for continued regulated trading activities of UK entities on own account in Germany.[18] However, this specific measure will not cover the regulated activity of 'proprietary trading' (*Eigenhandel*), i.e. 'dealing on own account' that is provided as a service for others. 'Proprietary trading' includes, in particular, the activities of market makers and systematic internalisers. High-frequency trading is deemed to be a case of 'proprietary trading' (even if not provided as a service for others) and will therefore not benefit from the specific relief measure either.

6.2.3 National Approach to Authorisation

6.21 Pursuant to the explanatory statement in the government's draft of the Brexit-StBG, the German federal government expects UK institutions to either terminate the relevant business relationships with its German clients, obtain a German licence (by establishing a dependent branch) or transfer the respective business to a provider licensed in Germany before the end of the national transitional periods. Due to the described limitations and shortcomings of both the general transitional regime and the specific relief measure under the Brexit-StBG, however, UK market participants will have to take into consideration potential German licensing requirements already from the withdrawal date.

6.2.3.1 Competent authorities

6.22 Germany participates in the Single Supervisory Mechanism (**SSM**) established in the eurozone. Therefore, with respect to credit institutions that conduct at least deposit business and lending business (**CRR credit institutions**), the supervisory responsibilities are shared between the European Central Bank (**ECB**) and BaFin as the national competent authority:[19] The ECB directly supervises significant CRR credit institutions, whereas BaFin, in principle, directly supervises less significant CRR credit institutions. With respect to all CRR

---

[17] Section 64m(2) KWG in conjunction with s. 64x(8) Sentence 1 KWG.

[18] The German government published a draft bill in September 2019 introducing a new exemption from the licensing requirement for all non-EEA entities dealing on own account as a member or participant of a trading venue. However, the government's draft exemption does not cover dealing on own account (i) by means of 'direct electronic access' to a German trading venue and (ii) with certain derivatives and emissions allowances (or derivatives thereof). The specific Brexit relief measure covers the latter cases as well and, therefore, will remain relevant for UK entities.

[19] See Art. 6(4) of Regulation (EU) No. 1024/2013 (**SSM Regulation**).

credit institutions regardless of their significance, however, only the ECB grants and withdraws an authorisation and ultimately assesses notifications of the acquisition and disposal of qualifying holdings.

Outside the scope of the SSM, BaFin remains responsible for the authorisation of other credit institutions[20] and for the authorisation of investment firms, insurance undertakings, payment and electronic money institutions as well as fund management companies. Also, BaFin authorises and supervises dependent branches of institutions from third countries. The German Central Bank (Deutsche Bundesbank—**Bundesbank**) assists both the ECB and BaFin in their supervision.

6.23

6.2.3.2 Territorial scope of German licensing requirements

UK institutions without a physical presence in Germany will not be exempted from the German licensing requirements. Anyone wishing to conduct banking business or to provide financial services in Germany commercially or on a scale which requires commercially organised business operations requires written authorisation.[21] Based on the administrative practice of BaFin set out in related guidance notices,[22] the regulated activities can be conducted 'in Germany' not only if the provider has its registered office or ordinary residence inside Germany. Pursuant to BaFin, if the provider has its registered office or ordinary residence outside of Germany, the licensing requirement will be triggered if the provider *targets the German market* in order to offer banking products or financial services repeatedly and on a commercial basis to German residents. BaFin has given examples of typical scenarios giving rise to a licensing requirement such as the use of brokers in Germany, websites aimed at the German market and advertisement of specific services.

6.24

6.2.3.3 Reverse solicitation exemption

Certain cross-border services from the UK, however, will not trigger the licensing requirements. BaFin has generally recognised an exemption in case of a reverse solicitation scenario, i.e. cross-border services of a third country provider requested at the *own exclusive initiative* of a German client. This exemption is based on the so-called freedom to provide requested services (*passive Dienstleistungsfreiheit*) defined as the right of persons and entities domiciled in Germany to request the services of a foreign entity on their own initiative. Such exception is explicitly stipulated for requested investment services and activities under MiFID II.[23] In its related guidance notices, BaFin states that such exemption may also cover maintaining an existing relationship without a German licence.[24]

6.25

However, it should be noted that the exact scope of the reverse solicitation exemption (in particular, in relation to an existing relationship) has become subject to political debate. ESMA has been rather restrictive in recent publications on the reverse solicitation

6.26

---

[20] The scope of the definition of a 'credit institution' under German law is wider than the scope of the definition set out in the CRR (only one type of banking business needs to be conducted).

[21] Section 32(1) Sentence 1 KWG.

[22] BaFin, 'Notes regarding the licensing for conducting cross-border banking business and/or providing cross-border financial services' dated 5 April 2005 (last amended 11 March 2019).

[23] Art. 42 MiFID II.

[24] See n. 22.

exemption and has excluded the sale of other services and products in case of a one-off investment service.[25]

6.2.3.4 Exemption of cross-border services in the individual case

6.27 The explanatory statement of the Brexit-StBG mentions that the general powers of BaFin remain unaffected by the transitional rules. For third country entities, such general powers include an exemption in the individual case: on application, BaFin may grant a non-EEA institution that intends to provide regulated services in Germany on a cross-border basis an exemption from the German licensing requirement if the institution does not require additional supervision by BaFin due to the supervision by the competent authority in its home country.[26]

6.28 The German regulator, however, has discretion as to the granting of such exemption. The explanatory statement of the Brexit-StBG gives two examples for exemptions that BaFin may grant following Brexit: a transitional exemption until a licence has been granted and an exemption for purposes of the orderly run-off of business—both examples are rather interim measures. Also, the Brexit-StBG will introduce a specific relief measure limited to 'proprietary business' (*Eigengeschäft*) as described. BaFin may be rather reluctant to grant exemptions under general rules going beyond the scope of the specific measure. So far, BaFin has not publicly announced that it will be willing to grant UK institutions individual exemptions under the general third country rules.

6.2.3.5 Administrative guidance for licence applications

6.29 In case a UK entity cannot rely on any of the described exemptions, it will have to establish a dependent branch or an independent subsidiary that applies for a German licence. Such application will have to comprise comprehensive information and documentation as required by the regulators.

6.30 On their websites, BaFin and Bundesbank have each published administrative guidance specifically for UK institutions that intend to apply for a German licence. In particular, BaFin has provided a list of frequently asked questions (**FAQs**) on Brexit[27] and offers a contact form for financial services providers wishing to move their registered office or operations to Germany. BaFin confirms in its FAQ, for example, that it already accepts applications for a licence as third country branch by UK entities which, however, will only become effective upon a hard Brexit.

6.31 Other administrative materials relate to applications for a licence in general. With respect to credit institutions, BaFin and Bundesbank have issued a guidance notice on the granting of an authorisation.[28] Specific details of the submission process and of the contents of the application can also be found in a checklist provided by BaFin.[29]

---

[25] ESMA, 'Questions and Answers on MiFID II and MiFIR investor protection and intermediaries topics' (dated 28 March 2019), Topic 13, Question 4.
[26] Section 2(5) KWG.
[27] BaFin, 'FAQs on Brexit' (last updated 24 March 2017).
[28] BaFin/Bundesbank, 'Guidance notice on the granting of authorisation to conduct banking business pursuant to s. 32(1) of the German Banking Act', 31 December 2007 (only available in German).
[29] BaFin, 'Checklist: Authorisation as a credit institution, 20 August 2017' (last amended 14 November 2017).

6.32 With respect to investment firms, Bundesbank has published a corresponding guidance notice on the granting of an authorisation.[30] However, it should be noted that the application procedure with respect to investment firms has been harmonised on the European level under MiFID II: when applying for an authorisation as investment firm, applicants must provide the information set out in a Commission Delegated Regulation[31] and must use a standard application form attached to a Commission Implementing Regulation.[32] Although the statutory German rules relating to the application procedure thus have been replaced by directly applicable European law, BaFin has published additional guidance notes regarding the information to be filled in the European standard forms on its website.

6.2.3.6 Substance requirements in Germany

6.33 With respect to the Brexit-driven licensing applications in Germany, manifold individual or general issues may arise for the UK group entities. As in other EU27 Member States, however, one of the crucial points is the required substance of the new subsidiary or branch in Germany. BaFin has placed importance on institutions setting up and maintaining appropriate governance structures and a functioning risk management system. The German regulator requires that internal control procedures as well as an independent risk control and compliance function are established in Germany. The special functions of risk control, compliance and internal auditing must be adequately equipped both in terms of personnel and technology. Furthermore, these functions must also be granted a full, unlimited right to information. Generally, staffing requirements are discussed in connection with the application procedures, in particular the amount of time for which the members of the management body are present and available on site in Germany.

6.3 France

6.3.1 Introduction

6.34 In the event of a no-deal Brexit, France has not put in place contingency measures such as a national transitional regime for UK credit institutions and investment firms. After exit day,[33] UK credit institutions and investment firms will be subject to the standard regime applicable in France to non-EEA firms, pursuant to which a non-EEA credit institution or investment firm must be licensed by French authorities in order to carry out banking transactions or provide investment services in France, unless it falls within one of the few exemptions available (see below).

---

[30] Bundesbank, 'Notice on the granting of authorisation to provide financial services pursuant to s. 32(1) of the German Banking Act', 6 July 2018.
[31] Delegated Regulation (EU) 2017/1943.
[32] Implementing Regulation (EU) 2017/1945.
[33] The day on which the UK leaves the EU, at the time of writing this is 31 January 2020 at 11:00 pm (GMT).

6.3.2 French Competent Authorities

6.35 The Autorité de contrôle prudentiel et de résolution (**ACPR**) is responsible for approving and supervising credit institutions and investment firms, including French branches of non-EEA credit institutions.[34] As France participates in the SSM, French incorporated credit institutions are formally approved by the ECB.[35] As part of the approval process of investment firms run by the ACPR, the programme of activities of investment firms must be submitted to and approved by the Autorité des marchés financiers (**AMF**).[36]

6.3.3 French Approach to a No-Deal Brexit

6.36 The ACPR introduced at the end of 2016,[37] i.e. far before the initial exit day,[38] a simplified fast-track procedure designed to allow UK institutions, that conducted prior to exit day regulated activities in France by using the EU passport, a streamlined application procedure if they wished to create a French entity and seek a licence in France as an investment firm, payment institution, electronic money institution, or insurance company (but not as a credit institution). Under this procedure, a French licence could be sought on the basis of a specific, shorter, and simplified application form, and the whole procedure could be run in English (while the French language is usually the working language of French authorities). As this procedure was designed to target activities that were already under the supervision of the UK authorities, the ACPR relied on information previously provided by UK firms to the UK authorities in relation to their pre-existing French activities and presumably on feedback from the UK authorities themselves. This simplified fast-track procedure is said to have been used by a rather large number of investment firms since 2016 and has led to licensing on shorter timescales.

6.37 This simplified French fast-track procedure has not been made available to credit institutions in relation to their banking activities, as the ECB remains the competent authority. The AMF has implemented a similar procedure for asset management companies (which do not qualify as investment firms).[39]

6.38 As the fast-track procedure has been in place for some time, France has not introduced any national transitional measures for UK participants after exit day. In addition, the fast-track procedure is expected to cease to operate when the UK leaves the EU. As a result, after exit day any non-EEA entity, whether or not it had pre-existing activities in France, will have to seek a licence as an investment firm under the standard procedure.

---

[34] Art. L. 612-1 and Art. L. 612-2 of the Code Monétaire et Financier (**CMF**).
[35] Art. L. 511-10 of the CMF.
[36] Art. L. 532-1 and Art. L. 532-48 of the CMF.
[37] 'The Autorité de contrôle prudentiel et de résolution (ACPR) and the Autorité des marchés financiers (AMF) are simplifying and speeding up licensing procedures in the context of BREXIT', press release, jointly issued by the ACPR and AMF, on 28 September 2016.
[38] 29 March 2019.
[39] 'The AMF is creating a dedicated welcome programme for management firms and FinTech companies based in the UK: AGILITY', AMF press release, 28 September 2016.

However, France has introduced a limited number of specific temporary relief measures in the event of a no-deal Brexit. The following is a summary of the applicable regime as from exit day. **6.39**

6.3.4 Continuity of Contracts

After a no-deal Brexit, UK credit institutions and investment firms will lose the benefit of the EU passport and will no longer be able to carry out regulated activities in France. As a result, a potential cliff-edge risk has been feared by the industry and its regulators with respect to the continuity of existing cross-border contracts. The European Banking Authority (EBA) expressed its concerns in its opinion of 25 June 2018,[40] and urged financial institutions to identify the existing or future contracts (including derivative contracts) that were going to be affected[41] by the loss of benefit of the EU passport. Indeed, the performance of existing contracts after exit day may amount to the provision of regulated services or ancillary services or actions. The ACPR indicated in June 2018[42] that contracts entered into prior to Brexit remain valid and must be performed in good faith. In February 2019, the French government took measures,[43] only applicable in the event of a no-deal Brexit, providing that the ACPR would keep the power to control, and impose sanctions on, UK credit institutions and investment firms which, after exit day, perform obligations pursuant to existing contracts entered into prior to Brexit, or for any breach of French regulations they committed prior to exit day.[44] However, a report of the French Treasury on these measures[45] stated that the loss of the EU passport will prevent UK firms from entering into new contracts after exit day. The latter statement highlights the strict application of the French monopoly (see below) to third country (non-EEA) firms. **6.40**

With regard to the continuity of master agreements used for the provision of financial services (such as ISDA agreements), a French ordinance[46] provides that in the event of a no-deal Brexit and for a period of twelve months from exit day, French or EU companies that have entered prior to exit day into a master agreement with a UK credit institution or investment firm will be deemed to accept that such master agreement be substituted with a new master agreement to be entered into with a French or EU credit institution or investment firm, provided the latter belongs to the same group as the initial UK credit institution or investment **6.41**

---

[40] 'Opinion of the European Banking Authority on preparations for the withdrawal of the United Kingdom from the European Union' dated 25 June 2018 (EBA/Op/2018/05).
[41] 'Opinion of the European Banking Authority on preparations for the withdrawal of the United Kingdom from the European Union' dated 25 June 2018 (EBA/Op/2018/05), p. 6.
[42] 'Mesures destinées à faire face aux effets du BREXIT', ACPR press release, June 2018.
[43] Ordinance n°2019-75 dated 6 February 2019 relating to the preparatory measures of the withdrawal of the United Kingdom from European Union for financial services, as amended by Ordinance n°2019-236 dated 27 March 2019.
[44] 'Rapport au Président de la République relatif à l'ordonnance n° 2019-75 du 6 février 2019 relative aux mesures de préparation au retrait du Royaume-Uni de l'Union Européenne en matière de services financiers', JORF n°0032, 7 February 2019.
[45] 'Brexit : Mesures de préparation en matière de services financiers en cas de Brexit sans accord, Adoption of the ordinance pertaining to measures of preparation to the United Kingdom's withdrawal from the European Union in the area of financial services', Direction Générale du Trésor press release, 26 February 2019.
[46] Ordinance n°2019-75 dated 6 February 2019 relating to the preparatory measures of the withdrawal of the United Kingdom from European Union for financial services, as amended by Ordinance n°2019-236 dated 27 March 2019.

firm, the terms and conditions of the new master agreement are identical to the previous one (with the exception of governing law, jurisdiction clause, and minor adaptations resulting from such changes) and a few formal conditions are met.

6.3.5 French Monopoly

6.42 French law provides for the French banking monopoly and the French investment services monopoly which forbid any entity other than a licensed entity from carrying out, in the normal course of its business, respectively banking activities[47] and investment services[48] in France, unless it benefits from one of the few exemptions available. The French banking monopoly appears wider-reaching and stricter than in most other EU countries insofar as virtually all lending activities are caught by it.[49]

6.3.6 Territorial Application of the French Monopoly

6.43 The French banking and investment services monopolies apply on a territorial basis, only to those activities deemed to be carried out in France. French law does not define the criteria to be considered to establish the localisation of activities in France and, according to case law, this issue is to be assessed on an ad hoc basis by French courts, using the totality of circumstances test so as to assess the extent to which, pursuant to relevant criteria, there are relevant contacts with France. Criteria to be considered may include (this list is not exhaustive): where the characteristic performance of the agreement has taken place, where parties are located or the agreement with the client is deemed to be entered into or performed, how and where contact between the parties was established, whether active marketing took place in France, the willingness to target French clients and enter/develop the French market, where the due diligence, know-your-customer/anti-money laundering process is conducted, and/or where an account is held or receives delivery of funds or securities.[50]

6.3.7 Reverse Solicitation Exemption

6.44 In relation to investment services only (and not banking activities), third country credit institutions and investment firms may rely on the general reverse solicitation exemption, available irrespective of Brexit.[51] Under this exemption, an unlicensed entity may provide an investment service in France, provided that the client's request has not been solicited, whether directly or indirectly, on a personal basis and the regulated investment service that

---

[47] Art. L. 511-5 of the CMF.
[48] Art. L. 531-1 of the CMF.
[49] 'Rapport sur le monopole bancaire' (Haut Comité Juridique de la Place financière de Paris, dated 14 March 2016), p. 95.
[50] 'Rapport sur le monopole bancaire' (Haut Comité Juridique de la Place financière de Paris, dated 14 March 2016), pp. 68 to 70.
[51] Art. L. 532-51 of the CMF.

is provided has been specifically and explicitly requested by the client.[52] Provided the required conditions are met, the reverse solicitation exemption would allow an unlicensed UK firm to continue providing existing services or to provide a new service after Brexit in France. The assessment of whether or not reverse solicitation exists is very much an ad hoc factual assessment, which parties should be able to prove.

6.3.8 Standard Procedure for Non-EEA Entities Following Exit Day

6.45 As France has not introduced any transitional relief, following Brexit, any UK credit institution[53] and investment firm[54] will need to follow the standard procedure in place for the licensing of non-EEA entities. The procedure for a new authorisation as a credit institution or investment firm will require a comprehensive application file. It will usually take about six to twelve months for a bank,[55] less for an investment firm.[56] There is no indication from French authorities that a UK credit institution or investment firm would be treated differently than other non-EEA entities after a no-deal Brexit.

6.3.9 French Guidelines in Relation to the Use of Third Party Employees or Technical Means

6.46 Once a UK entity establishes a licensed operation in France, the question arises as to the use by the French licensed operation of third party employees or technical means, whether or not located outside the EEA. The ACPR has not issued general or specific rules or guidelines on the use by French operations of UK owned entities of third party employees or technical means. Any such arrangements will need to be described in detail in the initial licensing application file and the programme of activities that the entity must provide as part of the application file. The ACPR will assess whether the employees and technical means provided for are adequate and proportionate to the proposed programme of activities and prospective turnover and will require a reasonable level of presence in France. With respect to this issue, the ACPR is said to agree to and follow in practice very closely the principles laid down by the EBA,[57] the ECB, and the ESMA.

6.3.10 Required Substance in France

6.47 Although a local substance is required in order to establish a credit institution or investment firm in France, it is possible in practice to organise arrangements designed to allow a French operation to rely on non-French entities or employees, provided these arrangements do

---

[52] Art. 314-8 of the Règlement général of the AMF.
[53] Art. L. 511-10 of the CMF.
[54] Art. L. 532-1 of the CMF.
[55] Art. R. 511-2-1 of the CMF.
[56] Art. R. 532-3 of the CMF.
[57] 'Notice de conformité aux Orientations de l'Autorité bancaire européenne relatives à l'externalisation', ACPR press release, July 2019.

not lead to the creation of 'letter-box' or 'empty shell' entities in France[58] and provided that French operations retain overall responsibility for activities in France.[59] Such arrangements may take the form of 'outsourcing' or 'dual-hatting' arrangements. According to the ACPR, following exit day, UK activities in France must be transferred to entities fully capable of overseeing all risks, and running such arrangements in a way that allows them to control and monitor their activities and processes notwithstanding the implementation of such arrangements, and to carry out independent risk assessment and monitoring[60] by using governance and risk management processes that are adequate to the nature, scale, and complexity of their activities.[61] Compliance with these requirements is to be assessed on a case-by-case basis by the ACPR.

6.3.11 Outsourcing Arrangements

6.48 The ACPR expects banks and investment firms to implement efficient risk control processes within France. These risk control processes must ensure proper monitoring by the management of the French bank or investment firm in compliance with applicable regulatory requirements.

6.49 In addition, any outsourcing arrangement implemented must ensure the operational independence of the bank or investment firm, and provide for efficient contingency procedures guaranteeing continuity of the bank's or investment firm's activities. Local oversight of the outsourced activities or services and full access by supervisors to relevant information are essential features that an outsourcing arrangement must have. Outsourcing arrangements are assessed and reviewed by the ACPR on a case-by-case basis.[62]

6.50 According to the ACPR and the ECB, branches in third countries should be used primarily to meet local needs, and not to perform critical functions for a bank or investment firm established in France or to provide services to operations or clients in other countries.[63]

6.3.12 'Dual-hatting' within Group Entities

6.51 The ACPR also scrutinises 'dual-hatting' arrangements. The ACPR will ensure that UK banks and investment firms established in France have sufficient staff (including the number of employees and the time devoted to such functions) located in France and perform required functions, including in relation to risk management and front office.[64]

---

[58] 'Rapport sur le Brexit, activités bancaires et services d'investissement' (Haut Comité Juridique de la Place financière de Paris, 15 October 2018), 'Opinion of the European Banking Authority on preparations for the withdrawal of the United Kingdom from the European Union', dated 25 June 2018 (EBA/Op/2018/05).
[59] EBA Guidelines on outsourcing arrangements, 25 February 2019 (EBA/GL/2019/02).
[60] Consultation Paper, EBA Draft Guidelines on outsourcing arrangements, 22 June 2018 (EBA/CP/2018/11).
[61] Relocating to the euro area, ECB, 31 May 2018.
[62] Relocating to the euro area, ECB, 31 May 2018.
[63] Relocating to the euro area, ECB, 31 May 2018, 'Rapport sur le Brexit, activités bancaires et services d'investissement' (Haut Comité Juridique de la Place financière de Paris, 15 October 2018).
[64] Relocating to the euro area, ECB, 31 May 2018.

6.52 Any 'dual-hatting' arrangement implemented should guarantee a local and independent organisation dealing with key functions such as risk control, compliance, and internal audit, with local responsibilities and efficient reporting lines to local management.[65] Any such arrangement must ensure that the management body of a French bank or investment firm devotes adequate resources and sufficient time to management of risk issues, independent of operational functions.[66]

6.4 Netherlands

6.4.1 Introduction

6.53 The Netherlands has seen quite a number of licence applications since the announcement of Brexit. The Netherlands has mostly been selected by trading venues and parties that deal for own account ('proprietary traders') as the place to establish their EU27 entity. The reasons we often hear are that Amsterdam offers good facilities with the presence of good infrastructure (Schiphol and good public transportation), quality of life, the fact that everyone speaks (proper) English, and that the regulators have longstanding experience with these kinds of financial institutions, with Euronext being the world's oldest exchange.

6.54 One other factor is that the strict Dutch bonus cap rules (under Dutch law the bonus is capped to a maximum of 20% of the annual fixed salary) in principle do not apply to such entities. The bonus cap rules do apply to other financial institutions such as credit institutions, insurers and asset managers.

6.4.2 Dutch Brexit Legislation

6.4.2.1 Dutch Brexit Act

6.55 On 16 November 2018, the Dutch Minister of Justice and Security (*Minister van Justitie en Veiligheid*) submitted a legislative proposal to the Dutch Parliament proposing changes to a number of laws and regulations in the Netherlands in preparation for Brexit (the **Dutch Brexit Act**).

6.56 The explanatory notes to the Dutch Brexit Act provide that the proposal is a product of an inventory that was carried out to see whether Dutch laws needed to be amended as a result of Brexit. This inventory was based on the fact that the withdrawal of the UK will lead to the loss of its EU membership, irrespective of whether consensus will be reached on a withdrawal agreement or the UK leaves the EU without an agreement in place (no-deal Brexit). For most cases, it turned out that the existing legislative frameworks offer sufficient freedom to be able to act quickly and adequately in each of the currently foreseen scenarios. Therefore, the Dutch Brexit Act only contains technical amendments to Dutch legislation that are strictly necessary and need to enter into effect as of a no-deal Brexit.

---

[65] Relocating to the euro area, ECB, 31 May 2018.
[66] Relocating to the euro area, ECB, 31 May 2018.

6.57 In view of the complexity and the amount of legislation possibly affected by Brexit, the Dutch legislator believes it to be important that quick legislative action can be taken in cases of urgent, unforeseen issues resulting from Brexit. This only insofar as is necessary for the proper implementation of a Brexit-related binding EU legal act or to avoid unacceptable consequences. Therefore, the Dutch Brexit Act contains a generic provision making it possible to quickly take necessary legislative action by means of a general administrative order or ministerial decree instead of by changing the law. These emergency legislative actions will in principle have a transitional nature, meaning that they will generally apply only temporarily and/or will be substituted by a more structural/formal legislative action.

6.58 It is important to note that neither the Dutch Brexit Act nor the explanatory notes thereto include (or mention) changes or measures aimed specifically at the financial sector. However, the aforementioned generic provision can also be used as a basis for legislative actions that may need to be taken in the financial sector. In addition, the Dutch government and the Dutch regulatory authorities have been focusing on the possible implications of Brexit.

6.4.2.2 Exemption for investment firms

6.59 In February 2019 a transitional regime has been published for investment firms (*beleggingsondernemingen*) with their seat in the UK in case of a no-deal Brexit. For other financial institutions such as banks, regulated markets and insurers, no transitional regimes have been proposed (yet). This would mean that in case of a no-deal Brexit, these financial institutions will be treated as third country firms under the Act on the Financial Supervision (*Wet op het financieel toezicht*, **AFS**) and in principle require authorisation in order to continue to provide regulated services within the Netherlands.

6.60 The amendments to the Exemption Regulation AFS (*Vrijstellingsregeling Wft*, the **Exemption Regulation**) in relation to the (temporary) exemption for investment firms based in the UK was published in the Dutch government gazette (*Staatsblad*), stipulating that Article 10 of the Exemption Regulation will apply to investment firms with their seat in the UK if the UK and the EU have not entered into an agreement on the exit of the UK from the EU.

6.61 The consequence of this exemption is that investment firms with their seat in the UK are exempted from the licence obligation for providing investment services and/or the investment activity of dealing on own account in the Netherlands, insofar provided to professional investors or eligible counterparties. A condition is that the investment firm will need to be supervised in the UK and it will need to notify the Netherlands Authority for the Financial Markets (*Autoriteit Financiële Markten*, the **AFM**). The investment firm will largely be exempted from the prudential and ongoing conduct of business requirements as set out in the AFS.

6.62 The exemption will apply to investment firms from the UK acting on a cross-border basis or via a branch office in the Netherlands. The fee for the notification to the AFM is €4,400.

6.63 The date of entry into force of this exemption can be set by means of a ministerial decree (where necessary retroactively). This means that any registration of UK investment firms is currently still conditional to such ministerial decree in case of a no-deal Brexit. If there is a deal on Brexit and a transitional regime for investment firms, registration under this exemption will not take place.

Despite the aforementioned conditionality, UK investment firms are nevertheless urged to register themselves with the AFM as soon as possible. The notification form that needs to be used for this purpose is available on the AFM's website.   **6.64**

6.4.3 Dutch Regulators

In the Netherlands the so-called twin peaks model has been in place since March 2002. This means that there are two regulators which are both responsible for supervising the Dutch financial markets and the players on that market.   **6.65**

6.4.3.1 Netherlands Authority for the Financial Markets
The AFM is responsible for supervising the financial institutions to comply with the conduct of business rules. This means that the AFM supervises the conduct of the financial institutions relating to savings, investment, insurance, loans, pensions, capital markets, asset management, accountancy and financial reporting. In addition, the AFM grants the licence in relation to investment firms, collective investment fund managers, and financial services providers.   **6.66**

6.4.3.2 Dutch Central Bank
The Dutch Central Bank (*De Nederlandsche Bank*, the **DNB**) is responsible for supervising the financial institutions to comply with the prudential requirements. In addition, the DNB grants the licence in relation to credit institutions (together with the European Central Bank), payment services providers, (re)insurers, pension funds, clearing and settlement institutions.   **6.67**

6.4.3.3 Ministry of Finance
The Dutch of Finance (**Minister**) is the Dutch legislator but is also responsible for granting licences to operators of regulated markets. After a licence has been granted, the AFM is responsible for the ongoing supervision of the licensed regulated markets.   **6.68**

6.4.4 Licence Obligation and Exemptions

Under Dutch law, a licence obligation exists in principle and (in short), if services are provided to entities or persons in the Netherlands or if trading activities for own account of such trader take place on Dutch trading venues. A licence should be obtained prior to providing the services or undertaking the activities in the Netherlands.   **6.69**

6.4.4.1 Initiative test/reverse solicitation
No licence (or European passport) is required if a non-Dutch financial institution is contacted by a Dutch entity or resident. The non-Dutch financial institution should not be   **6.70**

marketing its services to Dutch entities or residents. There is no explicit guidance on the conditions to be able to rely on reverse solicitation.

6.4.4.2 Exemption to the licence obligation

6.71 The AFM can exempt trading venues from their licence obligation. This exemption should be used for trading venues outside the EU for activities that are similar to a regulated market or a multilateral trading facility (MTF). The trading venue must demonstrate that it meets the licence requirements prescribed by the AFS in order to qualify for the exemption. This can be tricky because most provisions are based on European legislation.

6.4.5 Licence Application Procedure

6.4.5.1 Regulated market

6.72 A regulated market may not be operated or managed without a licence in the Netherlands. A regulated market should apply for a licence from the Minister. The Minister provides the AFM with the data for the licence application and requests the AFM to render its advice. The Minister will only decide on the licence application after the Minister has received AFM's advice. It is not a legal requirement that the Minister requests advice from the AFM, however, in practise this is always requested. In principle the Minister should decide on the application no later than eight weeks of receipt of the licence application. Should the Minister request additional information, then the general decision period does not start until the information is provided. Any subsequent changes to the information supplied in the licence application need to be provided to the AFM directly.

6.4.5.2 Investment services

6.73 Article 1:1 of the AFS gives a list of the various investment services and investment activities. To provide investment services means providing services to clients relating to financial instruments. Performing investment activities means: (i) to deal on own account; and (ii) to operate an MTF or an OTF.

6.74 According to the AFS, an investment firm is not allowed to perform investment services or activities in the Netherlands without the proper licence. The AFS states that the AFM shall in principle decide on the licence application within thirteen weeks of receipt of the application. Should the AFM request additional information, this period shall not start until the information is provided. However, the AFM has to make a decision within six months of receipt of the licence application.

6.4.5.3 Substance

6.75 A very important aspect for UK firms to consider when seeking to establish a presence in the Netherlands is substance: how many persons will the new Dutch entity have on the ground in the Netherlands? The ESMA has published its opinions which set out that the newly established entities in the EU27 Member States should not be so-called letterbox entities and what is allowed in relation to outsourcing back to the UK.

6.76 No explicit guidance has been provided by the Dutch regulators on how many persons on the ground are required. This will depend on the circumstances of the to-be regulated entity. All regulators of the EU27 Member States have to report to ESMA on what kind of entities have applied for a licence and on certain aspects such as the number of people who will work in their Member State. This to ensure a level playing field. For trading venues, a (seemingly) arbitrary number of ten persons has been agreed to be sufficient, although these persons do need to have a certain degree of seniority. For investment firms the AFM looks at the core business and in relation to the activities of such core business there need to be sufficient persons on the ground. For instance, in relation to proprietary firms the AFM will want to know the number of traders. Trading nowadays is often done electronically. The AFM also regards the persons in charge of risk management and risk monitoring as traders, even persons from IT could be regarded as traders. However, this needs to be discussed within the Dutch regulator(s) upfront.

6.4.5.4 Licence fees

The AFS provides that the regulators can charge costs to companies in relation to the activities the regulators will carry out. The Decree on payment of financial regulation (*Besluit bekostiging financieel toezicht*) determines that the AFM and the DNB can charge the applicant the costs relating to the processing of a licence application. The rates can be found in a costs regulation (*kostenregeling*) and will be established by the Minister every year. **6.77**

6.4.6 Declaration of No Objection

6.4.6.1 Investment firm

An investment firm will only be granted a licence if the shareholders, direct or indirect, have been approved by the DNB, taking into account the need to ensure the sound and prudent management of the investment firm. A declaration of no objection (**DNO**) needs to be obtained from the DNB to acquire 10% or more of the undertaking's issued capital or shares carrying the right to exercise voting rights (**a qualifying holding**) in an investment firm established in the Netherlands. **6.78**

The integrity of the applicant or holder of a DNO must be beyond all doubt. The DNB also considers whether:

  (i) the applicant is suitable, also taking into account its reputation;
 (ii) the applicant is financially stable;
(iii) participating has a negative effect for the prudential compliance of the investment firm;
 (iv) there are good reasons to assume that the qualifying holding is linked to money laundering or terrorist financing;
  (v) the applicant provided incomplete or incorrect information.

The DNO does not have any requirements relating to the experience of an applicant and the applicant's expertise is therefore not tested. **6.79**

Article 3:100 (a) of the AFS does not determine what the DNB must do if the integrity of the potential shareholder is not beyond all doubt. There are no legal provisions stating that the DNB must refuse an application for a DNO if the applicant is not beyond all doubt. The DNB **6.80** will also have to demonstrate that the fact that the integrity of the applicant is not beyond all doubt is in conflict with the sound and prudent management of the investment firm.

6.81 A big burden which is also different from most other EU Member States is that DNB requires audited financial statements in relation to all (in)direct shareholders that need to apply for a DNO. This also applies for entities that in their home jurisdictions are not legally required to have their annual financial statements audited.

6.4.6.2 Regulated market

6.82 A DNO is required to exercise a qualifying holding in a regulated market. This declaration can be obtained from the Minister. The Minister will decide on the application after the AFM has rendered its advice on the application. An application for a DNO will be refused if:

(i) it leads to a non-transparent control structure which could obstruct the supervision;
(ii) the influence conflicts with the AFS interests; and
(iii) it would pose a threat to sound and prudent management.

6.83 It is not explicitly stated in the AFS that the shareholder of a regulated market should be 'trustworthy'. MiFID II states that the shareholders should be suitable. The Dutch legislator stated that the DNO provides a framework for the 'test of suitability'. In our view this means that the integrity of the shareholder is tested beyond all doubt. The regulated market needs to decide which (directors) of the shareholders have actual influence on the day-to-day operations of the regulated market. Only those (directors of) shareholders will need to be screened. In order to determine that the shareholders are suitable the AFM has decided that the shareholders have to complete a suitability matrix.

6.84 The Dutch legislator states that a DNO that has been granted under the provisions of article 5:32 (d) of the AFS, is also a declaration of no objection for an MTF and OTF if the market operator operates both trading venues.

6.85 Based on a mandatory decision, the AFM has certain powers regarding the holders of a DNO in regulated markets. The most important power is that the AFM grants a DNO to potential shareholders of a market operator, unless this would result in fundamental changes to shareholders' structure of the market operator. Should this be the case, then the Minister grants the declaration of no objection after the AFM has rendered its advice.

6.86 The AFM needs to observe the Policy Regulation declarations of no objection regulated markets (*Beleidslijn verklaringen van geen bezwaar gereglementeerde markten*, the **Policy Regulation**) when exercising its powers under the mandatory decision. The Policy Regulation states that the considerations taken into account to assess the application are broadly worded in order to anticipate any: (i) specific circumstances of a certain case; and (ii) changing market circumstances.

6.4.7 Enforcement powers of regulators

6.87 Most of the enforcement powers regulators can use for the supervision of investment firms and regulated markets can be found in Part 1 of the AFS. The AFM and the DNB may also use some general enforcement instruments. They can give a decision that includes guidelines that must be followed by the investment firm or regulated markets. Decisions can also cover fines and penalties. The AFM and the DNB can also withdraw the licence or prohibit a systematic internaliser to systematically internalise client orders.

Moreover, the AFM has the power to suspend, interrupt or delete a transaction in certain financial instruments on a trading venue.   **6.88**

A decision to use an enforcement power by the regulator is an administrative decision according to the General Administrative Law Act. (*Algemene wet bestuursrecht*) Therefore, a trading venue has the right to a writ of objection. The writ of objection must be in writing and sent within six weeks after publication of the decision to the AFM or the DNB. The regulator will reconsider its decision. Appeal can be made against the decision on the writ of objection at the administrative court of Rotterdam. Against the pronouncement of the court of Rotterdam appeal can be made within six weeks at the higher court (*College van Beroep voor het bedrijfsleven*).   **6.89**

6.5 Ireland

6.5.1 Background

Since the United Kingdom voted on 23 June 2016 to leave the European Union (**Brexit**) the Irish government has been preparing for the possibility of a no-deal Brexit. During this period, Ireland has seen a sharp increase in the number of regulated financial services firms that have chosen to locate their EU head offices in Ireland thereby maintaining access to the internal market.[67]   **6.90**

We discuss in this chapter some of the measures taken by the Irish government in relation to Brexit, the treatment under Irish law of non-European Economic Area investment firms seeking to engage in investment activities or to provide investment services in Ireland and the regulatory authorisation process in Ireland for certain types of firms.   **6.91**

6.5.2 Brexit Contingency Planning

The government published its Brexit contingency plan[68] on 19 December 2018 which was updated in January 2019 and again in July 2019. In the financial services area, the planning involved extensive engagement between the Central Bank of Ireland (**Central Bank**) and regulated firms, engagement with UK firms seeking to relocate to Ireland, engagement with the European Supervisory Authorities, implementation of a limited number of legislation   **6.92**

---

[67] Between 23 June 2016 and 1 August 2019 there were sixty-eight AIFMs, thirty-two UCITS management companies, and twenty-seven MiFID firms established out of a total of 193 AIFMs, 108 UCITS management companies, and 106 MiFID firms according to the Central Bank's registers.

[68] 'Preparing for the Withdrawal of the United Kingdom from the European Union Contingency Action Plan', available at: <https://www.dfa.ie/brexit/getting-ireland-brexit-ready/governmentcontingencyactionplan>

enactments in key areas and making extensive guidance available to the public on the impact of Brexit.

6.93 The Irish government enacted the Withdrawal of the United Kingdom from the European Union (Consequential Provisions) Act, 2019 (the **Brexit Omnibus Act**) on 17 March 2019. This is an omnibus piece of legislation crossing the remit of nine different government departments. Its stated purpose is to reduce the possibility of a serious disturbance in the Irish economy and in the sound functioning of Irish markets in the event of a hard Brexit. In the financial services sphere, the Brexit Omnibus Act facilitates a temporary designation for certain UK payment and settlement systems (including CREST which is the settlement system for Irish equities listed on Euronext, Ireland's stock exchange) in the event of a hard Brexit.[69] UK systems will have three months after a hard Brexit within which to apply for recognition, which is expected to last for nine months. The Act also provides that insurance undertakings that meet certain conditions will be deemed to be authorised for three years following the withdrawal of the UK for the purposes of running their existing portfolio as well as also establishing a temporary domestic run-off regime for certain insurance intermediaries for the same period, providing certainty to Irish policy holders holding insurance contracts underwritten by UK insurers.

6.5.3 Authorisation of AIFMs, UCITS Management Companies, and MiFID Investment Firms in Ireland

6.94 The Central Bank is responsible for the authorisation and supervision of financial intermediaries in Ireland, including alternative investment fund managers (**AIFMs**), UCITS management companies and MiFID investment firms.[70]

6.95 The Central Bank's powers to authorise and supervise AIFMs, UCITS management companies and MiFID investment firms derive primarily from the European Union (Alternative Investment Fund Managers) Regulations, 2013, as amended (in relation to the authorisation of Alternative Investment Fund Managers) (the **AIFM Regulations**) which implemented Directive 2011/61/EU, as amended (the **AIFM Directive**); the European Communities (Undertakings for Collective Investment in Transferable Securities) Regulations, 2011 as amended (in relation to the authorisation of UCITS Management Companies) (the **UCITS Regulations**) which implemented Directive 2009/65/EC (as amended), Commission Directive 2010/43/EU and Commission Directive 2010/44/EU (collectively, the **UCITS Directive**); and the European Union (Markets in Financial Instruments) Regulations, 2017 (in relation to the authorisation of investment firms (including the operators of MTFs and OTFs), regulated markets and data reporting service providers) (the **MiFID Regulations**), which implemented Directive 2014/65/EU and Commission Delegated Directive (EU)

---

[69] This complements the European Commission's decision in December 2018 to grant temporary equivalence under EU law to central securities depositories and central counterparties based in the UK. This is intended to allow Irish participants continued access to these designated systems.

[70] The term AIFM also refers to 'internally managed AIF' and the term 'UCITS management company' also refers to 'self-managed' UCITS unless otherwise indicated.

2017/593 (collectively, the **MiFID Directive**) as well as from the various Central Bank Acts 1942 to 2015.

6.96 These individual pieces of legislation set out the requirement for authorisation and the key requirements which a firm must meet before it can be authorised. The more detailed requirements and the required processes are set out in legislation, various pieces of Central Bank guidance and Central Bank application forms.[71]

6.97 The opinions issued by the European Securities Markets Authority (ESMA) in 2017[72] and the emergence of ESMA's Supervisory Coordination Network have seen the Central Bank pay heightened attention to UK-based firms seeking to relocate entities, activities, or functions to Ireland.

6.98 The Central Bank operates a risk-based system of regulation in Ireland called the Probability Risk Impact System (**PRISM**) which ranks firms as low, medium–low, medium, medium–high, and high based on the risks they pose to the economy and the consumer. The Central Bank allocates regulatory resources and attention to such firms accordingly. The Central Bank operates what it describes as an 'outcome focussed risk-based' approach to regulatory applications.[73] A firm's anticipated PRISM rating has an impact on the approach which the Central Bank will take to the firm's application. All investment funds and most AIFMs and UCITS management companies, and all but the largest and most complex of MiFID investment firms, are currently designated as low or medium–low by the Central Bank.

6.99 The Central Bank has developed on its website a series of FAQs for financial services firms considering relocating their operations from the UK to Ireland.

6.5.4 Treatment of Third Country Firms under Irish Law

6.100 It is possible for non-EU firms to carry out certain activities under certain circumstances under the MIFID Regulations and the AIFM Regulations and each of those Regulations contain their own rules as regards the treatment of third country firms. A third country firm will not be within scope of the UCITS Regulations.

---

[71] Commission Delegated Regulation (EU) 2017/1943 with regard to regulatory technical standards on information and requirements for the authorisation of investment firms which, together with regulatory guidance and the associated Central Bank application form, is available at: <https://www.centralbank.ie/regulation/industry-market-sectors/investment-firms/mifid-firms/authorisation-process>. See also <https://www.centralbank.ie/regulation/industry-market-sectors/funds-service-providers/ucits-management-companies/ authorisation-process. https://www.centralbank.ie/regulation/industry-market-sectors/funds-service-providers/aifm/authorisation>

[72] 'General Principles to Support Supervisory Convergence in the Context of the United Kingdom Withdrawing from the European Union', 31 May 2017 (ESMA 42-110-433) which addresses cross-sectoral regulatory and supervisory arbitrage risks that arise as a result of increased requests from financial market participants seeking to relocate in the EU27 within a relatively short period of time and Opinion to support supervisory convergence in the area of investment management in the context of the United Kingdom withdrawing from the European Union of 31 July 2017 (ESMA 34-45-344) which sets out principles based on the objectives and provisions of the UCITS Directive and AIFM Directive, which are applied to the specific case of relocation of entities, activities, and functions following the UK's withdrawal from the EU.

[73] See <https://www.centralbank.ie/regulation/how-we-regulate/brexit-faq#heading-What-is-the-Central-Banks-approach-to-authorisation-1219956092>

6.5.4.1 Providing services to, or engaging in investment activities with, Irish clients under MIFID

6.101 According to Article 46 of MiFIR,[74] a third country firm may provide investment services to, or engage in investment activities with, per se professional clients and eligible counterparties without the establishment of a branch, subject to registration with ESMA. This is contingent on the existence of a positive equivalence determination in respect of the third country jurisdiction. In the absence of a positive equivalence determination, national regimes apply. The adoption of an equivalence determination triggers the transitional provision of Article 54 of MiFIR according to which firms may continue to provide cross-border services under the national regime without seeking registration with ESMA for a period of three years.

6.102 For the purposes of determining whether a firm is required to seek authorisation as an investment firm in Ireland or not, an investment firm whose head or registered office is in a third country (i.e. outside of the European Economic Area) will not be regarded as operating in the Republic of Ireland if the firm provides investment services to, or engages in investment activities with, eligible counterparties or per se professional clients as defined under the MIFID Regulations without the establishment of a branch in the Republic of Ireland.[75] Importantly, this 'safe harbour' for third country firms applies only where the target client is a per se professional client or eligible counterparty, and not to retail or so-called elective professional clients.

6.103 A third country firm will not be able to rely on this safe harbour unless certain conditions are met:[76]

(a) the firm is subject to authorisation and supervision in the third country where the firm is established and the firm is authorised so that the competent authority of the third country pays due regard to any recommendations of the Financial Action Task Force in the context of anti-money laundering and countering the financing of terrorism; and

(b) cooperation arrangements that include provisions regulating the exchange of information for the purpose of preserving the integrity of the market and protecting investors are in place between the Central Bank and the competent authorities where the third country firm is established.

6.104 A third country firm intending to provide investment services or perform investment activities in Ireland to retail clients or to elective professional clients must establish a branch in Ireland.[77] Such a branch must obtain a prior authorisation from the Central Bank in accordance with conditions (a) and (b) above and the following conditions—

(c) there is sufficient initial capital at free disposal of the branch;
(d) one or more persons are appointed to be responsible for the management of the branch;

---

[74] Reg. 600/2014 of the European Parliament and of the Council.
[75] Reg. 5(4) of the MiFID Regs.
[76] These are set out in Reg. 5(5) of the MiFID Regs.
[77] Reg. 48(1) of the MiFID Regs.

(e) the third country where the third country firm is established has entered into an agreement with Ireland, which fully complies with the standards laid down in Article 26 of the OECD Model Tax Convention on Income and on Capital and ensures an effective exchange of information in tax matters, including, if any, multilateral tax agreements; and

(f) the firm belongs to an investor-compensation scheme.[78]

Where an eligible counterparty or a per se professional client established or situated in the Republic of Ireland initiates at its own exclusive initiative the provision of an investment service or activity by a third country firm, Article 46(5) of MiFIR obliges all Member States to disapply Article 46 of MiFIR to the provision of that service or activity by the third country firm to that person. Where a retail client or an elective professional client established or situated in the Republic of Ireland initiates, at their own exclusive initiative, the provision of an investment service or the performance of an investment activity by a third country firm, the requirement to establish an authorised branch does not apply to the provision of that service or the performance of that activity by the third country firm.[79] **6.105**

Third country firms may be required to meet certain legislative criteria which apply to delegates of Irish AIFMs[80] and Irish UCITS management companies[81] and, if the third country firm is proposing to manage the assets of any Irish regulated fund, it will be required to seek the pre-clearance of the Central Bank to do so. **6.106**

6.5.4.2 Third country firms as AIFMs under the AIFM Directive

A third country firm managing one or more alternative investment funds (AIFs) is currently not required, or entitled, to seek authorisation as an AIFM in the Republic of Ireland (as is the case in each Member State at the moment). This will only change, if and when the European Commission, on the advice of ESMA, legislates to extend the scope of the AIFM Directive to include third country AIFMs as envisaged by Articles 67 of the AIFM Directive. **6.107**

6.5.4.3 Third country firms marketing AIFs under the AIFM Regulations

When marketing one or more AIFs to professional investors that are resident or established in Ireland (**Irish professional investors**), a third country AIFM will be required to observe the marketing rules of the Republic of Ireland which apply under Regulation 43 of the AIFM Regulations. Article 42 of the AIFM Directive imposes certain minimum requirements in that regard but each Member State is entitled to impose stricter rules in this area. Regulation 43 transposes Article 42 faithfully from the AIFM Directive and the Irish government has imposed no further requirements on third country AIFMs in this regard. The AIFM is required to notify the Central Bank in advance of its intention to market the relevant AIF or AIFs to Irish professional investors by completing and filing with the Central Bank a straightforward regulatory form based on a template developed by ESMA. There is **6.108**

---

[78] The investor compensation scheme must be authorised or recognised in accordance with European Directive 97/9/EC of the European Parliament and of the Council of 3 March 1997 on investor-compensation schemes.
[79] Reg. 51 of the MiFID Regs.
[80] Reg. 21 of the AIFM Regs. and Arts. 77 and 78 of Commission Delegated Regulation (EU) No. 231/2013 of 19 December 2012.
[81] Reg. 23 of the UCITS Regs.

currently no fee associated with this filing. Once the Central Bank has processed the form, it confirms to the AIFM that it may commence marketing the relevant AIFs in Ireland.

6.109   The Central Bank allows the marketing of shares of non-EU alternative investment funds to retail investors in Ireland subject to the prior approval of the Central Bank.[82]

6.5.5 Key Requirements for Authorisation in Ireland

6.5.5.1 The influence of ESMA on the authorisation requirements

6.110   While the Central Bank must decide whether to authorise an applicant AIFM, UCITS management company or MiFID investment firm, the Central Bank does, however, engage with its peers in ESMA in relation to applications through the forum of the Supervisory Coordination Network (**SCN**). ESMA established the SCN as a forum for discussion among national EU regulators regarding market participants seeking to relocate entities, activities, or functions to the EU27, with the objective of promoting consistency in the approach of national regulators.

6.111   ESMA issued an opinion on 31 May 2017[83] setting out general principles aimed at fostering consistency in authorisation, supervision and enforcement relating to the relocation of entities, activities, and functions from the UK. In addition, ESMA published three further opinions on 13 July 2017[84] setting out sector-specific principles in the areas of investment firms, investment management and secondary markets, aimed at fostering consistency in authorisation, supervision and enforcement related to the relocation of entities, activities, and functions from the United Kingdom. ESMA recommended, among other things, that national regulators should apply additional scrutiny to situations where relocating entities, even those of smaller size employing simple investment strategies and having a limited range of business activities, do not dedicate at least three locally based full-time employees (or equivalent to employees) (including time commitments at both senior management and staff level) to the performance of portfolio management and/or risk management functions and/or monitoring of delegates. ESMA recommended that national regulators should assess the requirements for human and technical resources on a firm-by-firm basis taking into account, in particular, a number of criteria, including the size of the business (value of assets under management), number of (sub-)funds and share classes, complexity of investment strategies pursued, type and range of asset classes invested in, geographical spread of investments, use of leverage, frequency of investment activities, cross-border management or marketing activities, type and range of functions performed internally and delegated, whether the firm is seeking to be authorised to carry out additional services set out in Article 6(3) of the UCITS Directive and Article 6(4) of the AIFM Directive, number and type of investors, frequency of investor subscriptions and redemptions and geographical distribution of marketing activities.

---

[82] Such marketing may take place pursuant to Reg. 44 of the AIFM Regs. but only in accordance with the conditions set out by the Central Bank in Part III of Chapter 1 of the Central Bank's AIF Rulebook.
[83] See n.72.
[84] See n.72.

6.112 The Central Bank has adopted the ESMA opinions of 31 May 2017 and 13 July 2017 and does so as a matter of policy with all ESMA opinions, guidelines and recommendations.[85] These recommendations from ESMA and in particular the criteria which ESMA recommended national regulators have regard to in the context of applications for regulatory authorisations, now form an important component of the Central Bank's regulatory application process.

6.113 The ESMA opinions are further discussed in Chapter 5 of this book.

6.5.5.2 Head office and registered office in Ireland

6.114 The Central Bank will not authorise an investment firm, an AIFM,[86] or a UCITS management company unless it is a body corporate with its registered office and its head office in Ireland.[87]

6.115 The Central Bank interprets head office to mean the location of the mind and management of the applicant firm and the place where the day-to-day decisions about the direction of the applicant firm's business are taken.[88] The Central Bank expects that there should be a significant senior management presence in Ireland to ensure that full authority and effective control of the applicant firm rests within the head office.[89] The Central Bank considers that indications of this include:

- decision-making at board and committee level taking place within Ireland;
- significant senior management presence in Ireland; and
- financial control, legal and compliance, and risk management functions located within the head office.

6.116 The Central Bank tends not to permit a firm's compliance officer or risk officer to also be a director of a firm.[90]

6.5.5.3 Substance in Ireland
(a) Irish resident directors, directors to direct the business, and independent directors

6.117 AIFMs, UCITS management companies, and MiFID investment firms are required to have at least two Irish resident directors on their boards. There is no maximum number of directors.

---

[85] The Central Bank issued a public statement on 31 July 2018, which is available on the Central Bank's website, welcoming the ESMA opinions and confirming that the opinions 'reflect the views expressed consistently by the Central Bank'.

[86] In the case of an AIFM unless and until Arts. 35 and 37 of the AIFM Directive are activated by the European Commission as described earlier, which would permit the Central Bank to authorise non-EU AIFMs under certain circumstances.

[87] In the case of MiFID investment firms, as set out in Reg. 7 of the MiFID Regs.; in the case of AIFMs, as set out in Reg. 9(1)(a) of the AIFM Regs.; in the case of a UCITS management company, as set out in Reg. 17 of the UCITS Regs.

[88] The Central Bank's stated policy on this in the case of MiFID firms is illustrative of its general policy. See Central Bank's 'Guidance on Completing an Application for Authorisation under the European Union (Markets in Financial Instruments) Regulations 2017'.

[89] Central Bank's 'Guidance on Completing an Application for Authorisation under the European Union (Markets in Financial Instruments) Regulations 2017'.

[90] This is a function of the Central Bank's policy of requiring three lines of defence to be built into a regulated firm's organisational structure.

6.118 The AIFM Regulations, UCITS Regulations, and MIFID Regulations set out that the conduct of the authorised entity should be decided by at least two senior managers.[91] In practice, the Central Bank will apply this requirement in what it considers to be a proportionate manner, depending on the nature, scale, and complexity of the firm. Larger and more complex firms can expect to be required to have two Irish resident executive directors on the Board, one of whom will be the firm's managing director or chief executive officer, who are involved in the day to day running of the firm's business. For smaller and less complex firms, the Central Bank can be flexible as regards its interpretation of this requirement though will still require a managing director/chief executive officer to be in place. For internally managed AIFs and self-managed UCITS, the Central Bank has tended not to require full-time executives and adopts a more flexible approach to its interpretation of this requirement.

6.119 The Central Bank requires all AIFMs, UCITS management companies, and MiFID investment firms to have at least one independent non-executive director on the board of directors. This director will be the chairman of the board of directors unless otherwise agreed with the Central Bank. A minimum of two independent directors may be required for investment firms with a PRISM rating of medium or higher.

6.5.5.4 AIFMs and UCITS management companies: managerial functions[92]

6.120 The Central Bank has identified six managerial functions for AIFMS and UCITS management companies, being capital and financial management; operational risk management; fund risk management; investment management; distribution; and regulatory compliance. The Central Bank requires firms to identify an individual, known as a designated person, who will be responsible for monitoring and overseeing the managerial function assigned to him or her. The Central Bank expects firms to allocate each legal and regulatory obligation applicable to the AIFM or UCITS management company to a specific managerial function. Designated persons can be directors or employees of the firm. Alternatively, they can be seconded to the firm, on a full- or part-time basis, from another firm such as the investment manager or a firm which specialises in the provision of designated persons. It is possible for a designated person to oversee more than one managerial function, however, he or she will not be permitted to perform the investment management managerial function in addition to either risk function.

6.5.5.5 AIFMs and UCITS management companies: senior management location rule

6.121 The Central Bank's so-called location rule requires that an AIFM or a UCITS management company[93] conduct a preponderance of its management in the EEA or such other country as the Central Bank may, taking into account criteria regarding effective supervision, determine and advise by notice published on the website of the Central Bank.[94] Such determination may be changed, including if circumstances change.

---

[91] Reg. 9(1)(a) of the AIFM Regs., Reg. 17(3) of the UCITS Regs., and Reg. 17(8) of the MiFID Regs.

[92] The detailed requirements regarding managerial functions are set out in the Central Bank's Fund Management Company Guidance, which is available on the Central Bank's website.

[93] This rule appears in Reg. 100 of the Central Bank (Supervision and Enforcement) Act 2013 (s. 48(1)) (Undertakings for Collective Investment in Transferable Securities) Regs. 2015. This rule is applied by the Central Bank to AIFMs in practice pending a planned update being made to the Central Bank's AIF Rulebook.

[94] The Central Bank has stated that in the event that the UK leaves the EU, it will continue to permit UK-resident directors and designated persons to be treated as if they were resident in the EEA for the purpose of this rule.

Where an AIFM or a UCITS management company has a PRISM impact rating of medium–low or above, the AIFM or UCITS management company shall have at least— **6.122**

(i) three directors resident in Ireland or, at least, two directors resident in Ireland and one designated person resident in Ireland,
(ii) half of its directors resident in the EEA or such other country as determined by the Central Bank, and
(iii) half of its managerial functions performed by at least two designated persons resident in the EEA or such other country as determined by the Central Bank, or

Where an AIFM or a UCITS management company has a PRISM impact rating of low, the AIFM or UCITS management company shall have at least—

(i) two directors resident in Ireland,
(ii) half of its directors resident in the EEA or such other country as determined by the Central Bank, and
(iii) half of its managerial functions performed by at least two designated persons resident in the EEA

6.5.5.6 Fitness and probity regime

The Central Bank operates a system of direct regulation of persons holding responsible positions in financial firms which is one of the corner-stones of regulation in Ireland and an important aspect of the regulatory application process.[95] The fitness and probity regime applies to persons in senior positions (referred to in the legislation as Controlled Functions (CFs) and Pre-Approval Controlled Functions (**PCFs**)) within regulated financial service providers which include all AIFMs, UCITS management companies, and MIFID investment firms.[96] **6.123**

Firms are obliged to ensure that their senior personnel comply with the fitness and probity regime. The regime requires the approval in advance by the Central Bank of persons holding PCFs, and imposes ongoing responsibilities on CFs and PCFs and the firms appointing them. **6.124**

6.5.5.7 Financial control, compliance, and risk management

As set out above under 'Head Office and Registered office in Ireland', the Central Bank considers that a firm's financial control, legal and compliance and risk management functions should be located within the firm's head office in Ireland. **6.125**

In practice, the Central Bank will look for firms to have one or more part-time or full-time employees assume the role of compliance officer and risk manager.[97] For smaller and less **6.126**

---

[95] The fitness and probity regime applies to all regulated financial services providers under the Central Bank Reform Act 2010.
[96] Ireland currently does not have any regime equivalent to the UK's senior managers regime, however, in an interview with the Financial Times in May 2019, Derville Rowland, Director General of Financial Conduct in the Central Bank, called for Ireland to bring in a similar framework.
[97] In the case of an internally managed AIF or a self-managed UCITS, the historic position has been that these functions could be carried out, effectively, by designated persons, however, the time commitments expected by the Central Bank from designated persons have increased significantly over the past number of years, making this practice challenging from a resources and costs perspective.

complex firms the Central Bank will consider allowing one person to assume the two roles, though, following ESMA's statement on that matter in its July 2017 opinion, this practice is under some pressure.[98] The Central Bank does not require firms to have an in-house legal resource. The Central Bank does not tend to require smaller or less complex firms to have an in-house financial controller and allows firms to outsource the function provided that there is a senior manager within the firm who takes responsibility for the area.

6.5.5.8 Staffing

6.127 With respect to staffing other than senior managers, financial controllers, compliance officers, or risk officers, the Central Bank will expect the applicant firm to set out a detailed staffing plan for the three years following the firm's authorisation. In assessing the firm's proposed staffing levels, the Central Bank will want to see that the firm's regulated activities are carried out by a sufficient number of sufficiently experienced and qualified staff and the Central Bank will have regard to the nature, scale, and complexity of the firm's business. The Central Bank seeks to implement ESMA's recommendations in its July 2017 opinion in this regard.[99]

6.5.6 The Authorisation Process

6.5.6.1 Initial contact with the Central Bank

6.128 The Central Bank requires all applicants for MIFID, UCITS Management Company, or AIFM licences to make initial contact with the Central Bank prior to submitting an application. The initial contact is expected to be made by email.

6.5.6.2 Key facts document (KFD)

6.129 Applicant firms must complete a template KFD, available on the Central Bank's website,[100] before submitting a formal application. The KFD is intended to be a summary of the firm's proposal covering its background, the reason why the firm intends to establish a presence in Ireland, its business model, organisational structure, key management and staff, significant shareholders, and financial projections covering three years. The purpose of the KFD is to identify any material issues with the firm's proposed application before the formal application is made.

6.130 The Central Bank tends to rigorously analyse, and comment upon, the KFD prior to the submission of a complete application for authorisation. The Central Bank reverts to the applicant firm with written comments on the KFD within twenty working days of receipt of the KFD, and, once it receives a response to its comments, arranges a face-to-face meeting with the applicant to discuss the application.

---

[98] ESMA Opinion to support supervisory convergence in the area of investment management in the context of the United Kingdom withdrawing from the European Union (ESMA 34-45-344) 'Combining the risk, compliance and/or internal audit functions should generally be avoided as this is likely to undermine the effectiveness and independence of these control functions' (para. 33).

[99] See section 6.5.5.1 above.

[100] AIFMs and UCITS management companies use the same KFD which is available from the Central Bank. The MiFID KFD is broadly similar.

6.5.6.3 Preliminary meeting with the Central Bank

6.131 A preliminary meeting will be held with all applicant firms in advance of an application being made. The completed KFD will form the basis for the preliminary meeting. At this meeting, the applicant firm will be informed of the Central Bank's authorisation process and timeframes. The Central Bank will advise the applicant firm of significant issues that are apparent at this juncture that might negatively impact the Central Bank's determination of any application.

6.5.6.4 Application

6.132 Applications are made via the Central Bank's ORION online system.

6.133 The application process for AIFMs and UCITS management companies run along similar lines. An application for authorisation as an AIFM or UCITS management company is made by submitting the following to the Central Bank:

   (i) completed application form;
   (ii) detailed programme of activity;
   (iii) details of minimum capital, three-year financial projections and detailed assumptions on which projections are based;
   (iv) all information regarding ownership structure;
   (v) information of the remuneration policies and practices;
   (vi) information on the firm's target clients and proposed business;
   (vii) ancillary documents (including confirmation of capital and statement of responsibility);
   (viii) organisational chart;
   (ix) fully completed online individual questionnaires for all PCF holders, including directors.

6.134 In the case of a MIFID investment firm, the application form tracks the requirements of Commission Delegated Regulation (EU) 2017/1943 with regard to regulatory technical standards on information and requirements for the authorisation of investment firms and is broadly similar to the requirements which apply to AIFMs and UCITS management companies.

6.5.6.5 Timing

6.135 Regulation 17(11) of the UCITS Regulations and Regulation 9(5) of the AIFM Regulations provide that a proposed fund management company shall be informed whether or not authorisation has been granted within six months or three months respectively of the date of receipt of a complete application. The MiFID Regulations oblige the Central Bank to issue a determination on an application for authorisation as an investment firm within six months of receipt of a complete application.

6.136 In practice, the Central Bank will issue comments to the applicant firm within forty working days of receipt of the complete application. Provided that the applicant firm responds within twenty working days of receiving the first comments from the Central Bank, a second round of comments will be issued to the applicant firm within twenty working days. The applicant firm must respond within ten working days of receiving the second round of comments from the Central Bank.

6.137 It is expected that all issues/comments will be addressed in the applicant firm's second submission of comments and therefore the Central Bank will not review more than three submissions before reaching a decision on the application.

6.138 An application is only considered complete when it includes completed application form, all relevant individual questionnaires/declarations, and a comprehensive business plan. The quality of the application is important when it comes to minimising the time it will take the Central Bank to process an application. A well-thought-out application that adheres to the statutory requirements, the Central Bank's guidance, and accurately reflects the requirements of the applicable regulatory application form and will be processed efficiently.

7
The UK Supervisory Regime in the Post-Brexit Environment

Michael Thomas and James Roslington

7.1 Introduction

Much of the pro-Brexit rhetoric ahead of the June 2016 referendum on the United Kingdom's exit from the European Union was centred on the concept of 'taking back control'. This slogan was widely credited to Dominic Cummings, the campaign director of the pro-Brexit lobby group, Vote Leave, and recurred as a leitmotif in campaign literature and the speeches of leading pro-Brexit voices.[1] 'Taking back control' included reasserting national sovereignty over lawmaking powers that had gradually been ceded to the EU since 1973.

7.01

Consequently it is arguable that the vote to leave the European Union was fundamentally a legal issue, based on the concept that rules for the United Kingdom should be made in the United Kingdom. In essence, the Brexit vote rejected a form of transnational law, which was seen by pro-Brexit voters as remote and elitist, in favour of a return to sovereign law-making, in which UK laws could be tailored more closely to the perceived needs of the British economy and society.[2]

7.02

During the referendum campaign, the call to 'take back control' in the legal sphere was summarised in another slogan: the appeal to remove 'Brussels red tape'. Pro-Brexit campaigners mooted a 'bonfire of regulation' in which a post-Brexit UK would have the freedom to jettison impractical and burdensome EU laws, such as the Working Time Directive and the Common Agriculture Policy. For the UK's financial services industry, Brexit would mean an opportunity for the UK government to embark on a round of deregulation, boosting the City of London to become an ultra-competitive offshore financial centre, a 'Singapore-on-Thames'.[3] As Theresa May later claimed, 'we would have the freedom to set the competitive tax rates and embrace the policies that would attract the world's best companies and biggest investors to Britain. And—if we were excluded from accessing the Single Market—we would be free to change the basis of Britain's economic model.'[4] Pro-Brexit voices in the City called for the removal of regulatory obstacles to the UK's competitiveness, such as the AIFMD framework for regulating fund managers and the bonus cap and other restrictions on remuneration.

7.03

---

[1] Henry Mance and George Parker, 'Combative Brexiteer Who Took Control of Vote Leave Operation', *Financial Times* (14 June 2016).
[2] Ralf Michaels, 'Does Brexit Spell the Death of Transnational Law?' (2016) 17 *German Law Journal* 51–61.
[3] For an earlier example of this view, see Kwasi Kwarteng et al., *Britannia Unchained* (London: Palgrave, 2012).
[4] 'Theresa May's Brexit Speech in Full', *Daily Telegraph* (17 January 2017), available at: <https://www.telegraph.co.uk/politics/2017/01/17/theresa-mays-brexit-speech-full>, accessed 4 November 2018.

7.04 In the months that followed the vote by the UK to leave the European Union, UK regulators had to grapple with the practicalities of 'taking back control'. This chapter will explore how UK regulators essentially adopted a pragmatic, technical solution that did not initially result in any major shift towards deregulation. The chapter argues that, under the premiership of Theresa May, the UK government was unwilling to make a definitive political decision to amend significantly the future shape of UK regulation, while UK regulators displayed a strong preference in favour of the regulatory status quo. The prospects for deregulation also faltered due to the potential need to maintain regulatory equivalence with EU laws, as well as fears of possible retaliatory action by the EU. In addition, the tight timetable imposed by Article 50 of the Treaty on the European Union, and its subsequent limited extension, reduced the time available to introduce radical new legislation.

7.05 The technical solution adopted by the UK government and regulators involved the wholesale transposition of EU legislation into UK law, and the formal arrogation of EU powers to UK bodies; in the crisp language of the parliamentary draughtsman, 'for "ESMA" substitute "the FCA"'. The plans put forward by HM Treasury, the Bank of England, the Prudential Regulation Authority, and the Financial Conduct Authority did not propose radical changes to the overall nature of the pre-Brexit regulatory environment, and their representatives repeatedly and publicly stated their desire not to engage in a 'bonfire of regulation'.

7.06 The UK government has had to deal with complicated issues around the onshoring of regulatory powers and cooperation between UK and EU regulators. The European Supervisory Authorities (ESAs) are responsible for preparing technical standards as well as certain categories of non-legislative materials, such as regulatory guidance and template forms. The UK government and regulators had to decide how to treat existing materials of this kind, and how UK regulators may interpret them in the future. In addition, the onshoring of supervisory functions previously held by the ESAs has led to new responsibilities and functions for UK regulators.

7.07 To date, therefore, the onshoring of lawmaking powers has been restricted by the UK government's plan under the premiership of Theresa May to 'convert and preserve' EU-derived law in UK law. Nevertheless, the UK's decision to leave the European Union is a constitutional revolution. It is clear that the restoration of lawmaking powers to UK legislative bodies and regulators will have a major impact for years to come. In particular, the appointment of Boris Johnson as prime minister in July 2019 spurred a resurgence in calls for greater deregulation of the financial services industry, which may, in time, lead to a more profound reform of the UK's regulatory framework.

7.2 The Entangled Nature of the UK and EU Frameworks

7.08 Since the UK's accession to the European Economic Community (EEC) in 1973, the UK and European frameworks for financial services law and regulation have become increasingly entangled. As a result, the contemporary UK rules for financial services comprise a bedrock of pre-EEC legal norms encrusted with European-derived legislation and overlaid with UK-specific requirements and concepts.

In particular, the growth of EU power over the financial services industry since the late 1990s has resulted in a complex entanglement of EU and UK rules, institutions, and powers. The classical elegance of the EU's legislative vocabulary has to a certain extent hidden the sprawling and tentacular nature of its powers; in reality, this entanglement of the European project with the UK's residual sovereign powers explains why Brexit will require a major reform of the UK's legislative and regulatory framework for financial services.

7.09

To disentangle this legislative morass has been a mammoth task. Following the 2016 referendum on leaving the EU, it was estimated that there were over 12,000 EU regulations in force, and that EU legislation had been implemented in the UK by around 7,900 statutory instruments.[5] In particular, financial services in the UK are largely framed by a complex matrix of EU legislation, particularly the Single Market directives.[6] This has represented a vast body of law to be nationalised. For example, the Markets in Financial Instruments Directive II (**MiFID II**) legislative package alone contains forty-two sets of administrative rules supported by non-legislative guidance, Q&As, and template forms. The Capital Requirements Directive IV (**CRD IV**) package, another regulatory behemoth, contains a similar mix of rules and guidance, with a single piece of legislation, the Capital Requirements Regulation (**CRR**) running to over 500 Articles.

7.10

7.2.1 The Growing Influence of Europe from the Late 1990s

From the late 1990s, the UK financial services industry experienced an intensified penetration of UK financial services law by EU rules. The 1999 Financial Services Action Plan (**FSAP**) drove the 'Europeanisation' of financial services by imposing greater harmonisation on the EU's fragmented financial markets.[7] This resulted in a significant reform of financial services legislation between 1999 and 2005. Existing laws were revised and expanded in increasingly complex and wide-ranging legislative packages that affected every area of the UK's financial services industry. During these years, EU legislators adopted the Markets in Financial Instruments Directive (**MiFID**), the Market Abuse Directive, the Prospectus Directive, the Transparency Directive,[8] and the Banking Consolidated Directive,[9] all of which had a major impact on the UK industry. Work also began to develop the Solvency II legislative package in order to replace a total of fourteen existing directives relating to insurance.[10]

7.11

Admittedly, this intensification of EU power was a two-way process; the dominant role of the City of London and the depth of the UK's sectoral expertise meant that the UK

7.12

---

[5] Department for Exiting the European Union, *Legislating for the United Kingdom's Withdrawal from the European Union* (March 2017) (Cm 9446) 14.
[6] The Single Markets Directives consist of the Capital Requirements Directive IV; Solvency II Directive; Markets in Financial Instruments Directive II, the Insurance Distribution Directive, the Mortgage Credit Directive, the Undertakings for Collective Investment in Transferable Securities Directive, and the Alternative Investment Fund Managers Directive.
[7] See the definition of 'Europeanization' in T. A. Borzel and T. Risse, 'Europeanization: The Domestic Impact of European Union Politics', in K. E. Jørgensen, M. A. Pollack, and B. Rosamund, *Handbook of European Union Politics* (London: SAGE, 2007), pp. 483–504.
[8] Directives 2003/6/EC, 2003/71/EC, and 2004/109/EC.
[9] Directive 2000/12/EC, subsequently recast and amended as Directive 2006/48/EC.
[10] Directive 2009/138/EC.

government played a key part in assisting the integration of EU law and influence into the UK's financial services legal and regulatory framework. In particular, from the late 1990s, the UK government promoted the City of London as a successful model for the EU's financial markets, and positively embraced the coordination of financial services regulation at the European level. Indeed, UK officials and negotiators had a decisive role in shaping the EU's financial services policy in recent years.[11] Nevertheless, the overall result was to produce a complex web of national and supranational legislation which has proved extremely difficult and time-consuming to disentangle.

7.2.2 The Shift towards 'More Europe' after the 2007–8 Financial Crisis

7.13 The penetration of UK financial services law by EU regulation intensified further after the 2007–8 global financial crisis. The need to respond to the financial crisis led to the declarations of the G20 Pittsburgh summit in 2009. The G20 protocol highlighted the need for regulators to manage risks more closely and take a more interventionist approach in order to ensure financial stability. The outcome was to result in a decisive shift of regulatory power in favour of the EU. As commentators have observed, in the aftermath of episodes such as the Icelandic banking collapse and the rescue of Fortis, EU policymakers shifted their stance in favour of 'more Europe' by issuing an even greater volume of legislation at the EU level and awarding greater powers to EU institutions.[12]

7.14 The drive towards 'more Europe' provided the impetus for a wide range of EU legislation, including rules to implement the G20 Pittsburgh protocol. These measures were designed to control Europe's financial markets more closely, in order to protect investors and ensure the resilience and transparency of the financial system. The new rules included the vast and wide-ranging MiFID II package, the European Markets Infrastructure Regulation (EMIR), the Short Selling Regulation, the Benchmarks Regulation, and the Securities Financing Transactions Regulation.[13] In addition, the Basel III reforms to bank capital, liquidity, and leverage led to the equally large CRD IV and CRR package. The aftermath of the eurozone crisis spurred the creation of the Single Supervisory Mechanism and Single Resolution Mechanism in 2014 and 2015, as well as the Bank Recovery and Resolution Directive (**BRRD**).

7.2.3 The Growing Power of the ESAs

7.15 Another important outcome of the global financial crisis was the rise of the EU's so-called super-regulators, the ESAs. The ESAs were established in January 2011 under the 2010 ESA Regulations, replacing the previous EU Committees of securities regulators, banking

---

[11] Ferran, Ellis, 'Crisis-Driven Regulatory Reform: Where in the World is the EU Going?', in Ferran et al, *The Regulatory Aftermath of the Global Financial Crisis* (Cambridge: Cambridge University Press, 2017), 24–5.
[12] Niamh Moloney, *EU Securities and Financial Markets Regulation* (Oxford: Oxford University Press, 2014), p. 1014.
[13] See Ferran, 'Crisis-Driven Regulatory Reform'; Niamh Moloney, 'EU Financial Market Regulation After the Global Financial Crisis: "More Europe" or More Risks?' (2007) 47 *Common Market Law Review* 1317–83.

European Systemic Risk Board (ESRB) includes:	Joint Committee of ESAs
• ECB and central bank governors • ESA chairs • European Commissioner • National representatives	• EBA • ESMA • EIOPA

National competent authorities, including FCA and PRA

Figure 7.1 The European system of financial supervision

supervisors, and insurance and pensions regulators.[14] The ESAs comprise the European Banking Authority (**EBA**), the European Securities and Markets Authority (**ESMA**), and the European Insurance and Occupational Pensions Authority (**EIOPA**) (see Figure 7.1). The EBA was originally based in London but moved to join the ESMA in Paris following the UK's referendum on leaving the European Union, while the EIOPA is located in Frankfurt.

The ESAs were set up in order to drive EU-wide supervision and dispute resolution mechanisms.[15] They are intended to foster a common supervisory culture and help to coordinate responses to EU-wide challenges.[16] As a matter of principle and in order to protect the existing institutional balance within the EU (the so-called *Moroni* doctrine), they are not empowered to take discretionary decisions unless the appropriate conditions apply.[17] Nevertheless, the formal limits on their role mask the growing influence of the ESAs, both at the level of the Member States and in international financial governance.[18] **7.16**

The ESAs are not themselves legislators, but can be mandated to provide technical advice to the European Commission or to propose technical standards for the Commission to adopt. The ESAs may also adopt 'soft law' arrangements in form of guidelines, recommendations, and Q&As.[19] The ESAs also have powers to intervene in the affairs of Member States as a matter of last resort. Niamh Moloney has highlighted the growing expertise and role of the ESAs in shaping EU financial governance from the 'bottom up'.[20] **7.17**

The role of the ESAs in issuing the EU's 'soft law' has been critical to the most recent round of EU lawmaking. The EU's 'soft law' has proved to be increasingly important in interpreting national legislation; it has been persuasively argued that the EU has 'hardened' soft law by encouraging financial institutions to treat its Level 3 guidelines and recommendations as **7.18**

---

[14] Regulation (EU) No. 1093/2010 establishing the EBA, Regulation (EU) No. 1094/2010 establishing the EIOPA, and Regulation (EU) No. 1095/2010 establishing the ESMA.

[15] Ellis Ferran, 'Regulatory Parity in Post-Brexit UK–EU Financial Regulation', in Kern Alexander, Catherine Barnard, Ellis Ferran, Andrew Land, and Niamh Moloney, *Brexit and Financial Services: Law and Policy* (Oxford: Hart, 2018), pp. 1–37.

[16] See Regulation (EU) No. 1093/2010 of the European Parliament and of the Council of 24 November 2010 establishing a European Supervisory Authority (European Banking Authority), Arts. 29 and 31. The Regulations establishing ESMA and EIOPA contain similar provisions.

[17] See Niamh Moloney, *EU Securities and Financial Markets Regulation* (3rd edn, Oxford: Oxford University Press, 2014); Case 9/56 *Meroni v. High Authority of the ECSC* [1957–9] ECR 133.

[18] Niamh Moloney, 'International Financial Governance, the EU, and Brexit: The "Agencification" of EU Financial Governance and Its Implications' (2016) 17(4) *European Business Organization Law Review* 451–80.

[19] Christopher Brummer, *Soft Law and the Global Financial System: Rule Making in the 21st Century* (2nd edn, Cambridge: Cambridge University Press, 2015).

[20] Niamh Moloney, 'EU Financial Governance after Brexit: The Rise of Technocracy and the Absorption of the UK's Withdrawal', in Alexander et al., *Brexit and Financial Services*, pp. 61–114.

near-binding.[21] As the ESA Regulations state, the ESAs can issue guidelines and recommendations, which are subject to 'comply or explain' requirements. This function of issuing regulatory guidance has been removed from national regulators in favour of an EU-wide approach.

7.2.4 Accelerating Loss of National Discretion

7.19 In addition to these changes, recent years have seen an increasing loss of power by national governments and regulators in favour of the EU through other means. For example, EU regulations have increasingly replaced directives as the legislative instrument of choice for new initiatives. Unlike directives, EU regulations have direct effect in Member States so that they do not need to be implemented in domestic legislation in order to become effective. EU legislative packages now commonly consist of a directive and regulation, such as CRD IV and the CRR or MiFID II and the Markets in Financial Instruments Regulation (MiFIR). Similarly, legislation previously promulgated by way of a directive has been replaced by regulations, such as the replacement of the Prospectus Directive by the Prospectus Regulation[22] or the replacement of the Market Abuse Directive by the Market Abuse Regulation (MAR). This may encourage harmonisation of national legislation, but it has also to a large extent removed national discretion.

7.20 Furthermore, the use of reporting requirements as a regulatory tool has been harmonised throughout the EU. EMIR, MiFID II, and CRD IV have imposed reporting requirements, requiring increasingly standardised formats and templates for a broader scope or reporting, using more sophisticated and complex technology. Some of this reporting is at the level of national regulators, but connectivity to the relevant ESA is also required. This has provided another point of connection between regulation by the Member State and by the EU institutions.

7.3 UK Framework for Financial Services Legislation and Regulation

7.21 The UK institutions that legislate and regulate the financial services industry, including the implementation of EU rules, are set out in Figure 7.2.

7.22 These UK institutions have been heavily implicated in the implementation of EU law in the UK. This is because Parliament enacted the European Communities Act 1972 (ECA) to ensure that much of EU law applied in the UK. The ECA provided for the supremacy of EU law in the UK, and ensured that UK courts must follow the rulings of the Court of Justice of the European Union (CJEU). Specifically, section 2(1) of the ECA states that EU regulations are directly effective in the UK. This means that EU regulations apply in the UK without the

---

[21] Abraham Newman and David Bach, 'The European Union as Hardening Agent: Soft Law and the Diffusion of Global Financial Regulation' (2014) 21(3) *Journal of European Public Policy* 430–452.
[22] Regulation (EU) 2017/1129.

Parliament
The UK Parliament is the bicameral legislative body for the United Kingdom, with extensive legislative powers to pass primary and secondary legislation in the form of Acts of Parliament and statutory instruments.

HM Treasury
HM Treasury is the government ministry responsible for economic and finance policy, including the oversight of financial services policy and preparation of legislation.

Financial Policy Committee
• The Financial Policy Committee, which is a sub-committee of the Court of Directors of the Bank of England, provides oversight for ensuring financial stability. • Specifically, it is mandated to identify systemic risks to the stability of the financial system, and to make recommendations to the PRA and FCA to take action to preserve financial stability.

PRA
• The Prudential Regulation Authority is a subsidiary of the Bank of England. • The PRA is responsible for the prudential regulation of firms that are systematically important, including banks, building societies, insurance companies, and certain large investment firms, known as 'dual-regulated firms', for which the PRA provides prudential regulation whereas the FCA provides conduct of business regulation. • It has powers to monitor the firms that it supervises in order to assess the risk of failure and any subsequent impact on the financial system. The PRA maintains a set of regulatory requirements in the PRA Rulebook.

Financial Conduct Authority
The Financial Conduct Authority is responsible for regulating conduct of business requirements for all UK regulated firms. The FCA is required to co-operate with the PRA in the supervision of dual-regulated firms. The FCA also maintains the FCA Handbook of Rules and Guidance.

Payment Services Regulator
The Payment Services Regulator was created in 2015 to promote competition and innovation in payment systems, and ensure they work in the interests of the organisations and people that use them.

Figure 7.2 UK institutions responsible for financial services

need for additional implementing legislation or rules to be passed in the UK. In contrast, section 2(2) requires that EU directives must be implemented in UK legislation in order to be effective in the UK.

Consequently, from 1973, UK legislative and regulatory authorities embedded EU rules within the national framework for financial services rules. This was done by implementing EU directives directly in primary legislation or in regulatory rules, although the approach taken varied over time. During the mid 2000s, the FSA adopted an approach of 'intelligent copy-out', which aimed to use the language of EU Directives as far as practicable as the basis for implementing the requirements in FCA rules. This was intended to avoid 'gold-plating', that is, placing any unintended additional obligations on UK firms.[23] However, the copying-out of EU texts led firms to complain of a lack of clarity and guidance from the FSA, especially in relation to the implementation of MiFID in 2006 to 2007.

7.23

---

[23] HM Treasury and Financial Services Authority, *Joint Implementation Plan for MiFID* (May 2006) 6.

7.24 Following complaints from the industry on the regulatory burden, the UK government committed to avoiding 'gold-plating' EU law where possible. When transposing EU law, the UK government stated its intention to ensure that, except in exceptional circumstances, the UK should not go beyond the minimum requirements of the measure being transposed.[24] The European Commission similarly identified gold-plating as an obstruction to the Single Market.[25]

7.25 In some cases, such as the UK's implementation of MAR, given the increasing use of regulations by the Commission as the legislative instrument of preference, the FCA resorted to deleting large sections of the Handbook and inserting only cross-references to the relevant EU instrument.

7.26 The increasingly harmonised nature of EU law has led to an even more entangled connection between UK and EU rules.

7.4 A 'Bonfire of Regulation'?

7.27 The extent and pervasive impact of European rules in relation to the UK's financial services industry led to a number of complaints among market participants. The costs of introducing EU rules were widely criticised, for example, in the response to the FSA's assessment that implementing MiFID would lead to a one-off cost of up to £1.2 billion and annual costs of £120 million for the industry as a whole.[26] Likewise, the regulatory burden imposed by EU requirements has been vociferously challenged by sectors of the industry, for example in response to EU rules on alternative investments and in relation to remuneration.[27]

7.28 Consequently, one of the major elements in pro-Brexit thinking has been to encourage a 'bonfire of regulation' in which the UK's exit from the European Union will enable the UK to remove costly and burdensome European rules. The former Conservative leader Iain Duncan Smith has argued that Brexit will 'reduce the cost on business and on individuals by reducing regulations which will improve our competitiveness, our productivity and therefore ultimately our economy'.[28] Similarly, Jacob Rees-Mogg, the influential chairman of the pro-Brexit European Research Group, has stated that, after Brexit, the UK 'will be free to make its own laws and conclude its own trade agreements, free to take back control of its immigration policy and no longer obliged to pay "Eurogeld" in return for the dubious privilege of following EU laws'.[29]

---

[24] HM Government, *Guiding Principles for EU Legislation* (BIS/13/774) (2013); HM Government, *Transposition Guidance: How to Implement European Directives Effectively* (February 2018), p. 7.

[25] European Commission, 'Commission Staff Working Document on Call for Evidence: EU Regulatory Framework for Financial Services' (SWD/2016/0359) (23 November 2016).

[26] FSA, *The Overall Impact of MiFID* (November 2006).

[27] E. Ferran, 'After the Crisis: The Regulation of Hedge Funds and Private Equity in the EU', *European Business Organization Law Review* 12 (2011) 379–414; E. Ferran, 'New Regulation of Remuneration in the Financial Sector in the EU', *European Company and Financial Law Review* (2012) 1–34.

[28] Iain Duncan Smith, 'We Need to Have a "Root and Branch" Review of EU Regulations before the 2020 General Election', *Daily Telegraph*, 28 March 2017, available at: <https://www.telegraph.co.uk/news/2017/03/27/need-have-root-branch-review-eu-regulations-2020-general-election>, accessed 5 July 2019.

[29] Jacob Rees-Mogg, 'Mrs May Has Made Many Promises on Brexit, Now She Must Keep Them', *Daily Telegraph*, 2 July 2018, available at: <https://www.telegraph.co.uk/politics/2018/07/01/history-bodes-tory-prime-minister-defies-party-theresa-may>, accessed 5 July 2019.

7.29 In the context of financial services, this viewpoint has encouraged a view of the City of London as historically geared towards 'light-touch' regulation in comparison to the rules-driven nature of the EU project. According to this view, the UK financial services industry is 'built on an ethic of free trade and competition over centuries' and therefore many in the industry 'consider that success has been constrained by the prescriptive nature of EU legislation, one in which EU lawmaking tends to impose a single "rule book", or one insensitive to the diversity of the sector. They want the government to move quickly and decisively to the new arrangements for access for our trade to global and EU markets, just as other successful systems (such as the US and Australia) now have'.[30]

7.30 An influential interpretation of this view has been to argue that post-Brexit UK should aim to become an offshore financial centre, a 'Singapore-on-Thames'. In this view, Brexit represents an opportunity become a world financial centre that is no longer shackled by the protectionist impulses of the EU.[31] Brexit will allow the UK government to remove unnecessary and burdensome regulatory requirements and to rationalise UK laws. For example, this would allow the UK to redraft EU-derived laws in common law style to ensure greater certainty, to cease the purposive interpretation of legislation, and to move away from inappropriate decision-making by the European courts. Specific proposals have included the removal of the market structure rules in MiFID II, the bonus cap under CRD IV, the fund manager rules under AIFMD, EU rules on processes for indirect clearing, and the commodity position limits imposed by MiFID II.[32]

7.31 During the premiership of Theresa May (2016–19), political and legislative pressures negated these proposals. The enormous number of EU-derived laws applicable in the UK affects all areas of national life. The two-year timetable set by Article 50 of the Lisbon Treaty meant that it was not practicable to engage in a wide-ranging redrafting of EU-derived financial services laws in the UK. This would potentially have been a huge exercise, and lack of parliamentary time militated against any radical approach to legislative reform.

7.32 It was also perceived that unilateral deregulation might place the UK out of step with the current global consensus. International standard-setting bodies such as the International Organization of Securities Commissions (**IOSCO**) and the International Association of Insurance Supervisors (**IAIS**) have been influential in promoting regulatory convergence in recent years. The overall direction of travel in the aftermath of the global financial crisis appears to be towards closer cooperation and convergence. It has been argued that any significant attempt at deregulation might place the UK outside this global consensus.

7.33 This policy stance was evident in the public statements of UK policymakers and regulators, who repeatedly insisted that they did not intend to move towards creating a new Singapore off northern Europe. Stephen Barclay, the then City minister, sought to

---

[30] Sheila Lawlor, 'Preface', in Barnabas Reynolds, *A Blueprint for Brexit: The Future of Global Financial Services and Markets in the UK* (Politeia, 2016).
[31] David P. Blake, 'Brexit and the City' (22 May 2018), available at SSRN: <https://ssrn.com/abstract=3183017> or <http://dx.doi.org/10.2139/ssrn.3183017> accessed 19 November 2018.
[32] Reynolds, *Blueprint for Brexit*.

reassure the other EU Member States that Brexit would not lead to 'heavy deregulation' in the UK, even if no deal was reached on the terms of the departure.[33] The FCA Chief Executive Andrew Bailey affirmed that the UK did not intend to engage in a 'race to the bottom on deregulation'. Bailey stated that 'the stakes are simply too high in terms of our public interest objectives'.[34] Likewise, Christopher Woolard, the FCA director of strategy and competition, explicitly rejected the idea of a 'Singapore-on-Thames', stating that the EU's regulations followed principles which the FCA itself agreed with.[35] The chair of the FCA, Charles Randall[36] and the chair of the PRA, Sam Woods, equally warned against a 'bonfire of regulation'.[37]

7.34 Coming from a similar policy outlook, officials in the EU made near-identical arguments. A senior official at the Deutsche Bundesbank warned that it was necessary 'to avoid a regulatory race to the bottom at all costs', urging UK regulators to 'turn a blind eye to demands for deregulation and lax supervision'.[38] Similarly, a senior official at the ECB stated that it would 'resist any supervisory or regulatory race to the bottom', affirming that 'any bank that moves to the Euro area will have to meet our standards, regardless of whether it comes from the UK or any other place'.[39]

7.35 A further policy consideration was the likelihood of the need for some form of regulatory equivalence with the EU after Brexit. According to this line of thinking, the need to ensure that UK standards are maintained roughly at parity with those of the EU militates against any serious attempt at deregulation for the time being. As John Armour has noted, the UK will have a body of law substantively similar to EU law on exit day, which would to all intents and purposes be equivalent. However, this is likely to lead to a problem of divergence, as the UK could 'fall behind' unless it issues new laws to 'keep up' with the EU. Equivalence is subject to periodic monitoring, and the European Commission has powers to withdraw equivalence.[40]

7.36 The prospect of the UK deregulating its financial services sector was noted by policymakers in the EU. A policy document for the ECON Committee warned that the UK could transform the City of London into an offshore financial centre by minimising tax and regulatory costs. According to the study, this would require many changes to the UK's regulatory and

---

[33] 'City Minister Rules Out Brexit Bonfire of Regulation', *FT Adviser*, 5 December 2017, available at: <https://www.ftadviser.com/regulation/2017/12/05/city-minister-rules-out-brexit-bonfire-of-regulation>, accessed 5 July 2019.

[34] Andrew Bailey, 'Why Free Trade and Open Markets in Financial Services Matter' (6 June 2017), available at: <https://www.fca.org.uk/news/speeches/why-free-trade-and-open-markets-financial-services-matter>, accessed 5 July 2019.

[35] 'FCA Rules Out Brexit Bonfire of Regulation', *FT Adviser*, 10 October 2017, available at: <https://www.ftadviser.com/regulation/2017/10/10/fca-rules-out-brexit-bonfire-of-regulation>, accessed 5 July 2019.

[36] 'City Watchdog Boss Rejects Call for Financial Services Deregulation Post-Brexit', *City A.M.*, 2 October 2019, available at: <http://www.cityam.com/264370/city-watchdog-boss-rejects-calls-financial-services>, accessed 5 July 2019.

[37] 'BoE Deputy Warns Against "Bonfire of the Regulations" after Brexit', *Financial Times*, available at: <https://www.ft.com/content/d9ab6862-09a3-11e8-8eb7-42f857ea9f09>, accessed 5 July 2019.

[38] Andreas Dombret, 'The Possible Impact of Brexit on the Financial Landscape' (24 February 2017), available at: <https://www.bis.org/review/r170228a.htm>, accessed 5 July 2019.

[39] Sabine Lautenschläger, 'Caution Should Be the Life of Banking' (22 March 2017), available at: <https://www.ecb.europa.eu/press/key/date/2017/html/sp170322.en.html>, accessed 5 July 2019.

[40] John Armour, 'Brexit and Financial Services' (2017) 33(1) *Oxford Review of Economic Policy*.

supervisory framework, which risk creating a lack of equivalence with the EU's legal regime. From the EU's point of view, 'in political terms, an offshore financial centre close to the borders of Europe implying certain tax constructions seems not to be a very attractive outlook.'[41] It is likely that UK policymakers have also taken into account the possibility of a hostile response by the EU to any unilateral action by the UK. According to media reports, the EU is prepared to take retaliatory measures in advance of any attempt at deregulation by the UK.[42]

Any attempt to remove EU law from the statute book also poses a conceptual problem. It has been argued that, even though the formal role of EU law may be removed after Brexit, judicial interpretation will inevitably continue to be guided by 'European' concepts, such as the use of purposive interpretation. In order to understand EU-derived law, it will still be necessary to take into account EU interpretations and standards, for example in order to resolve a textual dispute.[43] 7.37

7.5 The EU (Withdrawal) Act 2018

The initial lack of political will to enact a 'bonfire of regulation' is evident in the instrument of the UK's departure from the EU, the European Union (Withdrawal) Act 2018 (the 'EU Withdrawal Act'), which received royal assent on 26 June 2018. As the policy document for the Great Reform Bill, which resulted in the EU Withdrawal Act, made clear, the policy approach was designed to transfer EU legislation directly into UK law, only amending the legislation to the extent needed for it to continue properly to apply in the UK. In the words of the UK government proposal, this was described as the 'converting and preserving' approach.[44] 7.38

In the adoption of the vast body of the EU's *acquis communautaire* into UK law, the UK's foremost policy concern has been to ensure the proper 'onshoring' of EU law. 'Onshoring' is the expression used by HM Treasury and the FCA to refer to the need to ensure that the EU-derived aspects of the UK legal system remained effective and continued to function after the UK left the EU. 7.39

The principal mechanism by which the EU Withdrawal Act is intended to achieve this is by repealing the ECA, thereby ending the formal role of EU law in the UK. This is a critical step, because, as noted above, the ECA has ensured that much EU law applied in the UK: the ECA ensured that EU regulations were directly effective in the UK, and required the national legislature to implement EU directives in UK legislation. The repeal of the ECA will mean that much of the EU law that effective in the UK will fall away. 7.40

---

[41] Directorate-General for Internal Policies of the Union, *Implications of Brexit on EU Financial Services: Study for the ECON Committee* (2017).
[42] Alex Barker and Jim Brunsden, 'EU Seeks Powers to Stop Post-Brexit Bonfire of Regulation', *Financial Times* (1 February 2018), available at: <https://www.ft.com/content/9052ed50-06d5-11e8-9650-9c0ad2d7c5b5>, accessed 5 July 2019.
[43] Ian Forrester, 'European Union Law after Brexit' (2018) 23(1) *Judicial Review* 45–64.
[44] Department for Exiting the EU, *EU (Withdrawal) Bill: Factsheet 2: Converting and Preserving Law*.

7.5.1 Retained EU Law

7.41 The EU Withdrawal Act is intended to ensure that EU directives already implemented in UK law and regulation are preserved after Brexit as 'retained EU law'. In order for retained EU law to remain effective, the EU Withdrawal Act provides powers to UK legislative bodies to make secondary legislation to amend the relevant legislative texts.

7.42 This only applies to 'direct EU legislation' that is in effect on exit day. It does not apply to legislation that has not yet been enacted, and any new EU legislation or amendments to pre-exit legislative texts will not be adopted by the UK under the EU Withdrawal Act, including where the CJEU has decided that a provision is invalid. However, the UK government and UK regulators have the powers to enact laws or rules in order to update laws, especially in the case of legislation that is needed to complete a particular EU-derived legislative package that is not yet complete.

7.5.2 Retained EU Case Law

7.43 According to the EU Withdrawal Act, EU retained law should continue to be interpreted in accordance with 'retained EU case law'.[45] 'Retained EU case law' is defined as 'principles laid down by, and any decisions of, the European Court, as they have effect on EU law immediately before exit day'. However, the UK Supreme Court is able to depart from a decision of the CJEU.[46] UK courts will not be bound by any new case law issued by the CJEU after exit day, but they 'may have regard' to such decisions.[47]

7.5.3 Remedying Deficiencies in Retained Law

7.44 Importantly, UK legislators have powers under section 8 of the EU Withdrawal Act to make initial modifications. UK legislators will be able to issue statutory instruments in order to remedy 'deficiencies' in retained EU law for up to two years after exit day.[48] The UK government stated that it expected around 800 items of secondary legislation would be needed in order to resolve deficiencies of this kind.[49]

7.45 However, in keeping with the publicly stated desire to avoid a 'bonfire of regulation', the power to amend deficiencies in EU retained law is severely restricted by the EU Withdrawal Act. Amendments may only be made where:

(a) there is a failure of retained EU law to operate effectively or there is another deficiency in the retained EU law; and

---

[45] EU Withdrawal Act, s. 6(3).
[46] Ibid., s. 6(4).
[47] Ibid., ss. 6(1) and (2).
[48] Ibid., s. 8(8). The European Union (Withdrawal Agreement) Bill provided that, if there was an implementation period, changes to retained EU law to amend 'deficiencies' in the legislation would be made by the later date of 31 December 2022, rather than 29 March 2021.
[49] HM Government, The EU (Withdrawal) Bill Receives Royal Assent (26 June 2018), available at: <https://www.gov.uk/government/news/the-eu-withdrawal-bill-receives-royal-assent>, accessed 5 July 2019.

(b) the failure or deficiency is a result of the UK's withdrawal from the EU.[50]

7.46 Consequently, the statutory instruments are not intended to make policy changes. 'Deficiency' is expressly defined in section 8(2) of the EU Withdrawal Act, which has the effect of restricting the scope of changes that may be made to the following:

(a) changes to provisions that have no practical application after the UK has left the EU;
(b) changes to provisions that confer functions on EU entities;
(c) changes which contain EU references that are no longer appropriate;
(d) reciprocal arrangements between the UK and the EU or the EU Member States that are no longer in place or appropriate.

7.47 Significantly, a 'deficiency' does not arise because the EU has subsequently amended the relevant law.[51]

7.48 The UK government may expand the categories of what is considered a 'deficiency' in the future.[52] In addition, the UK government will have broad powers to issue provisions that it considers appropriate to 'prevent, remedy or mitigate' a deficiency. This may involve providing UK authorities with powers previously exercised by EU authorities.[53] However, there are limits on these powers. The powers cannot be used to:

(a) create public authorities;
(b) increase taxation; or
(c) make retrospective provision.[54]

7.5.4 Powers of UK Parliament to Make Secondary Legislation

7.49 The EU Withdrawal Act contains specific provisions on the making of secondary legislation. In general terms, statutory instruments are made by Parliament using either the 'affirmative' or 'negative' procedure. The 'affirmative' procedure, which is relatively uncommon, requires a statutory instrument to be approved expressly by the House of Commons and the House of Lords. In contrast, the 'negative' procedure requires only a minister's signature, and remains effective in the absence of express disapproval by either House.

7.50 Given the significant implications of lawmaking in this area, special restrictions have been imposed in Schedule 7 of the EU Withdrawal Act on the making of secondary legislation. This requires that the affirmative procedure must be used for any statutory instrument that provides for any function of an EU entity making a legislative instrument to be exercised instead by a UK authority, except in the case of urgency. In addition, where the negative procedure is to be used for the adoption of a statutory instrument, this must be reviewed by committees of the House of Commons and the House of Lords.

---

[50] EU Withdrawal Act, s. 8(1).
[51] Ibid., s. 8(4).
[52] Ibid., s. 8(3)(b).
[53] Ibid., s. 8(6).
[54] Ibid.

7.51 Section 7 of the EU Withdrawal Act imposes additional controls on making further changes to EU-derived law after the initial modifications have been made under section 8. This is defined as 'retained direct principal EU legislation' and 'retained direct minor EU legislation'. This was inserted as a result of political debate in Parliament, and is likely to make it significantly more difficult to amend retained EU legislation.

7.52 'Retained direct principal EU legislation' (that is, any EU regulation that is treated as retained EU law and which is not 'EU tertiary legislation' (that is, rules made pursuant to an EU regulation or directive)) should be treated as if it is UK primary legislation. This can only be amended by:

- (a) an Act of Parliament;
- (b) secondary legislation under the EU Withdrawal Act; or
- (c) a 'Henry VIII' power in primary legislation or by secondary legislation if the amendment is 'supplementary, incidental or consequential'. A 'Henry VII power' is a power granted in primary legislation that allows secondary legislation to amend primary legislation.

7.53 'Retained direct minor EU legislation' (that is, any other kind of direct EU legislation that is treated as retained EU law) is treated as if it is UK secondary legislation. It can be amended by:

- (a) an Act of Parliament;
- (b) secondary legislation under the UK Withdrawal Act; or
- (c) under a Henry VIII power in prior primary legislation, or by powers granted by prior legislation, provided that the amendment is consistent with retained direct principal EU legislation.

7.6 Statutory Instruments under the EU Withdrawal Act

7.54 A series of statutory instruments have been adopted by Parliament under the EU Withdrawal Act to make the appropriate changes to EU retained law. As currently drafted at the time of writing (25 November 2019), the statutory instruments are intended to make necessary changes to UK law and regulation required in the event of a 'no-deal' Brexit (that is, where there is no withdrawal agreement between the UK and the EU on exit day, and the UK becomes a third country after Brexit).[55]

7.55 The statutory instruments have been made in accordance with the processes required by the EU Withdrawal Act 2018. Most have been made using the negative procedure, but some have followed the affirmative procedure as required by the EU Withdrawal Act.

7.56 The current versions of the statutory instruments assume that there will be no withdrawal agreement in place, so the statutory instruments are intended to ensure that the UK legal

---

[55] 'HM Treasury's approach to financial services legislation under the European Union (Withdrawal) Act', available at: <https://www.gov.uk/government/publications/financial-services-legislation-under-the-eu-withdrawal-act>, accessed 5 July 2019.

and regulatory framework will continue to function in the event of a 'no-deal' Brexit. The changes will therefore reflect that the UK will treat EU Member States as 'third countries' with effect from exit day.

However, if there is a withdrawal agreement between the UK and the EU, the statutory instruments are likely to be required, but they may need to be deferred, revoked or amended to reflect the terms of the withdrawal agreement and the terms of the future relationship between the UK and the EU. The UK government has stated that it may make further changes to the statutory instruments by way of the European Union (Withdrawal Agreement) Bill. **7.57**

In addition, HM Treasury has stated that the UK government may exceptionally provide the EU and Member States with special status rather than as third countries. This would be considered in order to: **7.58**

(a) minimise disruption and avoid material unintended consequences for the continuity of service provision to UK customers and investors;
(b) protect the existing rights of UK customers; and
(c) ensure financial stability.[56]

7.7 Minimising Disruption

Much of the UK government's concern has been to minimise disruption and, if possible, avoid a 'no deal' Brexit. In particular, the UK has planned for: **7.59**

(a) a transitional period (known as the 'implementation period') that would follow the agreement of a bilateral withdrawal agreement; and
(b) temporary transitional relief for firms if a 'no deal' scenario occurs.

7.7.1 Implementation Period in the Event of a UK–EU Withdrawal Agreement

In March 2018, the UK government and the EU announced that they had agreed to an implementation period of twenty-one months commencing on 29 March 2019 until 31 December 2020. The implementation period would be effective if there was a UK–EU withdrawal agreement in place, and would allow the parties to negotiate the detail of the future relationship to be in place by the end of the transition period. **7.60**

During the implementation period, it would be intended that EU law continues to apply in the United Kingdom, and UK and EU firms would continue to have access to each other's financial markets. This would provide individuals and businesses with certainty and avoid the disruption of a 'no deal' scenario. **7.61**

---

[56] HM Treasury, 'HM Treasury's approach to financial services legislation under the European Union (Withdrawal) Act', available at: <https://www.gov.uk/government/publications/financial-services-legislation-under-the-eu-withdrawal-act>, accessed 5 July 2019.

7.62 The UK government set out further detail on its approach to implementing Brexit in its July 2018 White Paper.[57] The White Paper explained that, provided that the UK and EU enter into a withdrawal agreement, there would be an implementation period during which the UK would remain part of the Single Market in financial services. This would allow firms to continue to operate on the same basis as before exit day. EU law would continue to apply in the UK, and the UK government would be required to implement new EU laws, during the implementation period. As a result, firms would need to apply any new EU rules adopted from 29 March 2019 until 31 December 2020. It would be expected that EU laws would cease to apply in the UK at the end of the implementation period.

7.63 The EU Withdrawal Act specifies that EU laws will cease to be effective in the UK on exit day. The UK government therefore proposed a European Union (Withdrawal Agreement) Bill to amend the EU Withdrawal Act in order that EU law would cease to be effective in the UK at the end of the implementation period rather than on exit day. The UK government expected that the implementation period would take place, and that the transfer of EU law into UK law as 'retained EU law' would not take place until 31 December 2020.[58]

7.64 However, subsequent defeats of the UK government in Parliament led to amendments of the proposed timing. Initially, the EU Withdrawal Act was amended so that exit day would be delayed to 22 May 2019 or, if parliamentary approval was not forthcoming, 12 April 2019.[59] Subsequently, the EU Withdrawal Act was amended again to change the definition of 'exit day' to refer to 31 October 2019.[60] Following further political debate in Parliament, the 'exit date' was extended to 31 January 2020.[61]

7.7.2 Temporary Transitional Powers for UK Regulators in the Event of a 'No Deal' Brexit

7.65 HM Treasury announced in October 2018 that it intended to provide financial services regulators with temporary transitional powers, which will only be used in the event of a no-deal Brexit.

7.66 These powers allow the Bank of England, the PRA and the FCA to waive or modify firms' regulatory obligations where those obligations have changed as a result of onshoring EU financial services rules. For example, if onshoring results in a regulatory requirement applying to firms for the first time on exit day, the relevant UK regulator is able to waive or modify the requirement. The intention behind these temporary powers is to ensure continuity for firms on and after exit day.[62]

---

[57] Department for Exiting the European Union, *Legislating for the Withdrawal Agreement between the United Kingdom and the European Union* (July 2018), available at: <https://www.gov.uk/government/publications/legislating-for-the-withdrawal-agreement-between-the-united-kingdom-and-the-european-union>, accessed 5 July 2019.
[58] Ibid.
[59] European Union (Withdrawal) Act 2018 (Exit Day) (Amendment) Regulations 2019.
[60] European Union (Withdrawal) Act 2018 (Exit Day) (Amendment) (No. 2) Regulations 2019.
[61] European Union (Withdrawal) Act 2018 (Exit Day) (Amendment) (No. 3) Regulations 2019.
[62] SI 2019/632. See HM Treasury, *Proposal for a Temporary Transitional Power to be Exercised by UK Regulators* (8 October 2018), available at: <https://www.gov.uk/government/publications/proposal-for-a-temporary-transitional-power-to-be-exercised-by-uk-regulators>, accessed 5 July 2019.

7.67 Notwithstanding the availability of these powers, the FCA has stated that there are some areas where it would not be consistent with its statutory objectives to grant temporary transitional relief. In these areas, the FCA has stated that firms should begin preparing to comply with their changed obligations prior to Brexit. This affects the following areas:

(a) MiFID II transaction reporting;
(b) EMIR reporting obligations;
(c) information and disclosure requirements applying to EEA Issuers that have securities traded or admitted to trading on UK markets;
(d) contractual recognition of bail-in under the BRRD;
(e) the market-making exemption under the Short Selling Regulation;
(f) use of credit ratings issued or endorsed by FCA-registered credit ratings agencies after exit day; and
(g) securitisations that UK originators or sponsors wish be considered simple, transparent, and standardised under the Securitisation Regulation.[63]

7.68 Similarly, the Bank of England and PRA have confirmed that they will *not* provide transitional relief in relation to the following areas. Consequently, the PRA considered that firms would need to be ready to comply with these changes by exit day, in the event that there is no implementation period:

(a) contractual recognition of bail-in under the BRRD;
(b) stay in resolution rules;
(c) rules relating to depositor protection under the Financial Services Compensation Scheme;
(d) provisions that contain already contain specific transitional or savings provisions;
(e) exemptions for central banks and other bodies from certain requirements;
(f) certain obligations relating to the Securitisation Regulation;
(g) legislative references to EU International Accounting Standards;
(h) the use by firms of technical information produced by the PRA after Brexit;
(i) obligations for central counterparties under MiFIR and EMIR;
(j) arrangements for settlement finality protection to be extended to financial market infrastructure providers not governed by UK law and third country central banks; and
(k) arrangements for the recognition of third country central securities depositories.[64]

7.8 Allocation of Powers to UK Regulators

7.69 New lawmaking powers for UK regulators are set out in the Financial Regulators' Powers (Technical Standards etc.) (Amendment etc.) (EU Exit) Regulations 2018 (the

---

[63] See https://www.fca.org.uk/news/statements/brexit-what-we-expect-firms-now, accessed 5 July 2019 and ch. 3, FCA, Brexit Policy Statement: Feedback on CP 18/28, CP 18/29, CP 18/34, CP 18/36, and CP 19/2 (PS 19/5) (February 2019) (hereafter 'FCA, PS 19/5').

[64] Bank of England and PRA, *CP 25/18*, ch. 4; Bank of England and PRA, 'The Bank of England's Amendments to Financial Services Legislation under the European Union (Withdrawal) Act 2018 (PS 5/19)' (February 2019) (hereafter, 'Bank of England and PRA, PS 5/19 (February 2019)'), s. A.

'Financial Regulators' Powers SI').[65] These powers were made under section 8 of the EU Withdrawal Act.

7.70 The purpose of the Financial Regulators' Powers SI was to ensure that the FCA, PRA, Bank of England, and the PSR have the power to amend EU-derived rules in their rule books and any existing EU technical standards that have been adopted in UK law in accordance with the EU Withdrawal Act.

7.71 These limited powers are intended to allow UK regulators to correct 'deficiencies' in legislation rather than to effect any policy changes.

7.72 The Financial Regulators' Powers SI sets out the powers of UK regulators to make 'EU exit instruments' which amend EU Regulations containing technical standards to ensure that they continue to be effective after Brexit. Part 2 of the Financial Regulators' Powers SI specifies which UK regulator will be the appropriate regulator with powers to amend the relevant EU regulation by issuing an 'EU exit instrument' (see Figure 7.3).

7.73 The UK regulators also have the power, under Part 3 of the Financial Regulators' Powers SI, to make standards instruments containing new technical standards or modify, amend, or revoke existing technical standards that have been domesticated into UK law.

7.74 Where the PRA and the FCA, or the FCA and the Bank of England are the appropriate regulators, neither may make an exit instrument which amends an EU regulation unless:

(a) the other regulator has been consulted on the proposal to divide the EU regulation into two parts; or
(b) if the relevant EU regulation is not being divided, the other regulator consents to any amendments being made.

7.75 Any EU exit instruments are subject to HM Treasury approval.

7.9 The Bank of England's Approach to Onshoring

7.76 HM Treasury has delegated powers to the Bank of England and the PRA to amend their existing rules and ensure that technical standards can be implemented in the UK. These changes would only take effect if there is no implementation period agreed between the UK and the EU as part of a UK–EU withdrawal agreement.

7.77 On the other hand, if there is an implementation period, the Bank of England would expect the changes to take effect from the end of the period. However, further changes may be made to reflect changes to rules and technical standards during the implementation period and the provisions of the EU Withdrawal Act.[66]

7.78 The Bank of England and the PRA have proposed to use the temporary transitional powers to ensure that firms do not generally have to prepare to implement any onshoring changes

---

[65] SI 2018/115.
[66] Bank of England and PRA, 'The Bank's Approach to Amending Financial Services Legislation under the EU (Withdrawal) Act 2018 (CP 15/28)' (October 2018) (hereafter 'Bank of England and PRA, *CP 15/28*').

Powers of UK regulators under the Financial Regulators' Powers SI
Financial Conduct Authority The FCA is the appropriate regulator for EU Regulations related to the following legislation: • Alternative Investment Fund Managers Directive • Credit Ratings Agencies Regulations • European Markets Infrastructure Regulation • European Social Entrepreneurship Fund Regulation • European Venture Capital Funds Regulation • Insurance Distribution Directive • Market Abuse Regulation • MiFID II Directive • MiFIR • Mortgage Credit Directive • Packaged Retail and Insurance-Based Investment Products Regulation • Payment Services Directive • Prospectus Directive • Short Selling Regulation • Transparency Directive • UCITS
Prudential Regulation Authority The PRA is the appropriate regulator for the EU Regulations related to the following legislation: • Capital Requirements Directive • Capital Requirements Regulation • Central Securities Depositories Regulation • Institutions for Occupational Pensions Provision Directive • Solvency II
Bank of England The Bank of England is the appropriate regulator for Regulations related to the following legislation: • Bank Recovery and Resolution Directive • Central Securities Depositories Regulation • European Markets Infrastructure Regulation
PRA and FCA Both the PRA and FCA are appropriate regulators for Regulations related to the following legislation: • Bank Recovery and Resolution Directive • Capital Requirements Directive • Capital Requirements Regulation • EMIR • Financial Conglomerates Directive
FCA and Bank of England Both the FCA and the Bank of England are appropriate regulators for Regulations related to the following legislation: • MiFIR • EMIR
Payment Services Regulator The PSR is the appropriate regulator for tthe following legislation: • Interchange Fee Regulation

Figure 7.3 Powers of UK regulators under the Financial Regulators' Powers SI

by exit day. They recognised that it would be challenging for firms to comply with onshoring changes where no specific transitional arrangement was agreed.

7.79 The Bank of England and the PRA have delegated powers under the Financial Regulators' Powers Regulations. The Bank and PRA have stated that 'the Bank and PRA will not be making amendments that are unrelated to the UK's withdrawal from the EU as part of this process. Therefore, the proposed changes do not reflect any change in Bank or PRA policy, except to reflect the UK's withdrawal from the EU.'[67]

7.10 The FCA's Approach to Onshoring

7.80 After the UK's exit from the EU, the FCA will be able to make its own changes to technical standards in accordance with its statutory powers. The Financial Regulators' Powers SI includes a list of EU regulations for which UK regulators are the appropriate regulators after Brexit. According to the FCA, this will result in the following changes:

(a) **Credit rating agencies.** Amendments are required to technical standards including cross-cutting changes. The requirement to receive reports on credit ratings will be transferred from ESMA to the FCA.

(b) **Fund management.** The FCA intends to amend technical standards associated with AIFMD and the UCITS Directive.

(c) **EMIR.** The FCA will make consequential changes to EU regulations on the format and detail of applications for registration as trade repositories.

(d) **MiFID II.** The FCA has reviewed the 44 technical standards associated with MIFID II, and intends to make mostly non-material amendments, including cross-cutting. The FCA has specific concerns with RTS 22 (transaction reporting) and RTS 23 (instrument reference data), and intends to establish an onshored transaction reporting regime. Nine technical standards will be removed as they relate to obligations that will cease on leaving the EU.

(e) **Short selling.** Most of the changes to technical standards are cross-cutting changes and minor consequential changes, such as the obligation on ESMA to publish shares traded on EU venues that are exempt from the Short Selling Regulation as principally traded outside the EU, will be transferred to FCA, which will publish the list of shares principally traded outside UK.

(f) **Capital requirements.** Onshoring changes will be required to technical standards. The FCA will share this responsibility with the PRA.[68]

7.11 The PSR's Approach to Onshoring

7.81 The PSR has set out its approach to financial services legislation under the EU Withdrawal Act. According to the PSR, it will be tasked with amending and maintaining the technical standards made under the Interchange Fee Regulation. These powers are linked to the PSR's

---

[67] Bank of England and PRA, *CP 25/18*, p. 4.
[68] FCA, *CP 18/28*, ch. 5; FCA, PS 19/5, chs. 6, 8, and 9.

role as the main competent authority for the Interchange Fee Regulation in the UK.[69] The PSR subsequently consulted on changes to the Interchange Fee Regulation, with the amendments adopted by way of an EU exit instrument in early 2019.[70]

7.12 The UK Regulators' Approach to Non-Legislative EU Materials

7.82 In the context of Brexit, the UK regulators have had to decide how to deal with a large number of non-legislative materials, including Level 3 EU guidelines, template forms, and Q&A documents. Although these are in form of 'soft law', they are highly influential in the UK, and are frequently relied upon by practitioners and their professional advisers in order to interpret EU law. EU regulators and firms are currently under an obligation to 'make every effort to comply' with non-legislative material of this kind. National competent authorities are not bound by such material, but they must inform the relevant ESA if they do not intend to comply with them, on a 'comply or explain' basis.

7.83 Currently the ESAs do not maintain an exhaustive list of guidelines or recommendations, but they are generally available on the relevant ESA's website. Prominent examples include ESMA's guidance on MiFID II and EMIR, as well as earlier CESR guidance on MiFID I.

7.84 The EU Withdrawal Act will not incorporate these materials into UK law. It does not preserve as 'retained EU law' any guidelines, recommendations, FAQs or other non-binding pre-Brexit Level 3 pronouncements by the European Commission or the ESA. Specifically, HM Treasury has stated that it intends to delete the obligation to make every effort to comply with them.[71] Given their non-binding nature, to do so is unnecessary.

7.85 Nevertheless, the Bank of England and the PRA have recognised that these non-legislative materials will continue to be relevant, and stated that:

(a) it is expected that firms and financial market infrastructures (FMIs) will 'continue to "make every effort to comply" with any Guidelines and Recommendations that they are currently expected to comply with, to the extent that they remain relevant after the UK's withdrawal from the EU'.[72] This approach is set out in a Statement of Policy on 'Interpretation of EU Guidelines and Recommendations: Bank of England and PRA approach after the UK's withdrawal from the EU'.[73]

---

[69] PSR, *The PSR's Approach to Financial Services Legislation under the European Union (Withdrawal) Act* (27 June 2018), available at: <https://www.psr.org.uk/psr-publications/news-announcements/PSR-approach-financial-services-legislation-under-EU-withdrawal-act>, accessed 5 July 2019.

[70] See https://www.psr.org.uk/psr-publications/consultations/cp18-3-onshoring-EU-regulatory-technical-standards-under-the-IFR> and https://www.psr.org.uk/psr-publications/policy-statements/onshoring-eu-regulatory-technical-standards-under-ifr>, accessed 5 July 2019.

[71] HM Treasury, *Guidance: Regulations relating to the European Supervisory Authorities and the European Systemic Risk Board* (9 October 2018), available at: <https://www.gov.uk/government/publications/regulations-relating-to-the-european-supervisory-authorities-and-the-european-systemic-risk-board/regulations-relating-to-the-european-supervisory-authorities-and-the-european-systemic-risk-board>, accessed 5 July 2019.

[72] Bank of England and PRA, *CP 25/18*, ch. 5.

[73] Bank of England and PRA, Interpretation of EU Guidelines and Recommendations: Bank of England and PRA approach after the UK's withdrawal from the EU (April 2019) (hereafter Bank of England and PRA, 'Interpretation of EU Guidelines and Recommendations').

(b) they do not propose to reproduce and make amendments to the content of individual guidelines and recommendations ahead of exit day. However, 'firms and FMIs should interpret them in light of onshoring changes that are being made to financial services legislation' under the EU Withdrawal Act.

7.86 The relevant guidelines have been listed by the Bank of England and PRA. However, they note that the list is not exhaustive, and that, for example, guidelines made by predecessor committees to the ESAs (that is, Committees of European Banking Supervisors (**CEBS**), European Insurance and Occupational Pensions Supervisors (**CEIOPS**), and European Securities Regulators (**CESR**)) may continue to be relevant unless they have been revoked or replaced. The Bank of England and PRA have also confirmed that they do not expect firms to comply with guidelines where the UK has previously informed the EU authorities that it does not intend to comply with them; the CP contains a list of these guidelines. As is the case with new EU legislative changes, any changes to guidelines or recommendations by EU authorities will not automatically apply in the UK after exit day.[74]

7.87 The FCA has set out its approach to existing non-legislative materials, which is similar to that of the Bank of England and the PRA. It intends to issue non-Handbook guidance on this approach, which will specify that:

(a) The FCA recognises value of Level 3 material and considers that it will continue to be relevant.
(b) The FCA expects financial institutions and other market participants to continue to apply ESA guidelines and recommendations.
(c) References to other non-legislative materials, such as European Commission Q&As and ESA opinions, may continue to be relevant, and the FCA will continue to have regard to these as appropriate.
(d) The FCA expects to continue to apply ESA guidelines and recommendations that relate to the FCA's functions, to the extent that the FCA already complies with them.[75]

7.88 The FCA has stated that it does not intend to carry out a detailed, line-by-line review of the Level 3 materials. It expects financial institutions to interpret materials 'sensibly and purposively, taking into account the UK's withdrawal from the EU, the provisions of the EU Withdrawal Act and amendments made to relevant legislation in the withdrawal process'.[76]

7.89 However, the FCA proposes to change a specific reference to the EBA guidelines in relation to the bonus cap. This refers to a notional discount rate that can be applied to variable remuneration awarded to material risk takers to calculate the bonus cap. The discount rate relies on inflation and interest rates produced by Eurostat, a European Commission entity based in Luxembourg, which may not be provided after exit day. This has instead been replaced by a Handbook note reference.[77]

---

[74] Bank of England and PRA, 'Interpretation of EU Guidelines and Recommendations'. See also Bank of England and PRA, *CP 25/18*, ch. 5.
[75] FCA, *CP 18/28*; FCA, *PS 19/5*, ch. 10.
[76] FCA, *CP 18/28*, p. 36; FCA, *PS 19/5*, ch. 10.
[77] FCA, *PS 19/5*, ch. 10.

7.13 The Impact of Brexit on the FCA Handbook

7.90 The FCA rules will need to be amended to be consistent with the new legal framework following the UK's exit from the European Union. The FCA may amend its Handbook using powers under the Financial Regulators Powers SI. This means that there is no formal requirement for the FCA to issue a public consultation, although the FCA has chosen to do so, or a cost–benefit analysis. Any amendments to be made by the FCA must nevertheless be approved by HM Treasury.

7.91 The FCA has identified a number of 'cross-cutting issues', that is, issues that affect multiple parts of the FCA Handbook and technical standards. In particular, this will involve amending the FCA Handbook by:

(a) replacing references to EU law;
(b) deleting provisions related to passporting rights; and
(c) removing references to EU Member States, EU institutions, and the sharing of information with ESAs and other competent authorities.[78]

7.92 In addition to cross-cutting issues, the FCA has proposed the following changes:

(a) **Changes to prudential standards.** The FCA intends to amend prudential standards, including to remove preferential treatment for exposures originating from EU Member States.
(b) **Changes to COBS.** The FCA will make a number of amendments to COBS. For example, it will amend COBS 1 so that COBS will apply to EEA firms that obtain FCA or PRA authorisation in same way as any UK-authorised third country firm. It will remove the statement in COBS 2 firms can rely on information from EEA authorised firms, for example for the purposes of suitability or appropriateness assessments. The distinction in COBS 3 between EEA and non-EEA local authorities for purposes of the elective professional client assessment will be removed.
(c) **Fund management rules.** The FCA intends to make a number of consequential changes to FUND and COLL to reflect the removal of EU law.
(d) **MiFID II.** The FCA will also make changes to the Handbook to reflect the onshoring of MiFID II.[79]

7.14 The Impact of Brexit on the PRA Rulebook

7.93 The PRA issued near-final rules containing changes to the PRA Rulebook and onshored technical standards after Brexit.[80] The amendments are intended to fix deficiencies in the PRA Rulebook, and relation to Binding Technical Standards (BTS) that will be onshored into UK law.

---

[78] FCA, *CP 18/28*, ch. 3; FCA, *PS 19/5*, ch. 4.
[79] FCA, *CP 18/28*, ch. 4; FCA, *PS 19/5*, ch. 6.
[80] Bank of England and PRA, *The Bank of England's amendments to financial services legislation under the European Union (Withdrawal) Act 2018* (June 2019) (updating April 2019) (PS 5/19). See also PRA, *UK Withdrawal from the EU: Changes to PRA Rulebook and Onshored Binding Technical Standards* (October 2018) (CP 26/18).

7.94 The PRA's consultations and policy statements, issued with the Bank of England, set out the proposals on how existing non-binding PRA materials, including supervisory statements, statements of policy and the PRA approach documents should be interpreted after Brexit. The changes proposed by the PRA are amendments to ensure an operable legal framework after the UK withdraws from the EU.

7.95 Like the FCA, the PRA may only use the powers delegated under the EU Withdrawal Act to fix 'deficiencies', and cannot make policy changes unrelated to the UK's withdrawal from the EU. The PRA is not required to issue a public consultation, but has chosen to do so to help keep stakeholders informed.

7.96 In particular, the PRA proposed detailed changes in relation to the following areas:

(a) contractual recognition of bail-in and stay in resolution;
(b) technical standards for risk mitigation techniques for OTC derivatives not cleared by a central counterparty;
(c) ring-fenced banks;
(d) location of branch assets for PRA-regulated insurers;
(e) location of admissible assets for non-Solvency II firms;
(f) exposure of credit unions to EEA credit institutions;
(g) prudential rules for firms in the UK temporary permissions regime; and
(h) FSCS protection.

7.15 The Overseas Persons' Exclusion after Brexit

7.97 The UK has traditionally had a liberal approach to overseas firms wishing to operate in the UK. This approach is exemplified by the 'overseas persons' exclusion', which was previously in the Financial Services Act 1986 and subsequently passed into the FSMA framework. This exclusion is a UK-specific rule that is not part of EU law.

7.98 The overseas persons' exclusion allows non-UK firms to carry on certain regulated activities in the UK, subject to certain conditions. As a general rule, it is prohibited for a person to carry on regulated activities in the UK unless that person is authorised or exempt.[81] Broadly, the UK Regulated Activities Order (**RAO**) provides an exclusion to allow an overseas person to carry on the following regulated activities, provided it does not do so from a permanent place of business in the UK:

(a) dealing in investments as principal;
(b) dealing in investments as agent;
(c) arranging deals in investments;
(d) making arrangements with a view to transactions in investments;
(e) arranging, entering into or administering a home finance transaction;
(f) operating a multilateral trading facility;
(g) operating an organised trading facility;
(h) advising on investments; and
(i) agreeing to carry on a regulated activity.[82]

---

[81] FSMA, s. 19.
[82] RAO, Art. 72. For FCA guidance on the overseas persons exclusion, see ch. 2.9 in the Perimeter Guidance sourcebook in the FCA Handbook.

The exclusion is generally available if the overseas person carries on the regulated activity: **7.99**

(a) with or through an authorised firm, or a person that is exempt from authorisation; or
(b) following a legitimate approach (that is, an approach made to or from a UK client that does not breach UK rules on financial promotions).

The overseas persons' exclusion has been an important element of the UK's liberalised financial markets. In particular, it has allowed firms from key non-EEA jurisdictions in the Americas, Africa, Asia, and Australia, which have not had EEA passporting rights, to operate in the UK. As a result, during previous episodes of regulatory change, the UK government has defended the overseas persons' exclusion. For example, the UK government chose not to apply the provisions of Article 39 of the MiFID II Directive, which would have provided the UK with a more comprehensive third country regime for MiFID investment services, partly because of concerns that this would undermine or otherwise limit the overseas persons' exclusion.[83] **7.100**

During the UK's negotiations on Brexit, UK policymakers and regulators stated their intention to maintain the overseas persons' exclusion as an important means of access for firms within and outside the EEA post-Brexit. The Chief Executive of the FCA, Andrew Bailey, cited the overseas persons' exclusion as an example of the UK's approach to open financial markets that is independent of the EU's regulatory framework. He praised the exclusion as a 'sensible and proportionate way to support stable global markets'.[84] **7.101**

Consequently, it appears unlikely that the UK government will seek to amend the overseas persons' exclusion as a result of Brexit. Nevertheless, following the appointment of Boris Johnson as prime minister in July 2019, it is possible that the UK government will implement a more wide-ranging reform of the UK's regulatory framework, which may conceivably include changes to the overseas persons' exclusion. **7.102**

7.16 Reallocation of Supervisory Powers

UK regulators will exercise supervision over EEA firms as a result of the UK Temporary Permissions Regime which will allow EEA firms to continue operating in the UK for a time-limited period after exit day in the event of a 'no deal' scenario.[85] The Temporary Permissions Regime is intended to allow EEA firms wishing to continue to operate in the UK sufficient time to apply for full authorisation from UK regulators. If this regime was not in place, it would mean that EEA firms would lose their EEA passporting rights on exit day without having the necessary permissions to carry on regulated activity. **7.103**

---

[83] HM Treasury, *Transposition of the Markets in Financial Instruments Directive II: Response to the Consultation* (February 2017) 5.
[84] Andrew Bailey, 'Brexit: What Does It Mean for Financial Markets to Be Open?' (24 April 2018), available at: <https://www.fca.org.uk/news/speeches/brexit-what-does-it-mean-financial-markets-be-open> accessed 19 November 2018.
[85] FCA, *Temporary Permissions Regime for Inbound Firms and Funds* (October 2018) (CP18/29).

7.104 The creation of the Temporary Permissions Regime means that UK regulators will exercise direct supervisory powers over inbound EEA firms for the first time. These firms will previously have been supervised primarily by their home state regulators. EEA firms requiring a temporary permission are expected to notify the relevant UK regulator. This is expected to be a significant increase in the regulatory responsibilities of UK regulators.

7.105 The UK has also issued legislation to ensure that existing contractual obligations not covered by the Temporary Permissions Regime can continue in force. The Financial Services Contracts Regime (FSCR) is intended to ensure that, where an incoming EEA firm fails to apply for a temporary permission or fails to secure authorisation after the end of a permission, the firm can service its UK contracts in order to wind down its UK business. As a result, UK regulators will be responsible for supervising the run-off of this business, and will also be able to extend the period of such run-off, subject to approval from HM Treasury.

7.106 In addition, the UK is expected to leave the ESAs after Brexit. Consequently, the roles carried on by the ESAs are to be reallocated among the UK regulators after Brexit. This means that, for example, UK regulators will become responsible for certain kinds of entities that have previously been supervised by the ESAs or by EU home state regulators:

(a) The FCA will become responsible for supervising UK trade repositories and credit rating agencies that have previously been supervised at the EU level by ESMA.

(b) The Bank of England is responsible for regulating central counterparties (**CCPs**) and central securities depositories (**CSDs**). After Brexit, the Bank of England will be responsible for supervising non-UK CCPs and CSDs, including those from EU Member States, subject to the application of the Temporary Permissions regime.

7.107 Previously, non-EEA firms have been allowed to operate in the EEA following an equivalence decision under third country regimes. After Brexit, UK regulators will become responsible for making assessments under which non-UK legal and regulatory jurisdictions are deemed to be equivalent. For example:

(a) After Brexit, the European Commission's function of making equivalence decisions under the CRR for third country regimes will be transferred to HM Treasury. The PRA will become responsible for providing HM Treasury with technical assessments of third country regimes.

(b) Similarly, the Commission's power to make equivalence decisions under EMIR will pass to HM Treasury, while the FCA rather than ESMA will be responsible for recognising non-UK trade repositories and the Bank of England will be responsible for the application and timing of the clearing obligation.[86]

7.108 There are a number of areas in which equivalence decisions will be important. For example, following the UK's onshoring of EU legislation, UK legislation will include a UK-specific share trading obligation similar to that in Article 23 of MiFIR. This will require investment firms to trade shares admitted to trading on a UK trading venue on certain categories of

---

[86] See <https://www.gov.uk/government/publications/draft-over-the-counter-derivatives-central-counterparties-and-trade-repositories-amendment-etc-and-transitional-provision-eu-exit-regulations/draft-over-the-counter-derivatives-central-counterparties-and-trade-repositories-amendment-etc-and-transitional-provision-eu-exit-regulations>, accessed 5 July 2019.

UK venue or equivalent third country venues. It is possible that this may conflict with the EU's share trading obligation, particularly where shares are dual listed in the UK and an EU Member State, or where the UK branch of an EEA firm is subject to both UK and EU obligations. Similar concerns apply in respect of the derivatives trading obligation in Article 28 of MiFIR. It will be important for UK regulators to consider making equivalence decisions in tandem with their EU partners in order to avoid conflicts of this kind.

In addition, there are a number of technical functions performed by the ESAs that will need to be transferred to UK regulators. For example, the MiFID II transparency regime relies on functions including a series of calculations that are performed by ESMA. In the event of a 'no-deal' Brexit scenario, ESMA would cease to perform these functions which would need to be transferred to the FCA. The Markets in Financial Instruments (Amendment) (EU Exit) Regulations 2018 provides the FCA with temporary powers that can be exercised for a transitional period of up to four years to ensure that the MiFID transparency regime can continue to operate after exit day in the event of a 'no-deal' Brexit. 7.109

7.17 Regulatory Cooperation

As a result of Brexit, the UK will no longer be subject to the ESAs' intervention powers including cross-border mediation. The loss of the supervisory mediation and dispute resolution mechanisms of ESAs means that the UK may lose concrete solutions to common regulatory problems.[87] In principle, third countries may participate in ESAs as an observer, but are subject to financial contributions and staff obligations, and this only applies to third countries that adopt and apply EU law, such as the EFTA EEA states, so this is not likely to be suitable for the UK.[88] Instead, like other third country supervisors, the UK is required to enter into non-binding arrangements with the EU for supervisory cooperation, information sharing, and participation in supervisory colleges.[89] 7.110

From the outset, UK regulators have made clear the need for continued cooperation with EU authorities. In the absence of the framework provided by the EU system of financial supervision, Andrew Bailey of the FCA called for an 'optimal framework' for the outcome, including regulatory cooperation and information sharing.[90] Similarly, the Bank of England and PRA confirmed that, even though the existing arrangements for participation in EU supervisory colleges and joint decision-making will be removed, the UK will continue to participate in bilateral and multilateral cooperation mechanisms. The UK regulators will rely on existing FSMA provisions to support supervisory cooperation with third countries, and UK regulators will participate in global supervisory colleges and crisis management groups.[91] 7.111

These arrangements were formalised in memoranda of understanding (MoUs) agreed in early 2019 between the FCA, PRA, and EU regulators. The MoUs provide for continued 7.112

---

[87] Ellis Ferran, 'Regulatory Parity'.
[88] EBA Regulation, Arts. 75(3), 75(1).
[89] Ibid., Arts. 33(1), 75(2).
[90] Andrew Bailey, letter to Andrew Tyrie MP, 28 October 2016.
[91] Bank of England and PRA, *CP 25/18*, p. 8.

cooperation and the exchange of information after the UK leaves the EU, including in the event of a 'no-deal' Brexit. The MoUs consist of the following:

(a) A multilateral MoU between the FCA and EU and EEA national competent authorities covering supervisory cooperation, enforcement, and the exchange of information.
(b) An MoU between the FCA and ESMA covering the supervision of credit rating agencies and trade repositories.
(c) An MoU between the FCA, PRA, and EBA covering supervisory cooperation and the exchange of information.[92]

7.18 Treatment of 'In Flight' Legislation

7.113 The UK government has previously indicated that it intends to allow HM Treasury, in the event of a 'no deal', to implement and amend so-called in-flight legislation (that is, EU legislation that has not been adopted prior to exit day). The EU Withdrawal Act does not permit the implementation of 'in flight' legislation. The Financial Services (Implementation of Legislation) Bill was intended to provide HM Treasury with the necessary powers.[93] The Bill only covered EU legislation that is implemented on a date up to two years after exit day.

7.114 Under the Bill, the relevant legislation consisted of:

(a) the settlement discipline regime under the CSDR (Articles 6 and 7);
(b) the Delegated Cash Penalties Regulation;
(c) provisions of the Prospectus Regulation that came into force on 21 July 2019 and any secondary EU legislation adopted by the European Commission before that date;
(d) the reporting obligation under the Securities Financing Transactions Regulation;
(e) the proposed revisions to the EU Capital Requirements Directive, Capital Requirements Regulation and BRRD, published by the European Commission on 23 November 2016 (known as the 'risk reduction package');
(f) the proposed CCP Recovery and Resolution Regulation published by the European Commission on 28 November 2016;
(g) the proposed revisions to EMIR and the related changes to the regulations establishing the ESAs on third country CCP authorisation and supervision (known as 'EMIR Refit' and 'EMIR 2.2') published by the European Commission on 13 June 2017;
(h) the proposed prudential regime for EU investment firms and related changes to CRR, CRD, and MiFID II;
(i) the proposed directive on cross-border distribution of collective investment funds;

---

[92] See <https://www.fca.org.uk/news/press-releases/fca-agrees-mous-esma-and-eu-regulators-allow-co-operation-and-exchange-information> and <https://www.fca.org.uk/news/press-releases/pra-and-fca-agree-memorandum-understanding-mou-eba>

[93] The Bill was not passed before the dissolution of Parliament in November 2019, and fell away as a result, meaning that maintaining alignment with the EU after Brexit will require new primary legislation (see further, House of Commons library briefing paper 7628 (13 August 2019) entitled 'Brexit and Financial Services').

(j) the proposed directive on the issue of covered bonds and covered bond supervision and related changes to the CRR;
(k) the proposed regulation on the promotion of the use of SME growth markets; and
(l) the proposed revisions to various EU pieces of legislation aimed at strengthening the EU's framework for preventing money laundering and terrorist financing, published by the Commission on 12 September 2018.[94]

7.19 Impact of a 'No-Deal' Scenario

If no bilateral mechanism is agreed to apply after Brexit, WTO law especially the General Agreement on Trade in Services will apply between the UK and EU alongside and in addition to any bilateral agreements. A bilateral agreement will make some but not all aspects of WTO redundant, but some WTO rights and obligations will continue to apply. It has been noted that, from experience of other free trade agreements, even if a deep and comprehensive trade agreement exists between two trading partners, they almost always prefer to settle trade disputes via the WTO. However, the WTO has a limited oversight role and its law has untested and uncertain application.[95]

7.115

In a 'no deal' Brexit, the UK would be a third country in relation to the EU and would fall under third country regimes. Most third country regimes rely on the equivalence of the third country's regulatory and supervisory regime, which is determined unilaterally by European Commission. In event of a no-deal Brexit, the UK may seek to apply for equivalence, which would require close co-operation between the UK and EU authorities. For example, equivalence under MiFID II would require a cooperation agreement between ESMA and the competent authority of the third country whose regulatory and supervisory framework has been recognised by the European Commission as equivalent. As a minimum, this would require a mechanism for the exchange of information, and procedures for coordination of supervisory activities and on-site inspections.[96] It will also be necessary for UK authorities to carry out a similar assessment regarding the equivalence of the EU's regulatory and supervisory framework, as required by the UK's onshored legislation.

7.116

It is possible that the UK will be subject to the existing third country framework. For example, the CRD IV third country regime provides for consolidated supervision by third country supervisory authority (Article 127(1), CRD IV), which states that a competent national authority may determine that a third country supervisory authority is responsible for consolidated supervision if its supervisory framework is equivalent to that of the EU.

7.117

7.20 Conclusion

The initial response of the UK government was not to engage in a 'bonfire of regulation' as a result of the UK's referendum to leave the European Union. As this chapter has argued,

7.118

---

[94] HM Treasury, Financial Services (Implementation of Legislation) Bill: Updated Policy Note (February 2019).
[95] Andrew Lang, 'The "Default Option"? The WTO and Cross-border Financial Services Trade after Brexit', in Alexander et al., *Brexit and Financial Services*, pp. 155–217.
[96] MiFIR, Art. 47.

there was little appetite at the UK regulators for significant deregulation of the UK's financial services industry. Equally, at the international level, there was no real impetus to deregulate. The regulatory direction of travel at international bodies such as IOSCO, IAIS, and the Basel Committee is towards regulatory convergence, and there is a perception that the concept of 'light-touch' regulation has been largely discredited after the 2007–8 global financial crisis.

7.119 UK policymakers are also subject to short- to medium-term political concerns about sparking a 'trade war' in financial services with EU. The mutually beneficial dynamic of cross-border trade in financial services means that UK regulators consider that regulatory cooperation will be needed, and lawmakers may be wary of losing equivalence or encouraging retaliation by the EU.

7.120 Within the European Union, the role of the ESAs looks likely to expand. Having been operational since 2011, they have become to a large extent 'battle-hardened' by the experience of carrying out the Commission's instructions in relation to MiFID II, Solvency II, and other significant pieces of legislation. Moloney has suggested that that the loss of UK expertise at this stage is not likely to be as critical for the ESAs as it would have been at the outset. The ESAs are likely to become more powerful inside Europe without the UK acting as a restraining influence and in particular they are likely to play a crucial role in driving towards a more explicitly 'European' agenda, for example, towards closer financial and banking union.[97]

7.121 Nevertheless, despite the initial lack of momentum towards a 'bonfire of regulation', divergence between the UK and the EU may be more likely in the future. In particular, a severe political crisis in EU–UK relations or an economic crisis that calls into question the ethos of the UK's current regulatory framework could equally encourage a more radical approach. In particular, the appointment of Boris Johnson as prime minister in July 2019 led to increased calls for deregulation which may in time lead to a shift in government policy.

7.122 Ultimately, therefore, Brexit may represent an opportunity for sectors within the UK financial services industry. Firms may find that UK regulators outside the constraints of the EU framework become more responsive and transparent and better able to respond to UK-specific conditions, in contrast to the 'black box' of EU decision-making. At the very least, the onshoring of legislation and institutional power will mean that firms deal with lawmakers and regulators who are more directly accountable to the industry which they regulate.

---

[97] Moloney, 'International Financial Governance'.

8

PRA Approach to the Authorisation of International Branches and Subsidiaries

Clive Cunningham, Katherine Dillon, and Alison Matthews

8.1 Introduction

Under the UK regulatory framework, an overseas bank, (re)insurer, or other financial services firm (or group) that is seeking access to UK clients and markets has three options for doing so: **8.01**

- provision of services into the UK remotely on a cross-border basis (without a UK office or other place of business);
- establishment of a regulated UK branch; or
- incorporation of a regulated UK legal entity (e.g. a subsidiary company).

At present, the EEA single market for financial services means that scenarios one and two are possible for EEA firms on a semi-automatic basis under passporting arrangements. A large number of EEA banks, (re)insurers, and investment firms are currently operating in the UK through either or both of the UK branch and cross-border services passports.   **8.02**

The UK government is proceeding on the basis that passporting arrangements will ultimately cease following Brexit.[1] The key consequence of this for EEA banks and other financial services firms will be the need (subject to any applicable transitional arrangements agreed, if any) to obtain UK licences in order to continue to carry on regulated activities 'in the UK'.   **8.03**

This chapter focuses on the position of EEA incorporated firms (and 'overseas firms' generally) seeking to carry on banking activities from a UK place of business (scenarios two and three above). The position of (re)insurers is also considered in sections 8.8 and 8.9. We use the term 'overseas firm' in this chapter to refer to firms incorporated outside the UK but which carry on regulated activities from a UK place of business (which will include EEA firms once passporting rights cease).[2] A licence from the UK Prudential Regulation Authority (**PRA**) will always be required in these circumstances.   **8.04**

---

[1] There is nothing in the draft Withdrawal Agreement [https://assets.publishing.service.gov.uk/government/uploads/system/uploads/attachment_data/file/840655/Agreement_on_the_withdrawal_of_the_United_Kingdom_of_Great_Britain_and_Northern_Ireland_from_the_European_Union_and_the_European_Atomic_Energy_Community.pdf] or Political Declaration [https://assets.publishing.service.gov.uk/government/uploads/system/uploads/attachment_data/file/840656/Political_Declaration_setting_out_the_framework_for_the_future_relationship_between_the_European_Union_and_the_United_Kingdom.pdf] to indicate an intention to replicate the existing passporting arrangements across all financial services, and implementation of existing EU 'equivalence' regimes would not achieve that.

[2] The PRA and FCA use the terms 'overseas firm', 'overseas branch', and 'third country firm' to describe firms whose head office is outside the UK; we have used 'overseas firm' to avoid confusion with overseas (non-UK) branches of UK firms and the EU third country regime.

8.05 The position for cross-border services is more complex and will need to be assessed on a case-by-case basis. The PRA does not in general grant licences for pure cross-border financial services activity into the UK,[3] although in some circumstances cross-border activity will not fall within the UK regulatory perimeter. Relevant exclusions may also enable overseas firms with no UK presence to continue to service UK clients and participate in UK markets. Detailed consideration of the UK legal position for cross-border services is therefore outside the scope of this chapter.

8.06 As at December 2017, there were 160 branches of international banks operating in the UK, of which 77 were EEA branches operating under the passporting regime. Branches of international banks accounted for approximately 30% (£4 trillion) of the total assets of the UK banking system in 2017. As at December 2017, there were 110 branches of international insurers in the UK, of which 80 were EEA branches.

8.07 Once passporting ceases, EEA banks and (re)insurers seeking to maintain a UK presence post-Brexit must apply for authorisation from the PRA to operate either as a branch or a subsidiary—in common with other 'overseas' or 'third country' banks from outside the EEA. Authorisation applications will be determined by the PRA in consultation with the UK Financial Conduct Authority (FCA), which already regulates passported EEA bank and (re)insurer branches for conduct of business purposes. The FCA is the primary licensing authority for most UK and overseas financial sector firms, other than banks, (re)insurers, and certain systemically important 'designated' investment firms. A branch may be the preferred route for most overseas firms, for the reasons discussed in section 8.2 below. In practice, however, the PRA will decide whether a branch structure is acceptable. The availability of the branch route will depend on whether the proposed UK business model falls within the PRA's stated risk appetite for branch authorisation. If it does not, it may require the application to establish a separate UK subsidiary.

8.1.1 PRA Approach to Bank Branches

8.08 In relation to banks, the PRA first published a supervisory statement in 2014 (unconnected with Brexit), setting out its risk appetite thresholds for overseas retail and wholesale branches (the '2014 SS').[4] This confirmed that business models judged to be outside the PRA's stated risk appetite would be expected to apply for subsidiary authorisation.

8.09 The PRA has recently updated the 2014 SS in the context of Brexit planning and the need for EEA branches to obtain direct PRA authorisation before passporting arrangements expire. The PRA first proposed its revised policy in a consultation paper published in December 2017.[5] This consultation did not propose a fundamental departure from the PRA's branch risk appetite policy as outlined in the 2014 SS, although it contained further emphasis on

---

[3] This is the same with the FCA, with limited exceptions for consumer credit licences.
[4] PRA, 'SS10/14: Supervising International Banks: The PRA's Approach to Branch Supervision' (30 September 2014) <https://www.bankofengland.co.uk/-/media/boe/files/prudential-regulation/supervisory-statement/2014/ss1014> accessed 30 October 2018 (as for all websites cited, unless otherwise stated).
[5] PRA, 'CP29/17: International Banks: The PRA's Approach to Branch Authorisation and Supervision' (20 December 2017) <https://www.bankofengland.co.uk/-/media/boe/files/prudential-regulation/consultation-paper/2017/cp2917.pdf>

the strength of supervisory cooperation mechanisms, more detail on the boundary of permitted retail activities for branches, and comprehensive discussion of the PRA's approach to systemic branches.

8.10 The revised draft supervisory statement included in the December consultation paper was subsequently confirmed by the PRA (with some clarifications) in March 2018, in the policy statement 3/18 and revised supervisory statement 1/18 (SS1/18).[6] SS1/18 is now applicable to passported EEA bank branches seeking to operate in the UK post-Brexit, existing overseas firms authorised as such by the PRA and prospective applicant overseas firms.[7]

8.11 Helpfully for existing overseas firms (i.e. non-EEA entities), the PRA has clarified that it does not expect its revised approach to wholesale branches to affect any existing authorised overseas firms.[8]

8.1.2 PRA Approach to (Re)insurer Branches

8.12 As discussed in section 8.8, the PRA's approach under the Solvency II Directive to third country insurance and pure reinsurance branches is set out in SS44/15, which was issued in November 2015[9] and was supplemented in November 2018 by a new supervisory statement, SS2/18.[10]

8.1.3 Transitional Arrangements and Timing Considerations

8.13 It is currently expected that the UK's formal exit from the EU will take place on 31 January 2020, following the extensions agreed by the UK and EU to the original exit date of 29 March 2019. The UK government's official policy materials published during 2018 emphasised its expectation that a deal would be agreed with the EU under which a transitional period will apply until 31 December 2020 (as was provisionally agreed between the EU and UK on 14 November 2018). However, this position formed part of both Withdrawal Agreement

---

[6] PRA, 'PS3/18: International Banks: The PRA's Approach to Branch Authorisation and Supervision' (29 March 2018) (hereafter PRA, 'PS3/18') [Comment: Check consistency throughout of 'hereafter PRA, ' ... ... ']<https://www.bankofengland.co.uk/-/media/boe/files/prudential-regulation/policy-statement/2018/ps318>; PRA, 'SS1/18: International Banks: The PRA's Approach to Branch Authorisation and Supervision' (28 March 2018) (hereafter PRA, 'SS1/18') <https://www.bankofengland.co.uk/-/media/boe/files/prudential-regulation/supervisory-statement/2018/ss118.pdf>

[7] In principle, PRA SS1/18 (n. 6) applies both to banks and to PRA-designated systemically important investment firms, although the current population of these firms is limited to a small number of UK-authorised entities. It is assumed that any potential branch entrants to this category would be reviewed in accordance with the PRA's general approach, insofar as relevant. Systemically important investment firms are certain firms that do not have deposit-taking permissions but do have permission to deal as principal and which have been designated as systemically important by the PRA based on thresholds specified in the Financial Services and Markets Act 2000 (PRA-regulated Activities) Order 2013 (SI 2013/556).

[8] PRA, 'PS3/18' (n. 6), para. 1.6.

[9] PRA, 'SS44/15: Solvency II: Third-Country Insurance and Pure Reinsurance Branches' (27 November 2015) (hereafter PRA, 'SS44/15: Solvency II') <https://www.bankofengland.co.uk/-/media/boe/files/prudential-regulation/supervisory-statement/2015/ss4415> accessed 18 November 2018.

[10] PRA, 'SS2/18: International Insurers: The PRA's Approach to Branch Authorisation and Supervision' (28 March 2018) (hereafter PRA, 'SS2/18: International Insurers') <https://www.bankofengland.co.uk/-/media/boe/files/prudential-regulation/supervisory-statement/2018/ss218.pdf?la=en&hash=7028E1E5523C1C1309A3DE73206132EB5C75EBDB>

'deals' agreed provisionally between the UK and EU but subsequently rejected by the UK Parliament).[11] Following the repeated rejection of these deals by the UK Parliament, and the [subsequent] general election, the prospect of a formal transitional arrangement is currently unclear.

8.14 In parallel with these developments the UK government has developed detailed contingency plans for a 'no deal' Brexit, in which no transitional period will apply and reciprocal passporting rights for financial services firms will cease immediately upon exit.[12] The Bank of England (BoE), PRA, and FCA are also actively involved in contingency plans to minimise disruption to UK markets, firms and their clients in the event of a no-deal scenario.

8.15 A key component of this is the development of a UK statutory 'temporary permissions regime' (TPR). This will enable EEA firms currently passporting into the UK to continue operating in the UK (with deemed UK authorisation) for up to three years after exit, pending full authorisation from UK regulators. The PRA and FCA published statements[13] outlining their approach to the TPR for EEA firms. The PRA and FCA also published consultations in October 2018 setting out their intentions in more detail.[14] This was followed in February and April 2019 by further packages of materials from the FCA, PRA and BoE clarifying the intended approach and including draft rules; and in July 2019 by updated 'near-final' rules and related EU exit instruments from the BoE and PRA[15,16] The deadline for notifications to enter the PRA's TPR was 12 April 2019 and has not been extended since (in contrast with the FCA, which has extended the period until 30 January 2020). Existing EEA bank branches have in general already submitted draft business plans to the PRA to enable the PRA to scrutinise banks' post-Brexit business models. The PRA is

---

[11] UK Government, '19 October Draft Agreement on the Withdrawal of the United Kingdom of Great Britain and Northern Ireland from the European Union and the European Atomic Energy Community', Art. 126 <https://assets.publishing.service.gov.uk/government/uploads/system/uploads/attachment_data/file/840655/Agreement_on_the_withdrawal_of_the_United_Kingdom_of_Great_Britain_and_Northern_Ireland_from_the_European_Union_and_the_European_Atomic_Energy_Community.pdf>

[12] HM Treasury, 'Banking, Insurance and Other Financial Services If There's No Brexit Deal' (23 August 2018) <https://www.gov.uk/government/publications/banking-insurance-and-other-financial-services-if-theres-no-brexit-deal/banking-insurance-and-other-financial-services-if-theres-no-brexit-deal>

[13] PRA, 'Temporary Permissions and Recognition Regimes' (24 July 2018) (hereafter PRA, 'Temporary Permissions') <https://www.bankofengland.co.uk/news/2018/july/temporary-permissions-and-recognition-regimes>; FCA, 'The Temporary Permissions Regime for Inbound Passporting EEA Firms and Funds—Our Approach' (10 October 2018) <https://www.fca.org.uk/markets/eu-withdrawal/temporary-permissions-regime>

[14] PRA, 'CP 18/29: Temporary Permissions Regime for Inbound Firms and Funds' (8 October 2018) (hereafter PRA, 'CP 18/29: Temporary Permissions Regime') <https://www.fca.org.uk/publication/consultation/cp18-29.pdf>; PRA, 'CP 26/18: UK Withdrawal from the EU: Changes to PRA Rulebook and Onshored Binding Technical Standards' (25 October 2018) (hereafter PRA, 'CP 26/18': UK Withdrawal from the EU') <https://www.bankofengland.co.uk/-/media/boe/files/prudential-regulation/consultation-paper/2018/cp2618-complete.pdf?la=en&hash=2A1C385C5C157974FDDE36FC5D72F515AD667AA1 accessed 18 November 2018.

[15] PRA, 'CP18/19: UK withdrawal from the EU: Changes following extension of Article 50' (25 July 2019) (hereafter, PRA 'CP18/19). The PRA has not finalised these rules because it may need to make additional amendments before 31 January 2020. https://www.bankofengland.co.uk/-/media/boe/files/prudential-regulation/consultation-paper/2019/cp1819-complete.pdf?la=en&hash=573F7920C9CFF71114674FE54707645F9CF4C247

[16] In particular, PRA PS 5/19: 'The Bank of England's Amendments to Financial Services Legislation under the European Union (Withdrawal) Act 2018' (February 2019) (hereafter PRA, 'PS5/19') [https://www.bankofengland.co.uk/-/media/boe/files/paper/2019/the-boes-amendments-to-financial-services-legislation-under-the-eu-withdrawal-act-2018.pdf?la=en&hash=1B26AA88A7DCA56C731498A74DB2B688EC79CD58] and FCA PS 19/5: FCA Brexit Policy Statement (February 2019) (hereafter FCA, 'PS19/5'). [https://www.fca.org.uk/publication/policy/ps19-05.pdf]

continuing to progress application discussions despite the potential extra time offered by the formalisation of the TPR plans and the delay to exit day. This has given the PRA the opportunity to take a more considered and strategic approach to the assessment of EEA firms' authorisation applications and to focus initially on the larger and more systemic banks. The FCA is also actively involved in the PRA-led authorisation discussions with EEA applicant banks.[17]

In principle, PRA 'third country branch' authorisation is expected to be granted to EEA banks before the expiry of the TPR. However, if a formal transitional period is agreed between the UK and EU as part of any Brexit deal, the PRA has stated that firms should assume that that direct 'overseas firm' PRA authorisation for EEA firms would not take effect until the end of the transitional period (even if decided positively by the PRA during such period).[18] In the event that no transitional period is agreed, however, the TPR will enable currently passported EEA firms to continue carrying on regulated activities in the UK pending direct PRA authorisation (although this will have potentially significant compliance implications, as discussed below). **8.16**

The BoE, PRA, and FCA will have temporary relief powers to modify (e.g. switch off) certain obligations of currently passported EEA firms within the TPR regime (as described at 8.7.3 and 8.8.2 below). **8.17**

Alongside the TPR, the UK government has introduced the Financial Services Contracts Regime (**FSCR**) to allow for the orderly wind down of the UK regulated activities of EEA firms that do not enter the TPR or that leave the TPR without full UK authorisation.[19] The FSCR will automatically apply to EEA passporting firms that do not join the TPR but have pre-existing contracts in the UK which they would need a permission to service. The FSCR will provide two discrete mechanisms: **8.18**

- *Supervised run-off*—for EEA firms with UK branches or top-up permissions in the UK, and firms who entered the TPR but did not secure a UK authorisation at the end; and
- *Contractual run-off*—for remaining incoming services (no UK branch) firms.

The FSCR is time limited: fifteen years for insurance contracts and five years for other contracts. Firms in the FSCR will be expected to run off, close out, or transfer obligations arising from contracts that exceed the time limit, prior to the end of the regime. **8.19**

While the process and timing considerations may still change depending on any final agreement with the EU, it is assumed for the purposes of this chapter that a 'hard Brexit' outcome will ultimately apply and that the current passporting regime (or anything similar) will not continue. **8.20**

---

[17] As PRA-authorised firms are jointly regulated by both the PRA and the FCA, applications for PRA authorisation will be considered by the PRA in consultation with the FCA.

[18] PRA, 'Dear CEO letter to all firms authorised and regulated by the PRA' (25 October 2018) <https://www.bankofengland.co.uk/-/media/boe/files/prudential-regulation/letter/2018/update-to-firms-on-the-boes-regulatory-approach-and-firm-preparations-for-eu-withdrawal.pdf?la=en&hash=3E85FCA4466E0AF2ED240B4466A719300D8FCC80>.

[19] See the Financial Services Contracts (Transitional and Saving Provision) (EU Exit) Regulations 2019 (SI 2019/405).

8.1.4 Remaining Chapter Summary

8.21 The following sections of this chapter are focused on discussion of the PRA's approach to the authorisation of overseas firms, including the circumstances in which a subsidiary is expected to be mandatory, based on the PRA's updated supervisory statements, as follows:

- general differences between branches and subsidiaries;
- banks:
  ○ PRA's approach to significant retail activities;
  ○ PRA's general approach to branch authorisation and supervision (absent significant retail activities);
  ○ PRA's approach to systemic wholesale branches;
  ○ application process for overseas firms; and
  ○ transition to overseas branch or UK subsidiary status—implications for EEA banks.
- (re)insurers:
  ○ PRA's general approach to authorisation of overseas (re)insurers; and
  ○ PRA's approach to UK branches of overseas insurers—factors to be considered.

8.2 General Differences between Branches and Subsidiaries

8.22 Unlike a UK-incorporated subsidiary, a UK branch of an overseas firm forms part of a legal entity incorporated outside the UK. A UK branch therefore has no separate legal personality from the 'head office' firm, although it is typically a UK taxable presence and for legal and economic purposes able to operate as a distinct booking centre. From a prudential regulation perspective, branches of banks do not attract regulatory capital requirements in the UK; and although liquidity requirements may in principle be imposed at branch level, under the current UK regime this is generally limited to reporting requirements.[20] The Solvency II Directive establishes a regime for EEA branches of third country direct insurers, which does include prudential requirements applying at a branch level (or in some cases at the level of one or more EEA branches together).

8.23 Under a branch model, financial resources are generally available at both the UK branch and head office level, which avoids 'trapped' capital and generally leads to cheaper funding costs for the branch business. By contrast, a UK subsidiary would need to be separately capitalised and both parent and subsidiary would need to meet the requirements of the prudential regime on a solo entity basis, as well as being potentially subject to consolidated group prudential requirements. A branch will have its own management but will typically have a reporting line to the head office board rather than a distinct, stand-alone board.

---

[20] PRA, 'SS1/17: Supervising International Banks: The PRA's Approach to Branch Supervision—Liquidity Reporting' (23 February 2017) <https://www.bankofengland.co.uk/-/media/boe/files/prudential-regulation/supervisory-statement/2017/ss117>

8.24 For most banks and (re)insurers, there are therefore few economic incentives to choose the subsidiary route voluntarily. While the PRA does have greater supervisory control over overseas firm branches than it does over passported EEA branches, its level of oversight and powers is still far less than with a subsidiary. This is particularly so in relation to a branch's financial resources, ownership and governance arrangements, all of which generally remain regulated by the home supervisor.

8.25 Overseas branches and subsidiaries must both meet the PRA's threshold conditions for authorisation, including as to adequacy of financial and operational resources and suitability for supervision. The practical difference is that the PRA's assessment of UK branch authorisation applications will be conducted at the level of the whole firm and not only the UK branch. The PRA's view on the quality and transparency of the home country regulatory framework is therefore critical to whether a particular firm is permitted to operate from a branch; the same is true of the PRA's relationship with the home state supervisor.

8.26 In SS 1/18, the PRA has provided a helpful diagram illustrating the PRA's policy approach to international banks in accessible flowchart format.

8.27 We have reproduced this in Figure 8.1 as a quick-reference aid to the policy considerations discussed below and the questions that overseas banks will need to ask themselves in establishing or reviewing their UK presence.

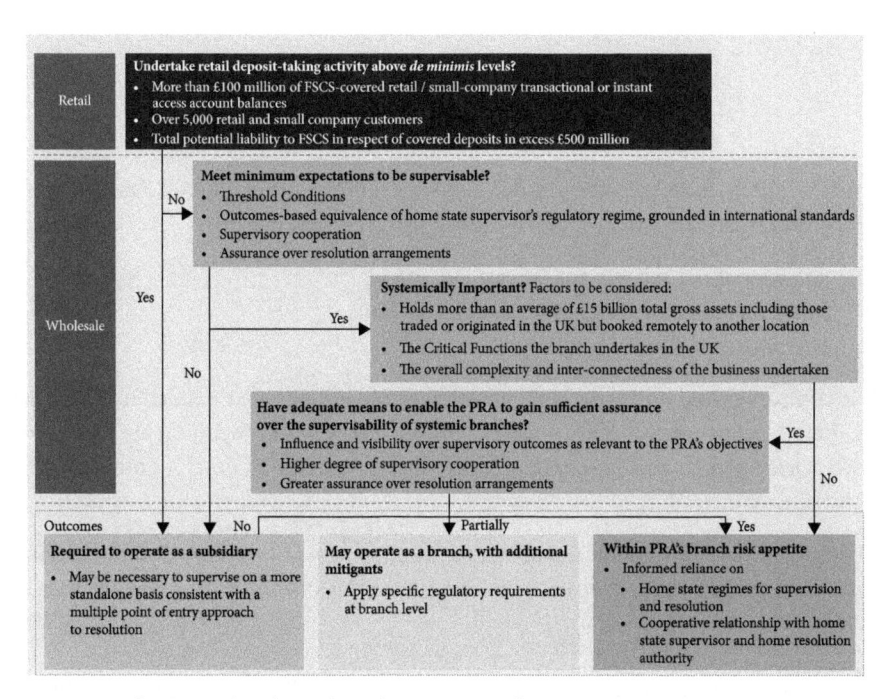

Figure 8.1 PRA's approach to branch authorisation and supervision
Source: PRA SS1/18 (28 March 2018). Reproduced with the permission of the Bank of England.

8.3 Banks: PRA's Approach to Significant Retail Activities

8.28 The first question an overseas firm seeking to establish a bank branch in the UK should consider is whether it intends to accept UK retail or other insured deposits (i.e. deposits covered by the UK Financial Services Compensation Scheme (**FSCS**).[21]

8.29 If the answer is yes, the next question is on what scale. If the bank intends to take significant UK retail or other insured deposits, it should assume that it will need to establish a UK subsidiary.

8.30 The test for 'significant "retail"' has three component *de minimis* thresholds:

- size of retail deposit base:
  ○ £100 million of retail and small company transactional or instant access account balances covered by the UK FSCS: or
  ○ 5,000 retail and small company customers (transactional or instant access accounts);
- size of FSCS-protected deposit base: FSCS liability of >£500m.

8.31 These are alternative and not cumulative thresholds; an overseas firm whose UK deposit base exceeds any one or more of the tests above can expect to fall outside the PRA's risk appetite for branches.

8.32 The terms of reference for the 'retail' thresholds are described further in paragraphs 8.06–8.15.

8.3.1 Size of Retail Deposit Base

8.33 A 'small company' is defined under s. 381 and s. 382 of the Companies Act 2006 as (broadly) a company that satisfies two or more of the following conditions:[22]

(a) turnover of not more than £10.2m;
(b) balance sheet total of not more than £5.1m; and
(c) not more than fifty employees.

Public companies and most regulated financial services firms are excluded from the definition. 'Retail' depositors for these purposes (other than small companies) are not expressly defined (discussed further at paragraph 8.40 below). 'Transactional account' is not expressly defined; instead, the PRA states that:

> the PRA starts from the understanding that an account, whilst it may have transactional functionality, is only considered a 'transactional account' if withdrawals from it have been

---

[21] The Financial Services Compensation Scheme established under FSMA, s. 213 insofar as applicable to deposits.
[22] Note that the full definition of this must also be calculated in accordance with conditions relating to the relevant financial year(s) and the threshold for parent/group companies.

made nine or more times within a three month period, but it may additionally consider other factors. The PRA will continue to take a pragmatic, judgement-based view as to whether the accounts are transactional in practice.[23]

FSCS-covered accounts refers to the aggregate retail and small company transactional or instant access account balances covered by the FSCS. Overseas firms are required to calculate the aggregated FSCS-covered balances on a per-customer basis under the PRA's single customer view rules.[24] This does not currently apply to passported EEA branches, although EEA banks are subject to similar home state rules implementing the EU Deposit Guarantee Schemes Directive.[25]

8.3.2 Size of FSCS-Protected Deposit Base

8.34 Even if an overseas bank falls short of both of the above size of retail deposit base thresholds, it will be a candidate for subsidiarisiation if the total potential liability to the FSCS in respect of FSCS 'covered deposits' is over £500 million.

8.35 This test differs from the pure 'retail' and 'small company' deposit-based tests above, because the scope of the FSCS extends to deposits from other entity types, including some larger corporates.

8.36 Eligibility for FSCS coverage is defined based on negative scope. The following are not covered:[26]

- Deposit types excluded based on status of depositor: banks, investment firms, financial institutions, insurers, reinsurers, investment funds, pension funds (subject to exclusions), and public authorities other than small local authorities.
- Deposits arising out of a transaction in connection with which there has been a criminal conviction for money laundering.
- Deposits for which the holder and any beneficial owner have not been verified in accordance with anti-money laundering requirements.
- Banks' own funds (i.e. capital instruments).
- Banks' issued debt securities and liabilities arising out of own acceptances and promissory notes.

8.37 Any deposit that is not excluded will be within scope of the FSCS. FSCS coverage is generally limited to £85,000 per depositor in aggregate for all eligible deposits; however, coverage up to £1,000,000 also extends to 'temporary high balances' held for certain specified purposes (such as property purchases and certain compensation payments).

---

[23] PRA, 'SS1/18' (n. 6), p. 13.
[24] PRA, 'Rulebook for CRR Firms' (30 March 2015) <http://www.prarulebook.co.uk/rulebook/Media/Get/db8bc539-1fac-49e4-9601-2c78832323e4/PRA_2015_39/pdf> Depositor Protection Part, ch. 12.
[25] Council Directive 2014/49/EU of 16 April 2014 on deposit guarantee schemes [2014] OJ L173/149 (hereafter Deposit Guarantee Scheme Directive).
[26] See PRA Rulebook (n. [25]), Depositor Protection Part, especially chs. 4 and 10.

8.3.3 How Should Banks Assess Their Position under the Updated 'Significant Retail' Approach?

8.38 The PRA stresses that the updated approach set out in SS 1/18 does not represent a fundamental change from the 2014 SS. The revised SS does provide more detail on the applicable 'retail' thresholds and a clearer statement that banks whose UK deposit activity is above one or more of the *de minimis* thresholds will be expected to establish subsidiaries.

8.3.4 Which Customers?

8.39 Overseas firms seeking PRA authorisation will need to assess the extent of their 'retail' activity and be in a position to discuss this with the PRA.

8.40 Identifying which customers are 'retail' and 'small companies' will likely require some additional diligence. Some account holders' categorisation may not be entirely clear. In particular, the meaning of 'retail' deposits is not expressly clarified in SS 1/18 (or the 2014 SS). 'Retail' depositor in this context is evidently intended to refer to a category of account holder that is not a small company and is narrower than the population of FSCS-eligible depositors. It seems reasonable to assume that this category includes accounts held by or on behalf of natural persons, but it is unclear whether it would also include (for example) limited partnerships and trust accounts (or indeed all categories of entity that are not 'wholesale depositors' under the definition used in the PRA's bank application form).[27]

8.3.5 Which Accounts?

8.41 The process of establishing which accounts should qualify as 'transactional' will require review of account usage and withdrawal activity (and may need ongoing monitoring). If the usage-based status is material to whether a particular bank may exceed the *de minimis* thresholds, then it is likely that the PRA would want to discuss this in more detail with the bank.

8.42 It is also unclear in the SS what the PRA's approach is likely to be in circumstances where a UK-authorised branch inadvertently or temporarily exceeds these thresholds. This would presumably trigger discussions with the PRA and the relevant bank may be expected to reduce its retail deposit base or take steps to establish or transfer the balances to an authorised subsidiary.

---

[27] PRA, 'Application form for banks—notes' (March 2018) <https://www.fca.org.uk/publication/forms/application-for-authorisation-banks-notes.pdf> para. 3.1.3; 'wholesale depositor' category includes banks, large companies (i.e. not small companies), large mutual associations, governments, supranationals, local authorities, and affiliates of the deposit-taker.

8.4 'Wholesale' Banks: PRA's General Approach to Branch Authorisation and Supervision (Where No Significant Retail Activities)

Banks whose UK retail and covered deposit presence is expected to remain below the *de minimis* thresholds (referred to for simplicity as 'wholesale' banks) should follow the PRA's stated 'general approach' to branch risk appetite. These banks still face possible mandatory subsidiary risk: the PRA may insist on this outcome if it considers that an overseas applicant bank may not meet the PRA's threshold conditions for authorisation under the reduced supervisory oversight offered by a branch structure. **8.43**

In contrast with the retail/FSCS tests, which are fixed quantitative thresholds, the PRA's approach to wholesale banks is a more holistic, cumulative approach that imports both quantitative and qualitative factors. Barriers to wholesale branching might arise because of the overseas bank's home country regulatory and supervisory framework. If the home country regime and/or supervisory cooperation arrangements are judged by the PRA to be materially deficient, the subsidiary route is likely to be the only viable option. **8.44**

8.4.1 The Wholesale or 'General Approach' to Branch Authorisation and Supervision

In determining whether an overseas wholesale bank can become UK authorised as a branch, the PRA will consider the following factors: **8.45**

- Will the UK branch meet the PRA and FCA's statutory threshold conditions for authorisation?
- Does the bank's home state supervisor (HSS) meet minimum equivalence standards?
- Are adequate cooperation arrangements in place between the PRA and the HSS?
- Will the PRA (together with the BoE in its capacity as UK resolution authority) have appropriate assurance over resolution arrangements for the UK branch?

The interpretation of these various factors is explained below. If the answer to any of these questions is no, the overseas bank may be required to establish a subsidiary. This is a more likely conclusion for banks with 'systemic' UK businesses, for which the standards for assessing the above factors will be higher. **8.46**

The PRA makes clear that not all banks from the same jurisdiction can necessarily expect the same outcome. This illustrates the interaction of both jurisdictional and bank-specific factors in the PRA's decision-making process, which will vary according to the size and activities of the bank in question, as well as the local regulatory framework and HSS relationship. This holistic PRA decision-making makes it difficult (bar the most extreme cases) for banks to predict whether a subsidiary will be required, although recent examples may assist in forming expectations. **8.47**

The PRA's approach to authorised branches that meet 'systemic' thresholds is discussed further in section 8.5. Wholesale branches that are deemed to be systemic but permitted to **8.48** operate as branches may be subject to additional requirements under the PRA's systemic branch regime (discussed further at paragraph 8.73).

8.4.2 The PRA's and FCA's Threshold Conditions for Authorisation

8.49 All applicants for PRA authorisation will need to satisfy both the PRA and FCA's statutory threshold conditions for authorisation on an ongoing basis.

8.50 While this chapter focuses on the authorisation requirements for banks and other PRA-authorised firms, it is important that overseas firm applicants are aware of the FCA's role in the authorisation process and in ongoing supervision. As the PRA has emphasised,[28] a bank can only be authorised where both the PRA and the FCA's threshold conditions are met.

8.4.3 PRA

8.51 The PRA's statutory threshold conditions for banks are as follows:[29]

- **Legal status**—deposit-takers must be bodies corporate or partnerships.
- **Location of offices**—a UK-incorporated corporate body must maintain its head offices and, if one exists, its registered office in the United Kingdom.
- **Prudent conduct of business**—the applicant must conduct its business in a prudent manner, which includes having appropriate financial and non-financial resources.
- **Suitability**—the applicant must satisfy the PRA that it is a 'fit and proper' person with regard to all circumstances to conduct a regulated activity.
- **Effective supervision**—the applicant must be capable of being effectively supervised by the PRA.

8.52 In the context of a branch authorisation application, the authorisation is granted to the legal entity as a whole, but having regard to its UK branch presence. The threshold conditions must be satisfied on this basis.

8.53 The first two conditions are basic requirements that are either assumed to be met or will not be relevant (i.e. the location condition does not apply to branches, although the branch will need to be UK registered as such under UK corporate law requirements). The PRA's assessment will therefore focus on the more substantive, subjective threshold conditions (i.e. the last three at paragraph 8.51).

8.54 It is potentially more challenging for the PRA to reach a positive assessment on these factors in a branch scenario in which responsibility for prudential resources, group structuring, and the banks' controlling shareholders and affiliates will rest primarily with the home state regulator. In this context, the PRA must have sufficient confidence in the regulatory requirements and supervisory approach applicable in the branch's home state to be satisfied that its threshold conditions will be met on a continuing basis. For example, in a subsidiary

---

[28] PRA, 'SS1/18' (n. 6), para. 2.7.
[29] FSMA, Part IV and Sch. 6.

scenario the PRA would have direct responsibility for determining compliance with prudential requirements (including approval of the bank's individual capital and liquidity adequacy assessments (ICAAP and ILAAP), and have powers to prescribe additional requirements. For a UK branch, these requirements would be primarily the responsibility of the home state supervisor, although the PRA will need to scrutinise the local requirements and individual bank resources in order to be satisfied that the 'prudent conduct of business' condition is met.

8.4.4 FCA

The FCA's threshold conditions are as follows: **8.55**

- **Effective supervision**—the firm must be capable of being effectively supervised by the FCA.
- **Appropriate non-financial resources**—the firm's non-financial resources must be appropriate in relation to the regulated activities it seeks to carry on, having regard to the FCA's operational objectives.
- **Suitability**—the firm must be a 'fit and proper' person. Its management must have adequate skills and experience and act with integrity (fitness and propriety). The firm must have appropriate policies and procedures in place and appropriately manage conflicts of interest.
- **Business model**—the firm's strategy for doing business must be suitable for a person carrying on the regulated activities it undertakes or seeks to carry on and does not pose a risk to the FCA's objectives.

The FCA's threshold conditions are to some extent similar to the PRA's, but with differences reflecting the regulators' respective remits. The FCA focuses less on structural and financial conditions and places greater scrutiny on bank-level rather than systemic factors, including systems and controls, and conduct of business requirements. **8.56**

FCA input and engagement in the overseas bank authorisation and supervision process has been an important part of the ongoing process for passported EEA branches seeking PRA authorisation. Examples of areas in which the FCA has demonstrated a particular interest during the application process have included adequacy of IT systems and controls, outsourcing arrangements, anti-money laundering policies and procedures, and approach to cross-border booking models. **8.57**

8.4.5 Equivalence Standards

In practice, it will not be possible for the PRA to have confidence in the viability, compliance standards, and supervisability of an overseas branch without confidence in the adequacy of the overseas bank's local regulatory and supervisory framework. This is particularly so for areas in which the PRA's supervisory remit is more limited, including capital and other prudential regulation, recovery and resolution arrangements, ownership and governance. The PRA will also need sufficient reassurance over the ability and willingness of the HSS under **8.58** the local regime to exchange information, to preserve confidentiality and to cooperate on investigative and enforcement matters.

8.59 It is clear from the PRA's commentary on equivalence that 'equivalent' need not mean 'identical'. The benchmark for assessment will generally be applicable international standards rather than the specific detail of the UK or EU regime. The PRA cites peer reviews carried out by the International Monetary Fund (IMF), the Financial Stability Board (FSB), and the Basel Committee on Banking Supervision (BCBS) of compliance with international banking standards as core assessments of equivalence, although the PRA will also take its own practical experiences into account. Evidence of the UK branches licensed in the UK indicates that the PRA may be willing to adopt a relatively flexible approach to assessing equivalence, since there are current examples of UK branches of banks from jurisdictions in which material gaps remain regarding adherence to international standards.

8.60 The degree of equivalence expected will be considered by the PRA in the context of the branch's relative systemic importance and the scope of its UK business. As an example, the PRA could expect a bank that intends to conduct and book significant derivatives trading activity in the UK to be subject to prudential and mandatory clearing requirements for derivatives that are more closely aligned with the relevant UK regimes regulating derivatives trading than a bank focused principally on deposits and payments activity.

8.61 The PRA explains that equivalence assessments are reviewed periodically, but there has been no indication in recent commentary from the PRA (or indeed the UK government) that a stricter approach will be followed in future, particularly given the incentives for the UK to preserve an open, inclusive approach to inward investment by overseas firms. It is assumed that EEA banks will generally satisfy equivalence standards, as UK and EU law will remain substantially aligned at the point of Brexit and at least in the short term thereafter.

8.4.6 Supervisory Cooperation Arrangements

8.62 The strength of cooperation arrangements with a bank's home state supervisor has always been a key factor for the PRA in assessing whether to permit branches for overseas banks. The nature and extent of cooperation expected by the PRA is based on principles set out in the Basel Committee's 'Core Principles for Effective Banking Supervision', which the PRA regards as being founded on 'an open, transparent and proactive exchange of information and views with the home state supervisor and a collaborative approach including the support where necessary of the home state supervisor in the delivery of PRA's objectives'.[30] The PRA expects to be able to engage in continuing open and transparent supervisory dialogue with each relevant HSS, either with other regulators in a college format, or bilaterally as appropriate.

---

[30] PRA, 'SS1/18' (n. 6), para. 3.9.

8.63 In practice, the PRA expectations translate into the following minimum requirements:[31]

- Clear acceptance from the HSS of its prudential responsibility for UK branches, which should include:
  ◦ a clear agreement with the HSS on the split of responsibilities for prudential supervision of branches of firms headquartered within its jurisdiction, with provision for periodic reviews to ensure reciprocal compliance by the PRA and HSS; and
  ◦ confirmation from the HSS on an individual bank basis that the relevant bank meets the PRA's threshold conditions at legal entity level.
- A memorandum of understanding or equivalent document, setting out expectations for supervisory information exchange, including:
  ◦ arrangements for the protection of confidential information; and
  ◦ documentation of the minimum information required from the HSS for effective branch supervision.
- Arrangements for ongoing dialogue with the HSS on a periodic and incident-specific basis, including:
  ◦ regular updates on risks facing the firm and risk management practices;
  ◦ responsive cooperation by the HSS to questions and requests from the PRA, particularly in stress scenarios and/or to address perceived threshold condition risks; and
  ◦ proactive disclosure by the HSS on significant events affecting the firm, particularly where this could affect threshold condition compliance.

8.64 For EEA banks, extensive cooperation arrangements are currently in place between the PRA, the European Central Bank (**ECB**), and other EEA supervisors, as part of the single market for financial services. By contrast, in the post-Brexit regulatory framework, there is currently a vacuum for formal bilateral agreements between the PRA and EEA supervisors. The PRA has confirmed, however (both in public statements and in bilateral discussions with EEA banks), that it expects to be able to implement supervisory cooperation agreements even in a no-deal Brexit scenario. On 20 March 2019, the PRA and FCA announced the agreement of a template memorandum of understanding with the ECB, which sets out the expectations for supervisory cooperation and information-sharing arrangements between UK and EU/EEA national authorities and would take effect in a no-deal scenario.[32]

8.65 Although the PRA initially requested all EEA bank branches to consider and plan for both the branch and subsidiary options,[33] the PRA has since confirmed bilaterally with EEA banks that they may proceed on the assumption that a branch structure may be maintained (although the supervisory approach is expected to differ depending on the size and complexity of individual branches).

---

[31] Ibid., para. 3.10.
[32] <https://www.bankofengland.co.uk/-/media/boe/files/prudential-regulation/letter/2017/contingency-planning-for-the-uk-withdrawal-from-the-eu>
[33] PRA, 'Contingency Planning for the UK's Withdrawal from the European Union' (7 April 2017) <https://www.bankofengland.co.uk/-/media/boe/files/prudential-regulation/letter/2017/contingency-planning-for-the-uk-withdrawal-from-the eu.pdf?la=en&hash=86E380D94B9FEBD49999ACE2AB3FD9B799C3A76C>

8.4.7 Assurance over Resolution Arrangements

8.66 The PRA can be expected to take at least some interest in the resolution arrangements governing most overseas banks seeking to operate in the UK. For branches that will carry out 'critical functions' in the UK, the PRA will look for a higher degree of assurance over the resolution arrangements covering the UK branch.

8.67 'Critical functions' will include the following, where carried out on such a scale that withdrawal of the function could adversely affect UK financial stability or the safety and soundness of PRA-supervised firms: retail banking, corporate banking, payments, clearing and settlement, custody, intra-financial system borrowing and lending, and investment banking.[34]

8.68 The PRA (together with the BoE as UK resolution authority) will consider the following factors in relation to UK branch resolvability:

- equivalence of the home state resolution regime with the UK regime (which derives from the Bank Recovery and Resolution Directive and FSB global standards);[35]
- credibility and feasibility of the firm/group resolution strategy, including the approach to removal of barriers to resolution and engagement with host state supervisors;
- alignment of the resolution strategy with the PRA's objectives and the need for continuity of UK critical functions;
- willingness of the home state resolution authority to share and discuss the resolution plan with the PRA, including implications for the UK branch; and
- ability of the PRA to rely on the HSS and home resolution authority to execute the intended resolution strategy and to coordinate with HSSs.

8.69 Ultimately, however, the PRA emphasises that despite the information and assurances given by the home resolution authority, the PRA may nonetheless insist on subsidiarisation if it suspects that in practice the home resolution authority will prioritise national interests at the expense of UK depositors and creditors. While a home state depositor preference regime would present a clear impediment to a branch authorisation, the PRA will also take account of softer country risk considerations associated with the risks of short-notice legislative change to enable depositor preference, particularly in a financial crisis or stress scenario, and the related risk of discrimination against UK branch creditors arising on a de facto basis in the event of the wider firm failure. The PRA's position in this respect is not new and was outlined in detail in the 2014 SS. This position reflects the PRA's experience during a period of eurozone financial stress in 2012–13, which saw attempts by regulators of distressed banks to bail in retail deposits above the €100,000 deposit guarantee scheme limit.

8.70 Consistent with the PRA's general approach, the PRA will focus on the greatest risks to UK financial stability and the standards applied will also reflect the branch's systemic importance. If the risks cannot be mitigated to a reasonable confidence level through home state information and assurance, a subsidiary will likely be required.

---

[34] PRA, 'SS1/18' (n. 6), box 3, p. 12.
[35] FSB, 'Key Attributes of Effective Resolution Regimes for Financial Institutions' (15 October 2014) <http://www.fsb.org/wp-content/uploads/r_141015.pdf>

8.4.8 Considerations for Banks

The qualitative, judgement-based approach prescribed by the PRA under the general approach makes it more difficult for banks to assess the likely outcome, particularly given the recent updates to the PRA's policy and the current regulatory and political uncertainty surrounding Brexit. However, many current passported EEA branches are likely to be aware of the PRA's evolving approach through ongoing discussions with the PRA. **8.71**

The PRA has also confirmed that a new approach is not expected in itself to affect any existing overseas banks' authorised UK branches. The updated approach will be relevant for overseas banks seeking to increase their UK footprint or retail deposit base. Current Brexit planning trends, however, tend to be in the opposite direction, with more international banks looking to move operations from the UK to elsewhere in the EEA. **8.72**

8.5 Banks: PRA's Approach to 'Systemic' Wholesale Branches

For wholesale branches that the PRA perceives to be systemic in nature but otherwise within its branch risk appetite, the 'systemic branch' designation facilitates a compromise solution between regular branch status and requiring a subsidiary. **8.73**

8.5.1 Which Branches Qualify as 'Systemic'?

The PRA will consider both quantitative and qualitative factors in making this judgement, to assess whether the size, complexity, and interconnectedness indicate that the failure of the bank could have significant consequences for financial stability in the UK. **8.74**

The description of the PRA's approach in these areas highlights the following factors as the starting point: **8.75**

- whether the branch holds more than an average of £15 billion total gross assets including those traded or originating in the UK but booked remotely to another location;
- whether the branch undertakes critical functions (such as retail banking, custody or clearing and settlement) in the UK and on what scale; and
- the overall complexity and interconnectedness of the business undertaken in the branch, for example, whether it provides significant operational services or is otherwise interconnected to a systemically important UK bank.

In outlining the thinking behind these indicators, the PRA emphasises that: **8.76**

- The £15 billion gross assets figure is only indicative and will not automatically result in systemic designation (although the PRA will also consider future potential to exceed the threshold).
- Where an overseas bank or group maintains multiple UK bank branches, the PRA will form a view based on the aggregated UK branch footprint and may also take into account the assets of any investment firm branches (if any).

- Booking models should be (among others):
  ○ clearly outlined and rationalised, showing broad alignment of risk and returns at the entity level;
  ○ supported by robust systems and controls, with oversight by risk and senior management accountability; and
  ○ not an impediment to recovery and resolution of the branch.
- Complexity considerations will include an evaluation of the overall group structure (including the number of UK branches and whether branching is direct from the head office or via intermediate subsidiaries).
- The PRA's judgement on the 'supervisability' of the branch will be important. This will take into account any barriers presented by structural complexity and the level of transparency over the wider firm and group.

8.5.2 How Is the Supervisory Experience Different from Non-Systemic Branches?

8.77 The PRA's expectations on supervisory cooperation standards are higher for systemic branches. For these branches, the PRA would expect clear agreement with the HSS on a programme of regular structured engagement. The PRA requires this to extend beyond mere information sharing. It should enable the PRA to contribute to the supervisory strategy for the overall firm and to participate actively in supervisory work on strategic priorities agreed with the HSS. The PRA would also expect greater reassurance on operational continuity in resolution and operational resilience generally and cooperation from the HSS in mitigating identified risks to UK financial stability. The practical implications of this enhanced supervisory cooperation for the branch would depend on the circumstances, but in general systemic branches should expect more regular and intrusive PRA scrutiny of their UK business.

8.78 The PRA will also consider imposing specific regulatory requirements on systemic branches in circumstances where concerns arise that cannot readily be remedied by discussions with the firm and the HSS. The PRA gives the following examples of actions that could be taken to mitigate perceived systemic risk:

- enhanced governance requirements, including additional accountable senior managers in finance, risk or operations, and/or a local oversight board;
- additional branch-specific liquidity requirements; and
- additional reporting and information disclosures to the PRA.

8.79 For EEA branches, the PRA currently has powers under EU law to designate certain passported branches as 'significant'. The criteria and implications for this are prescribed by EU law[36] and are not identical to the 'systemic branch' approach for overseas branches, but the practical implications for branches and the HSS relationship are broadly comparable.

---

[36] Under Council Directive 2013/36/EU of 26 June 2013 on access to the activity of credit institutions and the prudential supervision of credit institutions and investment firms [2013] OJ 176/338, Art. 51 (hereafter Capital Requirements Directive).

8.5.3 Booking Models

The PRA's expectations on booking models highlighted at paragraph 8.76[37] are not exclusive to systemic wholesale branches: they apply more widely to UK branches and subsidiaries with material wholesale activity. A very similar set of principles for booking models was outlined by the FCA in a 'Dear CEO' letter published in August 2018.[38] This reiterates that these expectations are common to all firms and remain of particular interest to the PRA and FCA against the background of Brexit restructuring activity. In contrast with the recent commentary from the ECB and other EU authorities on booking models,[39] however, the FCA has emphasised that it is 'open to a broad range of legal entity structures or booking models' and is not seeking to mandate or prohibit any particular models. Both this letter and the recent experience of EEA banks' authorisation discussions with the PRA and FCA illustrate that the regulators are applying careful scrutiny to this area.

8.80

8.6 Banks: Application Process

All applicants for PRA authorisation, including overseas firm applicants, are encouraged to engage in early stage preapplication discussions with the PRA before completing an application. This will be particularly important for banks intending to pursue a branch structure but whose business model and/or home state regime is such that the bank risks falling outside the PRA's branch risk appetite. Up-front, proactive engagement with the PRA will enable banks to understand early on in the process whether a subsidiary will be required, whether systemic branch designation will apply and any particular pressure points from the PRA's perspective that may place significant business change or diligence demands on the bank before it is able to obtain authorisation. It also enables 'scene-setting' for the future business, pre-empting potential concerns, and establishing a constructive relationship with the PRA and the FCA.

8.81

Firms are expected to prepare and be ready to discuss the following minimum information at the first meeting:[40]

8.82

(a) business plan—including what products and services will be offered, how they will be offered, and the target market;
(b) sources of funding—how the business proposes to fund its activities, and whether there are any investors and/or funding in place; and
(c) corporate governance—details of structure, board, senior management, and governance arrangements, as far as they are known.

---

[37] PRA, 'SS1/18' (n. 6), box 5, p. 16.
[38] FCA, 'Cross-Border Booking Arrangements' (8 August 2018) <https://www.fca.org.uk/publication/correspondence/dear-ceo-letter-cross-border-booking-arrangements.pdf>
[39] ECB, 'Supervisory Expectations on Booking Models' (August 2018) <https://www.bankingsupervision.europa.eu/banking/relocating/shared/pdf/ssm.supervisoryexpectationsbookingmodels_201808.en.pdf>
[40] PRA, 'New Firm Authorisation' (undated) <https://www.bankofengland.co.uk/prudential-regulation/authorisations/new-firm-authorisation>, section entitled 'The Pre-application Stage'

8.83 The application documents comprise a core application form, regulatory business plan, various other specific forms, and a large number of supporting documents. Some of these supporting documents will be readily obtainable from the head office and others will need to be produced or tailored to the UK branch (such as branch compliance monitoring programme, governance charts and individual senior management approval applications). Other supporting documents listed in the application will not be required for an overseas branch (for example: controller forms, recovery, and resolution plan), although the PRA may request some details on prudential or structural information from the HSS or directly from applicants. Before a bank submits an application, the PRA will typically seek to focus in some detail on the draft business plan and the material questions in the draft application form.

8.84 As explained in section 8.1, the new authorisation process is already underway for UK branches of EEA banks. It is understood that all such banks have been given approval to seek authorisation as branches and that the PRA has not mandated subsidiarisation for any passported EEA branches.

8.85 The PRA's website indicates that less preapplication scrutiny may be needed for firms that are already operating in the UK or whose business is known to the PRA. In practice, however, recent experience of the PRA's ongoing interaction with passported EEA branches has shown that this is far from a simple rebadging exercise. In most cases (bar the smallest most straightforward applications), the PRA has held multiple preapplication meetings, has reviewed, and commented on several iterations of business plans, and in some cases has requested detailed follow-up analysis and supporting documents.

8.86 The comparatively intense scrutiny reflects the relative lack of visibility that the PRA has had to date over the businesses of passported branches.

8.87 The PRA engages in regular dialogue with the HSS—in particular the ECB—throughout the application discussion process. As the PRA must (from a legal perspective) authorise the whole firm, it needs comprehensive information from both the applicant and its HSS in order to assess satisfaction of the threshold conditions, particularly with respect to prudential and resolution arrangements. At the same time, however, the PRA has focused in detail on understanding how the wider firm's policies, procedures and resources translate specifically to the UK branch, and on obtaining clarity on branch-specific roles, capabilities, and arrangements. The core areas of PRA focus for EEA branches have generally been consistent with the three core areas highlighted above; i.e. business plan, branch funding profile and corporate governance.

8.88 The PRA and FCA have also focused on the adequacy of branch systems and controls relating to IT, outsourcing and business continuity. It has been made clear that even in areas of regulation that are nominally identical between the UK and elsewhere in the EU (such as outsourcing requirements) the UK regulators will not presume compliance with the UK standards and will be prepared to scrutinise EEA banks' branch arrangements.

8.89 The application process for EEA passported banks has also proved challenging in the context of the legal and practical uncertainties generated by the end of the passporting regime and the imperfect alignment between EU regulatory concepts and the UK domestic near-equivalent concepts. All applicants are expected, as part of the application form, to complete a 'permissions' profile[41] outlining the scope of the banking and investment services intended to be carried on by the firm in the UK.

For EEA bank applicants this may raise difficult questions over how regulated activities carried on in (or into) the UK under the services passport (i.e. cross-border) should be accommodated. Where an EEA bank has exercised both the branch and services passports from the same entity, the PRA has indicated that both the branch-based and cross-border activities should be included within scope of the UK branch authorisation (to the extent that authorisation is required). This may not be necessary in all circumstances; a closer examination of activities carried on from outside the UK might lead to the conclusion that no licence will be needed for some formerly passported activities. This conclusion could arise as a result of available exemptions, the territorial scope of the UK regulatory perimeter, or a lack of mandatory regulation (for some passported banking services,[42] notably non-retail lending). For cross-border services that do trigger UK licensing requirements, however, the need to accommodate these activities within the branch licence also raises questions over whether such services will affect the PRA's supervisory approach (including systemic designation), and the extent to which UK conduct of business requirements will apply to these services. These considerations are particularly relevant for EEA banks that provide cross-border services to UK retail clients (for example, retail mortgage lending on EEA residential property). **8.90**

8.7 Banks: Implications of the Transition to Overseas Branch or Subsidiary Status

8.7.1 UK Branches

The transition for EEA banks from passported branch status to UK-authorised status (after being in the TPR regime, if relevant) will present a substantially increased compliance burden and is likely to require changes to branch systems and controls, and governance arrangements. **8.91**

In very high-level terms, the following areas are particularly likely to present a challenge for EEA banks transitioning to UK-authorised status: **8.92**

8.7.1.1 PRA rules

- **Depositor protection**: the UK depositor protection rules apply in full to non-passported UK branches (in contrast with the current position for passported branches, which are subject to home state depositor protection rules).
- **Remuneration**: UK branches must comply with the UK remuneration requirements (in addition to home state rules). The UK rules are derived from the EU regime but are super-equivalent in certain limited respects.

---

[41] That is, a set of matrices showing the regulated activities, investment types, and client types intended to be covered as part of the branch authorisation.
[42] Capital Requirements Directive, Annex I (n. 37).

8.7.1.2 PRA and FCA rules

- **Senior Managers and Certification Regime (SMCR):** current passported EEA branches are not required to obtain PRA approval for any individuals performing senior management functions (SMFs) and FCA approval is only required for the branch manager and MLRO. Non-passported UK branches will need PRA *and* FCA approval for the branch manager and potential new approval for certain other key functions, including compliance.
- **Reporting:** Additional periodic reporting requirements will apply, including (as applicable) in relation to liquidity data, single customer view[43] reports for insured deposits, close links, client assets, and remuneration data. The scope of ad hoc disclosure requirements to the FCA will also increase.

8.7.1.3 FCA Rules

- **Custody and client money:** the FCA's client assets rules will apply (in addition to any applicable home state rules) to UK branches that hold or control client money, or hold custody assets (i.e. safeguarding and administration).
- **Compensation:** FSCS rules and levies on compensation for investment services will apply.

8.93 The change is likely to have greatest impact for currently passported EEA branches that take FSCS-covered deposits and/or hold client money or custody assets. The systems requirements applicable to the holding of these funds and assets are complex and detailed, and can be challenging to implement from an operational perspective.

8.7.2 UK Subsidiaries

8.94 The increased compliance burden will be significantly exacerbated for any overseas firms or groups that opt for or are directed by the PRA to take the subsidiary route. All of the PRA and FCA's rules will apply, insofar as relevant to the bank's UK business. Further consideration of the impact of transition to subsidiarisation is outside the scope of this chapter.

8.7.3 TPR Implications

8.95 Under the TPR arrangements it is contemplated that deemed 'overseas firm' status will in principle become effective immediately post-Brexit (assuming no transitional period). If this outcome were introduced without further modification to the UK regulatory regime, this would result in all of the enhanced compliance requirements described above

---

[43] PRA Rulebook (n. 25) defines this as 'a single, consistent view of a depositor's aggregate eligible deposits with a firm which contains the information required by [Rule] 12.9 [of the Rulebook], but excludes from view those accounts included in the exclusions view'.

becoming 'switched on' from exit date. Recognising the practical challenges this presents, the UK government has committed to provide the BoE, PRA, and FCA with temporary relief powers to modify (e.g. switch off) the obligations of currently passported EEA firms within the TPR regime. This power will be exercised through legal directions. The aim is "to ensure that the UK's regulatory regime is flexible enough to support firms as they adjust to altered regulatory requirements in the unlikely event that there is no [UK–EU agreed] implementation period".[44]

If the UK leaves the EU without an agreed implementation period, both the FCA's and the BoE/PRA's current intention is that their transitional directions will take effect from exit day for a maximum period of fifteen months (but some of the PRA transitionals are only for three months). The transitional period will be extendable up to a maximum timeframe of two years from exit. **8.96**

Despite the temporary relief powers, the PRA broadly expects EEA branches within the TPR to comply from exit day with the same rules that apply to other branches of third country (non-EEA) firms. This will include (among others) UK depositor protection requirements and the SMCR (subject to limited modifications in the latter case to allow for temporary deemed approval).[45] The PRA plans to allow only limited temporary transitional derogations from third country branch rules, to mitigate the challenge for EEA firms of immediate compliance with certain PRA rules in the following areas: remuneration rules (where they go beyond CRD IV requirements); branch level profit and loss reporting; and status disclosure requirements for retail business.[46] **8.97**

This contrasts with the more flexible proposed FCA approach to the compliance framework for EEA firms under the TPR outlined in the FCA's policy materials. The FCA characterises the TPR compliance regime as a 'bridge' to the full application of FCA rules.[47] EEA firms will be expected under the TPR to comply with (1) all FCA rules which currently apply to them; (2) all EU-derived FCA rules which implement a requirement of an EU directive which are currently reserved to the firm's home state(but allowing the firm to comply on a 'substituted compliance' basis—i.e. compliance with the equivalent home state rule in respect of its UK business will be deemed compliance with FCA rules); and (3) certain additional UK-specific requirements believed to be necessary for consumer protection purposes. Under category (2), there are notable exceptions, where substituted compliance will not be permitted, including for transaction reporting under the onshored version of the Markets in Financial Instruments Regulation.[48] The FCA plans to allow only limited transitional relief to TPR firms (for example in relation to post-trade reporting obligations).[49] **8.98**

---

[44] HM Treasury, 'Proposal for a Temporary Transitional Power to Be Exercised by UK Regulators' (8 October 2018) <https://www.gov.uk/government/publications/proposal-for-a-temporary-transitional-power-to-be-exercised-by-uk-regulators/proposal-for-a-temporary-transitional-power-to-be-exercised-by-uk-regulators>
[45] PRA, 'CP 26/18: UK Withdrawal from the EU' (n. 14), pp. 17–18.
[46] PRA, 'PS5/19' (n. 16) (February 2019) (hereafter PRA, 'PS5/19') (Table A on p.20).
[47] FCA, 'CP 18/29: Temporary Permissions Regime for Inbound Firms and Funds' (10 October 2018), p. 7 <https://www.fca.org.uk/publication/consultation/cp18-29.pdf> accessed 18 November 2018.
[48] Regulation 600/2014/EU.
[49] FCA, 'PS19/5' (n. 16).

8.7.4 FSCR

8.99 Instead of the TPR, the FSCR may be available (but only for up to five years) to EEA banks that have decided to run off their existing contracts (and not to enter into any new business in the UK).

8.8 Overseas (Re)insurers: General PRA Approach to Authorisation

8.100 Consistent with the position for banks, an overseas (re)insurer that wishes to access the UK market has three options:

- provision of services from overseas without establishing a permanent presence in the UK;
- establishment of a UK branch; and
- establishment of a UK subsidiary, which is authorised by the PRA to conduct insurance business in the UK.

8.101 Currently, passporting rights mean that EEA (re)insurers can conduct business in the UK under the first or second of these scenarios without obtaining authorisation from the PRA.

8.102 Again as for banks, Brexit does not mean that EEA (re)insurers will no longer be able to conduct business in the UK. The loss of passporting rights does mean, however, that they will not be able to conduct business in the UK without obtaining authorisation here. The need for authorisation arises if, as a matter of fact, a (re)insurer is carrying on regulated activities 'in the UK'.

8.103 When an international insurance group establishes a UK subsidiary, that subsidiary will need to be authorised by the PRA in the same way as any other UK (re)insurance company. The process for obtaining authorisation is the same for all UK companies irrespective of ownership.

8.104 This chapter will not discuss in detail the authorisation process and requirements applying to UK applicants, including those that are UK subsidiaries within an EEA-headquartered group. It will focus, instead, on the PRA's approach to UK branches of overseas (re)insurers (including EEA (re)insurers post-Brexit), which also require authorisation from the PRA for those of their activities that are carried on in the UK and regulated under the Financial Services and Markets Act 2000 (**FSMA**). In addition, because the primary focus of this chapter is on the authorisation of UK branches and subsidiaries, the consequences of Brexit for an EEA (re)insurer operating in the UK on a cross-border services basis is only considered very briefly below. We understand, however, that an EEA (re)insurer that currently passports into the UK on a services basis but that requires authorisation for its activities post-Brexit will, in practice, be expected to establish a branch in the UK.

8.105 Much of the discussion on the authorisation of banks earlier in this chapter applies equally to (re)insurers and will not be repeated here. For example:

- (Re)insurers applying for authorisation in the UK will have to meet relevant statutory threshold conditions which are similar, but not identical, to those applying to banks.
- Discussion about the general differences between branches and subsidiaries in section 8.2 above also applies to (re)insurers.
- The process of applying for PRA authorisation as a (re)insurer is likely to match very closely the process followed by banks, albeit that different types of firm will raise different concerns from a supervisory perspective. Each will need to be considered on its own merits.

8.8.1 PRA Approach to EEA (Re)insurers Post-Brexit

8.106 The rules applying to EEA (re)insurers seeking authorisation in the UK post-Brexit will, for the most part at least, be the same as the requirements applying to third country (re)insurers now.

8.107 In December 2017, the Treasury, PRA and FCA sought to clarify their approach, post-Brexit, to financial services firms that have their head office outside the UK. In the first instance, they published the following which are particularly relevant to (re)insurers:

- PRA consultation paper (CP30/17) on its approach to third country insurers;[50] and
- a separate 'Dear CEO letter'.[51]

8.108 Evidence given to the House of Commons Treasury Select Committee in January 2018 in the context of its Solvency II inquiry also shed light on the PRA's thinking.[52]

8.109 CP30/17 described the PRA's policy towards authorising and supervising non-UK (re)insurers (including EEA (re)insurers post-Brexit) carrying on (or considering carrying on) insurance business in the UK that do not benefit from passporting rights. The PRA also proposed to issue a new supervisory statement supplementing SS44/15 'Solvency II: third-country insurance and pure reinsurance branches'.

8.110 The PRA subsequently published a policy statement (PS4/18)[53] confirming its approach, accompanied by a new supervisory statement (SS2/18).[54] SS2/18 was broadly in the same form as consulted upon subject to one significant change which is discussed below.

---

[50] PRA, 'CP 30/17: International Insurers: The PRA's Approach to Branch Authorisation and Supervision' (20 December 2017) <https://www.bankofengland.co.uk/-/media/boe/files/prudential-regulation/consultation-paper/2017/cp3017>.

[51] FCA, 'Firms' Preparations for the UK's Withdrawal from the European Union: Planning Assumptions' (20 December 2017) <https://www.bankofengland.co.uk/-/media/boe/files/prudential-regulation/letter/2017/firms-preparations-for-uk-withdrawal-from-the-eu>.

[52] PRA, 'Interim Response to the Treasury Select Committee's Response on Solvency II' (3 January 2018) <https://www.parliament.uk/documents/commons-committees/treasury/Correspondence/2017-19/PRA-Interim-Response-Solvency-II.PDF>.

[53] PRA, 'PS4/18: International Insurers: The PRA's Approach to Branch Authorisation and Supervision' (29 March 2018) <https://www.bankofengland.co.uk/-/media/boe/files/prudential-regulation/policy-statement/2018/ps418.pdf>.

[54] PRA, 'SS2/18: International Insurers' (n. 10).

8.111 On 5 March 2019, the PRA and FCA announced that they had agreed memoranda of understanding with EIOPA and EU/EEA supervisory authorities regarding supervisory cooperation and information sharing arrangements to apply in the event of a 'no deal' Brexit.[55]

8.8.2 TPR Implications

8.112 The TPR will apply to (re)insurers as well as to banks and the same general approach being taken to EEA firms entering the TPR is that they will be treated in the same way as other third country firms. The PRA and FCA will have the same powers in relation to TPR (re)insurers as if they were fully authorised firms. The firms will be subject to the same obligations and supervisory framework as if they were fully authorised firms.

8.113 Some of the rules of the TPR will, however, be different from those that would normally apply to third country firms where necessary to ensure that they are effective and operable. In particular, the PRA has said that it will make use of its temporary transitional power to give relief to firms who may struggle to meet some of the PRA's requirements immediately after the UK leaves the EU. For example, the PRA plans to use this power in relation to the following:

- branch solvency and minimum capital requirements for insurance branches (although they would be expected to comply with branch security deposit requirements);
- certain reporting obligations which involve the segregation of branch data and the reporting and review of this data where this is not already required; and
- composites rules for insurance branches[56].

8.114 Brexit-related rule changes being made to the FSCS will make special provision for (re)insurers that are in the TPR.

8.8.3 FSCR

8.115 Instead of the TPR, the FSCR may be available (for up to fifteen years) to EEA (re)insurers that have decided to run off their existing contracts and not to write any new business in the UK.

8.9 Overseas (Re)insurers: PRA Approach to UK Branches—Factors to Be Considered

8.116 SS44/15 is addressed to non-EEA (re)insurance undertakings that have a UK branch. It expands on the PRA's general approach to supervision as set out in its Insurance Approach

---

[55] See <https://www.bankofengland.co.uk/-/media/boe/files/news/2019/march/boe-and-fca-agree-mou-with-eiopa-and-eu-insurance-supervisors.pdf>

[56] PRA, 'PS5/19' (Table A on p. 20).

document,[57] by explaining its expectations of firms in relation to certain specific matters, including the following:

- The PRA expects considerable importance to be attached to calculating branch own funds to ensure that branch policyholders enjoy the same level of protection as policyholders of an undertaking situated in the EU.
- The PRA will expect to be given sufficient information to make an assessment of the adequacy of the worldwide financial resources of the non-EEA (re)insurance undertaking.

Post-Brexit, the requirements of SS44/15 will continue to apply to all third country (re)insurers with a UK branch, including EEA (re)insurers. 8.117

8.9.1 New Factors to Be Considered by PRA

SS2/18 introduces a number of new factors which the PRA will take into account alongside its long-established requirements for third country branch authorisation. It notes that its approach is 'anchored in its statutory objectives' and includes an assessment of the 'supervisability' of the insurer. In particular, the PRA will consider, and need to be satisfied that: 8.118

- the home jurisdiction's prudential supervision regime is 'broadly equivalent';
- the firm is capable of being supervised effectively by the HSS;
- the whole firm is able to meet the threshold conditions (as discussed above);
- there is sufficient supervisory cooperation with the HSS (this factor is particularly important);
- UK policyholders will be given 'appropriate' priority in an insolvency scenario and there is no discrimination against policyholders whose business is written in the UK on a winding up of the insurer; and
- the firm is able to meet relevant PRA rules, including SMCR requirements applicable to the relevant individuals responsible for the branch.

Two additional factors the PRA will use in its assessment of a branch, but which are not to do with 'supervisability', are: 8.119

- the scale of UK branch activity that is covered by the FSCS and whether the PRA is satisfied that insurers liable to pay into the FSCS would be able to absorb that amount of loss; and
- the impact of the failure of a firm with a UK branch on the wider insurance market and financial system in the UK.

In summary, the PRA will, in some circumstances at least (discussed further below), require overseas firms to conduct their UK business through a local subsidiary instead of through a branch. 8.120

---

[57] PRA, 'The PRA's Approach to Insurance Supervision' (31 October 2018) <https://www.bankofengland.co.uk/-/media/boe/files/prudential-regulation/approach/insurance-approach-2018.pdf?la=en&hash=4055BBB0B728E1F9E536AB09D69107D01236C658>

8.9.2 Scale of UK Branch Activity Covered by the FSCS

8.121 Where a firm is likely to have more than £500 million of FSCS-protected liabilities, the PRA's default approach will be to require that firm to subsidiarise. In CP30/17, the PRA proposed that this threshold should be set at just £200 million, but this was increased in response to comments.

8.122 Given the requirement for industry to pick up any FSCS costs associated with an insurer failing, the PRA has argued that it needs to have greater oversight over a firm that poses greater systemic risk to the UK. It believes that the levels of FSCS-protected liabilities a branch has provide a 'straightforward measure' of that risk.

8.123 In the context of Brexit, the PRA's change in policy may mean that an EEA (re)insurer that currently operates through a UK branch without PRA authorisation will have to transfer that business to a UK subsidiary (which may itself need authorisation if it is a new company) under the relevant home state's law on transfers of business. This is likely to be considerably more complex and costly than simply applying for a new branch authorisation in the UK and it may take much longer. On an ongoing basis, subsidiarisation is also likely to be considerably more onerous than operating through a UK branch.

8.9.3 Impact of Branch Failure on the Wider Insurance Market and Financial System

8.124 Where a branch's FSCS-protected liabilities fall below the £500 million threshold, the PRA may nonetheless require the business to subsidiarise because of the systemic risk it brings to the UK. The risk a firm poses to the PRA's objectives in this context will be assessed according to the:

- ability of policyholders to obtain substitute products offering a similar level of protection;
- branch's importance in the market, looking particularly at market share in a niche market;
- level of connectivity of a branch in the industry it operates within; and
- significance of the UK operations to the firm's overall business.

8.125 The PRA argues that a retail life business is most likely to be regarded as 'systemic' in these terms. This is because the failure of a single business will usually affect the ability of a large number of policyholders to receive benefits from annuity and other long-term insurance policies for many years.

8.126 Insurers operating in the commercial sector may also be required to subsidiarise if they have a large market share in a niche market, leaving policyholders with little hope of finding alternative cover if that insurer fails.

8.9.4 Cross-border Services Business

8.127 PRA comments on Brexit have primarily been directed at UK branches of EEA (re)insurers and have not discussed in any detail EEA insurers that currently carry on activities in the UK under the services passport. In CP25/18, however, the PRA stated (paragraph 3.2(a)): "European Economic Area (EEA) firms that were able to provide services into the UK through passporting arrangements will need to seek authorisation to continue to be able to do so after exit day."

8.128 This may suggest on its face that all (re)insurers operating on a freedom of services basis in the UK would need to obtain full authorisation to be able to continue their activities post-Brexit. Looking more closely at the context of that comment, however, it seems to be aimed more generally at EEA firms that currently passport into the UK, including those operating through a UK branch, rather than specifically being directed at cross-border services activity. In CP26/18, the PRA stated: "The aim of the TPR is to allow firms that currently access the UK market via the EU passporting regime to continue to operate in the UK for a limited period after withdrawal while they seek authorisation from UK regulators."

8.129 In other words, the TPR is designed for (re)insurers that rely on passporting rights to access the UK market, which may include (re)insurers who conduct business in the UK on a services basis only without a UK branch. By implication, however, it is not intended for use by firms that fall outside the territorial jurisdiction of the FSMA regime. The FCA appears to have recognised this distinction (albeit that its comments are not directed particularly at (re)insurers). In CP18/29, it stated as follows in response to the question 'Is a temporary permission needed to continue to access the UK market?' (paragraph 2.30):

> Depending on the activities a firm is undertaking it may not come within the UK regulatory perimeter. For example, depending on the facts that apply to a firm and the activities it is undertaking, firms without an establishment of permanent place of business in the UK may not be carrying on a regulated activity in the UK.

8.130 The better view would appear to be, consistent with the FCA's comments, that EEA (re)insurers who can satisfy themselves that their activities fall outside the UK regulatory perimeter post-Brexit should not require UK authorisation here.

9

The UK's Senior Managers, Certification and Conduct Regime

Charlotte Henry

9.1 Introduction

Further to paragraph 1.8, it is not yet known at the time of writing this chapter whether the United Kingdom (UK) will leave the European Union (EU) with a deal, with no deal, or will not leave at all (i.e. if there is a second referendum with a different outcome or revocation of Article 50 of the Treaty on the Functioning of the European Union (TFEU)). This chapter assumes that there will either be 'a deal' (with resultant transitional arrangements) or 'no deal' (with resultant temporary arrangements) (collectively **Brexit**). 9.01

Based on this assumption, there are a number of impacts that Brexit will have on the current regime in the UK that applies to entities regulated by the UK's Prudential Regulation Authority (**PRA**) and/or the UK's Financial Conduct Authority (**FCA**) (collectively, the **UK Regulators**), known as the Senior Managers, Certification and Conduct Regime (**SMCR**). 9.02

This chapter explores the following key impacts: 9.03

- applicability of different SMCR regimes;
- responsibility for changing regulatory requirements during Brexit;
- practical implications of moving between regimes;
- responsibility for cross-border business into the UK;
- impact on certification and conduct regimes;
- insourcing and outsourcing; and
- enforcement against non-UK resident senior managers.

9.2 Summary of the Relevant Background

By way of summary background, the SMCR is the regime implemented by the UK Regulators to aim to increase individual accountability within UK financial services firms. It was first introduced for banks in March 2016 applying to UK-incorporated banks, UK branches of third country banks and UK branches of EEA banks. It has been applied to other sectors of the UK financial services market since then and will be proportionately applied to all but a few of the remaining UK financial services firms with effect from 9 December 2019. 9.04

The SMCR focuses on three layers of individuals within financial services firms—senior managers (those who need to be approved by or notified to the relevant UK Regulator), certified or certification staff (those who need to be certified as fit and proper by the financial 9.05

services firm itself) and conduct staff (who are all remaining staff within financial services firms, with some exceptions).

9.06 The key principles of the SMCR are as follows:

(a) **senior managers**—increase the transparency of the accountabilities of senior managers through written statements of responsibilities clearly identifying the function(s) they hold, their prescribed responsibilities within or to the organisation and their wider accountabilities;

(b) **certified/certification staff**—for those who can cause significant harm to a firm or who are material risk takers (and who are not already senior managers), increasing the robustness of oversight over their fitness and propriety by requiring in-scope firms to certify them as being fit and proper and to review that certification at a minimum annually;

(c) **conduct staff**—for all staff working in the UK financial services industry (with some exceptions), including senior managers and certification staff, ensuring there is a minimum standard of conduct set through the introduction of conduct rules that each staff member must individually comply with; and

(d) **firm-wide requirements**—for in-scope firms, increase the transparency of the role and responsibilities of senior managers and certified staff and their interaction/responsibilities in relation to the governance and oversight structures within the firm, the first, second and third lines of defence and other group entities (where applicable) through a management responsibilities map.

9.07 While the principles of the SMCR are applied consistently across the UK's financial services industry, the detailed requirements that apply to a particular firm can differ depending on the type of sector that it is in (e.g. banking, insurance, etc.), its structure (e.g. subsidiary, branch), whether it meets particular tests so as to fall into one category or another (e.g. enhanced, core or limited scope firms) and depending on whether it is dually regulated by both UK Regulators or solo regulated.

9.3 Applicability of Different SMCR Regimes with Brexit

9.08 As the SMCR applies differently across the wide variety of UK financial services firms, this chapter focuses primarily on financial services firms which are banks.

9.09 Turning now to consider how Brexit will impact on SMCR, firstly, it adds even more complexity to SMCR requirements. For example, with Brexit, an entity may be changing from being a 'UK branch of an EEA entity' to being considered (for SMCR purposes) to be a 'third country branch'. This means that the same entity will switch from being subject to the SMCR requirements that applied to EEA branches to those that apply to third country branches. The suite of possible switches includes:

(a) EEA firms which are not banks or insurers and which have a branch in the UK - regardless of the transitional arrangements (**Transitional**) (if the UK leaves the EU with a deal) or the temporary permissions regime (**TPR**) (if the UK leaves the EU without a deal), these branches are subject to the Approved Persons Regime until the extended SMCR comes into effect on 9 December 2019.[1] After this date, such a firm in either the TPR or Transitional will be automatically converted to the FCA SMCR regime as it applies to EEA branches. Following the FCA's approval of an EEA firm's application for authorisation as a third country branch, the FCA SMCR for third country non-bank branches will apply.

(b) EEA firms which are not banks or insurers and which have a subsidiary incorporated and authorised in the UK—the subsidiary will be subject to the Approved Persons Regime until the extended SMCR comes into effect on 9 December 2019 and thereafter subject to either the SMCR regime applicable to limited, core, or enhanced firms depending on what test the subsidiary meets.

(c) EEA firms which are not banks or insurers and provide cross-border business into the UK—in the TPR, these firms are subject to the Approved Persons Regime until the SMCR comes into effect on 9 December 2019. Thereafter these firms will be automatically converted to the FCA SMCR regime as it applies to EEA firms conducting cross-border services until the date on which they exit the TPR. Under the threshold conditions set out in Schedule 6 of the Financial Services and Markets Act 2000 (**FSMA**), a third country entity cannot be authorised in the UK where it is only intending to carry on regulated activities on a cross-border basis in the UK (i.e. it will have no establishment or physical presence within the UK). Notwithstanding this, the FCA has authorised such firms in the past and some appear on the Financial Services Register although its position on this point is changing with Brexit.

(d) EEA banks with a branch in the UK - in the Transitional, the current FCA and PRA SMCR regimes applicable to EEA branches will continue to apply until the branch is reauthorised.[2] For the purposes of an EEA bank's authorisation with the PRA and FCA, the PRA/FCA SMCR as applied to third country bank branches will apply.

(e) EEA banks with a branch in the UK - in the TPR, there is currently a multitude of different SMCR requirements as the FCA and PRA have adopted different approaches to the treatment of EEA banks and their SMCR obligations. During the TPR:

  (i) Under the FCA's approach, EEA banks with a UK branch remain subject to the FCA's current SMCR regime for EEA branches until reauthorisation. In summary, only two senior manager functions (SMFs) apply (the MLRO (SMF17) and the EEA Branch Senior Manager (SMF21)) and there is no requirement for prescribed responsibilities to be allocated.

  (ii) Under the PRA's approach, some of the PRA senior manager functions that apply to third country bank branches will apply (Head of Overseas Branch function (SMF19), Chief Finance Officer (SMF2), Chief Risk Officer (SMF4), Head of Internal Audit (SMF5), Group Entity Senior Manager (SMF7), Chief Operations Officer (SMF24) if a branch has individuals performing those roles and, on a risk-based decision, it is appropriate to allocate them).

---

[1] Bank of England and Financial Services Act 2016, s. 21, which, as at the time of writing, has yet to be commenced for the non-bank/non-insurance sector.

[2] 'Application of SMCR to Firms in TPR—Clarification of PRA and FCA Proposals', PRA webpage available at <https://www.bankofengland.co.uk/-/media/boe/files/prudential-regulation/report/application-of-smcr-to-firms-in-tpr-clarification-of-pra-and-fca-proposals>

Branches have twelve weeks from entry into the TPR to submit these SMFs to the PRA for deemed or full approval. In order to limit the compliance burden on EEA bank branches, the PRA has tweaked the SMCR prescribed responsibilities that normally apply to third country bank branches and introduced two prescribed responsibilities that only apply during this period. These two prescribed responsibilities are: (i) the existing 'responsibility for the firm's compliance with the UK regulatory system applicable to the firm', (which does not extend to include compliance with any PRA requirements for which transitional relief has been granted until the expiry of the relief) and (ii) the bespoke new responsibility of:

> where the firm has applied for permission under Part 4A of FSMA to carry on a regulated activity, until such time as the application has been determined or withdrawn, the responsibility for managing the process of obtaining such permission (including, without limitation, the completion and submission of the firm's application and providing the PRA with such co-operation and with all accurate and up to date information that it may reasonably require in order to determine whether the requirements for authorisation have been met).

The above creates a hybrid version of the SMCR, whereby the FCA/PRA apply different types of SMCR regime and different requirements to the same branch. Following reauthorisation these firms will move from the hybrid SMCR regime to the full third country bank branch SMCR regimes of the PRA and FCA.

(f) EEA banks with bank subsidiaries incorporated and authorised in the UK—regardless of the Transitional or the TPR, they are subject to the current SMCR regime that has been applicable to them since March 2016 which continues.

(g) EEA banks and/or their subsidiaries conducting cross-border business into the UK—in the TPR, the FCA has no additional SMCR requirements. However, the PRA has proposed that these firms will, with appropriate modifications, be subject to the SMCR regime for third country branches. Under this modified version of the SMCR, these firms will be required to have one or more individuals approved to perform the Head of Overseas Branch function (SMF19). Depending on the circumstances of these firms (i.e. the nature and risks involved in their cross-border business into the UK), the PRA expects these firms to also have additional SMFs (such as SMF4—Chief Risk Officer function). As these entities do not have branches in the UK (and therefore may not have submitted an application for authorisation as a third country branch), these entities will need to seek deemed approval from the PRA for persons to fulfil the relevant SMF roles within the firm during the TPR. These firms have twelve weeks from entering into the TPR to apply for deemed approval for their proposed senior manager(s). The PRA will also apply the Certification Regime and the requirements in relation to regulatory references to these firms during the TPR. This is discussed more later in this chapter.

9.10 Therefore, depending on the entity type and structure, Brexit has the potential to create additional complexity for firms in introducing hybrid arrangements and for firms in moving into different regimes depending on whether they are in the Transitional or the TPR. This is particularly a challenge for groups where senior managers may have responsibilities for the UK entity and be subject to different requirements at different times for the same entity.

9.3.1 Deemed Approval for SMFs

Deemed approval is where the PRA treats an individual as approved whose SMF application has been submitted. Submission is conducted in one of two ways—either the authorisation application is submitted, which also includes full SMF applications for relevant individuals who will hold the SMFs, or the streamlined TPR process for 'deemed approval' to perform a SMF is followed. In both scenarios, the PRA conducts a basic fit and proper assessment of the individual to be deemed approved, leaving the comprehensive assessment to be conducted at the time the authorisation application is considered. The streamlined TPR process for deemed approval includes an adapted version of the Short Form A (the UK form that seeks approval for a senior manager) with a short Statement of Responsibilities. The PRA will provide a notice conferring deemed approval but has not, at the time of writing, confirmed whether such individuals will appear on the Financial Services Register. As firms are required to only put forward individuals as SMF where they are satisfied they meet their own fit and proper requirements, firms will likely need to conduct a fuller fit and proper assessment on such SMFs (even if the PRA will conduct a basic fit and proper assessment initially). This is proving challenging for EEA firms conducting purely cross-border business into the UK (discussed below) where such UK fit and proper assessment requirements/criteria may not be embedded into the business.

9.11

9.3.2 Challenges

In relation to paragraph 9.09 above, this is causing the market some challenges. A few of those challenges, relating to UK branches of EEA banks, in the TPR, are discussed below:

9.12

(a) As the FCA SMCR regime for third country bank branches does not apply until reauthorisation, SMF 16 (Compliance Officer) is not available as a senior manager function during the TPR (this is due to it only becoming an available SMF for third country bank branches). Notwithstanding this, as discussed above, there are prescribed responsibilities that need to be allocated, including the new prescribed responsibilities set out above, one of which relating to the branch's compliance with its regulatory requirements. Although this prescribed responsibility is likely to naturally fit within the job description/responsibility of the branch's Compliance Officer, it is unable to be allocated to the Compliance Officer as they will not be an approved SMF. It will, therefore, need to be allocated elsewhere with the accompanying system and control changes, reporting line changes, etc. that this may encompass. Following the branch's reauthorisation, this will need to be unwound so that the prescribed responsibilities are reallocated to the senior manager who holds the actual overall accountability for these areas within the branch (i.e. likely to be the Compliance Officer—SMF16).

(b) As a hybrid SMCR regime applies during the TPR, the EEA branch manager will be responsible: (i) for their accountabilities under their existing FCA SMF function (SMF21); (ii) their accountabilities under the new deemed PRA SMF function (SMF19); and (iii) it is anticipated that they will also be responsible for the additional PRA prescribed responsibilities that only apply during the hybrid SMCR period. This adds a layer of complexity to what is essentially the same role and the PRA has issued clarification on the overlapping requirements on the branch manager during this period.[3]

(c) In addition, the branch manager may have to take responsibility for any cross-border business conducted under the firm's cross-border permissions during the TPR if senior managers with accountability for those cross-border services have not been identified and submitted for approval. This is discussed later in this chapter.

(d) Finally, the additional prescribed responsibility of 'where the firm has applied for permission under Part 4A of FSMA to carry on a regulated activity, until such time as the application has been determined or withdrawn, the responsibility for managing the process of obtaining such permission (including, without limitation, the completion and submission of the firm's application and providing the PRA with such co-operation and with all accurate and up to date information that it may reasonably require in order to determine whether the requirements for authorisation have been met)' is causing some challenges. The reauthorisation application is technically an application of the legal entity, so is submitted by the firm (not by the branch) (**Head Office**). Where the application process is primarily led by individuals within the Head Office, they may not be approved under the PRA SMCR regime in order to have this responsibility allocated to them and, even if they were, the PRA has stated that it expects that this responsibility to be allocated to the Head of Overseas Branch (SMF19). Also the scope of the prescribed responsibility is proving challenging for those entities that are also subject to supervision by the ECB/JST who have, on occasion, made specific requests of in-scope entities which can, on the face of them and in practice, appear at odds with this responsibility.

9.4 Responsibility for Changing Regulatory Requirements during Brexit

9.13 In the various applicable SMCR regimes that could apply during Brexit (discussed above), senior managers need to ensure, among other items, that their various areas of accountability comply with regulatory requirements. The universe of regulatory requirements that apply to firms during the TPR will change and will change again after a firm comes out of the TPR/the Transitional ends, and, in some cases, the requirements that apply differ between the UK Regulators. This adds to what is already a complex picture for in-scope senior managers in understanding what they are responsible for complying with at a point in time and the resultant individual accountability that they have for those responsibilities.

---

[3] Ibid.

The FCA's approach to broader regulatory requirements for an EEA firm's UK business during the TPR is to maintain the status quo, subject to only slight modifications. This is discussed in more detail in Chapter 7 but, in summary, EEA firms must comply with the following rules during the TPR:[4] **9.14**

(a) all FCA rules which currently apply;
(b) all FCA rules which implement a requirement of an EU directive, which are currently reserved to the firm's home state (i.e. Home State Rules). The FCA has stated that it intends to accept 'substituted compliance' in respect of these rules (i.e. if EEA firms can demonstrate that they continue to comply with equivalent home state rules in respect of their UK business then such firms will be deemed to comply with the FCA's rules); and
(c) certain additional rules which the FCA believes are necessary to provide appropriate consumer protection or relate to funding requirements.

By contrast, the PRA's approach is different. The PRA requires UK branches of EEA banks to comply with the regulatory requirements that apply to third country bank branches as if they were a third country branch from 'exit day', subject to modifications.[5] The PRA has recognised that it may be challenging for EEA firms to comply immediately after exit day with some of the regulatory requirements and has therefore provided for transitional relief for certain aspects of the requirements (including some aspects of the PRA remuneration rules).[6] See Chapter 7 for a fuller analysis. **9.15**

A senior manager's responsibilities will, therefore, be constantly changing and the scope continually increasing with the changes to reasonable steps considerations that this entails. **9.16**

9.5 Practical Implications of Moving between Regimes

As discussed above, firms need to be ready to comply with the full regulatory requirements that apply to them in time for when they come out of the TPR. This is discussed more fully in Chapter 8, but, in summary, there are three circumstances by which firms will exit the TPR: **9.17**

(a) when the application for authorisation in the UK as a third country branch is determined—either approved or rejected/withdrawn. Under the TPR Regulations, the statutory time limits for the UK Regulators to process authorisation applications from EEA passporting firms has been temporarily extended from six and twelve months for complete and incomplete applications respectively to three years, and so the PRA will have until at least the end of the initial TPR period to consider a reauthorisation application;

---

[4] FCA Consultation Paper 18/29 (Temporary permissions regime for inbound firms and funds) October 2018 and FCA Policy Statement PS19/5 (Brexit Policy Statement and Transitional Directions) February 2019.

[5] PRA Consultation Paper 26/18 (UK withdrawal from the EU: Changes to PRA Rulebook and onshored Binding Technical Standards) October 2018 and Bank of England Policy Statement/PRA Policy Statement PS5/19 (The Bank of England's amendments to financial services legislation under the European Union (Withdrawal) Act 2018) April 2019 (updated June 2019).

[6] Direction made by the PRA under Part 7 of the Financial Services and Markets Act 2000 (Amendment) (EU Exit) Regulations 2019.

(b) when the PRA exercises its own powers to cancel a deemed permission (or, if a firm has a deemed variation, to vary the permission so that there are no longer any activities covered by that deemed variation). This includes the PRA's use of its power—provided to the PRA in the TPR Regulations—to cancel a firm's deemed Part 4A permission under the TPR, if that EEA firm does not submit an application within the first two years of TPR for authorisation as a third country branch; or

(c) when the TPR period ends (i.e. three years from exit day, subject to any extensions by HM Treasury).

9.18 As a firm may not remain in the TPR for the entire three-year initial period, firms will need to be ready to comply with the full regulatory requirements at any time before their reauthorisation application is determined. As at the date of writing, the FCA has indicated that it will start to consider applications for authorisations for EEA firms from October 2019 (subject to exit day being further delayed). The PRA has not provided any similar indication publicly but has been communicating likely timing directly to firms.

9.19 With the uncertainty on timing for when a firm will potentially need to comply with different regulatory requirements (discussed above), it is likely that firms may need to consider complying with the regulatory requirements ahead of time (i.e. front-running compliance) in order to allow sufficient time for the changes to fully embed.

9.20 Moving between the regime that currently applies to a firm, to the one that will apply during the TPR, to the one that will apply once they are authorised can involve a significant amount of work. It not only potentially impacts on the identification of senior managers, certified persons, prescribed responsibilities and allocating overall responsibilities, it could also impact on all aspects of the UK branch activity and the interaction between the UK branch and that of the Head Office. The practicalities that may need to be considered include:

(a) the sufficiency of local branch governance structures and, to the extent needed, formalising (where appropriate) whatever body will exercise local governance;
(b) the sufficiency of branch oversight arrangements and committees;
(c) the sufficiency of the lines of defence;
(d) reporting lines, including into the branch general manager;
(e) local ownership of local business areas, activities, functions;
(f) the sufficiency of management information that senior managers receive including ensuring, for those firms organised along global business lines where management information is provided vertically, that there is sufficient management information also provided horizontally across the branch;
(g) information flows and support from Head Office back into the branch; and
(h) formalising any support provided by Head Office to the branch (e.g. IT systems).

9.6 Responsibility for Cross-border Business into the UK

9.21 For some UK branches, there is a combination of activity done from the UK branch (under passported permissions for the branch and, in some cases, domestic top-up permissions) and activity done on a purely cross-border basis into the UK (which may have benefitted from passport permissions for services). For cross-border business (where this is not also conducted from the UK branch), once the UK branch of an EEA bank is reauthorised as a third country branch, all passported permissions that are held by the EEA bank for services will cease to have legal effect within the UK (subject to modifications for the Contractual Run-Off Regime and Supervised Run-off Regime for historic pre-exit day activities). The EEA bank will not be able to conduct any new cross-border activities into the UK where that activity is regulated unless: (i) the activity is conducted by relying on the permissions of the UK branch; or (ii) there is an exemption that can be relied on.

9.22 While the permissions granted by the UK Regulators to the legal entity following its authorisation as a third country branch will be on a single entity basis, it is important to note that in light of the threshold conditions, it is principally expected that the permissions will be used for UK branch business. Notwithstanding this, it appears to be the case that post-Brexit an EEA bank can still conduct certain regulated activities into the UK on a cross-border basis by relying on the permissions of the UK branch. In terms of SMCR impact, although the regime is primarily concerned with accountability for branch business,[7] the UK Regulators have to date expected that cross-border business comes within the SMCR regime. If senior managers within the UK branch are unable to have adequate oversight and control over the regulated activities conducted cross-border so as to be comfortable with accountability for that business, it may be necessary for an individual or individuals in the Head Office of an EEA bank to become a senior manager for these purposes. Even then, the UK Regulators expect that relevant senior management within the UK branch maintain an appropriate level of oversight and control over the cross-border activities to ensure any risks to the UK branch are identified, monitored, and controlled/mitigated. The level of oversight and operational control that is expected is proportionate depending on the nature, extent, and materiality of the regulated activities/services being conducted into the UK. However, it is envisaged that, among other items, there is an element of reporting from these senior managers into the UK branch manager and other branch senior managers where appropriate.

9.23 Cross-border activity can also be conducted by other group entities. There are typically three options explored for group entities to continue to provide regulated activities which do not fall within an exemption/exclusion into the UK post-Brexit, namely:

(1) establishing a branch in the UK and applying for authorisation as a third country branch—the SMCR impact for which is discussed above;
(2) becoming an appointed representative of an entity which has already been granted a Part 4A permission—the SMCR impact for which is discussed below; or
(3) dual-hatting relevant group employees—the SMCR impact for which is discussed below.

---

[7] PRA Consultation Paper 26/18 (UK withdrawal from the EU: Changes to PRA Rulebook and onshored Binding Technical Standards) October 2018.

9.6.1 Appointed Representatives

9.24 In order to carry on regulated activities in the UK, a firm must be either an authorised person, or an exempt person in relation to the relevant regulated activities. A person will be an exempt person if, among other options, they are an appointed representative. An appointed representative is an entity/person contractually permitted to carry on regulated activities on behalf of an authorised person with the authorised person accepting regulatory responsibility for the activities of that appointed representative. Appointed representatives themselves are not directly subject to SMCR requirements as they are outside the scope of the regime. In terms of SMCR impact, should an entity in the same group as the UK branch wish to become an Appointed Representative so as to rely on the UK branch permissions, this type of arrangement comes with increased risks for the authorised firm (and is subject to any change in the FCA's position on whether Appointed Representatives can be non-UK entities/persons). As, in this scenario, the appointed representative will be outside the UK, they could be unfamiliar with UK regulatory requirements. In addition, as UK branch senior management will be accountable for the activities/actions of the appointed representative, the branch's senior management will want sufficient oversight and robust systems and controls in place to monitor the activities of the appointed representatives.

9.6.2 Dual-Hatting

9.25 Dual-hatting refers to relevant individuals being employed by/seconded to, and working for, two entities - in this context, the group entity conducting cross-border activities into the UK and the authorised UK branch. When the individual is wearing the hat of the group entity, they are within the accountability net of the group entity and when they are wearing the hat of the UK branch, they are within the accountability net of the UK branch. Due to the substance requirements for this arrangement to be effective (e.g. the employment and tax aspects), and the level of oversight that senior managers within the UK branch would need to exercise over any dual-hatted individuals, these models can be challenging to operate in practice in compliance with SMCR requirements. With Brexit, these arrangements are being reconsidered by various European regulators. In addition, the UK Regulators generally wish to understand the impact of the arrangements on the branch's business model (as submitted to the UK Regulators as part of the authorisation process) and how any potential conflicts of interest are mitigated.

9.7 Impact on Certification and Conduct Regimes

9.26 The approach to applying the requirements of the Certification and Conduct Regimes to firms in the Transitional or the TPR is similar to that set out for the application of the requirements to senior managers discussed above.

9.27 During the Transitional, the Certification and Conduct Regimes will continue to apply to EEA firms in the same manner as prior to exit day.

9.28 For EEA firms that enter into the TPR, the FCA is proposing that firms comply with the requirements as they apply to EEA firms prior to exit day. The PRA is, again, adopting a different approach to that of the FCA requiring firms to comply with the requirements for third country branches and, in addition, applying the requirements to EEA firms providing cross-border business only. The PRA has amended the scope of the Certification and Conduct regimes so that they not only apply to business carried out from a UK branch but also to 'activities in the UK' to capture those firms conducting cross-border business. Notwithstanding this extension, the PRA is, at the time of writing, considering using its temporary transitional relief to not apply these requirements in certain circumstances. Similar to the discussion in relation to senior managers above, firms have found this aspect challenging for similar reasons. For firms conducting both activities from a UK branch and cross-border business, the process to identify any new certification staff can be difficult where, for instance, the reporting line from a certification staff member who could, for example, be in Head Office does not eventually report into a senior manager (where, for example, the in-scope senior managers are only in the UK branch). In addition, for these firms it can be difficult deciding how wide or narrow to scope the universe of conduct staff, particularly in Head Office. For firms conducting cross-border business only, with the requirements in relation to the certification regime and conduct regime being new to them, if the PRA proceeds with applying these aspects to them in the TPR, additional challenges could arise with the lack of appropriate regulatory infrastructure to support complying with these regimes.

9.8 Insourcing and Outsourcing

9.29 The UK Regulators, and in particular the PRA, have typically expected EEA firms to formalise their existing outsourcing arrangements and other important systems and controls (such as business continuity planning and disaster recovery (BCP/DR)) for the purposes of their application for authorisation as a third country branch. With Brexit, the UK Regulators have typically extended this expectation to also apply to any 'insourcing' arrangements provided within a legal entity—e.g. services provided by Head Office to a UK branch. This approach is having an impact on SMCR compliance including in the following ways:

(a) on occasion, firms have been requested to provide an attestation to a UK Regulator that the services that are being provided/received on an outsourced or insourced basis are robust, have had no issues, etc.; and
(b) the UK Regulators have generally required oversight of these arrangements to be included within scope of the relevant senior manager's Statement of Responsibilities.

9.30 In relation to attestations that have been requested, firms have had to consider the most appropriate provider of those attestations where, for instance, it may not be within the accountability of a senior manager approved under the SMCR.

9.31 In relation to accountability arrangements, this has proved particularly challenging for EEA firms, notably in determining which senior manager(s) should take responsibility for these services. The UK branch is typically the receiver of the services which are generally under the responsibility of others in the Head Office or group. There are broadly three options that EEA firms could consider in allocating accountability for outsourcings and insourcings which, in summary, are:

(a) appointing senior manager(s) within the Head Office to have accountability for these risks/systems to the UK Regulators;
(b) allocating accountability for these risks/systems to the existing/proposed senior manager population in the UK branch (e.g. to the SMF19); or
(c) a combination of (a) and (b) so that accountability for these risks/systems are split between some new senior managers in the Head Office and existing senior managers in the UK branch.

9.9 Enforcement against non-UK Resident Senior Managers

9.32 The UK SMCR has always had extraterritorial application in a number of respects including the potential for non-UK-based senior managers to be within scope of the regime. It has always been an interesting question with the current regime of how the UK Regulators would, in practice, enforce their powers against a non-UK senior manager. One of the impacts of Brexit on SMCR compliance by firms is that there is the potential for an increased number of senior managers who are located outside the UK to come within scope of the UK SMCR regime. As discussed earlier in this chapter, accountability for cross-border business, accountability for outsourcings/insourcings and converting to comply with SMCR requirements for third country firms (as opposed to EEA firms) is likely to result in a greater number of non-UK senior managers being subject to the SMCR regime. Therefore, this question is of even greater importance with Brexit including how the enforceability of the powers might alter with Brexit when considering the regulator cooperation that may be needed and enforcement of judgments, etc. once the UK is outside of the EEA. This part of this chapter explores, at a high level, what powers the UK Regulators hold in relation to non-UK senior managers and how those powers might be exercised.

9.33 During the TPR, the FCA and PRA will have the same powers in relation to an EEA firm as if they were authorised under Part 4A of FSMA. Therefore, entities in the TPR will be subject to the same rule-making powers and supervisory framework as if they were a Part 4A FSMA authorised firm (i.e. a UK-incorporated authorised firm) and these powers will continue once a firm comes out of the TPR and is authorised as a third country firm.

9.9.1 Supervisory Powers

9.34 The UK Regulators' supervisory powers in relation to senior managers, including non-UK senior managers, includes, in summary:

(a) assisting in a deep dive or other firm systematic framework analysis;
(b) attending interviews requested by the UK Regulators or relevant persons acting on their behalf;

(c) responding to queries raised by or on behalf of the UK Regulators (including investigations by third parties); and

(d) where requested, providing an attestation to the UK Regulators (discussed above in relation to outsourcings/insourcings).

As all senior managers (together with all other in-scope Certification and Conduct Staff) must comply with the Conduct Rules—one of which is being open and honest with the regulators—all senior managers including non-UK senior managers would be expected to be an active and cooperative participant in any of the supervisory work noted above.

9.9.2 Enforcement Powers

The UK Regulators also have the ability to take enforcement action against a senior manager, including a non-UK senior manager, in a number of circumstances which can broadly be grouped into the following categories which are summaries of more detailed tests:

(a) where the behaviour of the senior manager is considered to amount to a material breach of relevant regulatory requirements. For example, where a senior manager has not complied with aspects of the UK regulatory regime which are not specific to the SMCR, they will be at risk of enforcement action;

(b) where a senior manager is considered to have breached conduct requirements.[8] These include where, for those areas where a senior manager is accountable (as recorded in his/her Statement of Responsibilities), the senior manager did not take such steps as a person in the senior manager's position could reasonably be expected to take to avoid a contravention occurring (or continuing). Taking 'reasonable steps' is one way that a senior manager can mitigate incurring any personal liability to the UK Regulators; and

(c) where the standards expected of a senior manager have not been met. For example,
   (i) where the UK Regulators conclude that an individual is not a 'fit and proper' person to perform the SMF function which is assessed in accordance with the FCA's standards;[9]
   (ii) where a senior manager has not complied with the Conduct Rules applicable to senior managers;[10] or
   (iii) where a senior manager carries out a controlled function without approval.

The categories above can be cumulatively applied—for example, were a senior manager to engage in insider dealing, in addition to being prosecuted under market abuse provision, that senior manager may be subject to enforcement under SMCR requirements (e.g. failing to act with integrity).

---

[8] FSMA, s. 66A (for action by the FCA) and s. 66B (for action by the PRA).
[9] FIT Sourcebook in the FCA Handbook, <https://www.handbook.fca.org.uk/handbook/FIT/1/1.html>
[10] COCON Sourcebook in the FCA Handbook, <https://www.handbook.fca.org.uk/handbook/COCON/1/1.html>

9.38 As well as personal liability to the UK Regulators, a senior manager can also (theoretically) trigger committing a criminal offence under FSMA as part of the SMCR. This offence would be committed when a decision causes a financial institution to fail. In order to commit the offence of causing a financial institution to fail, the following would need to be satisfied:[11]

> A person ('S') commits an offence if—
> (a) at a time when S is a senior manager in relation to a financial institution ('F'), S—
>   (i) takes, or agrees to the taking of, a decision by or on behalf of F as to the way in which the business of a group institution is to be carried on, or
>   (ii) fails to take steps that S could take to prevent such a decision being taken,
> (b) at the time of the decision, S is aware of a risk that the implementation of the decision may cause the failure of the group institution,
> (c) in all the circumstances, S's conduct in relation to the taking of the decision falls far below what could reasonably be expected of a person in S's position, and
> (d) the implementation of the decision causes the failure of the group institution.

9.39 It should be noted in this context that a 'financial institution' is 'an institution which is incorporated in, or formed under the law of any part of, the United Kingdom'. Therefore, senior managers of UK branches of EEA banks would not be at risk of committing this offence.

9.9.3 Enforcement Tools

9.40 The UK Regulators have a number of enforcement 'tools' which they can employ when taking action against an individual and these will remain regardless of the different SMCR regimes potentially applying in connection with Brexit. These include:

(a) *Issuing a private warning*: the UK Regulators have the power to issue a private warning to an individual at any point in an investigation;

(b) *Making a public statement*: the UK Regulators can publish a statement about a senior manager's misconduct and that they have taken enforcement action. They are not required to agree the wording of the public statement before it is made although, in practice, this is usually agreed by the parties;

(c) *Withdrawing or suspending approval or placing limitations or restrictions on it*: the UK Regulators can withdraw their approval for a person to carry out a senior manager function or suspend their approval, which in essence revokes their status such that that individual can no longer carry on that role at that regulated entity. They can also impose limitations or restrictions on any approval;

(d) *Issuing a Prohibition Order*: the UK Regulators can prevent an individual from carrying on a controlled function at any other authorised entity; and

(e) *Levying fines*: the UK Regulators can impose a penalty of such amount as they consider appropriate in accordance with their internal calculation formula which changes from time to time. Currently, the calculation is made up of two elements: to

---

[11] Financial Services (Banking Reform) Act 2013, as amended, s. 36.

deprive the individual of any benefit received as a result of the breach and as a punitive measure to reflect the seriousness of the breach. The size of the fine relating to the seriousness of the breach will, depending upon its seriousness, be a certain percentage of the senior manager's salary (earned during the period of investigation or alleged misconduct) in accordance with criteria set by the UK Regulators. This fine may be increased or decreased subject to any aggravating or mitigating factors relating to the breach. The fine may also be increased if the UK Regulators believe that it is necessary as a deterrent to future breaches and may be discounted if the individual comes to an early settlement or, in some circumstances, if the individual is suffering from serious financial hardship.

9.9.4 Practical Enforcement against non-UK Resident Senior Managers

If the UK Regulators wished to take the enforcement action described above or seek to bring court proceedings for any related offences, the UK Regulators would have certain practical hurdles to overcome with non-UK resident senior managers which may be further exacerbated by Brexit. **9.41**

9.9.4.1 Private and public warnings, withdrawal or suspension of approval, placing limitations or restrictions on approval, and Prohibition Orders

If the enforcement process were to find against an individual senior manager, that senior manager could appeal to the FCA's Upper Tribunal which is a court. That appeal process would involve a rehearing of the facts as well as considering legal requirements. If an individual was unsuccessful in the Upper Tribunal, that senior manager could appeal up through the English court system. These subsequent appeals would be on matters of law only. **9.42**

If the senior manager based outside the UK chose not to dispute enforcement proceedings, the UK Regulators would not be prevented from pursuing due enforcement process and reaching a conclusion in the normal course. Additionally, if a senior manager chose not to respond to enquiries of the UK Regulators, or chose not to cooperate with an investigation, that senior manager would risk committing a further offence under FSMA. **9.43**

9.9.4.2 Enforcing fines outside the UK

It is possible that the UK Regulators might impose a fine on a senior manager who is located in another jurisdiction. Should the senior manager not pay the fine, the relevant regulator could seek to take action through the courts to attach payment to any assets of that individual which are in the UK. If there are no assets in the UK, seeking the payment of the fine would be treated in the same way as enforcing any UK judgment in a foreign jurisdiction. First, a court order would need to be obtained in the UK, and then it would be sought to be recognised in the country in which the (likely former) senior manager is located and a judgment obtained in that jurisdiction with a successful foreign judgment being enforced in accordance with local law in that jurisdiction. This could involve seeking payment of the cost/fine and/or seizing assets of the individual in that jurisdiction. **9.44**

9.9.4.3 Commence court proceedings

9.45 In order to bring court proceedings against a non-UK resident senior manager, for civil proceedings, the court proceeding can be held without the senior manager needing to be present. Any judgment obtained as a result of those civil proceedings will be binding on the senior manager (*in absentia*) and, if it involves an award of costs, the same process as for seeking payment of a regulatory fine (discussed above) would apply. In order to bring criminal proceedings against a non-UK resident senior manager, this would be treated in the same way as any criminal proceeding that is sought to be brought against a non-resident individual. Namely, an extradition order will be sought and potentially granted to seek to have the non-resident individual extradited from the country in which they are located and brought to the UK to face trial.

9.9.5 Other Consequences

9.46 If any of the above action is taken, there could be additional consequences for the senior manager including the likelihood that the UK Regulators would contact their counterpart regulators in the EEA which may affect an individual's standing in their home jurisdiction. Although, as discussed in Chapter 7.16, this may become more difficult for the UK Regulators post exit day. In addition, a number of EEA jurisdictions routinely seek to verify whether certain key individuals within a financial services firm have been subject to enforcement action or investigation in another jurisdiction. Therefore, action taken by UK Regulators may impact on an individual's ability to work in the financial services sector in other EEA states.

9.47 Ordinarily, the FCA would need to enlist the assistance of a foreign regulator in order to seek to hold a non-UK resident senior manager to account and potentially other bodies (e.g. the court) depending on the nature of the issue. This could prove challenging and may see the UK Regulators change their approach to liability of non-UK resident senior managers.

10
Markets in Financial Instrument Directive II (MiFID II)/Markets in Financial Instruments Regulation (MiFIR)

Nico Leslie and Aaron Taylor

10.1 Introduction

10.1.1 From MiFID to MiFID II

In 2004 the European Union introduced the Markets in Financial Instruments Directive (MiFID) as part of its efforts to create a harmonised single market for financial trading.[1] MiFID has had a profound impact on the regulation of financial trading platforms in the United Kingdom over the past decade, and has now been superseded by a new Directive effective from 3 January 2018. This new Directive was formally adopted by the European Union on 12 June 2014 and is known colloquially as 'MiFID II'.[2] Like the original MiFID, MiFID II applies to investment firms and 'market operators'.[3]

10.01

Alongside MiFID II, the European Union passed two further Regulations: the European Market Infrastructure Regulation (EMIR); and the Markets in Financial Instruments Regulation (MiFIR). The purpose of EMIR was to impose closer regulation on over-the-counter (OTC) derivatives, including a requirement for clearing through a central counterparty and an obligation to report to a trade repository, and it officially came into force on 16 August 2012 (although many provisions remained suspended until 10 April 2014). The purpose of MiFIR was broadly to ensure that all financial trading would be conducted on exchanges, on multilateral trading platforms (MTFs), or through organised trading facilities (OTFs). MiFIR entered into force on 3 January 2018, on the same date as MiFID II.

10.02

EMIR and MiFIR, being regulations, are directly effective in English law.[4] By contrast, MiFID II, being a directive, required domestic implementing legislation.[5] MiFID II contains

10.03

---

[1] Note that on 20 October 2011, following its review of MiFID, the European Commission adopted legislative proposals for MiFID II consisting of a recast directive and new regulation. The principal impact MiFID II is expected to have in regulation of exchanges and clearing houses is summarised in W Blair, G Walker & S Willey (Eds.), *Financial Markets and Exchanges Law* (2nd edn, OUP: Oxford, 2013) at [4.175]–[4.184].
[2] Directive 2014/65/EU. See Hudson 2013, [7.82]–[7.83].
[3] Directive 2014/65/EU, Art. 1(1) which also notes that it applies to data reporting service providers. 'Market operators' are defined in Art. 4(1)(18) as 'a person or persons who manages and/or operates the business of a regulated market. The market operator may be the regulated market itself.' Note that MiFID II also provides regulators with a power to intervene in the case of overly large derivatives positions by other market participants: MiFID II, Arts. 61, 72, and 83.
[4] Under the European Communities Act 1972, s. 2.
[5] See e.g. Financial Services and Markets Act 2000 (Markets in Financial Instruments) Regulations 2017.

a number of provisions empowering the European Commission to make secondary legislation in the form of delegated acts, regulatory technical standards (RTS), and implementing technical standards (ITS).

10.1.1.1 The scope of the new directive

10.04 MiFID II contains numerous detailed provisions, most of which fall outwith the focus of this chapter. It covers most aspects of financial markets, from controls on high-frequency trading and the positions held in commodities derivatives, to the infrastructure of clearing houses and trading exchanges. The directive has five principal goals: (1) ensuring financial products are traded on regulated venues; (2) increasing transparency; (3) limiting speculation on commodities; (4) adapting rules to new technologies; and (5) reinforcing investor protection.[6]

10.05 The increasing complexity of financial markets, and the technologies that underpin them, has given rise to a division of functionality between (1) exchanges, (2) clearing houses, and (3) payment and settlement systems. The regulation of each of these has been significantly affected by MiFID II.

10.06 This chapter will focus primarily on market infrastructure. In the authors' view, the regulation of market infrastructure is likely to be among the most contentious—and most important—questions arising out of the Brexit negotiations. The legal issues affecting the regulation of market infrastructure once the UK has ceased to be a Member State of the EU can, broadly, be grouped into three categories: (1) applicability of EU regulation to UK firms; (2) access requirements; and (3) definitional questions. These are discussed at paragraphs 10.65 to 10.81.

10.07 Since MiFID II has been implemented in domestic law, it remains possible for its provisions to remain on the statute book, in their current form or with amendment. The extent of their amendment will depend upon the extent to which the UK wishes to maintain regulatory 'equivalence' with the EU (a matter discussed below). That is probably a political, rather than a legal, question.

10.1.1.2 Structure of the chapter

10.08 This chapter is divided into three sections: (1) the regulation of trading exchanges and other markets across the EU under MiFID II; (2) the ability of EU and non-EU parties to have access to or 'operate' exchanges and markets under MiFID II; and (3) the potential impact of Brexit on both of the above issues. Section 10.3 also contains a case study considering the steps understood to have been taken by a major international investment bank to protect its UK- and EU-based operations in the light of the matters discussed in this chapter.

---

[6] See, for example, the summary provided to accompany the directive (Document 32014L0065), available at <https://eur-lex.europa.eu/legal-content/EN/TXT/HTML/?uri=LEGISSUM:240405_3&from=EN>

10.2 Regulation under MIFID II

10.2.1 The Structure of MIFID II

MiFID II is divided into seven titles, with four annexes. Title I sets out the scope of the directive and defines a large number of key terms. Title II, governing investment firms, constitutes almost half of the directive. It has four chapters, the first three of which set out the rules for the (1) authorisation, (2) operating conditions, and (3) rights of investment firms. The fourth chapter addresses the provision of investment services and activities by firms established outside the EU (third country firms). Title III concerns regulated markets, including access to regulated markets and clearing and settlement arrangements. Title IV sets out position limits in commodity derivatives. Title V sets out the rules for data reporting services providers. Title VI concerns national supervisory authorities. Title VII sets out the power of the Commission to adopt delegated acts under the directive.

10.09

10.2.2 Exchanges and Clearing Houses

10.2.2.1 Exchanges
Exchanges provide a vital infrastructure to facilitate trade in specific products, and share a number of key characteristics: (1) membership is limited to persons admitted to the exchange; (2) contracts on the exchange are standardised; (3) a market is provided, whereby members buy or sell at a given price the contracts on offer on the exchange; (4) when a contract is entered into, the counterparty to the trade does not matter (and is usually unknown), and the contract is in fact between the respective exchange members (as buyer or seller) and the exchange (as seller or buyer);[7] (5) the exchange will usually settle trades via 'netting', which involves balancing all the buys and sells of a given member in respect of a given contract, and obliging the member only to pay and perform the difference; and (6) exchanges facilitate settlement by both seller and buyer.

10.10

10.2.2.2 Clearing houses
(a) The role of clearing houses
Transactions, whether on-exchange or OTC, will require performance through delivery of the payment or securities that the parties have traded. In its simplest form, the settlement of a securities transaction will involve two systems: a payment settlement system for the transfer of payment; and a securities settlement system for the transfer of the traded securities. This means that both parties (or their respective nominees or custodians) will have to be participants in the same settlement systems. However, in practice this is rarely necessary, because most securities transactions are settled by a clearing house.

10.11

---

[7] This is because one of the key functions of exchanges is to provide clearing services, whereby counterparty risk can be eliminated. Absent such systems, were A and B to contract with one another, each would run the risk of the other not performing. Note that exchanges, via clearing houses, originally operated as mere administrators or at most guarantors to trades, before evolving to step into the places of the buyers and sellers in their own capacity: see J Huang, *The Law and Regulation of Central Counterparties* (Hart: London, 2010), [3.1.3].

10.12 The reason for using a clearing house is not only to avoid administrative difficulties, but above all to avoid the risk that the other party will not perform its side of the transaction. Clearing houses operate by novating the contract entered between the parties, meaning that they will then seek performance of each party's obligations directly from that party. Typically, clearing houses will net off the transactions between the parties, such that each party is only required to pay the balance.[8] This function is of considerable importance to the smooth operation of global markets, and is also reflected in the calculation of 'margin' payments.

(b) Clearing houses' exposure to default

10.13 Given that clearing houses assume the counterparty risk in a huge number of securities transactions, they are in a potentially exposed position. It is for this reason that risk management is an essential feature of modern clearing houses. Typically, the clearing houses will require a participant to post 'margin' or collateral for the trades it enters. The level of that margin is continuously monitored so as to cover the risk of default.[9] In the case of a shortfall, the clearing house will also be able to draw upon a common default fund comprised of the margin posted by all clearing house participants, and finally upon its own capital.[10] In terms of the regime upon the insolvency of a member, this is governed by Part VII of the Companies Act 1989 at the UK domestic level, which stipulates that a recognised body's default rules[11] will take precedence over general UK insolvency law in relation to market contracts and the posting of margin. At a European level, Directive 98/26/EC (the 'Settlement Finality Directive') creates a pan-European legislative framework for ensuring the finality of settlement in payment settlement and securities settlement systems.[12] The effect is that the insolvency laws of one Member State will not prejudice the enforcement of collateral under a settlement system designated by another.[13]

10.2.2.3 Application of MiFID II to financial trading infrastructure

(a) Distinguishing between on-exchange and OTC markets

10.14 This chapter focuses on the impact of MiFID II on the market infrastructure for the trading of securities and other financial instruments. A central distinction must be made, between (1) 'on-exchange' markets, and (2) markets that exist on an OTC basis.[14]

10.15 On-exchange markets provide an organisational structure and a set of pre-agreed rules that govern transactions made between members. These markets are characterised by a high degree of price disclosure (including continuous updating of prices)[15] and by a trading,

---

[8] Ibid.
[9] Ibid., [3.2.1]; note that the clearing houses will usually look to the assessment of the rating agencies, but may in some cases apply their own risk management tools.
[10] Ibid., [3.2.2].
[11] All recognised bodies are required to have such default rules: FSMA (Recognition Requirements for Investment Exchanges and Clearing Houses) Regulations 2001, Sch. 1 paras. 10 and 24–28.
[12] In England and Wales, see the Financial Collateral Arrangements (No. 2) Regulations 2003 (as amended, including by the Financial Markets and Insolvency (Settlement Finality and Financial Collateral Arrangements (Amendment) Regulations 2010. See, generally, L. Gullifer (ed), *Goode and Gullifer on Legal Problems of Credit and Security* (6th edn, London: Sweet & Maxwell, 2017), ch. 6, s. 5.
[13] Note that transfer orders comprise all instructions to make a payment or transfer title to securities: Settlement Finality Directive, Art. 2.
[14] The phrase 'over the counter' is used only once in the directive, in Recital 4.
[15] Blair, Walker & Willey 2012, [1.91].

clearing, and settlement infrastructure according to which the exchange seeks to match offers to buy and offers to sell without the buying and selling counterparties having to interact with one another.[16]

By contrast, OTC markets have no physical location or formal organisational structure. In general, they involve individual counterparties contracting with each other on a bilateral basis to negotiate trades,[17] with the 'market' emerging out of the number of regular participants and common contracts involved.[18] OTC markets lack the trading, clearing, and settlement functions provided by an exchange.[19] Note, however, that there is increasing convergence in terms of the execution of on-exchange and OTC transactions.[20]

10.16

10.2.3 The Regulation of Markets under MiFID II

10.2.3.1 Markets and trading platforms

MiFID II regulates *markets* in financial instruments rather than the *persons* active in those markets,[21] though the directive contains rules governing entitlement to operate particular markets.

10.17

Following MiFID II there are five principal venues in which a securities transaction can be executed: (1) on a regulated market;[22] (2) on an MTF;[23] (3) on an OTF;[24] (4) with a 'systematic internaliser';[25] or (5) OTC.

10.18

Of these, regulated markets and MTFs have much in common. Both are essentially multilateral systems bringing together multiple third-party buying and selling interests in financial instruments, which result in contracts between buyers and sellers reached according to non-discretionary rules; in other words, they are 'exchanges'. By contrast, OTFs and systematic internalisers are not 'exchanges' because the operator/internaliser has a discretion over the execution of trades that are placed on its platform. OTC transactions, as we have seen, fall wholly outside the definition of an 'exchange'.

10.19

(a) Regulated markets
Article 4(1)(21) defines a 'regulated market' as follows:

10.20

> a multilateral system operated and/or managed by a market operator, which brings together or facilitates the bringing together of multiple third-party buying and selling interests in financial instruments—in the system and in accordance with its non-discretionary

---

[16] Ibid., [1.92]–[1.94].
[17] Note however that there may be standardised features of such OTC transactions. So, for example, ISDA master agreements (a standard terms master contract for OTC derivative transactions published by the ISDA) are used in a very large number of derivatives transactions worldwide. Even though these transactions will be on the same standard terms, each individual contract is discrete to the transacting parties. See, generally, A. Hudson, *The Law on Financial Derivatives* (5th edn, (London: Sweet & Maxwell, 2012), [2.94]–[2.106].
[18] Blair, Walker & Willey 2012, [1.83].
[19] But note that price information providers, such as Reuters, do exist (ibid., [1.83]–[1.84]).
[20] Ibid., [10.48]–[10.51].
[21] See Art. 2(1)(j).
[22] See Art. 4(1)(21).
[23] See Art. 4(1)(22) (relying, in turn, on the definition of 'multilateral system' in Art. 4(1)(19)).
[24] See Art. 4(1)(23).
[25] See Art. 4(1)(20).

rules—in a way that results in a contract, in respect of the financial instruments admitted to trading under its rules and/or systems, and which is authorised and functions regularly and in accordance with the provisions of Title III.

(b) Multilateral trading facilities

10.21 Article 4(1)(22) defines a 'multilateral trading facility' or 'MTF' as:

> a multilateral system, operated by an investment firm or a market operator, which brings together multiple third-party buying and selling interests in financial instruments—in the system and in accordance with non-discretionary rules—in a way that results in a contract in accordance with the provisions of Title II.

(c) Organised trading facilities

10.22 Article 4(1)(22) defines an 'organised trading facility' or 'OTF' as:

> a multilateral system which is not a regulated market or an MTF and in which multiple third-party buying and selling interests in bonds, structured finance products, emission allowances or derivatives are able to interact in the system in a way that results in a contract in accordance with the provisions of Title II.

10.23 The key difference between an OTF and an MTF is the extent of the discretion that an OTF operator enjoys over the execution of trades. If an organiser executes clients' orders, it will be deemed to be exercising discretion (incompatible with being an MTF) if it decides if, when, and how much of two or more orders it wants to match within its system. In exercising that discretion, OTF operators will be subject to the conduct of business requirements under MiFID II, including as to best execution, client order handling, and conflicts of interest.

(d) Systematic internalisers

10.24 **A new category** Some firms do not seek to operate as a multilateral trading facility, but are *in practice* execution venues for financial instruments (including possibly for the execution of orders from retail clients). A 'systematic internaliser' is 'an investment firm which, on an organised, frequent and systematic basis, deals on its own account by executing client orders outside a regulated market, an MTF or an OTF without operating a multilateral system'.[26] Thus, systematic internalisers are those execution venues that operate in parallel to, and may compete with, regulated markets and multilateral trading platforms.

10.25 This raises a point of some controversy, as systematic internalisers do not themselves choose their status—unlike regulated markets or multilateral trading facilities—but are nonetheless subject to regulatory requirements imposed by MiFID II. The key requirement is that an investment firm caught so categorised is required to publish firm quotes for all shares that are admitted to trading on a regulated market, for which the firm is a systematic internaliser, and for which there is a liquid market.[27] Although the firm will still retain a

---

[26] Art. 4(1)(20).
[27] Art. 27(3). The requirement of a liquid market means that, e.g., it does not extend to shares on AIM (as this is not a regulated market) or any type of bond, even if these bonds are traded on a regulated market: see Blair, Walker & Willey 2012, [14.68]–[14.71] (discussing the original MiFID).

discretion as to which investors it chooses to give access to its quotes, it is likely that firms dealing in certain financial instruments or markets will be reluctant to do this. Designation as a 'systematic internaliser' may therefore prove a matter of real commercial significance to those firms.

Classification difficulties The motivation behind the 'systematic internaliser' designation has been to establish clear and transparent prices for shares across all types of execution venues. However, in practice, there are difficulties with the application of the test. One problem has been in establishing what types of shares are 'liquid' for the purposes of Article 27. Another has been in the implementation of price quotes where clients wish to improve on the price that has been given (something that would not be possible on a conventional exchange). These difficulties are still at large, and it is unclear whether the systematic internaliser designation has had any significant effect on the transparency of pre-trade data.[28]   **10.26**

Brexit difficulties Moreover, a further and potentially even more significant issue has arisen specifically in the context of Brexit. As has been seen, under MiFID II a firm is considered a systematic internaliser if the volume of activity that it carries out exceeds a certain quantitative threshold. This calculation is complex and varies according to the type of financial instrument involved and the liquidity of the market for that instrument. However, a common component across all financial instruments is that firms should compare the amount of client orders they are internalising against the total trading activity of that instrument within the EU.   **10.27**

The potential difficulty post-Brexit is clear. It is well known that a significant proportion of EU trading activity in all financial instruments takes place in the UK, and the applicable thresholds were set taking that activity into account. If the UK data is removed from the total EU activity, then the absolute threshold lowers. This reduction is likely to bring far more firms across the EU into the regime for 'systematic internalisers' and could therefore extend the pre-trade transparency regime to less-liquid parts of the EU market. Equally, if the UK data is removed and the UK is forced to continue to use the existing 'systematic internaliser' thresholds to achieve equivalence, then its firms may also face lower absolute thresholds. That would result in many more UK-based firms being brought into the 'systematic internaliser' regime and being subject to additional transparency requirements.   **10.28**

This difficulty is likely to arise whatever form of Brexit is agreed; the calculation specifically references total EU trading data, such that any form of legal exit from the EU (whatever the precise terms of that exit) would impact on the calculation itself. The position is not insoluble, of course, since a reappraisal of the appropriate thresholds could remedy the potentially excessive reach of the 'systematic internaliser' designation; however, such a reappraisal will require time, and is unlikely to be fully worked out by the time of the UK's exit from the EU. It will also raise challenging questions as to how UK firms might achieve equivalence under a recalibrated regime.   **10.29**

---

[28] See further ibid., [14.68]–[14.77] for a full discussion of these issues (in the context of the original MiFID).

(e) OTC trading

10.30 Trades not on a regulated market, an MTF, an OTF or a systematic internaliser are OTC. As we saw above, this is an ever-narrowing definition. Although OTC trades fall outside the regime of MiFID II, many of them will be covered by the regulatory framework introduced by EMIR.[29] This regulation was introduced as part of an effort inter alia to reduce counterparty and operational risk in the OTC derivatives market, a market which had been identified as a contributing factor to the financial crisis. As such, it requires many classes of derivative transaction to be cleared through a central counterparty and to be reported to a trade repository, with a view to improving transparency and risk management processes.[30] In the case of a no-deal Brexit, investment firms based in the UK will be considered third country counterparties but will still fall under the same reporting requirements where transactions are executed with EU investment firms.[31]

10.3 Rights of Operation and Access

10.3.1 Authorisation of Exchanges in the UK

10.3.1.1 Listing of securities on an exchange

10.31 The admission of securities to listing on an official stock exchange is governed by Directive 2001/34/EC (the 'Listing Directive'),[32] which has been implemented in England and Wales by the Financial Services and Markets Act 2000 (Disclosure of Confidential Information) (Amendment) (No. 2) Regulations 2001. The Listing Directive provides that Member States shall ensure that securities may not be admitted to official listing on any stock exchange situated or operating within their territory unless the conditions laid down by the directive are satisfied, such as in relation to minimum market capitalisation, the publication of accounts, and the publication of prospectuses.[33]

10.32 The Listing Directive also creates a 'single passport' regime for issuers of securities, with the aim of increasing transparency and investor protection. Issuers must disclose information on their financial circumstances and details of the securities to be issued. Once approved

---

[29] EU Regulation 648/2012, Arts. 6, 9, and 52.

[30] It applies to all derivatives that involve financial counterparties, central counterparties (CCPs) or trade repositories. As for non-financial counterparties, these are caught only where they trade with a financial counterparty or where their positions exceed a designated clearing threshold (i.e. a monetary value): Art. 10.

[31] See Statement of the European Securities and Markets Authority dated 7 March 2019, p. 4.

[32] See also Directive 2003/71/EC on the prospectus to be published when securities are offered to the public or admitted to trading (the 'Prospectus Directive'). The Prospectus Directive, Art. 20 provides that the competent authority of the home Member State of issuers having their registered office in a third country may approve a prospectus for an offer to the public or for admission to trading on a regulated market, drawn up in accordance with the legislation of a third country. The Prospectus Directive has been repealed and replaced by a substantially similar Regulation (EU) 2017/1129, most of the provisions of which come into force on 21 July 2019.

[33] Listing Directive, Art. 5(a). Note that even after the departure of the United Kingdom from the European Union, it is likely that the effect of the Listing Directive will be broadly replicated under any subsequent regime.

and distributed, the prospectus benefits from mutual recognition across the EU. Article 41 provides for reciprocity arrangements with non-member states.

(a) The UK Listing Authority (the 'competent authority')
Article 105(1) of the Listing Directive requires Member States to ensure that the directive is applied and to appoint one or more 'competent authorities' for the purposes of the directive. In the United Kingdom, the competent authority is the Financial Conduct Authority (FCA), acting as the UK Listing Authority.[34]

10.33

(b) Recognised investment exchanges and recognised overseas investment exchanges
Recognised investment exchanges Section 285(1)(a) of the Financial Services and Markets Act 2000 (FSMA) defines a 'recognised investment exchange' as 'an investment exchange in relation to which a recognition order is in force'. Section 286(1)(a) of FSMA authorises the Treasury to make regulations setting out the requirements which must be satisfied by an investment exchange if it is to qualify for a recognition order from the FCA.

10.34

The recognition requirements in respect of investment exchanges are contained in the Financial Services and Markets Act 2000 (Recognition Requirements for Investment Exchanges and Clearing Houses) Regulations 2001.[35] Recognised investment exchanges are listed under that head in the FCA Register. There are presently seven such exchanges listed on the Register.[36]

10.35

Recognised overseas investment exchanges Under section 292(2) of FSMA, the FCA may make a recognition order in respect of an overseas investment exchange, provided that it appears to the FCA that the investment exchange satisfies the requirements of section 292(3) of FSMA. Recognised overseas investment exchanges are listed under that head in the FCA Register; there are presently seven such exchanges listed.[37]

10.36

Designated investment exchanges In addition to status as a recognised investment exchange, there is an additional category of designated investment exchange that is recognised by the FCA. An investment exchange that does not carry on regulated activities in the UK and is not a regulated market may apply to the FCA to be included in the FCA's list of designated investment exchanges (if it meets certain consumer protection standards). Designation allows firms to be treated in the same way as recognised investment exchanges for the purposes of certain conduct of business and regulatory rules.[38]

10.37

---

[34] FSMA, s. 73A. Originally, the competent authority for the UK was the London Stock Exchange (LSE). Since the LSE produced listing rules for its own purposes, implementing the Listing Directive through the LSE was attractive, and was typically the course followed in other Member States. However, in light of the LSE's decision to demutualise and convert into a public company, it was considered necessary to create an independent listing authority and this regulatory function was transferred from the LSE to: (1) the FSA, via the Official Listing of Securities (Change of Competent Authority) Regulations 2000, SI 2000/968; and then (2) to the newly formed FCA via the Financial Services Act 2012.

[35] SI 2001/995, as amended.

[36] See https://register.fca.org.uk/ (under the 'Exchanges, markets and prohibited individuals tab'); the relevant exchanges are: ICE Futures Europe; London Stock Exchange plc; London Metal Exchange Ltd; NEX Exchange; CME Europe Ltd; BATS Trading Ltd; Euronext London Ltd.

[37] Ibid.; the relevant exchanges are: Australian Securities Exchange Ltd; Chicago Board of Trade; EUREX; the NASDAQ; New York Mercantile Exchange Inc; SIX Swiss Exchange AG; Chicago Mercantile Exchange.

[38] See Blair, Walker & Willey 2012, [4.172].

10.3.2 Authorisation of Trading Infrastructure in the EU

10.3.2.1 Authorisation of exchanges in the EU

(a) 'Investment firms' and 'market operators'

10.38 A 'market operator' is 'a person or persons who manages and/or operates the business of a regulated market. The market operator may be the regulated market itself'.[39] An 'investment firm' is 'any legal person whose regular occupation or business is the provision of one or more investment services to third parties and/or the performance of one or more investment activities on a professional basis'.[40] If a body provides investment services, it will be considered an investment firm, and so may not operate on regulated markets.

(b) The provisions for the authorisation of investment firms and regulated markets are different

10.39 Both an investment firm and a regulated market must be authorised by its home Member State's 'competent authority'.[41] In the case of regulated markets, it is the regulated market, and not the operator of that market, who has to be authorised.

10.40 The 'competent authority' means the authority designated by each Member State in accordance with Article 67 of MiFID II.[42] Of course, MiFID II does not envisage the competent authority of *every* Member State authorising each investment firm or regulated market. That responsibility lies with the 'home Member State', defined in Article 4(1)(55) of the directive as the Member State where the investment firm has its registered office (if a company or market), or its head office (if a natural person or if a company or market without a registered office).

10.41 Other Member States, where an investment firm or regulated market may carry on business, are referred to as 'host Member States' and are defined as the Member State, other than the home Member State, in which an investment firm has a branch or performs services and/or other relevant activities.[43]

10.42 Title II to MiFID II sets out the rules regarding the authorisation and functioning of an investment firms (Articles 9–32) and regulated markets (Articles 44–47). The relevant conditions require that firms and markets have sufficient expertise and competence, and be managed by persons of good repute. Further, a number of disclosure, organisational, and compliance requirements are set out.

10.3.2.2 Authorisation of clearing houses and settlement systems in the EU
(a) Clearing houses and payment and settlement systems

10.43 Clearing houses, as we saw above, are CCPs that take on the counterparty risk in all transactions between members *before* settlement. By contrast, settlement systems are systems intended to deal with the transfer of title (or other interest) in securities between the counterparties *after* settlement.[44] In the context of securities trading, settlement systems will

---

[39] MiFID II, Art. 4(1)(18).
[40] Ibid., Art. 4(1)(1).
[41] Ibid., Art. 5(1) in the case of investment firms, and ibid., Art. 44(1) in the case of regulated markets.
[42] Ibid., Art. 4(1)(26).
[43] Ibid., Art. 4(1)(56).
[44] Blair, Walker & Willey 2012, [12.63].

usually operate alongside a payment system, such that both the relevant payment and title to the relevant security can be exchanged simultaneously.

Indeed, clearing houses may themselves act as operators of the settlement systems they use, by making and applying rules to ensure the smooth processing of transactions. An example of this close relationship is the payment system operated by LCH.Clearnet. While LCH.Clearnet itself is a clearing house, it has contractual arrangements in place with a number of third-party banks. These banks operate a payment system that is devised and supervised by LCH.Clearnet, and is known as the Protected Payment Scheme (PPS). Thus, while the infrastructure for this payment system is not owned by LCH.Clearnet, it enjoys effective control. **10.44**

(b) The impact of MiFID II on clearing and settlement systems
Article 18(6) of MiFID II imposes an obligation on Member States to 'require that investment firms and market operators operating an MTF or an OTF clearly inform its members or participants of their respective responsibilities for the settlement of the transactions executed in that facility' and to 'require that investment firms and market operators operating an MTF or an OTF have put in place the necessary arrangements to facilitate the efficient settlement of the transactions concluded under the systems of that MTF or OTF'. **10.45**

10.3.3 Access for EU Investment Firms to Trading Infrastructure in other Member States

10.3.3.1 'Passporting' for investment firms
MiFID II provides wide rights to investment firms to gain access to other Member States, albeit with some formal regulatory requirements. If any investment firm wishes to provide services or activities within the territory of another Member State for the first time to change the range of services or activities it already provides there,[45] or if it wishes to establish a branch in that Member State,[46] it must communicate the information regarding these activities to the competent authority of its home Member State, who will forward this information on to the relevant host Member State.[47] **10.46**

The host Member State is obliged to ensure that any investment firm authorised and supervised by the competent authorities of another Member State in accordance with MiFID II may freely perform investment services and/or activities as well as ancillary services within their territories, provided that such services and activities are covered by its authorisation,[48] and providing it has a relevant 'passport'. The passporting process is undertaken simply by giving notification of the firm's intentions to the competent authority in its home Member State.[49] **10.47**

---

[45] MiFID II, Art. 34(2).
[46] Ibid., Art. 35(2).
[47] Ibid., Arts. 34(3) and 35(3), respectively. Under Art. 35(3), the competent authority must, within three months, either pass on the information to the host Member State (in which case the branch may be established) or decline to do so under Art. 35(5) (in which case it must give reasons for that decision).
[48] Ibid., Arts. 34(1) and 35(1), respectively.
[49] Blair, Walker & Willey 2012, [14.54]–[14.55]; see also the Banking Consolidation Directive 2000/12/EC and the Investment Services Directive 93/22/EEC. The procedure for passporting into the UK is set out in FSMA, Sch. 3.

10.3.3.2 Cross-border operation of multilateral trading facilities and regulated markets

10.48 The provisions regarding the cross-border operation of MTFs are contained in Articles 36–38 of MiFID II. If the operator of an MTF wishes to provide those services in another country, it must 'passport' that activity by notification to the competent authority in its home Member State in the same way as applies to investment firms.[50] MiFID II then ensures that the operator will be allowed to access appropriate clearing or settlement arrangements with a central counterparty or clearing house in the host Member State.[51]

10.49 By contrast, regulated markets are not themselves able to offer services cross-border. However, this does not mean that regulated markets cannot provide services to investment firms outside of their home Member State. Instead, investment firms are able to apply for cross-border access to the regulated markets of different Member States.[52] It is in this way that the firms and markets of different Member States can interact. One common example is where a regulated market sets up screens in another Member State by which a properly authorised investment firm can monitor and access the market.[53]

(a) Access to the regulated markets of other Member States

10.50 By Article 36(1) of MiFID II, Member States shall require that investment firms from other Member States which are authorised to execute client orders or to deal on own account have the right of membership or have access to regulated markets established in their territory either directly (by setting up branches in the host Member States) or by becoming remote members or having remote access to the market where a physical presence is not required.[54]

10.51 A regulated investment exchange can *choose* whether a market it operates is classified as a 'regulated market' or a 'multilateral trading facility'. The LSE has sought regulated market status for its main market, but not for the Alternative Investment Market (AIM).

10.3.3.3 Access to clearing houses and settlement systems

10.52 Although MiFID II does not address obligations linked to clearing and settlement, Article 37(1) stipulates that investment firms from other Member States should be accorded the same access to central counterparty, clearing and settlement systems as domestic firms. Provision is also made to allow investment firms to designate which settlement system they wish to employ for transactions on a given regulated market, subject to regulatory approval.

10.53 This emphasis on free access to clearing and settlement systems is also extended to regulated markets: Article 55 requires Member States to allow regulated markets to enter into arrangements with clearing houses or settlement systems in other Member States, except where to do so would threaten the orderly functioning of the market.

---

[50] Blair, Walker & Willey 2012, [6.62]–[6.65].
[51] MiFID II, Art. 38(1).
[52] Blair, Walker & Willey 2012, [6.62]–[6.65].
[53] Note that any such trading performed under the systems of the regulated market will be governed by the public law of the regulated market's home Member State: MiFID II, Art. 44(4).
[54] Ibid., Art. 36(1)(b).

10.3.4 Access for Non-EU Investment Firms to Trading Infrastructure in the EU

10.3.4.1 Limited access for third country firms

A 'third country firm' is defined as 'a firm that would be a credit institution providing investment services or performing investment activities or an investment firm if its head office or registered office were located within the Union'.[55] **10.54**

Third country firms can gain access to the EU market in two ways: (1) cross-border, where there is regulatory equivalence between the third country and the EU;[56] or (2) by establishing an authorised branch in a Member State. **10.55**

(a) Cross-border provision of services subject to regulatory equivalence
Under Article 3(1)(c)(iii) of MiFID II: **10.56**

> Member States may choose not to apply this Directive to any persons for which they are the home Member State, provided that the activities of those persons are authorised and regulated at national level and those persons:
>
> [....] (c) In the course of providing that service, are allowed to transmit orders only to:
>
> [...] (iii) branches of investment firms or of credit institutions authorised in a third country and which are subject to and comply with prudential rules considered by the competent authorities to be at least as stringent as those laid down in this Directive, in Regulation (EU) No 575/2013 or in Directive 2013/36/EU.

The effect of this provision is that Member States may allow third country firms to deal with bodies established in that Member State *without* establishing a branch in that Member State, but only if the relevant third country has a regulatory regime of its own which is 'at least as stringent' as the EU regime.[57] The directive therefore requires (at least) regulatory equivalence between the third country and the EU before a third country firm can be permitted access to the market of a Member State. 'Stringency', for these purposes, must be judged according to the aims of the directive (for example, transparency, investor protection, and reduction of systemic risk). **10.57**

Third country firms that have access to the markets of a Member State in this way 'do not enjoy the freedom to provide services and the right of establishment in Member States other than the one in which they are established'.[58] **10.58**

(b) Establishing a branch in a Member State
Under Article 39 of MiFID II, 'A Member State may require that a third country firm intending to provide investment services or perform investment activities with or without any ancillary services to retail clients or to professional clients within the meaning of Section II of Annex II in its territory establish a branch in that Member State.' **10.59**

---

[55] Ibid., Art. 4(57).
[56] Such cross-border access for third country firms was among the most controversial topics in the negotiations over MiFID II.
[57] Note that this provision applies only to professional clients and eligible counterparties established in the home Member State, not to retail clients. Consequently, third country firms must establish a branch in a Member State in order to offer services to retail clients in that Member State.
[58] See ibid., Recital 109.

10.60 Where a third country firm seeks to establish a branch in accordance with Article 39, the provision of services for which the third country firm requests authorisation must be subject to authorisation and supervision in the third country where the firm is established,[59] there must be in place cooperation agreements (including as to the exchange of information) must be in place between the competent authorities of the relevant Member State and the third country in which the firm is established,[60] the branch must have suitable management in place,[61] and the branch must have sufficient capital at its free disposal.[62] Further, the third country firm must comply with the substantive provisions on investment firms within MiFID II.[63] It must therefore, in effect, itself demonstrate equivalence to the MiFID II regulatory regime.

10.61 The Member State may withdraw an authorisation if it has not been made use of within twelve months, if the firm has not provided investment services for the preceding six months, if the investment firm no longer meets the relevant condition set out above or obtained the authorisation by making false statements, has 'seriously and systematically infringed the provisions adopted pursuant to this Directive governing the operation conditions of investment firms', or otherwise as provided for under the national law.[64]

10.62 Firms which have established a branch in a Member State under these provisions, and which also come from a third country which is deemed to have regulatory equivalence to the EU, may provide services to eligible counterparties across the EU without establishing any further branches.[65]

10.4 The Potential Impact of Brexit

10.4.1 Introduction

10.63 Since the United Kingdom's vote to leave the European Union on 23 June 2016, the impact of MiFID II has been one of the most closely watched topics of negotiation, as it sets out the parameters for the future relationship between the UK and EU financial markets. Given the economic importance of the financial services industry, this is a sensitive issue both for the UK and the EU27.

10.64 From the perspective of the UK, the financial services sector is of vital economic importance. In 2017, it contributed £119bn to the UK economy and was the source of 1.1m jobs.[66] From the perspective of the EU, the UK is a major source of financial services, with highly liquid and sophisticated capital markets and limited regulatory hurdles. Maintaining minimal regulatory barriers is therefore of mutual concern. Nonetheless, some of the EU27

---

[59] Ibid., Art. 39(2)(a).
[60] Ibid., Art. 39(2)(b). Details of this competent authority, and all other relevant details of the firm, must be provided to the host Member State (ibid., Art. 40).
[61] Ibid., Art. 39(2)(d).
[62] Ibid., Art. 39(2)(c).
[63] Ibid., Art. 41(2).
[64] Ibid., Art. 43.
[65] Ibid., Art. 47(3). The branch remains subject to the supervision of the Member State in which it is established.
[66] House of Commons Briefing Paper SN06193, *Financial Services: Contribution to the UK Economy*, 25 April 2018.

states have economic incentives to diminish the importance of the City of London in favour of their own financial hubs, and the ECB has repeatedly called for euro clearing to be moved to the eurozone (a move which has been pre-empted by Euroclear and some major banks).

10.4.2 Key Areas of Impact

10.4.2.1 Three types of concern
In the authors' view, MiFID II-related issues arising from Brexit can be grouped into three categories: **10.65**

(1) **Applicability of EU regulation to UK firms.** One key concern is the extent to which the European regulatory regime(s) will continue to apply to UK firms after Brexit.
(2) **Access requirements.** Two issues are of particular importance: (1) access of investment firms to the EU through 'passporting' or a determination of regulatory equivalence; (2) authorisation of UK-based clearing houses to conduct euro clearing.
(3) **Definitional questions.** Some clarity will be required as to whether the UK, or UK-based firms, falls within certain relevant definitions post-Brexit. One example is the calculation of 'total trading in the Union' for the purposes of determining whether a firm is classified as a 'systematic internaliser' under the directive (an issue discussed in paragraphs 10.26–10.29).[67] Such definitional questions should permit of relatively straightforward answers, through Commission decisions or other delegated legislation where necessary; the European Securities and Markets Authority (ESMA) has already announced that it intends to suspend and recalibrate various thresholds and calculations on this basis, should the UK leave the EU without a deal.[68]

The remainder of this chapter focuses on the first and second of these categories, before concluding with a study of the measures understood to have been taken by certain banks to protect their clients from Brexit-related disruption. **10.66**

10.4.2.2 Applicability of EU regulation to UK firms
(a) Legal status of MiFID II and MiFIR after Brexit
Section 3(1) of the European Union (Withdrawal) Act 2018 provides that 'Direct EU legislation, so far as operative immediately before exit day, forms part of domestic law on and after exit day'. Unsurprisingly, section 2(1) provides that domestic legislation of European origin remains in force after exit day. Consequently, MiFID will remain in force after Brexit through its domestic implementing legislation, and MiFIR will continue to apply, for the time being at least, under s.3(1). **10.67**

---

[67] Another related concern is whether EU-wide authorisations granted by the FCA will continue to apply to the relevant authorised body. For example, if a data reporting service provider is authorised in the UK (under MiFID II, Art. 59), that authorisation allows the relevant provider to carry out those activities throughout the EU (under Art. 60(2)). UK-authorised data reporting service providers will be concerned to maintain this EU-wide authorisation once the UK ceases to be a 'home Member State'.
[68] See ESMA statement of 5 February 2019.

10.68 On 27 June 2018, HM Treasury and the Bank of England each released a statement concerning financial regulation in the immediate aftermath of Brexit. The Treasury's statement said:

> During the implementation period, common rules will continue to apply. The UK will continue to implement new EU law that comes into effect and the UK will continue to be treated as part of the EU's single market in financial services. This will mean that access to each other's markets will continue on current terms and businesses, including financial services firms, will be able to trade on the same terms as now until 31 December 2020.[69] UK firms will need to comply with any new EU legislation that becomes applicable during the implementation period.

10.69 The real impact of Brexit, therefore, is unlikely to be a sudden legislative change, but rather how existing laws will apply to the UK. Even if the UK leaves the MiFID II and MIFIR regimes untouched, it appears inevitable that it will no longer be being treated as a Member State, but will instead be seen as a 'Third Country'. Consequently, even if regulatory standards in the UK and the EU remain coterminous, cross-border economic activity will no longer benefit from the mutual recognition, non-discrimination and passporting regimes built into MiFID II and MIFIR. The suddenness of the UK's shift to Third Country status will depend upon the terms of any transitional arrangements governing the 'implementation period', if any. These may be uncertain until the eve of the UK's departure from the EU.

(b) The effect of future EU legislation

10.70 **UK firms may be new bound by EU regulations during the implementation period** The UK government's current understanding, as reflected in the Treasury statement quoted above, is that, under the terms of any transitional arrangements applicable during the implementation period, new EU regulations coming to effect during that period will bind UK firms. That may give rise to compliance costs to UK firms, but will also help to ensure regulatory equivalence between the UK and the EU as at the end of the implementation period.

10.71 **Protection from excessive regulation** Under the Investment Exchanges and Clearance Houses Act 2006 (IECHA), the FCA is authorised to prevent the implementation of any proposed regulation which it deems to be 'excessive'.[70] This Act was passed in response to fears that the LSE might be acquired by a US-based company, and that as a consequence all shares traded on the LSE might become subject to US securities regulation.[71]

10.72 In summary, the IECHA provides that where a regulatory provision connected with an investment exchange or connected clearing services is proposed, and that provision goes beyond what is required under UK or EU law, the FCA can decide not to implement it if it considers the provision to be unnecessary or disproportionate.[72] This means that, even if

---

[69] At the time of that statement, it appeared to be provisionally agreed between the UK and the EU27 that the implementation period would end at the end of 2020.

[70] Note that these powers are incorporated, by IECHA, s. 1, directly into the FSMA.

[71] A Hudson, *The Law and Regulation of Finance* (2nd edn, Sweet & Maxwell: London, 2013), [5-67]. See the statements by the Economic Secretary to the Treasury on 13 September 2006 (Hansard (House of Commons) vol. 449, cols. 125WS–126WS).

[72] FSMA, s. 300A–D.

the non-EU regulator does still implement the provision in question, no English court will enforce it.[73]

After the end of the implementation period, new EU regulations will not bind UK institutions. Consequently, if EU regulations having an effect on UK institutions are held to exceed UK law, it will be open to the FCA to refuse to implement those regulations. This might be a politically contentious issue, since a decision not to enforce EU standards would have an effect on the UK's regulatory equivalence. **10.73**

10.4.2.3 Access requirements
(a) Passporting or equivalence
One of the major advantages of the European regime is the relative ease of obtaining a 'passport' allowing a firm based in one Member State to provide financial services throughout the Union.[74] The mechanism for obtaining such a passport was set out in paragraphs 10.46 to 10.47. This mechanism provides considerable advantages over that applicable to firms from third states (set out in paragraphs 10.54 to 10.62), which—unless the third state maintains 'regulatory equivalence' with the EU—must establish an authorised branch in a Member State. **10.74**

Following Brexit, the UK will become a 'third state' for the purposes of MiFID II, in the absence of any agreement to the contrary in respect of the implementation period.[75] Given the inconvenience that would result to UK investment firms if they were required to establish a branch in every Member State in which they wished to operate, the UK government has indicated its intention to maintain 'regulatory equivalence' although it is far from clear that an attempt to maintain such 'equivalence' would receive the EU's approval. By way of example, on 30 June 2019 a similar equivalence granted to Switzerland by the European Commission expired, leaving Swiss firms without access to European stock exchanges. In retaliation, Switzerland has banned EU-based banks from trading in Swiss stocks other than on the Swiss stock exchange. **10.75**

The Markets in Financial Instruments (Amendment) (EU Exit) Regulations 2018 were made on 19 December 2018.[76] This statutory instrument seeks to maintain regulatory equivalence under MiFID II[77] by: **10.76**

(1) transferring regulatory functions from ESMA to the FCA and PRA, and from the European Commission to HM Treasury;
(2) giving the FCA and PRA the power to make binding technical standards;
(3) empowering HM Treasury to make equivalence decisions for third country regimes after Brexit. Equivalence determinations made by the Commission before the UK exits the EU will be followed automatically;

---

[73] Hudson 2013, [5-71]; for a fuller discussion of the IECHA, see ibid., [5-67]–[5-73].
[74] See Blair, Walker & Willey 2012, [6.62]–[6.65] and [14.54]–[14.55]; see also the Banking Consolidation Directive 2000/12/EC and the Investment Services Directive 93/22/EEC. The procedure for passporting into the UK is set out in FSMA, Sch. 3.
[75] At the time of writing, it appears that no such special agreement has been reached, but that the EU has agreed to make an 'equivalence' determination, effective as at the moment the UK exits the EU.
[76] Available at: <http://www.legislation.gov.uk/uksi/2018/1403/pdfs/uksiem_20181403_en.pdf>
[77] This is, of course, subject to determination (and renewal thereafter) by the Commission.

(4) amending the Data Reporting Services Regulations 2017 to establish a temporary authorisation regime for EEA-authorised data reporting services providers meeting relevant conditions;

(5) providing that, in respect of some financial instruments and market data, the EU is not to be treated as a third state. Examples include the trading of EEA emission allowances, exclusion of energy forwards from the definition of 'financial instruments', the exemption from authorisation for commercial firms trading commodity derivatives, and treatment of Undertakings for Collective Investment in Transferable Securities (UCITS) in the EU as automatically non-complex instruments, so that they can continue to be sold to UK retail clients;

(6) granting powers to the FCA in respect of the MiFID II transparency regime during an implementation period of four years, and requiring UK branches of EU firms to provide post-trade transaction reports to the FCA rather than their home state regulator.

10.77 The EEA Passport Rights (Amendment, etc., and Transitional Provisions) (EU Exit) Regulations 2018 came into force on 6 November 2018. This instrument creates a temporary permissions regime, under which EEA firms operating in the UK, and which are authorised under the regime, will be deemed to be compliant with UK regulations if they can demonstrate compliance with the corresponding provisions of MiFID II.[78]

10.78 There is an ongoing dialogue between ESMA and the FCA concerning the share trading obligations found in art.23 MIFIR, in the event that the UK is not granted the status of regulatory equivalence. That article requires investment firms to conclude transations in shares admitted to trading on a regulated market on a regulated market, MTF, systematic internaliser, or equivalent third country trading venue. That obligation does not apply to transactions in shares which are traded in the EU on a non-systematic, ad hoc, irregular and infrequent basis. Following a negative reaction from the FCA to its earlier position,[79] ESMA has announced that this trading obligation will only apply to shares with an EU27 ISIN—that is, shares issued by firms incorporated in the EU - but not to shares issued by firms incorporated in the UK.[80] The FCA remains concerned that 'a number of shares with EU-27 ISINs have both a listing, as well as their main or only significant centre of market liquidity, on UK markets', giving rise to overlapping obligations under MIFIR and UK domestic legislation.[81]

(b) Euro clearing

10.79 It had been a major issue of concern, both for the UK financial services industry and EU investment firms, whether EU banks and companies would be authorised, by the EU, to continue using UK-based clearing houses to process derivatives trades. European banks

---

[78] This does not apply to aspects of MiFID II for which supervisory responsibility is reserved to the host state regulator (e.g. conduct of business obligations for branches).

[79] The ESMA Statement of 19 March 2019 is avaiable at: <https://www.esma.europa.eu/sites/default/files/library/esma70-155-7329_public_statement_trading_obligation_shares.pdf>; the FCA response of the same date is available at: <https://www.fca.org.uk/news/statements/fca-statement-share-trading-obligations>.

[80] Statement of 29 May 2019, available at: <https://www.esma.europa.eu/sites/default/files/library/esma70-154-1204_revised_public_statement_trading_obligation_shares.pdf>

[81] Statement of 29 May 2019, available at: <https://www.fca.org.uk/news/statements/fca-update-share-trading-obligations>

and non-financial companies account for 14% of LCH's interest-rate derivatives business. The Bank of England estimates that EU-based companies have OTC derivatives contracts with a notional value of £69tn at UK clearing houses. Of these, $41tn will mature after March 2019.[82]

The European Commission has sought to alleviate concerns that there may be a sudden withdrawal of authorisation for UK-based clearing houses. Such sudden withdrawal might leave EU firms unable to hedge their market exposure, or at least give rise to a significant increase in trading costs.[83] The wholesale removal of authorisation would also cause considerable harm to the UK financial services industry. The Commission vice-president with responsibility for the euro had assured markets that, in the absence of some more comprehensive agreement on the issue, the Commission would provide short-term authorisation to UK-based clearing houses so long as the UK maintains regulatory equivalence. This was formalised by the Commission on 19 December 2018, via a decision that the UK's regulatory framework for clearing houses would be considered equivalent on a temporary and conditional basis until 30 March 2020.[84] In a keynote speech given on on 15 November 2019, the European Commission Vice-President and European Commissioner for Financial Stability, Financial Services and Capital Markets Union announced that that end-date would be extended.[85] However, the threat of future disruption, or of an attempt by the EU to diminish the role of UK-based derivatives clearing houses where European firms transact, cannot be discounted. 10.80

Further to that Decision, ESMA announced on in February and March 2019 its decision that three clearing houses (LCH Limited, ICE Clear Europe Limited, and LME Clear Limited) and one central securities depository (Euroclear UK and Ireland Ltd) had been established in accordance with EMIR and applicable European regulation and would be granted equivalence.[86] That equivalence is to take effect on the eventual date of Brexit. 10.81

(c) Recognition of EU-based clearing houses in the UK

The Central Counterparties (Amendment, etc., and Transitional Provision) (EU Exit) Regulations 2018 came into force on 14 November 2018. These Regulations amend the relevant parts of EMIR in relation to EU-based CCPs, in three significant ways: 10.82

(1) Transferring ESMA's functions relating to the recognition of third country CCPs to the Bank of England. In its explanatory note on the regulations,[87] HM Treasury says that it 'expects that jurisdictions that have already been assessed as equivalent by the EU will also be found equivalent by the UK'.

---

[82] See Bank of England's Financial Policy Committee Statement dated 3 October 2018, available at: <https://www.bankofengland.co.uk/-/media/boe/files/statement/fpc/2018/financial-policy-committee-statement-october-2018.pdf?la=en&hash=A10878A3FF65433E1296FD552C4406C9D28ACAC2>

[83] The statement cites estimates suggesting that every basis point increase in the cost of clearing interest rate swaps could cost EU businesses around €22bn annually (ibid.).

[84] Commission Decision 2018/2031 of 19 December 2018.

[85] Available at: <https://ec.europa.eu/commission/presscorner/detail/en/SPEECH_19_6285>

[86] See ESMA's statement of 18 February 2019 in respect of LCH Limited, ICE Clear Europe Limited, and LME Clear Limited, available at: <https://www.esma.europa.eu/press-news/esma-news/esma-recognise-three-uk-ccps-in-event-no-deal-brexit>; and its statement of 1 March 2019 recognising Euroclear UK and Ireland Ltd, available at: <https://www.esma.europa.eu/press-news/esma-news/esma-recognise-uk-central-securities-depository-in-event-no-deal-brexit>

[87] Available at <https://www.legislation.gov.uk/uksi/2018/1184/pdfs/uksiem_20181184_en.pdf>.

(2) Empowering the Bank of England to determine the recognition of non-UK CCPs before exit day, with those decisions taking effect on exit day as if they were made under Article 25 EMIR (provided that the other conditions under retained Article 25 EMIR have also been satisfied).

(3) Establishing a 'Temporary Recognition' regime, enabling third country CCPs to continue their activities in the UK for a limited period after exit day if they are currently able to provide those activities in the European Union under EMIR, and have notified the Bank of England (before exit day) that they intend to continue doing so in the United Kingdom.

Nonetheless, concerns remain. In particular, on 5 April 2019 the Futures Industry Association (**FIA**), together with other major organisations such as the International Swaps and Derivatives Association (**ISDA**), wrote to HM Treasury outlining their concerns at the need for the UK to recognise EEA-exchange traded derivatives, both so as to avoid them being classed as OTC derivatives and so as to preserve the ability of UK counterparties to execute OTC derivatives on EEA trading venues. These steps were thought to avoid a cliff edge upon a 'no-deal' Brexit.[88]

10.4.3 Case Study

10.83 By way of conclusion, it is perhaps helpful to explain how certain major investment banks are understood to have set about preparing for the post-Brexit financial environment. The process involves a series of legal and practical steps designed to ensure that client trading is not disrupted in the event of either a disorderly Brexit or post-Brexit regulatory divergence.

10.84 The first step is for the relevant bank to identify an alternative and appropriately licensed European trading entity, most likely in France or Germany, for client trading that has hitherto been performed by the bank's UK entity. The second step is to identify clients that are likely to be affected. This will involve (1) identifying clients with potentially relevant trading within the EU (such as an asset manager based in Milan, Italy), and then (2) determining whether that entity's regulator is likely to require its trading to be conducted through an EU entity. In this respect, it is understood that different European regulators have adopted a range of stances as to whether trading in certain products can be continued from London in the event of, for example, a 'hard' Brexit.

10.85 Once it is determined that a client performs relevant trading, and that there is a potential regulatory concern, the sample bank will write to the customer to 're-paper' its existing contractual arrangements with the UK entity. The purpose is to set up an entirely parallel contractual architecture between the client and the European entity. This does not yet, however, amount to a novation of the parties' existing contracts: the purpose is to ensure that contracts are in place so that, if novation becomes necessary, this can be performed seamlessly

---

[88] Letter of 5 April 2019 from the FIA, ISDA, the Alternative Investment Management Association, the Association for Financial Markets in Europe, the Associazione Intermediari Mercati Finanziari, the European Federation of Energy Traders, ICI Global, the Securities Industry and Financial Markets Association's Asset Management Group, and UK Finance to Mr Charles Roxburgh, the Second Permanent Secretary to HM Treasury.

in due course. As to the governing law of those contracts, this would remain English law (or whatever other national law was applicable to the original contract).

10.86 However, in order to allow the European entity to take a novation of relevant client trades (and accept new trades), that entity will typically need to be expanded and restructured so that it can service clients to the same level as the UK entity. Affected banks are likely to increase the scale of these preparations from the beginning of 2019. Further, they will be required to ensure that the European entity is properly capitalised, both for regulatory reasons (under MiFID II and EU Directive 2013/36) and so that the client does not face increased counterparty risk as a result of the transfer of its trades. This may be achieved through a range of measures, including intra-bank guarantees. Once all these steps have been taken, trading can be migrated with minimal disruption to the client.

11
Capital Requirements Directive (CRD IV)/ Capital Requirements Regulation (CRR)

Stuart Willey

11.1 Introduction

This chapter examines the likely impact of Brexit on aspects of European legislation that impose prudential and related requirements on regulated financial entities, such as banks and investment firms. This is a very broad topic and the issues highlighted in this chapter reference some specific material policy and practical outcomes for financial businesses both in the UK and in the remaining countries of the EU (hereafter the 'EU27'). The eventual outcome of the current Brexit stand-off and possible further negotiations between the UK and the EU on behalf of the EU27 is not currently known and may remain unclear following the publication of this book. Even if a settlement between the EU and the UK is eventually reached, some of the issues identified here are likely to persist and surface in the post-Brexit regulatory environment or alternatively will be issues for negotiation during the implementation or transitional period (assuming the UK and the EU27 enter a withdrawal agreement).

Wherever relevant, reference is made to the published UK legislation made under the European Union Withdrawal Act 2018 (the legislation intended to transpose the existing body of directly applicable EU law into UK domestic law and otherwise to ensure that, post-Brexit, the UK has a properly functioning body of financial regulatory law). The UK government continues, as part of its hard-Brexit contingency preparations, to make a series of statutory instruments (SIs) in order to onshore directly applicable EU financial services legislation. These SIs are not intended to make policy changes, except to the extent necessary to accommodate the UK's position outside of the EU and to provide for a smooth transition. This chapter, however, focuses on what appear to be the principal issues at stake and how they impact the prudential regulation of banks and investment firms and is not an exhaustive account of the transposition of existing EU financial regulatory law to the UK's own body of prudential and related requirements.

The issues addressed in this chapter include:

1. the loss of passporting rights for banks;
2. the UK's approach to the authorisation and supervision of EU27 banks;
3. future collaboration and information sharing among bank supervisors;
4. setting capital buffer requirements;
5. the establishment of intermediate holding companies;
6. the impact of Brexit on risk weights of EU and UK exposures and liquidity;
7. remuneration controls;

8. supervision of banking groups and consolidation; and
9. securitisation requirements.

11.2 How Does the CRD IV/CRR Regime Differ from Other Sectors in Respect of Passporting and Equivalence Tests?

11.2.1 EU Financial Services

11.04 EU legislation attempts to create a single market across the EEA in financial services, at least from a regulatory perspective. This legislation is set out in sectoral and product frameworks. Each framework can include the obligations relating to authorisation for firms operating in that sector, structural and organisational obligations applicable to those firm, conduct rules applicable to the firm and their staff, and the external reporting requirements. The Capital Requirements Directive (2013/36/EU) (hereafter **CRD IV**) and the Capital Requirements Regulation ((EC) 575/2013) (hereafter **CRR**) sets out the sectoral framework applicable to credit institutions.

11.05 There are a various sectoral frameworks for other types of financial services firms, including: investment firms under the Markets in Financial Instruments Regulation (Regulation (EU) 600/2014) (hereafter **MiFIR**) and the Markets in Financial Instruments Directive (2014/65/EU) (hereafter **MiFID II**); alternative investment fund managers under the Alternative Investment Fund Managers Directive (2011/61/EU) (hereafter **AIFMD**); management companies of retail funds under the UCITS V Directive (2014/91/EU); and insurance firms under the Solvency II Directive (2009/138/EC) (hereafter **Solvency II**). There are also product frameworks, such as for derivatives under the European Market Infrastructure Regulation (Regulation (EU) 648/2012) (hereafter **EMIR**) or securities lending under the Securities Financing Transactions Regulation (Regulation (EU) 2015/2365).

11.2.2 Barriers to a Single Market

11.06 Although the EU sectoral and product frameworks have had a positive impact on the integration of financial markets and regulatory standards across the EEA, some areas still create fragmentation. These include:

1. the absence of a single market in securities laws, insolvency laws and tax laws;
2. differing implementation of European directives and varying interpretations of EU rules; and
3. inconsistent third country regimes in sectoral and product frameworks.

11.07 Critically, since the inception of the European project, securities, insolvency, and tax laws have been within the competence of individual Member States. Therefore, until further integration or standardisation is undertaken, these areas will continue to present challenges in creating a fully integrated single market in financial services across the EEA.

Varied implementation and interpretation of EU rules by Member States pose a challenge. This challenge is being tackled through the increased use of EU regulations, rather than directives, so that they are automatically applicable to EEA member states. **11.08**

The focus of this chapter is on the passport available to credit institutions under CRD IV, the third country regimes under CRR and the impact of Brexit on those areas. **11.09**

11.2.3 Financial Services Passport

EU credit institutions have legal rights under CRD IV to provide certain services across the EEA. Article 33 of CRD IV provides that: **11.10**

> Member States shall provide that the activities listed in Annex I may be carried out within their territories, in accordance with Article 35, Article 36(1), (2) and (3), Article 39(1) and (2) and Articles 40 to 46 either by establishing a branch or by providing services, by any credit institution authorised and supervised by the competent authorities of another Member State, provided that such activities are covered by the authorisation.

This allows credit institutions to passport the banking services and activities listed in Annex 1 of CRD IV, and for which they have been authorised to undertake in their home state, to clients and counterparties across the EEA. These include the following services and activities: taking deposits or other repayable funds; lending; payment services; trading on own account or for customers; and safe custody services. **11.11**

Other sectoral legislation also provides passports to firms. Investment firms can passport across the EEA under MiFID II. Article 34(1) of MiFID II provides that: **11.12**

> any investment firm authorised and supervised by the competent authorities of another Member State in accordance with this Directive, and in respect of credit institutions in accordance with Directive 2013/36/EU, may freely provide investment services and/or perform investment activities as well an ancillary services within their territories, provided that such services and activities are covered by its authorisation.

This allows investment firms to passport investment services and activities listed in Annex I of MiFID II, and for which they have been authorised to undertake in their home state, to clients and counterparties across the EEA. These include the following services and activities: execution of client orders; dealing on own account; portfolio management; and investment advice. **11.13**

Passporting is also available to other financial services firms, such as EEA AIFMs seeking to manage and market EEA funds across the EEA and UCITS Management Companies seeking to manage and market UCITS across the EEA. **11.14**

As set out above, under the sectoral frameworks, firms authorised in one EEA member state have the right to passport their activities and services across the EEA through the establishment of branch in the relevant Member State or on freedom of services basis from their member state of authorisation. **11.15**

11.16 The ability of EEA firms to use the passport has deepened the integration of European markets and, as firms are no longer required to create subsidiaries in each EEA member state, reduced the legal and commercial costs of conducting business. This has reduced the barriers to entry for market participants and removed regulatory overlap, as each EEA member state recognises the standards of other EEA member states.

11.2.4 Impact of Brexit on Passporting

11.17 Once the UK has left the EU (or after any transitional period agreed between the UK and EU), UK-incorporated firms will no longer be able to passport their services from the UK across the EEA. This will be the case unless the UK firm obtains national licences in each EEA member state or exemptions from EU and national licensing requirements are available.

11.18 A UK credit institution that seeks to provide banking services to EU clients will be required to become authorised under CRD IV or within individual EEA member states. If the UK credit institution is seeking to operate from a single EEA base in order to service clients from multiple EEA member states, thereby benefiting from the passport, the UK credit institution will need to incorporate an entity in an EEA member state.

11.19 As discussed above, such a new EEA entity could then benefit from the financial services passport, subject to obtaining the relevant authorisations and making the relevant notifications to regulators under the CRR/CRD IV regime. This will incur the substantial costs involved in capitalising a new entity, staffing and resourcing, setting up new operations, and obtaining the relevant licences.

11.20 UK credit institutions not seeking to set up a new EEA legal entity, but with substantial business in particular EEA member states, would need to consider whether it is permissible to obtain individual licences in a given EEA member state. This may be achievable through the establishment of an authorised branch in the particular EEA member state. Article 39 of MiFID anticipates that where individual Member States require a third country firm to establish a branch in that Member State, the relevant firm must become authorised under that Member State's rules. Third country firms operating in this way will not however be able to use the branch to passport across the EEA.

11.21 The only other way third country firms could operate in the EEA is under the relevant sectoral or product framework's third country regime or in reliance on possible individual member state regimes that may provide flexibility of interpretation and approach. The next section considers this further.

11.2.5 Third Country Regimes

11.22 Under some EU financial services sectoral and product frameworks, there are third country regimes that permit firms from outside the EEA to provide certain services to clients and counterparties in the EEA. These regimes do not exist across the broad range of EU financial services legislation, do not have consistent application or requirements and are at the full discretion of European institutions, mainly the European Commission.

Under MiFIR, third country firms can provide investment services or perform investment activities across the EEA without a branch registered with the European Securities and Markets Authority (hereafter **ESMA**), subject to the following conditions: **11.23**

1. the European Commission has adopted an equivalence decision, pursuant to Article 47(1) of MiFIR, in relation to the third country of the third country firm;
2. the third country firm is authorised in the jurisdiction of its head office to provide investment services or activities to be provided in the EEA and is subject to effective supervision and enforcement ensuring a full compliance with the requirements applicable in that third country; and
3. there are cooperation arrangements in place, pursuant to Article 47(2) of MiFIR between ESMA and the competent authorities of the third country.

Points 1 and 3 require the European Commission and ESMA to take positive action in order for this third country regime to apply. Further, once an equivalence decision is in place, they have the power to withdraw the equivalence and registration. **11.24**

Banks in the UK may also wish to consider the scope of specific banking laws of an EEA member state which may not for example require a banking licence to the held for the purpose of non-deposit-taking banking activities such as commercial lending. Where a country adopts a more limited approach to regulating banking activities this may extend to third country banks. The definition of 'credit institution' for the purposes of CRD IV refers to an undertaking the business of which is to take deposits or repayable funds from the public.[1] This therefore leaves open the possibility that while deposit taking will universally require a banking licence other so-called banking activities such as for example commercial lending and the provision of guarantees may not. **11.25**

Another example of a third country regime sits under EMIR. Third country central counterparties (**CCPs**) are able to provide clearing services to EU firms where they have been recognised under Article 25 of EMIR. For third country CCPs to benefit from this third country regime, certain conditions—similar to those set out above in relation to investment firms under MiFIR—must be satisfied. EMIR has been in force since August 2012, with the first mandatory clearing obligation (in relation to G4 currency interest rate swaps) coming into force in in June 2016. The first recognition decisions in respect of third country CCPs took effect in April 2015.[2] The time between the regulation coming into force and the ability of third country CCPs to provide clearing services, demonstrates that the third country recognitions can take several years. **11.26**

EMIR also has a broader equivalence regime under Article 13, which allows the European Commission to deem a third country as equivalent for the purposes of clearing, risk **11.27**

---

[1] See CRD IV, Art. 3(1) and point (1) CRR, Art. 4(1)
[2] ESMA, 'List of Third-Country Central Counterparties Recognised to Offer Services and Activities in the Union' (as of 21 August 2018), ESMA70-152-348 <https://www.esma.europa.eu/sites/default/files/library/third-country_ccps_recognised_under_emir.pdf>

mitigation and reporting requirements. In a scenario where a third country has equivalence, firms could satisfy these EMIR obligations through the relevant arrangements in the third country. However, to date, this broader equivalence regime has only been used in one instance (in 2017), specifically for non-cleared OTC derivatives transactions in the US. The decision alleviates the regulatory burden for EU and US companies by allowing market participants to comply with only one set of rules and to avoid duplicative or conflicting rules.[3] However, equivalence decisions only cover non-cleared OTC derivatives and not the other requirements under EMIR.

11.28 These examples demonstrate the piecemeal approach to third country equivalence. A large gap in the third country regimes in EU legislation relates to banking. Under the CRR/CRD IV regime, there is no method of granting equivalence for third country firms seeking to provide banking services in the EEA as there is for third country investment firms seeking to provide investment services under MiFID or third country CCPs seeking to provide clearing services under EMIR.

11.29 There is no mechanism to grant equivalence to the UK in respect of the CRR/CRD IV regime. Therefore, UK credit institutions will need to consider whether they need to subsidiarise in the EEA or obtain potential branch authorisations in individual EEA member states if they wish to provide banking services to EEA clients and counterparties.

11.30 Although CRR does not contain a sectoral equivalence framework, it does provide for other third country recognition procedures, which will be affected by Brexit. These relate to the treatment of:

1. exposures to UK entities; and
2. exposures to UK CCPs.

11.31 Without an amendment to the European Commission's decision relating to exposures, EEA institutions may no longer be able to apply the same risk weights to their exposures to UK institutions arising from OTC derivatives as such exposures may now be treated as exposures to UK corporates (as opposed to UK investment firms and credit institutions.[4] Similarly, without a recognition of UK CCPs under EMIR or an amendment to the European Commission's decision relating to transitional periods on CCP exposures, EEA institutions would no longer be able to treat exposures to UK CCPs as exposures to 'Qualifying CCPs', and so would have to apply a higher capital charge in respect of derivative exposures cleared though UK CCPs. In view of the latter, ESMA announced that it would recognise three UK CCPs—LCH Limited, ICE Clear Europe Limited, and LME Clear Limited—to limit disruption.[5] Finally UK banks may also look at the scope of an EEA country's banking law to see if beyond deposit taking there is a need for a licence to undertake banking activities including by way of example commercial lending and providing guarantees.

---

[3] European Commission Implementing Decision on Equivalence arrangements of US CFTC regime for the purposes of Article 11 of EMIR ((EU) 2017/1857), 13 October 2017 <https://eur-lex.europa.eu/legal-content/EN/TXT/PDF/?uri=CELEX:32017D1857&from=EN>

[4] Implementing Decision (EU) 2016/2358. CRR, Arts. 107, 114, 115, 116, and 142.

[5] ESMA, 'ESMA to Recognise Three UK CCPs in the Event of a No-Deal Brexit', ESMA71-99-1114 (18 February 2019) <https://www.esma.europa.eu/press-news/esma-news/esma-recognise-three-uk-ccps-in-event-no-deal-brexit>

11.32 In summary, UK credit institutions will lose the ability to provide their banking products and services across the EEA from the UK using a passport. Outside any agreement between the UK and EU covering banking services, UK credit institutions will need to establish a new credit institution in order for that new entity to use a passport. Alternatively, UK credit institutions need to consider whether they can obtain licences or exemptions from individual member states in which their clients and counterparties are based. Absent decisions made by the European Commission, it will become more expensive for EEA entities to have exposures to UK entities and CCPs that have not been granted recognition.

11.3 The Handling of Prudential Requirements under the UK's Authorisation of EU Bank Branches

11.3.1 Current Framework

11.33 The Prudential Regulation Authority (**PRA**) is responsible for the prudential regulation of banks, building societies, credit unions, insurers, and major investment firms. One of the PRA's primary objectives is to promote the safety and soundness of firms. The PRA is required to pursue its general objective primarily by seeking to avoid adverse effects on financial stability resulting from the way firms run their business, and by preventing disorderly failure.[6]

11.34 Under the CRR/CRD IV regime, the home state supervisor of an EEA credit institution is responsible for the prudential supervision of the whole firm, including any branches of that bank in other EEA member states. EEA credit institutions operating in the UK through a branch currently do so under the right of establishment pursuant to Article 33 of CRD IV (following an Article 35 of CRD IV notification to the home member state). EEA credit institutions exercising their passporting rights into the UK only require authorisation from the PRA (and potentially the FCA) where they seek to undertake activities that go beyond the scope of their passport in the UK. In these circumstances, such EEA credit institutions would need to apply for the relevant 'top-up' permissions from the PRA and/or FCA.

11.35 Even though the PRA lacks direct prudential supervision over EEA credit institutions, pursuant to its general objectives, it still needs to ensure that the UK branches of such firms do not adversely affect the UK's financial stability. Existing powers in CRD IV assist host state regulators in the EEA. Under Article 51 of CRD IV, if the PRA considers that a UK branch of an EEA credit institution is important to UK financial stability, it has the ability to designate the branch as 'significant'. In such a scenario, the EEA home state regulator will be required to supply the PRA with additional information about the EEA credit institution and consult the PRA on various issues such as emergency planning.

11.36 The PRA will consider a credit institution as significant where it undertakes a 'critical function' in the UK. PRA defines 'critical function' as a function whose disruption or withdrawal

---

[6] Bank of England, 'The Prudential Regulation Authority's Approach to Banking Supervision' (March 2016) <https://www.bankofengland.co.uk/-/media/boe/files/prudential-regulation/approach/banking-approach-2016.pdf?la=en&hash=67655137353DEB7FFF88F5726EE81FE2F8B750F7>

could have an adverse material impact on financial stability in the UK and the safety and soundness of firms supervised by the PRA.

11.3.1.1 Impact of Brexit

11.37 After Brexit, the UK will no longer be subject to the CRR/CRD IV framework, though, it will through the 'onshoring' legislation referred to above, have implemented the same requirements into the UK *acquis*. Therefore, UK branches of EEA credit institutions will no longer have the ability to passport their services and activities into the UK (at least after the expiry of the temporary permissions regime). EEA credit institutions that wish to operate in the UK would need to apply for authorisation in order to carry on any regulated activities in the UK.

11.38 EEA credit institutions intending to operate in the UK would need to consider whether they could operate through a branch or whether they would be required to incorporate a subsidiary. The UK regulatory authorities are open to hosting branches of international credit institutions, but the method of operation depends very much on the scale and scope of activities undertaken by the credit institutions in the UK and the ability of the PRA to supervise the firm effectively. Where an EEA credit institution seeks authorisation in the UK through a branch, PRA authorisation will apply to the firm as a whole (and not just its UK branch).

11.3.2 UK Authorisation

11.39 For the PRA to authorise an international bank as a branch, the following conditions must be satisfied:

1. that the whole firm meets the PRA's threshold conditions;
2. there is a sufficient degree of equivalence of the firm's home state regulatory regime;
3. there is appropriate supervisory cooperation between the home state supervisor and resolution authority; and
4. appropriate assurance over the resolution arrangement for the firm and its UK operations.

11.40 Section 55B and Schedule 6 FSMA 2000 set out the relevant threshold conditions[7] for PRA-authorised firms. For a firm incorporated outside the UK, these broadly comprise:

1. a firm's business to be conducted in a prudent manner—in particular that the firm maintains appropriate financial and non-financial resources;
2. the firm itself to be fit and proper, and be appropriately staffed; and
3. the firm and its group to be capable of being effectively supervised.

11.41 When determining whether these conditions have been satisfied, the PRA has scope to rely on the home state supervisor's opinion about an EEA credit institution's compliance with the relevant conditions.

11.42 When assessing the equivalence of a home state's regulatory regime, the PRA will focus on the supervisor's powers, approach to supervising firms and groups, confidentiality, and

---

[7] There are also FCA threshold conditions that would apply to dual-regulated firms.

information sharing. The PRA will also consider the supervisor's independence and competence in other areas. These considerations are benchmarked against the UK regulatory framework and international standards.[8]

11.43 In respect of supervisory cooperation, the PRA is guided by the Basel Committee's Core Principles for Effective Banking Supervision. The PRA will require confirmation from the international bank's home state supervisor that the whole firm meets the PRA's threshold conditions and require a specific agreement with the home state supervisor on the split of responsibilities for prudential supervision. The PRA will also require open and transparent exchange of supervisory information.

11.44 Resolution arrangements are a key factor in the PRA's review of the firm and in determining its risk appetite to authorise the firm. Where the UK branch performs (or will perform) critical functions as described above, the PRA alongside the Bank of England (as the resolution authority) will assess a number of points, including:

1. the alignment and credibility of the firm's group resolution strategy;
2. the equivalence of the firm's home state resolution regime and ability of the PRA to rely on the home state authority to execute the firm's resolution strategy; and
3. willingness of the home state resolution authority to share the group resolution plan with the PRA.

11.45 Although EEA and UK regulatory regimes will be practically equivalent on Brexit day, the PRA would still have to assess whether EEA firms meet the above the requirements and can obtain authorisation to operate as a branch in the UK.

11.46 There are also other important factors to consider on the nature a branch's activities and a firm's ability to obtain authorisation as a branch in the UK. These relate to whether the firm will be:

1. undertaking significant retail activities; and
2. a systemic wholesale branch.

11.3.3 Retail Activities

11.47 If a firm's UK branch intends to undertake retail deposit-taking beyond the PRA's prescribed thresholds, they will be required to operate as a subsidiary.[9] The relevant thresholds for the branch to consider are:

1. a maximum of £100 million in retail or small company transactional or instant access account balances covered by the Financial Services Compensation Scheme (**FSCS**);
2. over 5,000 retail and small company customers; or
3. total potential liability to the FSCS in respect of covered deposits in excess of £500 million.

---

[8] The PRA will base its analysis on the IMF's Financial Sector Assessment Programme review, the FSB's peer reviews, and Basel Committee's Regulatory Consistency Assessment Programme reviews.
[9] The PRA will also consider the firm's plans for growth.

11.3.4 Systemic Wholesale Branches

11.48 If a firm's UK branch is a systemic wholesale branch, the PRA will need to be satisfied that there are adequate means to enable it to gain sufficient assurance over the supervisability of the branch. This will include the PRA's influence and visibility over the supervisory outcomes of the firm, the degree of supervisory cooperation between the PRA and the firm's home state supervisor, and assurances on the firm's home state resolution arrangements. Where the PRA is satisfied about the above conditions, it may allow the firm to operate a branch in the UK. Where the PRA is only partially, or is not, satisfied, it may allow the firm to operate as branch with specific mitigants and regulatory requirements at a branch level or require the firm operate as a subsidiary.

11.49 A branch may be categorised as 'systemically important' where:

1. it holds more than an average of £15 billion total gross assets (including those traded or originated in the UK but booked remotely to another location);
2. it undertakes critical functions (discussed above); and/or
3. the PRA considers that the overall complexity and interconnectedness of the firm's business warrants further review.

11.4 Collaboration and Information Sharing

11.50 CRD IV imposes obligations on member states to ensure that national laws require competent authorities to cooperate in the supervision of banks and of investment firms, including through the sharing of confidential information. As mentioned in Section IX ('Supervision of banking groups and consolidation'), in the case of banking groups, such cooperation must be taken forward through so-called regulatory colleges of relevant supervisors from across the EU. In particular, these cooperation and information sharing requirements are intended to facilitate the efficient and effective supervision of cross-border businesses. Following Brexit, a number of legal, policy, and practical issues would need to be addressed if such cooperative arrangements are to continue. It is currently unclear what approach the UK regulators intend to take towards rebuilding such cooperative structures in relation to prudential supervision.

11.51 The potential impact of Brexit on supervisory cooperation with EU27 supervisors can be seen most markedly in the Capital Requirements (Amendment) (EU Exit) Regulations 2018 (the '**CR Amendment Regulations**'), which will come into effect on Brexit day. The regulations substantially amend the UK Capital Requirements Regulations 2013,[10] which give effect to the UK's obligations derived from CRD IV. For example, Part 4 of the UK Capital Requirements Regulations 2013 ('PRA and FCA: cooperation and coordination') is simply deleted, as are Regulations 22–33, which

---

[10] Capital Requirements Regulations 2013 No. 3115.

currently oblige UK regulators to engage with EU supervisory colleges. On their face, these provisions imply a complete withdrawal of the UK regulators from cooperation with EU27 bank and investment firm supervisors in relation to prudential supervision. Beyond these organisational changes, there are further legal challenges. For example, the ability for regulators to share information to which banking confidentiality applies may be restrained by statutory obligations to disclose relevant information as derived from CRD IV, and which currently stand to be deleted. This is also a consideration for banks themselves who, if they are to disclose confidential client information, need to have confidence that such disclosures are being made within a framework of legal obligations which may extend beyond the immediate regulator to whom information is provided. Such considerations derived from bank secrecy laws may apply with equal force to EU27 banks in relation to their ability to disclose otherwise confidential information to UK regulators.

11.52 There have been efforts to retain certain information sharing provisions in UK law. On Brexit day, the Public Record, Disclosure of Information and Co-operation (Financial Services) (Amendment) (EU Exit) Regulations 2019 (the '**Cooperation Amendment Regulations**') will amend Part 23 of FSMA,[11] which imposes duties of confidentiality on UK regulators. The Cooperation Amendment Regulations will change Part 23 to take account of the removal of the information sharing obligations derived from CRD IV and other provisions of EU law. This will allow the so-called gateways facilitated by Part 23 that permit the disclosure of confidential information to EU supervisors to survive Brexit.

11.53 Also removed by the CR Amendment Regulations are those provisions of UK law that confer on EU supervisors the ability to carry out on the spot inspections of UK branches of EU established institutions. Since the UK is fostering the prospect of EU27 bank branches becoming authorised by the UK regulators (see Section II ('How does the CRD IV/CRR regime differ from other sectors in respect of passporting and equivalence tests?')) it follows that post-Brexit EU27 supervisors will require similar access to the UK premises and records of bank branches.

11.54 The FCA has agreed memoranda of understanding (**MoUs**) with national competent authorities and ESMA to allow for continued close cooperation after Brexit.[12] Its multilateral MoU with EU27 and EEA supervisors covers supervisory cooperation, enforcement and information exchange, and its bilateral MoU with ESMA covers supervision of credit rating agencies and trade repositories. As is consistent with other MoUs agreed between the UK regulators and non-EU supervisors and enforcement agencies, these MoUs are non-binding undertakings.

---

[11] Financial Services and Markets Act 2000.
[12] ESMA, 'ESMA and EU Securities Regulators Agree No-Deal Brexit MoUs with FCA', ESMA71-99-1096 (1 February 2019) <https://www.esma.europa.eu/sites/default/files/library/esma71-99-1096_esma_and_eu_securities_regulators_agree_no-deal_brexit_mous_with_fca.pdf>

11.5 Setting Capital Buffer Requirements

11.55 CRD IV sets out requirements for EU Member States in relation to setting so-called 'capital buffers'[13] which include capital conservation, countercyclical, globally systemic financial institution and systemic risk buffers. These capital buffer provisions may require Member States to be able to 'recognise' and apply countercyclical and systemic risk buffers that may be established by other Member States and by third countries. Such recognition can arise when an institution's assets (or 'exposures') are located in a country other than where the institution is established and allows for the judgement taken by the authorities in that other country as to the macro-economic conditions to be applied by the domestic supervisor. The UK framework for these CRD IV provisions are contained in a UK SI[14] and followed the EU framework, which included elaborate comitology between EU Member States and conferred roles on the European Systemic Risk Board. The CR Amendment Regulations reorganise these requirements and to an extent simplify them, since the EU27 will be considered as third countries going forward, although the ability to recognise and apply the risk buffers imposed in respect of third countries continues.

11.6 EU Intermediate Holding Company Regime

11.6.1 Reforms under CRD V Package

11.56 In November 2016, the European Commission set out proposals to amend key aspects of the EU's banking and resolution regimes. These included proposed amendments to CRD IV, CRR, Bank Recovery and Resolution Directive (2014/59/EU), and the Single Resolution Mechanism. Many of the proposed amendments addressed the outstanding parts of the Basel Committee's agreement on post-crisis reforms. The proposals included amendment of Directive 2013/36/EU—so called CRD V and of Regulation 575/2013—so called CRR 2.

11.57 The final texts of CRD V and CRR 2 were adopted by the Council of the EU on 14 May 2019, and were published in the Official Journal on 7 June 2019.[15] The majority of the provisions will apply from June 2021, although some measures will be subject to phase-in.

11.58 The European Commission has described the package of reforms as an important step towards the completion of the European post-crisis regulatory reforms. Some of the amendments originate from the Basel Committee's reforms. Others however derive from EU-specific proposals, such as the requirement for large non-EU banks to establish an intermediate holding company (IHC) in the EU where they have two or more EU credit institutions or investment firms in their group.[16]

---

[13] Directive 2013/36/EU, Art. 128.
[14] Capital Requirements (Capital Buffers and Macro-Prudential Measures) Regulations 2014 (SI 2014/No. 894).
[15] Regulation (EU) 2019/876 and Directive (EU) 2019/878.
[16] CRD V, Art. 1(9) which adds a new Art. 21b to CRD.

11.59 The European Commission's rationale for the new IHC requirement is to strengthen and simplify the resolution of non-EU groups in the EU. However, market commentary indicates that, although a new IHC at the top of the group for EU purposes may simplify resolution due to consolidated oversight, it is more likely that these amendments are a reaction and retaliation to similar US rules.[17]

11.60 It is questionable whether these EU IHC requirements were necessary, given the existing powers of competent authorities in the EU under Article 127 of CRD IV. Competent authorities have discretion to determine that a third country's supervisory and prudential framework is not equivalent and to take certain actions. These actions include the ability to require the third country group to establish an EU financial holding company or mixed financial holding company and apply the provisions on consolidated supervision to that EU holding company.

11.6.2 Threshold and Application

11.61 When it comes into application, the new Article 21b of CRD will require certain non-EU groups to hold their EU credit institutions and investment firms under a single EU IHC. This IHC will need to be authorised as an EU credit institution or investment, pursuant to the new Article 21a of CRD.

11.62 A non-EU group will be subject to the IHC requirements when:

1. it has two or more credit institutions or investment firms in the EU; and
2. the total value of assets in the EU of the third country group is at least €40 billion.

11.63 The total value of assets in the EU under 2 above will include:

1. the total assets of each EU credit institution and investment firm of the third country group, as resulting from their consolidated balance sheet; and
2. the total assets of each branch of the third country group authorised in the EU.

11.64 The conditions for the total assets are very broad and more onerous than the US IHC regime. While the EU IHC regime includes branch assets, the US IHC regime sets a *de minimis* threshold of $50 billion in US non-branch or agency assets.[18]

11.65 The €40 billion threshold is similar to the 'significant threshold' in the Single Supervisory Mechanism (SSM),[19] which brings significant institutions under the direct prudential supervision of the European Central Bank. It should be noted that although the SSM's significant threshold considers the assets of the relevant EU institution, unlike the new EU IHC threshold, it does not include branch assets.[20]

---

[17] Alex Barker et al., 'EU to Retaliate against US Bank Capital Rules', *Financial Times* (21 November 2016) <https://www.ft.com/content/26078750-b003-11e6-a37c-f4a01f1b0fa1>; Huw Jones, 'Foreign Banks Face New EU Set-up to Allow More Scrutiny', *Reuters* (4 September 2017). <https://www.reuters.com/article/eu-banks-regulations/foreign-banks-face-new-eu-set-up-to-allow-more-scrutiny-idUSL8N1LL1RO>
[18] Title 12, US Code of Financial Regulations, s. 252.153.
[19] Single Supervisory Mechanism Regulation (Council Regulation (EU) 1024/2013) and Single Supervisory Mechanism Framework Regulation (Regulation (EU) 468/2014) (hereafter '**SSM Framework Regulation**').
[20] SSM Framework Regulation, Art. 50.

11.6.3 Impact on Third Country Groups

11.66 Under the EU IHC regime, there may be more than one IHC where this is necessary to accommodate mandatory requirements for the separation of activities imposed by the rules of third country supervisory authorities. Therefore, where the relevant conditions are met, non-EU groups breaching the threshold will need to consider whether an existing EU holding entity or parent company would qualify to be authorised as an EU IHC. If not, they would need to establish a new EU IHC and obtain authorisation.

11.67 There also appears to be an asymmetric impact, such that some third countries fall within the scope of the EU IHC regime but not others. A non-EU G-SIB with group entities representing (for example) €5 billion in total assets is in scope. Conversely, a non-GSIB with EU group entities representing €30 billion in total assets falls outside the scope of the EU IHC requirements.

11.6.4 Impact of Brexit

11.68 Unless Brexit day is delayed beyond June 2021, the amendments to CRD IV will not be in application by the time the UK exits the EU. Further, if there is an EU/UK transitional period in place and these amendments come into force during that period, the UK will need to implement the changes into the UK *acquis*. In this scenario, the UK would not be a third country for EU legislative purposes until the expiry of the transitional period. Market participants are already in the process of restructuring their European groups to ensure they are able to operate in the UK and EU after Brexit. The EU's IHC amendments add a layer of complexity to these plans in terms of where assets are held and whether the creation of an additional entity or entities in the EU to mitigate the loss of market access and passporting in the EU could inadvertently bring such non-EU groups within the scope of the IHC requirements.

11.69 Post-Brexit (or transitional period), UK banking groups could become subject to the EU's IHC requirements. Therefore, the possible options for UK banking groups are: comply with the rules; consolidate EU entities into one; or reduce the total assets held in the EU. UK banking groups (and other non-EU banking groups) may also have to consider whether the UK will introduce its own standalone regime after Brexit or the expiry of the transitional period. If the UK were to do so and there were no equivalence measures in place for non-UK regimes, global banking groups with presences in the EU, UK, and US may have to comply with three IHC regimes.

11.7 Impact of Brexit on Risk Weights of EU and UK Exposures and Liquidity

11.70 Another consequence of the UK becoming a third country post-Brexit (and if no equivalence assessment is made by the European Commission in respect of the UK) is that UK exposures will no longer receive preferential treatment by the EU. Similarly, the CR

Amendment Regulation will remove preferential treatment of EU exposures from a UK perspective in the event of no mutual equivalence.

Currently, under CRR, EU assets and assets of third countries deemed equivalent by the European Commission are treated preferentially. In particular, EU sovereign debt denominated in the currency of the sovereign is subject to a 0% risk weight, meaning that firms are not required to hold capital against such exposures. This zero-risk weight rule—based on a Basel standard—was subject to heavy criticism, particularly during the eurozone debt crisis. The sharp drop in the market value of government bonds in Spain, Portugal, Ireland, and Greece highlighted that sovereign debt can carry high risks (particularly if the relevant state's fiscal situation is not sufficiently strong to support its banking sector). Efforts to amend the zero-risk weight rule for sovereign debt and thereby close the so-called doom loop have been unsuccessful, largely on political grounds, due to the potential financial implications of disincentivising investors from holding debt of governments with lower credit ratings. **11.71**

It seems likely, therefore, that the zero-risk weight rule will continue at least in the short term when the UK is a third country. This poses the question: what risk weight will be assigned to the UK's exposures post-Brexit? If the PRA assigns a zero-risk weight to the UK's credit risk, can this risk weight be used by a German bank, for example? Article 114(1)–(2) of CRR specifies that, as a starting point, exposures to central governments and central banks of third countries shall be assigned a 100% risk weight, unless a credit assessment by a nominated external credit assessment institution (**ECAI**) is available (in which case, the risk weight corresponds to the assessed credit quality; from 0% for credit quality 1 to 150% for credit quality 6). **11.72**

However, Article 114(7) of CRR states that when the competent authority of an 'equivalent' third country assigns a risk weight to exposures to their central government and central bank (denominated and funded in the domestic currency) that is lower than that prescribed by CRR, EU institutions may risk-weight such exposures in the same manner. Therefore, the treatment of sterling-denominated exposures towards the UK central government and central bank depends on the European Commission making an equivalence assessment in favour of the UK or a nominated ECAI making a credit assessment available. Neither option provides a clear route to maintaining the zero-risk weight rule for UK exposures in EU27 institutions post-Brexit. The issue with the latter option is that, as confirmed by ESMA earlier this year,[21] credit rating agencies established in the UK will no longer be considered established in the EU. Consequently, ESMA will withdraw these entities' registration with effect from Brexit day, in accordance with Articles 14 and 20 of the Credit Ratings Agencies Regulation (Regulation (EC) 1060/2009) (hereafter '**CRA Regulation**') (subject to any transitional arrangement that may be contained in a possible withdrawal agreement). **11.73**

Article 4(1) of the CRA Regulation specifies that credit rating agencies established in the EU need to be registered and supervised by ESMA in order for their ratings to be recognised **11.74**

---

[21] ESMA, 'Endorsement of Credit Ratings Elaborated in the United Kingdom in the Event of a No-Deal Brexit', ESMA33-5-735 (15 March 2019) <https://www.esma.europa.eu/press-news/esma-news/esma-clarifies-endorsement-uk-credit-ratings-in-case-no-deal-brexit>

for regulatory purposes in the EU. Therefore, as a consequence of the deregistration of UK credit rating agencies, EU institutions will no longer be able to use ratings issued by UK credit rating agencies for regulatory purposes unless such ratings are endorsed by an EU27 CRA. The effect that this will have on the treatment of UK exposures is unclear at this stage. In the insurance context, the European Insurance and Occupational Pensions Authority suggested that UK exposures and/or UK credit rating agencies could be transferred to an EU27 Member State to mitigate against the uncertainty.

11.75 The potential loss of preferential treatment for EU assets would also apply to the liquidity regime, where EU27 central bank-backed assets, and assets representing claims on or guaranteed by EU27 governments, would automatically become third country assets requiring ECAI credit assessments. This could incentivise the dumping of exposures to EU27 central banks and governments, and the take-up of similar UK exposures, in order to meet UK liquidity ratio requirements.

11.8 CRD Remuneration Provisions: Variable Remuneration

11.8.1 Background

11.76 The CRD IV provisions on remuneration are likely to attract scrutiny post-Brexit, particularly in relation to whether or not the UK will continue to retain the CRD IV 'bonus-cap' restrictions as part of its retained EU law.

11.77 Under Article 94(1)(g) of CRD IV, Member States' competent authorities are required to ensure that financial institutions set 'appropriate ratios' between the fixed and variable components of total remuneration. The variable component cannot exceed 100% of the fixed component of the total remuneration for each individual—with Member States given discretion to adopt a lower maximum percentage. Member states could, however, allow the shareholders or owners of the institution to approve a higher maximum level of the ratio between the fixed and variable components of remuneration, provided the overall level of the variable component does not exceed 200% of the fixed component of the total remuneration for each individual. In addition, for the purpose of calculating the ratio between the variable and fixed component of remuneration, Member States have discretion to allow institutions to apply a 'discount rate' (in accordance with EBA guidelines)[22] to a maximum of 25% of the variable remuneration, provided it is paid in instruments that are deferred for a period of no fewer than five years.

11.78 In addition to the variable remuneration provisions, CRD IV also requires institutions to maintain robust governance arrangements, including remuneration policies and practices that are consistent with, and which promote, sound and effective risk management (Article 74(1) of CRD IV). Article 75(2) of CRD IV also required the EBA to issue guidelines on sound remuneration policies that comply with the principles in Articles 92 to 95 of the Directive (including the provisions on variable remuneration). The EBA guidelines on

---

[22] EBA Guidelines on the applicable notional discount rate for variable remuneration, EBA/GL/2014/01 dated 27 March 2014.

sound remuneration policies were published in December 2015 (the '**EBA Guidelines**').[23] The EBA Guidelines make clear that the variable remuneration cap under Article 94(1)(g) of CRD IV should apply to all institutions as well as to their subsidiaries within the scope of prudential consolidation.

11.8.2 UK Regulatory Approach to Implementation of CRD IV Remuneration Requirements

11.79 Following publication of the EBA Guidelines, the PRA and FCA notified the EBA that they would seek to comply with all aspects of the EBA Guidelines, except for the provision that the variable remuneration cap must be applied to all firms subject to the CRD. Instead, the PRA and FCA favoured a proportionate, risk-based approach when applying the bonus cap in accordance with Article 92 of CRD IV, which provides that 'competent authorities shall ensure that ... institutions comply with the following principles [including the bonus cap] in a manner and to the extent that is appropriate to their size, internal organisation and the nature, scope and complexity of their activities'. On this basis, the PRA and FCA took the view that a proportionate approach may include not applying the variable remuneration requirement in its entirety based on the size, internal organisation and the nature, scope, and complexity of the activities of the firm in question. Consequently, the PRA and FCA's position was that all large and systemically important CRD-regulated firms must continue to apply the bonus cap, while in parallel retaining the PRA and FCA's original approach of only requiring smaller firms to determine an appropriate ratio between fixed and variable remuneration for their business, without formally applying the bonus cap.

11.80 The PRA and FCA's objection to the EBA's interpretation reflected a previous challenge by the UK government as to the legitimacy of the variable remuneration cap in Article 94 of CRD IV. On 25 September 2013, the UK government issued a statement noting that it had lodged a legal challenge with the European Court of Justice on the 'bonus cap' provisions. This was on the basis that the 'bonus cap' provisions were not fit for purpose as they did not improve stability across the banking system, but instead led to an increase in fixed salaries, which would achieve the opposite effect. The UK government sought to annul Article 94(1)(g) on the grounds that:

1. the provision had an inadequate treaty legal base;
2. the provision was disproportionate and failed to comply with the principle of subsidiarity;
3. the provision had been brought into effect in a manner that infringed the principle of legal certainty; and
4. the assignment of tasks and powers to the EBA in respect of this provision was *ultra vires*.

11.81 Following the hearing in September 2014, Advocate General Jääskinen delivered an opinion in November 2014, which suggested that all of the UK government's grounds for challenge

---

[23] EBA Final Report, 'Guidelines on Sound Remuneration Policies under Articles 74(3) and 75(2) of Directive 2013/36/EU and Disclosures under Article 450 of Regulation (EU) No 575/2013', EBA/GL/2015/22 (21 December 2015).

should be rejected and that the ECJ should dismiss the action. Following publication of the opinion by the ECJ, the UK government determined that it would no longer pursue the legal action. However, in seeking to limit the scope of application of the bonus cap provisions to large and systemically important CRD-regulated firms, in direct opposition to the EBA Guidelines, the PRA and FCA approach could be seen as an indication that they remained unconvinced of the value of imposing the bonus cap requirements.

11.8.3 UK Current Position on Bonus Cap

11.82 While there has been little official commentary on the matter since the UK government sought to withdraw its legal action, there continue to be indications that UK authorities remain opposed to the bonus cap, and that moves may be considered post-Brexit to restrict or remove the cap.

11.83 On 29 November 2017, following a speech to mark the two-year anniversary of the FICC Markets Standards Board, the Governor of the Bank of England noted a number of areas where the UK could seek to 'roll back' regulations after Brexit.[24] This included the variable remuneration cap under CRD IV, as well as elements of insurance regulation and the application of the full weight of rules on challenger banks and building societies. Mr Carney noted that these were 'things we don't think are necessary' and that 'there are areas we would make changes but within the context of maintaining the overall levels of resilience'.

11.84 However, there may be practical obstacles to any attempt to restrict or repeal the CRD IV bonus cap post-Brexit. One of the key obstacles may be the impact of the equivalence regime. Under Article 46 of MiFIR, investment firms incorporated in a third country are (in theory) permitted to provide investment services to eligible counterparties and professional clients in the Union without the establishment of a branch, provided that the Commission has adopted an equivalence decision under Article 47 of MiFIR for that third country. This equivalence decision would determine whether the legal and supervisory arrangements of that third country ensure that authorised firms comply with legally binding prudential and conduct of business requirements that have 'equivalent effect' to the requirements set out in MiFID II, MiFIR, CRR, and CRD IV. This regime might be available post-Brexit even in circumstances where no withdrawal agreement is reached. However, this would be dependent upon the Commission adopting the decision that the UK-authorised firms remained subject to 'equivalent' prudential and conduct of business requirements.

11.85 In December 2017, the Commission published proposals for the reform of existing prudential requirements for investment firms as contained in CRR and CRD IV. The proposals introduced a new regulation (the Investment Firms Regulation (IFR))[25] and a directive

---

[24] Mark Carney, 'Turning Back the Tide', speech given to the FICC Market Standard Board, 'Two Years on from the Fair and Effective Markets Review' (29 November 2017) <https://www.bankofengland.co.uk/-/media/boe/files/speech/2017/turning-back-the-tide-speech-by-mark-carney.pdf?la=en&hash=E6DC8F0093FF3ED65C249C0B5A7968A453567CCE>

[25] Presidency Compromise Proposal for a Regulation of the European Parliament and of the Council on the prudential supervision of investment firms and amending Regulations (EU) No. 575/2013, (EU) No. 600/2014, and (EU) No. 1093/2010 (2017/0359 (COD)) <https://eur-lex.europa.eu/legal-content/EN/TXT/?uri=COM:2017:0790:FIN>

(the Investment Firms Directive (**IFD**))[26] on the prudential requirements applicable to investment firms. The European Parliament adopted the legislation in April 2019, with the Council expected to follow later this year. It is expected that IFR and IFD will apply from the first quarter of 2021.

11.86   Under Article 61(2) of the IFR, it is proposed that Article 47 of MiFIR is amended to provide further restrictions on the circumstances in which a third country's prudential and conduct of business requirements can be regarded as having 'equivalent effect'. For example, the changes introduce a requirement that, when assessing services performed by third country firms in the EU that are likely to be of systemic importance, the prudential and business conduct requirements may only be considered to have equivalent effect after a 'detailed and granular assessment'. For the purposes of conducting this assessment, the Commission must also assess and take into account the supervisory convergence between the third country concerned and the EU.

11.87   This tightening-up of the equivalence assessment process could potentially provide the Commission with grounds to conclude that the UK regime was not 'equivalent' in circumstances where there is even a slight deviation from the existing European *acquis*. For example, if the UK were to seek to remove the variable remuneration caps from adopted European law following Brexit, then the Commission might conclude that the UK prudential regime was no longer 'equivalent' following the 'detailed and granular' assessment. In any case, the threat of such an assessment being reached (either before or after the UK obtaining an 'equivalence' decision) may provide enough of a chilling effect for the UK to avoid making any changes to the variable remuneration cap in the immediate future.

11.88   However, there are signs that the European authorities may be starting to question the value of seeking to ensure that the UK retains equivalent bonus cap provisions. In December 2017, Andrea Enria, head of the European Banking Authority, noted that in his view if the UK was to remove the bonus cap then it could still be deemed robust enough in the eyes of European policymakers to allow cross-border dealing. Mr. Enria noted that he 'wouldn't say that the bonus cap is a key component for judging a system equivalent'.[27]

11.89   There are also signs that the Commission's stance on variable remuneration caps may be starting to soften. In particular, the amendments to the prudential regime for investment firms in the IFD represent a change in stance on variable remuneration caps, at least in relation to their application to investment firms. Article 28(2) of the IFD effectively removes the fixed 100% (or 200%) limit for the ratio between fixed and variable remuneration. In its place will be a requirement for Member States to 'ensure that investment firms set the appropriate ratios between the variable and the fixed component of the total remuneration in their remuneration policies, taking into account the business activities of the investment firm and associated risks'. This move away from prescriptive limits towards affording Member States discretion to impose 'appropriate ratios' represents a more proportionate approach by the Commission to the imposition of variable remuneration caps.

---

[26] Presidency Compromise Proposal for a Directive of the European Parliament and of the Council on the prudential supervision of investment firms and amending Directives 2013/36/EU and 2014/65/EU (2017/0358 (COD)) <https://data.consilium.europa.eu/doc/document/ST-7460-2019-ADD-1/en/pdf>

[27] Lucy McNulty, 'EBA Chair Calm on UK Plans to Bin Bonus Cap' (*Financial News*, 20 December 2017) <https://www.fnlondon.com/articles/eba-chair-calm-on-uk-plans-to-bin-bonus-cap-20171220>

Whether a similar approach may be taken by the Commission on bonus caps in relation to credit institutions remains to be seen. However, in light of this change in approach in relation to investment firms, it is possible that there may be some room for movement for the UK when determining its own approach to retention of variable remuneration caps post-Brexit.

11.9 Supervision of Banking Groups and Consolidation

11.90 The CR Amendment Regulations aim to ensure that the UK continues to have a functioning financial services regulatory regime in any Brexit scenario. The CR Amendment Regulations were made in exercise of the powers in section 8(1) of the EU (Withdrawal) Act 2018 to address failures of retained EU law to operative effectively and other deficiencies arising from the UK's withdrawal from the EU.

11.91 The majority of rules imposed under CRR and CRD IV have been in force since January 2014. The PRA and FCA each implemented CRD IV in respect of the firms under their supervision, while CRR, as a regulation, has direct effect in the UK. Under CRR, banking groups are required to carry out consolidation for regulatory capital and liquidity purposes at Member State level, irrespective of whether or not the group's ultimate parent is located in the EU or a third country. As such, all UK groups are currently carrying out consolidation under their UK parent entity. The purpose of consolidation is to capture risk to group regulated entities at the level of the consolidated group that are not captured through solo entity regulation.

11.92 The relevant sections of the Financial Groups Directive (2002/87/EC) (hereafter **Financial Groups Directive**) and CRD IV are implemented in the UK by the General Prudential Requirements chapter of the FCA Handbook (GENPRU) and in 'CRR Firms' in the PRA Rulebook. In accordance with GENPRU 3.2.3G, UK regulators may defer to group consolidation carried out by a third country regulator where the EEA regulated entities in the third country group are subject to supervision by a competent authority equivalent to supervision under the Financial Groups Directive (for financial conglomerates) or CRD IV (for banking or investment groups).

11.93 The Financial Groups Directive sets out the process for establishing equivalence with respect to third country financial conglomerates,[28] whereas CRD IV does so with respect to third country banking and investment groups[29] (aside from CAD investment firms[30] only, which fall under Article 143 of the Banking Consolidation Directive (2006/48/EC)). GENPRU 3.2 does not apply to incoming EEA or treaty firms, UK- or EEA-authorised banks, insurers, or designated investment firms, UCITS qualifiers or investment companies with variable capital. Therefore, certain groups with an EU (non-UK, post-Brexit) parent entity and consolidating supervisor do not currently have a separate layer of UK liquidity

---

[28] Financial Groups Directive, Art. 18(1).
[29] Ibid., Arts. 127(1) and (2).
[30] A CAD investment firm is defined in the FCA Handbook as a firm that is subject to the requirements of MiFID (or which would be if its head office were in an EEA state) but excludes a bank, building society, credit institution, local firm, and exempt CAD firm.

consolidation. Instead, such groups apply the consolidated liquidity requirements under CRR on a cross-EU basis.

11.94 This poses the question: post-Brexit, how will equivalence of third country banking groups be assessed in the UK for consolidation purposes? Moreover, how will UK banking groups be treated in the EEA for consolidation purposes?

11.95 Under CRR, the European Commission may deem a third country's regulatory or supervisory regime to be equivalent to those of EU27 Member States' regimes in terms of their approaches to (amongst other things) credit risk and exposures to central banks and governments and large financial sector entities. Following Brexit, the European Commission's jurisdiction will no longer extend to the UK. Consequently, HM Treasury will assume the European Commission's role from a UK perspective with regard to equivalence assessments for third countries. The PRA, on the other hand, shall assume the role of the European Banking Authority (**EBA**) in providing technical assessments of third country regimes. The European Commission's existing equivalence decisions[31] will be incorporated into UK law by the European Union (Withdrawal) Act and will continue to apply to the UK's regulatory and supervisory relationship with the relevant third countries.

11.96 The CR Amendment Regulations amend the geographical scope of all group consolidation provisions in CRR to restrict consolidation to the UK. This amendment acknowledges that the UK will become a third country post-Brexit and will fall outside of the joint supervisory framework that calculates consolidated capital requirements on both national and EU levels. As such, the UK regulators will no longer be able to act as the EU consolidated group supervisor for a UK group with EU business. More importantly, this will also subject EU banks operating in the UK to a new layer of UK-specific capital and liquidity consolidation, which the PRA shall oversee.

11.97 In terms of which UK regulatory authority—the PRA or the FCA—shall assume the role of consolidating supervisor, the CR Amendment Regulation states that a determination will be made by reference to four cases:

(1) PRA-authorised UK parent institutions that are required to comply with CRR requirements on a consolidated basis;
(2) FCA-authorised UK parent institutions that are required to comply with CRR requirements on a consolidated basis;
(3) UK parent financial holding companies or UK parent mixed financial holding companies that have a PRA-authorised subsidiary institution; and
(4) circumstances where none of the institutions are controlled by a UK parent financial holding company or UK parent mixed financial holding company that are required to comply with CRR requirements on a consolidated basis.

11.98 In cases 1 and 3, the PRA shall be the consolidating supervisor, whereas the FCA shall assume this role in cases 2 and 4. The PRA and FCA may vary the determination of the consolidated supervisor by written agreement, if they consider that the outcome would be

---

[31] European Commission, 'Equivalence/Adequacy Decisions Taken by the European Commission as of 29/10/2018' (20 May 2019) <https://ec.europa.eu/info/sites/info/files/overview-table-equivalence-decisions_en.pdf>

inappropriate (i.e. by having regard to the importance of the PRA-authorised persons and the FCA-authorised persons concerned).

11.99 Notwithstanding the multilateral MoU, it is not yet clear how and to what extent supervisory cooperation will continue between UK and EU27 regulatory authorities post-Brexit. Supervisory cooperation is well entrenched within the financial markets infrastructure of EU cross-border banking and insurance group supervision. As the Chief Executive Officer of the PRA, Sam Woods, stated: 'There is a quite highly developed institutional and regulatory architecture around this business of supervisory cooperation and the best example of that is this thing called the JRAD process, which is the Joint Risk Assessment and Decision.'[32] Under the Joint Risk Assessment and Decision process, a regulatory 'college' is formed, which comprises of the group supervisor, the supervisor of a subsidiary and the supervisor of a significant branch. Colleges are permanent, though flexible, coordination structures that bring together regulatory authorities involved in the supervision of a banking or insurance group to enable exchanges of information between home and host authorities and to decide issues such as capital requirements.[33]

11.100 CRD IV[34] allows supervisors of non-EEA entities to participate in regulatory colleges where appropriate and subject to the confidentiality requirements that are equivalent, in the opinion of all EEA college members, to those provided for by European legislation. The EBA Guidelines[35] further clarify that membership of non-EEA supervisors in regulatory colleges should take due account of:

1. the obligation for the consolidating supervisor to gather the opinion of EEA members of the college as to the equivalence of the confidentiality provisions in the third country concerned; and
2. the necessity of ensuring consistency across colleges, in terms of equivalence to CRD IV of confidentiality requirements applicable in a given third country.

11.101 Therefore, pending any equivalence assessment being made regarding the UK's confidentiality requirements with reference to CRD IV, the participation of the PRA and FCA in regulatory colleges post-Brexit depends on a productive dialogue taking place with the EU consolidating supervisor, in accordance with the EBA's guidance and as detailed in Section IV ('Collaborating and Information Sharing').

11.102 The UK level group consolidation change described above in relation to capital would also apply for the purposes of the level of liquidity consolidation. Applied in isolation to a UK bank in a wider EU group post-Brexit, where the group liquidity consolidation requirements have previously been met at EU level, this could result in costly fragmentation and sclerosis of liquidity pools.

---

[32] Chapter 6, European Union Select Committee (House of Lords), 'Brexit: The Future of Financial Regulation and Supervision' 11th Report of Session 2017–19, HL Paper 66 (27 January 2018) <https://publications.parliament.uk/pa/ld201719/ldselect/ldeucom/66/6609.htm >
[33] EBA definition: <https://www.eba.europa.eu/supervisory-convergence/supervisory-colleges>
[34] CRD IV, Art. 131(a).
[35] Committee of European Banking Supervisors, 'CEBS' Guidelines of the Operational Functioning of Supervisory Colleges (GL 34)' (15 June 2010) <https://www.eba.europa.eu/documents/10180/16094/CollegeGuidelines.pdf/586871d7-414a-45bd-88f0-e185e59a76fe>

11.10 Securitisation

11.10.1 Background

Prior to January 2019, Articles 404 to 410 of CRR (the '**CRR risk retention regime**') set out the 'risk retention' rules applicable to credit institutions and investment firms that are within scope of CRD IV. These rules, which have been superseded by the Securitisation Regulation (discussed below), provided that any such entity must only become exposed to the credit risk of a securitisation position where the originator, sponsor, or original lender for the securitisation had explicitly disclosed that it would retain a material net economic interest in the securitisation of at least 5%. There were five different ways in which the originator, sponsor and original lender could retain the 5% interest, however the most commonly used were:

1. retention of at least 5% of the nominal value of each of the tranches sold or transferred to the investors (a 'vertical slice');
2. retention of the 'first loss tranche' (i.e. the most subordinated tranche in the securitisation) so that the retention equals, in total, no less than 5% of the nominal value of the securitised exposures ('first loss' retention).

11.103

The purpose of the risk retention rules under CRR and now the Securitisation Regulation is to ensure that the originator, sponsor, or original lender behind the securitisation retains sufficient 'skin in the game'. The intent is to ensure that the creators of the exposures underlying the securitisation retain at least some of the risk in those exposures, with the hope that this will discourage the creation of poor-quality exposures that are created solely for the purpose of being securitised.

11.104

For these purposes, an 'originator' is defined as an entity which:

11.105

1. itself or through related entities, directly or indirectly, was involved in the original agreement which created the obligations or potential obligations of the debtor or potential debtor giving rise to the exposure being securitised; or
2. purchases a third-party's exposures for its own account and then securitises them.

A 'sponsor' under CRR was defined as an institution that established and managed an asset-backed commercial paper programme or other securitisation scheme that purchased exposures from third-party entities. For these purposes, an 'institution' included either credit institutions or investment firms that were subject to the requirements of MiFID II. Consequently, an investment firm established in a third country that was not subject to the requirements of MiFID II was not able to act as a risk retainer for CRR purposes.

11.106

The nature of CRR risk retention regime was essentially that of an indirect obligation. The regime did not impose any obligations directly on the originator, sponsor, or original lender of the securitisation—rather the obligations were imposed on any authorised EEA institutions that sought to invest in the securitisation. Authorised institutions that invested in a securitisation where there was no valid disclosure concerning risk retention, or that had not conducted appropriate due diligence on the risks of the securitisation, were effectively

11.107

penalised through the imposition of punitive 'risk weightings' on such non-compliant securitisation positions. These punitive risk-weightings could be as high as 1,250%, vastly increasing the amount of capital that an investing EEA institution would require in order to maintain its exposure to the securitisation (and causing a corresponding impact on the liquidity of such exposures amongst EEA-based institutions).

11.10.2 Securitisation Regulation and Brexit

11.108 The CRR risk retention regime formed part of a patchwork of different risk retention regimes across European sectoral legislation. In addition to the CRR regime, there were also separate similar (but not identical) regimes applicable to alternative investment fund managers under the AIFMD and to insurance firms under the Solvency II.

11.109 These regimes were harmonised for the first time with the entry into effect of the Securitisation Regulation ((EU) 2017/2402) (the '**Securitisation Regulation**') on 1 January 2019. The Securitisation Regulation applies the same risk retention rules to credit institutions, investment firms, fund managers and insurance firms. In addition, the Securitisation Regulation changed the nature of the risk retention obligation. Under Article 6 of the Securitisation Regulation, originators, sponsors, and original lenders are under a direct obligation to retain an ongoing material net economic interest of not less than 5% in the securitisation. This direct risk retention obligation applies to all originators, sponsors, and original lenders that are established in the EEA, along with the continuation of the indirect obligation for EEA institutional investors to verify that the originator, sponsor, or original lender retains an interest in accordance with Article 6. For originators, sponsors, or original lenders established outside of the EEA, there is no direct obligation, but EEA-based investors continue to be subject to punitive risk weightings if they invest in a securitisation where there is no valid disclosure by the originator, sponsor, or original lender concerning risk retention.

11.110 It is worth noting that a side product of this move to a combined direct and indirect risk retention obligation is that the definition of 'sponsor' has changed to allow an entity that is a non-EEA credit institution or investment firm to be regarded as a 'sponsor' for risk retention purposes. In particular, the reference to 'credit institution' in the definition of sponsor now refers to 'a credit institution, whether located in the Union or not'. The reference to 'investment firm' has also removed the previous language about being an investment firm subject to the requirements of MiFID II, again indicating that the definition of sponsor has extended to non-EEA investment firms. This could prove to be a very helpful change for UK-based sponsors, as such entities would be able to continue to act as sponsors post-Brexit, despite the fact that they would become third country entities. However, post-Brexit, such entities would (under the European *acquis*) no longer be regarded as EEA-based sponsors and so would not be subject to the direct risk retention obligation under Article 6 of the Securitisation Regulation. They would, however, remain subject to the equivalent obligation as incorporated into the UK *acquis*.

11.111 A further change under the Securitisation Regulation is the introduction of a regime for 'simple, transparent and standardised securitisations' (hereafter '**STS securitisations**').

The purpose of the STS regime is to provide a more risk-sensitive prudential treatment for simple securitisation structures, to distinguish such instruments (and their regulatory capital treatment) from more complex, opaque, or risky instruments. The Securitisation Regulation imposes lengthy and detailed conditions that have to be complied with in order for a securitisation to qualify as an STS securitisation. However, provided these obligations are met, then an EEA institutional investor in a securitisation can benefit from preferential regulatory capital treatment. For CRD IV firms, this preferential treatment has been provided for in amendments to Chapter 5 of Title II of CRR as a result of the CRR Amendment Regulation ((EU) 2017/2401).

One of the key requirements in order for a securitisation to be considered as an STS securitisation is that the originator, sponsor, or original lender has to be established in the EU. Post-Brexit, this will effectively prohibit securitisations with UK-based originators, sponsors, or original lenders from being regarded, or from continuing to be regarded, as STS securitisations. This could have a significant impact on existing positions held by European institutions in STS securitisations where the originator, sponsor, or original lender is based in the UK, with the result that such exposures will lose the benefit of the preferential regulatory capital treatment. This, in turn, would impact the liquidity of such instruments in the European market. However, such instruments would not necessarily become subject to any punitive risk weightings, as it would still be possible for a non-STS securitisation to otherwise comply with the risk retention obligations in the Securitisation Regulation. 11.112

The Securitisation (Amendment) (EU Exit) Regulations 2019 will amend the Securitisation Regulation as implemented in the UK from Brexit day. As described in HM Treasury's explanatory text,[36] the amendment seeks to remedy the deficiencies caused as a result of onshoring the Securitisation Regulation. For example, the obligation under Article 18 of the Securitisation Regulation that originators, sponsors, and original lenders of an STS securitisation have to be established in the EU will be amended in stages: 11.113

1. Securitisations recognised as STS in the EU before Brexit day, and added during a subsequent two-year transition period, will continue to be recognised as STS in the UK.
2. Thereafter, asset-backed commercial paper (**ABCP**) cross-border securitisations will be eligible for STS recognition in the UK where the sponsor is located in the UK, even where the SSPE and/or originator are located outside the UK. Non-ABCP cross-border securitisations will be eligible for UK STS recognition where the sponsor and originator are located in the UK.

However, this puts the UK in the position of operating a parallel regime where UK entities have to comply with detailed STS securitisation requirements, but without the benefit of being able to market such interests to European investors as an STS securitisation. The continued operation of such a parallel regime may, therefore, be of limited value. 11.114

It remains possible that the UK could, in due course, seek to distinguish the UK STS securitisation regime from the equivalent European regime. For example, the UK could 11.115

---

[36] HM Treasury, Securitisation (Amendment) (EU Exit) Regulations 2019: explanatory information (19 December 2018) <https://www.gov.uk/government/publications/draft-securitisation-amendment-eu-exit-regulations-2019/the-securitisation-amendment-eu-exit-regulations-2019-explanatory-information--2>

consider simplifying the currently very detailed conditions required in order for a securitisation to qualify as an STS securitisation. Either way, there is scope for the UK to adopt innovative approaches to the regulation of equivalent STS securitisation structures post-Brexit, especially given the limited benefits of maintaining the existing European requirements.

12
Bank Recovery and Resolution Directive (BRRD)

Jan Putnis and Chris Hurn

12.1 Introduction

Notwithstanding recent UK government and EU Commission efforts to agree a Withdrawal Agreement and Political Declaration (discussed in detail in Chapter Two), there remains considerable uncertainty over the final terms on which the UK will leave the EU (if at all). In the absence of certainty over the future legal relationship between the UK and the EU once the UK leaves the EU, this chapter assumes that the UK will, at that point, become a third country for the purposes of the BRRD and that the UK will treat EU Member States as third countries for the purposes of the UK's recovery and resolution regime (the **UK Regime**). On that assumption, Brexit may have a profound impact on the tools available to UK and EU regulators and resolution authorities relating to the recovery and resolution of failing banks, building societies, and systemically important investment firms., under legislation made by the UK government under the European Union (Withdrawal) Act 2018 (as amended) (the **Withdrawal Act**),[1] once the UK leaves the EU the legal and regulatory framework that provides for the UK recovery and resolution regime will operate independently of the equivalent EEA framework.

12.1

Despite the UK government's stated aim of ensuring that the UK Regime retains the policy aims of the current, pan-EEA recovery and resolution framework, inevitably, the post-Brexit UK Regime will look and may operate very differently as regards the recovery and resolution of institutions and groups that have an EEA presence. This is due in part to the fact that the UK will regard EEA member states as third countries for the purposes of its regime. It is also a consequence of the fact that UK regulatory authorities will no longer be required to participate in the operational and procedural mechanisms under EU law that ensure cooperation among EEA resolution authorities.

12.2

As a practical matter, the UK is expected to continue to engage with international counterparts, but the removal of legal requirements in this area will reduce legal certainty considerably. This chapter highlights this change and discusses its potential impact on the conduct of recovery and resolution activity by UK regulators and resolution authorities.

12.3

---

[1] Save where indicated otherwise, the terms of that Act and the powers granted to the UK government under that Act are outside the scope of this chapter.

12.2 Background to the UK Regime

12.2.1 UK Framework

12.4 The UK Regime is set out primarily in the Banking Act 2009 (as amended, the **Banking Act**).

12.5 The preparatory work that led to the Banking Act began in 2007, in response to the 2007–9 global financial crisis, and was led by HM Treasury, the Bank of England (the **BoE**), and the Financial Services Authority, the predecessor regulator to the Prudential Regulation Authority (the **PRA**), and the Financial Conduct Authority (the **FCA**).[2] That crisis saw the failure of a number of financial institutions, including, in the UK, Northern Rock and Bradford & Bingley and the injection of public money into a number of others, including, most notably, the Royal Bank of Scotland and Lloyds/HBOS Groups. In common with their overseas counterparts, the UK authorities lacked the tools to resolve such institutions in an orderly fashion. As a result, the UK, among other EU Member States, was forced to bail out a number of these institutions at great cost to taxpayers.

12.6 In parallel with the development of the Banking Act in the UK, other states and international bodies began work on similar national and international measures. For example, at leaders' summits in 2008 and 2009, the G20 identified a need to, 'lay the foundation for reform to help ensure that a global crisis, such as [the GFC], does not happen again',[3] and to, 'develop resolution tools and frameworks for effective resolution of financial groups to help mitigate the disruption of financial institution failures and reduce moral hazard in the future'.[4] The Financial Stability Board (the **FSB**) published a paper entitled 'Key Attributes of Effective Resolution Regimes for Financial Institutions' (the **Key Attributes**) in October 2011, which were endorsed by the G20 leaders in November 2011.[5]

12.2.2 BRRD Framework

12.7 At an EU level, recovery and resolution tools are set out in the Bank Recovery and Resolution Directive (the **BRRD**)[6] and its associated delegated acts, technical standards, and guidelines (the **BRRD framework**), a significant proportion of which is directly effective in the UK.

12.8 The BRRD entered into force on 2 July 2014. Member States were required to implement the BRRD by 31 December 2014, and to put into effect the majority of the provisions of the BRRD from 1 January 2015.

---

[2] HM Treasury, the Bank, and the FSA published a discussion paper, *Banking Reform—Protecting Depositors*, in October 2007. The paper explored ways to strengthen the then existing framework for financial stability and depositor protection.

[3] G20 leaders' Washington summit declaration, p. 1.

[4] G20 leaders' Pittsburgh summit final declaration, p. 9.

[5] The FSB adopted the Key Attributes in October 2011. The Key Attributes were updated on 15 October 2014 (see: <https://www.fsb.org/wp-content/uploads/r_141015.pdf>).

[6] Directive 2014/59/EU of the European Parliament and of the Council of 15 May 2014 establishing a framework for the recovery and resolution of credit institutions and investment firms and amending Council Directive 82/891/EEC, and Directives 2001/24/EC, 2002/47/EC, 2004/25/EC, 2005/56/EC, 2007/36/EC, 2011/35/EU, 2012/30/EU, 2013/36/EU, and Regulations (EU) No. 1093/2010 and (EU) No. 648/2012, of the European Parliament and of the Council.

12.9 On 9 February 2018, a decision[7] was adopted by the EEA Joint Committee that will incorporate the BRRD into the EEA Agreement, subject to the decision being published in the EU Official Journal. The effect of incorporating the BRRD into the EEA Agreement will be to apply the BRRD to all non-EU EEA states.[8] It is assumed that this will occur. This chapter therefore discusses the BRRD framework in terms of it being an EEA-level framework.

12.10 In broad terms, the tools and powers provided by the BRRD can be divided into three areas:

1. preparation and prevention: the preparation of recovery and resolution plans, resolvability, and intragroup financial support arrangements;
2. early intervention: the powers of prudential regulators to impose certain requirements on institutions experiencing severe financial difficulties, before resolution actions become necessary; and
3. resolution tools: the tools and powers of resolution authorities necessary to facilitate the resolution of a failing institution and its holding company, such as the powers to sell the institution or holding company or all or part of its business, and powers to 'bail in' creditors.

12.11 The BRRD provides for cooperation among EEA prudential regulators and resolution authorities in a number of areas within the BRRD framework. As we discuss in this chapter, UK government amendments to the UK Regime will remove UK requirements for UK regulators to cooperate with and consider the views of their EEA counterparts.

12.12 The BRRD empowers the European Commission to adopt delegated acts in certain areas. The delegated acts adopted by the European Commission in accordance with the BRRD are delegated regulations, which are directly effective in Member States, and do not therefore need to be implemented separately into domestic law.

12.13 The BRRD also requires the European Banking Authority (the **EBA**) to produce regulatory technical standards and implementing technical standards for adoption by the European Commission (together, **BTS**), and to issue guidelines and recommendations in certain areas. BTS have direct effect in Member States. Guidelines and recommendations are not binding, but competent authorities and institutions must make every effort to comply with them.

12.2.3 UK Implementation of the BRRD Framework

12.14 Where necessary, the UK government has implemented the BRRD framework into domestic UK legislation by way of a number of statutory instruments, including, by way of supplement and amendment to the Banking Act, the Bank Recovery and Resolution Order 2014 (as amended, the **BRRO**),[9] and the Bank Recovery and Resolution (No. 2) Order 2014 (as amended, the **BRRO2**).[10] Parts of the BRRD framework have also been implemented in PRA and FCA rules.

---

[7] Joint Committee Decision No. 021/2018.
[8] Iceland, Lichtenstein, and Norway.
[9] Bank Recovery and Resolution Order 2014 (SI 2014/3329).
[10] Bank Recovery and Resolution (No. 2) Order 2014 (SI 2014/3348).

12.15 The BRRO amended, among other things, the Banking Act, to align the UK Regime with the BRRD, and to extend the powers of the BoE to intervene in failing institutions before resolving them. It also amended the Financial Services and Markets Act 2000 (FSMA), to implement the requirements of the BRRD as regards the powers of the successors to the FSA, the PRA, and the FCA.

12.16 The BRRO2 sets out the powers of the BoE, the PRA, the FCA, and HM Treasury when performing their functions under the UK Regime, including in relation to cooperation with their counterparts in other EU Member States and with third countries.

12.3 Overview of UK Legislation That Will Amend the UK Regime

12.17 The UK government has used powers granted to it under the Withdrawal Act to make a number of regulations seeking to address deficiencies in what will become retained EU law in the UK Regime.

12.18 The following paragraphs summarise measures that will amend the statutory and regulatory basis of the UK Regime. References in this chapter to statutory and regulatory provisions should be construed as those provisions as amended by those measures.

12.3.1 The BRR Brexit Regulations

12.19 The Bank Recovery and Resolution and Miscellaneous Provisions (Amendment) (EU Exit) Regulations 2018 were made on 20 December 2018 (the **BRR Brexit Regulations**).[11] The BRR Brexit Regulations amend the Banking Act, among other pieces of primary UK legislation,[12] and certain pieces of secondary legislation, including the BRRO2. The BRR Brexit Regulations also revoke certain retained EU law[13] and amend other retained EU law.[14]

12.20 The main aim of the BRR Brexit Regulations is to ensure that the UK Regime is 'legally and practicably workable on a standalone basis'[15] following Brexit. Therefore, the BRR Brexit Regulations propose a number of amendments to retained EU law to cure deficiencies that will arise as a result of the UK no longer being part of the EU. The UK Regime will, however, retain the policy aims of the BRRD and continue to be consistent with the FSB Key Attributes.[16]

12.21 Despite the UK government's statement regarding continuity of policy under the post-Brexit UK Regime, two types of amendments made by the BRR Brexit Regulations will make fundamental changes to the way that the UK Regime operates in relation to the BRRD

---

[11] Bank Recovery and Resolution and Miscellaneous Provisions (Amendment) (EU Exit) Regulations 2018 (SI 2018/1394).
[12] Insolvency Act 1986 and Financial Services (Banking Reform) Act 2013.
[13] Commission Delegated Regulation (EU) 2015/63; Commission Delegated Regulation (EU) 2016/1434; Commission Delegated Regulation (EU) 2017/867.
[14] Commission Delegated Regulation (EU) 2016/778 and Commission Delegated Regulation (EU) 2016/860.
[15] BRR Brexit Regulations: Explanatory information, para. 3, published by HM Treasury on 8 October 2018.
[16] See paragraph 12.6. The current version of the Key Attributes was published on 15 October 2014.

framework as implemented in the EU. One of those types of amendments is that the UK will treat EU Member States as third countries under the UK Regime. In turn, the UK will treat EU-led resolutions of banks as third country-led resolutions. This means, for example, that there will be no automatic recognition in the UK of the exercise of powers by resolution authorities in the EU.

Another crucial type of amendment in this regard is that the BRR Brexit Regulations revoke the UK implementation of BRRD requirements relating to operational and procedural mechanisms that EU Member State regulators must use to cooperate with each other. For example, the provisions in UK law that require the UK's participation in the framework provided by the cross-border group resolution provisions in the BRRO2 will be removed.[17] That framework comprises rules on cross-border coordination (e.g. participation in resolution colleges), cooperation (e.g. in accordance with framework agreements with third countries adopted by the EBA), and notification (e.g. to other EEA resolution authorities). The new third country status for EU Member States and the removal of the UK from aspects of the BRRD framework that relate to cross-border cooperation are discussed further below.

12.3.2 The Regulators' Powers Regulations

The Financial Regulators' Powers (Technical Standards etc.) (Amendment etc.) (EU Exit) Regulations 2018 (the **Regulators' Powers Regulations**),[18] which were made on 25 October 2018, give the BoE, the PRA, the FCA, and the Payment Systems Regulator powers to address deficiencies arising from the UK's withdrawal from the EU in specified EU regulations[19] and in EU-derived provisions in the regulators' respective rulebooks.[20] The Bank is the appropriate regulator for certain EU regulations,[21] and both the PRA and the FCA are the appropriate regulators for certain other EU regulations.[22] In each case, those EU regulations are BTS made in relation to the BRRD.

12.3.3 Regulators' Transitional Powers

The Bank, the PRA, and the FCA have powers to give transitional directions waiving or modifying firms' UK regulatory obligations where those obligations have changed as a result of the onshoring of EU legislation under the Withdrawal Act.[23] Those existing powers therefore go further than the regulators' powers under section 138A of FSMA to modify or waive regulatory rules.

---

[17] BRRO2, Part 16.
[18] SI 2018/1115.
[19] Defined in Reg. 2(l) of the Regulators' Powers Regulations as the EU Regulations or parts of EU Regulations forming part of retained EU law which are specified in the schedule to that instrument.
[20] Defined in Reg. 2(f) of the Regulators' Powers Regulation as the rules and other enactments made by the FCA, the PRA, or the BoE which fall within the definition of 'EU-derived domestic legislation' within the meaning the Withdrawal Act, s. 2(2).
[21] Regulators' Powers Regulation, paras. 104–113 (inclusive) of the schedule.
[22] Ibid., paras. 124–125.
[23] Pursuant to Part 7 ('Transitional Powers of the Financial Regulators') of the Financial Services and Markets Act 2000 (Amendment) (EU Exit) Regulations 2019.

12.3.4 Guidelines and Recommendations

12.25 Guidelines and recommendations of European Supervisory Authorities such as those of the EBA are not incorporated into UK domestic law by the Withdrawal Act, and HM Treasury has stated that it intends to revoke the regulations requiring UK authorities and firms to make every effort to comply with them. However, the BoE and the PRA continue to expect firms to make every effort to comply with guidelines and recommendations which are relevant to regulatory requirements that will apply to them following Brexit.[24]

12.3.5 BRRD II

12.26 On 20 May 2019, a directive containing a package of amendments to the BRRD was published in the Official Journal of the EU (**BRRD II**).[25] BRRD II came into force on 27 June 2019, and Member States are required to implement the majority of the provisions in the directive by 28 December 2020.

12.27 Under the Financial Services (Implementation of Legislation) Bill, which fell when Parliament was dissolved in advance of the 2019 UK general election, HM Treasury would have been empowered to make corresponding or similar provisions in UK law to reflect forthcoming EU financial services legislation in the event that the UK leaves the European Union without a deal.[26] At the time of writing, it is not clear whether the Bill will be reintroduced in the next Parliament and HM Treasury has not made the regulations required to implement BRRD II in the UK. However, the following sections describe the key amendments to the BRRD that will be brought about by the BRRD II and assumes that those changes will ultimately be implemented in the UK Regime. We should note, however, that this might not happen.

12.4 What the UK Regime Will Look Like after Brexit

12.4.1 Overview of the Regime

12.28 The purpose of the UK Regime for banks is to address the situation where all or part of the business of a bank has encountered, or is likely to encounter, financial difficulties.[27] The UK Regime consists of the stabilisation options,[28] the bank insolvency procedure,[29] and the bank administration procedure.[30]

---

[24] Joint Bank of England and PRA Statement of Policy, 'Interpretation of EU Guidelines and Recommendations: Bank of England and PRA Approach after the UK's Withdrawal from the EU', 18 April 2019, para. 2.1.

[25] Directive (EU) 2019/879 of the European Parliament and of the Council of 20 May 2019 amending Directive 2014/59/EU as regards the loss-absorbing and recapitalisation capacity of credit institutions and investment firms and Directive 98/26/EC.

[26] Financial Services (Implementation of Legislation) Bill, s. 1.

[27] Banking Act, s. 1(1).

[28] Ibid., ss. 11, 12, 12ZA, 12A, and 13.

[29] Ibid., Part 2. The bank insolvency procedure is currently subject to the requirements of the Credit Institutions (Reorganisation and Winding up) Regulations 2004 (SI 2004/1045), which implement Directive 2001/24/EC on the organisation and winding up of credit institutions. In summary, those regulations determine, for the purposes of English law, the EEA state that will oversee insolvency proceedings for institutions, and the extent of the Banks's powers as regards those proceedings.

[30] Banking Act, Part 3.

12.29 The UK Regime applies principally to undertakings with permission under Part 4A of FSMA to accept deposits,[31] such as UK banks, excluding credit unions[32] (absent an order from HM Treasury including them within the application of the UK Regime)[33] and other types of institution that are excluded by an order made by HM Treasury[34] (such as insurers that have permission under FSMA to accept deposits).[35]

12.30 The UK Regime also applies in modified ways to: (1) building societies;[36] (2) systemically important investment firms;[37] (3) recognised central counterparties;[38] (4) banking group companies;[39] (5) banks not regulated by the PRA;[40] and (6) UK branches of third country institutions[41] (together with UK banks and the undertakings in (1) to (5) (inclusive), **Institutions**).[42]

12.4.2 Preparatory Measures: Recovery Plans

12.31 The basic obligations in the UK Regime relating to the preparation, assessment and review[43] of recovery plans,[44] group recovery plans,[45] the relevant PRA, and the FCA

---

[31] Ibid., s. 2(1).
[32] Ibid., s. 2(2)(b).
[33] Ibid., s. 89.
[34] Ibid., s. 2(2)(c).
[35] Banking Act 2009 (Exclusion of Insurers) Order 2010, Art. 2.
[36] Defined in s. 2(2)(a) of the Banking Act by reference to s. 119 of the Building Societies Act 1986. Section 84 of the Banking Act applies Part 1 of that Act to building societies in a modified way. Parts 2 and 3 of that Act apply to building societies in a modified way pursuant to the Building Societies (Insolvency and Special Administration) Order 2009, which was made by the Treasury under ss. 130 and 158 of the Banking Act.
[37] Defined in the Banking Act, s. 258A and Art. 2(1) of the Banking Act 2009 (Exclusion of Investment Firms of a Specified Description) Order 2014 as a UK institution which is (or, but for the exercise of a stabilisation power, would be) an investment firm for the purposes of Regulation (EU) No. 575/2013 of the European Parliament and of the Council as it had effect on the day on which the BRR Brexit Regulations were made, that is required for the purposes of Directive 2013/36/EU of the European Parliament and of the Council of 26 June 2013 on access to the activity of credit institutions and the prudential supervision of credit institutions and investment firms, amending Directive 2002/87/EC and repealing Directives 2006/48/EC and 2006/49/EC (**CRD IV**) to have an initial capital of €750,000 or more, but excluding an institution that is also a bank, a building society or a credit union. Section 89A of the Banking Act applies Part 1 of that Act to such firms in a modified way.
[38] Defined in s. 89G of the Banking Act by reference to s. 285 of FSMA. Sections 89B to 89G of the Banking Act apply Part 1 of that Act to recognised central counterparties in a modified way.
[39] Sections 81AA–81D of the Banking Act apply Part 1 of that Act to banking group companies in a modified way. The term 'banking group company' is defined in s. 81D of the Banking Act and includes certain companies in the same group as a bank that are not banks themselves.
[40] This type of firm would fall within the definition of 'bank' in the Banking Act, but would not carry on any activity which is a PRA-regulated activity for the purposes of FSMA. It is not currently possible for a firm to be a UK bank but not regulated by the PRA. However, ss. 83A, 129A, and 157A of the Banking Act apply Parts 1, 2, and 3 of that Act, respectively, to such firms in a modified way.
[41] The term 'third country institution' is defined in s. 89H(7) of the Banking Act (as amended by the BRR Brexit Regulations, Sch.1, para. 41(4)(b)) as: 'an institution established in a country or territory other than the United Kingdom that would, if it were established within the United Kingdom, be regarded as a bank, building society, credit union or investment firm'. Section 89JA (as amended by the BRR Brexit Regulations) applies Part 1 of the Banking Act to branches of third country institutions in a modified way.
[42] Unless otherwise stated, references in this chapter to provisions of the UK Regime should be read as references to those provisions as modified in accordance with the Banking Act to suit the relevant type of firm.
[43] BRRO2, Arts. 7, 11–32 (inclusive) and 33–35 (inclusive).
[44] Defined in Art. 2(1) as 'a document which provides for measures to be taken by an institution authorised by the PRA or FCA which is not part of a group, following a significant deterioration in the financial position of the institution, in order to restore its financial position' (ibid.).
[45] Defined in Art. 2(1) as, 'a document which provides for measures to be taken in relation to a relevant group to achieve the stabilisation of the group as a whole, or of any institution within the group, where the group or the institution is in a situation of financial stress, in order to address or remove the causes of the financial stress and restore the financial position of the group or institution' (ibid.).

rules[46] will be amended to apply solely to UK undertakings and UK supervisory and commercial activities. This will be achieved principally through the removal of references to the EEA and to EEA supervisory authorities. For instance, the term 'group', which is currently defined for these purposes as a 'group constituted by an EEA parent undertaking and its subsidiaries', will be amended to mean 'a parent undertaking and its subsidiaries'.[47]

12.32 As at present, Institutions will be required to draw up, maintain, and submit recovery plans,[48] and, if they are a UK parent undertaking of a group that is subject to consolidated group supervision, group recovery plans (if relevant),[49] to the PRA and/or the FCA (as appropriate). Subject to the PRA/FCA power to require the inclusion of additional information in those plans,[50] Institutions will be required to prepare recovery plans containing at least the information set out in section A1 of the BRRO2 and Commission Delegated Regulation 2016/1075 (the **Delegated Regulation**).[51]

12.33 Schedule A1 of the BRRO2 consolidates the information listed in Section A of the Annex to the BRRD ('Information to be included in recovery plans') and the other requirements relating to the content of recovery plans set out Articles 5 to 9 of the BRRD. There is no indication at the time of writing that those requirements will be amended as they apply in the UK in connection with Brexit.

12.34 The consolidation generally replicates the current BRRD requirements (as implemented), save that Schedule A1 will require Institutions to ensure that their recovery plans include the following additional information:

(1) evidence that the management body of the Institution has assessed and approved the plan before the plan is submitted to the appropriate regulator—the BRRD and the relevant current PRA rules[52] only require Institutions to ensure that their management bodies oversee, assess, and approve recovery plans prior to submission;

(2) an appropriate framework of indicators established by the Institution which identifies the points at which the appropriate actions referred to in the plan may be taken—the BRR Brexit Regulations insert the word 'appropriate' before 'framework', which arguably sets a higher standard for Institutions to meet in this regard than under the pre-Brexit rules; and

(3) details of appropriate arrangements which the Institution has put in place for the regular monitoring of the indicators referred to above—at present, Institutions are only required to have in place such arrangements, not provide the details of those arrangements in their recovery plans.[53]

---

[46] In the Recovery Plans Part of the PRA Rulebook and in IFPRU 11.2 ('Individual recovery plans'), IFPRU 11.3 ('Group recovery plans'), and IFPRU 11 Annex 1 of the FCA Handbook of Rules and Guidance (the **FCA Handbook**).
[47] Defined in BRRO2, Art. 2(1).
[48] Recovery Plans Part of the PRA Rulebook, ch. 2 and IFPRU 11.2 in the FCA Handbook, respectively.
[49] Recovery Plans Part of the PRA Rulebook, ch. 3 and IFPRU 11.3 in the FCA Handbook, respectively.
[50] BRRO2, Art. 7(3).
[51] Onshored pursuant to the Withdrawal Act, s. 3 and amended by Annex B of the Technical Standards (Bank Recovery and Resolution) (Amendment etc.) (EU Exit) (No. 1) Instrument 2019.
[52] BRRD, Arts. 5(9) and 7(7) and Recovery Plans Part of the PRA Rulebook, ch. 5, respectively.
[53] BRRD, Art. 9(1) and Recovery Plans Part of the PRA Rulebook, ch. 6.

12.35 Institutions will be required to base their recovery plans on certain assumptions, such as the assumption that the Institution or group concerned will not have access to or receipt of extraordinary public financial resources,[54] and to stress-test their recovery plans against a range of scenarios of severe macroeconomic and financial stress relevant to the firm's or the group's specific conditions.[55] EBA guidance on the range of those scenarios[56] will continue to be relevant to UK banks. Recovery plans and group recovery plans must also set out a framework of indicators which identify the points at which actions identified in the recovery plan may be taken.[57]

12.36 The appropriate regulator will be required[58] to assess recovery plans against the criteria set out in:

(1) Schedule A1 of the BRRO2, to determine whether such plans would be reasonably likely to be effective and implemented quickly and effectively in situations of financial stress and, as far as possible, without any material adverse impact on the financial system of the United Kingdom;[59] and
(2) the Delegated Regulation.[60]

12.37 Where an Institution is part of a consolidation group, the appropriate regulator will need to conduct its assessment of the group recovery plan in cooperation with the BoE and the PRA or the FCA where either is not the appropriate regulator but supervises a group entity that is an authorised person under FSMA.[61] This cooperation will require the exchange of information (for instance, the duty to transmit a copy of the group recovery plan to the BoE and the PRA or FCA as appropriate).[62]

12.38 Although consistent with the UK government's stated aim of amending UK legislation to work independently of EU legislation post-Brexit, the fact is that the UK regulators will no longer be required to share recovery plans with their EEA counterparts or take into account their recommendations in relation to recovery plans—as is the case prior to Brexit—where groups contain relevant EEA regulated firms. Cross-border cooperation on the assessment of recovery plans is an important aspect of the EEA recovery planning regime in the BRRD. It seems logical that UK regulators would, in practice, engage in similar cross-border cooperation post-Brexit. However, in the absence of a legal requirement to do so, it is uncertain that such cooperation will continue and opportunities to deepen cooperation may not arise so readily.

---

[54] Recovery Plans Part of the PRA Rulebook, ch. 2.5 and IFRPU 11.2.10R in the FCA Handbook, respectively.
[55] Recovery Plans Part of the PRA Rulebook, ch. 2.10 and IFPRU 11.2.9G (in respect of individual recovery plans) and IFPRU 11.3.11G (in respect of group recovery plans) in the FCA Handbook, respectively, implement the requirement in BRRD, Art. 5(6).
[56] On 18 July 2014, the EBA issued, 'Guidelines on the Range of Scenarios to Be Used in Recovery Plans'.
[57] Recovery Plans Part of the PRA Rulebook, ch. 6 and IFPRU 11.2.12R in the FCA Handbook, respectively.
[58] BRRO2, Art. 12(1).
[59] Ibid., Art. 13(1).
[60] Delegated Regulation, Arts. 17–21 (inclusive).
[61] BRRO2, Arts. 16–32 (inclusive).
[62] Ibid., Art. 17.

12.4.3 Preparatory Measures: Resolution Planning

12.39 As with recovery planning, the substance of the current provisions relating to resolution planning[63] are retained save to the extent they require cross-border cooperation with EEA counterpart regulation and resolution authorities. For instance, the BoE will still be required to draw up[64] and review[65] resolution plans[66] and group resolution plans[67] on the basis of information provided for that purpose by the relevant Institution (as required by the relevant PRA[68] or FCA rules)[69] or the appropriate regulator.[70]

12.40 The Bank must also ensure that resolution plans cover the information requirements set out in Schedules 2 and 2A of the BRRO2 and any additional information covered by Schedule 2B of the BRRO2 that it determines is required.[71] In so doing, the BoE must also assess the resolvability[72] of the Institution or group concerned, with particular regard to ensuring the continuity of the Institution's or the group's critical functions[73] and the potential impact of such a resolution on the UK economy and financial system.

12.41 Although consistent with the UK government's stated aim of ensuring that the UK Regime functions effectively without relying on EU legislation or regulatory arrangements, and despite there being no obvious policy intent to avoid cross-border cooperation, inevitably, removing the relevant requirements for such cooperation creates a risk that international coordination in this area will diminish or be lacking. For instance, the fact that the BoE will not be required specifically[74] to consider the potential impact of a resolution plan on the economies or financial systems of EEA states could mean that potential adverse effects of UK resolution plans on the EEA go unconsidered. It is of course also the case that reciprocal

---

[63] Ibid., Arts. 8, 37, and 40.
[64] Ibid., Arts. 37 and 40.
[65] Ibid., Arts. 53–54.
[66] Defined in Art. 2(1) as a 'document which makes provision relating to the resolution action to be taken in the event that an institution or other person meets the conditions for resolution' (ibid.).
[67] Defined as a 'document which makes provision for—(a) taking resolution action in respect of the group, whether at the level of the parent undertaking or of an institution within the group; or (b) co-ordinating the application of resolution tools and the exercise of resolution powers by resolution authorities in respect of group entities that meet the conditions for resolution' (ibid.).
[68] Resolution Pack Part of the PRA Rulebook, ch. 2.
[69] IFPRU 11.4 in the FCA Handbook.
[70] BRRO2, Art. 37(3).
[71] Ibid., Art. 8.
[72] Required by Arts. 59–82 (inclusive) (ibid.). 'Resolvability assessment' is defined in Arts. 59(2) and 61(2) (ibid.) as an assessment of the extent to which it would be feasible and credible to apply the resolution tools, exercise resolution powers, or take insolvency proceedings in respect of the Institution or group entities concerned while avoiding to the maximum extent possible any significant adverse effect on the financial system of the UK or the continuity of the Institution's or group's critical functions, and interpreted in accordance with Art. 6 of Commission Delegated Regulation (EU) 2016/778 (onshored pursuant to the Withdrawal Act, s. 3 and amended by the BRR Brexit Regulations, Sch. 5, para. 1).
[73] Defined in the Banking Act, s. 3(1) as:

> activities, services or operations the discontinuance of which is likely (wherever carried out)—to lead to the disruption of services that are essential to the economy of the United Kingdom, or to disrupt financial stability in the United Kingdom, due to the size, market share, external and internal connectedness, complexity of cross-border activities of a bank or a group which includes a bank (with particular regard to the substitutability of those activities, services or operations).

[74] Pursuant to BRRO2, Sch. 2B, the Bank will be required to consider the extent to which: (a) the impact of the entity's resolution on the financial system and on confidence in financial markets can be adequately evaluated; and (b) the resolution of the entity could have a significant direct or indirect adverse effect on the financial system, market confidence, or the economy, among other things.

binding cooperation obligations under which EEA resolution authorities provide information to the BoE will, absent specific agreement to the contrary, also cease to have effect when the UK leaves the EU.

12.42 The Bank will also not be required to consult EEA resolution authorities where the resolution plan relates to an Institution with a significant branch located in an EEA state or to a group with one or more subsidiary undertakings located in an EEA state. Instead, as at present, the BoE may consult the relevant EEA resolution authorities as it may any other third country authorities in relation to the drawing up of resolution plans.[75] However, in the event of a dispute, the BoE will not be obliged to refer the matter to a higher authority, as it currently is in relation to referrals of disputes to the EBA. Although it seems likely that the BoE would continue to bear in mind the potential impact of faulty or inadequate resolution plans on overseas financial systems, there will be no requirement in the BRRO2 for the BoE to do so.

12.4.4 Preparatory Measures: Intragroup Financial Support Arrangements

12.43 Under the post-Brexit UK Regime, cross-border groups will continue to be permitted to provide intragroup financial support, albeit that the relevant rules[76] will be significantly broadened to include agreements between a relevant parent undertaking[77] and one or more group subsidiaries[78] established in any country other than UK (rather than any country other than an EEA state as is the case under the current UK Regime) (**Support Agreements**).

12.44 Under the post-Brexit rules, a group may not enter into a Support Agreement unless the terms of the agreement meet certain conditions[79] and the consolidating supervisor has approved the agreement.[80] The consolidating supervisor will be the competent authority responsible for the exercise of supervision on a consolidated basis of: (a) a UK parent institution; or (b) an institution controlled by a UK parent financial holding company or a UK parent mixed financial holding company.[81] The competent authority for these purposes will be:

(1) the PRA, in respect of PRA-authorised persons;
(2) in relation to a MiFID investment firm, the authority designated before exit day (as defined in the Withdrawal Act) by the UK in accordance with Article 67 of MiFID II (i.e. the FCA or the PRA); or
(3) the FCA, in respect of any other person.[82]

---

[75] Ibid., Art. 40(7).
[76] Ibid., Part 7.
[77] Defined in Art. 83(2) as a UK parent institution, a financial holding company, a mixed financial holding company, or a mixed-activity holding company established in the UK (ibid.).
[78] Defined as an undertaking which is: (a) a subsidiary of a relevant parent undertaking; and (b) an institution or financial institution (ibid.).
[79] Group Financial Support Part of the PRA Rulebook, ch. 2.1.
[80] Ibid., ch. 2.2.
[81] Defined in the Glossary to the PRA Rulebook.
[82] For definition, see ibid.

12.45 This means that only UK regulators, as opposed to relevant EEA regulators as at present, will be able to approve Support Agreements in relation to UK banks after Brexit. Similarly, an Institution intending to provide financial support will be required to notify: (a) the PRA; and (b) the FCA where it is the consolidating supervisor, rather than: (i) the PRA; (ii) where different, its EEA consolidating supervisor; (iii) where different to the PRA and the EEA consolidating supervisor, the competent authority of the group member receiving the financial support; and (iv) the EBA before providing that support.[83]

12.46 In line with the approach of creating a standalone UK Regime, the BRR Brexit Regulations also remove obligations on UK competent authorities to cooperate with their EEA counterparts when reviewing Support Agreements.[84]

12.4.5 Early Intervention

12.47 In keeping with the approach taken in other areas, the BRR Brexit Regulations retain in an amended form the early intervention powers[85] that the PRA and the FCA have as consolidating supervisors in respect of UK group entities,[86] while removing obligations and powers of the PRA and the FCA in relation to EEA regulators and non-UK firms.[87] Those are powers to intervene where an Institution breaches, or is likely in the near future to breach, its regulatory capital requirements, by taking one or more measures for early intervention.[88]

12.4.6 Resolution: Conditions

12.48 The PRA and the BoE must be satisfied that certain general conditions set out in the Banking Act are met before making use of the stabilisation options (described in paragraphs 12.4.7–12.4.13 below).[89] In summary, those conditions relate to whether the Institution may continue to carry on its business, either because it is failing, or is likely to fail, to satisfy the threshold conditions in FSMA,[90] or because it is, or in the near future will be, insolvent, in each case without the application of one or more stabilisation options.

12.49 The BoE must also be satisfied that certain other conditions are met. In summary, those conditions are that: (a) it is not reasonably likely that the Institution will take action to correct its position; (b) the exercise of the power is necessary; and (c) one or more of the BoE's special resolution objectives would not be met to the same extent by the winding up of

---

[83] Group Financial Support Part of the PRA Rulebook, ch. 6.
[84] BRR Brexit Regulations, Sch. 3, paras. 84–89 (inclusive) and 91–96 (inclusive).
[85] BRRO2, Arts. 107–120 (inclusive).
[86] For instance, the BRR Brexit Regulations, Sch. 3, para. 60(4) inserts a new definition of 'relevant measure' in BRRO2, Art. 107 that retains in onshored form the measures for early intervention set out in BRRD, Art. 27(1) to which the BRRO2 previously referred.
[87] BRR Brexit Regulations, Sch. 3, paras. 62–65 (inclusive).
[88] Defined in BRRO2, Art. 107.
[89] Banking Act, s. 7.
[90] As defined by FSMA, s. 55B(1) for which the PRA is treated as responsible under sub-s. (2) of that section.

the Institution (whether under the bank insolvency procedure provided by Part 2 of the Banking Act or otherwise).[91]

The Bank may also exercise certain stabilisation powers in respect of a banking group company[92] if certain conditions are met.[93] Post-Brexit, satisfaction of those conditions will no longer depend (in part) on determinations made by EU resolution authorities. **12.50**

12.4.7 Stabilisation Options: Overview

The five stabilisation options, which are not expected to change substantively in connection with Brexit, are transfer to a private sector purchaser,[94] transfer to a bridge bank,[95] transfer to an asset management vehicle,[96] the bail-in option;[97] and transfer to temporary public ownership.[98] **12.51**

Those stabilisation options may be achieved through the exercise of one or more of the 'stabilisation powers' by the BoE, which are the resolution instrument powers,[99] the share transfer powers,[100] and the property transfer powers.[101] **12.52**

The Bank also has the power to recognise or refuse all or part of third country resolution action in respect of a third country institution or third country parent undertaking.[102] Post-Brexit, institutions and parent undertakings established in the EEA will be third country institutions and parent undertakings for the purposes of those powers. Consistent with the approach to amendments made to other aspects of the UK Regime, the BoE will no longer be required to consider the potential impact of recognising third country resolution actions on the EEA.[103] **12.53**

12.4.8 Stabilisation Options: Bail-in

The Banking Act gives the BoE broad powers to bring about the absorption of the losses of, and to recapitalise, a failing Institution (i.e. to bail in its creditors) using the firm's own resources. This would be achieved by cancelling, transferring, or diluting the firm's capital **12.54**

---

[91] Banking Act, s. 7.
[92] Defined in the Banking Act, s. 81D as an undertaking which is (or, but for the exercise of a stabilisation power, would be) in the same group as a bank or third country institution, and which meets any other criteria set by HM Treasury for that purpose.
[93] The Group Conditions are set out in ss. 81B–81BA (inclusive) of the Banking Act (as amended by paras. 30–32 (inclusive) of the BRR Brexit Regulations, Sch. 1).
[94] Banking Act, s. 11.
[95] Ibid., s. 12.
[96] Ibid., s. 12ZA.
[97] Ibid., s. 12A.
[98] Ibid., s. 13.
[99] Ibid., ss. 12A(2) and 48U–48W (inclusive).
[100] Ibid., ss. 15, 16, 26–31 (inclusive), and 85.
[101] Ibid., ss. 33 and 41A–46 (inclusive).
[102] Ibid., ss. 89H, 89I, and 89J.
[103] For instance, the Bank will be required to consider whether recognition would have an adverse impact on the financial stability of the UK only, rather than another EEA state also (ibid., s. 89H(4) (as amended by the BRR Brexit Regulations, Sch. 1, para. 41(2)).

instruments.[104] The Bank may also cancel or modify any liability owed by the Institution save for liabilities that are excluded in accordance with the Banking Act (e.g. covered deposits).[105]

12.55 Institutions and qualifying parent undertakings[106] of those Institutions are required to include in agreements for liabilities (except excluded liabilities) governed by the law of a third country, a contractual term by which the creditor or party to the agreement creating the liability recognises that liability may be subject to the exercise of a bail-in power by the BoE and agrees to be bound by any reduction of the principal or outstanding amount due, conversion or cancellation that is effected by the exercise of those powers by the BoE (the **Article 55 Requirement**).[107] As noted above, in many respects, EEA states will be treated as third countries under UK law after the UK has ceased to be a member of the EU. However, a transitional provision in the relevant PRA and FCA rules provides that the Article 55 Requirement will not apply to contracts made before exit day that are governed by the law of an EEA State unless and until their terms are materially amended.[108]

12.56 The Article 55 Requirement does not apply where an EEA resolution authority determines that the relevant liabilities or instruments can be subject to write down and conversion powers by EEA resolution authorities pursuant to the law of a third country or to a binding agreement with that third country.[109] In light of the post-Brexit UK process for recognising EEA resolution actions which, post-Brexit, will be treated in the same way as all third country resolution actions are treated under section 89H of the Banking Act, there is a risk that the Single Resolution Board and/or other resolution authorities in the EEA could take the view that this exemption cannot reliably be used by EEA banks (or their subsidiaries) which are party to contracts governed by English law. This will be a particular problem for contracts and securities issued by EEA banks existing at the time when the UK withdraws from the EU because the terms of such contracts generally cannot be amended without counterparty consent, which in the context of securities issues may be impossible to obtain, and may in any event be costly to seek. More generally, however, the Article 55 Requirement could ultimately discourage some EEA banks from contracting and issuing securities under English law post-Brexit.

12.57 Given the volume of issuance of securities under English law, in the long term, this could threaten an important stream of work for the legal services sector in the UK, although at the time of writing, this is not yet happening. A provision which makes clear that the UK will recognise EEA resolution actions would be an important step in avoiding this, again,

---

[104] Ibid., s. 6B.
[105] Ibid., s. 48B.
[106] Defined in FSMA, s. 192B.
[107] So-called because this requirement originates in BRRD, Art. 55.
[108] The Contractual Recognition of Bail-in Part of the PRA Rulebook. In addition, that Part of the PRA Rulebook previously required that in respect of a liability that is an additional tier 1 (AT1) or tier 2 (T2) capital instrument, firms must provide an independent legal opinion regarding the enforceability and effectiveness of the required contractual term. The PRA has made a minor amendment, to provide firms with certainty that this requirement will now only apply where the requirement to add the contractual term also applies. As such, there will be no requirement for a legal opinion in respect of EEA law governed AT1 or T2 capital instruments that were issued before the UK's departure from the EU (unless they are subsequently materially amended).
[109] BRRD, Art. 55(1).

although at the time of writing, this does not appear likely. In addition, without action EEA resolution authorities could require banking groups which, as part of their Brexit planning, are novating existing English law contracts to EEA banking subsidiaries, where applicable, to include terms recognising bail-in within these contracts; this would impose a significant burden on those groups and may not be attractive to the relevant contractual counterparties. From the reverse perspective, it should be considered how the relevant PRA and FCA rules could be modified to ease compliance of UK Institutions and qualifying parent undertakings with Article 55 of the BRRD (as transposed into UK law) in respect of contracts they make with counterparties under EEA law.

12.58 Under BRRD II,[110] the Article 55 Requirement will be amended to address instances where it is impracticable for an institution[111] (a **BRRD Institution**) or one of the entities referred to in point (b), (c), or (d) of Article 1(1) of the BRRD[112] (together with BRRD Institutions, **BRRD Undertakings**) to include those contractual terms in agreements or liabilities (excluding unsecured liabilities in certain capital and debt instruments) that would otherwise be covered by the requirement. If a BRRD Undertaking makes such a determination, it will be required to notify its resolution authority of that determination, at which point the Article 55 Requirement will be suspended in respect of the relevant contracts and liabilities.[113] BRRD II mandates the EBA to develop draft regulatory technical standards (RTS) further specifying the conditions under which it would be legally or otherwise impracticable for a BRRD Institution to include the relevant contractual term. It is assumed that the UK will onshore those RTS or otherwise adopt rules reflecting the RTS.

12.59 The UK already operates a similar exclusion to the Article 55 Requirement, which provides that the requirement does not apply in respect of an unsecured debt liability where it would be impracticable for the Institution to comply with it in respect of that liability.[114] It is possible that the UK will expand this exclusion to be consistent with the BRRD II exclusion from the Article 55 Requirement.

12.4.9 MREL Reforms: External TLAC

12.60 BRRD II will make a number of changes in relation to the requirement of BRRD Undertakings to maintain a minimum requirement for own funds and eligible liabilities expressed as a percentage of the total liabilities and own funds of the institution (**MREL**)[115] and determined by the BoE in accordance with certain eligibility requirements.[116]

---

[110] BRRD II, Art. 1(21).
[111] Defined in BRRD, Art. 2(1)(23) as a credit institution (i.e. a bank) or an investment firm.
[112] Those entities are, in summary: (a) a EU financial institution that is a subsidiary of a credit institution or investment firm, or of a company referred to in point (b) or (c), and is subject to group supervision applied to its parent undertaking; (b) EU holding company financial holding companies, mixed financial holding companies and mixed-activity holding companies; and (c) EU parent financial holding companies, parent financial holding companies, parent mixed financial holding companies and parent mixed financial holding companies.
[113] BRRD, Art. 55(2) (as amended by BRRD II, Art. 1(21)).
[114] Contractual Recognition of Bail-in Part of the PRA Rulebook, ch. 2.1.
[115] BRRO2, Art. 122.
[116] Ibid., Art. 123 and Commission Delegated Regulation ((EU) 2016/1450) (onshored pursuant to section 3 of the Withdrawal Act and amended by Annex E of the Technical Standards (Bank Recovery and Resolution) (Amendment etc.) (EU Exit) (No. 1) Instrument 2019).

The purpose of MREL is to provide adequate loss-absorbing capital and eligible liabilities for the bail-in tool to be applied effectively. Currently, the term 'own funds' is defined in the BRRO2[117] by reference to the Capital Requirements Regulation (the **CRR**),[118] which defines own funds as being the sum of Tier 1 capital[119] and Tier 2 capital.[120] The term 'eligible liabilities' means the liabilities and capital instruments that do not qualify as Common Equity Tier 1 (**CET1**) or Additional Tier 1 (**AT1**) or Tier 2 capital instruments, and are not excluded from the scope of the bail-in tool.[121]

12.61 One such change is that calculation of MREL will be aligned with the new external total loss-absorbing capacity (**TLAC**) requirement that will be introduced by a parallel package of reforms to the CRR (**CRR II**).[122]

12.62 As the first recital to BRRD II explains, on 9 November 2015, the FSB published the TLAC Term Sheet (the **TLAC Standard**), which was endorsed by the G20 in November 2015. The objective of the TLAC Standard is to ensure that global systemically important banks, referred to in BRRD II as global systemically important institutions (**G-SIIs**),[123] more commonly known as banks that are 'too big to fail', have the loss-absorbing and recapitalisation capacity necessary to help ensure that, in, and immediately following, a resolution, those institutions can continue to perform critical functions without putting public funds or financial stability at risk.

12.63 The TLAC Standard contemplates 'internal' and 'external' TLAC. Institutions to which the new external TLAC requirements apply (see below), will be required from 27 June 2019 to 31 December 2021[124] to satisfy the following requirement for own funds and eligible liabilities:

(1) a risk-based ratio of 16%, representing the own funds and eligible liabilities of the institution expressed as a percentage of the total risk exposure amount; and
(2) a non-risk-based ratio of 6%, representing the own funds and eligible liabilities of the institution expressed as a percentage of the total exposure measure,[125]

provided that, from 1 January 2022, those ratios will increase to 18% and 6.75%, respectively (the **External TLAC Standard**).[126]

12.64 The External TLAC Standard will apply to each resolution entity within a G-SII. A 'resolution entity' is an entity to which resolution tools will be applied in accordance with the

---

[117] BRRO2, Art. 2(1).
[118] Regulation (EU) No. 575/2013 of the European Parliament and of the Council of 25 June 2013 on prudential requirements for credit institutions and investment firms and amending Regulation (EU) No. 648/2012.
[119] Defined in CRR, Art. 25 as the sum of Common Equity Tier 1 capital and Additional Tier 1 of an institution.
[120] Defined Art. 71 (ibid.) as the sum of an institution's Tier 2 items (defined in Art. 62 (ibid.)) after the deductions referred to in Art. 66 and the application of Art. 79 (ibid.).
[121] Banking Act, s. 3(1).
[122] Regulation (EU) 2019/876 of the European Parliament and of the Council of 20 May 2019 amending Regulation (EU) No. 575/2013 as regards the leverage ratio, the net stable funding ratio, requirements for own funds and eligible liabilities, counterparty credit risk, market risk, exposures to central counterparties, exposures to collective investment undertakings, large exposures, reporting and disclosure requirements, and Regulation (EU) No. 648/2012.
[123] BRRD, Art. 2(1)(83c) (inserted by BRRD II, Art. 1(1)(e)).
[124] CRR, Art. 494 (amended by CRR II, Art. 1(128)).
[125] CRR, Art. 494 (amended by CRR11, Art. 1(128)).
[126] CRR II, Art. 92a (inserted by CRR11, Art. 1(47)).

resolution strategy for the G-SII, or in the case of a BRRD Institution that is not subject to consolidated supervision, that BRRD Institution for the purposes of its solo resolution plan.[127] Depending on the resolution strategy, a resolution entity may be a parent company, an intermediate or ultimate holding company, or an operating subsidiary. A G-SII may have one or more resolution entities.

12.65 Under BRRD II, resolution authorities will also be required to identify resolution groups when drawing up group resolution plans. A 'resolution group' is defined as a resolution entity and its subsidiaries that are not resolution entities themselves, subsidiaries of other resolution entities, or entities that are established in a third country that are not included in the resolution group in accordance with the resolution plan and their subsidiaries. A resolution group may also comprise credit institutions permanently affiliated to a central body (an arrangement that is not used in the UK and that involves credit institutions being affiliated to a central body which supervises them) and the central body itself when at least one of those credit institutions or the central body itself is a resolution entity, and their respective subsidiaries.[128]

12.66 BRRD II will also amend the MREL requirement to align it with the External TLAC Standard insofar as it will be expressed as a percentage of the total risk exposure amount of the entity and of the total exposure measure of the relevant entity (**Standard MREL**).[129] Standard MREL for a resolution entity that is a G-SII or part of a G-SII will consist of the external TLAC requirement that applies to it and any institution-specific additional requirement for own funds and eligible liabilities determined by the resolution authority in accordance with the BRRD.[130] Resolution entities will be required to comply with Standard MREL from 1 January 2024.[131]

12.67 A specific MREL regime will be introduced in relation to resolution entities that are not G-SIIs and that are part of a resolution group with assets exceeding €100 billion (the **Top-Tier Bank MREL**). These entities are referred to as 'top tier' banks.[132] Top-tier banks will be subject to a risk-based MREL ratio of 13.5% and a non-risk-based ratio of 5% when implemented.[133] Resolution authorities will also have the discretion to apply the Top-Tier Bank MREL to resolution entities that are not top tier banks where they determine that those entities are reasonably likely to pose a systemic risk in the event of their failure.[134]

12.68 BRRD II also provides powers for resolution authorities to impose additional institution-specific requirements for own funds and eligible liabilities for resolution entities of G-SIIs and EU material subsidiaries of non-EU G-SIIs (the **G-SII Add-on**), which will of course mean that EU resolution authorities may, post-Brexit, apply the G-SII Add-on to institutions that are material subsidiaries of UK G-SIIs. This would be in addition to the TLAC minimum requirement. That power may only be exercised where a G-SII's TLAC requirement is insufficient to ensure that the G-SII is able to absorb losses and be recapitalised

---

[127] BRRD, Art. 2(1)(83a) (inserted by BRRD II, Art. 1(1)(e)).
[128] BRRD, Art. 2(1)(83b) (inserted by BRRD II, Art. 1(1)(e)).
[129] BRRD, Art. 45 (amended by BRRD II, Art. 1(17)).
[130] BRRD, Art. 45d (inserted by BRRD II, Art. 1(17)).
[131] BRRD, Art. 45m(1) (inserted by BRRD II, Art. 1(17)).
[132] BRRD II, Recital 10.
[133] BRRD, Art. 45c(5) (inserted by BRRD II, Art. 1(17)).
[134] BRRD, Art. 45c(6) (inserted by BRRD II, Art. 1(17)).

under the relevant resolution strategy.[135] It is presumed that the BoE will be given the power to impose the G-SII Add-on in respect of UK G-SIIs and UK material subsidiaries of non-UK G-SIIs.

12.69 Resolution entities will be required to ensure that the resolution group complies with aggregate Top-Tier Banks MREL and the G-SII Add-on (if applicable) requirements imposed on the group (i.e. on a consolidated basis)[136] from 1 January 2022.[137]

12.4.10 MREL Reforms: Eligible Liabilities

12.70 BRRD II will also replace the current BRRD definition of 'eligible liabilities'[138] (the UK implementation of which is discussed in paragraph 12.60) with a more tightly defined definition of eligible liabilities[139] that is aligned with the definition of that term for the purpose of calculating TLAC requirements.[140] In summary, eligible liabilities will include, subject to certain exceptions:

(1) instruments that:
   (a) do not qualify as CET1, AT1, or Tier 2 items; and
   (b) are fully paid-up, unsecured instruments with a residual maturity of at least one year, that are not owned by the institution that issues the instrument or an entity in the issuer's group or funded by a resolution entity, and that are not subject to set-off or netting arrangements that would undermine their capacity to absorb losses, among other characteristics; and
(2) Tier 2 instruments with a residual maturity of at least one year, to the extent that they do not qualify as Tier 2 items.[141]

12.4.11 MREL Reforms: Internal TLAC

12.71 CRR II will also amend the CRR to introduce an internal TLAC requirement for BRRD Institutions that are material subsidiaries of non-EU G-SIIs and that are not resolution entities, which will require them to hold at all times own funds and eligible liabilities equal to 90% of the External TLAC Requirement (the **Internal TLAC Requirement**).[142] Post-Brexit, from a UK perspective, Institutions that are not resolution entities and that are material subsidiaries of non-UK G-SIIs will be subject to the Internal TLAC Requirement.

12.72 BRRD II will introduce a corresponding requirement for BRRD Institutions that are subsidiaries of a resolution entity or a third country resolution entity, but are not themselves resolution entities, to meet the MREL requirement by issuing certain types of eligible

---

[135] BRRD, Art. 45d (inserted by BRRD II, Art. 1(17)).
[136] BRRD, Art. 45e (inserted by BRRD II, Art. 1(17)).
[137] BRRD, Art. 45m (inserted by BRRD II, Art. 1(17)).
[138] BRRD, Art. 2(71a).
[139] Set out in BRRD, Art. 45b (inserted by BRRD II, by Art. 1(17)).
[140] CRR, Arts. 72a and 72b (inserted by CRR II, Art. 1(31)).
[141] Tier 2 items and Tier 2 instruments are defined in CRR, Arts. 62 and 63, respectively.
[142] CRR, Art. 92b (inserted by CRR II, Art. 1(47)).

debt instruments and equity to entities in the same resolution group (**Internal MREL**).[143] Resolution authorities will have discretion, after having consulted the competent authority, to apply Internal MREL to BRRD Entities. Resolution authorities will also be given powers to write down or convert Internal MREL into CET1 capital instruments (or both) if the issuer reaches the point of non-viability.[144] It is anticipated that the UK will implement this power by adding to the bail-in powers in the Banking Act. It is important to note in this regard that Internal MREL instruments must be issued to group entities, whereas instruments issued to meet the External TLAC Standard may not be held by group entities. Internal MREL therefore requires the creation a level of loss-absorbing capacity within groups, the aim of which is to enable the recapitalisation of BRRD Institutions that have issued Internal MREL through realising intragroup losses (i.e. at the level of the resolution entity). Institutions will be required to comply with Internal MREL from 1 January 2024.[145]

12.4.12 Stabilisation Options: Moratorium Tool

12.73 BRRD II will also give EEA resolution authorities the power if certain conditions are satisfied and they have consulted the relevant competent authorities, to impose a moratorium on the payment and delivery obligations of any entity that is subject to the BRRD framework.[146] The conditions include that the exercise of the power is necessary to determine whether to take a resolution action in respect of the resolution entity or to choose which resolution action to take. As with other areas of the BRRD framework, the use of this power will be likely to involve cross-border cooperation. Based on the currently anticipated amended form of the UK Regime following Brexit, it seems unlikely that the BoE will be required to consult with EEA competent authorities before applying the moratorium power.

12.4.13 Government Stabilisation Tools

12.74 The UK government has powers under the Banking Act in extraordinary circumstances to provide funding to resolve failing Institutions. This may be achieved by taking an Institution into temporary public ownership or by participating in the recapitalisation of the Institution in exchange for CET1, AT1, or Tier 2 instruments.[147] It is not anticipated that these powers will change in connection with Brexit.

12.4.14 Cross-border Group Resolution

12.75 Aside from the UK's automatic participation in EEA cross-border cooperation measures (such as EBA resolution colleges)[148] falling away at the point of Brexit, the BoE, PRA and

---

[143] BRRD, Art. 45f (inserted by CRR II, Art. 1(17)).
[144] BRRD, Arts. 59 and 60 (amended by BRRD II, Art. 1(23)–(24)).
[145] BRRD, Art. 45m(1) (inserted by BRRD II, Art. 1(17)).
[146] BRRD, Art. 33a (inserted by BRRD II, Art. 1(12)).
[147] Banking Act, ss. 9, 13, 78A, 228, 229, 256A, and 257.
[148] BRRD, Arts. 87–92 (inclusive).

FCA will no longer be required under UK law to participate in the cross-border group resolution procedures and mechanism in the BRRD. The UK will also lose the benefit of non-binding cooperation arrangements with third countries that the EBA has entered into under Article 97 of the BRRD. The Bank, the PRA, and the FCA will also no longer be required under UK law to consider entering into arrangements with equivalent third country authorities in order to implement those framework agreements.[149]

12.76 The potential impact of this loss of cross-border cooperation arrangements has been noted as an area of particular legal and practical uncertainty.[150] HM Treasury has stated, however, that the BoE will continue to be able to cooperate with its EEA counterparts on the basis that FSMA and the Banking Act will continue to provide for this.[151] This cooperation is called for by the FSB Key Attributes, which as HM Treasury notes in its *Banking Act 2009: Special Resolution Code of Practice* (the **Code**), 'promote co-operation between resolution authorities through mutual recognition of resolution action, subject to certain conditions such as considering the impact on financial stability in other jurisdictions and that resolution authorities are strongly encouraged to achieve a cooperative solution, helping to ensure third country resolution is successful'.[152] The Code also provides that, for significant UK subsidiaries and branches of non-EEA banks, 'if the banking group in question is a Globally Systemically Important Financial Institution (**G-SIFI**), the BoE will be a member of the Crisis Management Group (**CMG**) for that banking group'.[153] The Treasury has confirmed that, consistent with the UK's current approach to third country headquartered G-SIFIs, UK authorities will continue to participate in CMGs for EU-headquartered G-SIFIs, and that the UK authorities will continue to be permitted to share information with their CMG counterparts.[154]

12.77 In addition, the Banking Act provisions that relate to the recognition of third country resolution actions[155] will not apply in relation to the application of resolution tools, the exercise of a resolution power or the enforcement of crisis management or prevention measures by EEA States prior to Brexit. This provision is described as a transitional measure; the import of which would be that without that provision, such actions would not be recognised automatically in the UK under the EU cross-border recognition regime that is in place prior to Brexit.

12.78 It is unclear whether this approach is appropriate given the interconnectedness of the UK and EU financial services sectors. In particular, the loss of automatic recognition of EEA state-led resolution actions could undermine effective cross-border cooperation on

---

[149] BRR Brexit Regulations, Sch. 3, para. 114 omits Art. 244 of the BRRO2, which currently sets out the requirement on the Bank, PRA, and FCA to make arrangements with equivalent authorities in third countries in line with EBA framework cooperation arrangements if the Bank, the PRA, or the FCA concludes that entering into such arrangements would facilitate the more effective performance of their resolution functions, and doing so would be more effective than any other bilateral or multilateral arrangements.

[150] For instance, Financial Markets Law Committee, '"Onshoring" Statutory Instruments Comment Series: Bank Recovery and Resolution', October 2018.

[151] HM Treasury's policy note on the draft Bank Recovery and Resolution and Miscellaneous Provisions (Amendment) (EU Exit) Regulations 2018, published 8 October 2018 (the **BRR Brexit Regulations Policy Note**), para. 3.

[152] The Code, para. 10.14.

[153] Ibid., para. 10.7.

[154] BRR Brexit Regulations Policy Note, para. 3.

[155] Banking Act, s. 89H.

resolution as the process of recognising EEA state-led resolution actions in this way could become overly cumbersome.

12.79 One way that the cross-border resolution of institutions and groups could be hampered is in the deletion of provisions in the BRRO2 relating to the BoE's participation in resolution colleges established under the BRRD. It would be helpful for the UK to be able to continue to participate in those colleges in addition to the BoE's current role on CMGs. However, irrespective of what is provided for in UK legislation, following Brexit, the BoE would not be able to continue to participate resolution colleges as it currently does; it may only participate as an observer. In order for the BoE to continue to participate in the relevant resolution colleges as an observer, it must: (1) make a request to observe; and (2) then receive an invitation to do so.[156] Based on the current proposed amendments to the BRRO2, it is not clear how the BoE would have the power to request to observe at EU resolution colleges. Nevertheless, in relation to G-SIFIs, in many respects it is the CMGs which have proved to be the most important forum in which resolution authorities have discussed cooperation and resolution planning matters.

12.4.15 Depositor Preference

12.80 The UK's departure from the EU will affect the position of depositors in EEA branches of UK banks in the creditor hierarchy on insolvency. These deposits will no longer qualify for protection under the Financial Services Compensation Scheme, will no longer rank *pari passu* with deposits at UK branches of the same UK bank and will cease to be exempt from the BoE's application of the bail-in tool.[157] Similarly, deposits at UK branches of EEA banks are likely to rank behind deposits booked in EEA branches of those banks on insolvency, albeit that this will depend on the precise detail of how relevant EEA member states continue to implement the BRRD in their national laws.

12.5 Conclusion

12.81 The UK's departure from the EU is a watershed moment in cross-border regulatory cooperation and leaves many questions unanswered about how UK and EU resolution authorities will work together to help prevent, and mitigate the effects of, banking crises in the future. While some of the infrastructure of cooperation in the BRRD can be replicated informally, for example through the continued involvement of the BoE in CMGs, other aspects of the BRRD regime, including most notably the automatic cross-border recognition of certain decisions and resolution actions, will come to an end.

12.82 The consequences of this decoupling will evolve according to how many banks and banking groups straddle the UK and the EU. The more UK–EU and EU–UK cross-border banking

---

[156] BRRD, Art. 88(3).
[157] BRR Brexit Regulations. The PRA acknowledged these points in its consultation paper CP 26/18 ('UK Withdrawal from the EU: Changes to PRA Rulebook and Onshored Binding Technical Standards') (October 2018), para. 8.22.

groups there are, the greater will be the need for sound regulatory cooperation and certainty about recognition of resolution actions. One effect of the UK's departure from the EU has been the need for global and UK-based banks to ensure that they have appropriately regulated entities in the EU from which to carry on business that is regulated in EU Member States. As a result, there are now more such entities than previously, many of them designed to carry on business that would previously have been conducted on a cross-border services basis from the UK in reliance on EU passporting. In addition, some such entities that existed prior to the UK referendum on EU membership have become much more substantial, heavily capitalised subsidiaries than before in order to accommodate the additional EU business they will be carrying on.

12.83 It follows, somewhat ironically, that the case for deeper cooperation between UK and EU resolution authorities is now greater than ever before, and at a time when the UK is disconnecting from the BRRD regime which, for all its imperfections, mandates a level of cooperation and mutual recognition of resolution actions that has not been achieved elsewhere in the world.

13
European Markets Infrastructure Regulation (EMIR) and Euro Clearing

Bob Penn

13.1 Introduction

This chapter discusses some implications of Brexit for those classes of market participant and activity regulated under the European Market Infrastructure Regulation[1] (EMIR). It is current as at 24 November 2019. **13.01**

As noted in Chapter 1, the political and regulatory environment remains uncertain and highly fluid. In the context of this chapter, it should in particular be noted that a large proportion of the UK law and regulation described is not yet in effect and may be subject to change. **13.02**

13.1.1 EMIR

EMIR is a European Union (EU) regulation which seeks to establish a framework throughout the EU for the regulation of derivatives trading and post-trade activities. Derivatives are financial contracts whose value is derived from one or more underlyings (which may include property, indices, or other factors) and include options, futures, and contracts for differences. Derivatives may be entered into on an over-the-counter (OTC) basis or traded over an exchange (**exchange-traded**), and may be cleared by a clearing house or uncleared. Although a relatively recent innovation, OTC derivatives have become widely used by businesses to manage risk in the last two decades. **13.03**

The derivatives market serves important economic purposes, such as enabling market participants to hedge exposures, invest and manage risks, and is of systemic relevance due to its size and the interconnectedness between financial institutions that are also active in other key financial markets and market infrastructures. A resilient and well-functioning derivatives market is an important component of the financial markets and broader global economy. **13.04**

The financial crisis of 2008 exposed significant weaknesses in the OTC derivatives market, including the build-up of large counterparty exposures between market participants which were not appropriately risk-managed; limited transparency concerning levels of activity in **13.05**

---

[1] Regulation (EU) No. 648/2012 of the European Parliament and of the Council of 4 July 2012 on OTC derivatives, central counterparties and trade repositories: <http://eur-lex.europa.eu/LexUriServ/LexUriServ.do?uri=OJ:L:2012:201:0001:0059:EN:PDF>

the market and overall size of counterparty credit exposures; and operational weaknesses which demonstrated the need for further standardisation and automation.

13.06 In response, in 2009 and following the G20 leaders agreed to reforms in the OTC derivatives market to achieve central clearing and, where appropriate, exchange or electronic trading of standardised OTC derivatives; reporting of all transactions to trade repositories; and higher capital as well as margin requirements for non-centrally cleared transactions.

13.07 EMIR represents part of the EU's implementation of the G20 commitments. It provides for:

(a) the authorisation and supervision of central counterparties (**CCPs**);
(b) the registration and supervision of trade repositories;
(c) the mandatory clearing of standardised OTC derivatives on CCPs;
(d) the mitigation of operational and counterparty risk by persons transacting uncleared OTC derivatives, including requirements to place collateral against the risk of counterparty default (**margin**); and
(e) the reporting of information about derivatives trades to trade repositories.

13.08 EMIR therefore primarily affects three classes of market participant: persons dealing in derivatives (**counterparties**); trade repositories; and CCPs. Counterparties will often also fall to be regulated under other aspects of EU law, including national law implementing the recast Markets in Financial Instruments Directive (**MiFID II**) and the Markets in Financial Instruments Regulation (**MiFIR**), which regulate the provision of investment services and provide for the application of an obligation on certain counterparties to trade certain classes of derivatives on a qualifying trading venue, and the Capital Requirements Regulation (**CRR**), which establishes capital and liquidity requirements for EU banks and investment firms. These, and the implications of Brexit for the regulation of counterparties subject to them, are considered separately in this volume.

13.1.2 Territoriality

13.09 The derivative trading environment is global. It is common for wholesale market dealings in derivatives to occur between counterparties in different jurisdictions. Further, where transactions are reported, cleared, or traded on an exchange, transactions may involve other parties (a trade repository, exchange, or clearing house). The parties could be in different jurisdictions either inside or outside the EU. Regulating an inherently international market poses challenges for legislators and regulators, whose jurisdiction and remit is almost inevitably national (or in the case of the EU, regional) rather than global. Regulation of international market activity inevitably poses questions around whether, and how, to regulate foreign participants and raises tensions between the need to ensure a level playing field between domestic and foreign market participants, and the risk of closing off access to (or of) foreign market participants by imposing requirements on them which are over-burdensome or inconsistent with applicable foreign requirements, which could have negative implications for liquidity and for the real economy.

13.10 EMIR seeks to manage this tension by providing for concepts of recognition and equivalence of certain non-EU (**third country**) actors, and by capturing certain transactions between third country counterparties where they have a direct, substantial, and foreseeable effect in the EU or where necessary to prevent evasion. As is discussed further below, these concepts—and their application—would become key to continuing interaction between market participants in the EU27 and the UK following Brexit.

13.1.3 Sources

As an EU regulation, EMIR is directly applicable and legally binding in all EU Member States without any national implementing legislation. EMIR includes extensive provision for secondary legislation by way of delegated regulations, regulatory technical standards (**RTS**) and implementing technical standards (**ITS**), much of which has now been made.

13.11

Both EMIR and the secondary legislation give rise to a significant number of interpretative difficulties which are unaddressed in the legislation. The EU Commission (the **Commission**) has published frequently asked questions (**FAQs**) providing responses to market participants' most common questions about EMIR.[2] The European Securities Markets Authority (**ESMA**) also publishes a questions-and-answers document[3] (**ESMA Q&As**), which is updated regularly and provides guidance on a number of issues.

13.12

13.1.4 EMIR REFIT

In order to ensure its consistent and effective application, Article 85 of EMIR requires that the Commission review and, if appropriate, submit proposals to amend EMIR within specified timeframes. The review of EMIR was included in the 2016 EC Regulatory Fitness and Performance Programme (**EMIR REFIT**) and, on 4 May 2017, the Commission published a proposal to amend EMIR. The amended EMIR regulation (known colloquially as **EMIR REFIT 2.1**) was published in the Official Journal of the European Union on 28 May 2019 and entered into force on 17 June 2019.[4] On 13 June 2017, the EC published a second proposal to amend EMIR (colloquially known as **EMIR REFIT 2.2**) which was further amended in September 2017 as part of the EU's package of proposals to strengthen the European System of Financial Supervision. The UK proposals relating to the 'onshoring' of EMIR (as discussed below) take account of changes arising to EMIR as a result of the EMIR REFIT 2.1 changes which came into force prior to 31 October 2019, which at the time the relevant proposals were made or last updated was the anticipated date on which the UK was to exit the EU (**exit day**). Following the deferral of exit date, which at the time of writing is anticipated on or shortly before 31

13.13

---

[2] <https://ec.europa.eu/info/files/emir-frequently-asked-questions_en>
[3] <https://www.esma.europa.eu/sites/default/files/library/esma70-1861941480-52_qa_on_emir_implementation.pdf>
[4] Regulation (EU) 2019/834 of the European Parliament and of the Council of 20 May 2019 amending Regulation (EU) No 648/2012 as regards the clearing obligation, the suspension of the clearing obligation, the reporting requirements, the risk-mitigation techniques for OTC derivative contracts not cleared by a central counterparty, the registration and supervision of trade repositories and the requirements for trade repositories: <https://eur-lex.europa.eu/legal-content/EN/TXT/PDF/?uri=CELEX:32019R0834&from=EN>

January 2020, it is anticipated that the UK legislation discussed below will be further amended to take account of any further changes which come into force under EMIR REFIT before exit date.

13.1.5 UK Supervisory Responsibility for EMIR

13.14 Responsibility for supervising the obligations of UK market participants under EMIR is split between the Bank of England, Prudential Regulation Authority (**PRA**) and Financial Conduct Authority (**FCA**). The precise delineation of responsibilities is set out in Regulation 6 of the Financial Services and Markets Act 2000 (Over the Counter Derivatives, Central Counterparties and Trade Repositories) Regulations 2013.[5] In broad terms, this allocates responsibility to the Bank of England for the regulation of CCPs; to the PRA with respect to EMIR's provisions relating to margin and clearing to the extent applicable to PRA-authorised firms; and to the FCA with respect to the regulation of trade repositories and to the supervision of counterparties (including third country entities) otherwise.

13.2 The EU Withdrawal Act and 'Onshoring'

13.2.1 Background

13.15 As EU regulations, EMIR and its secondary legislation are directly applicable in the UK by virtue of the European Communities Act 1972 (the ECA). The ECA confirmed the UK's membership of the European Economic Community (as then was) and gave EU law supremacy over UK domestic law. In particular, section 2(1) of the ECA ensures that rights and obligations in some types of EU law, including EU regulations, are directly applicable in the UK legal system. This means that they apply directly without the need for the UK Parliament to pass specific domestic implementing legislation. The removal of the doctrine of the supremacy of EU law is a key element of the UK's departure from the EU.

13.16 At the time of writing, the UK and EU have negotiated and agreed a draft withdrawal agreement under Article 50 of the Treaty on European Union (TEU) (the **withdrawal agreement**)[6] which contemplates a transitional arrangement under which the UK would continue to participate in the Single Market for a period of time, pending negotiation of an agreement of the future relationship between the UK and EU. It remains unclear whether the agreement will be ratified by the UK Parliament.

13.17 To plan for the possibility that the withdrawal agreement may not be ratified, the UK government passed the European Union (Withdrawal) Act 2018 (EUWA) as a contingency measure to ensure that the legislative mechanism exists to exit the EU on exit day.

---

[5] SI 2013/504.
[6] <https://ec.europa.eu/commission/sites/beta-political/files/draft_withdrawal_agreement_0.pdf>

13.2.2 EUWA

The principal purpose of the EUWA is to provide a functioning statute book on the day the UK leaves the EU in order to ensure that legal certainty, continuity, and stability is retained as the UK exits from the EU. The EUWA performs a number of functions, including: **13.18**

(a) repealing the ECA with effect from exit day;
(b) converting EU law as its stands on exit day into domestic law and preserving laws made in the UK to implement EU obligations;
(c) creating temporary powers to make secondary legislation to enable corrections to be made to the laws that would otherwise no longer operate appropriately once the UK has left;
(d) bringing to an end the jurisdiction of the Court of Justice of the EU in the UK;
(e) providing for Parliament's oversight of the outcome of the government's negotiations with the EU on the withdrawal agreement and the framework for the future relationship between the EU and the UK; and
(f) enabling domestic law to reflect the content of the Article 50 withdrawal agreement once the UK leaves the EU.

Because the EUWA operates on the assumption that the UK will leave the EU on exit day, if a transitional arrangement is ratified extending the time that EU law applies in the UK, a new Act of Parliament will be required to provide for changes to the EUWA to save the effect of the ECA during that period. Any further legislation made will be unlikely to affect the substance of the issues discussed below: it is anticipated that a similar approach to the onshoring of EU legislation discussed below will be taken, but its effect may be delayed to the end of the transitional period rather than the point of exit. **13.19**

13.2.3 Incorporation of EMIR and Delegated Legislation in UK Law

Absent further legislation, on repeal of the ECA directly applicable EU law, including EMIR and its secondary legislation, would cease to apply in the UK, leaving the UK without much of its legal framework (including for the regulation of derivatives activities). In order to avoid this consequence, the EUWA provides for the retention of most in-force EU law, as it stands on exit day, by incorporating it as a freestanding body of domestic law. This new body of law will replicate several different sources of EU law. **13.20**

The category of source relevant to EMIR is direct EU legislation. This is defined in section 3(2) to include all EU regulations, decisions, or tertiary legislation, and certain parts of the EEA agreement that has effect in EU law immediately before exit day. The EUWA subdivides direct EU legislation into two categories: **13.21**

(a) retained direct 'principal' EU legislation (broadly, EU regulations (which are not also EU tertiary legislation); and
(b) retained direct 'minor' EU legislation (broadly EU tertiary legislation and EU decisions).

13.22 EMIR is retained direct principal EU legislation for the purposes of the EUWA. The RTS, ITS and delegated regulations set out above are retained direct minor legislation. The EUWA sets out rules that govern how those two categories of law can be modified or repealed and by what type of conventional domestic legal instrument.

13.23 Section 3 of the EUWA provides that (subject to certain exceptions which are not relevant in respect of EMIR) direct EU legislation, so far as operative immediately before exit day, forms part of domestic law on and after exit day. This has the effect of incorporating the relevant legislation on the statute book following repeal of the ECA.

13.2.4 Ensuring EMIR Operates Effectively and Correcting Deficiencies

13.24 It will be clear that the mere incorporation of EU regulations into UK law would not create a workable framework for the UK regulation of derivatives markets. EMIR provides for an EU, not a UK, framework, involving EU institutions and concepts. It would not be appropriate to have ESMA be the regulator of UK trade repositories post-exit, for example.

13.25 To deal with this, section 8 of the EUWA gives ministers of the Crown a power to make secondary legislation to deal with any failure of retained EU law to operate effectively or any other 'deficiency' in retained EU law that would arise on exit in retained EU law. The term 'deficiency' is intended to capture the following plus any deficiency not listed below but which is of a 'similar kind' to those listed:

(a) provisions that have no practical application after the UK has left the EU;
(b) provisions on functions that are currently being carried out in the EU on the UK's behalf, for example by an EU agency;
(c) provisions on reciprocal arrangements or rights between the UK and other EU Member States that are no longer in place or are no longer appropriate;
(d) any other arrangements or rights, including through EU treaties, that are no longer in place or no longer appropriate; and
(e) EU references that are no longer appropriate.

13.26 Section 8 provides the government with powers to amend deficiencies to prevent, remedy or mitigate any failure of retained EU law to operate effectively or any other deficiency in retained EU law which arises from the UK's withdrawal from the EU for up to two years after exit day. Section 8(5) provides that secondary legislation made under the power in this section can do anything an Act of Parliament might to deal with deficiencies. This includes altering Acts of Parliament where appropriate and subdelegating the power to a public authority where they are best placed to deal with the deficiencies—for example, the Bank of England, the PRA, and/or the FCA (as applicable) in the context of financial services, as further discussed below. The power is subject to restrictions under section 8(7): for example, it cannot be used to impose or increase taxation or fees, make retrospective provision, create a relevant criminal offence, establish a public authority or amend the Human Rights Act 1998.

13.27 With respect to financial services regulation, responsibility for exercising the powers conferred by section 8 falls to HM Treasury. In July 2018 HM Treasury published a statement setting out its approach to financial services legislation under the EUWA (the White Paper)[7] The general approach under the White Paper is discussed in Chapter 1.

13.2.5 Policy Choices in Creating Onshored Legislation

13.28 Onshoring EU legislation is not just about making EU legislation workable in a UK domestic context, however. It also involves making policy choices about the treatment of EU actors. In particular, a key policy question is whether, in onshoring EMIR, the UK should continue to confer broadly consistent treatment on EU counterparties, CCPs, and trade repositories with that which applies today, or whether the UK should default to treating such parties in the same way as third country counterparties, CCPs, and trade repositories. The White Paper indicates that the government's general approach is to apply the latter treatment, based in part on the likelihood that the EU will treat the UK as a third country post-exit. Paragraphs 1.17 and 1.18 of the paper state:

> 1.17 In the unlikely scenario that the UK leaves the EU without a deal, the UK would be outside the EU's framework for financial services. The UK's position in relation to the EU would be determined by the default Member State and EU rules that apply to third countries at the relevant time. The European Commission has confirmed that this would be the case.
>
> 1.18 In light of this, our approach in this scenario cannot and does not rely on any new, specific arrangements being in place between the UK and the EU. As a general principle, the UK would also need to default to treating EU Member States largely as it does other third countries, although there are instances where we would need to diverge from this approach, including to provide for a smooth transition to the new circumstances.

13.29 The approach paper recognises that, given the complex and highly integrated nature of the EU financial services system, deficiencies would not be adequately resolved by defaulting to existing third country frameworks alone. In such cases, a different approach might be needed to manage the transition to a stand-alone UK regime. This is the basis for a policy decision to introduce a transitional permissions regime for firms (discussed elsewhere in this volume). As discussed further below, similar relief is proposed for CCPs and more limited relief for trade repositories in the EEA Member States following Brexit (the EU27).

13.30 HM Treasury's policy therefore points to a general approach under which EU27 counterparties, CCPs, and trade repositories would be treated under onshored EMIR in the same way as third country CCPs and trade repositories respectively, subject to limited transitional relief. The implications of this are discussed further below.

---

[7] <https://assets.publishing.service.gov.uk/government/uploads/system/uploads/attachment_data/file/720298/HM_Treasury_s_approach_to_financial_services_legislation_under_the_European_Union__Withdrawal__Act.pdf>

13.3 Onshoring EMIR and the Delegated Legislation Made under It

13.31 As indicated above, onshoring is a two-stage process, involving the incorporation of EU legislation in the UK statute book and its amendment to deal with failures to operate effectively and to rectify deficiencies. At the time of writing, a series of statutory instruments (the SIs) have been made, or laid, onshoring EMIR. The following are the principal SIs relevant to onshored EMIR:

(a) Central Counterparties (Amendment, etc., and Transitional Provision) (EU Exit) Regulations 2018) (the **CCP SI**);[8]
(b) Trade Repositories (Amendment and Transitional Provision) (EU Exit) Regulations 2018 (the **Trade Repositories SI**);[9] and
(c) Over the Counter Derivatives, Central Counterparties and Trade Repositories (Amendment, etc., and Transitional Provision) (EU Exit) Regulations 2018 (the **EMIR SI**).[10]

In addition, the Over the Counter Derivatives, Central Counterparties and Trade Repositories (Amendment, etc., and Transitional Provision) (EU Exit) (No. 2) Regulations 2019 (the **EMIR REFIT SI**) was made on 29 October 2019.[11] A number of other statutory instruments make minor changes to onshored EMIR to correct deficiencies or amend the principal SIs.[12]

13.32 In broad terms, the CCP SI makes changes to EMIR relevant to the regulation of CCPs; the Trade Repositories SI makes changes relevant to the regulation of trade repositories; and the EMIR SI makes changes relevant to the regulation of counterparties and trade repositories. The CCP SI and Trade Repositories SI also provide for transitional relief for CCPs and trade repositories arising from the former ceasing to be authorised or recognised, and the latter ceasing to be registered or recognised, under onshored EMIR. The EMIR SI provides for transitional relief associated with the change in status of some intragroup counterparty relationships between UK and EU27 counterparties (from being relationships between EU counterparties under EMIR to being relationships between a UK counterparty and a third country counterparty). The EMIR REFIT SI makes amendments to the changes effected by EMIR REFIT to bring it into line with the policy approach discussed below, but only with respect to changes made under EMIR REFIT 2.1 which entered into force prior to the date of the EMIR REFIT 2.1 SI: further amendments will be needed to accommodate subsequent changes which have come into force between that date and exit date Salient aspects of each SI are discussed further below.

---

[8] SI 2018/1184.
[9] SI 2018/1318.
[10] SI 2019/335.
[11] SI 2019/1416.
[12] The Financial Services (Electronic Money, Payment Services and Miscellaneous Amendments) (EU Exit) Regulations 2019 (SI 2019/1416); The Financial Services (Miscellaneous) (Amendment) (EU Exit) Regulations 2019 (SI 2019/710); The International Accounting Standards and European Public Limited-Liability Company (Amendment etc.) (EU Exit) Regulations 2019 (SI 2019/685); The Securitisation (Amendment) (EU Exit) Regulations 2019 (SI 2019/660); The Financial Services Contracts (Transitional and Saving Provision) (EU Exit) Regulations 2019 (SI 2019/405).

13.33 The delegated legislation made under EMIR also requires onshoring, as it suffers from many of the same deficiencies identified above. The Financial Regulators' Powers (Technical Standards etc.) (Amendment etc.) (EU Exit) Regulations 2018[13] (the **Technical Standards SI**) delegates powers to amend the RTS, ITS, and delegated regulations (together **Binding Technical Standards**) to the Bank of England, the FCA, and/or the PRA, subject to the oversight of HM Treasury. The Bank of England, the PRA, and the FCA have made a series of instruments[14] under the Technical Standards SI intended to onshore the Binding Technical Standards. As with the EMIR REFIR 2.1 SI, these generally do not contemplate changes to the underlying EU legislation scheduled to take effect after the point at which they were made—meaning that where changes to the relevant EU legislation come into force between the date on which they were made and exit date, they will need to be updated to take account of the changes

13.34 Guidance also performs an important role in the interpretation of EMIR. The UK regulators have also indicated that they will generally continue to apply the existing Commission FAQs and ESMA Q&As, subject to interpreting them consistent with the changes wrought by the onshoring process.

13.35 In addition, as discussed in Chapter 1, the government brought forward legislation to allow regulators to grant some flexibility in applying new legislative requirements under the EUWA. In summary, the power, which is contained in Part 7 of the Financial Services and Markets Act 2000 (Amendment) (EU Exit) Regulations 2019 (the **Amendment SI**), is intended to enable the UK regulators to amend the effect of the onshored EU legislative ruleset (including EMIR) in order to provide temporary relief from changes to pre-exit practice. The FCA and PRA have generated directions (**Transitional Directions**) under the Amendment SI to provide for a so-called standstill of certain new or changed obligations arising from Brexit. These are discussed further in section 13.8.

13.36 For the remainder of this chapter, references to onshored EMIR are to EMIR, as incorporated into UK law and amended in accordance with the SIs. References to EMIR post-Brexit are to EMIR as it applies following exit. References to the EU27 are to the remaining members of the European Economic Area to which EMIR would continue to apply post-Brexit.

---

[13] SI 2018/1115.
[14] The following were issued on 18 April 2019 by the Bank of England and PRA (limited subsequent changes to the package were made on 13 June 2019): Technical Standards (European Market Infrastructure) (EU Exit) (No. 1) Instrument 2019, issued by the Bank of England and amending Delegated Regulations 1249/2012; 152/2013; 153/2013; and 484/2014; the Technical Standards (European Market Infrastructure) (EU Exit) (No. 2) Instrument 2019, issued by the Bank of England and amending Delegated Regulations 285/2014; 2015/2205; 2016/592 and 2016/1178; the Technical Standards (European Market Infrastructure) (EU Exit) (No. 3) Instrument 2019 issued by the PRA and amending Delegated Regulation 2016/2251. At the time of writing, the PRA has consulted on minor changes to the No. 3 Instrument in Consultation Paper 18/19 by way of a further instrument: the draft Technical Standards (European Market Infrastructure) (EU Exit) (No.4) Instrument. The FCA has issued four sets of technical standards: the Technical Standards (European Market Infrastructure Regulation) (EU Exit) (No. 1) Instrument 2019 and Technical Standards (European Market Infrastructure Regulation) (EU Exit) (No. 2) Instrument 2019, issued on 29 March 2019, and the Technical Standards (European Market Infrastructure Regulation) (EU Exit) (No. 3) Instrument 2019 and Technical Standards (European Market Infrastructure Regulation) (EU Exit) (No. 4) Instrument 2019 issued on 19 April 2019.

13.4 Implications of Exit and Onshoring

13.37 Exit and onshoring have a number of implications for market participants, both in terms of the treatment of UK market participants under EU law (to the extent that they have relationships with EU27 counterparties, CCPs, or trade repositories) and the treatment of EU27 market participants under UK law.

13.38 The regulatory framework that has been developed within the period of UK membership of the EU is a highly sophisticated (and complex) array of requirements regulating market participants and their activities. It has been created against a legislative backdrop requiring the removal of barriers to the free movement of services and capital within the EU and the equality of treatment of EU market participants, and reflects a number of policy choices to prefer the position of EU market participants relative to third country participants.

13.4.1 Exit

13.39 Without further changes to EU law, the status of UK market participants would change from being EU actors subject to the rights and preferential treatments conferred by EU law, to being third country actors. For the purposes of EMIR this carries with it changes to:

(a) licensing requirements, including requirements for authorisation or recognition of UK CCPs and for registration or recognition of UK trade repositories (similar issues also arise for UK counterparties in relation to licensing requirements under MiFID II);

(b) how EMIR applies to UK counterparties, for whom EMIR would largely be disapplied as a result of UK counterparties ceasing to be established within the EU (although certain requirements applicable to third country entities may apply in certain circumstances); and

(c) the application of EMIR's requirements to EU27 counterparties when dealing with UK counterparties, CCPs, and trade repositories, by reason of the change in status of the latter from EU to third country counterparties. Absent equivalence determinations or other transitional relief under EMIR, in particular, derivatives traded on UK markets would become OTC derivatives for the purposes of EMIR, and transactions cleared on UK CCPs would in principle need to meet the EMIR requirements applicable to OTC derivatives.

13.4.2 Onshoring

13.40 Similar considerations apply when considering how onshored EMIR applies to EU27 market participants. By reason of the general policy approach indicated in paragraph 13.30 above, EU27 market participants would also see a change in status under onshored EMIR relative to their pre-exit status. For the purposes of onshored EMIR, this carries with it similar issues as apply to UK market participants in relation to access to the EU, including changes to:

(a) licensing requirements, including requirements for authorisation or recognition of EU27 CCPs and for registration or recognition of EU27 trade repositories (similar issues also arise for EU27 counterparties in relation to licensing requirements under onshored MiFID II: these are discussed in Chapter 10 of this volume);
(b) the application of onshored EMIR's requirements applicable to EU27 counterparties, which would largely be disapplied as a result of EU27 counterparties not being established within the UK (although certain requirements applicable to third country entities would apply in certain circumstances); and;
(c) the application of onshored EMIR's requirements to UK counterparties when dealing with EU27 counterparties, by reason of the change in status of the latter from EU counterparties under EMIR to third country counterparties under onshored EMIR. Absent equivalence determinations under UK EMIR, in particular, derivatives traded on EU markets would become OTC derivatives for the purposes of UK EMIR, and transactions cleared on EU CCPs would need to meet the EMIR requirements applicable to OTC derivatives.

13.41 The CCP SI and Trade Repositories SI address licensing requirements for EU27 CCPs and trade repositories, respectively. The EMIR SI addresses some of the consequences of the application of onshored EMIR's requirements to UK counterparties dealing with EU27 counterparties.

13.5 CCP SI

13.5.1 Background

13.42 EMIR provides for the authorisation of EU established CCPs and the recognition of CCPs established in third countries. Under Article 25, third country CCPs that intend to provide clearing services to clearing members or trading venues established in the EU must be recognised by ESMA. ESMA can only recognise a third country CCP if various conditions are met. These include requirements that the European Commission have determined that the legal and supervisory arrangements of the third country in which the CCP is established are equivalent to those set out in EMIR, that the relevant CCP is authorised in the third country and is subject to effective supervision and enforcement, and that ESMA has established cooperation arrangements with the relevant third country regulatory authority (Article 25(2)). At the time of writing, over thirty third country CCPs are recognised under EMIR.

13.43 Other regulatory consequences also flow from recognition for third country CCPs. A third country CCP must also be recognised in order to be eligible for the purposes of the clearing obligation under Article 4 of EMIR, which requires that certain transactions be cleared by an authorised or recognised CCP. Prudential consequences also potentially flow from recognised or authorised status under EMIR under the CRR for regulated credit institutions and investment firms which are users of CCP services. In particular, the CRR provides for preferential treatment of exposures to so-called qualifying CCPs (QCCPs) (defined in

Article 4(1)(88) of the CRR). Under the CRR, QCCP status requires authorisation or recognition under EMIR.

13.5.2 Amendments to Onshored EMIR

13.44 The CCP SI addresses failures and deficiencies arising from Brexit in relation to the recognition of third country CCPs under EMIR, once onshored.

13.45 For onshored EMIR to operate appropriately, the roles conferred on ESMA and the Commission need to move to be the responsibility of UK, rather than EU authorities. To ensure that the onshored EMIR operates effectively after exit day the CCP SI transfers the equivalence and recognition functions from ESMA to the Bank of England and from the Commission to HM Treasury respectively by amendments to Article 25.

13.46 Consistent with the policy position discussed above, the SI also provides that all non-UK CCPs, including CCPs established in the EU, are considered as third country CCPs for the purpose of the United Kingdom's post exit-day third country regime for CCPs by limiting the scope of the authorisation contemplated by Article 14 of EMIR to bodies corporate and unincorporated associations established in the UK.

13.47 As to the recognition of CCPs under onshored EMIR, there are therefore two categories of affected CCPs: those in third countries recognised under EMIR today (i.e. outside the EU), and those EU27-authorised CCPs which would fall to become third country CCPs under onshored EMIR.

13.48 With respect to the former, the CCP SI revokes the Commission Implementing Acts that relate to third country equivalence under Article 25 of EMIR. This means that at the point of exit recognised CCPs under EMIR would lose their recognition in the UK, as they would not be recognised under onshored EMIR, unless an implementing regulation is made by HM Treasury relating to the jurisdiction of the CCP, a cooperation arrangement is established between the CCP's home regulator and the Bank of England and an assessment has been made as to the effective supervision and enforcement in that jurisdiction, as contemplated by Article 25(2) of onshored EMIR. In a letter issued by the Bank of England in December 2017,[15] it indicated that it was commencing its assessments of equivalence and that 'if the relevant criteria under Article 25 are satisfied a non-UK CCP will be recognised and able to operate in the UK without discontinuity of service'. It therefore appears likely that, subject to the relevant cooperation arrangements being put in place, existing recognised CCPs would be eligible for recognition under onshored EMIR.

13.49 The position described in the preceding paragraph means that third country recognised CCPs would remain subject to a substantially identical regulatory regime applied by the UK as are applied by the EU today—albeit that the conditions for recognition would not yet be

---

[15] <https://www.bankofengland.co.uk/-/media/boe/files/letter/2017/letter-to-ccps.pdf?la=en&hash=544DA5A3C8759C5D16D66FC5C269452912B8EF3F>

satisfied. Conversely, onshoring results in EU27 CCPs being subject to recognition requirements for the first time. This is because on exit day the status of EU27 CCPs would change from being authorised under Title III of EMIR, under which they may provide services into the UK as of right, to being third country CCPs without authorisation or recognition under onshored EMIR.

13.50 Absent transitional relief, both non-EU27 CCPs and EU27 CCPs would therefore become unable to provide clearing services to trading venues or clearing members established in the UK under Article 25 of onshored EMIR. (The same is true as regards a UK CCP seeking to provide clearing services to trading venues or clearing members established in the EU 27 under EMIR.)

13.51 This poses so-called cliff-edge risks—the risk that, prior to or at the point of exit, the lack of requisite regulatory status would cause a migration of UK counterparties' cleared derivative positions from EU27 CCPs (and of EU27 counterparties' cleared positions from UK CCPs) pending recognition. A key element of the cliff effect risks arises from the possibility that, notwithstanding that the UK and EU are integrated markets operating on the basis of highly harmonised standards today, no mechanism would be in place to provide for equivalence assessments or cooperation arrangements in advance of exit day. Any gap between exit day and recognition would cause significant market disruption as affected CCPs would be required temporarily to exit the UK market, requiring the short-term migration or termination or very large positions.

13.5.3 Transitional Relief: Temporary Deemed Recognition

13.52 To mitigate this risk Part 6 of the CCP SI provides transitional relief for CCPs by way of temporary deemed recognition, and mechanisms to facilitate equivalence assessments and recognition in advance of exit day. Regulations 17 to 19 provides for a temporary recognition regime to provide a fallback for non-UK CCPs to be deemed recognised under onshored EMIR pending equivalence decisions being made. In order to qualify for the regime a CCP must be recognised, authorised, or within the transitional regime for nationally recognised CCPs under Article 89(4) of EMIR at exit day, have notified the Bank of England in advance of exit day of its intent to provide clearing services in the UK following exit day, and if it has submitted an application for recognition in advance of exit day, not have had the application determined by the Bank of England.

13.53 The effect of deemed recognition is to recognise the applicant in respect of those services, activities, and classes of financial instrument within its application which is licensed to perform under EMIR or performs at exit day. CCPs with deemed recognition would need to apply for recognition within six months of exit day or lose their deemed recognition. Otherwise, deemed recognition lasts until the earlier of three years following exit day, the loss of the CCP's authorisation under EMIR, the determination of the CCP's application for recognition or a direction by the Bank of England that the CCP is to cease to be deemed recognised. Recognition would result in a CCP being recognised for the purposes of EMIR and the CRR.

13.5.4 Mechanisms to Facilitate Equivalence Assessments and Recognition in Advance of Exit Day

13.54 In order further to support continuity of services by non-UK CCPs, Articles 12–16 of the CCP SI provide the Bank of England with powers to receive applications and assess and make decisions on the recognition of non-UK CCPs before exit day—with those decisions taking effect on exit day as if they were made under Article 25 EMIR (provided that the other conditions under Article 25 EMIR have also been satisfied).

13.5.5 Other Changes to CCP Regulation

13.55 More broadly, the CCP SI and technical instrument relating to the various Binding Technical Standards which establish the prudential and other supervisory standards for CCPs are subject to a number of minor technical amendments reflecting wider changes associated with the onshoring process (for example changes from EU to UK accounting standards). These do not impose substantive changes to the regulatory regime for UK CCPs.

13.5.6 Recognition of UK CCPs under EMIR

13.56 The continued recognition of UK CCPs under EMIR is also highly important post-Brexit. EU market participants are dependent on UK CCPs for clearing services, and the potential loss of recognition has been a long-standing source of financial market anxiety associated with cliff-edge effects. Responding to this concern the European Commission issued an implementing decision[16] under Article 25(6) of EMIR on 19 December 2018 recognising the UK as equivalent for purposes of Article 25 on exit date (assuming a hard Brexit), to permit EU counterparties to continue to clear through the UK CCPs until 30 March 2020: the Commission has informally indicated that it will further extend recognition until 30 March 2021[17]. ESMA has also provided comfort to market participants that it will adopt recognition decisions in relation to the major UK CCPs following exit date.[18]

13.6 Trade Repository SI

13.6.1 Background

13.57 Similar issues arise in respect of trade repositories as are discussed above in relation to CCPs. Title VII of EMIR provides a regulatory framework for trade repositories established in the EU, which are required to be registered with ESMA to provide trade repository

---

[16] Commission Implementing Decision (EU) 2018/2031, amended by Commission Implementing Decision (EU) 2019/544.
[17] https://ec.europa.eu/commission/presscorner/detail/en/SPEECH_19_6285
[18] <https://www.esma.europa.eu/press-news/esma-news/esma-recognise-three-uk-ccps-in-event-no-deal-brexit>

services. To ensure that transactions are reported to trade repositories Article 9 of EMIR requires that counterparties and CCPs report their derivative contracts (including modifications and terminations) to a trade repository that is either registered, or is a third country trade repository recognised under EMIR. As of November 2019, there are nine registered trade repositories, five of which are incorporated in the UK.

Article 77 of EMIR provides for the recognition of third country trade repositories. In order to be recognised, a third country trade repository must be recognised by ESMA. In order to be recognised, the Commission must have issued an implementing regulation recognising its home jurisdiction as having an equivalent and enforceable regulatory and supervisory framework; the home jurisdiction must have entered into an international agreement with the EU regarding mutual access to and exchange of information on derivative contracts (so as to ensure that the EU has immediate and continuous access to that information); and a cooperation agreement must be in place between the home jurisdiction and ESMA. Possibly because of the difficulties associated with meeting the conditions for recognition, as at the date of writing there are no recognised third country trade repositories under EMIR. **13.58**

13.6.2 Amendments to Onshored EMIR

For onshored EMIR to operate appropriately, the roles conferred on ESMA and the Commission need to move to be the responsibility of UK, rather than EU authorities. To ensure that the onshored EMIR operates effectively after exit day the Trade Repositories SI transfers the equivalence and recognition functions from ESMA to the FCA and from the Commission to HM Treasury, respectively. **13.59**

Regulation 2 of the Trade Repositories SI also limits registration of trade repositories to those established in the UK by amending Article 55 of EMIR, thereby rendering EU27 trade repositories ineligible for registration under onshored EMIR. EU27 trade repositories would therefore fall outside the scope of the registration regime and would need to be recognised under Article 77 of onshored EMIR in order to provide trade repository services to UK counterparties. **13.60**

A key role of trade repositories is to make information available to the public sector to enable them to discharge their functions. Article 81 of EMIR establishes requirements for trade repositories to make information available to various EU and national authorities. Reflecting the narrower geographic scope of onshore EMIR, Regulation 3 of the SI limits the requirement to the FCA, the Bank of England, and the Pensions Regulator. **13.61**

To ensure continuity of trade repository services, Chapter 1 of Part 3 of the Trade Repository SI permits applicants to submit an advance application for registration as a trade repository to the FCA. This may be granted registration in advance of exit day to take effect on and from exit day. This would allow new trade repositories to apply for registration before the FCA takes over the de facto powers over trade repositories under onshored EMIR. **13.62**

Chapter 3 of Part 3 permits UK entities that are currently registered with ESMA as trade repositories to retain their registered trade repository status in the UK on exit day by providing notification in the form prescribed by the FCA before exit day. This would permit **13.63**

UK registered trade repositories to receive trade reports from UK counterparties in scope of the onshored EMIR reporting obligation as it would apply in the UK from exit day.

13.6.3 Transitional Relief: Temporary Deemed Recognition for UK Affiliates

13.64 Chapter 2 of Part 3 provides limited transitional relief for EU27 entities that are currently registered with ESMA as trade repositories (EU27 repositories). EU27 repositories would not be eligible to become registered trade repositories in the UK under onshored EMIR, and (unlike the transitional regime for EU27 CCPs and most other categories of regulated EU27 market participant) there is no transitional licensing provided for them. Instead, Regulation 9 provides that a UK affiliate of an EU27 repository will be deemed to be a registered trade repository in the UK on and after exit day, provided it has submitted a complete advance application for registration, for a period of up to three years after exit day pending the outcome of its advance application for registration.

13.6.4 Other Changes to Trade Repository Regulation

13.65 More generally, the Trade Repository SI and technical instrument relating to the various Binding Technical Standards which establish the supervisory standards for trade repositories are subject to a number of minor technical amendments reflecting wider changes associated with the onshoring process (for example changes from EU to UK accounting standards). These do not involve substantive changes to the regulatory regime for UK trade repositories.

13.7 EMIR SI

13.66 The EMIR SI makes a variety of changes to the scope of EMIR and to the obligations of counterparties and supervision of trade repositories, and provides for transitional relief in respect of certain intragroup obligations. It also makes consequential changes to the Financial Services and Markets Act 2000 (Over the Counter Derivatives, Central Counterparties and Trade Repositories) Regulations 2013[19] and to FSMA.

13.7.1 Scope and Exemptions

13.67 EMIR applies on a pan-European basis to CCPs and their clearing members, to financial counterparties, to trade repositories, to non-financial counterparties, and to trading venues, subject to certain exemptions. In order to narrow the scope of application of onshored EMIR the EMIR SI amends the key definitions of trading venue, financial counterparty and

---

[19] SI 2013/16.

non-financial counterparty in Articles 4(1)(4), (4)(1)(8), and 4(1)(9) respectively so as to limit their scope to venues and counterparties established in the UK, and alternative investment funds managed by alternative investments fund managers which are authorised or registered in the UK and also narrows the exemptions.

Similarly, Article 1(4)(a) of EMIR exempts various classes of counterparty, including the members of the ESCB and other Member States' bodies performing similar functions and other Union public bodies charged with or intervening in the management of the public debt. The EMIR SI limits this exemption to the Bank of England and other public bodies in the UK charged with or intervening in the management of the public debt. **13.68**

A number of consequences flow from these changes in scope: **13.69**

(a) As a result of the narrowing of the counterparty definition, EU27 counterparties would not be directly regulated under onshored EMIR. Onshored EMIR generally would not apply to such counterparties, with one exception. The clearing obligation under Article 4 of EMIR and the risk mitigation requirements under Article 11 of EMIR apply to third country entities where both of the following conditions are satisfied:
   (i) each counterparty is established in a third country and would be subject to the clearing obligation if it were established in the EU; and
   (ii) the contract has a direct, substantial and foreseeable effect within the EU or where such an obligation is necessary or appropriate to prevent the evasion of any of the provisions of EMIR (Articles 4(1)(a)(v) and 11(12): Commission Delegated Regulation 285/2014 further elaborates the latter condition).

Onshored EMIR and the Binding Technical Standard onshoring Regulation onshoring Regulation 285/2014 replicate these requirements, subject to substituting the references to the EU with references to the UK. Accordingly, where an EU counterparty would be subject to the clearing obligation were it established in the UK and contracts with another third country entity which satisfies the condition, then it would be within the scope of Articles 4 and 11 if the second condition above is met. The reverse situation would apply in relation to UK counterparties under EMIR.

(b) Relationships between UK counterparties and EU27 counterparties would attract regulatory obligations under each of EMIR and onshored EMIR. UK counterparties party to OTC derivatives with EU counterparties would need to identify and recategorise their EU27 counterparties, identify the onshored EMIR requirements applicable to the relationship and put in place appropriate procedures to meet those requirements. Again, the reverse situation would apply to the EU counterparty under EMIR in each case.

(c) With respect to trading venues, as a result of the narrowing of the trading venue definition, EU27 trading venues would not be trading venues under onshored EMIR. Onshored EMIR generally would not apply to such venues. EU27 trading venues therefore would lose the benefit of access rights to UK CCPs conferred by Article 7 of EMIR, and the obligation to provide data feeds to UK CCPs required by Article 8 of EMIR. Again, the reverse would be true of UK trading venues under EMIR.

(d) The narrowing of scope of the exemption so as to exclude EU27 central banks and public bodies would have the effect of subjecting UK financial counterparties, when dealing with such central banks and public bodies, to the risk mitigation and clearing requirements under onshored EMIR unless HM Treasury were to exercise its power to make regulations under Article 1 of onshored EMIR to amend the exemptions so as restore the status quo. Again, the reverse would be true of the Bank of England and other UK bodies under EMIR unless the Commission exempts them under Article 1 of EMIR. To enable temporary exemptions to be granted on exit date, the Equivalence Determinations for Financial Services and Miscellaneous Provisions (Amendment etc.) (EU Exit) Regulations 2019[20] (the **Temporary Equivalence Regulations**) empower HM Treasury to exempt the ESCB and EU27 central banks and public bodies from the scope of UK EMIR at any time up to one year from exit date. HM Treasury has exercised its power under the Temporary Equivalence Regulations to exempt the EU27 and other EEA central banks[21]. The Commission has made a corresponding exemption in respect of the position of the Bank of England and Debt Management Office under EMIR[22].

13.70 Another key exemption under EMIR relates to the application of the clearing obligation under Article 4 of EMIR to pension scheme arrangements. Until 17 August 2018 OTC derivatives with pension schemes were exempt from the clearing obligation under Article 89(1) of EMIR. This captured arrangements with various species of EU pension scheme arrangement (defined in Article 2(10)). This exemption has been continued under EMIR REFIT 2.1. In onshoring EMIR HM Treasury has narrowed the definition of pension schemes to UK pension schemes only. To continue to permit EU27 pension schemes to benefit from exemption under onshored EMIR, the EMIR REFIT SI amends Article 89 of onshored EMIR to provide exemption for arrangements with EU27, as well as UK, pension schemes until 18 June 2023.

13.71 Further exemptions exist to the clearing obligation for certain transactions with 'securitisation special purpose entities' (SSPEs) and 'covered bond entities'. These concepts are narrowed under onshored EMIR to capture SSPEs qualifying under the onshored Securitisation Regulation, and UK incorporated covered bond vehicles rather than EU ones. In the case of the former, the Securitisation (Amendment) (EU Exit) Regulations 2019[23] provides a transitional regime for SSPEs qualifying under the EU Securitisation Regulation to continue to benefit from the exemption for two years: in the case of the latter there is equivalent transitional relief under the FCA 'standstill' direction discussed in section 13.8 below, meaning that qualifying transactions with EU covered bond entities would continue to benefit from exemption for the duration of the standstill.

---

[20] 2019/541.
[21] The OTC Derivatives, Central Counterparties and Trade Repositories Exemption Directions 2019 and The OTC Derivatives, Central Counterparties and Trade Repositories Exemption (No.2) Directions 2019.
[22] Commission Delegated Regulation EU) 2019/460.
[23] SI 2019/660.

13.7.2 Definition of OTC Derivative: Exclusion of EU27 Exchange-Traded Derivatives

One of the key definitions in EMIR is the definition of OTC derivative in Article 2(1)(7). This is defined under EMIR so as to capture a derivative the execution of which does not occur on a regulated market within the definition of Article 4(1)(4) of MiFID or a third country market considered to be equivalent to a regulated market under Article 2a. The SI amends the definition so as to replace the reference to a regulated market with a reference to a UK regulated market. Absent equivalence determinations of the EU27 regulated markets, exchange-traded derivatives traded on EU27 regulated markets (**EU ETDs**) therefore would fall to be OTC derivatives under onshored EMIR. This has a number of potential consequences:

13.72

(a) The application of obligations in onshored EMIR would vary dependent upon an entity's categorisation as a financial counterparty or non-financial counterparty. For non-financial counterparties, EMIR distinguishes between entities that take positions in OTC derivative contracts that exceed a specified clearing threshold (calculated on a group basis) (**NFC+**) and entities that do not (**NFC-**). For purpose of the determination of whether a counterparty exceeds the mandatory clearing threshold under Article 10(3) of onshored EMIR, EU27 ETDs would need to be included. This could cause some non-financial counterparties to exceed the clearing threshold as a result of exit and therefore become NFC+, with consequences for their regulatory obligations under EMIR.

(b) EU27 ETDs could become subject to the mandatory clearing obligation under Article 4 of onshored EMIR with respect to derivatives of a class of OTC derivatives that has been declared subject to the clearing obligation (currently, the classes declared subject to the clearing obligation include certain interest rate and credit default derivatives) if concluded in the circumstances contemplated by Article 4(1)(a) of onshored EMIR. Where the mandatory clearing obligation applies a counterparty would be obliged to clear the derivative on a CCP that is authorised or recognised under onshored EMIR to clear that class of OTC derivatives and listed in the Bank of England's register of authorised and recognised CCPs. In practice EU27 ETDs are already cleared: in light of the provision for the temporary deemed recognition regime for EU27 CCPs above, the clearing obligation should be satisfied assuming the relevant EU27 CCP for the EU27 ETD in question has sought to benefit from the regime.

(c) Risk mitigation requirements under Article 11 of onshored EMIR should not apply, however, assuming that the ESMA Q&As are followed in the UK following exit. These include a question and answer on the application of EMIR's risk mitigation requirements which confirms that the risk mitigation requirements apply only to OTC derivatives that are not cleared on a CCP, irrespective of that CCP's status under EMIR.

(d) Consequences could also follow under onshored MiFIR. Under Article 21 of onshored MiFIR, certain derivatives that are subject to the clearing obligation in EMIR must be traded on UK trading venues or, provided HM Treasury has adopted an equivalence decision, third country trading venues (the **trading obligation**). Were EU27 ETDs to be OTC derivatives subject to the clearing obligation for the purpose of onshored EMIR, it is possible that they could also fall to be subject to the trading obligation.

13.73 It is anticipated that the EU27 regulated markets would be granted equivalence by exit day or other relief would be granted to avoid the consequences set out above. To facilitate the grant of equivalence at exit, the Temporary Equivalence Regulations empower HM Treasury to make a temporary equivalence determination up to one year from exit date under Article 2a of UK EMIR in order to provide continuity while the formal process for making an equivalence determination is undertaken. In advance of any determination it appears that the 'standstill' discussed below in section 13.8 would enable market participants to continue to regard EU27 ETDs as not being OTC derivatives pending any determination by HM Treasury.

13.74 The issues above also apply with respect to the definition of OTC derivatives under EMIR following exit, insofar as the EU may not recognise UK exchanges under Article 2a of EMIR.

13.7.3 Definition of OTC Derivative: C6 Energy Derivatives

13.75 A further technical issue associated with the scope of the definition of the term 'derivative' arises by reason of the so-called REMIT carve-out. The term derivative for the purpose of EU EMIR is derived from points (4)–(10) of section C of Annex I to MiFID II. This includes, in paragraph C(6): 'Options, futures, swaps, and any other derivative contract relating to commodities that can be physically settled provided that they are traded on a regulated market, a MTF, or an OTF, except for wholesale energy products traded on an OTF that must be physically settled.'

13.76 To be eligible to the exemption set out in section C(6) of Annex I of MiFID II and not to be considered as a financial instrument, a derivative contract must meet three conditions: it must qualify as a wholesale energy product, it must be traded on an organised trading facility (OTF) and it must be physically settled.

13.77 As a result of the narrowing of the definition of the term OTF to capture only UK OTFs post-Brexit, certain physically settled wholesale energy products traded on an EU OTF will cease to be excluded from derivative status under amendments to the UK Financial Services and Markets Act 2000 (Regulated Activities) Order 2001, as amended. Such instruments would be brought within the scope of UK EMIR (but not EU EMIR). Similar considerations arise for physically settled wholesale energy products traded on a UK OTF and not on an EU OTF under EU EMIR. Article 89a of onshored EMIR empowers the FCA to provide transitional relief in respect of such products by exempting contracts from the clearing and risk mitigation obligations for NFC+s (or NFC+s as at 3 January 2018 which subsequently become authorised, and hence FCs) and from the calculation of the clearing threshold, until 3 January 2021.

13.7.4 Exemptions for Intragroup Transactions

13.78 EMIR exempts certain intragroup transactions from the clearing obligation under Article 4 and margin obligations under Article 11(3). Article 3 provides a definition of intragroup transactions for this purpose, capturing certain transactions with affiliates established in the EU or in a third country for which the Commission has adopted an implementing act under Article 13(2). Article 4 exempts all intragroup transactions from the clearing obligation. Article 11 provides for a series of exemptions for intragroup transactions between parties in different jurisdictions based on notifications and, in certain cases, positive decisions by the competent authorities.

13.79 Article 3 of onshored EMIR limits the first limb of the definition of intragroup transaction in Article 3 to capture affiliates established in the UK, rather than the EU. This would have the effect of taking transactions between a UK counterparty and an EU27 counterparty, which currently fall within the definition under EMIR, outside of the definition under onshored EMIR—in turn applying the clearing obligation and margin obligations to arrangements which are currently exempt.

13.80 The EMIR SI also removes the exemptions applicable to counterparties in different Member States in Article 11 of onshored EMIR, reflecting the treatment of EU27 counterparties as third country counterparties post-exit.

13.81 These changes would impact UK firms which are currently trading via intragroup exemptions as it would disproportionately increase their costs. In order to continue the current treatment of such relationships Article 84 of the EMIR SI therefore establishes a temporary intragroup exemption regime which would ensure that intragroup transactions continue to be exempted from the clearing and margin requirements where this is the case pre-exit, including under Articles 4 and 11 of EMIR and under the delegated regulations on the clearing obligation, pending the making of regulations under Article 13(2) relating to EU27 Member States. This regime would last three years from exit subject to extension by HM Treasury in certain circumstances. Article 85 also enables applications for exemptions in advance of an equivalence determination being made.

13.7.5 Clearing Obligation

13.82 Under Article 4 of onshored EMIR, UK counterparties within the scope of the clearing obligation pre-exit would be obliged to clear certain derivative contracts through CCPs which are authorised or recognised by the Bank of England after exit. Given the availability of transitional recognition for CCPs under the CCP SI, the change in requirement should not result in regulatory disruption to the ability of UK counterparties subject to the clearing obligation to continue existing clearing arrangements for the transitional period, although other considerations may affect EU27 CCPs' willingness to continue to offer clearing services to UK participants post-exit.

13.83 For all financial counterparties and NFC+, the power to set the clearing obligation for different types of asset classes would be transferred from ESMA to the Bank of England, which would also be responsible for maintaining a public register of the classes of OTC derivatives subject to the clearing obligation. The Bank would also be empowered to specify the timing for any phase-in of any new clearing obligations to apply to PRA regulated entities, while the FCA would have the power to specify the timing of entry of any changes to the clearing obligation for other counterparties. Following EMIR REFIT 2.1, Article 6a of onshored EMIR provides for a power for the Bank of England to suspend the clearing obligation under certain circumstances for up to twelve months with the consent of HM Treasury. This power—and process for exercising it—diverges in a number of respects from EMIR REFIT 2.1.

13.84 The Bank of England has indicated as part of its webpages on Brexit[24] that it does not intend to make immediate changes to the classes of OTC derivative to which the existing EU clearing obligation applies. Consistent with this approach, the technical standards instrument issued by the Bank of England relating to the clearing Binding Technical Standards (Commission Delegated Regulations 2015/2205, 2016/592, and 2016/1178) make various technical amendments to the rules to reflect the narrower scope of the application of onshored EMIR and the intragroup exemptions referred to above, but do not make substantive changes to the clearing obligation.

13.7.6 Reporting Obligation

13.85 The EMIR SI amends Article 9 of EMIR to require that UK counterparties and CCPs entering into derivatives would be obliged to report details of those trades to a trade repository that has been registered, or recognised, by the FCA after exit. The responsibility for further specifying reporting requirements would be transferred from EU institutions to the relevant UK regulators, with the Bank of England responsible for setting them for CCPs and the FCA responsible for all other firms.

13.86 This would require counterparties and CCPs to report trades entered into before, and that were outstanding on, 12 February 2014 and trades entered into on and after that date, to a trade repository that has been registered or recognised by the FCA. Because of the lack of transitional recognition of EU27 trade repositories under the onshoring regime, UK counterparties that, in advance of exit day, are reporting to EU27 trade repositories would be required to migrate their reporting arrangements to a UK trade repository (which may be a UK affiliate of an EU27 trade repository which has sought transitional relief under the Trade Repositories SI).

13.87 Article 9(4) of EMIR provides that a disclosure made to a trade repository or to ESMA does not amount to a breach of any restriction on disclosure of information. One effect of onshoring would be to limit the effect of Article 9(4) of onshored EMIR so as to apply as a matter of UK, rather than EU, law. UK counterparties to derivatives with EU27 counterparties would need to reassess whether the discharge of their reporting obligations will amount to a breach of EU law restrictions post-exit and obtain any necessary consents to disclosure.

---

[24] <https://www.bankofengland.co.uk/eu-withdrawal/information-on-the-effect-of-the-uks-withdrawal-from-the-eu-on-fmi-supervision>

13.88 The EMIR SI also amends Article 9 to introduce a power for the FCA, where there is no registered or recognised trade repository available to record the details of a derivative contract, to require submission of reporting direct to it or to suspend the reporting obligation for a period of up to one year (extendible by HM Treasury) with the agreement of HM Treasury. Under this power, the FCA would also be empowered to require firms to report previous trades undertaken during the suspension period once the suspension ends. EMIR REFIT 2.1 makes a number of changes with effect from 18 June 2020 to Article 9 of EMIR to permit one party to a transaction to report ('single sided reporting'): because those changes are effective after the date of the EMIR REFIT 2.1 SI they have not been onshored.

13.7.7 Risk Mitigation Obligations

13.89 The risk mitigation requirements are largely dealt with by the RTS. As a result, beyond the changes to the intragroup exemptions discussed in section 13.7.4 above, the EMIR SI does not make changes to the risk mitigation obligations save to transfer responsibility for technical standards. Responsibility for technical standards associated with the margin obligation would become the dual responsibility of the PRA with respect to PRA regulated entities and the FCA with respect to other counterparties. The EMIR SI also introduces powers for the PRA and FCA to make technical standards in relation to the criteria for intragroup exemptions under Article 11 on the same basis. Other powers under the article are conferred on the FCA.

13.90 The onshoring Binding Technical Standards dealing with the risk mitigation obligations provide for substantive changes to the margin requirement under Delegated Regulation 2015/2205 (the **Risk Mitigation RTS**). Consistent with the approach of treating the EU27 in the same way as third countries, the Bank of England Technical Standards (European Market Infrastructure) (Amendment etc.) (EU Exit) (No. 3) Instrument modifies the onshored Risk Mitigation RTS to conform the treatment of collateral issued by EU issuers with that of third country issuers. This would significantly affect the eligibility of EU-issued collateral and the treatment of such collateral, including rendering EU-issued covered bonds and UCITS funds ineligible as collateral and materially affecting the treatment of other EU-issued collateral. In order to provide transitional relief with respect to the changes to margining, the Instrument includes a new Article 35A which is intended to permit the treatment of EU-issued collateral in the same way as pre-Brexit for a specified period. This is stated to commence at exit date and end on 30 June 2020. It is unclear whether the specified period will be extended to be consistent with the approach taken by the regulators to the standstill discussed below.

13.91 Consistent with the approach taken by the Withdrawal Act to legislation which takes effect following exit date, the Instrument also amends the Risk Mitigation RTS to delete references to the final stage of implementation of the margining requirements (applicable where both counterparties have, or belong to groups each of which has, an aggregate average notional amount of non-centrally cleared derivatives that is above €8 billion and below €750 billion), which comes into effect under EU EMIR on 1 September 2020. Further legislation will be needed if the UK is to follow the EU approach in this regard.

13.7.8 Trade Repository Regulation

13.92 The EMIR SI makes a number of technical amendments to revoke provisions relating to the supervision of trade repositories, including as to registration, appeals, fines, supervisory fees, penalties, and other supervisory requirements, and replace them with provisions that align with those already contained in FSMA concerning supervision and enforcement, including applying the criminal offence of misleading the FCA to trade repositories that apply for registration and recognition from the FCA after exit.

13.93 The EMIR SI also transfers the power to make equivalence decisions for trade repositories under Article 75 from the Commission to HM Treasury, and the power and functions to recognise non-UK trade repositories from ESMA to the FCA. It removes the requirement as set out in Article 75(2) for an international agreement concerning the cross-border transfer of data.

13.8 Standstill

13.94 As described in the preceding sections, the effect of the onshoring SIs and Binding Technical Standards is to make material changes to the substantive and procedural obligations of CCPs, trade repositories, and counterparties, but to defer the effect of many of the most material changes through transitional relief, and to confer discretion on HM Treasury to provide equivalence determinations with respect to the EU Member States which would further mitigate the risk of disruption to cross-Channel derivatives activity.

13.95 Notwithstanding the provisions designed to mitigate the impact of onshoring, the industry has repeatedly indicated that implementation would be highly challenging given the breadth and complexity of the changes. In recognition of the difficulty of implementing changes across the full scope of financial services legislation by exit date, Part 7 of the Amendment SI empowers each of the Bank of England, the PRA, and the FCA to amend the effect of the onshored EU legislative ruleset (including EMIR) in order to provide temporary relief from changes to pre-exit practice by way of Transitional Directions. Regulation 198 of the Amendment SI provides that each regulator may direct that a relevant obligation to which a person is subject is not to apply to the person, or is to apply to the person with modifications specified in the direction, for up to two years from exit date. For this purpose, a 'relevant obligation' is defined in Regulation 199 as an obligation, in relation to a regulator and a person, if the following conditions are met:

(a) the obligation is imposed by or under an enactment;
(b) the obligation is not an excluded obligation (none of the obligations under EMIR fall under the categories of excluded obligation);
(c) the regulator has responsibility for supervising, or has other functions relating to, the person's compliance with the obligation; and
(d) as a result of the operation of an exit instrument (which term includes the SIs and Binding Technical Standards), the obligation begins to apply in the person's case, or applies in the person's case differently from how it would, but for the exit instrument, apply in the person's case.

13.96 Each regulator has produced a draft Transitional Direction[25] affecting the application of requirements which it is responsible for supervising. As responsibility for supervision of obligations under EMIR is split among all three of the regulators, each is relevant.

13.97 All three Transitional Directions share a number of common elements. Each will have the same duration, lasting from exit date to 30 December 2020. Each 'switches off' new relevant obligations and changes to existing relevant obligations to the extent they arise from onshoring, subject to certain exceptions set out in the Transitional Direction. The 'switch off' is achieved by providing that where a relevant obligation:

(a) begins to apply to a person, the relevant obligation shall not apply to that person; and
(b) applies to a person differently from how it would but for an exit instrument, the obligation is modified so that a person does not breach it if he or she complies with the obligation as it applied immediately before exit day, provided that such obligation must be construed in such a way that compliance with it would achieve the same result as it did immediately before exit day but in the context of the United Kingdom no longer being a Member State, with such adaptations to EU references as may be necessary.

13.98 Each Transitional Direction also provides that reporting obligations to EU institutions or recipients are to be read as requirements to report to their UK equivalents.

13.8.1 Scope

13.99 The approach to scoping relevant obligations under the Transitional Directions differs as between the FCA on one hand and the Bank of England and PRA on the other.

13.100 The Bank of England and PRA Transitional Directions purport to apply to all relevant obligations within the scope of their supervisory remit, subject to the exceptions. These capture all obligations which each regulator supervises under EMIR.

13.101 By contrast, the FCA takes the reverse approach: paragraph 3.1 of the FCA Transitional Direction is limited in its application to legislation set out in Annex A to the Direction. Annex A states that it applies to relevant obligations in the legislation specified in column (2) of the Annex. Row 15.1 of that Annex applies to EMIR, and provides guidance to the effect that the standstill does not apply to certain provisions of EMIR—although the effect of the instrument is not to apply the standstill at all other than in respect of Article 4 (discussed in the next paragraph). This stands in contradiction with other public statements made by the FCA whch suggest that the FCA intends that the standstill should apply to all obligations under onshored EMIR except reporting.[26]

---

[25] The Bank of England Transitional Direction is contained in Appendix 2 to CP18/19. The PRA Transitional Direction is contained in Appendix 1 to CP18/19. The FCA Transitional Direction was appended to Policy Statement 19/5: following the regulators' announcement in July 2019 that the standstill would be extended to the end of December 2020 was updated in September 2019 to reflect the revised end date and published on its website: <https://www.fca.org.uk/publication/handbook/draft-transitional-direction.pdf and https://www.fca.org.uk/publication/handbook/draft-transitional-direction-annex-a.pdf>

[26] For example, the FCA published a statement entitled 'Brexit – What We Expect Firms and Other Regulated Persons to Do Now' on 1 February 2019 (<https://www.fca.org.uk/news/statements/brexit-what-we-expect-firms-now>) in which it stated:

13.102 Row 15.2 of Annex A extends the application of the covered bond exemption under Article 4 of onshored EMIR to EU covered bonds for the duration of the standstill notwithstanding the narrowing of the covered bond exemption under Article 129 of onshored CRR to UK covered bonds.

13.8.2 Exceptions

13.103 The exceptions exist to preserve those elements of the onshoring process which are necessary to the functioning of the system post-Brexit. These differ slightly among the three directions. Relevant exceptions in the context of EMIR include obligations:

(a) to which a specific transitional or savings provision contained in an exit instrument, or another direction made by the Bank of England, applies or would apply if it were for the same period as the direction, including the transitional provisions contained in Articles 89(5A) and 89a of onshored EMIR;

(b) which begins to apply in a person's case or applies in the person's case differently as a result of the operation of an equivalence direction or equivalence determination (this would capture changes made as a result of the Treasury making a determination of equivalence under Article 13 of onshored EMIR, for example);

(c) relating to the definition of OTC derivative in Article 2 of EMIR; and

(d) in the case of the Bank of England Transitional Direction only, Article 25 of EMIR.

13.8.3 Effect

13.104 The intended effect of the standstill under the Transitional Directions is to create an environment in which market participants' obligations should not change but for the substitution of UK for EU reporting obligations. The exceptions complicate this position somewhat, as they give rise to the possibility that provisions within (or subject to) the exceptions could be (or become) inconsistent with the pre-Brexit position: however, in practice as the various transitional provisions and equivalence powers effectively mirror the pre-Brexit position, there should generally be no change where they prevail over the standstill. There are two exceptions to this outcome, both derived from the carve-out from the standstill relating to the definition of OTC derivative under Article 2 of onshored EMIR:

(a) first, as discussed at paragraphs 7.7 and 7.8 above: if HM Treasury were not to exercise its power to provide for equivalence of EU27 regulated markets the changes

> The Treasury has published legislation to give the UK financial regulators a power to make transitional provisions connected to changes to financial services legislation. If the UK leaves the EU without an agreement, we intend to use this power broadly to ensure that firms and other regulated entities can generally continue to comply with their regulatory obligations as they did before exit day for a temporary period.
>
> There are some areas where it would not be consistent with our statutory objectives to grant transitional relief. In these areas only, we expect firms and other regulated persons to begin preparing to comply with changed obligations now. The following persons should refer to the Annex of this statement for more information:
>
> […]
>
> Firms subject to reporting obligations under EMIR.

discussed in those paragraphs would come into effect on exit date regardless of the standstill; and

(b) second, as discussed at paragraphs 7.10 to 7.12, the changes to the derivatives within scope of onshored EMIR will take effect regardless of the standstill—requiring counterparties to derivatives which are newly brought within the scope of onshored EMIR to take action to ensure that they comply with the relevant obligations in respect of those contracts from exit date.

13.9 Implications for Market Participants

13.105 Withdrawal from the Single Market would inevitably bring with it transitional challenges as market participants adapt to the creation of frictional barriers between the EU27 and the UK. Migration to third country status on the part of the UK as regards the EU, and vice versa, inevitably would entail substantial changes to regulatory obligations: assuming that onshoring proceeds as contemplated by the SIs, UK and EU27 market participants face substantial compliance exercises to map their changed regulatory obligations as a result of exit, with particular regard to relationships that cross the English Channel, where there would be inevitable changes resulting from the change in status of their counterparties.

13.106 As has been widely discussed, Brexit also risks substantial disruption—including where licensing requirements create new barriers to access. With respect to onshored EMIR, the UK government's approach to the provision of transitional relief to permit continued access on the part of EU market participants to the UK, in particular, should mitigate the most significant regulatory risks of disruption to UK markets at the point of exit to the extent within its powers. In particular, the proposed standstill contemplated by the Transitional Directions and transitional relief proposed under the onshoring legislation and regulation should substantially mitigate the UK regulatory burdens arising from UK onshoring at the point of Brexit, and also preserve access of EU market participants to UK liquidity on broadly the same terms as today. Market participants will need to effect changes to reporting arrangements—including amendments to contracts governing reporting as well as IT systems and processes to manage reporting to UK repositories—at exit date, but will have until the end of 2020 to prepare for full implementation. The key question from the UK legal perspective in the meantime will be whether HM Treasury will grant equivalence to the EU27 Member States for purposes of onshored EMIR, in order to ease the continued conduct of cross-Channel derivatives activity. The question of the UK approach to margin requirements will also likely gain more prominence given the magnitude of the changes, and their impact on margining between UK and EU27 counterparties.

13.107 The approach taken by the EU to the parallel issues arising for its markets arising from Brexit will also be critical, however. There has been considerable industry pressure for the EU to provide transitional relief for UK CCPs to avoid a mass migration of cleared positions from the UK CCPs in advance of exit day. This has resulted in transitional relief provided by the EU for transactions cleared on UK CCPs, but it is not clear that this will be extended beyond March 2021. Even if it is, but it seems unlikely that the other areas in which onshored EMIR provides transitional relief would be mirrored by the EU—creating considerable disincentives to cross-Channel activity. Further, other regulatory requirements which are outside the scope of EMIR—particularly the share and derivatives trading obligations under MiFIR, and the requirement for authorisation to conduct cross-border business under MiFID 2—are also relevant to firms' ability to conduct cross-Channel business efficiently post-Brexit. The general approach of the EU to such areas has been to refuse to provide concessions, or even equivalence assessments where available, pre-Brexit—meaning that some disruption to trading patterns is inevitable.

13.108 Future developments are also likely to pose further barriers to the cross-border provision of CCP services from the UK into the EU27 following Brexit. In particular, the EMIR REFIT 2.2 proposals contemplate a more intrusive approach to the recognition and supervision of systemic non-EU CCPs, with the possibility of withdrawal of recognition where a recognised CCP poses risks of sufficient magnitude to EU financial stability. This is widely perceived as an attempt to force clearing in euro-denominated transactions to migrate to the EU.

13.109 Longer term, it appears inevitable that political pressure in Europe to take back control of European financial markets will result in some migration of OTC derivatives trading and clearing activity from the UK to the EU27.

14

Benchmarks Regulation

Michael Thomas and Anahita Patwardhan[*]

14.1 Introduction

> Attempted manipulation of benchmarks and market prices, misuse of confidential information, misrepresentation to clients and attempted collusion have led to huge fines, reputational damage, diversion of management resources and the reining in of productive risk taking. Market effectiveness has been impaired. And public trust has been severely damaged.
>
> *Fair and Effective Markets Review*[1]

14.01 The aftermath of the 2008 financial crisis revealed a number of serious cases of manipulation affecting important benchmarks including LIBOR and EURIBOR.[2] There were also allegations of manipulation of energy, oil, and foreign exchange benchmarks.

14.02 Financial services regulators in the UK and worldwide became aware of the need for measures to improve the transparency, governance, and integrity of benchmarks. This led to a number of international and national initiatives to regulate benchmarks. The European Benchmarks Regulation[3] (the '**Benchmarks Regulation**') is the latest step in this series of initiatives to prevent benchmark manipulation and to protect the markets. It does so by imposing restrictions on entities which use benchmarks, and those which produce or contribute to benchmarks.

14.03 Brexit will not substantially change the way in which this regulation will apply. A hard Brexit will, however, have the effect of creating two separate regulatory regimes in the EU and the UK. This will create extra compliance hurdles for entities providing or using benchmarks on a cross-border basis.

14.04 This chapter covers the following matters:

- a summary of the history of the regulation of benchmarks in the UK (see section 14.2);
- a description of the way the regime is likely to apply in the UK post-Brexit (see section 14.3); and

---

[*] This chapter was prepared in July 2019. Please see section 14.5 for information on relevant updates that have occurred after this point.
[1] Bank of England, *Fair and Effective Markets Review* (June 2015). Available at: <https://www.bankofengland.co.uk/report/2015/fair-and-effective-markets-review---final-report>
[2] FCA, *Benchmark Enforcement* (22 April 2016). Available at: <https://www.fca.org.uk/markets/benchmarks/enforcement>.
[3] Regulation (EU) 2016/1011 of 8 June 2016 on indices used as benchmarks in financial instruments and financial contacts or to measure the performance of investment funds [2016] OJ L171/1 (hereafter Benchmarks Regulation).

- a description of the cross-border challenges that will be created as a result of Brexit (see section 14.4).

14.2 The History of the Regulation of Benchmarks in the UK

14.2.1 International Initiatives: IOSCO Principles

14.05 Financial benchmarks remained largely unregulated prior to 2013. In 2013, the Board of the International Organization of Securities Commissions (**IOSCO**) produced a set of ten high-level principles (the '**IOSCO Principles**')[4] aiming to create an overarching framework for benchmarks used in financial markets, addressing conflicts of interest, transparency, and openness. Although the IOSCO Principles are fairly high level and non-prescriptive, the concepts and policy considerations articulated by IOSCO have strongly influenced the development of legislation at the European level.

14.06 The IOSCO Principles cover the following areas:

- overall responsibility and oversight—the benchmark administrator should retain ultimate control for every aspect of the benchmark determination process; where a third party is involved in the benchmark determination process or where a third party acts as calculation agent, the benchmark administrator should oversee the activities of such third parties;
- conflicts of interest—benchmark administrators should document, implement, and enforce procedures and policies to identify, disclose, manage, mitigate, and avoid conflicts of interest;
- control framework and internal oversight—benchmark administrators should implement a tailored control framework for determining and distributing the benchmark; benchmark administrators should develop an oversight function to review and challenge every aspect of the benchmark determination process;
- benchmark design and data sufficiency—when designing a benchmark, benchmark administrators should seek to accurately and reliably represent the economic realities of the interest the benchmark measures and eliminate factors that might distort the value of the benchmark; benchmarks should be based on prices, rates, indices, or values that have been formed by an active market with observable bona fide, arm's-length transactions;
- transparency—benchmark administrators should publish a concise explanation detailing how the benchmark determination was developed; benchmark administrators should make available guidelines regarding the hierarchy of data inputs to make clear to users the manner in which data and expert judgement is used in producing a benchmark;
- periodic review—benchmark administrators should periodically review the conditions in the underlying interest that the benchmark measures;

---

[4] IOSCO, *Principles for Financial Benchmarks Final Report* (July 2013). Available at: <http://www.iosco.org/library/pubdocs/pdf/IOSCOPD415.pdf>

- quality of the methodology—benchmark administrators should publish information about the methodology of each benchmark and the rationale for any material change to methodology; benchmark administrators should introduce a code of conduct for benchmark submitters (those contributing input data to benchmarks), and implement procedures and policies for making necessary changes to benchmark methodology; and
- accountability—benchmark administrators should implement and publish complaints procedures, maintain records, undertake audits of compliance with the principles and the benchmark methodologies, and cooperate with relevant regulatory authorities.

14.07 The IOSCO Principles are intended to be used as recommended practice, both for benchmark administrators and for entities which submit input data to benchmark administrators. IOSCO expects that the IOSCO Principles may be applied in a proportional manner depending on the size and risks involved in the benchmark-setting process.[5]

14.08 The IOSCO Principles were endorsed in September 2013 by G20 leaders and have, since then, been applied by financial regulators, benchmark administrators, and submitters.[6]

14.2.2 UK Initiative: Regulation of Specified Benchmarks

14.09 Following widely reported benchmark-related misconduct, Martin Wheatley, the Financial Conduct Authority's (**FCA**) chief executive-designate was tasked with independently reviewing the setting and usage of LIBOR with the aim of introducing reform. The Wheatley Review[7] was published, and made several policy recommendations.

14.10 A key recommendation of the Wheatley Review was that the activities of submitting input data for, and the administration of, certain benchmarks should be regulated by the FCA. Given the importance of LIBOR to the efficient operation of financial markets and the apparent inadequacy of the existing governance arrangements, the Wheatley Review made the case that these activities should be brought within the regulatory perimeter.

14.11 This was achieved by introducing a number of new 'regulated activities' applicable to benchmarks.[8] These came into effect the day after the majority of the old Financial Services Authority's functions were transferred to the FCA and Prudential Regulatory Authority (**PRA**), on 2 April 2013. The new regulated activities comprised:

- administering the arrangements for determining a specified benchmark and collecting, analysing, or processing information for the purpose of determining a specified benchmark; and

---

[5] Ibid.
[6] IOSCO, *Statement on Matters to Consider in the Use of Financial Benchmarks* (5 January 2018). Available at <https://www.iosco.org/library/pubdocs/pdf/IOSCOPD589.pdf>
[7] Wheatley Review, *The Wheatley Review of LIBOR* (September 2012). Available at: <https://assets.publishing.service.gov.uk/government/uploads/system/uploads/attachment_data/file/191762/wheatley_review_libor_finalreport_280912.pdf>
[8] Financial Services and Markets Act 2000 (Regulated Activities) (Amendment) Order 2013, SI 2013/655. This added ss. 63O(1)(a) and 63O(1)(b) to the Financial Services and Markets Act 2000 (Regulated Activities) Order 2001.

- providing information in relation to a specified benchmark, to a person who has permission to carry on the activity specified in the bullet point above, for the purpose of determining the specified benchmark.

14.12 Any legal person performing either of these activities would need to be authorised by the FCA, or to be exempt.[9] Entities with the relevant authorised status would then also be subject to FCA requirements summarised in BENCH 2.1 of the FCA Handbook. These included meeting requirements in the FCA Handbook in relation to senior management arrangements (SYSC), statements of principle and codes of practice for approved persons (APER), and market conduct (MAR).

14.13 It was determined that the FCA would only regulate the provision of certain 'specified benchmarks'. Initially, LIBOR was the only specified benchmark. However, following the Fair and Effective Markets Review in 2015 (a comprehensive review of standards in wholesale fixed income, currency, and commodity markets carried out jointly by the FCA, the Bank of England, and HM Treasury),[10] the regulation of specified benchmarks in the UK was extended to seven further benchmarks from 1 April 2015: ICE Swap Rate, Sterling Overnight Index Average, Repurchase Overnight Index Average, WM/Reuters London 4 p.m. Closing Spot Rate, LBMA Gold Price, LBMA Silver Price, and the ICE Brent Index.[11]

The manipulation of benchmarks was also made a criminal offence in the UK from 1 April 2013.

14.14 Section 91 of the Financial Services Act 2012 created two offences:

- making a false or misleading statement in the course of arrangements for the setting of a relevant benchmark; and
- creating a false or misleading impression as to the price or value of any investment or the interest rate appropriate to any transaction where the impression may affect the setting of a benchmark.

14.15 The motivations of the person making the false or misleading statement or impression are immaterial under these offences, which carry a penalty of imprisonment or a fine or both.[12]

14.2.3 The Benchmarks Regulation

14.16 On 28 April 2016 the European Parliament approved the final text of the Benchmarks Regulation, and this was published by the European Council on 29 June 2016.

14.17 The Benchmarks Regulation came into effect on 1 January 2018.[13] However, the practical effect of the Benchmarks Regulation has been limited due to the application of transitional provisions (see sections 14.3.10 and 14.4.2.4).

---

[9] Financial Services and Markets Act 2000, s 19.
[10] Bank of England, *Fair and Effective Markets Review*.
[11] Benchmarks (Amendment) Instrument 2015.
[12] Financial Services Act 2012, s. 92.
[13] Certain requirements came into force prior to this date.

14.18 The Benchmarks Regulation essentially replaces the specified benchmarks regime described above, except that entities currently subject to the specified benchmarks regime will continue to be subject to those requirements until they are authorised or registered under the Benchmarks Regulation.

14.3 The Regulation of Benchmarks in the UK

14.3.1 The UK's Post-Brexit Approach to the Benchmarks Regulation

14.19 As of the date of writing,[14] the Benchmarks Regulation is directly applicable in the UK as a matter of EU law. In addition, when the Benchmarks Regulation came into effect, changes were made to UK domestic legislation and the FCA rules to facilitate the implementation of the Benchmarks Regulation. The current regime, as it applies in the UK, is therefore based on a mix of EU legislation and guidance and UK domestic law and regulation.

14.20 We expect that the regime that will apply in the UK post-Brexit will be nearly identical to the regime which currently applies in the UK. The UK statutory instrument relating to the replication of the Benchmarks Regulation into UK law was published on 25 March 2019 (the '**Brexit Benchmarks SI**')[15] and the changes set out in that statutory instrument will take effect on exit day if there is no implementation period. In line with other onshored EU financial services regulations, the Benchmarks Regulation itself will be copied into UK law with consequential amendments made to reflect the fact that it should operate as a purely domestic UK regime and not as a framework for a pan-EU regime. For example, amendments have been made to replace references to 'competent authorities' or to EU bodies, such as the European Securities and Markets Authority (**ESMA**) and the European Commission, with references to the FCA and HM Treasury. Similarly, references defining the territory of application of the regime have been amended, so that references to the 'Member States' or to the 'European Union' will be replaced with references to the 'United Kingdom'. In the paragraphs below, we refer to this process as the '**onshoring process**'. Chapter 6 (paragraphs 6.93–6.101) provide more information on the onshoring process.

14.21 In the paragraphs below, we have described how the Benchmarks Regulation currently applies in the EU, and have explained how we would expect the provisions to apply post-Brexit in light of the Brexit Benchmarks SI. While UK-located benchmark administrators seeking authorisation or registration will continue to apply to the FCA, the Brexit Benchmarks SI clarifies that the territorial scope of the onshored Benchmarks Regulation extends only to the UK and not to the whole of the EU. Further, it ensures that EU-located benchmark administrators are subject to the onshored third country regime, which requires third country benchmark administrators or benchmarks to become recognised or endorsed until the third countries' supervisory regimes are deemed equivalent under the relevant provisions in the Brexit Benchmarks SI. See section 14.4 for more information.

---

[14] July 2019.
[15] The Benchmarks (Amendment and Transitional Provision) (EU Exit) Regulations 2019 (SI 2019/657).

14.22 As a general point, a number of the terms used in the Benchmarks Regulation refer to terms defined in other areas of EU law (for example, in Directive 2014/65/EU). As part of the onshoring process, these references have, in some instances, been updated to refer to the equivalent onshored rules under UK law.

14.3.2 The Purpose of the Benchmarks Regulation

14.23 The Benchmarks Regulation introduces a common framework and consistent approach to benchmark regulation across the EU. Post-Brexit, we expect that this framework and approach will be applied on an equivalent basis within the UK.

14.24 The main objective of the Benchmarks Regulation is to ensure that benchmarks produced and used in the EU are robust, reliable, transparent, representative of the market within which they function, and are fit for purpose. In pursuit of those aims, the Benchmarks Regulation imposes requirements on:

- users of a benchmark within the EU (see section 14.3.5 below);
- benchmark administrators—that is, a natural or legal person that has control over the provision of a benchmark[16] and that in particular administers the arrangements for determining the benchmark, collects and analyses the input data, determines the benchmark, and publishes it[17] (a '**benchmark administrator**') (see sections 14.3.6 and 14.3.7 below); and
- contributors of input data[18] to a benchmark—meaning natural or legal persons that provide input data not readily available to a benchmark administrator, that is required in connection with the determination of a benchmark, and is provided for that purpose[19] (see section 14.3.9 below).

14.25 While the onshoring process will not change the structure and approach taken by the Benchmarks Regulation, one point that will change as part of the onshoring process is the territorial scope of the regime.

14.26 The Benchmarks Regulation currently applies to benchmarks used in the EU, including the UK. Post-Brexit, the Benchmarks Regulation will apply to benchmarks used in the EU, but not to those used in the UK. The UK benchmarks regime post-Brexit (comprising the onshored version of the Benchmarks Regulation) will only apply to benchmarks used in the UK. The effect of this change is that where a benchmark administrator is authorised under one regime (e.g. in the UK), it will not automatically be authorised for the purposes of the other regime (e.g. in the EU). This will create barriers to the use of benchmarks on a cross-border basis. See section 14.4 for more information.

---

[16] Benchmarks Regulation, Art. 3(1)(6).
[17] Ibid., recital 16.
[18] Meaning the data in respect of the value of one or more underlying assets, or prices, including estimated prices, quotes, committed quotes, or other values, used by an administrator to determine a benchmark (ibid., Art. 3(1)(14)).
[19] Ibid., Art. 3(1)(8).

14.3.3 The Meaning of a 'Benchmark'

Under the Benchmarks Regulation, a 'benchmark' is: (1) any index by reference to which the amount payable under a financial instrument[20] or a financial contract,[21] or the value of a financial instrument, is determined; or (2) an index that is used to measure the performance of an investment fund with the purpose of tracking the return of such index or defining the asset allocation of a portfolio or computing the performance fees.[22] **14.27**

In turn, an 'index' is defined as any figure: **14.28**

- that is published or made available to the public;
- that is regularly determined, entirely or partially, by the application of a formula or any other method of calculation, or by an assessment; and
- where this determination is made on the basis of the value of one or more underlying assets, or prices, including estimated prices, actual or estimated interest rates, or other values or surveys.[23]

These concepts will remain substantially unchanged under the UK regime following the onshoring process. In relation to the terms set out above, the Brexit Benchmarks SI amends the definitions of 'financial instruments'[24] and 'financial contracts'.[25] **14.29**

14.3.4 Scope of the Benchmarks Regulation

The Benchmarks Regulation does not apply where an index provider[26] is unaware (and could not reasonably have been aware) that an index it provides is being used for the specified purposes which would cause it to be deemed a benchmark.[27] **14.30**

In addition, the Benchmarks Regulation does not apply to:[28] **14.31**

- central banks;

---

[20] Meaning a financial instrument within the scope of Directive 2014/65/EU of 15 May 2014 on markets in financial instruments and amending Directive 2002/92/EC and Directive 2011/61/EU [2014] OJ L173/349 (hereafter Directive 2014/65/EU), s. C, Annex I.

[21] Meaning credit agreements as defined in Directive 2008/48/EC of 23 April 2008 on credit agreements for consumers and repealing Council Directive 87/102/EEC [2008] OJ L133/66, Art. 3(c) or Directive 2014/17/EU of 4 February 2014 on credit agreements for consumers relating to residential immovable property and amending Directives 2008/48/EC, and 2013/36/EU and Regulation (EU) No. 1093/2010 [2014] OJ L60/34 (hereafter Directive 2014/17/EU), Art. 4(3).

[22] Benchmarks Regulation, Art. 3(1)(3).

[23] Ibid., Art. 3(1)(1).

[24] Meaning an instrument specified in Part 1 of Sch. 2 to the Regulated Activities Order for which a request for admission to trading on a UK trading venue has been made or which is traded on a UK trading venue or via a systemic internaliser as defined in Art. 2(1)(12) of the Markets in Financial Instruments Regulation, Brexit Benchmarks SI, Art. 5(4).

[25] Meaning any credit agreement, which immediately before exit day, satisfied the definition of a credit agreement in EU Benchmarks Regulation, Art. 3(17)(h); a mortgage agreement as defined in FSMA, s. 423A; and a credit agreement as defined in Directive 2008/48/EC, Art. 3(c). Brexit Benchmarks SI, Art. 5(6) modifies Directive 2008/48/EC.

[26] An 'index provider' is a natural of legal person that has control over the provision of an index (Benchmarks Regulation, Art. 3(1)(2)).

[27] Ibid., Art. 2(2).

[28] Ibid.

- public authorities, where they contribute data to, provide or have control over the provision of, benchmarks for public policy purposes (including measures of employment, economic activity, and inflation);
- central counterparties, where they provide reference prices or settlement prices used for risk-management purposes and settlement;
- the provision of a single reference price for any financial instruments;[29]
- the press, other media, and journalists where they only publish or refer to a benchmark as part of their journalistic activities and have no control over the provision of that benchmark;
- a natural or legal person who grants or promises to grant credit in the course of its trade, business, or profession, but only in so far as that person publishes or makes available to the public its own variable or fixed borrowing rates set by internal decisions and applicable only to financial contracts[30] entered into by that person (or by a company within its group) with their respective clients; and
- commodity benchmarks based on submissions by contributors which are in majority non-supervised entities where the following two conditions apply:
  - the benchmark is referenced by financial instruments[31] for which a request for admission to trading has been made on only one trading venue,[32] or which are traded on only one such trading venue, and
  - the total notional value of financial instruments referencing the benchmark does not exceed €100 million.

14.32 With the exception of definitional amendments (to 'financial instruments', 'financial contracts', and 'trading venue'), and some changes of references from EU legislation to UK legislation in the Brexit Benchmarks SI, these concepts will remain substantially unchanged under the UK regime following the onshoring process.

14.3.5 Restriction on the Use of Benchmarks

14.33 Under the EU regime, where a supervised entity uses a benchmark or a combination of benchmarks in the EU, it must ensure that the benchmark or its benchmark administrator is listed on a register maintained by ESMA.[33] This will be the case where:

- the benchmark administrator is authorised or registered (see section 14.3.6 below); or
- the benchmark is produced by a third country benchmark administrator which has obtained equivalence or recognition, or which has had its benchmarks endorsed (see section 14.4.2).

---

[29] Meaning a financial instrument within the scope of Directive 2014/65/EU, s. C, Annex I. See also Brexit Benchmarks SI, Art. 4(b)(ii) which substitutes the reference of Directive 2014/65/EU with Sch. 2 of the Regulated Activities Order.
[30] Meaning credit agreements as defined in Directive 2014/65/EU, Art. 3(c) or Directive 2014/17/EU, Art. 3(4).
[31] Meaning a financial instrument within the scope of Directive 2014/65/EU, s. C, Annex I.
[32] As defined in Directive 2014/65/EU, Art. 4(1)(24). See also Brexit Benchmarks SI, Art. 4(b)(iii) which refers to a UK trading venue rather than a trading venue.
[33] Benchmarks Regulation, Art. 29(1).

The term 'supervised entity' in this context applies to credit institutions,[34] investment firms,[35] insurance undertakings,[36] reinsurance undertakings,[37] a UCITS or a UCITS management company,[38] an alternative investment fund manager (AIFM),[39] an institution for occupational retirement provision,[40] a creditor[41] for the purposes of credit agreements,[42] a non-credit institution[43] for the purposes of credit agreements,[44] a market operator,[45] a central counterparty,[46] a trade repository,[47] and a benchmark administrator.

14.34

Use of a benchmark[48] in this context refers to:

- the issuance of a financial instrument which references an index or a combination of indices;
- determination of the amount payable under a financial instrument or a financial contract by referencing an index or a combination of indices;
- being a party to a financial contract which references an index or a combination of indices;
- providing a borrowing rate[49] calculated as a spread or mark-up over an index or a combination of indices and that is solely used as a reference in a financial contract to which the creditor is a party; and
- measuring the performance of an investment fund through an index or a combination of indices for the purpose of tracking the return of such index or combination of indices, of defining the asset allocation of a portfolio, or of computing the performance fees.

ESMA has clarified that this would include (1) trading venues where the derivative is subject to a request for admission to trading on such trading venue or is traded on such trading venue;[50] (2) an investment firm acting in the capacity of a systematic internaliser where the derivative is traded via a systematic internaliser;[51] (3) a central counterparty where the derivative is cleared by such central counterparty (in each of (1)–(3), to the extent that

14.35

---

[34] As defined in Regulation (EU) 575/2013 of 26 June 2013 on prudential requirements for credit institutions and investment firms and amending Regulation (EU) No. 648/2012 [2013] OJ L176/1, Art. 4(1)(1).
[35] As defined in Directive 2014/65/EU, Art. 4(1)(1).
[36] As defined in Directive 2009/138/EC of 25 November 2009 on the taking up and pursuit of the business of Insurance and Reinsurance (Solvency II) [2009] OJ L335/1 (hereafter Directive 2009/138/EC), Art. 13(1).
[37] As defined in Directive 2009/138/EC, Art. 13(4).
[38] Each as defined in Directive 2009/65/EC of 13 July 2009 on the coordination of laws, regulations and administrative provisions relating to undertakings for collective investment in transferable securities (UCITS) [2009] OJ L302/32 (hereafter Directive 2009/65/EC), Art. 1(2).
[39] As defined in Directive 2011/61/EU of 8 June 2011 on Alternative Investment Fund Managers and amending Directives 2003/41/EC and 2009/65/EC and Regulations (EC) No. 1060/2009 and (EU) No. 1095/2010 [2011] OJ L174/1 (hereafter Directive 2011/61/EU), Art. 4(1)(b).
[40] As defined in Directive 2003/41/EC of 3 June 2003 on the activities and supervision of institutions for occupational retirement provision [2003] OJ L235/10, Art. 6(a).
[41] As defined in Directive 2014/65/EU, Art. 3(b).
[42] As defined ibid., Art. 3(c).
[43] As defined in Directive 2014/17/EU, Art. 4(1).
[44] As defined ibid., Art. 4(3).
[45] As defined in Directive 2014/65/EU, Art. 4(1)(18).
[46] As defined in Regulation (EU) 648/2012 of 4 July 2012 on OTC derivatives, central counterparties and trade repositories [2012] OJ L201/1, Art. 2(1).
[47] As defined ibid., Art. 2(2).
[48] Benchmarks Regulation, Art. 3(1)(7).
[49] As defined in Directive 2014/65/EU, Art. 3(j).
[50] Each as defined ibid., Art. 4(1)(24).
[51] Each as defined ibid., Art. 4(1)(20).

the relevant entity has set the relevant terms of the derivative and thus chosen the specific benchmark to be referenced); or (4) each party to a transaction of a derivative where none of points (1)–(3) applies, particularly if the parties trade on an organised trading facility that has not set the terms of the contract.[52]

14.36 This restriction will continue to apply to supervised entities in the UK following the onshoring process. However, the list of regulated financial institutions falling within the definition of 'supervised entity' has been amended in the Brexit Benchmarks SI. Credit institutions, investment firms, a UCITS or a UCITS management company have been replaced with CRR firms,[53] UK investment firms, UK UCITS, or management companies, respectively. Additionally, occupational pension schemes have been included in the definition of supervised entity.[54] In most cases, the effect of this has been to replace EU regulatory concepts with UK concepts. Similarly, for UK supervised entities, the relevant list of benchmarks and benchmark administrators will be maintained by the FCA (rather than ESMA).

14.3.6 Authorisation and Registration of Benchmark Administrators

14.3.6.1 Requirement to be authorised or registered

14.37 Under the Benchmarks Regulation, a person in the EU that intends to act as a benchmark administrator will need to apply to be authorised or registered.[55] The application must be made to the competent authority of the Member State in which the relevant person is located.

14.38 See section 14.3.6.2 for an explanation of the differences between authorisation and registration.

14.39 These requirements have already been implemented in the UK by introducing an additional regulated activity: administering a benchmark.[56] No person can carry on a regulated activity (or purport to do so) unless that person is authorised or exempt.[57] As a result, benchmark administrators must be authorised in the UK by the FCA in order to perform services in the UK.

14.40 When applying for authorisation or registration, the applicant must provide all information necessary to satisfy the FCA that the applicant has established all the necessary arrangements to meet the requirements of the Benchmarks Regulation.[58] ESMA has clarified that this means that any such applicant must be in a position to meet the requirements of the Benchmarks Regulation at the time of authorisation or registration and not before that date.[59] We expect that the FCA will continue to have regard to this helpful clarification

---

[52] ESMA, *Questions and Answers on the Benchmarks Regulation (BMR)* (version 13, 23 May 2019) (hereafter ESMA, *Q&A on Benchmarks Regulation*), question 5.2.
[53] This is a CRR firm as defined in Art. 4(1)(2A) of Regulation (EU) No. 575/2013 of the European Parliament and of the Council of 26 June 2013 on prudential requirements for credit institutions and investment firms and amending Regulation (EU) No. 648/2012, which is a credit institution referred to in point (a)(i) of that definition.
[54] Brexit Benchmarks SI, Art. 5(5).
[55] Benchmarks Regulation, Art. 34(1).
[56] Regulated Activities Order, Art. 63S.
[57] Financial Services and Markets Act 2000, s. 19.
[58] Benchmarks Regulation, Art. 34(4).
[59] ESMA, *Q&A on Benchmarks Regulation*, question 7.1.

post-Brexit, in light of its statement that it will continue to have regard to such EU non-legislative materials where and if they are relevant.[60]

14.3.6.2 The differences between authorisation and registration

14.41 An entity will need to be authorised or registered depending on the type of benchmark activities it is conducting, and the type of entity it is. Authorisation is a more extensive approval process reserved for higher risk activities, while registration is a more streamlined process applicable to lower-risk activities and activities conducted by entities which are already regulated.[61]

14.42 Entities which are authorised and registered are ultimately supervised in the same way and subject to the same requirements under the Benchmarks Regulation.[62]

14.43 Under the EU regime, a natural or legal person located in the EU that intends to act as a benchmark administrator will need to apply for registration if: [63]

- it is a supervised entity (other than a benchmark administrator) that provides or intends to provide indices which are used or intended to be used as benchmarks but only if (1) the rules which apply to the supervised entity do not prevent it from providing a benchmark activity and (2) none of the indices provided would qualify as a critical benchmark (see section 14.3.8 below); and
- it provides or intends to provide only indices which would qualify as non-significant benchmarks. See section 14.3.8 for more detail in relation to non-significant benchmarks.

14.44 A natural or legal person located in the EU that intends to act as a benchmark administrator and does not fall within one of the categories in the paragraph above will need to apply for authorisation.[64] These requirements will also be applied under the post-Brexit UK regime to persons located in the UK intending to act as benchmark administrators. The Brexit Benchmarks SI requires natural and legal persons in the UK (rather than the EU) to apply for authorisation and assigns the FCA as the responsible body for authorisation and registration applications.[65]

14.45 Authorisation is a more extensive process.[66] There is a detailed list of information that must be provided in an application for authorisation, including general information, organisational structure and governance information, information in relation to its conflicts of interest policies and procedures, information in relation to its internal control, oversight and accountability framework, a description of the benchmarks or families of benchmarks provided, information in relation to the input data and methodology and details of any outsourcing.[67]

---

[60] FCA Guidance, *Brexit: Our Approach to EU Non-Legislative Materials* (March 2019).
[61] Benchmarks Regulation, recital 48 provides the context for the provisions on authorisation and registration.
[62] ESMA, *Discussion Paper: Benchmarks Regulation* (15 February 2016), ch. 12.2.
[63] Benchmarks Regulation, Art. 34(1).
[64] Ibid.
[65] Brexit Benchmarks SI, Art. 31
[66] ESMA, *Final Report: Draft Technical Standards under the Benchmarks Regulation* (30 March 2017), ch. 10.2.
[67] Regulation (EU) 2018/1646 of 13 July 2018 supplementing Regulation (EU) 2016/1011 of the European Parliament and of the Council with regard to regulatory technical standards for the information to be provided in an application for authorisation and in an application for registration [2018] OJ L274/43, Annex I.

14.46 An application for registration is a more streamlined process than the authorisation process. This is appropriate as the applicant is already known to the relevant competent authority as a supervised entity, or in light of the benchmarks involved.[68] As a result, the information to be provided as part of an application for registration is reduced compared to the information required as part of the authorisation process.[69] It should be noted that there is not a single set of requirements applicable to all applications for registration as the requirements vary depending on the particular circumstances. The requirements are tailored for supervised entities providing non-critical benchmarks and non-supervised entities providing a mix of significant and non-significant benchmarks. In the circumstance where a supervised entity provides a mix of significant and non-significant benchmarks, the elements of information concerning the providing entity and the provision process remain the same, while those inherent to the particular benchmarks provided are subject to a different degree of granularity of required information (depending on the category to which the benchmarks belong).[70]

14.47 In order to reduce the burden on applicants sending duplicative information, ESMA has clarified that the information need not be provided by the applicant if the relevant competent authority would easily be in possession of it, or where the information is or will be required from the applicant by the Benchmarks Regulation apart from the application process.[71]

14.3.6.3 Impact of Brexit

14.48 The requirement for benchmark administrators located in the UK to be authorised or registered in the UK will not change as a result of Brexit. Similarly, the process for obtaining authorisation and registration in the UK will remain substantially unchanged as a result of the onshoring process. Following the onshoring process, the FCA will no longer be expected to notify ESMA when granting registration or authorisation, as is currently required under Article 34(7) of the Benchmarks Regulation.[72]

14.49 Once authorised or registered (as applicable), benchmark administrators will be included on an official public register of qualifying administrators and benchmarks established and maintained by ESMA.[73] Following the onshoring process, the FCA will establish and maintain a separate official public register for those benchmark administrators that it has authorised or registered in the UK and for third country benchmarks.[74]

14.50 Post-Brexit, the EU and the UK will operate separate regulatory regimes for benchmarks. In the absence of an agreement between the UK and the EU, benchmark administrators in the UK will be treated as third country benchmark administrators for the purposes of the EU regime, and will need to apply the provisions relevant to third country benchmark administrators. Benchmark administrators that are operating or providing services in the UK that are not authorised or registered by the FCA will need to consider whether they have the

---

[68] ESMA, *Final Report: Draft Technical Standards*, ch. 10.2.
[69] Regulation 2018/1646, Annex II.
[70] ESMA, *Final Report: Draft Technical Standards*, ch. 10.2.
[71] Ibid.
[72] Brexit Benchmarks SI, Art. 31(6)
[73] Benchmarks Regulation, Art. 36.
[74] Brexit Benchmarks SI, Art. 33.

appropriate status in the UK before continuing to operate or provide services in the UK. See section 14.4 for further detail.

14.3.7 Requirements Applicable to Benchmark Administrators

The Benchmarks Regulation imposes a number of different requirements on benchmark administrators themselves and the way in which they produce relevant benchmarks. Table 14.1 summarises the types of requirements that are applied.

14.51

Type of requirement	Examples
Governance and conflict-of-interest requirements	• Requirement to have a clear organisational structure with well-defined, transparent, and consistent roles and responsibilities for all persons involved in the provision of a benchmark.[1] • Requirement to take adequate steps to identify and to prevent or manage conflicts of interest. Any judgement or discretion in the benchmark process must be honestly and independently exercised.[2] • The provision of a benchmark must be operationally separated from any part of a benchmark administrator's business that may create an actual or potential conflict of interest.[3] In certain cases, an independent oversight function may need to be established.[4] • Detailed requirements for the benchmark administrator to establish and operate adequate policies and procedures, as well as effective organisational arrangements for the identification, disclosure, prevention, and mitigation of conflicts of interest in order to protect the integrity and independence of benchmark determinations.[5] • Ensure their employees have the necessary skills, knowledge, and experience for the duties assigned to them and be subject to effective management and supervision.[6] • Establish specific internal control procedures to ensure the integrity and reliability of an employee or person determining the benchmark.[7]
Oversight function requirements	• Requirement to have a permanent and effective oversight function to ensure oversight of all aspects of the provision of benchmarks, including robust procedures.[8] • The oversight function must be carried out by a separate committee or another appropriate governance arrangement.[9] • Detailed requirements for the oversight function including annual review of the benchmark's definition and methodology and assessment of internal and external audits or reviews and monitoring the implementation of identified remedial actions.[10]

(*Continued*)

Table 14.1 Continued

Type of requirement	Examples
Control framework requirements	• Requirement to have a control framework that ensures benchmarks are provided and published or made available in accordance with the Benchmarks Regulation.[11] • The control framework must be proportionate to the level of conflicts of interest, the extent of discretion in the provision of the benchmark, and the nature of the input data.[12] • Detailed requirements including management of operational risk, adequate and effective business continuity and disaster recovery plans, and contingency procedures.[13] • The control framework should be available to the relevant competent authority and, on request, to users.[14] • Benchmark administrators must also establish measures to ensure that contributors adhere to the code of conduct and comply with applicable standards for input data, and establish measures to monitor input data.[15]
Accountability framework requirements	• Requirement to have accountability framework covering keeping, auditing and review, and a complaints process.[16] • Requirement to designate an internal function to review and report compliance with the benchmark methodology and the Benchmarks Regulation.[17] • For critical benchmarks, requirement to appoint an independent external auditor.[18]
Record-keeping requirements	• Requirement to keep records of certain data for five years including input data and the use of such data; any exercise of judgement or discretion by the benchmark administrator; and changes in or deviation from standard procedures and methodologies.[19] • Records of telephone conversations or electronic communications with contributors or submitters must also be kept for three years.[20]
Complaints-handling mechanism	• Requirement to have in place and publish procedures for receiving, investigating, and retaining records concerning complaints.[21] • The complaints-handling policy must be made available and complaints must be investigated in a timely and fair manner. • Inquiries must be conducted independently of any personnel who may be or have been involved in the subject matter of the complaint.[22]

Table 14.1 Continued

Type of requirement	Examples
Outsourcing	• Requirement to not outsource functions in the provision of a benchmark where control or regulator supervision over the provision is materially impaired.[23] • The benchmark administrator remains fully responsible for outsourced functions or any relevant services and activities in the provision of a benchmark.[24] • Detailed requirements in the event that functions, services, or activities are outsourced including ensuring that such third party has the ability, capacity, and all relevant authorisations to perform such functions, services, or activities reliably and professionally, and the ability to terminate.[25]
Input data	• Detailed requirements in relation to input data including that input data accurately and reliably represents the market or economic reality that the benchmark is intended to measure.[26] • Input data must be verifiable[27] and (where relevant) obtained from a reliable and representative panel or sample of contributors.[28] • Transaction data should be used where available and appropriate.[29] • Requirement to publish clear guidelines regarding the types of input data, the priority of use, and the exercise of expert judgement.[30] • Input data must not be used where there are indications that the contributors do not adhere to the benchmark administrator's code of conduct.[31] • Requirements around contribution of input data by a 'front office' function.[32]
Methodology	• Requirement to use a robust and reliable methodology with clear rules.[33] • Detailed requirements in relation to the methodology including that it should be rigorous, continuous, and capable of validation including, where appropriate, back-testing against available transaction data.[34] • A range of factors must be taken into account in developing methodologies including the size and normal liquidity of the market, the transparency of trading, and the positions of market participants.[35]
Transparency of methodology	• Requirement to operate methodology transparently including publishing or making available the key elements of the methodology, details regarding the internal review and approval and the frequency of the view, and the procedures for consulting on any proposed material change.[36]
Reporting of infringements	• Requirement to establish adequate systems and effective controls to ensure the integrity of the input data in order to be able to identify and report to the competent authority any conduct that may involve actual or attempted manipulation of a benchmark.[37]

(*Continued*)

Table 14.1 Continued

Type of requirement	Examples
Code of conduct	• Requirement to develop a code of conduct for each benchmark where such benchmark is based on input data from contributors.[38] • The code must cover certain areas, for example, a clear description of the input data to be provided, identification of the contributors and submitters, and policies to ensure a contributor provides all relevant input data, systems, and controls that a contributor is required to establish.[39] • Benchmark administrators may develop a single code of conduct for each family of benchmarks they provide.[40]

[1] Benchmarks Regulation, Art. 4(1).
[2] Ibid.
[3] Ibid., Art. 4(2).
[4] Ibid., Art. 4(3).
[5] Ibid., Art. 4(6).
[6] Ibid., Art. 4(7).
[7] Ibid., Art. 4(8).
[8] Ibid., Art. 5(1).
[9] Ibid., Art. 5(4).
[10] Ibid., Art. 5(3).
[11] Ibid., Art. 6(1).
[12] Ibid., Art. 6(2).
[13] Ibid., Art. 6(3).
[14] Ibid., Art. 6(5).
[15] Ibid., Art. 6(4).
[6] Ibid., Art. 7(1).
[7] Ibid., Art. 7(2).
[18] Ibid., Art. 7(3).
[19] Ibid., Art. 8(1).
[20] Ibid., Art. 8(2).
[21] Ibid., Art. 9(1).
[22] Ibid., Art. 9(2).
[23] Ibid., Art. 10(1).
[24] Ibid., Art. 10(2).
[25] Ibid., Art. 10(3).
[26] Ibid., Art. 11(1)(a).
[27] Ibid., Art. 11(1)(b).
[28] Ibid., Art. 11(1)(d).
[29] Ibid., Art. 11(1)(a).
[30] Ibid., Art. 11(1)(c).
[31] Ibid., Art. 11(1)(e).
[32] Ibid., Art. 11(3).
[33] Ibid., Art. 12(1)(a) and (b).
[34] Ibid., Art. 12(1)(c).
[35] Ibid., Art. 12(2)(a).
[36] Ibid., Art. 13(1).
[37] Ibid., Art. 14(1).
[38] Ibid., Art. 15(1).
[39] Ibid., Art. 15(2).
[40] Ibid., Art. 15(3).

14.3.8 Benchmark Categories

14.52 The Benchmarks Regulation differentiates between categories of benchmarks, and imposes different requirements on each category. Benchmarks are categorised by reference to:

- their importance: as 'critical', 'significant', or 'non-significant'; and
- their subject matter: including regulated data, commodities, and interest rates.

14.53 The rules apply in slightly different ways depending on the category of benchmark. The next section explores these differences in further detail.

14.3.8.1 The categories of benchmark under the EU regime
(a) Critical benchmarks

14.54 The Benchmarks Regulation envisages the establishment of an official list of benchmarks deemed 'critical' which will be established and reviewed at least every two years.[75] This means that the list of critical benchmarks will be specified by the Commission under implementing acts. To qualify as 'critical', a benchmark must fulfil at least one of the following conditions:

- it is used directly or indirectly within a combination of benchmarks as a reference for assets[76] with a total value of at least €500 billion (on the basis of all the range of maturities or tenors of the benchmark, where applicable);[77]
- it is based on submissions by contributors the majority of which are located in one Member State and it is recognised as being critical in that Member State;[78] or
- it meets all three of the following criteria:
  - it is used directly or indirectly within a combination of benchmarks as a reference for assets[79] (the '**Reference Assets**') with a total value of at least €400 billion (on the basis of all the range of maturities or tenors of the benchmark, where applicable, but not exceeding the value of €500 billion);[80]
  - it has no or very few appropriate market-led substitutes[81] ('**Poor Substitutability**'); and
  - if the benchmark ceases to be provided or be reliable,[82] there would be significant and adverse impacts on market integrity, financial stability, consumers, the real economy or the financing of households or corporations in one or more Member States ('**High Failure Impact**').[83]

---

[75] Benchmarks Regulation, Art. 20(1).
[76] That is, for financial instruments or financial contracts or for the determination of the performance of investment funds.
[77] Ibid., Art. 20(1)(a).
[78] Ibid., Art. 20(1)(b).
[79] That is, for financial instruments or financial contracts or for the determination of the performance of investment funds.
[80] Ibid., Art. 20(1)(c)(i).
[81] Ibid., Art. 20(1)(c)(ii).
[82] That is, if it were provided on the basis of input data no longer fully representative of the underlying market or economic reality or unreliable input data.
[83] Ibid., Art. 20(1)(c)(iii).

14.55 Where a benchmark has Reference Assets totalling less than €400 billion but has Poor Substitutability and High Failure Impact, the competent authority may nevertheless direct that the benchmark should be recognised as critical.[84]

14.56 Where a benchmark administrator of critical benchmarks intends to cease providing those benchmarks, it must immediately notify its competent authority[85] and provide an assessment of how the benchmark will be wound down or transitioned to a new benchmark administrator.[86] The competent authority will make its own assessment of the cessation or transition, and may compel the benchmark administrator to continue publishing the benchmark until transfer or orderly cessation can be achieved, or the benchmark is no longer critical, for a maximum period of up to twenty-four months in total.[87]

14.57 Where the majority of contributors to a critical benchmark are supervised entities, the supervised contributors must give advance notice to the benchmark administrator if they intend to cease contributing input data, and the benchmark administrator must report to its competent authority on the implications for the benchmark's ability to measure the underlying market or economic reality. The competent authority will make its own assessment, and may compel the supervised entity to continue contributing input data for a maximum period of up to twenty-four months in total. It may also require the benchmark administrator to change its code of conduct, methodology, or other rules of the critical benchmark.[88]

(b) Significant benchmarks

14.58 A benchmark which does not meet the criteria to qualify as 'critical' is 'significant' where:

- it is used for Reference Assets with a total value of at least €50 billion[89] (on the basis of all the range of maturities or tenors of the benchmark, where applicable, over a period of six months);[90] or
- it has no or very few appropriate market-led substitutes and, if the benchmark ceases to be provided or be reliable,[91] there would be a significant and adverse impact on market integrity, financial stability, consumers, the real economy or the financing of households or businesses in one or more Member States.[92]

14.59 A benchmark administrator must immediately notify its competent authority when its significant benchmark falls below the €50 billion threshold mentioned above.[93]

14.60 Benchmark administrators of significant benchmarks have the option not to apply certain requirements[94] of the Benchmarks Regulation where they consider that applying them

---

[84] Ibid., Art. 20(1).
[85] Ibid., Art. 21(1).
[86] Ibid., Art. 21(1)(b).
[87] Ibid., Art. 21(3).
[88] Ibid., Art. 23.
[89] The European Commission will have power to adopt delegated acts in order to review the calculation method used to determine the €50 billion threshold in light of market, price, and regulatory developments as well as the appropriateness of the classification of benchmarks which serve as a reference to assets which total an amount close to the threshold. This review will take place every two years after the Benchmarks Regulation becomes applicable.
[90] Ibid., Art. 24(1)(a).
[91] That is, if it were provided on the basis of input data no longer fully representative of the underlying market or economic reality or unreliable input data.
[92] Ibid., Art. 24(1)(b).
[93] Ibid., Art. 24(3).
[94] These requirements are set out ibid., Art. 4(2)(c)–(e), 11(3), or 15(2).

would be disproportionate taking into account the nature or impact of the benchmark or the benchmark administrator's size.[95] A benchmark administrator who chooses to do this must immediately notify the competent authority and provide it with all relevant information confirming the benchmark administrator's proportionality assessment.[96] It is possible for the competent authority to overrule the benchmark administrator's decision where it deems this appropriate in light of a number of factors, including the vulnerability of the benchmark to manipulation and the benchmark's importance to financial stability.[97]

(c) Non-significant benchmarks

Benchmarks which are neither 'critical' nor 'significant' are 'non-significant' and benchmark administrators of such benchmarks have the option to disapply a greater number of requirements[98] of the Benchmarks Regulation.[99]

14.61

Where a benchmark administrator exercises its option to disapply specified requirements of the Benchmarks Regulation, it must publish and maintain a compliance statement explaining its decision.[100] This applies to benchmark administrators of both 'significant' and 'non-significant' benchmarks. Unlike benchmark administrators of significant benchmarks, benchmark administrators of non-significant benchmarks are not subject to having their decision overruled. However, the competent authority is entitled to request additional information and can require changes to the compliance statement.

14.62

The requirements for non-significant benchmarks largely differ from those for significant benchmarks on the basis that: (a) there is no assessment by the competent authority of the appropriateness of the exemptions elected by the benchmark administrator; (b) the compliance statement should be provided to the relevant competent authority; and (c) the competent authority may require additional information as well as changes to ensure compliance with the Benchmarks Regulation.[101]

14.63

(d) Regulated-data, commodity, and interest rate benchmarks

'Regulated-data benchmarks' are also exempted from certain requirements[102] of the Benchmarks Regulation.[103] Broadly, a regulated-data benchmark is one determined by the application of a formula from input data that is contributed entirely and directly from either the net asset values of investment funds or certain other regulated sources (such as trading venues, electricity and natural gas exchanges, auction platforms, approved reporting mechanisms, and approved publication arrangements).[104]

14.64

A separate and more concise set of rules[105] apply to the provision of 'commodity benchmarks' in place of the usual requirements (with the exception of the outsourcing rules),

14.65

---

[95] Ibid., Art. 25(1).
[96] Ibid., Art. 25(2).
[97] Ibid., Art. 25(3).
[98] These requirements are set out ibid., Arts. 4(2), 4(7)(c)–(e), 4(8), 5(2), 5(3), 5(4), 6(1), 6(3), 6(5), 7(2), 11(1)(b), 11(2)(b)–(c), 11(3), 13(2), 14(2), 15(2), 16(2), and 16(3).
[99] Ibid., Art. 26(1).
[100] Ibid., Arts. 25(7) and 26(3).
[101] ESMA, *Final Report: Draft Technical Standards*, ch. 7.2.
[102] These requirements are set out in Benchmarks Regulation, Arts. 11(1)(d)–(e), 11(2), 11(3), 14(1), 14(2), 15, and 16 (and Art. 8(1)(a) with reference to input data that are contributed entirely and directly as specified Art. 3(1)(24)).
[103] Ibid., Art. 17(1).
[104] The full definition of a regulated-data benchmark is set out ibid., Art. 3(1)(24).
[105] Ibid., Annex II.

unless the benchmark is a regulated-data benchmark or is based on submissions by contributors which are in majority supervised entities.[106] In addition, where a commodity benchmark is a critical benchmark and the underlying asset is gold, silver, or platinum then the usual requirements will apply instead of the separate rules for commodity benchmarks.[107]

14.66 Interest rate benchmarks are also subject to a separate set of rules[108] which apply in addition to or in substitution of the usual requirements.[109]

14.3.8.2 Adapting the categories of benchmarks for the UK regime

14.67 The range or types of benchmark category will not change materially as a result of the onshoring process.

(a) Critical benchmarks

14.68 The Brexit Benchmarks SI introduces an additional Article A20[110] which sets out the procedure that the FCA and HM Treasury must follow in order to specify a benchmark as critical under the onshored version of the Benchmarks Regulation. In particular, the FCA is required to conduct certain reviews and submit reports to the Treasury of their recommendations.

14.69 The Brexit Benchmarks SI amends Article 20[111] of the Benchmarks Regulation, which sets these conditions for specifying a benchmark as critical. The Brexit Benchmarks SI does not make any material changes to these conditions, however, within these conditions, it does omit references to 'Member States' in substitution for the 'United Kingdom'. The conditions therefore only take into account UK-specific factors.

14.70 Other amendments to this article relate to the transfer of functions away from ESMA and the Commission to the FCA and HM Treasury. Currently, under the Benchmarks Regulation, where the FCA considers that a benchmark should be recognised as critical under the Benchmarks Regulation, it is to notify ESMA and transmit to ESMA a documented assessment every two years. ESMA then has six weeks to issue an opinion on this and transmit it to the Commission.[112] Under the Brexit Benchmarks SI, the FCA is to provide a written report of its assessment to HM Treasury every two years and that the first such review should take place within the period of two years[113] beginning with exit day.

(b) Significant benchmarks

14.71 Article 24[114] of the Benchmarks Regulation, which refers to the conditions for specifying a significant benchmark, is also amended. There are similarly no substantive changes to the conditions sets out in the provision, except for the assessment being carried out by reference to the UK only.

---

[106] Ibid., Art. 19(1).
[107] Ibid., Art. 19(2).
[108] Ibid., Annex I.
[109] Ibid., Art. 18.
[110] Brexit Benchmarks SI, Art. 15
[111] Ibid., Art. 16
[112] Benchmarks Regulation, Art. 20(2)–(4)
[113] Brexit Benchmarks SI, Art. 16(7)–(8)
[114] Ibid., Art. 20

14.72 The thresholds for 'critical' and 'significant' benchmarks are subject to review every two years by the Commission. The Commission has the power to adopt delegated acts in order to review the calculation method used to determine the threshold in light of market, price, and regulatory developments, as well as the appropriateness of the classification of benchmarks which serve as a reference to assets which total an amount close to the relevant financial threshold. Under the Brexit Benchmarks SI, this review process will be undertaken by the FCA, who have to report their findings to HM Treasury. The Brexit Benchmarks SI states that the first such review should take place within the period of two years[115] beginning with exit day.

14.73 The Brexit Benchmarks SI does not make any amendments to Articles 17–19 of the Benchmarks Regulation, which set out the requirements relating to regulated-data benchmarks, interest rate benchmarks and commodity benchmarks.

14.3.9 Requirements Applicable to Benchmark Contributors

14.74 A supervised contributor is a supervised entity that contributes input data to a benchmark administrator located in the EU.[116] There are a number of requirements applicable to the benchmark administrator in relation to any input data obtained from contributors including, for example, to develop a code of conduct for each benchmark that clearly specifies the contributors' responsibilities with respect to input data.[117] The benchmark administrator must be satisfied that contributors adhere to the code of conduct on a continuous basis and at least annually and in case of changes.[118]

14.75 The Benchmarks Regulation imposes a number of governance and controls requirements on supervised contributors themselves. These include a requirement for the supervised contributor to ensure that the provision of input data is not affected by any existing or potential conflict of interest and that, where any discretion is required, it is independently and honestly exercised based on relevant information in accordance with the benchmark administrator's code of conduct.[119] In addition, the supervised contributor must have in place a control framework that ensures the integrity, accuracy, and reliability of all contributions of input data to the benchmark administrator including limits on who may submit data, appropriate training for submitters, conflicts measures including operational separation of employees where appropriate and consideration of how to remove incentives to manipulate any benchmark created by remuneration policies and record-keeping requirements.[120]

---

[115] Ibid., Art. 16(8).
[116] Benchmarks Regulation, Art. 3(1)(10).
[117] Ibid., Art. 15(1).
[118] Ibid. These provisions remain unchanged under the Brexit Benchmarks SI except for transfer of functions from ESMA to the FCA (see Art. 13).
[119] Benchmarks Regulation, Art. 16(1).
[120] Ibid. These provisions remain unchanged under the Brexit Benchmarks SI except for transfer of functions from ESMA to the FCA (see Art. 14).

14.76 The Brexit Benchmarks SI amends the definition of a 'supervised contributor' such that it is now defined as a supervised entity that contributes input data to a benchmark administrator located in the UK.[121]

14.3.10 Transitional Provisions

14.3.10.1 Transitional provisions: benchmark administrators

14.77 The Benchmarks Regulation contains a number of transitional provisions. These have had the effect of significantly limiting the practical impact of the Benchmarks Regulation thus far.

14.78 The transitional provisions are contained in Article 51 of the Benchmarks Regulation. There are five separate transitional provisions. Four of these are relevant to index providers based in the EU. These are considered below. There is a separate transitional provision which deals with third country benchmarks and their administrators, which is described in section 14.4.

14.79 Transitional provisions are proposed to be included in UK law as part of the onshoring process, although the relevant provisions have been substantially redrafted.[122]

14.80 The availability of transitional provisions may have the practical effect of delaying the impact of any changes in this area that may be caused by Brexit.

(a) Index provider providing a benchmark on 30 June 2016

- The first transitional provision applies to an index provider[123] that was providing a benchmark on 30 June 2016. An index provider which meets this requirement will only be required to apply for authorisation or registration by 1 January 2020. This effectively gives an index provider extra time before it will become subject to the Benchmarks Regulation. This provision also applies to updates and modifications of benchmarks already provided before 1 January 2018, as well as the provision of new benchmarks for the first time after 1 January 2018.[124] The transitional provision applies unless and until an application for authorisation or registration is refused.
- The Brexit Benchmarks SI has replaced the text of this transitional provision with new text. Under the new provisions in the Brexit Benchmarks SI, the following transitional provisions apply.[125]
    (i) An index provider providing a benchmark in the UK[126] on 30 June 2016 is required to apply for authorisation or registration on or before 31 December 2019 (rather than by 1 January 2020), in order to enable the benchmark to be used on or after 1 January 2020.

---

[121] Brexit Benchmarks SI, Art. 5(3).
[122] Ibid., Art. 42
[123] Any natural or legal person who has control over the provision of an index (Benchmarks Regulation, Art. 3(1)(2)).
[124] ESMA, *Q&A on Benchmarks Regulation*, question 9.1.
[125] Brexit Benchmarks SI, Art. 42(2).
[126] The transitional provision applies where the benchmark is provided in the UK.

(ii) A supervised entity may use such a benchmark in the period between exit day and one of the following dates:
    (1) if the index provider has made an application for authorisation or registration and the application has been refused, the date on which the provider has been notified of such refusal;
    (2) if the index provider has made an application for authorisation or registration and the application has been granted, the date on which the benchmark/administrator appears on the register;
    (3) if the index provider has not made an application, 31 December 2019.
    For the purposes of the chapter, we refer to this period as the '**relevant period**'.
(iii) There are provisions which make clear when the transitional provisions will cease to apply (e.g. if an application for authorisation or registration is approved or refused).

- As at the date of writing, there is a proposal in process to extend the transitional period for existing critical benchmarks until 2021. See [reference to separate chapter update] for more information.

(b) FCA option to register rather than authorise

- The second transitional provision enables a Member State to choose to register rather than authorise an index provider (see section 14.3.6.1 above). Where an index provider is applying for authorisation before 1 January 2020, the competent authority of the Member State in which the index provider has applied has the option to decide to register that index provider as an administrator (rather than to authorise the entity) even if it is not a supervised entity. This applies only where the index provider does not provide a critical benchmark, and the competent authority is aware that the indices are not widely used in the EU.[127]
- The Brexit Benchmarks SI proposes to amend this provision such that the FCA may only register an index provider who was providing a benchmark in the UK[128] on 30 June 2016 or an index provider that was providing a benchmark in the UK in the period beginning with 1 July 2016 and ending with 31 December 2017,[129] rather than any index provider who applies for authorisation before 1 January 2020. The transitional provision is also amended to refer specifically to the FCA (as opposed to 'competent authority') and to the UK instead of 'Member State'.

(c) Index provider providing an existing benchmark on 1 January 2018

- The third transitional provision applies where an index provider is providing an existing benchmark on 1 January 2018. The existing benchmark can be used by supervised entities until 1 January 2020 or, where the index provider has applied for authorisation or registration, unless and until that application is refused.[130] This applies to modifications and updates to existing benchmarks, but does not apply to any new benchmarks. The difference between this provision and the first provision is that

---

[127] Benchmarks Regulation, Art. 51(2).
[128] Please note this territorial limitation, the benchmark must have been provided in the UK.
[129] Brexit Benchmarks SI, Art. 42(3)
[130] Benchmarks Regulation, Art. 51(3).

this provision applies to index providers that started providing benchmarks after 30 June 2016.[131]
- The Brexit Benchmarks SI proposes to delete this transitional provision, and substantially replaces this concept with new drafting.
- Under the Brexit Benchmarks SI, a supervised entity may use a benchmark during the relevant period where such benchmark was provided by a UK index provider in the United Kingdom in the period beginning with 1 July 2016 and ending with 31 December 2017. It is worth noting that this is different from the language used in the Benchmarks Regulation. Whereas the transitional provisions in the Benchmarks Regulation (as clarified by the ESMA Q&A) refer to benchmarks which the index provider starts to provide between 30 June 2016 and 1 January 2018, the transitional provisions in the Brexit Benchmarks SI refer to benchmarks provided in the period beginning with 1 July 2016 and ending with 31 December 2017.[132]

(d) *Competent authority/FCA option to allow use of a benchmark which does not meet requirements under certain conditions*

- The fourth transitional provision applies where an existing benchmark does not meet the requirements of the Benchmarks Regulation. The competent authority of the Member State in which the index provider is located may permit an existing benchmark to be used if certain conditions are met. These apply if ceasing or changing that benchmark to fulfil the requirements of the Benchmarks Regulation would result in a force majeure event under, frustrate, or otherwise breach: (1) the terms of any financial contract[133] or financial instrument[134] or (2) the rules of any investment fund,[135] which references the benchmark. There is then a restriction on any financial instruments, financial contracts or, measurements of the performance of an investment fund adding a reference to such a benchmark after 1 January 2020.[136]
- The Brexit Benchmark SI removes reference to 'existing' benchmark and instead refers just to benchmark. This suggests that this transitional provision may be available for benchmarks which were provided after the implementation of the Benchmarks Regulation (i.e. which are not 'existing').

14.81 There is also a separate transitional provision which applies to benchmarks provided by entities based outside the EU (or, in respect of the onshored UK regime, the UK). See section 14.4.3.2, for more information. There have recently been changes made to this transitional provision, see [reference to chapter update].

14.82 The Brexit Benchmarks SI includes two new definitions: 'transition period' which means the period beginning with exit day and ending with 31 December 2019[137] and 'UK index provider' which means an index provider located in the United Kingdom.[138]

---

[131] ESMA, *Q&A on Benchmarks Regulation*, question 9.2.
[132] Brexit Benchmarks SI, Art. 42(2).
[133] Meaning credit agreements as defined in Directive 2014/65/EU, Art. 3(c) or Directive 2014/17/EU, Art. 4(3).
[134] Meaning a financial instrument within the scope of Directive 2014/65/EU, s. C Annex I.
[135] Meaning an AIF as defined in Directive 2011/61/EU, Art. 4(1)(a), or a UCITS as defined in Directive 2009/65/EC, Art. 1(2).
[136] Benchmarks Regulation, Art. 51(4).
[137] Brexit Benchmarks SI, Art. 42(8).
[138] Ibid.

14.3.10.2 Transitional provisions: supervised contributors

14.83 As noted in section 14.3.9, the Benchmarks Regulation includes governance and control requirements applicable to supervised contributors. Article 51 of the Benchmarks Regulation does not contain transitional provisions applicable to these governance and control requirements. This means that supervised contributors should comply with the applicable governance and control requirements[139] from 1 January 2018. This approach has also been confirmed by ESMA in its Q&A on the Benchmarks Regulation.[140] We expect the FCA to take the same approach as ESMA in light of their guidance that firms and market participants should continue to apply the guidelines issued by European Supervisory Authorities to the extent that they remain relevant, as they did before exit day.[141]

14.84 The Benchmarks Regulation also includes requirements on benchmark administrators to produce a code of conduct and to ensure that supervised contributors comply with that code of conduct (as noted in section 14.3.9).[142] During the transitional period, benchmark administrators may not have produced a code of conduct as benchmark administrators may not be authorised or registered during that period. As such, ESMA has clarified that supervised contributors should only comply with the applicable governance and control requirements to the extent these provisions are applicable without a code of conduct.[143]

14.4 Brexit and the Benchmarks Regulation: Cross-border Issues

14.4.1 Introduction

14.85 A Hard Brexit will create challenges for entities providing and using benchmarks in the UK and the EU.

14.86 As described in more detail above (in section 14.3.5), the Benchmarks Regulation contains a restriction on the types of benchmarks that a 'supervised entity' based in the EU is permitted to use for specified purposes.[144] A particular benchmark may only be used if (a) its benchmark administrator is based in the EU and is on ESMA's public register (see Article 26 of the Benchmarks Regulation), or (b) the benchmark itself is listed on that register.

14.87 As noted in section 14.3.5, restrictions on use under the Benchmarks Regulation will be replicated under UK law. This means that supervised entities based in the UK will only be able to use benchmarks for specified purposes where either (a) the benchmark administrator is on the FCA register and is located in the UK, or (b) the benchmark itself (for third country benchmarks) is on that register, subject to the transitional provisions in Part 3 of the Brexit Benchmarks SI.

14.88 Post-Brexit, these restrictions will make it more difficult for benchmarks administered in the UK to be used by EU entities and vice versa.

---

[139] Benchmarks Regulation, Art. 16(1).
[140] ESMA, *Q&A on Benchmarks Regulation*, question 6.1
[141] FCA Guidance, *Brexit*.
[142] Benchmarks Regulation, Art. 15(1).
[143] ESMA, *Q&A on Benchmarks Regulation*, question 6.1.
[144] Benchmarks Regulation, Art. 29.

14.4.2 The Impact of Brexit on benchmark administrators Based in the UK

14.89 In the absence of Brexit, a benchmark administrator based in the UK which is authorised or registered with the FCA would have been treated as authorised or registered in accordance with Article 34 of the Benchmarks Regulation. The benchmark administrator would have automatically been listed on ESMA's public register, and the benchmarks that they administer would have been capable of being 'used' by an EU supervised entity.

14.90 However, following a Hard Brexit, a benchmark administrator based in the UK which is authorised or registered in the UK will not be treated as authorised or registered in the EU. ESMA has issued a public statement which indicates that 'in case of a no-deal Brexit, UK administrators included in the 'ESMA register of administrators before the date of the no-deal Brexit will be deleted from the ESMA register' and will be considered to be third country administrators, subject to the transitional provisions in the Benchmarks Regulation (as detailed further below).[145] It will also not be possible for that benchmark administrator to become authorised or registered in the EU in accordance with article 34 of the Benchmarks Regulation.

14.91 Instead, a UK-based benchmark administrator will need to pursue one of the following three options to enable its benchmarks to be 'used' by supervised entities in the EU.

- The benchmark administrator may obtain an equivalence decision. See section 14.4.2.1 for more information.
- The benchmark administrator may obtain recognition. See section 14.4.2.1 for more information.
- The benchmark administrator may arrange for its benchmarks to be endorsed by a benchmark administrator within the EU. See 14.4.2.3 for more information.

14.4.2.1 Option 1: equivalence

14.92 A benchmark administrator based outside the EU and the benchmarks which they administer can be added to the ESMA register and used in the EU if the benchmark administrator is determined to be subject to equivalent supervision to that which would apply in the EU.[146] To achieve this status, the following conditions must be met.

- The Commission must have adopted an equivalence decision stating that the legal framework and supervisory practice of the third country (i.e. in this case, the UK) ensures compliance with equivalent requirements to the Benchmarks Regulation, taking into account whether the framework and supervisory practice ensures compliance with the relevant IOSCO Principles (see section 14.2.1). The Commission may adopt a decision that the legal framework and supervisory practice of the third country meets

---

[145] ESMA public statement, *Impact of Brexit on MiFID II/MiFIR and the Benchmark Regulation (BMR)—C(6) carve-out, trading obligation for derivatives, ESMA opinions on third-country trading venues for the purpose of post-trade transparency and position limits, post-trade transparency of OTC transactions, BMR ESMA register of administrators and 3rd country benchmarks* (7 March 2019). Available at <https://www.esma.europa.eu/sites/default/files/library/esma70-155-7253_public_statement_mifidii_bmr_provisions_under_a_no_deal_brexit.pdf>

[146] Benchmarks Regulation, Art. 30.

this requirement only in respect of specific benchmark administrators or specific benchmarks, or it may make a decision that the requirements are met generally.
- ESMA must have established a cooperation agreement with the relevant authority in the third country—in this case, the FCA. This cooperation agreement should cover topics such as the exchange of information between the regulators, the process by which the third country regulator will promptly notify breaches to ESMA, and procedures for coordinating supervisory activities (such as inspections). There are regulatory technical standards which specify the minimum content of these cooperation arrangements.[147]
- The benchmark administrator must be authorised or registered in the third country and must be subject to supervision by a third country regulator.
- Finally, the benchmark administrator must have notified ESMA of its consent to its benchmarks being used in the EU, confirmed which of its benchmarks may be used, and confirm the name of its regulator.

14.93 Given that the requirements under the Benchmarks Regulation will be copied into UK law, one could argue that the UK's legal and regulatory framework for benchmarks should arguably be regarded as equivalent in this context. However, the Commission is able to make equivalence decisions at its discretion, and it is not obliged to assess or to consider the position of any jurisdictions. This means the availability of this option will be at the Commission's discretion. ESMA will also need to have agreed a cooperation agreement with the FCA. Given this, until these arrangements have been put in place, this is not a viable option for an individual benchmark administration business seeking to provide its benchmarks to users in the EU.

14.94 ESMA also has the power to withdraw benchmark administrators and benchmarks from the register in certain circumstances.[148] In particular, where the benchmark administrator is acting in a way which is clearly prejudicial to the interests of the users of its benchmarks or to the orderly functioning of markets, or has seriously infringed requirements applicable to it in the third country (where the Commission had determined there was equivalence on the basis of such requirements). Before it withdraws an entity from the register, ESMA will first approach the relevant third country regulator and will only take action where the third country regulator does not take appropriate action to resolve the matter. That is, where the third country regulator does not take appropriate action to protect investors and the orderly functioning of the markets in the EU, or has failed to demonstrate that the benchmark administrator concerned complies with the requirements applicable to it in that third country.

14.4.2.2 Option 2: recognition

14.95 Before an equivalence decision has been made by the Commission (see section 14.4.2.1), supervised entities in the EU may use benchmarks provided by third country benchmark administrators if the benchmark administrator has acquired prior recognition by regulators in its Member State of reference.[149]

---

[147] Regulation (EU) 2018/1644 of 13 July 2018 supplementing Regulation (EU) 2016/1011 of the European Parliament and of the Council with regard to regulatory technical standards determining the minimum content of cooperation arrangements with competent authorities of third countries whose legal framework and supervisory practices have been recognised as equivalent [2018] OJ L274/33.
[148] Benchmarks Regulation, Art. 31.
[149] Ibid., Art. 32.

14.96 The Member State of reference is a concept which must be determined for each benchmark administrator in accordance with Article 32(4) of the Benchmarks Regulation. This sets out a series of tests for determining the Member State of reference for a particular benchmark administrator. In summary, where the benchmark administrator has group entities which are 'supervised entities' located in the EU, the Member State of reference will be determined based on the location of these group entities. Where the benchmark administrator does not have group entities that are supervised, the Member State of reference is determined based on tests linked to where the benchmarks are used in practice. For example, the Member State of reference will be determined depending on where the financial instruments which refer to such benchmarks are admitted to trading on a trading venue.[150] Where the instruments are not admitted to trading on an EU trading venue, the Member State of reference will be calculated on the basis of where the largest number of supervised entities using such benchmarks are based or (failing that) where a supervised entity that has agreed to use the benchmark is based.

(a) Requirements for recognition

14.97 To become recognised, the third country benchmark administrator must comply with most of the provisions of the Benchmarks Regulation.[151] It may achieve this by complying with IOSCO Principles where applicable, provided that these are applied in a way that is consistent with the requirements of the Benchmarks Regulation. To determine whether this condition is met, the Member State of reference can rely on an external auditor's report or on a certificate from the third country regulator of the relevant benchmark administrator (being, in the case of a UK benchmark administrator, the FCA).

14.98 The benchmark administrator must also appoint a legal representative in the Member State of reference. The legal representative is the role of a person which acts on behalf of the benchmark administrator when dealing with the authorities and any other person in the EU in relation to the benchmark administrator's obligations under the Benchmarks Regulation. Please note that the legal representative is not simply an entity which receives correspondence on behalf of the benchmark administrator, for which it would be possible to appoint a third party for a fee. The legal representative and the benchmark administrator will both be responsible for performing the oversight function relating to the benchmarks provided by the benchmark administrator. As the legal representative is required to take on actual responsibility for the benchmark administrator's benchmark activities, this role will typically be held by a group company in the Member State of reference. The rules on determining the legal representative for the Benchmarks Regulation do in some cases specify the identity of the legal representative for a particular benchmark administrator. For example, where the Member State of reference is determined by reference to the location of supervised entities in the benchmark administrator's group, the legal representative will be one of the supervised entities in the Member State of reference (see Article 34(2) of the Benchmarks Regulation).

14.99 Where the benchmark administrator is supervised in the UK, the competent authority in the Member State of reference may only recognise the relevant benchmark administrator

---

[150] That is, an EU regulated market, MTF, or OTF, each as defined under Directive 2014/65/EU.
[151] The relevant benchmark administrator does not need to comply with Benchmarks Regulation, Arts. 11(4), 16, 20, 21, and 23.

if the competent authority has entered into a cooperation agreement with the FCA which governs the exchange of information between the authorities.

14.100 The competent authority of the Member State of reference may only recognise the relevant benchmark administrator if it is satisfied that the effective exercise by the competent authority of its supervisory functions under the Benchmarks Regulation is neither prevented by the laws, regulations or administrative provisions of the third country where the benchmark administrator is located, nor, where applicable, by limitations in the supervisory and investigatory powers of that third country's supervisory authority.

(b) Process for obtaining recognition

14.101 benchmark administrators must apply to the competent authority of the Member State of reference for recognition. The relevant competent authority will have up to ninety working days following receipt of the application in which to respond. Regulatory technical standards indicate the type of information which should be provided with the application.[152]

14.102 Where the competent authority of the Member State of reference considers that the conditions for recognition are not met, it must refuse the application and provide reasons.

14.103 Where the competent authority of the Member state of reference considers that a benchmark does meet the requirements and falls within the significant or non-significant categories of benchmark, it must notify ESMA of this fact. ESMA must provide advice on the categorisation of the benchmark within one month of this notice. As part of this, ESMA can also provide advice on whether the relevant benchmarks meet the requirements for significant or non-significant benchmarks. During this time period, the timeline for the competent authority's response (i.e. the ninety working days) is paused.[153]

14.104 The competent authority may grant recognition even where ESMA's advice indicates that it should not do so. Where this is the case, ESMA will publicise this fact.[154]

14.105 Any decision by the competent authority to recognise a particular benchmark administrator must be notified to ESMA by that competent authority within five working days.[155]

14.106 The relevant regulator of the Member State of reference may suspend or withdraw a benchmark administrator's recognised status in certain circumstances. This includes where: it has well-founded reasons and documented evidence to suggest that (a) the benchmark administrator is acting in a manner that is clearly prejudicial to either users of its benchmarks or to the orderly functioning of the market, (b) the benchmark administrator has seriously infringed the requirements of the Benchmarks Regulation, or (c) the benchmark administrator has made false statements or used irregular means to obtain recognition.[156]

---

[152] Regulation 2018/1645 of 13 July 2018 supplementing Regulation (EU) 2016/1011 of the European Parliament and of the Council with regard to regulatory technical standards for the form and content of the application for recognition with the competent authority of the Member State of reference and of the presentation of information in the notification to European Securities and Markets Authority (ESMA) [2018] OJ L274/36.
[153] Benchmarks Regulation, Art. 32(6).
[154] Ibid.
[155] Ibid., Art. 32(7).
[156] Ibid., Art. 32(8).

14.4.2.3 Option 3: endorsement

14.107 Regulated EU entities[157] can also 'endorse' third country benchmarks for use within the EU where they have a 'clear and well defined role' in the control or accountability framework of the benchmark administrator and so are able to effectively monitor the provision of the benchmark. The endorsing entity must also meet other requirements, such as having the expertise necessary to monitor the provision of the benchmark effectively. They must also be able to show that there is an objective reason to provide the benchmark(s) in a third country and endorse them for use in the EU and that the provision of the endorsed benchmark(s) fulfils requirements at least as stringent as those in the Benchmarks Regulation.

14.108 The endorsing entity must make an application for endorsement to the relevant competent authority of that endorsing entity, and that authority will have ninety working days from receipt of the application to decide whether or not to authorise or refuse the endorsement.

14.109 Where an entity in the EU is permitted to endorse a third country benchmark administrator's benchmarks, the relevant benchmarks shall be treated as provided by the endorsing entity, and the endorsing entity will be fully responsible for the administration of the relevant benchmarks.

14.4.2.4 Transitional provisions

14.110 Article 51(5) of the Benchmarks Regulation contains a transitional provision which applies to benchmarks provided by administrators located in a third country where no equivalence decision has been adopted, the benchmark administrator has not been recognised, and the benchmark has not been endorsed. If a benchmark is already used in the EU on or before 1 January 2020,[158] as a reference for financial instruments,[159] financial contracts[160] or for measuring the performance of an investment fund,[161] its use shall continue to be permitted in certain circumstances. The circumstances are that the benchmark can only be used for financial instruments, financial contracts, and measurements of the performance of a fund which already reference the benchmark (or have already included a reference to such benchmark) prior to 1 January 2020.[162]

14.111 These transitional provisions will have the effect of limiting the impact of Brexit on UK benchmark administrators. ESMA has clarified that this provision will also be applicable to benchmarks provided by UK benchmark administrators deleted from the ESMA register because of a no-deal Brexit.[163] UK benchmark administrators can continue to have their benchmarks referenced in financial instruments where these financial instruments already reference their benchmarks prior to 1 January 2020. While this is not stated explicitly, this also suggests that their benchmarks can be used more widely until 1 January 2020, and after

---

[157] This applies to authorised or registered EU benchmark administrators, as well as to other supervised entities located in the EU.
[158] ESMA, *Q&A on Benchmarks Regulation*, question 9.3.
[159] Meaning a financial instrument within the scope of Directive 2014/65/EU, s. C of Annex I.
[160] Meaning credit agreements as defined ibid., Art. 3(c), or Directive 2014/17/EU, Art. 4(3).
[161] Meaning an AIF as defined in Directive 2011/61/EU, Art. 4(1)(a), or a UCITS as defined in Directive 2009/65/EC, Art. 1(2).
[162] Benchmarks Regulation, Art. 51(5).
[163] ESMA public statement, *Impact of Brexit on MiFID II/MiFIR and the Benchmark Regulation*.

that date they can continue to be used for instruments in which they were referenced prior to 1 January 2020.

As of the time of writing, the European Parliament has adopted a proposal to amend Article 51. The amendment, if enacted into law, will extend the transitional period for the use in the EU of a benchmark provided by a third country administrator until 31 December 2021 where the benchmark is already used in the EU.[164] Please see [reference to chapter update] for more information on the status of these updates.

14.112

14.4.3 The Impact of Brexit on Benchmark Administrators Based in the EU

14.4.3.1 The UK third country regime

We would expect benchmark administrators based within the EU to be in a similar position where their benchmarks are to be used by supervised entities in the UK. Benchmark administrators located in the EU will be subject to the UK's third country regime, requiring benchmark administrators or benchmarks to be approved via recognition or endorsement applications to the FCA until they are able to benefit from the equivalence provisions in the Brexit Benchmarks SI.

14.113

Benchmark administrators located outside the UK will be subject to the third country regime under the Brexit Benchmarks SI.[165] This essentially mirrors the regime in the EU, as described above. The benchmark or the benchmark administrator will need to benefit from equivalence,[166] recognition,[167] or endorsement[168] in the UK to be added to the FCA register. This would apply to third country benchmarks and benchmark administrators even if they already appear on the ESMA register, unless they have already been recognised by the FCA, or endorsed by UK benchmark administrators or supervised entities (with such endorsement authorised by the FCA) before exit day.

14.114

Under the Brexit Benchmarks SI, HM Treasury will be responsible for assessing the equivalence of third countries' regulatory regimes relating to benchmarks rather than the European Commission.[169] If HM Treasury makes a positive equivalence decision on a third country's supervisory regime, then it will be incumbent on the FCA to establish a suitable cooperation arrangement with the national competent authority of the third country.[170] Third country benchmark administrators may then notify the FCA of consent to use of their benchmarks in the UK[171] and these benchmark administrators will then be added to the FCA register along with the list of benchmarks they consent to the use of and administer.

14.115

---

[164] Available at <https://data.consilium.europa.eu/doc/document/ST-7724-2019-INIT/en/pdf>
[165] Brexit Benchmarks SI, Art. 5(13).
[166] Ibid., Art. 27.
[167] Ibid., Art. 29.
[168] Ibid., Art. 30.
[169] Ibid., Art. 27(2)(b).
[170] Ibid., Art. 27(4)(a).
[171] Ibid., Art. 27(2)(c).

14.4.3.2 Transitional provisions

14.116 The Brexit Benchmarks SI will replace the third country transitional provisions in the Benchmarks Regulation (described in section 14.4.2.4).[172] The following transitional provisions will apply instead.

- A supervised entity may use a benchmark issued by a third country administrator as a reference for a financial instrument, a financial contract or for measuring the performance of an investment fund in the United Kingdom from exit day to 31 December 2019.
- A benchmark can continue to be used on and after 1 January 2020 if it was used as a reference for a particular financial instrument, financial contract or used to measure the performance of a particular investment fund on 31 December 2019.
- These transitional provisions will not apply if before exit day, the third country administrator has made an application for authorisation or registration under the Benchmarks Regulation (i.e. under the EU regime) and this has been refused. Where such an application has been refused, the benchmark may continue to be used as a reference for a financial instrument, financial contract or used to measure the performance of an investment fund if it was used for that financial instrument, financial contract or investment fund prior to the refusal.
- These transitional provisions will also not apply from the point that the benchmark is on the FCA's register in certain circumstances.

There have been changes made to these transitional provisions since the date of publication of this chapter. Please see [reference to update] for more information.

14.4.3.3 Brexit-specific provisions

14.117 To prevent a sudden loss of UK access to benchmarks, the Brexit Benchmarks SI introduced some specific transitional provisions in light of Brexit. These are not based on provisions within the Benchmark Regulation, but appear to have been designed to limit the impact of Brexit.

- Benchmarks and administrators that have been authorised, registered, recognised, or endorsed by the FCA and appear on the ESMA register at exit day will be automatically copied into the FCA's register.
- In relation to benchmarks and administrators already appearing on the ESMA register at exit day and benchmarks provided by benchmark administrators already appearing on the ESMA register at exit day, a transitional provision in the Brexit Benchmarks SI will migrate these benchmarks and benchmark administrators temporarily from the ESMA register to the FCA register at 5 p.m. on exit day.[173] This allows these benchmarks and benchmarks provided by these benchmark administrators to continue to be used for a period of two years beginning with exit day.[174]
- Under the Brexit Benchmarks SI, where a benchmark administrator or a particular benchmark is removed from the ESMA register during the two-year period, it will also be removed from the FCA register if this is consistent with the FCA's strategic and

---

[172] Ibid., Art. 42(6).
[173] Ibid., Art. 51.
[174] Ibid., Art. 54.

operational objectives.[175] However, to avoid contractual frustration, a benchmark removed from the FCA register can continue to be used where reference to it was added prior to its removal from the register.[176]

14.4.4 The Impact of Brexit on Benchmark Administrators Based Outside the EU and the UK

14.118 The position for benchmark administrators based outside the EU and the UK will also be affected by Brexit.

14.119 In particular, a non-EU benchmark administrator which intends to provide benchmarks which are used in both the EU and the UK will now need to ensure that it is able to comply with the regime in the UK as well as the separate regime in the EU.

14.120 A non-EU benchmark administration which intends to provide benchmarks for use in the EU post-Brexit may need to reconsider the way in which it is able to access the EU market. For example, if it has or had intended to be endorsed by an entity within the UK (see section 14.4.2.3 above), this may not be sufficient to enable its benchmarks to be used in EU Member States post-Brexit.

14.121 A non-EU benchmark administrator planning to provide benchmarks for use in the UK post-Brexit, will need to comply with the UK regime on benchmarks, and will therefore need to obtain recognition, endorsement, or equivalence under the UK regime. The fact that it may have some status under the EU regime will not necessarily give it access to the UK market beyond the initial two-year period during which non-UK benchmark administrators and benchmarks, including non-EU third country benchmark administrators and benchmarks, from the ESMA register are migrated temporarily to the FCA register.

14.4.5 The Impact of Brexit on Users of Benchmarks in the EU

14.122 Supervised entities based in the EU which use benchmarks for certain specified purposes will need to ensure that these benchmarks continue to meet the relevant requirements post-Brexit. Where they use benchmarks produced by benchmark administrators in the UK, they will need to ensure that the relevant benchmark administrators are endorsed, recognised, or determined to be equivalent by the relevant UK bodies. In practice, this may mean that they will need to amend the licencing agreements for the benchmarks which they use to ensure that UK-based benchmark administrators are required to ensure they meet the relevant requirements. Alternatively, these EU supervised entities may be prevented from using certain benchmarks (and therefore potentially trading in certain contracts) where the relevant arrangements have not been made.

---

[175] Ibid., Arts. 58 and 59.
[176] Ibid., Art. 62.

14.4.6 The Impact of Brexit on Benchmark Users Based in the UK

14.123 Supervised entities in the UK will be in a similar situation where they use benchmarks provided by benchmark administrators outside the UK. These entities will need to ensure that benchmark administrators based outside the UK have the appropriate status in the UK before continuing to use these benchmarks by consulting the FCA register rather than the ESMA register. This will apply even where the supervised entity is seeking to use non-EU benchmarks. Non-EU benchmark administrators will need to be endorsed, recognised, or determined to be equivalent under the relevant UK rules. The fact that they have the relevant status in the EU does not imply the same status in the UK beyond the two-year transition period outlined in Part 3 of the Brexit Benchmarks SI. Furthermore, even if a benchmark administrator or a benchmark is removed from the ESMA register, and consequently the FCA register, during the transition period the benchmark may continue to be used in contracts where reference to it was added before its removal from the registers.

14.5 Updates after July 2019

14.124 Since the date on which Chapter 14 was prepared,[177] there have been a number of relevant legal and regulatory developments. This section provides a non-exhaustive summary of some of the key updates which are specifically relevant to Brexit.

14.125 The European Council has adopted the Low Carbon Benchmarks Regulation, which is a new regulation on climate change and benchmarks.[178] This will make several changes to the transitional provisions of the Benchmarks Regulation.[179] In particular:

- It will be possible for an index provider to continue to provide an existing critical benchmark until 31 December 2021 or (if the index provider has applied for authorisation) unless and until the application is refused.
- A separate transitional provision also applies to enable an existing critical benchmark to be used for the same period.
- Unless equivalence, recognition, or endorsement applies for a particular benchmark, it will be possible for a third country benchmark to be used for purposes which are within scope of the Benchmarks Regulation until 31 December 2021. This is essentially an extension of two years beyond the current date, and will operate to delay the impact of Brexit on UK administrators and those non-EU administrators which have a status with the FCA.

---

[177] July 2019.
[178] European Counsel. Regulation (EU) 2019/… of the European Parliament and of the Council amending Regulation (EU) 2016/1011 as regards EU Climate Transition Benchmarks, EU Paris-aligned Benchmarks and sustainability-related disclosures for benchmarks. Available at: <https://data.consilium.europa.eu/doc/document/PE-90-2019-INIT/en/pdf>
[179] Regulation (EU) 2016/1011 of 8 June 2016 on indices used as benchmarks in financial instruments and financial contacts or to measure the performance of investment funds [2016] OJ L171/1 (hereafter Benchmarks Regulation).

14.126 The Low Carbon Benchmarks Regulation is expected to be published in the Official Journal shortly after the date of this update.[180]

14.127 In this context, ESMA has provided a further statement on the effect of a hard Brexit on UK benchmark administrators.[181] This update confirms that those UK or non-EU administrators which are authorised, registered or have some other status with the FCA will be deleted from the EU register as a result of Brexit. However, such administrators would continue to be able to benefit from the third country transitional provisions in the Benchmarks Regulation.

14.128 There have also been similar changes made in the UK which will operate to delay the impact of a hard Brexit on non-UK administrators seeking to provide benchmarks in the UK. The UK Parliament has extended the transitional regime for third-country benchmarks that will apply in the UK in the event of a hard Brexit from 31 December 2019 to 31 December 2022.[182]

14.129 The extension will enable UK firms to use third-country benchmarks until the end of 2022, without the need for those benchmarks to be on the FCA register.

14.130 It will also give administrators of third-country benchmarks additional time to gain endorsement of specific benchmarks or recognition as an administrator.

14.131 The EU Commission is consulting on a review of the Benchmarks Regulation. As of the date of this update,[183] there are no confirmed actions or amendments from this consultation.

14.6 Conclusion

14.132 The regulatory regime applicable to benchmarks in the UK has evolved significantly in recent years. It has developed from a set of high-level guiding principles, to a regime requiring only a limited number of benchmark administrators to become authorised. The Benchmarks Regulation has created a significant expansion in the scope of benchmarks regulation. It has introduced a significant number of new requirements and a detailed regime which applies to benchmark administrators more widely.

14.133 Brexit will not reverse or change this trend of increased regulation. We expect that the UK will continue to apply the Benchmarks Regulation requirements post-Brexit. In the years following Brexit, there will be further issues to be addressed. In particular, while the two parallel UK and EU regimes may look substantially the same immediately post-Brexit due to the way in which the onshoring process will be conducted, there is a question as to

---

[180] [November 2019].

[181] ESMA. Public Statement: Impact of no-deal Brexit on the application of MiFID II/MiFIR and the Benchmark Regulation (BMR). October 2019. Available at: <https://www.esma.europa.eu/sites/default/files/library/esma70-155-8500_statement_brexit_mifid_remaining_issues_oct2019.pdf>

[182] The amendment was introduced in the Financial Services (Electronic Money, Payment Services and Miscellaneous Amendments) (EU Exit) Regulations 2019 (SI 2019/1212), which were made on 5 September 2019 and amend the Benchmarks (Amendment and Transitional Provisions) (EU Exit) Regulations 2019 (the Benchmarks Exit SI).

[183] [November 2019].

whether there will be a divergence of practice when applying the Benchmarks Regulation post-Brexit. The answer to this question may depend on the outcome of the political deal between the UK and the EU, and whether the UK considers that it would be preferable to align itself closely with the EU regime in order to increase the likelihood that a wide-ranging equivalence decision will be granted.

15

Alternative Investment Fund Managers Directive (AIFMD)

Jake Green

15.1 Summary

The Alternative Investment Fund Managers Directive 2011/61/EU (**AIFMD**) came into force on 21 July 2011 and came into effect in the UK via the Alternative Investment Fund Management Regulations 2013 (SI No. 1773) (the '**Regulations**') on 22 July 2013. **15.01**

At a high level, the legislative changes made by AIFMD can be categorised as (1) changes to the regulatory burden on the manager (known as the alternative investment fund manager, or **AIFM**) of alternative investment funds (**AIFs**), (2) changes to the rules on the promotion of AIFs to investors by the AIFM and/or other parties on its behalf, and (3) changes to the rules in relation to delegation of performance of activities in respect of the AIF by the AIFM to third parties (such as portfolio management). **15.02**

Although UK AIFMs, unlike some of their European counterparts, had been authorised and regulated in the UK,[1] AIFMD substantially altered and increased the regulatory burden on UK AIFMs. While a lot of the obligations under AIFMD were applied, in part, to managers prior to AIFMD, the administrative and cost burden of becoming authorised as an AIFM and ongoing compliance has been significant. There has been much criticism of AIFMD which is largely driven by the fact that AIFMD attempts to apply the same rules (which are retail in nature) to a wide universe of funds including both open-ended and closed-ended, listed and unlisted and which invest in a wide range of both illiquid and liquid strategies that may or may not create systemic risk to the wider financial system. It therefore essentially provided a retail protectionist framework to funds designed for non-retail/sophisticated investors. **15.03**

The key benefit for most EEA AIFMs of AIFMD was the introduction of the marketing passport that (in theory) allowed for AIFMs to 'market' funds (AIFs) throughout the EEA to professional investors without additional costs, disclosures or other obligations imposed on the AIFM. Once the AIFM had a fund approved by its home state regulator, it was free to market it throughout the EEA (following a simple notification process). For many EEA AIFMs, this meant little change given the relatively liberal UK overseas person regime but reduced the compliance burden of understanding the relatively complex UK rules around the promotion of 'fund-like' vehicles. **15.04**

---

[1] In the UK fund managers have always performed regulated activities under the UK domestic Regulated Activities Order including the establishment, operation, and winding up of collective investment schemes and portfolio management.

15.05 The fund management industry has become more global in the last few decades and the choice of location for both the AIFM and the AIF has been driven by questions of tax, regulation, location of the investor base and location of the asset base, among others.

15.06 It is therefore common for AIFMs to delegate some or all of 'portfolio management' (the investment management decisions) to a third party.

15.07 As an example, an EEA AIFM may delegate the purchase of US assets to a US affiliate. Many managers and fund vehicles have been established in Luxembourg and Ireland, where a substantial funds administration industry has grown. While the 'manager' (AIFM) may be in these jurisdictions, the portfolio management may be undertaken in the UK and/or the US (as examples) while the rest of the more administrative compliance (such as 'risk management') with AIFMD is performed in Luxembourg or Ireland.

15.08 This chapter will assess the: (1) impact of Brexit on UK AIFMs in respect of UK implementation of AIFMD; (2) the ability of UK AIFMs to offer their funds within the EEA; (3) the ability of EEA AIFMs to market AIFs to UK investors; and (4) the impacts on the delegation arrangements that exist between UK and EEA AIFMs.

15.09 This chapter does not explore the implications of Brexit for UCITS funds or UCITS managers. It also does not review the impact of Brexit on MiFID investment firms performing MiFID activities such as portfolio management, except where relevant in the context of delegation and distribution of alternative investment funds. Further discussion concerning the impact of Brexit on MiFID can be found in Chapter 10.

15.2 AIFMD on Brexit

15.10 Although the political situation may change the position of the UK government, on Brexit, AIFMD will essentially continue to apply to UK AIFMs.[2] This is set out in the Alternative Investment Fund Managers (Amendment) (EU Exit) Regulations 2018 (**UK Exit Regulations**) and Financial Services (Implementation of Legislation) Bill[3] (**In-Flight Rules**). The Bill which was published in February 2019 and was part of the wider UK attempt to replicate the current European framework on Brexit, absent any deal as well as any financial services legislation that had been published in the Official Journal of the EU, but were either: (1) not operative immediately before Brexit and so were not transferred onto the UK statute book, or were operative but reliant on non-operative clauses, and so had not been transferred onto the UK statute books by the onshoring process; or (2) were currently in negotiation, and could enter into the Official Journal up to two years after the UK left the EU.

---

[2] Alternative Investment Fund Managers (Amendment) (EU Exit) Regulations 2018.
[3] The Bill failed to complete its passage through Parliament before the end of the 2017–19 Parliamentary session. It is has not been confirmed whether the government intends to introduce a replacement Bill or to resuscitate the Bill. Any effort to resuscitate the Bill would require amendments to take account of EU legislation that came into force after the Bill was introduced but which will not come into effect before exit day, such as the Directive (EU) 2019/1160 and many of the provisions of the Regulation (EU) 2019/1156.

However, absent any transitional arrangements, the EEA will treat UK AIFs and AIFMs as third country (non-EEA) AIFMs and AIFs. There is a regime in place for these entities at present and this will apply to the UK as it does to managers in other jurisdictions such as Jersey, Guernsey, Singapore at present. **15.11**

Understanding the current regime is important for understanding how Brexit will affect AIFMs. The UK will essentially onshore AIFMD and the EEA will essentially transfer the application of AIFMD on UK AIFMs and AIFs to the non-EEA regime. It is therefore instructive to understand the AIFMD regime today for both EEA and non-EEA AIFMs. In essence, much of this regime will continue to apply to UK AIFMs, albeit the elements that apply will differ. **15.12**

15.3 AIFMD: an Overview of the Position Today

15.3.1 Background and Legislative Intent

The scope of AIFMD was deliberately broad and covers the management and marketing of AIFs. **15.13**

AIFMD focuses on regulating the AIFM rather than the AIF. **15.14**

Broadly it covers any fund vehicle that is not subject to UCITS although there are carve-outs for certain vehicles such as joint ventures and 'employee participation schemes'.[4] **15.15**

The asset class that the fund invests in does not affect the status of the vehicle as an AIF and, therefore, it captures private equity, hedge funds, real estate, and other managers. **15.16**

The primary purpose of AIFMD was to create a harmonised framework for the management of funds in the EEA.[5] It formed one aspect of the post-financial crisis legislation. AIFMD was in part driven by a concern that the activities of fund managers may also serve to spread or amplify risks through the financial system. Uncoordinated national responses make the efficient management of those risks difficult. AIFMD therefore aimed at establishing common requirements governing the authorisation and supervision of AIFMs in order to provide a coherent approach to the related risks and their impact on investors and markets in the European Union.[6] It also applies to members of the EEA. **15.17**

The legislative intent was also, as part of the wider EU Capital Markets Union plan, to create a pan-European market for funds through the 'marketing passport' similar to that which exists for UCITS funds. The marketing passport is designed to allow authorised managers in one jurisdiction to offer their funds to certain investors (broadly, professionals) in other jurisdictions without any additional obligations being imposed by the jurisdiction of the potential investor. **15.18**

---

[4] AIFMD, Art. 4(1)(a) provides the definition of an AIF.
[5] Ibid., recital (4).
[6] Ibid., recital (2).

15.3.2 Application of AIFMD to Managers

15.19 Before understanding the implications of Brexit, it is important to understand that managers are treated differently depending upon their size and their location. Broadly, AIFMD distinguishes between three types of fund managers:

(a) full scope managers or AIFMs; EEA managers with assets of €500m and above (or €100m and above if any AIF managed is leveraged) (**full scope AIFMs**);
(b) sub-threshold managers: EEA managers with assets of less than €500m (or €100m if the funds are unleveraged) (**sub-threshold AIFMs**); and
(c) non-EEA AIFMs—managers established outside the EEA (**non-EEA AIFMs**).[7]

15.20 The nature and extent of the application of AIFMD depends on which category the manager falls within.

15.3.3 Full Scope AIFMs

15.21 Full Scope AIFMs are subject to the entirety of AIFMD including rules around remuneration, capital requirements, the appointment of a depositary for oversight of the fund's assets and rules on marketing.

15.22 In the UK, the FCA is the competent regulator of full scope AIFMs and deals with the initial authorisation of the full scope AIFM as well as ongoing scrutiny.[8] Accordingly, the FCA notifies other regulators when the AIFM wishes to use its passport.

15.23 Other European regulators are the competent regulators of full scope AIFMs established in their jurisdiction. While there is a common set of rules in market practice, regulatory interpretation of guidance, the AIFMD itself and some gold-plating (particularly by the UK)[9] the application of AIFMD does vary to full scope AIFMs.

15.3.4 Sub-Threshold AIFMs

15.24 The regulation of sub-threshold AIFMs is largely left up to each jurisdiction and materially differs per jurisdiction.[10]

15.25 Sub-threshold AIFMs, which are regulated in the UK as small authorised AIFMs by the FCA, have to meet certain requirements in the AIFMD but these are less onerous than the rules for a full scope AIFM.

---

[7] Where a manager is established outside the EEA, it will not be authorised as an AIFM but will be authorised/registered pursuant to local rules. For the purposes of this chapter a reference to a non-EEA AIFM is a reference to the 'manager' entity that most resembles an AIFM, i.e. would be the AIFM if the entity was in the EEA.

[8] Art. 65 of the Regulations.

[9] For example, the UK has implemented the MiFID product governance rules for AIFMs (FCA PROD Handbook).

[10] AIFMD, Art. 3(2).

However, the sub-threshold AIFM does not benefit from the marketing passport and must rely on the national private placement regime in each jurisdiction. **15.26**

15.3.5 Non-EEA AIFMs

For AIFMs domiciled outside the EEA (for example, commonly Channel Island and US managers) the AIFMD only applies to the extent the fund is 'marketed' in the EEA. Therefore, if the manager does not 'market' the fund in the EEA, AIFMD does not apply. **15.27**

Clearly, in most non-EEA jurisdictions the concept of an 'AIFM' does not exist as this is a concept introduced by AIFMD. Therefore, in order to determine the entity that is most akin to the functions of an AIFM, the performance of portfolio management and risk management, is designated to the AIFM. In some jurisdictions this may be the general partner, while in others, it may be a regulated entity such as an SEC-authorised adviser. There is, however, no common view on who the AIFM should be. **15.28**

Non-EEA AIFMs do not benefit from the marketing passport and must rely on the national private placement regime (known commonly as 'NPPR' or 'Article 42') in each jurisdiction in order to 'market' the funds to European investors.[11] **15.29**

However, in some jurisdictions, NPPR/Article 42 does not exist or cannot be satisfied in practice (France and Italy often being cited as examples). **15.30**

Non-EEA AIFMs are required to comply with limited aspects of the AIFMD. These include: **15.31**

(a) certain investor transparency requirements such as the provision of pre-investment disclosures and ongoing annual reports to investors;
(b) portfolio company notifications and the asset-stripping rules when acquiring EEA companies; and
(c) ongoing periodic reporting to the regulator including information on the instruments it trades in, markets which it is a member of, and its principal exposures.[12]

15.3.6 Delegation Arrangement

Full scope AIFMs are required to perform a number of activities set out in the Annex of AIFMD (for example, recalculating or administration). AIFMD recognises that there are business efficiencies in delegating the performance of some of these activities to third parties.[13] **15.32**

The activities an AIFM is required to perform are the management functions (portfolio management and risk management) and the support or administrative functions. **15.33**

Delegation is permitted of all of these functions provided that the AIFM does not become a 'letterbox entity' and that the delegation is justified. **15.34**

---

[11] Ibid., Art. 42.
[12] Ibid., Art. 42(1)(a).
[13] Ibid., recital 30.

15.35 This means (in practice) that AIFMs must retain at least either risk management or portfolio management.

15.36 When delegating a management function to a third party, that third party must be authorised for the provision of asset management and subject to supervision. If they are not, then the Member State must approve the delegation.[14] The European Securities and Markets Authority (ESMA) July 2017 sectoral opinion on investment management in the context of Brexit sets out ESMA's expectations in relation to delegation of functions.[15] In short, it is clear that non-EU delegations will be in focus over the coming years. ESMA outlines its expectations for NCAs when carrying out their assessment of objective reasons provided for a delegation. In particular, ESMA states that delegation to non-EU entities can make oversight and supervision of delegated functions more difficult and it is clear that NCAs will be expected to police the ability of the AIFM to control and oversee the delegation. Small and light-touch AIFMs will likely be under increased pressure.

15.4 Marketing: Differences between the Passport and NPPR

15.4.1 What Is Marketing?

15.37 Before discussing how funds are offered to investors it is important to understand the concept of 'marketing'.

15.38 Unfortunately, for AIFMs, no guidance was provided as to the meaning of 'marketing'.[16] This has meant a divergent approach to the concept of 'marketing' in each jurisdiction.

15.39 In the UK, the position is that 'marketing' occurs when materially final form documentation is provided to investors such as the limited partnership agreement, private placement memorandum and subscription document.[17] Essentially if the document cannot be used by an investor to make an investment in the AIF, the documents do not constitute marketing (however there are anti-avoidance rules/guidance to prevent abuse of this sensible starting position).

15.40 Other jurisdictions take a more restrictive approach and the relevant authority states that marketing occurs at an earlier stage such as the provision of draft documents, pitch books and high-level sales talks. In some jurisdictions, in the context of a typical private fund raise, it is very difficult not to trigger the 'marketing' obligation at an early stage.

15.41 However, where an investor approaches a fund manager and requests to invest at its own initiative, this is known as a reverse solicitation. If EU investors are only admitted to a fund as a result of a reverse solicitation there has been no 'marketing' and therefore no requirement for any notification or passport under AIFMD.[18] In practice, it can be difficult to determine the boundary between a reverse solicitation or 'marketing'. Reverse solicitation is discussed further in 15.4.4 below.

---

[14] Ibid., Art. 20.
[15] ESMA Opinion to support supervisory convergence in the area of investment management in the context of the United Kingdom withdrawing from the European Union.
[16] The definition in Art. 4(1) provides for a wide degree of interpretation.
[17] FCA Perimeter Guidance 8.37 (AIFMD Marketing).
[18] Recital 70 AIFMD and Art. 4(1)(x) AIFMD on the definition of marketing that makes it clear marketing must be at the initiative of the AIFM or a third party.

15.4.2 Passport

The passport should provide a relatively easy way for AIFMs to ensure that they can access investors in all European jurisdictions. The FCA, as home state regulator, has competency to assess the application and informs the relevant jurisdictions that the AIF will be marketed. The FCA has twenty working days to make the relevant notifications.[19]

15.42

In theory other regulators cannot make comments or refuse an application but some jurisdictions are known for making demands for payment or amendments to the documents. Despite this, there have been some issues. Opaque and inconsistently applied fees can be charged by some jurisdictions. Some regulators have come back with comments or queries on the AIF or AIFM despite this being reserved to the home state regulator. However, in practice the passport has provided a useful way of accessing a wide range of European investors. This is especially so when compared to the process available to non-European 'AIFs' that rely on a patchwork of national regimes of varying complexity to market in.

15.43

15.4.3 Marketing without the Passport

For non-EEA AIFMs and sub-threshold AIFMs, the lack of passport does not outrightly prevent the marketing of funds. However, the ease and method with which this is done is dependent on each jurisdiction and may be difficult to achieve in practice.

15.44

In order for an AIF to be marketed under NPPR, there are some basic requirements under AIFMD. There must be cooperation agreements in place between the jurisdictions and the jurisdiction of the AIFM and AIF must not be listed as a non-cooperative country and territory by the Financial Action Task Force.[20] It must also comply with paragraph 15.31 above.

15.45

AIFMD allows jurisdictions to impose stricter obligations.[21] Non-EEA AIFMs are therefore subject to the individual rules of each jurisdiction in order to 'market' their funds. In some jurisdictions such as the UK and Luxembourg, this process is relatively straightforward. In other jurisdictions such as Germany and Denmark there are requirements such as the appointment of a 'depositary' to perform certain oversight functions (generally the fund's custodian and banks are appointed).

15.46

15.4.4 Reverse Solicitation

Given the relative difficulty of accessing some jurisdictions, costs of applications (and/or fear of the asset stripping provisions) some non-EEA AIFMs will only admit investors on the basis of a reverse solicitation.

15.47

---

[19] Art. 31 AIFMD.
[20] Art. 42(1)(b)–(c).
[21] Art. 42(2).

15.48 Given the relative ease and simplicity of using the passport, most EEA AIFMs simply notify the home state regulator of the jurisdictions that their investors will be admitted from rather than analysing the reverse solicitation issue.

15.49 A genuine reverse solicitation means that the manager can admit the investor without registering the fund under NPPR (or indeed the marketing passport). This can be a substantial cost and time saving.

15.50 In the context of funds, it can be difficult to easily establish that an investor has approached on a reverse solicitation basis. Member State regulators have made it clear that reverse solicitation should not be used as a mechanism for the avoidance of obligations under AIFMD.[22]

15.4.5 Where Does Marketing Take Place?

15.51 Determining where marketing takes place can often be a complex question. As an example, an AIFM may initially discuss an opportunity with a contact in the UK who passes the opportunity on to a group company in Germany that makes an investment on behalf of a French private family office, using a Luxembourg special purpose vehicle. Where marketing has taken place in this situation can be difficult to untangle, especially as different jurisdictions will have different (and contradictory) views. Additional questions can be raised based on the nature of the 'marketing' such as whether attendances at conferences where invariably some informal discussions may take place.

15.52 This is not problematic for full scope AIFMs which can simply apply for the marketing passport in all EEA jurisdictions. However, for non-EEA AIFMs, there is significant cost and time expense of registering. Identifying the relevant jurisdictions is a more important process. In particular, it is not always clear at the beginning of a fund raise exactly where investors may be based, which entity they may wish to invest into, etc., and what their tolerance is to stating that they have made a reverse solicitation.

15.4.6 Marketing by Third-Party Entities

15.53 It is relatively common for managers to appoint third-party entities to assist in the marketing of funds to investors in Europe. This may be another group entity (for instance a US manager gets its UK subadviser to assist with marketing to European investors) or the appointment of a specialist placement agent who has relationships with an investor base that would be difficult for the manager to reach.

15.54 The placement agent can only 'market' a fund that has been registered on behalf of the AIFM—if the fund is not registered it cannot be marketed.

15.55 There is a wide variety of views in Europe on whether 'marketing' consists of a regulated activity. It is clear that, if the third-party entity is heavily involved, it may be performing the

---

[22] PERG 8.37.11 and 8.37.12.

regulated activity of reception and transmission and therefore be required to be authorised as a MiFID investment firm. However, where the boundary lies between unregulated introduction/marketing services and the MiFID investment service of reception and transmission, varies widely.

As with marketing, where a MiFID investment service is performed there are also differing views on where the service occurs. For instance, the activity can be performed where the placement agent is, where the investor is based, or both. **15.56**

15.5 Cross-border Distribution of Collective Funds: Changes to Come

The rules relating to cross-border distribution of collective funds were published in the EU Official Journal in July 2019. These consist of a regulation setting out a harmonised framework in relation to aspects of cross-border distribution of funds;[23] and a directive on the cross-border distribution of collective investment funds, containing amendments to the UCITS IV directive and the AIFMD.[24] The regulation and the directive will come into force in August 2019 and the directive must be transposed into national law by August 2021. **15.57**

The rules are aimed at reducing barriers to the cross-distribution of funds (one of the aims of the Capital Markets Union). **15.58**

The regime applies to AIFMs authorised in the EU using the passporting regime to market their funds. The regime aims to reduce the uncertainty that managers face working out exactly when they are 'marketing' and the need to register their funds by introducing a new harmonised definition of pre-marketing (requiring notification where this is the case). **15.59**

As detailed above, under the current regime, a marketing passport is required for EEA AIFMs carrying out promotional activities that fall within the definition of marketing. No guidance has hitherto been provided by the European Commission or ESMA on the meaning of 'pre-marketing' in the AIFMD, leading to divergent treatment of pre-marketing activities by individual regulators. **15.60**

The new regime addresses this by introducing a definition of 'pre-marketing' as: **15.61**

(a) the provision of information or communication (direct or indirect) on investment strategies or investment ideas by a manager to a professional investor;
(b) designed to test the interests of the professional investor in an AIF (not yet established, or where established, not yet notified for marketing to the relevant regulator in accordance with AIFMD); and
(c) an activity that does not amount to an offer or placement to the potential investor to invest in the units or shares of that AIF.[25]

---

[23] Regulation (EU) 2019/1156 on facilitating cross-border distribution of collective investment undertakings.
[24] Directive (EU) 2019/1160 with regard to cross-border distribution of collective investment undertakings.
[25] Ibid., Art. 2(1).

15.62 The rules also provide that EU AIFMs may undertake pre-marketing, provided that the information provided to potential professional investors:

(a) is insufficient to allow investors to commit to acquiring units of shares of a particular AIF;

(b) does not amount to subscription forms/similar documents, whether in draft or final form; and

(c) does not amount to constitutional documents, prospectus, or offering documents of a not-yet-established AIF in final form.[26]

15.63 Within two weeks of beginning pre-marketing, an EU AIFM must send a letter to the national competent authority of its home Member State setting out:

(a) the Member States in which pre-marketing is being carried out/was carried out, together with information on the relevant time periods that marketing is taking place; and

(b) a brief description of the pre-marketing (including information on the investment strategies presented, and where relevant, a list of AIFs).[27]

15.64 Under the new regime, an EU AIFM marketing an EU AIF in a host Member State can discontinue marketing any or all of its AIFs by sending a denotification notice to its home regulator, provided the following conditions are fulfilled:

(a) it makes a blanket offer to repurchase or redeem, free of any charges or deductions, the AIF units or shares held by investors in that Member State. The offer must be publicly available for at least thirty working days (and be addressed individually to all investors whose identity is known);

(b) the intention to discontinue marketing is made public by means of a publicly available medium (including by electronic means);

(c) any contractual arrangements with financial intermediaries or delegates are modified or terminated with effect from the date of denotification.[28]

15.65 Once this has occurred, the AIFM will be required to notify the national competent authority of the home Member State of its intention to cease marketing. Once a denotification of a fund has been made, the AIFM must not engage in pre-marketing referred to in the notification or in respect of similar investment strategies or investment ideas for three years.

15.66 Reverse solicitation is also under attack. As detailed above, under current rules, an EU AIFM is usually required to submit a marketing notification where professional investors have chosen to invest in an AIF on their 'own initiative'. However, the new regime provides that any subscription by professional investors (to units or shares of an AIF referred to in the information provided in the context of pre-marketing, or of an AIF established as a result of the pre-marketing) made within eighteen months of the EU AIFM commencing

---

[26] Ibid., Art. 2(2).
[27] Ibid.
[28] Ibid., Art. 2(4).

pre-marketing will be viewed as the result of marketing. The AIFM will, in this case, be subject to applicable notification procedures under the AIFMD.

15.67 Importantly, with Brexit in mind, the new regime provides that pre-marketing on behalf of an authorised AIFM can only be carried out by UCITS management companies, MiFID investment firms (or tied agents of MiFID investment firms) or CRD IV credit institutions or another AIFM. Where this is the case, the third party will be subject to conditions set out in relation to pre-marketing.[29] This is likely to impact managers relying on UK investor relation teams to carry out marketing to EEA investors post-Brexit; third country managers and so-called hotel/rent-an-AIFM structures.

15.6 Impact of Brexit

15.68 On Brexit, unless the draft Withdrawal Agreement is ratified:

(a) UK AIFMs will be treated by the FCA as having to comply with AIFMD;
(b) EEA Member States will treat UK AIFMs as non-EEA AIFMs (as described above); and
(c) the UK will treat EEA AIFMs as non-EEA AIFMs.

15.69 The UK has put in place a temporary permissions regime which means that EEA AIFMs marketing AIFs into the UK on the day of Brexit will be able to do so on Brexit for a period of three years, which may be extended by one year.[30]

15.6.1 UK AIFMs in the UK

15.70 The 'UK Exit Regulations' will mean that the UK AIFMs will continue to perform their obligations in the UK. Essentially AIFMD is 'onshored' for UK AIFMs and will continue to apply.[31]

15.71 The only change, which is largely administrative, is that the requirement to notify the regulator of the acquisition of portfolio companies and the associated asset stripping rules will be limited to where that portfolio company is based (or is partly based) in the UK, rather than in the EEA.

15.72 There is also some question as to how UK AIFMs managing EEA (but not UK) AIFs will be dealt with on Brexit as the UK Exit Regulations suggest that the AIF must be registered both as a new AIF by the manager but also through an essentially duplicative national private placement regime.

---

[29] Ibid., Art. 2(3).
[30] Proposed SI, s. 78.
[31] The Alternative Investment Fund Managers (Amendment) (EU Exit) Regulations 2018: explanatory information.

15.6.2 UK AIFMs in the EEA

15.73 UK AIFMs will no longer be able to use the management or marketing passport as they will no longer be full scope AIFMs. Instead, as non-EEA AIFMs, the managers will therefore have to comply with the NPPR regimes in each European jurisdiction. It appears that the appropriate cooperation agreements will be in place to satisfy the obligations set out in Article 42 AIFMD (listed at paragraph 15.45 above). Unlike for the UK, there is no transitional regime in place or currently proposed at a European level. Each Member State will be able to apply its own rules to UK AIFMs but to date only Germany has stated that it will simply treat the UK AIFM as any other third country manager.

15.74 The ability of a UK AIFM to manage a non-EEA AIF is less clear. In some jurisdictions, it will be possible to manage new AIFs while others require all or some categories of AIFs to be managed by an EEA AIFM.

15.75 Therefore, for UK AIFMs, the outcome is:

(a) more difficulty accessing an European investor base (reliance on NPPR and reverse solicitation rather than passport); but

(b) no change to the type and level of regulation of being a UK AIFM, rather than EEA AIFM.

15.6.3 UK Distributors into the EEA

15.76 UK placement agents will find it more difficult to provide services into the EEA where the relevant regulator considers these to be regulated services. Most placement agents will either be AIFMs or MiFID investment firms. As the MiFID or AIFMD passport is removed they will not be able to provide services into these jurisdictions. Indeed, the new rules detailed in section 15.5 are a direct attack on UK distribution activity into Europe. The new regime sets outs the requirements for third-party pre-marketing of funds in the EU on behalf of an EU AIFM, requiring this to be carried out by certain EU-authorised entities, seemingly prohibiting third country placement agents/investor relations teams being involved in the process. This could be a material issue post-Brexit. As detailed above, the new regime also introduces new requirements in relation to reverse solicitation under the AIFMD regime, effectively restricting its use. So while on surface the rules appear designed to address uncertainties in the existing regime, some of the provisions suggest far-reaching negative consequences, particularly for UK managers post-Brexit.

15.77 This leads to the (odd) outcome whereby a US manager appears able to market pursuant to the NPPR regime, but the UK affiliate would not be able to assist.

15.6.4 EEA AIFMs in the UK

15.78 EEA AIFMs which are marketing AIFs in the UK prior to Brexit will continue to be able to do so under the temporary permissions regime.

EEA AIFMs will lose the passport for future AIFs and will therefore have to rely on the UK implementation of AIFMD. As noted above, this is a relatively simple process and while it will impose some additional costs and disclosure obligations, perversely, it will be easier for an EEA AIFM to be marketed in the UK than in most other European jurisdictions, given that most home state regulators review documentation in detail, while the UK is more akin to a notification process.

15.79

The UK will also continue to allow EEA AIFMs to manage vehicles in the UK that are AIFs even though the marketing passport no longer exists.

15.80

15.6.5 Delegation Arrangements

As AIFMD allows for the formal delegation of the functions of AIFMs to entities outside the EEA in theory there should be no issue with delegation arrangements continuing to apply. However, it is likely that delegation will come under more formal regulatory scrutiny to ensure that there is no attempt to 'bypass' European regulation. In particular, concerns about whether European AIFMs are letterboxes essentially delegating all performance to a UK entity will become more heavily scrutinised. As noted above, ESMA signalled its expectations in relation to this area in its July 2017 opinion on investment management. We consider that the use of 'host' or 'umbrella' AIFM structures will be curtailed in time. This will result in increased AIFM substance requirements in countries such as Luxembourg and Ireland.

15.81

15.7 The Future of AIFMD in the UK and Europe

It has been anticipated for a number of years that AIFMD will develop in such a way that may affect the relationship after Brexit.

15.82

15.7.1 Application in UK

Any future changes to, or the interpretation of, the AIFMD in the EEA, through amendments to legislation, opinions of the European Court of Justice or guidance from ESMA may lead to a divergence in approach.

15.83

There may also be requirements, however, for further legislative clarification or update if there are changes in EU law before exit day.

15.84

To an extent any divergence should be manageable as there is already a certain level of divergence between the approach of the UK Financial Conduct Authority and other European regulators. For instance, the appointment of third parties and whether these constitute a delegation or simply a third party assisting the manager has been interpreted differently across Europe. There may, however, have to be some form of clarification from regulators or further legislation to ensure that managers understand their obligations.

15.85

15.7.2 Passport

15.86 AIFMD makes provision for the passport to be extended in the future to non-EEA AIFMs.[32]

15.87 ESMA undertook an initial consideration of this in relation to a number of jurisdictions and made recommendations that the passport could be extended to some jurisdictions.[33]

15.88 The UK, given that it will essentially comply with AIFMD in full from the date of Brexit, would be a clear candidate for the awarding of the passport as it will be equivalent with AIFMD and more 'equivalent' than any jurisdiction where ESMA has already given a positive recommendation.

15.89 However, this process is unlikely to develop further. First, the UK was the jurisdiction that advanced this concept in the initial AIFMD negotiations. There is little appetite in any other EEA jurisdiction to implement this. Second, given the political nature of Brexit, there is even less appetite now to give British managers access to passports. Although not identical, equivalence under other European legislation including EMIR, Solvency II has been perceived to be political and power remains with the European Commission determine equivalence. The assessment criteria set out by ESMA in its initial advice is, although detailed, partly subjective.[34] Therefore, even if this process does progress, the general market view is that a passport for UK AIFMs via this procedure would be less effective than the current process.

15.90 As noted above, we will see new rules come in around the definition of marketing for EEA AIFMs managing EEA AIFs. These rules do not impact non-European managers (non-EU managers) that would currently operate under Article 42 (reverse solicitation). However, it is also the case that Member States are not meant to implement rules that disadvantage European AIFMs against third-party AIFs. Therefore, we expect to see similar rules being put into place with respect to marketing of non-European managed funds. Naturally, this is going to be a material additional burden for non-European managers (especially those that are reliant on UK distributors—for the reasons set out above). Naturally, this will also lead to more caution (or reassessment) being take vis-à-vis reverse solicitation (both for European managers and non-European managers).

15.7.3 AIFMD 2/1.2

15.91 The Commission is required to report on the functioning of the AIFMD and has been undertaking reviews.[35] However, there has not been any movement towards AIFMD 2/1.2 as had been expected by this point.

---

[32] These provisions are set out in Arts. 35, 37–41 AIFMD.
[33] ESMA's advice to the European Parliament, the Council and the Commission on the application of the AIFMD passport to non-EU AIFMs and AIFs (ESMA/2015/1236).
[34] Ibid.
[35] AIFMD, Art. 67.

15.92 There is some regulatory arbitrage between AIFMs and MiFID investment firms given the wholesale update of MiFID II recently undertaken. There has been some discussion in areas such as transaction reporting, product governance, and best execution of amending AIFMD so the same standards apply to AIFMs as do to MiFID investment firms. Whether this would be part of a wider amendment to AIFMD or a more minor update to 'level' the regulatory obligations remains to be seen.

16
Solvency II Directive (Solvency II)

Bob Haken and Isabella Jones

16.1 Introduction

16.1.1 Legislative Background

Until relatively recently, the regulation of the insurance industry at the European Union (EU) level was a patchwork of predominantly minimum harmonising rules spread across fifteen different sector-specific directives (not to mention the numerous directives of general application such as those relating to accounting). However, since 1 October 2018 there have for current purposes been only two relevant directives: the European Parliament and Council Directive (2009/138/EC) of 25 November 2009 on the taking-up and pursuit of the business of Insurance and Reinsurance (**Solvency** II) which covers insurers and reinsurers and the Directive of the European Parliament and of the Council (2016/97/EU) of 20 January 2016 on insurance distribution (**IDD**) which governs the sale of insurance, including by insurance intermediaries. In addition, there is one delegated regulation made under Solvency II.[1] Although the rules applicable to insurance and reinsurance (and consequently to the distribution of insurance and reinsurance) differ slightly, in this chapter the term 'insurance' includes reinsurance unless the context requires otherwise. The term 'insurer' as used in this chapter also includes Lloyd's managing agents, save in respect of the sections on group supervision. **16.01**

As with many other European financial services laws, Solvency II and the IDD create a single market for insurance and insurance distribution respectively through the use of passporting rights exercised by firms with their head office in a Member State of the EEA (in the case of Solvency II) or by firms established in a Member State of the EEA (in the case of the IDD). Again, as with other financial services laws, Solvency II (but not the IDD) includes a concept of third country equivalence (in fact three separate assessments of equivalence for different purposes), but unlike in some other cases equivalence under Solvency II does not per se grant market access. **16.02**

In the UK, the licensing requirements of Solvency II and the IDD have been implemented using 'intelligent copy out' (save where the relevant provisions merely restate existing and already implemented provisions of the predecessor directives) through the Financial Services and Markets Act 2000 (**FSMA**) and the Financial Services and Markets Act 2000 (Regulated Activities) Order 2001 SI 2001/544 (**RAO**), with other provisions being implemented primarily through the Rulebook of the Prudential Regulation Authority (the **PRA**), **16.03**

---

[1] Commission Delegated Regulation (2015/35/EU) of 10 October 2014 supplementing Directive 2009/138/EC of the European Parliament and of the Council on the taking-up and pursuit of the business of Insurance and Reinsurance (Solvency II) (hereafter Solvency II Regulations).

the Handbook of Rules and Guidance of the Financial Conduct Authority (the FCA) and the Solvency 2 Regulations 2015.[2]

16.04 In addition, the European Commission has adopted a number of implementing technical standards (**ITS**) and regulatory technical standards (**RTS**) and the European Insurance and Occupational Pensions Authority (**EIOPA**), the European Supervisory Authority responsible for insurance and insurance distribution, has issued a number of 'Level 3' guidance documents, which are not legally binding but which can have legal effect as they form the basis of the industry's legitimate expectation unless a particular national legislature or regulator has indicated that it does not intend to comply.

16.05 Where Solvency II and the IDD are minimum harmonising, the UK has on occasion decided to adopt more onerous regimes. The most notable of these relates to governance where the PRA's Senior Manager and Certification Regime imposes considerably more requirements on insurers than the comparable Solvency II governance regime (and from 9 December 2019 the FCA has applied similar requirements to insurance intermediaries which again are more onerous than the comparable IDD requirements). These areas of 'gold-plating' will of course remain unaffected by the UK's withdrawal from the EU.

16.06 Even where the UK and the remainder of the EU operate on the basis of the same underlying rules, there is a key philosophical difference in approach between the UK and most of the rest of the EU. The UK's regulatory regime is 'activity-based', which is to say that the determining factor in deciding whether UK regulation applies is the location at which the regulated activity takes place. Most of the rest of the EU instead operate a 'location of risk-based' approach for insurance, which instead looks at where the insured risk is located. This can lead to significant differences for cross-border insurance, and once the UK has left the EU will create an asymmetrical relationship.

16.07 This difference is amplified in the case of insurance distribution. The predecessor to the IDD, the Insurance Mediation Directive, did not attempt to set out in any detail how cross-border insurance mediation would operate. This led to considerable confusion, and in April 2006 the supervisory authorities of each Member State adopted the 'Luxembourg Protocol'[3] which among other things contained an approved 'workable' definition of freedom of services in the context of insurance mediation. However, in reality this amounted to little more than a description and it did little to ease the confusion. It had been hoped that the IDD would provide greater clarity in this area, but unfortunately this did not happen. Instead the Board of Supervisors of EIOPA adopted a decision[4] in September 2018 which updated and replaced the Luxembourg Protocol. Neither the Luxembourg Protocol nor the EIOPA decision considers the activities of third country insurance distributors.

16.08 To add to the confusion, there is currently a fundamental disagreement as to the scope of the IDD. Article 1(6) of the IDD provides that 'This Directive shall not apply to insurance

---

[2] SI 2015/575.
[3] Protocol Relating to the Cooperation of the Competent Authorities of the Member States of the European Union in Particular Concerning the Application of Directive 2002/92/EC of the European Parliament and of the Council of 9 December 2002 on Insurance Mediation.
[4] Decision of the Board of Supervisors on the cooperation of the competent authorities of the Member States of the European Economic Area with regard to Directive (EU) 2016/97 of the European Parliament and of the Council of 20 January 2016 on insurance distribution.

and reinsurance distribution activities in relation to risks and commitments located outside the Union ... This Directive shall not regulate insurance or reinsurance distribution activities carried out in third countries'. It has been argued that the second quoted sentence must relate to risks that are located within the Union since if it only related to third country risks, it would be superfluous given the first quoted sentence. On that basis, activities carried on in third countries relating to European located risks would not be subject to the IDD.

However, EIOPA has stated[5] that: **16.09**

> When assessing whether a specific UK intermediary or entity is providing distribution activities in the EU, competent authorities should take into account that only the consistent and uniform application of the IDD can guarantee the same level of protection for consumers and ensure a level playing field in the Union. Competent authorities should ensure that all intermediaries carrying out distribution activities which target EU27 policyholders and EU27 risks fall under the scope of the IDD.

While EIOPA did not cite the basis for this, other legal commentators have pointed to Article 16 of the IDD which requires Member States to ensure that insurers and intermediaries only use the services of other intermediaries if they are registered (implying that those other intermediaries, if legal persons, are required to have their registered office in a Member State).

In the absence of any clarity on what constitutes cross-border insurance distribution activity and the absence in any event of any concept of equivalence under the IDD, it seems likely that each Member State will adopt its own treatment of third country insurance intermediaries. This is of course frustrating for internationally active insurance intermediaries who are attempting to put in place structures that will meet regulatory requirements following Brexit, and who would rather adopt a single model that works across the remaining Member States. However, at the time of writing, there is still no clarity, so insurance intermediaries are having to assume that they will need to be locally authorised in each Member State in which they do any business (or form an intermediary established and registered in a Member State which will retain the ability to passport). Accordingly, insurance distribution is not considered further in this chapter. **16.10**

16.1.2 Preserving the *Acquis*

If the UK and the EU agree on the terms of a withdrawal agreement pursuant to Article 50 of Treaty on European Union (whether the provisionally agreed text published on 17 October 2019 or a new text that is yet to be agreed), it seems likely that there Govwill be an implementation or transitional period until at least 31 December 2020 during which the existing rules will continue to apply as if the UK were still a Member State. This is achieved by Article 127 of the provisionally agreed text which provides, inter alia and with a few minor exceptions, that: **16.11**

---

[5] Recommendations for the insurance sector in light of the United Kingdom withdrawing from the European Union, para. 30.

- Union law is applicable to and in the UK during the transition period and that Union law shall produce in respect of and in the UK the same legal effects as those which it produces in the Union and its Member States.
- Unless otherwise provided, during the transitional period, any reference to Member States in the Union law applicable pursuant to the Withdrawal Agreement, including as implemented and applied by Member States, shall be understood as including the UK.

16.12 Accordingly, if such an agreement is adopted, there will be no immediate consequences for the insurance industry of the UK's withdrawal from the EU. On the expiry of any implementation period, in theory the terms of a newly negotiated trade agreement will apply. It is impossible to predict what any such trade agreement will say, but it seems highly unlikely that the EU will deviate from its principle that a non-Member State cannot enjoy the benefits of the Single Market. The expectation therefore is that the position as regards the insurance sector following the expiry of an implementation period will not differ substantially from the position that would apply if the UK were to leave the EU without an agreed Withdrawal Agreement. The rest of this chapter therefore does not distinguish between the two scenarios.

16.13 As noted at paragraph 16.03, Solvency II and the IDD were implemented into domestic UK law in accordance with their respective deadlines for transposition and accordingly section 2(1) of the European Union (Withdrawal) Act 2018[6] (EUWA) provides that the UK implementing legislation continues to have effect in UK domestic law.[7] The effect of the Solvency II Regulations is preserved by virtue of section 3(1) EUWA and the various ITS and RTS (which are 'European tertiary legislation' for the purposes of the EUWA, being made under Articles 291 and 290 respectively of the Treaty on the Functioning of the European Union) are similarly preserved by the same section.

16.14 EIOPA's Level 3 guidance does not constitute a legal instrument and so is not preserved by the EUWA, although the legal effect as to legitimate expectation referred to at paragraph 16.04 is expected to continue.

16.15 As with other sectors, the UK government has unveiled a number of statutory instruments designed to correct 'defects' in the way in which retained European legislation will operate following the UK's withdrawal, the most significant of which for the insurance industry are:

- Credit Institutions and Insurance Undertakings Reorganisation and Winding Up (Amendment) (EU Exit) Regulations 2019;
- EEA Passport Rights (Amendment, etc., and Transitional Provisions) (EU Exit) Regulations 2018;
- Electronic Commerce and Solvency 2 (Amendment etc.) (EU Exit) Regulations 2019;
- Financial Conglomerates and Other Financial Groups (Amendment) (EU Exit) Regulations 2019;

---

[6] 2018 c.16.
[7] This preservation is required because the effect of repealing the European Communities Act 1972 would ordinarily be to repeal all subsequent legislation made pursuant to it, which would include all legislation implementing European directives.

- Financial Services and Markets Act 2000 (Amendment) (EU Exit) Regulations 2019;
- Friendly Societies (Amendment) (EU Exit) Regulations 2018;
- Insurance Distribution (Amendment) (EU Exit) Regulations 2019;
- Packaged Retail and Insurance-based Investment Products (Amendment) (EU Exit) Regulations 2019; and
- Solvency 2 and Insurance (Amendment etc.) (EU Exit) Regulations 2019.

16.2 The Position of European Insurers Operating in the United Kingdom

16.2.1 Licensing Issues

16.16 At present, EEAauthorised insurers who wish to access the UK market can adopt one (or a combination) of the following approaches:

- Use of the financial services 'passporting' regime to conduct business in the UK on either a freedom of establishment basis (with a physical presence in the jurisdiction as a branch) or a freedom of services basis pursuant to Solvency II and (in respect of distribution activities) the IDD.[8]
- Establish a subsidiary which is authorised by the PRA to conduct business in the UK.

16.17 However, the UK government has been clear from the outset that the decision to withdraw from the EU includes the UK leaving both the European Single Market and the Customs Union in favour of 'a new strategic partnership with the EU',[9] which aligns with the expectation that the EU will not allow non-Member States to enjoy the benefits of the Union without being a participating member.

16.18 As a consequence, on exit day the UK will become a 'third country' for the purposes of Solvency II and the remaining EEA Member States will similarly become third countries for the purposes of the UK regulatory regime. EEA insurers will therefore lose the ability to conduct cross-border business in the UK as a matter of fundamental right pursuant to the 'passporting' regime in the EU directives and will need to seek authorisation in the UK as a third country branch or, as discussed in the previous chapter and depending on the scale of their liabilities protected by the Financial Services Compensation Scheme, a subsidiary. Alternatively, such firms will be required to restructure to move the entirety of their regulated business outside of the UK to operate on a 'non-admitted' (or 'offshore') basis. This section addresses the UK regulatory landscape for EEA insurers in the immediate aftermath of Brexit when the remaining EU27 Member States become third countries for the purposes of UK regulation, including in the context of the UK authorities' response to mitigate the impact of ongoing political uncertainty.

---

[8] We note it is possible for incoming EEA insurers to conduct business on both a freedom of services and freedom of establishment basis—Commission Interpretative Communication (Freedom to provide services and the general good in the insurance sector) Official Journal C 043, 16/02/2000 P. 0005-0027.

[9] Policy paper, *The United Kingdom's Exit from, and New Partnership with, the European Union*, published 2 February 2017 (updated 15 May 2017).

16.2.1.1 Inbound EEA authorised insurers passporting into the UK

(a) UK regulatory landscape for insurers

16.19 The UK financial services regulatory regime is governed by FSMA which provides that it is an offence to carry on regulated activities *in the UK* by way of business unless authorised or exempt.[10] This is referred to as the 'general prohibition' and a breach is a criminal offence which can result in a fine or imprisonment for individuals of up to two years. In addition, contracts which are made by an unauthorised person carrying on a regulated activity in breach of the general prohibition are unenforceable against the innocent party[11] but, significantly, the innocent party can enforce the contract against the unauthorised person. In the context of insurance contracts, this means that the insured is entitled to recover claims regardless of whether the terms of the policy have been complied with (including payment of premium).

16.20 For insurers, the two key regulated activities that are captured by the FSMA regime are as follows:

- 'effecting contracts of insurance as principal'; and
- 'carrying out contracts of insurance as principal'.[12]

16.21 Paragraphs 16.35–16.40 consider the nature of activities which fall within the scope of 'effecting' and 'carrying out' contracts of insurance in more detail but (subject to a few limited exceptions) insurers conducting either of these activities in the UK require authorisation from the PRA pursuant to Part 4A of FSMA. Both the PRA and the FCA take responsibility for the ongoing regulation of insurers: the PRA from a prudential/risk perspective and the FCA from a conduct perspective.

(b) Passporting into the UK and the impact of Brexit

16.22 As noted at paragraph 16.16, the position differs for EEA authorised insurers as they have the right to operate throughout the Single Market under the principles of freedom to provide services and the freedom of establishment on the basis of their home state authorisation (without seeking separate authorisation from the relevant authority in each Member State) under Solvency II. For the purposes of the UK regulatory framework, EEA authorised insurers who are carrying on regulated activities in the UK pursuant to the passporting regime are treated as 'authorised persons', and therefore do not require separate authorisation from the PRA pursuant to FSMA to avoid breaching the general prohibition.[13]

16.23 Once passporting rights cease (either at the point at which the UK leaves the EU without a deal or at the end of any implementation period), EEA firms currently conducting business in the UK via a passport under the existing regime will no longer be appropriately authorised to conduct regulated activities in the UK. The repealing of passporting rights has been implemented through legislation made by the UK government (the EEA Passport Rights (Amendment, etc., and Transitional Provisions) (EU Exit) Regulations 2018), which assumes that there are no new specific arrangements in place between the UK and the EU

---

[10] FSMA, s. 19.
[11] Ibid., s. 26.
[12] RAO, Art. 10(1)–(2).
[13] FSMA, s. 31(1)(a) and Sch. 3.

after exit day. Accordingly, such firms will require a Part 4A permission pursuant to FSMA to be able to continue to operate in the UK as a third country branch.

(c) The temporary permission regime

While it is clear that EEA insurers who are proposing to continue carrying on insurance business in the UK after exit will need to apply for authorisation in the UK, the precise timing of when such authorisation is required hinges upon on the outcome of the political negotiations. The Bank of England has been clear that any such authorisation will only be required at the end of any implementation period[14] but this necessarily assumes that the UK government ratifies the Withdrawal Agreement in its current form (or at the very least a version which contemplates an implementation period) before the UK leaves the EU. As this is by no means a certain outcome, the UK authorities have been actively preparing for the impact of a 'no deal' scenario in which the Withdrawal Agreement is not agreed between the UK and EU27 by exit day, and as a consequence the implementation period does not materialise. 16.24

The UK government has therefore enacted into law a temporary permissions regime (TPR) to protect the many thousands of EEA firms currently operating in the UK via a passport from the potential cliff-edge scenario in which authorisation as a third country branch is required on short notice to continue carrying on regulated business in the UK without breaching the general prohibition. 16.25

Chapter 8 outlines the key features of the TPR for incoming EEA firms at paragraphs 8.12 – 8.18]. Paragraphs 16.27–16.33 explore the nuances of the regime particularly as relevant to insurers and should be read in conjunction with the corresponding sections in the previous chapter. 16.26

(i) Implementation of the TPR The TPR is designed to mitigate the impact of a 'no deal' Brexit and accordingly will only be necessary if there is no transition period. However, it is worth noting that the implementing legislation[15] provides that the majority of the relevant changes will come into force on 'exit day', which is defined by reference to the corresponding definition in the EUWA, as subsequently amended to reflect the Article 50 extension,[16] as 31 January 2020.[17] The UK government has stated[18] that it proposes to deal with this anomaly pursuant to the powers conferred on it by the EU (Withdrawal Agreement) Bill (once enacted). Accordingly, the relevant statutory instruments will be deferred as necessary so that, instead of coming into force on exit day, they come into force at the end of an implementation period. The Bill will also provide that this deferral can apply to statutory instruments made under enactments other than the EUWA. It therefore appears that the TPR is intended to be a flexible construct which, if necessary, could apply following an implementation period and we would suggest that it is likely to be as pertinent post 31 December 2020 as in any 'no deal' scenario on 31 January 2019. 16.27

---

[14] Bank of England, news release, 24 July 2018.
[15] EEA Passport Rights (Amendment, etc., and Transitional Provisions) (EU Exit) Regulations 2018.
[16] European Union (Withdrawal) (No.2) Act 2019.
[17] Ibid., s. 20(1)–(2).
[18] Letter from David Lidington MP (Minister for the Cabinet Office) to Baroness Taylor of Bolton in relation to treatments of no-deal statutory instruments in a deal scenario, dated 14 February 2019.

16.28 **(ii) Timing of authorisation** As noted above, the primary purpose of the TPR is to allow EEA firms currently passporting into the UK to continue their activities in the UK for up to three years after the UK leaves the EU with a possibility of extension for further 12 month periods, while preparing for authorisation as a third country branch in the UK by a particular 'landing slot', as communicated by the PRA. There is a timing distinction in the legislation between those who are applying for a new UK third country branch and those who are not going to apply for a third country branch (e.g. who are intending to run off or transfer business during that period). In cases where there is a branch application, the temporary permission can potentially last for up to three years. In cases where there is no application for a UK branch, the regulators can either specify a period for the run-off which is shorter than two years or withdraw the permission after two years.

16.29 **(iii) Requirement to apply for authorisation** Although there has been some uncertainty around the suitability of the TPR for firms who do not ever intend to submit an application for a third country branch but wish to continue writing new business, the PRA appear to have taken the view that the TPR is appropriate for firms who are currently conducting business via a branch in the UK and propose to do so for a limited time after exit day even where such firms are in the process of transitioning their UK business to other appropriately licensed vehicles (either within or outside of the UK). We note that, in practice, the PRA has generally been engaging with eligible firms on receipt of the required notice to enter the TPR with a view to discussing the most appropriate 'landing slot' (or exit date) in view of the general commercial strategy of the firm in question.

16.30 **(iv) Regulation in the TPR** Once in the TPR, EEA insurers will be treated as though they have a deemed Part 4A permission which will allow the PRA and FCA to continue to exercise the same degree of supervisory oversight as over any UK-authorised firm. The PRA has been consistently clear that firms in the TPR (and FSCR SRO, which is discussed below) will be expected to meet UK third country requirements from exit day.[19] The PRA has however recognised that certain requirements will have a phased implementation (or a relief period) to enable firms operating within the TPR to bring their organisational capabilities to the required standard. For example, Solvency II qualitative reporting will be subject to a relief period of six months, whereas branch SCR and MCR calculations and Solvency II quantitative reporting will be subject to a fifteen-month relief period, extendable to two years if warranted.[20] In terms of activities, TPR firms will be restricted to the scope of activities which they conducted immediately prior to exit day pursuant to the passport.

16.31 For pure reinsurance branches, the PRA has confirmed that there will not be a requirement to localise assets in the UK to represent branch capital requirements under either the current or proposed rules.

16.32 **(v) Cross-border business of TPR firms** It is clear that, in EIOPA's view, the EEA insurers who are operating as a UK branch in the TPR pursuant to a deemed Part 4A permission will not be able to conduct freedom of services from the UK branch into other EEA states as a matter of course. This view appears to be held notwithstanding the continued ability of the head office of the insurer to write cross-border risks on either a freedom of services basis or

---

[19] Consultation Papers (CP25/18 and 32/18).
[20] Bank of England Policy Statement, PRA PS5/19.

passported branch throughout the remaining EU27 Member States.[21] The approach of EEA regulators and the availability and scope of equivalent regimes becomes a critical question.

(d) Post-TPR

As the TPR is designed to be an interim measure, the Financial Services Contracts (Transitional and Saving Provision) (EU Exit) Regulations 2019 has been implemented to establish a regime for firms who either never enter the TPR or leave the TPR without authorisation (either because no application was made by the designated landing slot and the deemed Part 4A permission was cancelled, or any such application was denied) to allow such firms to wind down their UK regulated activities in an orderly manner. See section 16.4 for a more detailed analysis. 16.33

16.2.1.2 EEA authorised insurers conducting business in the UK on an offshore basis

Although it is technically possible from the perspective of UK regulation for EEA insurers to conduct business in the UK on an offshore basis due to the 'activities-based' nature of the UK regulatory regime, the EU regulators conversely tend to require that firms conduct their cross-border business pursuant to the passporting regime facilitated by the EU directives. Following Brexit this approach is likely to increase in significance for EEAauthorised insurers who do not propose to establish a third country branch or otherwise set up a standalone subsidiary in the UK after passporting rights are no longer applicable. 16.34

As discussed above, for insurers the key regulated activities are 'effecting' contracts of insurance as principal (which comprises, inter alia, the entry into new business[22] and matters preparatory to the binding of the policy)[23] and 'carrying out' contracts of insurance as principal (which captures activities in relation to an *existing* policy,[24] such as collecting premium and handling claims).[25] To reiterate, both 'effecting' and 'carrying out' contracts of insurance as principal are subject to regulation by the PRA and FCA in respect of UK operations[26] even in circumstances in which the underlying policyholders and/or risks are located outside of the UK. This is because the UK is an activities-based regime. As a consequence, an overseas insurer with UK policyholders may be able to keep outside of the UK regulatory perimeter if its activities do not stray (and are not deemed to stray by virtue of relationships with third parties) onshore. 16.35

A key question for EEA insurers will therefore be whether their proposed activities fall within the scope of 'effecting' and 'carrying out' contracts of insurance in the UK (thereby requiring authorisation from the PRA) and further if there are any factors, such as relationships with independent UK-based agents, which could effectively bring the EEA insurer onshore for the purposes of UK regulation. 16.36

---

[21] Solvency II, Arts. 147ff. refer only to the exercise of the freedom to provide services by 'insurance undertakings' without stipulating which establishment of the undertaking, whereas EIOPA and some EU regulators believe either that only the head office of an insurance undertaking can exercise this right, or alternatively that only the head office or a branch in another Member State can do so.
[22] *Re Whiteley Insurance Consultants* [2009] Bus LR 418.
[23] *Stewart v. Oriental Fire and Marine Insurance Company Ltd* [1985] QB 988.
[24] This was established in various cases which pre-date the current requirements in FSMA, but the recent case of *Re Whiteley Insurance Consultants (A Firm)* [2008] EWHC 1782 (Ch.) confirmed this remains correct under FSMA.
[25] *Scher v. Policyholders Protection Board* [1994] 2 AC 57.
[26] RAO, Art. 10(1)–(2).

(a) Applicable regulation and guidance

16.37 In contrast to the guidance published in the Perimeter Guidance Manual in the FCA Handbook in respect of insurance distribution activities, the regulators in the UK have not published any substantive direction as to what constitutes 'effecting' or 'carrying out' contracts of insurance (the Glossary refers to the RAO, which does not include a definition). In relation to the capacity of independent persons to bring non-UK insurers onshore, FSMA expands the concept of carrying on business in the UK by setting out certain additional scenarios in which a person who would not otherwise be regarded as carrying on a regulated activity in the UK shall, for the purposes of FSMA, be regarded as carrying it on in the United Kingdom.[27] One of the examples includes where the head office is not in the UK but 'the activity is carried on from an establishment maintained by him in the United Kingdom'.[28]

16.38 From a European perspective, on 16 February 2000 the European Commission issued the Interpretative Communication which is non-binding guidance setting out the view of the EC on various CJEU case law distinguishing between carrying on business on a freedom of services and freedom of establishment basis. The guidance also provides that where the following three cumulative conditions are met in relation to an independent third party, the Commission's view is that the insurer will be treated as having an establishment in the relevant Member State:

- the third party must be subject to the direction and control of the insurer it represents;
- it must be able to commit the insurer; and
- it must have received a permanent brief.

16.39 Although the Interpretative Communication does not represent law, it has been broadly adopted in the UK and will therefore be relevant for EEA insurers considering whether the scope of proposed activities require authorisation as a third country branch post-Brexit.

(b) Case law

16.40 The point has been addressed by a series of judgments which as a general rule pre-date the current FSMA regime although, absent any direction to the contrary, this case law is likely to be followed by courts applying FSMA. In summary, the following key principles have been established by the courts:

- 'effecting' encompasses more than purely binding and can include the 'negotiation of the terms of a contract';[29]
- the 'mere payment' of a claim (it being established by *Bedford Insurance Co Ltd v. Instituto de Resseguros de Brasil* [1985] QB 966 that paying claims is the primary activity forming part of the performance of obligations under an insurance contract) to a person in the UK is not enough by itself to result in a person carrying out insurance business in the UK;[30]

---

[27] FSMA, s. 418.
[28] Ibid., s. 418(5).
[29] *Stewart v. Oriental Fire and Marine Insurance Co Ltd.*
[30] *Scher and others v. Policyholders Protection Board (Nos. 1 and 2)* [1994] 2 AC 57.

- the activities of a UK-based agent in preparing a slip and confirming that the contract was bound following the decision by the reinsurer will bring the reinsurer onshore for the purposes of UK regulation;[31]
- using UK-based agents to refer risks to the insurers for binding within agreed guidelines and suggest premium rates and make recommendations to the insurers as to the acceptance of risk utilising their particular market expertise is capable of bringing the insurer onshore for the purposes of UK regulation;[32]
- regularity and substance of the activities in the UK is a relevant factor in considering whether such activities fall within the territorial scope of FSMA;[33]
- activities undertaken by an agent must be so 'extensive and important' as to constitute carrying out of insurance business on behalf of the relevant insurer(s) in the relevant jurisdiction;[34] and
- 'isolated non-recurrent activities' might not constitute the carrying on of insurance business if there was a lack of continuity or regularity in the undertaking of activities or if such activities were not integral to the way in which the insurer conducted its affairs.[35]

16.41 In practice, following Brexit it will be fundamental for EEA insurers who do not propose to seek authorisation from the PRA as a third country branch or subsidiary to consider carefully the scope of proposed activities in the UK including in the context of relationships with third parties.

16.3 The Position of UK Insurers Operating in Europe

16.3.1 Licensing Issues

16.42 For direct insurers (as distinct from reinsurers), Article 162 of Solvency II provides that 'Member States shall make access to the business referred to in the first subparagraph of Article 2(1) by any undertaking with a head office outside the Community subject to an authorisation'. That subparagraph refers to 'direct life and non-life insurance undertakings', whereas the second subparagraph goes on to refer to 'reinsurance undertakings which conduct only reinsurance activities', commonly known as pure reinsurers.

16.43 The distinction reflects a curious anomaly in the history of European legislation, as the predecessor directives similarly distinguished between direct insurers and pure reinsurers, without recognising that direct insurers may also write reinsurance (a scenario which while common in the UK was not generally found in other Member States). That lacuna continues as regards third country insurers as the combined effect of Article 2(1) (which distinguishes between *types* of insurer) and Article 162 (which purports to relate to the nature of the

---

[31] *DR Insurance Company v. Seguros America Banamex DR Insurance Company v. Imperio Companhia De Seguros* [1993] 1 Lloyd's Rep. 120.
[32] *Re Great Western Assurance Co SA and others.*
[33] *Financial Services Authority v. Fradley and Woodward* [2005] EWCA Civ. 1183
[34] *DR Insurance Company v. Seguros America Banamex DR Insurance Company v. Imperio Companhia De Seguros* [1993] 1 Lloyd's Rep. 120.
[35] *Secretary of State and for Trade and Industry v. Great Western Assurance Co SA* [1997] Lloyd's Rep. 377

insurance business) means that it is by no means clear how reinsurance written by an insurance undertaking (which is therefore not a pure reinsurer) falls to be treated.

16.3.1.1 Direct insurers

16.44 Focusing on what is clear for the moment, as noted Article 162 provides that third country insurers may access direct insurance business in the EU if they obtain authorisation to do so. Article 162 goes on to impose certain conditions to the grant of such an authorisation, including that the third country insurer establishes a branch in the territory of the Member State in which authorisation is sought.

16.45 The process therefore for a third country insurer wishing to write insurance covering risks in a particular Member State is to establish a branch in that Member State and seek authorisation of the branch. The relevant supervisory authority will then apply its own regime to the branch, including requirements as to governance, reporting, the establishment of technical provisions, and the applicable capital requirement. Solvency II requires that the third country insurer holds assets representing the minimum capital requirement (MCR)[36] applicable to the branch in the Member State in which the branch is established and assets representing the balance of the SCR[37] in the EU. An amount equal to one-quarter of the absolute floor for the MCR must be deposited as security.

16.46 It is clear however that such a branch does not have its own passporting rights, meaning that a branch of a third country insurer will only be permitted to write business in the Member State in which it is established. In order to write insurance business in another Member State, the insurer would need to apply for a separate authorisation from that other Member State, and would similarly need to establish a second branch. Solvency II does recognise that this may become overly onerous for third country insurers wishing to establish branches in more than one Member State, and it allows for certain simplifications,[38] such as the ability to calculate the SCR across all European branches collectively and a requirement for only one security deposit, but these can only be granted if all relevant supervisory authorities agree.

16.3.1.2 Pure reinsurers

16.47 For pure reinsurers, as noted, Article 162 does not apply. Article 174 sets a minimum standard as it requires that Member States do not apply a more favourable regime to third country reinsurers than that applicable to reinsurers with their head office in the Member State, and Article 175 envisages agreements with third countries governing cross-border reinsurance, but beyond those high-level requirements Member States are free to approach branches of third country reinsurers as they see fit.

16.48 This does seem to have been recognised by the European Commission which said on 8 February 2018[39] that 'UK reinsurance undertakings will have to comply, for their EU

---

[36] Solvency II provides for a risk-based capital requirement, the solvency capital requirement (**SCR**), which is calculated using either a standard formula, a bespoke internal model that has been approved by the insurer's supervisor; or a mixture of both. There is also an MCR set at a lower threshold. Breach of the MCR is designed, unless remedied quickly, to lead to a loss of the insurer's authorisation whereas breach of the SCR results in supervisory intervention designed to restore the SCR level of capital.

[37] Ibid.

[38] Ibid., Art. 167.

[39] 'Notice to stakeholders—Withdrawal of the United Kingdom and EU rules in the field of Insurance/Reinsurance'.

business, with the conditions set by the EU Member State in which they carry out their activity. These conditions cannot be more favourable than those applying to reinsurance companies from the EU, but they may be less favourable and may well differ between EU Member States.' It is likely therefore that most Member States will require branches of UK reinsurers, or insurers conducting only reinsurance business, to be authorised by the Member State in which the branch is located and that the governance, reporting and prudential requirements applicable to the branch will be similar to those imposed on domestic reinsurers.

If Solvency II has little to say on the subject of the establishment of branches by third country reinsurance undertakings, it says even less about the cross-border provision of reinsurance without a permanent establishment. Article 174 refers to the third country reinsurer 'taking-up or pursuing reinsurance activity' in the relevant Member State, which echoes the full title of the directive (Directive on the taking-up and pursuit of the business of Insurance and Reinsurance). Given the tendency to approach regulation on a location of risk, rather than location of activity, basis, most European regulators are likely to regard reinsurance provided to cedants in their jurisdiction other than through a permanent establishment as subject to Article 174 with the result that they will not treat it more favourably than they treat reinsurance with domestic reinsurers. **16.49**

The most significant limitation on the ability of a third country insurer to sell reinsurance to European cedants is actually an indirect one. For the cedant itself, if it is calculating its SCR in accordance with the standard formula, the Solvency II Regulations provide[40] that the risk mitigating effect of the reinsurance can only be taken into account if the reinsurer is: **16.50**

- an insurer with its head office in a Member State which complies with its own SCR;
- a third country insurer situated in a jurisdiction that has been deemed equivalent or temporarily equivalent for reinsurance purposes; or
- a third country insurer which is not situated in an equivalent jurisdiction, but which has a credit quality that has been assigned to credit quality step 3 or better (broadly a rating of at least BBB−).

An unrated or lowly rated reinsurer in a non-equivalent jurisdiction is therefore likely to find little appetite for its products among European cedants. **16.51**

Some Member States have gone further and will only allow reinsurance with third country reinsurers in very limited circumstances. The German Federal Financial Supervisory Authority (BaFin) has stated[41] that third country reinsurers must establish an authorised branch in Germany if they wish to carry on reinsurance business in Germany unless that third country has been assessed as equivalent for reinsurance or the contract is concluded by correspondence (*Korrespondenzversicherung*). Insurance by correspondence is a very narrow exclusion and it is in practice difficult to adhere to the strict requirements. Accordingly, for most practical purposes, a third country reinsurer will only be able to reinsure German cedants if it is in an equivalent jurisdiction. **16.52**

---

[40] Solvency II Regulations, Art. 211.
[41] Interpretative decision of the German Federal Financial Supervisory Authority dated 31 August 2016 'Conduct of reinsurance business in Germany by insurance undertakings situated in a third country'.

16.53 The indications[42] are that (with the exception of Poland), other Member States are comfortable with non-admitted reinsurance, or reinsurance offered by a third country reinsurer other than through a permanent establishment in that Member State.

16.3.2 The Effect of Equivalence under Solvency II

16.54 There are three distinct concepts of equivalence under Solvency II. The first arises where an insurance group which is subject to group supervision under Solvency II has a subsidiary insurance undertaking in a third country.[43] The default is that the third country subsidiary would have to revalue its assets and liabilities (and its contribution to the group SCR) on a Solvency II basis, but by way of exception if the third country is assessed as equivalent for these purposes, the local rules can be used instead and the result aggregated with the remainder of the group instead of being fully consolidated. This concept of equivalence is of extremely limited application and is not relevant to any question of market access.

16.55 The second equivalence assessment arises where a European insurer is part of a group that is headquartered in a third country.[44] Here, by default, the European supervisory authority would be required to exercise worldwide group supervision over the entire group. However, if the jurisdiction in which the parent undertaking has been assessed as equivalent for group supervision purposes, the European supervisory authority is entitled to rely on the group supervision exercised by the supervisory authority in the relevant third country. Relatively few internationally active insurance groups are headquartered in the UK, so it is not expected that the application of this equivalence assessment will change significantly following the UK's withdrawal from the EU, although we discuss the potential impact of overlapping regimes below.

16.56 The final equivalence assessment is much more important for the question of continued market access. In general, the credit that a European cedant can take for transferring insurance risk to a reinsurer based in a third country is based on an assessment of that reinsurer's credit rating and any security provided by the reinsurer to support its obligations. However, where that reinsurer is based in a jurisdiction that is equivalent for reinsurance purposes, Article 172 of Solvency II requires that those reinsurance contracts 'shall be treated in the same manner as reinsurance contracts concluded with undertakings' that are subject to Solvency II.

16.57 The original aim of this equivalence assessment was to allow cedants to take full credit for the risk transfer effected by the reinsurance contract. However, in the light of the UK's withdrawal from the EU, this provision is now being read as requiring European supervisory authorities to permit cross-border reinsurance of cedants based in their jurisdiction in circumstances where the reinsurer is based in an equivalent jurisdiction. That is clearly the analysis behind the BaFin interpretative decision referred to above.

---

[42] See for example the announcement from Lloyd's of London, 'Lloyd's Brussels to Write FAC and Non-Proportional XOL Treaty Reinsurance', 29 October 2018.
[43] Solvency II, Art. 227.
[44] Ibid., Art. 260.

16.3.2.1 Impact on direct insurers

16.58 As will have been seen, whether or not the jurisdiction of the insurer has been assessed as equivalent for Solvency II purposes has no relevance to continued market access for a direct insurer.

16.3.2.2 Impact on reinsurers

16.59 Conversely, if the UK were to be assessed as equivalent under Article 172, a UK reinsurer (and arguably a UK insurer) would be permitted to write reinsurance of European cedants without any additional authorisation requirement, although it should be noted that if it wished to do so through an establishment in the relevant Member State, that Member State's domestic law would govern any requirements applicable to the branch.

16.3.3 Multiple and Overlapping Group Supervision Regimes

16.60 Due to the licensing issues discussed above, most internationally active insurance groups have implemented restructuring projects to preserve their ability to write risks located in a Member State. This has often resulted in a group maintaining a UK insurer to write risks from the UK and the rest of the world, with a separate insurer domiciled and regulated in a continuing Member State.

16.61 Solvency II requires supervisory authorities to exercise supplementary (or group) supervision over insurance and mixed-activity insurance groups. That supervision, depending on the particular structure of the group concerned and subject to equivalence, needs to be exercised at the level of the ultimate parent undertaking in the EU and at the level of the ultimate worldwide parent undertaking. There are detailed rules in the directive prescribing which supervisory authority is to take on the role of group supervisor, but critically for these purposes only supervisory authorities from a Member State are eligible to fulfil the role.

16.62 Where a group currently has the PRA in the UK as its Solvency II group supervisor but also has an insurance undertaking in one or more continuing Member States, one effect of Brexit therefore will be that a different supervisory authority will be required to act as group supervisor. While most decisions affecting groups are discussed at the applicable college of supervisors and agreed collectively, there are a number of decisions which the group supervisor is empowered to make.

16.63 However, if the insurance group has retained a UK insurer, it will also be subject to group supervision under the UK regime. The Group Supervision Part of the PRA's rulebook (as amended by the PRA Rulebook: (EU Exit) Instrument 2019) requires the PRA to exercise group supervision at the level of the ultimate parent undertaking in the UK and at the level of the ultimate worldwide parent undertaking. Given the potential for overlap between this regime and the Solvency II regime described above, there will be a number of issues affecting such a group which need to be considered separately by both the PRA and the Solvency II group supervisor.

16.64 Some of these relate to the ongoing supervision of the group, such as those relating to group governance, policies, risk concentrations, and intragroup transactions. However, there are a number of key specific decisions or approvals which are considered in more detail below.

16.3.3.1 Worldwide group supervision

16.65 The most obvious of these relates to the need for worldwide group supervision itself. Unless the group supervision regime applicable to a third country ultimate parent undertaking has been assessed as equivalent (or temporarily equivalent), prima facie both the PRA and the Solvency II group supervisor are required to exercise worldwide group supervision. At the time of writing, only Bermuda and Switzerland had been approved as equivalent for these purposes.[45] As a result, groups headquartered in other third countries could find themselves subject to worldwide group supervision under the UK rules, the Solvency II rules, and whatever regime does apply in that third country.

16.66 In reality, all regulators are constrained by limited resource and in some cases by their legal ability to conduct effective group supervision over entities based in third countries. This manifests itself in the way in which group supervision is exercised. Solvency II allows the group supervisor to conduct group supervision either by applying Solvency II *mutatis mutandis* at the level of the third country ultimate parent undertaking or by applying 'other methods'.[46] In the UK at least, the PRA has made extensive use of 'other methods', in that it has granted waivers to a number of third country groups disapplying worldwide group supervision in its entirety in return for transparency of information at the group level and increased scrutiny and oversight of transactions between the Solvency II parts of the group and the third country parts. This has allowed international groups to avoid unnecessarily onerous duplication of the existing (albeit non-equivalent) group supervision at the parent level.

16.67 In a model where both the PRA and the Solvency II group supervisor are required to conduct worldwide group supervision or apply other methods, clearly there is a risk that there is a difference of opinion. In order to secure the benefits of only having one worldwide group supervisor a group will need to persuade both regulators on an ongoing basis that some form of other method is suitable.

16.3.3.2 Disapplication of European group supervision

16.68 A similar issue arises when the situation is reversed. If a group is headquartered in a jurisdiction that is equivalent for these purposes (currently Bermuda or Switzerland), the PRA and the Solvency II group supervisor are required not to conduct worldwide group supervision, but there is nothing in the directive which disapplies the group supervision at the level of the ultimate EEA parent undertaking (or for the PRA, the ultimate UK parent undertaking). Recognising that this may be an inefficient use of resource, EIOPA has stated[47] that the acting group supervisor may decide to exempt the European subgroup from group supervision 'on a case-by-case basis, where this would result in a more efficient supervision of the group and would not impair the

---

[45] By Commission Delegated Decision (EU) 2016/309 of 26 November 2015 and Commission Delegated Decision (EU) 2015/1602 of 5 June 2015, respectively.
[46] Solvency II, Art. 261.
[47] EIOPA guidelines on group solvency (EIOPA-BoS-14/181), guideline 5, paras. 1.14–1.16.

supervisory activities of the supervisory authorities concerned in respect of their individual responsibilities'.

As with the previous section, in order to benefit from this leniency groups with UK and European insurers will have to satisfy both the PRA and the Solvency II group supervisor that the test has been met.

16.3.3.3 Choice of method for group solvency

One of the key components of group supervision is the assessment of the adequacy of group own funds against a group SCR. The default method for calculating the group SCR is accounting consolidation, that is to say that the group prepares consolidated accounts at the level of the relevant parent undertaking on a Solvency II basis and determines the group SCR as if those accounts were the accounts of an insurer.

However another method is permissible if approved by the group supervisor.[48] This is the deduction and aggregation method. Broadly this requires groups to calculate the individual SCRs and own funds for each company within the group separately and then to aggregate them (while removing any double counting). This approach does not recognise any diversification benefits and so is not suitable for most groups, but in some circumstances where accounting consolidation produces a nonsensical or disproportionate result it can be appropriate.

As before, groups with UK and European insurers wishing to use the deduction and aggregation method will need to convince both the PRA and the Solvency II group supervisor that the exclusive application of accounting consolidation is not appropriate.

16.3.3.4 Group internal models

As with solo SCRs, a group SCR can be calculated using either the standard formula (set out in the Solvency II Regulations) or an internal model. Indeed, a group may use an internal model that has been approved at the level of the group to calculate not just its group SCR but also the solo SCRs of each insurer within the group.[49] In order to realise this efficiency, a group must submit an application to the group supervisor and the college of concerned supervisory authorities must 'do everything within their power' to reach a joint decision within six months.[50]

The internal model will include a policy on changes to the model, with a definition of what constitutes minor and major changes (and the approval of a model will include an approval of that policy). Any major changes to the model are subject to prior supervisory approval.[51]

In the scenario where a group has a UK insurer and a European insurer, it follows that any group internal model, and any major changes to that model, will need to be approved by both the PRA and the Solvency II group supervisor. Since the group cannot implement the change to the model until it has been approved, but is required to change the model if necessary to reflect changes in the risk profile or the underlying assumptions and calibrations,

---

[48] Solvency II, Art. 220(2).
[49] Ibid., Art 231.
[50] There are dispute resolution processes including a referral to EIOPA, but these are not considered here.
[51] Solvency II, Art. 115.

this creates the risk that a group may be in default of its obligations to one supervisor as a result of the failure by the other supervisor to reach the same decision.

16.4 Contract Continuity for Existing Business

16.4.1 How Does Brexit Affect Existing Contracts?

16.76 It is not just writing new business that can be problematic on a cross-border basis. One characteristic of insurance contracts is that performance of the contractual obligations can take a very long time. For long-term or life insurance, it is quite obvious that the insurer may only be called upon to pay a claim many years after the policy was purchased. However, even with non-life insurance there are some very long-tailed liabilities. This can happen either where a claim is complex and takes years to assess and agree or where a policy was written to cover losses arising in the policy period, irrespective of when the claim is actually brought. In the UK, employer's liability insurance, for example, is written on this basis, with the result that claims need to be made against the policy that was in force at the time the employee suffered the incident or was exposed to a harmful substance. As many of the claims are in respect of latent diseases caused by an employee's exposure to asbestos, for example, these tend to be brought decades after the policy was originally written.

16.77 EIOPA has noted[52] that although policies written before Brexit will in principle remain valid following Brexit, an insurer which has lost the right to conduct business by way of freedom of establishment and freedom to provide services may no longer be authorised to perform its obligations. The position is particularly acute when it comes to paying claims, as an insurer may be faced with a choice of refusing to pay the claim and thereby breaching its contract or paying a claim and breaching local law or regulation in the territory concerned. However, the issue arises for any policy which has not expired by the date of Brexit since maintaining cover, even if no claims ever materialise, could itself be a breach of law or regulation.

16.4.2 European Insurers Operating in the UK

16.78 At the point the Solvency II passporting rules cease to be applicable to the relationship between the UK and the EU, the UK will be a 'third country' for the purposes of Solvency II and the EEA members will become third countries for the purposes of the UK regulatory regime.

16.79 As set out above, the RAO distinguishes between 'effecting' contracts of insurance and 'carrying out' contracts of insurance. However, both are regulated activities and the position is therefore that EEA insurers who are currently 'carrying out' contracts of insurance in the UK pursuant to a Solvency II passport will, post-Brexit, require authorisation as a third country branch from the PRA. Without such a third country branch, and in the absence of

---

[52] In its opinion on service continuity in insurance in light of the withdrawal of the United Kingdom from the European Union, dated 21 December 2017.

alternative arrangements, the EEA insurer would commit a criminal offence in the UK if it sought to pay claims under existing contracts of insurance as part of carrying on business in the UK.[53]

16.80 Through the implementation of the legislation which establishes the TPR,[54] the UK authorities ensured that the ability of EEA insurers to conduct business in the UK will be preserved for a limited period after exit day in any post-Brexit scenario. However, while the TPR was primarily designed to allow incoming EEA insurers an appropriate amount of time to prepare an application for authorisation as a third country branch, the position for firms who were planning to exit the UK market was less clear.

16.81 The Financial Services Contract Regime (**FSCR**) has therefore been established pursuant to the Financial Services Contracts (Transitional and Saving Provision) (EU Exit) Regulations 2019 to act as a backstop to the TPR. As a consequence, EEA insurers who do not enter the TPR or who leave it without the necessary Part 4A permission will be able to service their pre-existing contracts for a limited period after exit day through two principal mechanisms: Supervised Run-Off (SRO) and Contractual Run-Off (CRO).

16.82 Unlike the TPR, the FSCR does not allow an eligible firm to carry out regulated activities in relation to new contracts (except in limited circumstances to service pre-existing obligations). In addition, firms falling within the scope of the FSCR are expected to run-off or transfer obligations arising from contracts that exceed the time limit of the regime (which for insurance contracts is fifteen years) before the end of the regime. Given the very long-tail nature of many insurance liabilities (particularly for life insurance), fifteen years may well prove insufficient to allow for run-off to expiry.

16.83 EEA insurers operating in the UK via a branch (or that held top-up permissions before the UK's exit from the EU and were operating under an FOE or FOS passport immediately before exit day) would enter the SRO. In contrast, the CRO applies to firms without a UK branch (i.e. which are operating in the UK under a freedom of services passport immediately before exit day) that do not apply to enter the TPR and do not hold a top-up permission. Notably, and again unlike the TPR, eligible firms for the SRO and CRO enter automatically.

16.84 However, certain firms in the SRO (and CRO firms may also be permitted to) will also be permitted to carry on regulated activities which are necessary to:

- reduce the financial risk of parties to pre-existing contracts and third parties affected by the performance of pre-existing contracts;
- transfer the property, rights, or liabilities under a pre-existing contract; and
- comply with legal and regulatory requirements.

16.85 Whereas firms in the CRO are effectively subject to a limited exemption to the general prohibition solely for the purpose of allowing the wind down of the UK regulated activities, firms in the SRO are deemed to be authorised as UK firms. Accordingly, the PRA will have the same powers in relation to firms in the SRO as with UK-authorised firms. As a

---

[53] FSMA, s. 26.
[54] The EEA Passport Rights (Amendment, etc., and Transitional Provisions) (EU Exit) Regulations 2018.

consequence, and similarly to the TPR, firms in SRO with an establishment in the UK will be required to comply with the same rules that apply to other third country branches. Firms in the SRO without a branch in the UK (cross-border service providers) will be subject to a more limited set of rules, including for PRA firms a more streamlined version of SM&CR. Similarly to the TPR, the transitional relief discussed in paragraph 16.30 will apply for firms in the SRO for certain periods to allow SRO firms time to ensure compliance.

16.4.3 UK Insurers Operating in the EU

16.86 The solution for most UK insurers with European risks has been to transfer their existing policies to an insurance undertaking which is established and authorised in a Member State. However, such a transfer is a lengthy and expensive process, and it had been hoped by many that there would be a legislative solution which would provide for contract continuity. However, neither the provisional text of the withdrawal agreement nor the draft political declaration on the future relationship considers the point. While EIOPA has identified contract continuity as an issue, it has not proposed any coordinated approach and instead has called on national supervisory authorities to take steps to ensure this does not cause a problem in practice.

16.87 In the absence of any European-level initiative to deal with contract continuity, several Member States have unilaterally adopted legislation providing for a period of 'run-off' to allow insurers time either to perform their obligations in full or to transfer the remainder of their obligations to another insurer. As these are national initiatives, there is considerable inconsistency in the solution offered, both as to duration and scope. The Irish Withdrawal of the United Kingdom from the European Union (Consequential Provisions) Bill 2019 for example allows insurers three years to cease insurance activity in Ireland provided the insurer continues to comply with the Irish general good requirements whereas the French Ordinance (No. 2019-75) allows an unlimited period in which to perform pre-existing obligations.

Index

accounting and audit 3.200–3.219
  see also **International Accounting Standards Board (IASB); International Auditing and Assurance Standards Board (IAASB); International Financial Reporting Standards Foundation (IFRSF); International Standards on Auditing (ISAs)**
Alternative Investment Fund Managers (AIFMs)
  AIF, definition of 14.80, 14.110, 15.15
  AIFMD, application of 15.19–15.20
  authorisation of:
    Ireland 6.94–6.99
  concept of 15.28
  definition of 6.94, 14.34
  EEA (in the UK) 15.78–15.80
  full scope 15.21–15.23
  management companies:
    managerial functions 6.120
    senior management location rule 6.121–6.122
  non-EEA 15.27–15.31
  sub-threshold 15.24–15.26
  UK (in the EEA) 15.73–15.75
  UK (in the UK) 15.70–15.72
  see also **Alternative Investment Fund Managers Directive (AIFMD)**
Alternative Investment Fund Managers Directive (AIFMD) 15.01–15.92
  on Brexit 15.10–15.12
  contemporary position 15.13–15.36
    application of AIFMD to managers 15.19–15.20
    background and legislative intent 15.13–15.18
    delegation arrangement 15.32–15.36
    full scope AIFMs 15.21–15.23
    non-EEA AIFMs 15.27–15.31
    sub-threshold AIFMs 15.24–15.26
  cross-border distribution of collective funds, changes to 15.57–15.67
  future in the UK and Europe 15.82–15.92
    AIFMD 2/1.2 15.91–15.92
    passporting 15.86–15.90
    UK application 15.83–15.85
  impact of Brexit 15.68–15.81
    delegation arrangements 15.81
    EEA AIFMs in the UK 15.78–15.80
    UK AIFMs in the EEA 15.73–15.75
    UK AIFMs in the UK 15.70–15.72
    UK distributors in the EEA 15.76–15.77
  marketing 15.37–15.56
    definition of 15.37–15.41
    location of 15.51–15.52
    passporting 15.42–15.43
    reverse solicitation 15.47–15.50
    by third-party entities 15.53–15.56
    without the passport 15.44–15.46
  summary of 15.01–15.09
  see also **Alternative Investment Fund Managers (AIFMs)**
Article 50 (of the TEU)
  extensions to 1.34–1.36, 1.69, 1.75, 6.08, 7.04, 16.27
  no-deal preparations 1.39
  notification 1.09–1.14, 1.17
  revocation of 9.01
  two-year timetable 7.31
  Withdrawal Agreement, ratification of 1.27, 1.29, 2.04, 4.11, 5.04, 5.07, 13.16, 13.18, 16.11
authorisation
  background to 5.01–5.09
  EBA Opinions 5.96–5.131
  ESMA Opinions 5.10–5.95
  EU approach to 5.01–5.141
  France 6.34–6.52
  Germany 6.04–6.33
  Ireland 6.90–6.138
  national approaches 6.01–6.138
  Netherlands 6.53–6.89
  Withdrawal Agreement and Political Declaration 5.132–5.141
  see also **European Banking Authority (EBA) Opinions; European Securities and Markets Authority (ESMA) Opinions; France; Germany; Ireland; Netherlands**
autonomy, principle of 1.21

backstop 2.10–2.11, 2.30
  alternative arrangements to avoid a hard border 1.33
  Withdrawal Agreement, renegotiation of 2.07
bail in 12.54–12.59
  see also **stabilisation options**
Bank of England
  BCBS membership 3.90
  benchmarks regulation 14.13
  binding technical standards 1.59–1.60, 13.33, 13.84, 13.90
  BIS membership 3.36
  CCPs, responsibility for regulation of 7.106, 10.81, 13.14, 13.48, 13.52–13.54, 13.85
  clearing obligations 7.107, 13.82–13.84
  contingency planning 8.14
  CPMI membership 3.72–3.73, 3.80–3.83
  Crisis Management Groups (CMGs) 3.51, 12.77
  CSDs, responsibility for regulation of 7.106
  EMIR, UK supervisory responsibility for 13.14, 13.26, 13.45, 13.61, 13.68–13.69, 13.95

Bank of England (cont.)
  Euro clearing statistics 10.78, 10.81
  financial crisis (2007–8) 12.05
  FSM membership 3.43, 3.51
  IAIS membership 3.141
  IMF membership 3.20
  implementation period of Brexit, effect on authorisation 16.24
  Markets Committee membership 3.180
  onshoring, approach to 7.76–7.79
  policy papers 1.67–1.68, 1.74–1.75
  as regulator of EU legislation 1.61
  resolution arrangements 11.44
  'roll back' of regulations post-Brexit 11.83
  stabilisation powers of 12.52
  stability, calls for post-referendum 1.02
  statement concerning financial regulation (2018) 10.68
  supervisory regime post-Brexit 7.05, 7.66, 7.71, 7.74, 7.94, 7.111
    guidelines 7.85–7.87
    transitional relief, plans for 7.68
  Transitional Directions 13.99–13.103
Bank for International Settlements (BIS) 3.30–3.37
  activities 3.37
  history 3.31–3.32
  membership 3.35–3.36
  structure 3.33–3.34
Bank Recovery and Resolution Directive (BRRD) 12.01–12.84
  background to 12.01–12.03, 12.82–12.84
  BRRD institution, definition of 12.58
  cross-border group resolution 12.76–12.80
  depositor preference 12.81
  early intervention 12.47
  government stabilisation tools 12.75
  MREL reforms:
    eligible liabilities 12.71
    external TLAC 12.60–12.70
    internal TLAC 12.72–12.73
  'own funds', definition of 12.60
  preparatory measures:
    intragroup financial support arrangements 12.43–12.46
    recovery plans 12.31–12.38
    resolution planning 12.39–12.42
  resolution conditions 12.48–12.50
  stabilisation options:
    bail in 12.54–12.59
    moratorium tool 12.74
    overview of 12.51–12.53
  UK legislation 12.17–12.27
    BRR Brexit regulations 12.19–12.22
    BRRD II 12.26–12.27
    context 12.17–12.18
    guidelines and recommendations 12.25
    regulators' powers regulations 12.23
    regulators' transitional powers 12.24
  UK regime 12.04–12.16
    BRRD framework 12.07–12.13
    overview of 12.28–12.30
    post-Brexit 12.28–12.81
    UK framework 12.04–12.06
    UK implementation of BRRD framework 12.14–12.16
banks
  banking groups:
    banking group company, definition of 12.30, 12.50
    supervision of 11.90–11.102
  branches:
    current framework 11.33–11.38
    impact of Brexit 11.37–11.38
    prudential requirements 11.33–11.49
    retail activities 11.47
    systemic wholesale branches 11.48–11.49
    UK authorisation 11.39–11.46
  definition of 12.30
  PRA approach:
    accounts 8.41–8.42
    application process 8.81–8.90
    booking models 8.80
    to branches 8.08–8.11
    branches and subsidiaries, differences between 8.22–8.27
    considerations for banks 8.71–8.72
    customers 8.39–8.40
    FCA rules 8.92
    FSCR 8.99
    FSCS- Protected Deposit Base 8.34–8.37
    non-systemic branches 8.77–8.79
    overseas branch 8.91–8.99
    PRA rules 8.92
    to (re)insurer branches 8.12
    retail deposit base 8.33
    significant retail activities 8.28–8.42
    significant retail approach 8.38
    subsidiary status 8.91–8.99
    supervisory experiences 8.77–8.79
    systemic branches, qualification for 8.74–8.76
    systemic wholesale branches 8.73–8.80
    TPR implications 8.95–8.98
    UK branches 8.91–8.93
    UK subsidiaries 8.94
    wholesale banks 8.43–8.72
  see also Basel Committee on Banking Supervision (BCBS); Capital Requirements Regulation (CRR); Core Principles for Effective Banking Supervision; Capital Requirements Directive (CRD IV); Prudential Regulation Authority (PRA)
Basel Committee on Banking Supervision (BCBS) 3.85–3.104
  activities 3.92–3.104
  capital measurement and standards 3.99–3.104
  Core Principles 3.94–3.98
  history of 3.86–3.87
  membership 3.89–3.91
  structure 3.88

benchmarks regulation 14.01–14.125
  authorisation and registration:
    distinction between 14.41–14.47
    impact of Brexit 14.48–14.50
    requirement for 14.37–14.40
  background to 14.01–14.04, 14.124–14.125
  benchmark administrators:
    accountability framework 14.51
    authorisation and registration of 14.37–14.50
    based in UK, impact of Brexit 14.89–14.112
    based outside EU and UK 14.118–14.121
    Brexit-specific provisions 14.117
    code of conduct 14.51
    complaints-handling 14.51
    conflict-of-interest 14.51
    control framework 14.51
    definition of 14.24, 14.34
    in the EU, impact of Brexit on 14.113–14.117
    EU equivalence regime 4.95–4.98
    governance 14.51
    infringements, reporting of 14.51
    input data 14.51
    methodology 14.51
    outsourcing 14.51
    oversight function 14.51
    record-keeping 14.51
    requirements applicable to 14.51–14.51
    transitional provisions 14.77–14.82, 14.110–14.112, 14.116
    UK third country regime 14.113–14.115
  benchmark contributors:
    input data, contributors of 14.24
    requirements applicable to 14.74–14.76
    supervised contributors 14.83–14.84
  benchmark users based in EU, impact of Brexit on 14.122
  benchmark users based in UK, impact of Brexit on 14.123
  Brexit and cross-border issues 14.85–14.123
    assessment of 14.85–14.88
  categories of benchmark 14.52–14.73
    adaptation for UK regime 14.67–14.73
    commodity benchmarks 14.64–14.66
    critical benchmarks 14.54–14.57, 14.68–14.70
    interest rate benchmarks 14.64–14.66
    non-significant benchmarks 14.61–14.63
    regulated-data benchmarks 14.64–14.66
    under EU regime 14.54–14.66
    significant benchmarks 14.58–14.60, 14.71–14.73
  definition of benchmark 14.27–14.29, 14.51
  endorsement 14.107–14.109
  equivalence 14.92–14.94
  history in the UK 14.05–14.18
    benchmarks regulation 14.16–14.18
    IOSCO principles and international initiatives 14.05–14.08
    UK initiative 14.09–14.15
  purpose of 14.23–14.26
  recognition 14.95–14.106
    process for obtaining 14.101–14.106
    requirements for 14.97–14.100
  restrictions on use of benchmarks 14.33–14.36
  scope of 14.30–14.32
  transitional provisions 14.77–14.84
    benchmark administrators 14.77–14.82, 14.110–14.112, 14.116
    competent authority/FCA options 14.80
    FCA option to register 14.80
    index provider (30 June 2016) 14.80
    index provider (1 January 2018) 14.80
  in the UK 14.19–14.84
    benchmark administrators, impact of Brexit 14.89–14.112
    post-Brexit approach 14.19–14.22
binding technical standards (BTS) 1.55, 1.59–1.60, 1.64, 1.66, 7.93, 12.13, 12.23
borrowing rate, definition of 14.34
branches *see* banks; Prudential Regulation Authority (PRA)
Brexit contingency planning 1.51, 1.69, 3.75, 5.128, 6.92–6.93
building societies 4.37, 11.33, 11.83, 12.01
  definition of 12.30
business continuity planning (BCP) 9.29

C6 energy derivatives 13.75–13.77
capital buffer requirements 11.55
  see also Capital Requirements Directive (CRD IV)/Capital Requirements Regulation (CRR)
capital markets *see* International Capital Market Association (ICMA)
capital measurement
  capital standards and 3.99–3.104
  see also Basel Committee on Banking Supervision (BCBS)
Capital Requirements Regulation (CRR) 3.104, 4.37, 7.10, 7.114, 12.60, 13.08
  see also Capital Requirements Directive (CRD IV)/Capital Requirements Regulation (CRR)
card institutions
  EBA 2017 Opinion 5.107–5.112
central banks 3.02–3.199
  Central Bank of Ireland *see* Ireland
  Dutch Central Bank *see* Netherlands
  statistics *see* Irving Fisher Committee on Central Bank Statistics (IFC)
  see also international standards
central clearing counterparties (CCPs)
  central counterparty, definition of 14.34
  qualifying CCPs 13.43
  recognition of 4.57–4.60
  statutory instruments (SIs) 13.42–13.56
    amendments to onshored EMIR 13.44–13.51
    background to 13.42–13.43
    equivalence assessments and recognition 13.54
    recognition of UK CCPs under EMIR 13.56

central clearing counterparties (CCPs) (cont.)
    regulatory changes 13.55
    transitional relief 13.52–13.53
    see also equivalence; European Markets Infrastructure Regulation (EMIR)
central security depository (CSDs)
    recognition of 4.57–4.60
    UK-authorised 1.48, 5.134–5.135, 6.02
    see also equivalence
Chequers Plan 1.20–1.21
clearing houses 10.11–10.13
    access to 10.52–10.53
    authorisation of, in the EU 10.43–10.45
    EU-based, UK recognition of 10.81
    exchanges and 10.10–10.16
    exposure to default 10.13
    MiFID, impact of 10.45
    payment and settlement systems 10.43–10.44
    role of 10.11–10.12
    see also Markets in Financial Instrument Directive II (MiFID II); settlement systems
clearing obligations see central clearing counterparties (CCPs); European Markets Infrastructure Regulation (EMIR)
Code of Good Practices on Transparency in Monetary and Financial Policies 3.26–3.29
    see also International Monetary Fund (IMF)
collaboration see Capital Requirements Directive (CRD IV)/ Capital Requirements Regulation (CRR)
collective funds
    cross-border distribution of 15.57–15.67
Commission de Surveillance du Secteur Financier (CSSF) 4.20
Committee on Payments and Market Infrastructures (CPMI) 3.68–3.84
    activities 3.75–3.84
    history of 3.69–3.70
    membership 3.73–3.74
    structure 3.71–3.72
    see also Principles for Financial Markets Infrastructures (PFMI)
Committees of European Banking Supervisors (CEBS) 7.86
commodity benchmarks see benchmarks regulation
Compendium of Standards see Financial Stability Board (FSB)
competent authorities
    benchmark administrators 14.80
    definition of 5.11, 5.97
    France 6.35
    Germany 6.22–6.23
    UK Listing Authority 10.33
Competition/Antitrust Law Guidelines for Members of the GFXC (Competition Guidelines) 3.135
    see also Global Foreign Exchange Committee (GFXC)
compliance
    authorisation requirements 6.125–6.126

consolidation 11.90–11.102
    see also Capital Requirements Directive (CRD IV); Capital Requirements Regulation (CRR)
contingency planning see Brexit contingency planning
contracts
    continuity of:
    European insurers operating in UK 16.78–16.85
    existing contracts, effect of Brexit on 16.76–16.77
    France 6.40–6.41
    Solvency II Directive 16.76–16.87
    UK insurers operating in EU 16.86–16.87
Controlled Functions (CFs) 6.123–6.124
Core Principles for Effective Banking Supervision (Core Principles) 3.94–3.98
    see also Basel Committee on Banking Supervision (BCBS)
Core Principles for Effective Deposit Insurance Systems 3.171–3.175
    see also International Association of Deposit Insurers (IADI)
corporate governance
    principles of 3.12–3.14
    see also Organisation for Economic Co-operation and Development (OECD)
Court of Justice of the European Union (CJEU) 2.09, 2.17, 2.22, 2.32, 4.34, 7.22, 7.42, 7.43, 16.38
credit agreements
    definition of 14.27, 14.29, 14.31, 14.34, 14.80, 14.110
    creditors 14.34
    non-credit institutions 14.34
credit institution, definition of 11.25, 14.34
credit intermediaries
    EBA 2017 Opinion 5.119
Credit Requirements Directive (CRD IV)/Capital Requirements Regulation (CRR) 11.01–11.115
    background to 11.01–11.03
    banking groups and consolidation, supervision of 11.90–11.102
    capital buffer requirements 11.55
    collaboration and information sharing 11.50–11.54
    CRD IV/CRR distinction, passporting and equivalence tests 11.04–11.32
        barriers to a single market 11.06–11.09
        EU financial services 11.04–11.05
        financial services passport 11.10–11.16
        passporting, impact of Brexit on 11.17–11.21
        third country regimes 11.22–11.32
    CRD remuneration provisions 11.76–11.89
        background to 11.76–11.78
        bonus cap, UK position on 11.82–11.89
        UK regulatory approach to implementation of 11.79–11.81
    CRR firms, definition of 14.36
    EU intermediate holding company regime 11.56–11.69
        Brexit, impact of 11.68–11.69
        reforms under CRD V package 11.56–11.60
        third country groups, impact on 11.66–11.67

threshold and application 11.61–11.65
originator, definition of 11.105
'own funds', definition of (CRD IV) 5.126
prudential requirements 11.33–11.49
   Brexit, impact of 11.37–11.38
   current framework 11.33–11.38
   retail activities 11.47
   systemic wholesale branches 11.48–11.49
   UK authorisation 11.39–11.46
risk weights of EU and UK exposures and liquidity: Brexit, impact of 11.70–11.75
securitisation 11.103–11.115
   background to 11.103–11.107
   regulation and Brexit 11.108–11.115
sponsor, definition of 11.105, 11.110

critical benchmarks *see* **benchmarks regulation**
critical function, definition of 11.36, 12.40
cross-border issues
benchmarks regulation 14.03–14.04, 14.85–14.123
bonus cap, removal of 11.88
booking models 8.57
CCP services, provision of 13.108
collective investment funds, distribution of 7.114
contracts, continuity of 6.40, 16.76
crisis management 3.75
cross-border services 6.101, 9.04, 9.06, 10.69
   banking 11.99, 12.40, 12.83
   from EEA into UK 4.04, 9.10, 9.11
economic integration 4.08
investment services 4.42, 5.51, 6.12, 6.62
licences 8.05
   from UK into EEA 4.01
   Netherlands 4.20
   passports 8.02, 8.90
   regulatory equivalence 10.56–10.58
   remote provision of 8.01
   service providers 16.85
   supervision of 11.50
   TPR firms 16.32
   UK legal position 8.05
   white-label business 5.87
data transfer 13.93
debt securities markets 3.225, 3.233
equivalence decisions 5.132
EU entities use of UK-based shared services or systems 5.124
Germany 6.12, 6.25
   licensing exemptions 6.25, 6.27–6.28
group structures, changes to 5.124
support agreements 12.43
information exchange/sharing 3.75, 3.122, 11.50
insurance and reinsurance 4.90, 16.06, 16.10, 16.47, 16.49, 16.57
   EEA (re)insurers operating in UK 8.104, 16.18, 16.34
management and marketing activities 5.85, 6.111
mediation 7.110
MiFID II 13.107
multilateral trading facilities 10.48–10.49
Netherlands 6.62
PRA approach 8.127–8.130
prudential rules 4.06
regulated activities 9.10
regulated markets 10.48–10.49
regulatory cooperation 7.119, 12.22, 12.38–12.41, 12.74, 12.82
resolution 3.51
   group resolution provisions 12.22, 12.76–12.80
securitisations 11.113
senior managerial responsibility for business into UK 9.03, 9.12, 9.21–9.25
   accountability 9.32
   appointed representative 9.24
   business conducted into the UK 9.22–9.23
   certification and conduct regimes 9.28
   dual hatting 9.25
subject to regulatory equivalence 10.56–10.58
third country firms, access for 10.55–10.58
United Kingdom:
   access to market infrastructures 5.124
   business 3.257
   regulated trading activities 6.18
see also **backstop**; **benchmarks regulation**
cross-sectoral opinion *see* **European Securities and Markets Authority (ESMA) Opinions**
customer communication 5.129, 5.131
Customs Union 2.11, 2.12, 5.08, 16.17

declaration of no objection (DNO)
Netherlands 6.78–6.86
   investment firm 6.78–6.81
   regulated market 6.82–6.86
delegated legislation
EMIR and UK law 13.20–13.23
onshoring of 13.31–13.36
delegation arrangements
AIFMD 15.81
ESMA Investment Management Opinion 5.89–5.95
deposit guarantee schemes 5.127
depositor preference 12.81
derivatives, definition of 13.75
see also **International Swaps and Derivatives Association (ISDA)**
directors
Ireland 6.117–6.119
   directors to direct the business 6.117–6.119
   independent directors 6.117–6.119
   Irish resident directors 6.117–6.119
disaster recovery (DR) 9.29
dispute resolution 2.13–2.19
dual hatting
French group entities 6.51–6.52
UK senior managerial responsibility 9.25
due diligence 5.56, 5.80, 11.107
ESMA Investment Firms Opinion 5.58–5.59
see also **outsourcing**
Dutch Brexit legislation *see* **Netherlands**

electronic money
  institutions 5.116–5.118
eligible liabilities, definition of 12.60, 12.71
  see also MREL
equivalence 4.01–4.109
  assessments and CCP SIs 13.54
  authorisation and 5.103–5.119
  background to 4.01–4.04
  banking framework 4.37–4.40
  benchmark regulation 14.92–14.94
    administrators 4.95–4.98
  central counterparties (CCPs):
    recognition of 4.57–4.60
  central security depository (CSDs):
    recognition of 4.57–4.60
  concept of 4.05–4.10, 4.36, 4.90, 16.02, 16.10, 16.54
  CRD IV/CRR regime 11.04–11.32
  current status and timing 4.11–4.13
  decisions 4.24–4.36
  EMIR and derivatives 4.61–4.65
  at the EU level 4.21–4.23
  insurance and reinsurance framework 4.89–4.94
  investment funds 4.66–4.87
  investment services 4.41–4.48
  issuers 4.99–4.109
  market infrastructure 4.49–4.56
  MiFID 10.74–10.77
  onshoring of EU law 4.14–4.17
  PRA approach 8.58–8.61
  principle of 5.114
  Solvency II Directive, effect under 16.54–16.59
    direct insurers, impact on 16.58
    reinsurers, impact on 16.59
  third countries and member states 4.18–4.20
euro clearing
  ECB call for move to eurozone 10.64
  MiFID 10.78–10.80
  UK-based clearing houses 10.65
  see also European Markets Infrastructure Regulation (EMIR)
European Banking Authority (EBA) Opinions 5.96–5.131
  EBA 2017 Opinion 5.98–5.127
    authorisation 5.103–5.119
    card institutions 5.107–5.112
    credit intermediaries 5.119
    deposit guarantee schemes 5.127
    Directive 2014/17 5.119
    electronic money institutions 5.116–5.118
    equivalence 5.103–5.119
    general 5.103–5.106
    internal governance 5.122–5.123
    internal model approvals 5.120–5.121
    investment firms 5.113–5.115
    non-credit institutions 5.119
    payment institutions 5.116–5.118
    purpose 5.98–5.102
    resolutions 5.124–5.126
    risk management 5.122–5.123
    scope 5.98–5.102
  EBA 2018 Opinion 5.128–5.131
    customer communication 5.131
    preparedness 5.130–5.131
    purpose 5.128–5.129
    risk assessment 5.130–5.131
    scope 5.128–5.129
  legal basis 5.96–5.97
European Free Trade Association (EFTA) 1.04, 7.110
European Insurance and Occupational Pensions Authority (EIOPA) 1.43, 1.52, 4.28, 7.15–7.16, 8.111, 16.04, 16.07–16.09, 16.32, 16.68, 16.73, 16.77, 16.86
Committee of European Insurance and Occupational Pensions Supervisors (CEIOPS) 7.86
European Market Infrastructure (EMI)
  regulation and derivatives 4.61–4.65
  see also **equivalence**; **European Markets Infrastructure Regulation (EMIR)**
European Markets Infrastructure Regulation (EMIR) 13.01–13.109
  background to 13.01–13.14
  CCP SI 13.42–13.56
    amendments to onshored EMIR 13.44–13.51
    background 13.42–13.43
    equivalence assessments and recognition pre-exit day 13.54
    regulatory changes 13.55
    transitional relief 13.52–13.53
    UK CCPs under EMIR, recognition of 13.56
  clearing members, definition of 5.138
  EMIR REFIT 13.13
  EMIR SI 13.66–13.93
    C6 energy derivatives 13.75–13.77
    clearing obligation 13.82–13.84
    definition of OTC derivative 13.72–13.74
    EU27 exchange-traded derivatives, exclusion of 13.72–13.74
    exemptions for intragroup transactions 13.78–13.81
    reporting obligation 13.85–13.88
    risk mitigation obligations 13.89–13.91
    scope and exemptions 13.67–13.71
    trade repository regulation 13.92–13.93
  exit and onshoring, implications of 13.37–13.41
    exit 13.39
    onshoring 13.40–13.41
  market participants, implications for 13.105–13.109
  onshoring:
    background to 13.15–13.17
    delegated legislation 13.20–13.23, 13.31–13.36
    effective operation of EMIR 13.24–13.27
    EU Withdrawal Act 13.15–13.30
    EUWA 13.18–13.19
    policy choices 13.28–13.30
  role and purpose of 13.03–13.08
  sources 13.11–13.12
  standstill 13.94–13.104
    effect 13.104
    exceptions 13.103
    scope 13.99–13.102

INDEX   419

territoriality 13.09–13.10
trade repository SI 13.57–13.65
　amendments to onshored EMIR 13.59–13.63
　background 13.57–13.58
　regulatory changes 13.65
　transitional relief 13.64
trading venues, definition of 5.138
UK supervisory responsibility for 13.14
European Securities and Markets Authority (ESMA) Opinions 5.10–5.95
　cross-sectoral opinion 5.12–5.35
　　EU entities, sound governance of 5.30–5.31
　　existing authorisations, no automatic recognition of 5.20
　　general principles 5.20–5.35
　　letter-box entities 5.24–5.27
　　monitoring by ESMA 5.34–5.35
　　purpose 5.12–5.19
　　relocations, reasons for 5.22–5.23
　　rigorous and efficient authorisation 5.21
　　scope 5.12–5.19
　　substance requirements 5.29
　　third countries, outsourcing and delegation to 5.28
　　Union law, enforcement and supervision of 5.32–5.33
　influence of ESMA 6.110–6.113
　Investment Firms Opinion 5.37–5.65
　　authorisation 5.41–5.46
　　critical functions/services, outsourcing of 5.60–5.62
　　due diligence 5.58–5.59
　　effective supervision 5.65
　　governance and internal controls 5.47–5.50
　　non-EU branches 5.63–5.64
　　operations, programme of 5.51
　　outsourcing 5.53–5.62
　　outsourcing arrangements, assessment of 5.53–5.57
　　proportionality 5.52
　　purpose 5.37–5.40
　　resources, financial and non-financial 5.51
　　scope 5.37–5.40
　　substance requirements 5.47–5.64
　Investment Management Opinion 5.77–5.95
　　delegation 5.89–5.95
　　governance and internal control 5.83–5.88
　　governance structures 5.85–5.86
　　internal control mechanisms 5.85–5.86
　　purpose 5.77–5.82
　　scope 5.77–5.82
　　sound governance 5.83–5.84
　　white-label business 5.87–5.88
　legal basis 5.10–5.11
　Secondary Markets Opinion 5.66–5.76
　　activities 5.71–5.76
　　purpose 5.66–5.70
　　scope 5.66–5.70
　Sector-Specific Opinions 5.36

Committee of European Securities Regulators (CESR) 7.83, 7.86
European Supervisory Authorities (ESAs) 1.06, 1.23, 1.43, 1.53, 1.63, 3.255, 4.28, 4.35, 7.06, 7.20, 7.82–7.87, 7.91, 7.106, 7.109, 7.110, 7.114, 7.120
　growing power of 7.15–7.18
European Union (Withdrawal) Act 2018
　background to 13.15–13.19
　EMIR:
　　delegated legislation in UK law 13.20–13.23
　　effective operation of 13.24–13.27
　　onshoring/onshored legislation 13.15–13.30
　　policy choices 13.28–13.30
　　UK supervisory regime post-Brexit 7.38–7.58
　　remedying deficiencies in retained law 7.44–7.48
　　retained EU case law 7.43
　　retained EU law 7.41–7.42
　　statutory instruments 7.54–7.58
　　UK parliamentary powers to make secondary legislation 7.49–7.53
Europeanization, definition of 7.11
exchange, definition of 10.19
exchange-traded derivatives 13.72–13.74
'exit day', definition of 7.64, 12.44, 16.27
exit instruments 13.95
external credit assessment institution (ECAI) 11.72–11.73, 11.75

fees *see* licensing
Financial Action Task Force (FATF) 3.53–3.67
　activities 3.59–3.67
　history 3.54–3.55
　membership 3.57–3.58
　structure 3.56
Financial Conduct Authority (FCA)
　benchmark administrators 14.80
　EU Withdrawal Impact Assessment 2.34–2.38
　FCA Handbook, impact of Brexit on 7.90–7.92
　onshoring, approach to 7.80
　PRA approach 8.55–8.57
　Rulebook 8.92
　　client money 8.92
　　compensation 8.92
　　custody 8.92
　　recovery plans 12.31
　　resolution planning 12.39
　Threshold Conditions for Authorisation 8.49–8.50
financial contracts, definition of 14.29, 14.32
financial counterparty, definition of 13.67–13.69
financial crisis 2007–8 3.102, 3.172, 3.253
　AIFMD 15.17
　benchmarks regulation 14.01
　BRRD 12.05
　'light touch' regulation 7.118
　OTC derivatives market 10.30, 13.05
　shifts towards Europe post- 7.13–7.14, 7.32
　　ESAs, influence of 7.15
financial instruments, definition of 10.76, 14.27, 14.29, 14.31–14.32, 14.80, 14.110

financial market infrastructures (FMIs) 3.79–3.83, 3.111, 7.85
Financial Services Action Plan (FSAP) 7.11
Financial Services Authority (FSA) 3.148, 4.04, 7.23, 7.27, 12.15
Financial Services Compensation Scheme (FSCS) 3.167, 3.175, 7.96, 8.28, 8.30, 8.40, 8.44, 8.92–8.93, 8.114, 8.119, 8.124, 11.47
   Protected Deposit Base, size of 8.34–8.37
   UK branch activity, scale of 8.121–8.123
Financial Services Contract Regime (FSCR) 6.01–6.02, 7.105, 8.18–8.19, 8.99, 8.115, 16.30, 16.81–16.82
Financial Stability Board (FSB) 3.38–3.52
   activities 3.44–3.52
      Compendium of Standards 3.47–3.52
      key attributes 3.50–3.52
   history 3.39–3.40
   membership 3.42–3.43
   structure 3.41
financial support arrangements 12.43–12.46
   see also Bank Recovery and Resolution Directive (BRRD)
Fiscal Transparency Code 3.23–3.25
   see also International Monetary Fund (IMF)
France 6.34–6.52
   Autorité de contrôle prudentiel et de resolution (ACPR) 6.35–6.36, 6.40, 6.46–6.51
   Autorité des Marchés Financiers (AMF) 6.35, 6.36–6.37
   competent authorities 6.35
   context 6.34
   contracts, continuity of 6.40–6.41
   'dual hatting' within group entities 6.51–6.52
   guidelines in relation to use of third-party employees or technical means 6.46
   monopoly 6.42–6.43
      territorial application of 6.43
   No-Deal Brexit, approach to 6.34, 6.36–6.41, 6.45
   outsourcing arrangements 6.48–6.50
   required substance 6.47
   reverse solicitation exemption 6.44
   standard procedure for non-EEA entities post-exit day 6.45
freedom of services 11.15
   cross-border services 8.128
   definition of 16.07
   insurance 16.07
   Solvency II Directive 16.16, 16.32, 16.38, 16.83
Futures Industry Association (FIA) 10.81
FX Global Code 3.130–3.134
   see also Global Foreign Exchange Committee (GFXC)

Germany 6.04–6.33
   authorisation:
      competent authorities 6.22–6.23
      cross-border services in the individual case, exemption of 6.27–6.28
      licence applications, administrative guidance for 6.29–6.32
      licensing requirements, territorial scope of 6.24
      national approach to 6.21–6.33
      reverse solicitation exemption 6.25–6.26
      substance requirements 6.33
   background 6.04–6.05
   Brexit legislation 6.06–6.20
      Brexit-Steuerbegleitgesetz (*Brexit-StBG*/Tax Act) 6.08–6.11, 6.13, 6.15–6.18, 6.21, 6.27–6.28
      Brexit-Übergangsgesetz (*BrexitÜG*/Transition Act) 6.07
      general transitional periods 6.12–6.14
      general transitional regime, scope of 6.09–6.11
      limitations of 6.15–6.17
      overview of 6.06–6.08
      proprietary business, specific relief measure for 6.18–6.20
   freedom to provide requested services (*passive Dienstleistungsfreiheit*), definition of 6.25
   Bundesanstalt für Finanzdienstleistungsaufsicht (BaFin) 6.04, 6.12–6.16, 6.19, 6.22–6.33, 16.52, 16.57
Global Foreign Exchange Committee (GFXC) 3.125–3.135
   activities 3.129–3.135
      Competition Guidelines 3.135
      FX Global Code 3.130–3.134
   background to 3.125
   history 3.126
   membership 3.127–3.128
   structure 3.127–3.128
government stabilisation tools 12.75
   see also Bank Recovery and Resolution Directive (BRRD)
governments 3.02–3.199
   see also international standards
groups
   definition of 12.31
   group recovery plans, definition of 12.31
   group resolution plans, definition of 12.39
   group subsidiaries, definition of 12.43
   intragroup transactions, definition of 13.78–13.79
   supervision regimes
      disapplication of 16.68–16.69
      group internal models 16.73–16.75
      group solvency, choice of method for 16.70–16.72
      multiple and overlapping 16.60–16.75
      worldwide group supervision 16.65–16.67
   see also Solvency II Directive (Solvency II)

hard Brexit scenario
   authorisation, EU approach to 6.01–6.03, 6.08
   benchmarks regulation 14.03, 14.85, 14.90
   clearing services 4.02
   CRD IV/CRR 11.01–11.02
   domestic transitional measures 6.02–6.03

Germany 6.08, 6.12, 6.30
Ireland 6.93
Netherlands 6.56
EMIR and Euro clearing 13.56
EU equivalence regime 4.02–4.03, 4.08
hard border in Ireland *see* **backstop**
MiFID II/MiFIR 10.83
passporting rights 4.03
PRA approach 8.20
temporary permissions regime 6.01
UK firms access to EU markets 4.08
see also **soft Brexit scenario; temporary permissions regime (TPR)**
home Member State, definition of 4.100, 10.40
home state supervisor (HSS) 8.45, 8.47, 8.58, 8.62–8.63, 8.68, 8.77–8.79, 8.83, 8.87, 8.118
host Member State, definition of 10.41

implementing technical standards (ITS) 10.03, 13.11, 13.22, 13.33, 16.04, 16.13
index
definition of 14.28, 14.30
index provider (UK)
definition of 14.82
information sharing *see* **Capital Requirements Directive (CRD IV)/ Capital Requirements Regulation (CRR)**
initiative test *see* **reverse solicitation**
Institute of Asset Management (IAM) 3.240–3.250
activities 3.243–3.250
IAM Handbook 3.247–3.248
strategic asset management plan 3.244–3.246
Subject Specific Guidelines (SSGs) 3.249–3.250
membership 3.241–3.242
structure 3.241–3.242
institution for occupational retirement provision, definition of 14.34
insurance 4.89–4.94
branch failure, impact on insurance market 8.124–8.126
definition of 16.01
direct insurers:
equivalence, impact on 16.58
licensing issues 16.44–16.46
European insurers operating in the UK, position of 16.16–16.41
licensing issues 16.16–16.41
Insurance Core Principles (ICPs) 3.145–3.148
insurance undertakings, definition of 14.34
UK insurers operating in Europe, position of 16.42–16.75
group supervision regimes 16.60–16.75
licensing issues 16.42–16.53
Solvency II Directive, effect of equivalence under 16.54–16.59
see also **equivalence; International Association of Insurance Supervisors (IAIS); licensing; reinsurance; Solvency II Directive (Solvency II)**
interest rate benchmarks *see* **benchmarks regulation**

intermediate holding companies (IHC) 11.56–11.69
impact of Brexit 11.68–11.69
impact on third country groups 11.66–11.67
reforms under CRD V package 11.56–11.60
threshold and application 11.61–11.65
see also **Capital Requirements Directive (CRD IV)/ Capital Requirements Regulation (CRR)**
International Accounting Standards Board (IASB) 3.200–3.211
activities 3.206–3.211
IFRS Standards 3.206–3.211
membership 3.202–3.205
structure 3.202–3.205
see also **accounting and audit**
International Association of Deposit Insurers (IADI) 3.164–3.175
activities 3.169–3.175
context 3.164–3.165
Core Principles 3.171–3.175
membership 3.166–3.168
structure 3.166–3.168
International Association of Insurance Supervisors (IAIS) 3.136–3.148
activities 3.143–3.148
context 3.136
history of 3.137–3.138
Insurance Core Principles (ICPs) 3.145–3.148
membership 3.141–3.142
structure 3.139–3.140
International Auditing and Assurance Standards Board (IAASB) 3.212–3.219
activities 3.218–3.219
membership 3.214–3.217
structure 3.214–3.217
see also **accounting and audit**
International Capital Market Association (ICMA) 3.225–3.234
activities 3.230–3.234
Primary Market Handbook 3.232
secondary market, rules and recommendations for 3.233–3.234
membership 3.227–3.229
structure 3.227–3.229
International Financial Consumer Protection Organisation (FinCoNet) 3.191–3.199
activities 3.199
history 3.192–3.194
membership 3.197–3.198
structure 3.195–3.196
International Financial Reporting Standards Foundation (IFRSF)
activities 3.206–3.211
IFRS Standards 3.206–3.211
membership 3.202–3.205
structure 3.202–3.205
see also **accounting and audit**
International Labour Organization (ILO) 3.09
International Monetary Fund (IMF) 3.15–3.29
activities 3.21–3.29

International Monetary Fund (IMF) (cont.)
  Code of Good Practices on Transparency in
      Monetary and Financial Policies 3.26–3.29
  Fiscal Transparency Code 3.23–3.25
  history of 3.16–3.17
  membership 3.19–3.20
  structure 3.18
International Organisation of Pension Supervisors
      (IOPS) 3.149–3.163
  activities 3.156–3.163
  background to 3.149
  guidelines and good practices 3.160–3.163
  history of 3.150–3.151
  membership 3.154–3.155
  Principles of Private Pension Supervision 3.157–3.159
  structure 3.152–3.153
International Organisation for Standardization
      (ISO) 3.244–3.249
International Securities Lending Association
      (ISLA) 3.235–3.239
  activities 3.238–3.239
  membership 3.236–3.237
  structure 3.236–3.237
international standards 3.01–3.258
  assessment of 3.01, 3.251–3.258
  central banks 3.02–3.199
  governments 3.02–3.199
  members of international bodies 3.02–3.199
  regulators 3.02–3.199
  UK firms participating in industry
      bodies 3.220–3.250
  see also accounting and audit; Bank for International
      Settlements (BIS); Basel Committee on
      Banking Supervision (BCBS); Committee
      on Payments and Market Infrastructures
      (CPMI); Financial Action Task Force (FATF);
      Financial Stability Board (FSB); Global Foreign
      Exchange Committee (GFXC); Institute of
      Asset Management (IAM); International
      Accounting Standards Board (IASB);
      International Association of Deposit Insurers
      (IADI); International Association of Insurance
      Supervisors (IAIS); International Auditing
      and Assurance Standards Board (IAASB);
      International Capital Market Association
      (ICMA); International Financial Consumer
      Protection Organisation (FinCoNet);
      International Financial Reporting Standards
      Foundation (IFRSF); International Monetary
      Fund (IMF); International Organisation of
      Pension Supervisors (IOPS); International
      Organization of Securities Commissions
      (IOSCO); International Securities Lending
      Association (ISLA); International Swaps
      and Derivatives Association (ISDA); Irving
      Fisher Committee on Central Bank Statistics
      (IFC); Markets Committee; Organisation for
      Economic Co-operation and Development
      (OECD)

International Standards on Auditing (ISAs) 3.219
  see also accounting and audit
International Standards on Combating Money
      Laundering and the Financing of Terrorism
      & Proliferation (Recommendations) 3.48,
      3.59–3.62
International Swaps and Derivatives Association
      (ISDA) 3.221–3.224
  activities 3.224
  membership 3.222–3.223
  structure 3.222–3.223
International Organization of Securities
      Commissions (IOSCO) 3.105–3.124
  activities 3.115–3.124
  background to 3.105
  history 3.106–3.107
  international initiatives 14.05–14.08
  membership 3.111–3.114
  objectives and principles 3.118–3.124, 14.05–14.08
  structure 3.108–3.110
investment exchanges 10.34–10.37
  overseas 10.34–10.37
investment firms
  authorisation of exchanges 10.38
  CAD investment firm, definition of 11.93
  declaration of no objection (DNO) 6.78–6.81
  definition of 5.37, 5.39, 14.34
  Dutch exemption for 6.59–6.64
  EBA 2017 Opinion 5.113–5.115
  non-EU firms' access to EU trading
      infrastructure 10.54–10.62
  Opinion see European Securities and Markets
      Authority (ESMA) Opinions
  passporting for 10.46–10.47
  systemically important investment firms, definition
      of 12.30
  see also Markets in Financial Instrument
      Directive II (MiFID II)
investment funds
  EU equivalence regime 4.66–4.87
investment management
  Opinion see European Securities and Markets
      Authority (ESMA) Opinions
investment services
  definition of 5.37
  Dutch licence application procedure 6.73–6.74
  EU equivalence regime 4.41–4.48
  Ireland 6.90–6.138
    AIFMs:
      authorisation of 6.94–6.99
      Directive (AIFMD) 6.107
      Regulations 6.108–6.109
      third country firms as 6.107
      UCITS management companies and 6.120–6.122
    authorisation process 6.128–6.138
      application 6.132–6.134
      Key facts document (KFD) 6.129–6.130
      timing 6.135–6.138
    authorisation requirements 6.110–6.127

INDEX

compliance 6.125–6.126
ESMA, influence of 6.110–6.113
financial control 6.125–6.126
fitness and probity regime 6.123–6.124
Head Office and registered office in Ireland 6.114–6.116
risk management 6.125–6.126
staffing 6.127
background to authorisation 6.90–6.91
Brexit Contingency Planning 6.92–6.93
Central Bank:
  initial contact with 6.128
  preliminary meeting with 6.131
MiFID:
  investment activities 6.101–6.106
  Investment Firms 6.94–6.99
  service provision 6.101–6.106
no deal Brexit, approach to 6.90
substance requirements 6.117–6.119
  directors to direct business 6.117–6.119
  independent directors 6.117–6.119
  Irish resident directors 6.117–6.119
third country firms under Irish law 6.100–6.109
  as AIFMs under AIFM Directive 6.107
  marketing AIFs under AIFM Regulations 6.108–6.109
  MiFID 6.101–6.106
UCITS management companies 6.120–6.122
  managerial functions 6.120
  senior management location rule 6.121–6.122
see also backstop; cross-border issues
Irving Fisher Committee on Central Bank Statistics (IFC) 3.183–3.190
  activities 3.190
  history 3.184–3.185
  membership 3.187–3.189
  structure 3.186
issuers
  EU equivalence regime 4.99–4.109

Key Attributes of Effective Resolution Regimes for Financial Institutions 3.48, 3.50, 3.51, 12.06, 12.20, 12.77
Key facts document (KFD) 6.129–6.130

legal certainty, principle of 11.80
letter-box entities 5.24–5.27, 5.55, 5.69, 5.81, 5.103, 6.47
  definition of 5.15
licensing
  European insurers operating in the UK, issues for 16.16–16.41
  case law 16.40–16.41
  EEA-authorised (re)insurers conducting UK business offshore 16.34–16.41
  EEA-authorised (re)insurers passporting into UK 16.19–16.33
  guidance and regulation 16.37–16.39
  TPR 16.24–16.32

UK regulatory landscape for (re)insurers 16.19–16.21
Germany:
  applications, administrative guidance for 6.29–6.32
  requirements, territorial scope of 6.24
Netherlands:
  application procedure 6.72–6.77
  exemption to licence obligation 6.71
  fees 6.77
  initiative test 6.70
  investment services 6.73–6.74
  obligation and exemptions 6.69–6.71
  regulated market 6.72
  reverse solicitation 6.70
  substance 6.75–6.76
UK insurers operating in Europe, issues for 16.42–16.53
  direct insurers 16.44–16.46
  pure reinsurers 16.47–16.53
'light-touch' regulation 7.29, 7.118
listing of securities
  on an exchange 10.31–10.37
    recognised investment exchanges 10.34–10.37
    recognised overseas investment exchanges 10.34–10.37
    UK Listing Authority (competent authority) 10.33
London Stock Exchange (LSE) 10.33, 10.51, 10.71

management companies
  managerial functions 6.120
  senior management location rule 6.121–6.122
Market Abuse Regulation (MAR) 1.02–1.03, 7.19, 7.25, 14.12
market infrastructure
  EU equivalence regime 4.49–4.56
market operators, definition of 10.01, 14.34
marketing
  concept of 15.37–15.38
  definition of 15.37–15.41, 15.59–15.60, 15.90
    pre-marketing, definition of 15.60–15.61
  location of 15.51–15.52
  passport 15.42–15.43
    passport and NPPR, distinction between 15.37–15.56
    without the passport 15.44–15.46
  reverse solicitation 15.47–15.50
  by third-party entities 15.53–15.56
Markets Committee 3.176–3.182
  activities 3.181–3.182
  history of 3.177–3.178
  membership 3.180
  structure 3.179
  see also **Monetary Policy Frameworks and Central Bank Market Operations**
Markets in Financial Instruments Directive (MiFID I) 1.02, 7.83
Ireland:
  investment activities 6.101–6.106
  Investment Firms 6.94–6.99
  service provision 6.101–6.106

Markets in Financial Instrument Directive II (MiFID II)/ Markets in Financial Instruments Regulation (MiFIR) 10.01–10.85
  authorisation of exchanges in the EU 10.38–10.42
    investment firms, provisions for 10.38–10.42
    market operators 10.38
    regulated markets, provisions for 10.39–10.42
  authorisation of exchanges in the UK 10.31–10.62
  authorisation of trading infrastructure in the EU 10.38–10.45
  background to 10.01–10.08
  branches, Member State establishment of 10.59–10.62
  Brexit, potential impact of 10.63–10.85
    access requirements 10.65, 10.74–10.81
    applicability of EU regulation, applicability to UK firms 10.65
    case study 10.82–10.85
    context 10.63–10.64
    definitional questions 10.65
    equivalence 10.74–10.77
    EU regulation, applicability to UK firms 10.67–10.73
    Euro clearing 10.78–10.80
    future EU legislation, effect of 10.70–10.73
    key areas of impact 10.65–10.81
    legal status post-Brexit 10.67–10.69
    passporting 10.74–10.77
    types of concern 10.65–10.66
  clearing houses 10.11–10.13, 10.43–10.44
    access to 10.52–10.53
    authorisation of EU 10.43–10.45
    EU-based clearing houses in the UK, recognition of 10.81
    exchanges and 10.10–10.16
    exposure to default 10.13
    impact of MiFID II on 10.45
    role of 10.11–10.12
  close links, definition of 5.45
  cross-border operation:
    of MTFs and regulated markets 10.48–10.51
    provision of services subject to regulatory equivalence 10.56–10.58
  eligible counterparties 6.102
  EU investment firms, access to Member State's infrastructure 10.46–10.53
  exchanges 10.10
    clearing houses and 10.10–10.16
  financial trading infrastructure, application to 10.14–10.16
  listing of securities on an exchange 10.31–10.37
    recognised investment exchanges 10.34–10.37
    recognised overseas investment exchanges 10.34–10.37
    UK Listing Authority (competent authority) 10.33
    MIFID II 10.09–10.30
  markets and trading platforms 10.17–10.30
    multilateral trading facilities 10.21

  organised trading facilities 10.22–10.23
  OTC trading 10.30
  regulated markets 10.20
  systematic internalisers 10.24–10.29
  from MiFID to MiFID II 10.01–10.08
  on-exchange vs OTC markets 10.14–10.16
  non-EU Investment Firms, access to EU trading infrastructure 10.54–10.62
  passporting for investment firms 10.46–10.47
  per se professional clients, definition of 6.102
  qualifying holding, definition of 5.45
  regulated markets of other Member States, access to 10.50–10.51
  rights of operation and access 10.31–10.62
  scope of new directive 10.04–10.07
  settlement systems 10.43–10.44, 10.52–10.53
    authorisation of EU 10.43–10.45
    impact of MiFID II on 10.45
  structure of 10.09
  third country firms, limited access for 10.54–10.62
Member State of Reference, definition of 4.100
memoranda of understanding (MoUs) 7.112, 11.54, 11.99
minimum capital requirement (MCR) 16.30, 16.45
Monetary Policy Frameworks and Central Bank Market Operations 3.182
  see also **Markets Committee**
monopoly
  France 6.42–6.43
  territorial application of 6.43
moratorium tool 12.74
  see also **stabilisation options**
mortgages 5.124, 8.90
  mortgage agreement, definition of 14.29
MREL (*minimum requirement for own funds and eligible liabilities expressed as a percentage of the total liabilities and own funds of the institution*)
  reforms:
    eligible liabilities 12.71
    external TLAC 12.60–12.70
    internal TLAC 12.72–12.73
  see also **Bank Recovery and Resolution Directive (BRRD)**
multilateral trading facilities (MTFs) 4.49–4.51, 6.09, 6.13, 6.71, 6.73, 6.84, 6.95, 10.02, 10.18–10.19, 10.21–10.24, 10.30, 10.45, 13.75
  cross-border operation of 10.48–10.51
  definition of 10.21, 14.96
  multilateral system, definition of 10.18
  OTFs distinguished 10.23
  see also **Markets in Financial Instrument Directive II (MiFID II)**
mutual recognition, concept of 2.25, 4.08, 10.32, 10.69, 12.77, 12.84

National Competent Authorities (NCAs)
  authorisation, rigorousness and efficiency of 5.21
  EU entities, sound governance of 5.30–5.31
  relocations, objective reasons for 5.22–5.23
  substance requirements 5.29

Union law, supervision and enforcement of 5.32–5.33
see also **European Securities and Markets Authority (ESMA) Opinions**
national private placement regimes (NPPRs) 4.69, 4.77–4.78, 15.29–15.30, 15.73, 15.75, 15.77
passporting distinguished 15.37–15.56
negotiations 1.13–1.19
Netherlands 6.53–6.89
Autoriteit Financiële Markten (AFM) 4.20, 6.61–6.64, 6.66–6.68, 6.71–6.77, 6.82–6.89
background to authorisation 6.53–6.54
Brexit legislation 6.55–6.64
Dutch Brexit Act 6.55–6.58
investment firms, exemption for 6.59–6.64
declaration of no objection (DNO) 6.78–6.86
investment firm 6.78–6.81
regulated market 6.82–6.86
licence application procedure 6.72–6.77
investment services 6.73–6.74
licence fees 6.77
regulated market 6.72
substance 6.75–6.76
licence obligation and exemptions 6.69–6.71
exemption to licence obligation 6.71
initiative test/reverse solicitation 6.70
no deal Brexit, approach to 6.59, 6.63
regulators 6.65–6.68
Dutch Central Bank (DNB) 6.67
enforcement powers of 6.87–6.89
Ministry of Finance 6.68
Netherlands Authority for the Financial Markets 6.66
Wet op het financieel toezicht (AFS) 4.20, 6.59–6.61, 6.71, 6.73–6.74, 6.77, 6.80, 6.82, 6.84, 6.87
New York model *see* **total exit model**
no deal Brexit
avoidance of disruption in event of 7.59, 7.61, 10.81
CCPs, issues for 4.02, 4.57–4.60
contracts, continuity of 6.40
definition of 5.05
deregulation and 7.33
Dutch approach to 6.59, 6.63
ESMA register of administrators 14.90, 14.111
French approach to 6.34, 6.36–6.41, 6.45
impact of no-deal scenario 7.115–7.117, 9.05, 16.24, 16.27
implications of 9.05
in-flight legislation 7.113
interim legislation for 5.05
Decision 2018/2030 5.134–5.136
Decision 2018/2031 5.137–5.138
Irish approach to 6.90
key issues 1.78, 9.01
memoranda of understanding (MoUs) 7.112
possible dates for 5.133
preparations for 1.39–1.77
supervisory cooperation agreements 8.64, 8.111
supervisory powers, reallocation of 7.103, 7.109
temporary permissions regime and 7.103, 9.05, 16.24, 16.27
temporary transitional powers for UK regulators in event of 7.65–7.75
temporary transitional relief for firms 7.59
United Kingdom:
benchmark administrators 14.90, 14.111
government contingency plans 8.14
legal and regulatory framework in event of 7.56
statutory instruments, role of 7.54, 16.27
as a third country, status as 9.05, 10.30
non-credit institutions 5.119
non-significant benchmarks *see* **benchmarks regulation**
Northern Ireland backstop *see* **backstop**
Norwegian model 1.04

Objectives and Principles of Securities Regulation 3.48, 3.118–3.124
on-exchange markets 10.14–10.16
onshoring
Bank of England, approach of 7.76–7.79
EMIR and delegated legislation 13.31–13.36
amendments to onshored EMIR 13.59–13.63
EU Withdrawal Act 13.15–13.30
EMIR, effective operation of 13.24–13.27
EMIR and delegated UK legislation 13.20–13.23
policy choices 13.28–13.30
FCA approach to 7.80
implications of 13.40–13.41
process of:
accounting standards 13.55, 13.65
AIFMD 15.10
benchmark regulation 14.20, 14.22, 14.25, 14.29, 14.32, 14.36, 14.48–14.49, 14.67, 14.79, 14.125
EMIR 13.34, 13.103
PSR's approach to 7.81
Organisation for Economic Co-operation and Development (OECD) 3.03–3.14
activities 3.09–3.14
corporate governance, principles of 3.12–3.14
history of 3.04–3.05
membership 3.07–3.08
structure 3.06
organised trading facilities (OTFs) 10.22–10.23
definition of 10.22–10.23, 10.30, 13.77, 14.96
MTFs distinguished 10.23
see also **Markets in Financial Instrument Directive II (MiFID II)**
outsourcing
ESMA Investment Firms Opinion 5.53–5.62
arrangements, assessment of 5.53–5.57
of critical functions/services 5.60–5.62
due diligence 5.58–5.59
French arrangements 6.48–6.50
over-the-counter (OTC)
derivatives, definition of 13.103–13.104
C6 energy 13.75–13.77
EU27 exchange-traded, exclusion of 13.72–13.74

over-the-counter (OTC) (*cont.*)
  markets 10.14–10.16
  trading 10.30
  see also European Markets Infrastructure Regulation (EMIR)
overseas firm, definition of 8.04
Overseas Persons' Exemption
  post-Brexit 7.97–7.102
'own funds', definition of 5.126, 12.60

parent undertakings, definition of 12.43, 12.55
passporting
  AIFMD 15.86–15.90
  CRD IV/CRR regime 11.04–11.32
    financial services passport 11.10–11.16
    impact of Brexit on 11.17–11.21
  definition of 4.71
  for investment firms 10.46–10.47
  marketing 15.42–15.43
  without passport 15.44–15.46
  MiFID 10.74–10.77
  NPPR distinguished 15.37–15.56
  UK EEA-authorised (re)insurers 16.19–16.33
    impact of Brexit 16.22–16.23
    post-TPR 16.33
    TPR 16.24–16.32
  see also marketing; temporary permission regime (TPR)
payment institutions 5.116–5.118, 6.09, 6.12, 6.16
Payment Systems Regulator (PSR) 1.60–1.61, 7.71
  onshoring, approach to 7.81
pension scheme arrangements (EU), definition of 13.70
  see also International Organisation of Pension Supervisors (IOPS); Principles of Private Pension Supervision
Political Declaration on the Future EU–UK Relationship 1.22–1.25, 2.20–2.38
  background to 2.20–2.22
  FCA EU Withdrawal Impact Assessment 2.34–2.38
  financial services, implications for 2.24–2.28
  future prospects 2.29–2.33
  structure 2.23
  Withdrawal Agreement and interim legislation 5.132–5.141
  see also Withdrawal Agreement
Pre-Approval Controlled Functions (PCFs) 6.123–6.124
preparedness *see* risk assessment
Primary Market Handbook 3.232
  see also International Capital Market Association (ICMA)
Principles for Financial Markets Infrastructures (PFMI) 3.79–3.84
  see also Committee on Payments and Market Infrastructures (CPMI)
Principles of Private Pension Supervision 3.157–3.159
  see also International Organisation of Pension Supervisors (IOPS)

proportionality
  benchmarks regulation 14.60
  ESMA Investment Firms Opinion 5.52
  principle of 4.35
proprietary business
  specific relief measure for 6.18–6.20, 6.28
Protected Payment Scheme (PPS) 10.44
protocols 2.10–2.11
Prudential Regulation Authority (PRA) 8.01–8.130
  background to 8.01–8.07
  bank branches, approach to 8.08–8.11
  banks:
    accounts 8.41–8.42
    application process 8.81–8.90
    booking models 8.80
    customers 8.39–8.40
    FCA rules 8.92
    FSCR 8.99
    FSCS-Protected Deposit Base 8.34–8.37
    overseas branches or subsidiary status 8.91–8.99
    PRA rules 8.92
    retail deposit base 8.33
    significant retail activities 8.28–8.42
    significant retail approach 8.38
    supervisory experiences vs non-systemic branches 8.77–8.79
    systemic branches, qualification for 8.74–8.76
    systemic wholesale branches 8.73–8.80
    TPR implications 8.95–8.98
    UK branches 8.91–8.93
    UK subsidiaries 8.94
  branches and subsidiaries, differences between 8.22–8.27
  overseas (re)insurers:
    branch failure, impact of 8.124–8.126
    cross-border services business 8.127–8.130
    EEA (re)insurers post-Brexit 8.106–8.111
    factors to consider 8.118–8.120
    FSCR 8.115
    PRA approach to authorisation 8.100–8.115
    TPR implications 8.112–8.114
    UK branch activity covered by the FSCS, scale of 8.121–8.123
    UK branches 8.116–8.130
  (re)insurer branches, approach to 8.12
  Rulebook 8.92
    depositor protection 8.92
    remuneration 8.92
    reporting 8.92
    single customer view reports 8.92
    SMCR 8.92
    impact of Brexit on 7.93–7.96
    parent mixed financial holding company 12.44
    recovery plans 12.31
    resolution planning 12.39
  timing considerations 8.13–8.20
  transitional arrangements 8.13–8.20

wholesale banks 8.43–8.72
  branch authorisation and supervision, general approach to 8.45–8.48
  considerations for banks 8.71–8.72
  equivalence standards 8.58–8.61
  FCA 8.55–8.57
  PRA 8.51–8.54
  PRA and FCA Threshold Conditions for Authorisation 8.49–8.50
  resolution arrangements, assurance over 8.66–8.70
  supervisory cooperation arrangements 8.62–8.65

recognised central counterparties, definition of 12.30
recognised investment exchange, definition of 10.34
recovery plans, definition of 12.31
Referendum (Brexit, 2016) 1.01–1.08
  bonfire of regulations 1.05, 7.118
  business impact assessments of 1.06
  campaign 1.18, 7.01–7.03
    Single Market access, issues around 1.18, 4.10
    'taking back control,' concept of 7.01–7.04
  concerns for UK financial institutions 4.01
  EBA HQ relocation in light of 1.50, 7.15
  EU legislation and regulations, complexity of 7.10
  equivalence, concept of 4.05, 4.07
  financial services legislation, effect on 1.02–1.03
  history and result of 1.01
  options for continuing business in UK 1.08
  options for future UK-EU relationship 1.04
  second referendum, debate surrounding 1.37, 9.01
  third country equivalence provisions 1.07
regulated-data benchmarks *see* benchmarks regulation
regulated markets
  authorisation of exchanges 10.39–10.42
  cross-border operation of 10.48–10.51
  definition of 10.20, 14.96
  Member State access 10.50–10.51
  MiFID II 10.20
  Netherlands 6.82–6.86
  licence application procedure 6.72
regulators
  BRR Brexit regulations *see* Bank Recovery and Resolution Directive (BRRD)
  Dutch *see* Netherlands
  international standards 3.02–3.199
regulatory technical standards (RTS) 1.48, 7.80, 10.03, 12.58, 13.11, 13.22, 13.33, 13.89, 13.91, 16.04, 16.13
reinsurance
  equivalence 4.89–4.94
  PRA approach 8.100–8.115
    EEA (re)insurers post-Brexit 8.106–8.111
    to (re)insurer branches 8.12
    UK branches 8.116–8.130
  reinsurance undertakings, definition of 14.34

Solvency II Directive 16.16–16.41
  case law 16.40–16.41
  EEA-authorised (re)insurers conducting UK business offshore 16.34–16.41
  EEA-authorised (re)insurers passporting into UK 16.19–16.33
  equivalence, impact on reinsurers 16.59
  guidance and regulation 16.37–16.39
  licensing issues for pure reinsurers 16.47–16.53
  UK regulatory landscape for (re)insurers 16.19–16.21
  see also equivalence; insurance; Prudential Regulation Authority (PRA); Solvency II Directive (Solvency II)
relevant measure, definition of 12.47
relevant obligation, definition of 13.95
remuneration
  CRD provisions 11.76–11.89
    background to 11.76–11.78
    UK position on bonus cap 11.82–11.89
    UK regulatory approach 11.79–11.81
Republic of Ireland (ROI) *see* Ireland
resolutions
  BRRD:
    conditions 12.48–12.50
    planning 12.39–12.42
  EBA 2017 Opinion 5.124–5.126
  resolution group, definition of 12.66
  resolution plans, definition of 12.39
  resolvability assessment 12.40
retail activities
  PRA's approach to 8.28–8.42
    accounts 8.41–8.42
    customers 8.39–8.40
    FSCS-Protected Deposit Base, size of 8.34–8.37
    retail deposit base, size of 8.33
    significant retail approach 8.38
    retail, definition of 8.40
    retail depositors, definition of 8.33
  see also Prudential Regulation Authority (PRA)
retained EU case law, definition of 7.43
reverse solicitation 15.47–15.50
  France 6.44
  Germany 6.25–6.26
  Netherlands 6.70
  see also marketing
risk
  assessment:
    EBA 2018 Opinion 5.130–5.131
  management:
    EBA 2017 Opinion 5.122–5.123
    Ireland 6.125–6.126
  mitigation obligations 13.89–13.91
  weights, impact of Brexit on 11.70–11.75
  see also Capital Requirements Directive (CRD IV); Capital Requirements Regulation (CRR); European Markets Infrastructure Regulation (EMIR)

INDEX

Secondary Markets Opinion *see* European Securities and Markets Authority (ESMA) Opinions
Sector-Specific Opinions *see* European Securities and Markets Authority (ESMA) Opinions
securities lending *see* International Securities Lending Association (ISLA)
securities listing *see* listing of securities
securitisation 11.103–11.115
   background to 11.103–11.107
   regulation and Brexit 11.108–11.115
   simple, transparent, and standardised (STS securitisations) 11.111–11.115
   special purpose entities (SSPEs) 11.113, 13.71
   see also Capital Requirements Directive (CRD IV); Capital Requirements Regulation (CRR)
Senior Managers, Certification and Conduct Regime (SMCR)
   regimes, applicability of 9.08–9.12
     challenges 9.12
     deemed approval for SMFs 9.11
senior management 9.01–9.47
   background to 9.01–9.07
   certification and conduct regimes 9.26–9.28
   cross-border business into UK, responsibility for 9.21–9.25
     appointed representative 9.24
     business conducted into UK 9.22–9.23
     dual hatting 9.25
   enforcement:
     against non-UK resident senior managers 9.32–9.47
     approval, suspension of 9.42–9.43
     consequences 9.46–9.47
     court proceedings 9.45
     fines 9.44
     powers 9.36–9.39
     prohibition orders 9.42–9.43
     tools 9.40
     warnings, public and private 9.42–9.43
   in-sourcing and outsourcing 9.29–9.31
   location rule 6.121–6.122
   moving between regimes, implications of 9.17–9.20
   regulatory requirements during Brexit, responsibility for 9.13–9.16
   senior manager functions (SMFs) 9.11
   supervisory powers 9.34–9.35
   see also management companies; Senior Managers, Certification and Conduct Regime (SMCR)
settlement systems 10.52–10.53
   authorisation of 10.43–10.45
   clearing houses and payment and 10.43–10.44
   MiFID, impact of 10.45
   see also clearing houses; Markets in Financial Instrument Directive II (MiFID II)
significant benchmarks *see* benchmarks regulation
significant retail approach *see* retail activities
sincere cooperation, principle of 2.22
Single Market
   access to 1.04, 1.18, 7.03, 16.17
   during transition period 1.23, 2.12, 7.62, 13.16, 13.105, 16.12
   third country regimes 4.23, 9.05
   alignment with 4.09
   barriers to 11.06–11.09
   directives 7.10
   for financial services 4.02, 7.62, 8.64, 10.01, 10.68, 11.04, 11.07, 16.02
   four freedoms of 1.15, 1.18, 4.18, 16.22
   integrity of 1.15
   passporting rights 1.06–1.07, 1.16, 2.12, 4.38, 4.71, 4.94, 6.01, 8.02, 16.22
Single Supervisory Mechanism (SSM) 6.22–6.23, 6.35, 11.65
small company, definition of 8.33
soft Brexit scenario 6.07
   see also hard Brexit scenario
Solvency II Directive (Solvency II) 16.01–16.87
   background to 16.01–16.15
     legislative 16.01–16.10
     preserving the *acquis* 16.11–16.15
   contract continuity for existing business 16.76–16.87
     European insurers operating in the UK 16.78–16.85
     existing contracts 16.76–16.77
     UK insurers operating in the EU 16.86–16.87
   European insurers operating in the UK 16.16–16.41
     case law 16.40–16.41
     EEA-authorised (re)insurers 16.19–16.41
     guidance and regulation 16.37–16.39
     licensing issues 16.16–16.41
     passporting into the UK 16.22–16.23
     temporary permission regime 16.24–16.33
     UK regulatory landscape for (re)insurers 16.19–16.21
   solvency capital requirement (SCR) 16.30, 16.46, 16.45, 16.50, 16.54, 16.70, 16.73
   UK insurers operating in Europe 16.42–16.75
     direct insurers, impact on 16.44–16.46, 16.58
     equivalence, effect under Solvency II 16.54–16.59
     group supervision regimes 16.60–16.75
     licensing issues 16.42–16.53
     pure reinsurers 16.47–16.53
     reinsurers, impact on 16.59
   see also groups; licensing; temporary permission regime (TPR)
stabilisation options
   bail in 12.54–12.59
   moratorium tool 12.74
   overview of 12.51–12.53
   see also Bank Recovery and Resolution Directive (BRRD)
International Financial Reporting Standards (IFRS) 3.206–3.211
   see also International Accounting Standards Board (IASB); International Financial Reporting Standards Foundation (IFRSF)

INDEX 429

statutory instruments (SIs)
  central counterparties (CCPs) 13.42–13.56
    amendments to onshored EMIR 13.44–13.51
    background to 13.42–13.43
    equivalence assessments and recognition 13.54
    recognition of UK CCPs under EMIR 13.56
    regulatory changes 13.55
    transitional relief 13.52–13.53
  trade repositories 13.57–13.65
    amendments to onshored EMIR 13.59–13.63
    background to 13.57–13.58
    regulatory changes 13.65
    transitional relief-temporary deemed recognition for UK affiliates 13.64
strategic asset management plan 3.244–3.246
  see also Institute of Asset Management (IAM)
Subject Specific Guidelines (SSGs) 3.249–3.250
  see also Institute of Asset Management (IAM)
subsidiaries
  branches, differences with 8.22–8.27
  UK 8.94
subsidiarity, principle of 11.80
substance requirements
  ESMA Investment Firms Opinion 5.47–5.64
  France 6.47
  Germany 6.33
  Ireland 6.117–6.119
  NCAs 5.29
  Netherlands 6.75–6.76
  see also European Securities and Markets Authority (ESMA) Opinions
supervised contributors, definition of 14.76
  see also benchmarks regulation
supervised entity, definition of 14.34, 14.36
Supervisory Coordination Network (SCN) 5.34–5.35, 6.110
supervisory regime 7.01–7.122
  assessment of 7.118–7.122
  background to 7.01–7.07
  disruption, minimisation of 7.59–7.75
  EU (Withdrawal) Act 2018 7.38–7.58
    deficiencies in retained law 7.44–7.48
    retained EU case law 7.43
    retained EU law 7.41–7.42
    statutory instruments 7.54–7.58
    UK parliamentary powers 7.49–7.53
  FCA Handbook, impact of Brexit on 7.90–7.92
  financial services legislation and regulation, UK framework for 7.21–7.26
  in flight legislation, treatment of 7.113–7.114
  implementation period 7.60–7.64
  no deal scenario:
    impact of 7.115–7.117
    temporary transitional powers for UK regulators 7.65–7.75
  non-legislative EU materials, UK regulators' approach to 7.82–7.89
  onshoring:
    Bank of England's approach to 7.76–7.79
    FCA's approach to 7.80
    PSR's approach to 7.81
  Overseas Persons' Exemption post-Brexit 7.97–7.102
  PRA rulebook, impact of Brexit on 7.93–7.96
  regulation 7.27–7.37
  regulatory cooperation 7.110–7.112
  supervisory powers, reallocation of 7.103–7.109
  UK and EU frameworks, entangled nature of 7.08–7.20
    ESAs, growing power of 7.15–7.18
    influence of Europe from late 1990s 7.11–7.12
    national discretion 7.19–7.20
    shift towards Europe post-2007–8 Financial Crisis 7.13–7.14
Swiss model 1.04
systematic internalisers 10.24–10.29
  definition of 14.29, 14.35
  see also Markets in Financial Instrument Directive II (MiFID II)
systemic branches see banks

'taking back control,' concept of 7.01–7.04
temporary permissions regime (TPR)
  authorisation:
    requirement to apply for 16.29
    timing of 16.28
  cross-border business of firms 16.32
  implementation of 16.27
  PRA 8.95–8.98
    overseas (re)insurers 8.112–8.114
  regulation in 16.30–16.31
  Solvency II Directive 16.24–16.32
third countries
  access limitations for firms 10.54–10.62
  benchmarks regulation 14.113–14.115
  CRD IV/CRR regime:
    intermediate holding companies 11.66–11.67
    passporting and equivalence tests 11.22–11.32
  EU equivalence regime 4.18–4.20
    third country equivalence, concept of 16.02
  Irish firms 6.100–6.109
    as AIFMs under the AIFM Directive 6.107
    marketing AIFs under the AIFM Regulations 6.108–6.109
    MiFID 6.101–6.106
  outsourcing and delegation to 5.28
  third country firms, definition of 10.54
  third country institutions, definition of 12.30
third parties
  employees, guidelines in relation to use of 6.46
  entities, marketing by 15.53–15.56
Tier 1/Tier 2 capital, definitions of 12.60, 12.72
total exit model 1.04
total loss-absorbing capacity (TLAC)
  external 12.60–12.70
  internal 12.72–12.73
  see also Bank Recovery and Resolution Directive (BRRD); MREL

trade repositories
  definition of 14.34
  regulation 13.92–13.93
  statutory instruments (SIs) 13.57–13.65
    amendments to onshored EMIR 13.59–13.63
    background to 13.57–13.58
    regulatory changes 13.65
    transitional relief-temporary deemed recognition for UK affiliates 13.64
  see also **European Markets Infrastructure Regulation (EMIR)**
trading infrastructure *see* **Markets in Financial Instrument Directive II (MiFID II)**
trading venue, definition of 5.67, 5.138, 13.67, 13.69, 14.29, 14.32, 14.35
transactional account, definition of 8.33
transition period 1.19, 1.23–1.24, 2.09, 2.12, 2.26, 4.12, 5.132, 6.12–6.14, 6.18, 7.60, 11.113, 14.123, 16.11, 16.27
  benchmarks regulation 14.77–14.84
    administrators 14.77–14.82
    authorisation and registration 14.80
    competent authorities 14.80
    EU administrators 14.116
    FCA options 14.80
    indexing providers 14.80
    supervised contributors 14.83–14.84
    UK administrators 14.110–14.112
  definition of 14.82
  Germany 6.12–6.14
    limitations of 6.15–6.17
    scope of regime 6.09–6.11
  temporary powers for UK regulators in event of no deal 7.65–7.75
  transitional relief 13.52–13.53, 13.64
Treasury Committee (TC) 8.108
twin peaks model 6.65

Undertakings for Collective Investments in Transferable Securities Directive (UCITS)
  definition of 14.80, 14.110

UCITS management companies 6.94–6.99
  definition of 6.94, 14.34
  managerial functions 6.120
  senior management location rule 6.121–6.122
United Kingdom (UK)
  Listing Authority 4.101, 4.105, 10.33
  senior manager's regime *see* **senior management**
  supervisory regime post-Brexit *see* **supervisory regime**

variable remuneration *see* **remuneration**

white-label business 5.80, 5.87–5.88
wholesale branches *see* **banks**
wholesale depositors, definition of 8.40
Withdrawal Act *see* **European Union (Withdrawal) Act 2018**
Withdrawal Agreement 1.22–1.25, 2.01–2.38, 5.132–5.141
  background to 2.01, 5.132–5.133
  Decision 2018/2030 5.134–5.136
  Decision 2018/2031 5.137–5.138
  deficiency, definition of (EU Withdrawal Act) 7.46, 13.25
  dispute resolution 2.13–2.19
  EU-derived domestic legislation, definition of 12.23
  FCA EU Withdrawal Impact Assessment 2.34–2.38
  financial services, implications for 2.12
  implementation period 7.60–7.64
  protocols 2.10–2.11
  ratification of 1.26–1.38, 2.02–2.06
  Regulation 2019/396 5.139–5.140
  Regulation 2019/397 5.141
  renegotiation 2.07–2.08
  retained direct minor EU legislation 7.51
  retained direct principal EU legislation 7.51
  structure 2.09–2.09
  see also **transition period**